T0178560

Lecture Notes in Computer Science 14496

The series Lecture Notes in Computer Science (LNCS), including its subseries Lecture Notes in Artificial Intelligence (LNAI) and Lecture Notes in Bioinformatics (LNBI), has established itself as a medium for the publication of new developments in computer science and information technology research, teaching, and education.

LNCS enjoys close cooperation with the computer science R & D community, the series counts many renowned academics among its volume editors and paper authors, and collaborates with prestigious societies. Its mission is to serve this international community by providing an invaluable service, mainly focused on the publication of conference and workshop proceedings and postproceedings. LNCS commenced publication in 1973.

Bin Sheng · Lei Bi · Jinman Kim ·
Nadia Magnenat-Thalmann · Daniel Thalmann
Editors

Advances in
Computer Graphics

40th Computer Graphics International Conference, CGI 2023
Shanghai, China, August 28 – September 1, 2023
Proceedings, Part II

Springer

Editors
Bin Sheng (iD)
Shanghai Jiao Tong University
Shanghai, China

Jinman Kim (iD)
University of Sydney
Sydney, NSW, Australia

Daniel Thalmann
Swiss Federal Institute of Technology
Lausanne, Switzerland

Lei Bi (iD)
Shanghai Jiao Tong University
Shanghai, China

Nadia Magnenat-Thalmann (iD)
MIRALab-CUI
University of Geneve
Carouge, Geneve, Switzerland

ISSN 0302-9743   ISSN 1611-3349 (electronic)
Lecture Notes in Computer Science
ISBN 978-3-031-50071-8   ISBN 978-3-031-50072-5 (eBook)
https://doi.org/10.1007/978-3-031-50072-5

This Springer imprint is published by the registered company Springer Nature Switzerland AG
The registered company address is: Gewerbestrasse 11, 6330 Cham, Switzerland

Paper in this product is recyclable.

Preface Lecture Notes in Computer Science (14496)

CGI is one of the oldest annual international conferences on Computer Graphics in the world. Researchers are invited to share their experiences and novel achievements in various fields of Computer Graphics and Virtual Reality. Previous recent CGI conferences have been held in Sydney, Australia (2014), Strasbourg, France (2015), Heraklion, Greece (2016), Yokohama, Japan (2017), Bintan, Indonesia (2018), and Calgary in Canada (2019). CGI was virtual between 2020 and 2022 due to the COVID pandemic. This year, CGI 2023 was organized by the Shanghai Jiao Tong University, with the assistance of the University of Sydney and Wuhan Textile University, and supported by the Computer Graphics Society (CGS). The conference was held during August 28 to September 1, 2023.

These CGI 2023 LNCS proceedings are composed of 149 papers from a total of 385 submissions. This includes 51 papers that were reviewed highly and were recommended to be published in the CGI Visual Computer Journal track. To ensure the high quality of the publications, each paper was reviewed by at least two experts in the field and authors of accepted papers were asked to revise their paper according to the review comments prior to publication.

The CGI 2023 LNCS proceedings also include papers from the ENGAGE (Empowering Novel Geometric Algebra for Graphics & Engineering) 2023 Workshop (11 full papers), focused specifically on important aspects of geometric algebra including surface construction, robotics, encryption, qubits and expression optimization. The workshop has been part of the CGI conferences since 2016.

We would like to express our deepest gratitude to all the PC members and external reviewers who provided timely high-quality reviews. We would also like to thank all the authors for contributing to the conference by submitting their work.

September 2023

Bin Sheng
Lei Bi
Jinman Kim
Nadia Magnenat-Thalmann
Daniel Thalmann

Organization

Honorary Conference Chairs

Enhua Wu — Chinese Academy of Sciences/University of Macau, China

Dagan Feng — University of Sydney, Australia

Conference Chairs

Nadia Magnenat Thalmann — University of Geneva, Switzerland

Bin Sheng — Shanghai Jiao Tong University, China

Jinman Kim — University of Sydney, Australia

Program Chairs

Daniel Thalmann — École Polytechnique Fédérale de Lausanne, Switzerland

Stephen Lin — Microsoft Research Asia, China

Lizhuang Ma — Shanghai Jiao Tong University, China

Ping Li — Hong Kong Polytechnic University, China

Contents – Part II

Reconstruction

Rendering and Animation

Colors, Painting and Layout

Synthesis and Generation

Reconstruction

Single-View 3D Reconstruction of Curves

Ali Fakih[✉][iD], Nicola Wilser, Yvan Maillot, and Frederic Cordier

Université de Haute Alsace, Mulhouse, France
ali.fakih@uha.fr

Abstract. This paper describes a method to generate a 3D curve from a planar polygonal curve. One application of such method is the modeling of trajectories of moving objects in 3D using sketches. Given a planar polygonal curve C_{2D}, our algorithm computes a 3D curve C_{3D} such that its orthogonal projection matches the input curve. The algorithm aims at minimizing the variation of the curvature along the reconstructed curve. The driving idea is to fit a set of ellipses to the input curve; these ellipses enable us to determine the osculating circles and thus the tangent at every point of the curve to reconstruct in 3D. The reconstruction of 3D curve using these tangents is then straightforward. The method is demonstrated with several examples.

Keywords: 3D Reconstruction · Curve · Osculating circles

1 Introduction

The field of computer graphics has made significant advancements in areas such as rendering and animation. However, a persistent challenge remains in accurately capturing user intentions for 3D modeling in a simple and intuitive manner. Interacting with users becomes complicated due to the limitations of two-dimensional interfaces, which do not properly accommodate our natural perception and thinking in a three-dimensional environment. One particularly challenging aspect is drawing 3D curves within a 2D input device. These curves are crucial in various applications such as defining the trajectories of moving objects or modeling of 3D objects. Several works have been proposed to address this problem, such as changing perspectives or requiring the artist to draw the shadow of the curve. However, most of these methods pose some constraints to the artists, leading to reduced efficiency. This paper intends to address this problem, in particular, the modeling of 3D curve from a single drawing. Unlike most of the existing methods, our approach does not require any other input or user interaction than the planar curve of the drawing.

The main idea of the method is driven by the following observation. Let C_{3D} be a 3D polygonal curve and $O_{3D,i}$ the osculating circle at the midpoint of a segment $e_{3D,i}$ of this curve. The osculating circle is the circle that has the same tangent and the same curvature as at the midpoint of $e_{3D,i}$. Let C_{2D}, $e_{2D,i}$ and $O_{2D,i}$ be the orthogonal projection on the (x, y) plane of C_{3D}, $e_{3D,i}$ and

B. Sheng et al. (Eds.): CGI 2023, LNCS 14496, pp. 3–14, 2024.
https://doi.org/10.1007/978-3-031-50072-5_1

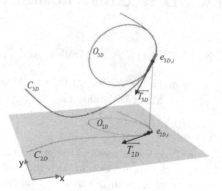

Fig. 1. The curve C_{3D} with its osculating circle O_{3D} at the midpoint of the edge $e_{3D,i}$. The curve C_{2D} which is the orthogonal projection of C_{3D} and the ellipse O_{2D} which is the orthogonal projection of the osculating circle $O_{3D,i}$.

$O_{3D,i}$ respectively. $O_{2D,i}$ is an ellipse whose tangent and curvature are equal to those of the curve C_{2D} at the midpoint of the segment $e_{2D,i}$ (see Fig. 1). Now, we are only provided the planar curve C_{2D} and our goal is to reconstruct the C_{3D} curve. Given a segment $e_{2D,i}$ of C_{2D}, we compute a set of ellipses whose curvature and tangent match those at the midpoint of $e_{2D,i}$. If we assume that this set of ellipses is large enough, one of these ellipses must be the projection of an osculating circle being very close to the actual osculating circle of the curve C_{3D} to reconstruct. We repeat this process of computing the set of osculating circle candidates for each segment of C_{3D}. Then, the problem comes down to selecting the best osculating circle for each segment such that the variation of curvature is minimized along the curve. This is a simple graph problem that is solved using Dijkstra's algorithm. These osculating circles are then used to determine the tangent for each segment and to compute the 3D coordinates of the points of C_{3D}.

The contribution of the paper is twofold. First, we propose the idea of fitting ellipses to the input planar curve; these ellipses are then used to determine the osculating circles and in turn, the orientation of the tangent at the midpoint of each segment of the 3D curve to reconstruct. The second contribution is a method to solve the optimization problem which aims at finding the optimal osculating circles such that the variation of the curvature along the 3D reconstructed curve is minimized. Usual approach would require solving a large nonlinear optimization using gradient-descent method. Instead, the solution space is discretized to form a graph, each node of this graph being a candidate for the osculating circles at the midpoint of each segment the curve. The edges of the graph correspond to the adjacency relationship between the segments. The solution of this optimization problem is then solved using the Dijkstra's algorithm.

The remainder of the paper is organized as follows. Section 2 reviews related works. Section 3 gives an overview of the approach. Section 4 describes our algorithm for fitting ellipses to a planar polygonal curve and Sect. 5 explains the process of computing the osculating circles from the ellipses. Section 6 describes the last step of the algorithm, which computes the coordinates of the 3D curve using the tangent of the osculating circles previously computed. Section 6 presents the results and Sect. 7 the conclusion

2 Related Works

Modeling a 3D curve can be done in two different ways, either using a 3D drawing interface or a 2D drawing interface.

2.1 Curve Modeling Using 3D Drawing Interfaces

A 3D drawing interface enables the artist to create the curve directly in 3D using a device that captures the movements of the hand in the 3D space. Different devices have been proposed such as using a smartphone [19], a HTC Vive controller [20] or other types of virtual reality controller [2], a virtual reality headset such as the Oculus Quest [15], or a hand tracking sensor [12]. The main limitation of this class of approaches is the use of a tracking device and/or a head-mounted display. This makes the modeling process not easy to setup and not as convenient as making a drawing, which only requires a pen and paper.

2.2 Curve Modeling Using 2D Drawing Interfaces

The second category is the use of a 2D drawing interface such as a tablet or a mouse. Sketching using a tablet is preferred by many designers since sketching is natural for them. In addition, these devices are usually cheaper than virtual reality devices. However, the main difficulty is to generate a 3D curve from the 2D curve drawn by the user; the third dimension is missing and the goal is to compute this missing information in a way to generate a 3D curve that looks natural and that matches the user's expectation. Researchers have proposed different approaches to recover this missing information.

One of the most common approaches is to process altogether the curves of the drawing. It is actually much easier to reconstruct in 3D a set of curves representing an object rather than a single curve. When all the curves are taken together, additional criteria such as parallelism, orthogonality, and symmetry between the curves can be used to facilitate the 3D reconstruction [11]. These methods have been proven to work very well. However, they fail when they are given a single curve; such a method cannot be used to reconstruct the trajectory of a dynamic object from a drawing.

Another common strategy to make the 3D reconstruction problem tractable is to make some assumptions about the curves to reconstruct. Some works have been done for the reconstruction of mirror-symmetric curves [8,10] or the reconstruction of curves around existing objects [13]. Other researchers focus their work on the reconstruction of specific shapes such as lower limb [17], anterior chamber [1] or specific curves such as the Helix [5,7]. Helices are 3D curves with constant curvature and torsion. The main drawback of these methods is that they are limited to special types of curves or to specific scenarios.

Finally, some works have been done for the curve reconstruction using multiple images or multiple viewpoints. The first strategy is to enable the artist to construct the curve interactively by drawing an initial version of the curve. The user then can change the viewpoint so that she/he can make some modifications in case the initial curve is not satisfactory [3]. Other researchers have proposed a method to reconstruct a curve given its drawing and its shadow on the floor plane [6]. Some work has also been done for the reconstruction of a curve given its two images [9] or the 3D reconstruction of objects using multiple viewpoints [4,21]. The strategy of using multiple viewpoints or images has been proven to work very well. However, they require the user to provide multiple images or some interaction during the reconstruction process.

In this paper, we aim at proposing a method for the modeling of a single 3D curve using a single-view drawing. No assumption such as symmetry or helix is made about the curve to reconstruct.

3   Overview

Our method takes as input a planar curve C_{2D} in the (x, y) plane and generates a 3D curve C_{3D} whose orthogonal projection onto the (x,y) plane matches the input C_{2D} curve and such that the change of curvature is minimized along this curve C_{3D}. The input curve C_{2D} is a polygonal curve composed of p points denoted $v_{2D,1}, v_{2D,2}...v_{2D,p}$. The set of $p-1$ segments is $e_{2D,1}, e_{2D,2}...e_{2D,p-1}$ with $e_{2D,i}$ being the segment connecting $v_{2D,i}$ to $v_{2D,i+1}$. This curve is assumed to be at least G1 continuous; it should not contain any sharp corners and the curvature can be accurately computed for every segment. The reconstructed 3D curve C_{3D} is composed of p points $v_{3D,1}, v_{3D,2}...v_{3D,p}$, each of these points corresponding to a point in the input curve C_{2D}. The segments are denoted $e_{3D,1}, e_{3D,2}...e_{3D,p-1}$.

The reconstruction is done iteratively, starting from the first segment $e_{2D,1}$ of the input curve C_{2D}. The driving idea is to fit a set of ellipses to each segment of the input curve, i.e. ellipses whose curvature and tangent match the curvature and tangent at the midpoint of the segment $e_{2D,i}$ (Fig. 2(b)). These fitted ellipses are then used to compute the set of candidates for the osculating circle at each segment of the curve C_{3D} (Fig. 2(c)). Next, we formulate an optimization problem that aims at finding the best osculating circle for each segment such that the change of curvature is minimized along the 3D reconstructed curve. This is done by building a graph whose nodes are the candidates for the osculating circles and by applying Dijkstra's algorithm. The last step is to compute the translation along the z-axis for each segment (Fig. 2(e)) using the tangent of the osculating circles previously computed (Fig. 2(d)).

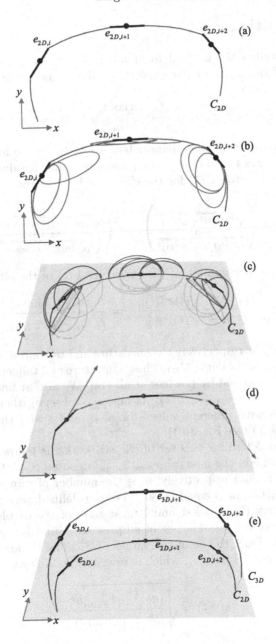

Fig. 2. Overview of the method. The input curve C_{2D} in with 3 adjacent segments $e_{2D,i}$, $e_{2D,i+1}$ and $e_{2D,i+2}$ (a). For the sake of clarity, only a subset of the segments is drawn. Ellipses are first fitted to the midpoint of each segment along the curve such that they have the same curvature and tangent as the corresponding midpoint (b). Candidates for the osculating circles at each midpoint are generated (c). These osculating circles are then used to estimate the tangent of the curve C_{3D} to reconstruct (d). Finally, the curve C_{3D} is reconstructed by lifting the points such as to satisfy the estimated tangent.

4   Ellipse Fitting

This section describes the method to fit a set of ellipses to the midpoint of a segment $e_{2D,i}$ of the input planar curve C_{2D}. The parametric equation of the ellipse is given as follows:

$$x(t) = a \cos t$$
$$y(t) = b \sin t \tag{1}$$

We assume that $a < b$. These parameters a and b are the half-length of the minor and major axes respectively. The parameter t has a value in the interval $0, 2\pi[$. The tangent vector $\boldsymbol{T}(t)$ for the ellipse of Eq. 1 is given as follows:

$$\boldsymbol{T}(t) = \begin{pmatrix} \frac{x'(t)}{\sqrt{(x'(t))^2 + (y'(t))^2}} \\ \frac{y'(t)}{\sqrt{(x'(t))^2 + (y'(t))^2}} \end{pmatrix} = \begin{pmatrix} \frac{-a\sin(t)}{\sqrt{(a\sin(t))^2 + (b\cos(t))^2}} \\ \frac{b\cos(t)}{\sqrt{(a\sin(t))^2 + (b\cos(t))^2}} \end{pmatrix} \tag{2}$$

We also provide the equation of the curvature $k(t)$ of the ellipse:

$$k(t) = \frac{||x'(t)y''(t) - y'(t)x''(t)||}{||(x'(t))^2 + (y'(t))^2||^{\frac{3}{2}}} = \frac{ab}{(a^2 sin^2(t) + b^2 cos^2(t))^{\frac{3}{2}}} \tag{3}$$

Let $k_{2D,i}$ and $\boldsymbol{T}_{2D,i}$ be respectively the curvature and tangent of at the midpoint of the segment $e_{2D,i}$ of the curve C_{2D}. These curvature and tangent are computed using the method proposed by Lewiner et al. [14]. We aim at finding the values of t, a, and b such that $k_{2D,i} = k(t)$. As one may observe, there is an infinite number of ellipses with different values for a, b, and t and that satisfies the equation $k_{2D,i} = k(t)$ (see Fig. 3(a)).

Our method to determine this set of ellipses works as follows. We compute a sampling of a and b in the interval $[r_{min}, r_{max}]$ denoted $S_a = \{a_1, a_2, \ldots, a_m\}$ and $S_b = \{b_1, b_2, \ldots, b_m\}$ respectively; m is the number of samples for a and b. In our implementation, m is equal to 30. The user-defined parameters r_{min} and r_{max} are respectively the smallest and largest radii of the osculating circles of the 3D curve to reconstruct. The set of ellipses are found by setting a to one of the values of Sa and b to one of the values of Sb. The value of t is found by solving the equation $k(t) = k_{2D,i}$, which is rewritten as follows:

$$sin(t) = \sqrt{\frac{(ab)^{\frac{2}{3}} - k_{v2D,i}^{\frac{2}{3}} b^2}{k_{v2D,i}^{\frac{2}{3}} (a^2 - b^2)}} \tag{4}$$

This equation has a solution if $\frac{ab}{b^2} \le k_{2D,i} \le \frac{ab}{a^2}$ with $a < b$. The inverse sine function gives two solutions for t. This set of ellipses that have been computed for a specific midpoint of the segment $e_{2D,i}$ along the input planar curve C_{2D} is denoted $S_{O,2D,i} = \{O_{2D,i,1} \ldots O_{2D,i,j} \ldots O_{2D,i,n}\}$ with n being the number of ellipses and $O_{2D,i,j}$ being an ellipse whose parameters are $a \in S_a$ and $b \in S_b$.

Note that our fitting algorithm is different from computing the osculating ellipse [18]. The osculating ellipse has a 4th-order contact at the midpoint of the segment $e_{2D,i}$ of the curve C_{2D}; this implies that the second derivatives of the curvature are equal [16]. In our case, the ellipses have only 2nd-order contact since we only require the curvatures and the tangent of the curves to be equal. As the 2nd-order contact is less restrictive, a large number of ellipses will be taken into account for next step to compute the osculating circles. If we compute the osculating ellipse and the part of curve has some noise, it could happen that this ellipse is not a good approximation of the osculating circle, making the reconstruction of the 3D curve very difficult.

5   Finding the Osculating Circles

The next step is to compute the osculating circles for each segment $s_{3D,i}$ of the curve C_{3D} using the set of ellipses $S_{O,2D,i} = \{O_{2D,i,1} \dots O_{2D,i,j} \dots O_{2D,i,n}\}$ that has been computed for each segment $s_{2D,i}$ of the curve C_{2D}. Each of these ellipses is the orthogonal projection of a circle with a specific radius and orientation with respect to the projection plane. Let $S_{O,3D,i} = \{O_{3D,i,1} \dots O_{3D,i,j} \dots O_{3D,i,n}\}$ be the set of circles whose orthogonal projection are the ellipses of the set $S_{O,2D,i}$; these are the candidates for the osculating circles at the midpoint of the segment $s_{3D,i}$. We now aim at selecting one of them such that the change of curvature is minimized along the C_{3D} curve.

Minimizing the change of the curvature implies that two neighboring segments $s_{3D,i}$ and $s_{3D,i+1}$ should have their osculating circle with similar radius, center, orientation and center. This means that we should select one circles in each set $S_{O,3D,i}$ and $S_{O,3D,i+1}$ such that the difference of the radius, orientation and center is the smallest possible. This is a combinatorial problem that we solve using Dijkstra's algorithm.

5.1   Construction of the Graph

We first build a graph whose nodes are the candidates for the osculating circles. The set of nodes is defined as the union of all the sets $S_{E,3D,i}$ for the midpoint of each segment $e_{3D,i}$ of the curve C_{3D} : $S_{O,3D,1} \cup S_{O,3D,2} \dots \cup S_{O,3D,m} = \{O_{3D,1,1} \dots O_{3D,i,j} \dots O_{3D,p,n}\}$. The edges of this graph correspond to the neighboring relationship between adjacent segments along the curve C_{3D}. An edge is put between two nodes $O_{3D,i,k}$ and $O_{3D,j,l}$ if the two corresponding segments $e_{3D,i}$ and $e_{3D,j}$ are adjacent along the curve C_{3D}. The construction of the graph as shown in Fig. 3.

A weight is associated with each edge to determine how similar the two osculating circles are. Let $O_{3D,i,j}$ and $O_{3D,i+1,k}$ be the osculating circles of two neighboring segments $e_{3D,i}$ and $e_{3D,i+1}$ respectively. Let $r_{3D,i,j}$, $c_{3D,i,j}$, $N_{3D,i,j}$ and $T_{3D,i,j}$ be the radius, center, binormal and tangent of the osculating circle $O_{3D,i,j}$ and $r_{3D,i+1,j}$, $c_{3D,i+1,j}$, $N_{3D,i+1,j}$ and $T_{3D,i,j+1}$ the radius, center, binormal and tangent vectors of the osculating circle $O_{3D,i+1,j}$. Let $\alpha_{i,j,i+1,k}$ be the angle between $N_{3D,i,j}$ and $N_{3D,i+1,j}$ and $\beta_{i,j,i+1,k}$ the angle between $T_{3D,i,j}$ and $T_{3D,i+1,j}$. The weight is calculated with a cost function $W_O(\ )$

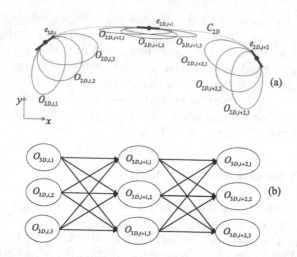

Fig. 3. The graph to compute the osculating circles. For the sake of clarity, the curve C_{2D} is composed of 3 segments only and a subset of the ellipses is shown.

which takes into account the difference of radii and center as well as the misalignment of the binormal and tangent of the osculating circles:

$$W_O\left(r_{3D,i+1,j}, r_{3D,i,j}, c_{3D,i+1,j}, c_{3D,i,j}, \alpha_{i,j,i+1,k}\right) = \delta\left((r_{3D,i+1,j} - r_{3D,i,j})^2\right.$$
$$\left. + |c_{3D,i+1,j} - c_{3D,i,j}|^2\right) + (1 - \delta)\left(\alpha_{i,j,i+1,k}^2 + \beta_{i,j,i+1,k}^2\right) \quad (5)$$

with δ being a user-defined parameter to put more weight on the radii and center difference or the binormal and tangent misalignment.

5.2 Using the Dijkstra's Algorithm to Compute the Osculating Circles

We use Dijkstra's algorithm to compute the optimal osculating circle for every segment $e_{3D,i}$ of the C_{3D} curve. For a given source node in a weighted graph, this algorithm finds the shortest path between that node and every other node. We have implemented a modified version of this algorithm as follows. The source is the set of osculating circle candidates $S_{O,3D,1} = \{O_{3D,1,1} \ldots O_{3D,1,j} \ldots O_{3D,1,n}\}$ of the first segment of the curve $e_{3D,1}$. The target is the set of osculating circle candidates $S_{O,3D,p-1} = \{O_{3D,p-1,1} \ldots O_{3D,p-1,j} \ldots O_{3D,p-1,n}\}$ of the last segment $s_{3D,p-1}$. Initially, all the nodes are in the unvisited node set, except those belonging to the source set $S_{O,3D,1}$. The nodes of this source set are given the distance 0. The algorithm works iteratively. It finds the unvisited node v with the minimal distance value; this distance value is computed using the weight of the associated edge. This node is then removed from the unvisited node set. The algorithm stops when one of the nodes of the target set $S_{O,3D,p-1}$ is visited.

The result of Dijkstra's algorithm is an approximation of the osculating circle for each vertex of the curve C_{3D}. These osculating circles provide an estimation of the tangent $T_{3D,i}$ at the midpoint of each segment $e_{3D,i}$ of the curve C_{3D}.

6   Reconstruction of the 3D Curve Using the Estimated Tangent at the Segments

The last step of the 3D reconstruction is to compute the z-coordinates of all the points $v_{3D,i}$ of curve C_{3D}. The x and y coordinates are the same as the corresponding point $v_{2D,i}$ in the curve C_{2D} since the curve C_{2D} is the orthogonal projection of C_{3D} onto the (x, y) plane.

The z-coordinates are computed iteratively starting from the first endpoint $v_{2D,1}$. Its z-coordinate is set to 0.0. The z-coordinate of a point $v_{2D,i+1}$ is computed by adding a value Δz_{i+1} to the z-coordinate of the previous point $v_{2D,i}$. This value Δz_{i+1} is defined using the estimated tangent $T_{3D,i}$ at the midpoint of the segment $e_{2D,i}$ as follows:

$$\Delta z_{i+1} = \frac{\|v_{2D,i+1} - v_{2D,i}\|}{\sqrt{(x_{T3D,i})^2 + (y_{T3D,i})^2}} z_{T3D,i}, \tag{6}$$

with $x_{T3D,i}$, $y_{T3D,i}$ and $z_{T3D,i}$ being the x, y and z coordinates of $T_{3D,i}$ respectively.

7   Results

Our method has been implemented in Python and has been tested with a variety of curves. The results are shown in Fig. 4. For each reconstruction, we provide the input curve, three views of the reconstructed 3D curve, and the graphs for the curvature and torsion of the reconstructed curve. These curvature and torsion values are calculated with respect to the arclength. The computation time ranges from 10 to 60 s depending on the number of points of the input curve. The number of points of all the curves ranges from 30 to 200.

7.1   Reconstruction of Helices, Spirals, and Hand-Drawn Curves

Helices are 3D curves whose curvature and torsion are constant. Figure 4(a) shows the reconstruction from a 2D curve which is the orthogonal projection of a helix with different orientations. The projected curve has been uniformly resampled before the reconstruction. The curvature and torsion of the helix are $4.65 \cdot 10^{-2}$ and $1.17 \cdot 10^{-2}$ respectively. As one may observe, the curvature of the reconstructed curve is very close to that of the helix. The value of torsion is less accurate. This is because the torsion of the curve is not taken into account during the reconstruction process. The reconstruction has been done with other curves. In Fig. 4(b), and Fig. 4(c), we apply the reconstruction to curves that are a 2D Euler spiral (b), and a hand-drawn curve (c). Similarly to the reconstruction of

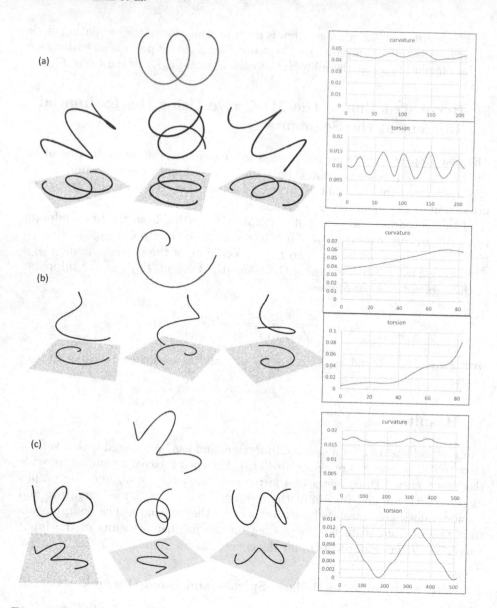

Fig. 4. Reconstruction using: the orthogonal projection of a helix with different orientation (a), 2D Euler spiral (b) and using hand-drawn curve (c).

helices, our algorithm is able to generate a 3D curve whose variation of curvature is small along the curve. Additional results are presented in the supplemental materials.

7.2   Limitations

The user is required to provide the lower and upper bounds of the helix parameters. The reconstruction fails in case these values are not properly set. One solution could be to compute a first reconstruction with large upper and lower bounds. These values can then be refined iteratively with trials and errors. The reconstruction does not work for some specific curves. The first case concerns curves with G_1 discontinuity, that is, curves with sharp corners. This is because our method requires the curvature values to be defined at every segment; this is needed for the ellipse fitting (see Sect. 4). The second case concerns connected segments whose curvature is null; this happens when the curve is composed of several points that are colinear. This set of consecutive colinear segments is actually the projection of a straight line in 3D; our method is not able to reconstruct straight lines in 3D since osculating circles are not defined for straight lines. On the other hand, our method handles a single segment whose curvature is null; these segments are usually located at the inflection point of the curve.

8   Conclusion

We have described a method to compute that generates a curve whose curvature variation is minimized and such that its orthogonal projection fits a planar polygonal curve. There are several paths of future work. One possible improvement would be to take into account the variation of the torsion in addition to the curvature. Another future work would be to extend the method to handle the reconstruction of close curves.

Acknowledgements. This research has been supported by the French Ministry of Higher Education, Research, and Innovation.

References

1. Ali, S.G., et al.: Cost-effective broad learning-based ultrasound biomicroscopy with 3D reconstruction for ocular anterior segmentation. Multimed. Tools Appl. **80**, 35105–35122 (2021)
2. Arora, R., Singh, K.: Mid-air drawing of curves on 3D surfaces in virtual reality. ACM Trans. Graph. (TOG) **40**(3), 1–17 (2021)
3. Bae, S.H., Balakrishnan, R., Singh, K.: ILoveSketch: as-natural-as-possible sketching system for creating 3D curve models. In: Proceedings of the 21st Annual ACM Symposium on User Interface Software and Technology, pp. 151–160 (2008)
4. Chen, J., Zhang, Y., Zhang, Z., Pan, Y., Yao, T.: 3D-producer: a hybrid and user-friendly 3D reconstruction system. In: Fang, L., Povey, D., Zhai, G., Mei, T., Wang, R. (eds.) CICAI 2022. LNCS, vol. 13606, pp. 526–531. Springer, Cham (2022). https://doi.org/10.1007/978-3-031-20503-3_43
5. Cherin, N., Cordier, F., Melkemi, M.: Modeling piecewise helix curves from 2D sketches. Comput. Aided Des. **46**, 258–262 (2014)

6. Cohen, J.M., Markosian, L., Zeleznik, R.C., Hughes, J.F., Barzel, R.: An interface for sketching 3D curves. In: Proceedings of the 1999 Symposium on Interactive 3D Graphics, pp. 17–21 (1999)
7. Cordier, F., Melkemi, M., Seo, H.: Reconstruction of helices from their orthogonal projection. Comput. Aided Geom. Design **46**, 1–15 (2016)
8. Cordier, F., Seo, H., Melkemi, M., Sapidis, N.S.: Inferring mirror symmetric 3D shapes from sketches. Comput. Aided Des. **45**(2), 301–311 (2013)
9. Fei Mai, Y.: 3D curves reconstruction from multiple images. In: DICTA, pp. 462–467 (2010)
10. Hähnlein, F., Gryaditskaya, Y., Sheffer, Alla, A.B.: Symmetry-driven 3D reconstruction from concept sketches. In: SIGGRAPH (Conference Paper Track), vol. 19, pp. 1–19 (2022)
11. Iarussi, E., Bommes, D., Bousseau, A.: BendFields: regularized curvature fields from rough concept sketches. ACM Trans. Graph. (TOG) **34**(3), 1–16 (2015)
12. Kim, Yongkwan, S.H.B.: SketchingWithHands: 3D sketching handheld products with first-person hand posture. In: UIST, pp. 797–808 (2016)
13. Krs, V., Yumer, E., Carr, N., Benes, B., Měch, R.: Skippy: single view 3D curve interactive modeling. ACM Trans. Graph. (TOG) **36**(4), 1–12 (2017)
14. Lewiner, T., Gomes Jr., J.D., Lopes, H., Craizer, M.: Curvature and torsion estimators based on parametric curve fitting. Comput. Graph. **29**(5), 641–655 (2005)
15. Li, W.: Pen2VR: a smart pen tool interface for wire art design in VR. In: STAG, pp. 119–127 (2021)
16. Rutter, J.: Geometry of Curves. CRC Press, Boca Raton (2000)
17. Shetty, V., et al.: CT-based 3D reconstruction of lower limb versus X-ray-based 3D reconstruction: a comparative analysis and application for a safe and cost-effective modality in TKA. Indian J. Orthop. **55**, 1150–1157 (2021)
18. Williamson, B.: An Elementary Treatise on the Differential Calculus: Containing the Theory of Plane Curves, with Numerous Examples. Longmans (1912)
19. Ye, H., Kwan, K., Fu, H.: 3D curve creation on and around physical objects with mobile AR. IEEE Trans. Visual Comput. Graphics **28**(8), 2809–2821 (2021)
20. Yu, E., Arora, R., Stanko, T., Bærentzen, J.A., Singh, K., Bousseau, A.: Cassie: curve and surface sketching in immersive environments. In: CHI, vol. 190, pp. 1–190 (2021)
21. Zhou, Y., Zhao, J., Luo, C.: A novel method for reconstructing general 3D curves from stereo images. Vis. Comput. **37**, 2009–2021 (2021)

Audio-Driven Lips and Expression on 3D Human Face

Le Ma[1,2], Zhihao Ma[1,2], Weiliang Meng[1,2(✉)], Shibiao Xu[3(✉)], and Xiaopeng Zhang[1,2]

[1] State Key Laboratory of Multimodal Artificial Intelligence Systems, Institute of Automation, Chinese Academy of Sciences, Beijing, China
weiliang.meng@ia.ac.cn
[2] School of Artificial Intelligence, University of Chinese Academy of Sciences, Beijing, China
[3] School of Artificial Intelligence, Beijing University of Posts and Telecommunications, Beijing, China
shibiaoxu@bupt.edu.cn

Abstract. Extensive research has delved into audio-driven 3D facial animation with numerous attempts to achieve human-like performance. However, creating truly realistic and expressive 3D facial animations remains a challenging task, as existing methods often struggle to capture the subtle nuances of anthropomorphic expressions. We propose the Audio-Driven Lips and Expression (ADLE) method, specifically designed to generate highly expressive and lifelike conversations between individuals, complete with essential social signals like laughter and excitement, solely based on audio cues. The foundation of our approach lies in the revolutionary audio-expression-consistency strategy, which effectively disentangles person-specific lip movements from dependent facial expressions. As a result, our ADLE robustly learns lip movements and generic expression parameters on a 3D human face from an audio sequence, which represents a powerful multimodal fusion approach capable of generating accurate lip movements paired with vivid facial expressions on a 3D face, all in real-time. Experiments validates that our ADLE outperforms other state-of-the-art works in this field, making it a highly promising approach for a wide range of applications.

Keywords: Face Expression · Lips Movement · Fusion

1 Introduction

Over the past few years, virtual reality technology has experienced remarkable advancements, thanks to innovations such as 3D human body pose estimation [13,14] and 3D video technology [26]. There have been significant improvements in audio-driven 3D facial animation, but achieving realistic, human-like performance is still a challenging problem, especially for generating natural expressions and lip motions simultaneously on the 3D human face [25]. While

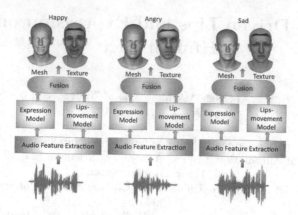

Fig. 1. Our Audio Driving Lips and Expression (ADLE) architecture can predict facial coefficients for 3D face animation only based on the audio. Face images are rendered from coefficients generated by the FLAME [17] model, and here we show 3 expressions generated by our ADLE.

some methods exist for re-targeting lip motion and expression to a character model via audio controls, these often result in unnatural-looking lip movements. Moreover, current 3D face animation methods pay little attention to estimating the 3D properties of faces from audio.

In this context, we propose a new architecture called Audio-Driven Lips and Expression (ADLE), which can generate accurate lip movements and real expressions from an audio sequence and the FLAME model [17]. Our novel approach uses a multimodal fusion strategy based on our groundbreaking audio-expression-consistency technique. This disentangles person-specific lips from dependent expressions, enabling our method to robustly learn lip movements and generic expression parameters on a 3D human face from an audio sequence. In the field of cartoon animations or virtual worlds featuring non-realistic avatars, excessively detailed facial features may not take center stage. Instead, we can effectively express emotions through minimalist facial animations.

Our ADLE approach outperforms other state-of-the-art methods in generating anthropomorphic 3D face animation with accurate lip movements and rich expression details, including happy and surprised states. Our work has the potential to revolutionize the way we create lifelike 3D facial animations, bringing a new level of realism and expressiveness to the art of visual storytelling, especially in VR headsets and eye tracking on several developer-focused AR/VR devices. The architecture of our ADLE is illustrated in Fig. 1.

In summary, the main contributions of our work are:

- We propose a new architecture 'ADLE' to learn an animatable anthropomorphic 3D face model from the audio sequence, which takes advantage of the locality and shift invariance in the frequency domain of the audio signal and automatically generates accurate lip movements and vivid facial expressions on the 3D face from audio in real-time.

- We build an audio-to-expression dataset by collecting 3D facial expression sequences together with audio, which has 6 females, 6 males and 8 emotions. Unlike any existing public datasets, it can train audio-to-expression models with lips movements.
- We implement comprehensive experiments for our ADLE, validating that our method can outperform other state-of-the-art methods.

2   Relate Work

Traditional Audio-Driven Animation: Traditional audio-driven methods produce lip movements of acceptable quality for low-fidelity stylized avatars. Ezzat et al. [8] utilize machine learning techniques to develop a speech animation module that generates realistic video output. Early works in this field, such as those by Vougioukas et al. [16] and Cosker et al. [6], also demonstrate audio-driven animation on photorealistic avatars using active appearance models and offline methods to synthesize coherent texture maps and stitch various facial regions together. Different from the work of [23], our approach involves using speech signals to exclusively regulate the movement of the upper half of the face, then blend lip movement. Moreover, we add the texture mapping on the 3D face to validate the effectiveness of our ADLE visual results.

Deep Learning Audio-Driven Animation: **Audio-to-lips dataset.** The B3D(AC)2 dataset [9] comprises a vast collection of audio-4D scan pairs of 40 spoken English sentences, but it suffers from noticeable artefacts. On the other hand, the 4DFAB dataset [4] has only 9-word utterances per subject, and the mesh quality is inferior. In comparison, VOCASET [7] includes 255 unique sentences, 12 subjects, and 480 sequences of approximately 3–4 s each. The sentences were chosen from a variety of standard protocols to ensure maximum phonetic diversity. To enable training on a large number of sentences and subjects, VOCASET shares some sentences across subjects and has some sentences spoken by only one subject. Additionally, VOCASET offers higher-quality scans, with 4D scans captured at 60fps, and alignment information.

Audio-to-Expression Dataset. The expression data can be obtained from various sources such as D3DFACS [5], which can have similar neighbouring frames in 3D sequences without associated speech or audio sequences. To address this, Li et al. [17] propose the FLAME model (Faces Learned with an Articulated Model and Expressions) that separates identity, pose, and facial expression representation, similar to human body models [19]. Additionally, FaceWareHouse [3] is a 3D facial expression database that provides facial geometry of 150 subjects with diverse ages and ethnic backgrounds. The Basel Face Model (BFM) [20] expresses different identities' faces as linear combinations of principal components. However, none of these datasets contains audio sequences that correspond to their 3D facial models of expressions, limiting their use in expression model training.

Audio-and-Image-Driven Animation Methods. Hai et al. [21,22] propose 3D facial animation methods that use a deep learning framework to generate facial expressions from audio signals only. Zhang et al. [27] present a talking face generation method that takes both audio signals and a short target video clip as input to synthesize a photo-realistic video of the target face with natural lip movements. Abdelaziz et al. [12] introduce a novel deep-learning approach for driving animated faces using both acoustic and visual information. However, these methods have limitations in terms of incomplete facial animation, specifically in regards to lip movement and expression, and also rely on both audio and image information for facial animation, whereas our method only employs audio signals for generating 3D facial animation.

3   Method

To improve the handling of 3D facial animation, it is commonly agreed that the face deformation can be represented by a restricted subspace, and 3D Morphable Models (3DMM) [2] can be learned from a limited number of 3D facial datasets in a neutral expression. Many state-of-the-art approaches [24] based on 3DMM rely heavily on such priors and have shown impressive results. However, these methods have limited generalizability in modeling the restricted low-dimensional subspace for our 3D facial animation. On the other hand, FLAME (Faces Learned with an Articulated Model and Expressions) [17] is an advanced model for face representation that expands the 3DMM and is more suitable for 3D face animation. The FLAME model [17] combines linear blend skinning (LBS) for head and jaw motion with linear PCA spaces to represent expression shape variations.

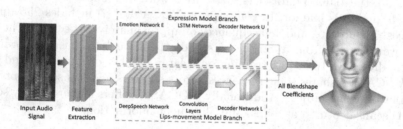

Fig. 2. Our 'Audio-Driven Lips and Expression' (ADLE) architecture. After the feature extraction on the input audio signal, two branches include the lips-movement model branch and the expression model branch are employed to generate the final face animation.

3.1   Overview

Although the audio signal strongly correlates with lip and lower-face movements, generating talking faces based on only these movements results in stiff and unnatural animations. To overcome this issue, we propose a new architecture called Audio-Driven Lips and Expression (ADLE) that produces natural-looking facial animations with realistic lip movements and expressions based on speech. To generate lip movements, our ADLE uses an arbitrary speech signal and a static character mesh (like FLAME) to output natural-looking lips movements with good lip closure, similar to the VOCA model [7]. However, the animation still appears stiff without expression. To address this, we use our expression model in ADLE to learn emotional feature vectors from the speech and generate 3D facial expressions that mainly act on the upper half of the face, resulting in a more natural and realistic 3D facial animation. Figure 2 illustrates our ADLE architecture.

3.2 Feature Extraction

Since the shape of the audio signal directly affects the produced sound, it is crucial to accurately extract the features that represent the phoneme being produced. The state-of-the-art technique in this field is Mel-frequency cepstral coefficients (MFCCs), which is used to extract audio features for our speech recognition task. The resulting MFCCs can then be fed into both the lips movement and expression models in parallel, as illustrated in Fig. 2.

3.3 Lips Movements

The objective for generating lip movements is to create a realistic talking mouth that varies in shape and motion depending on the speaker's audio input. To achieve this, we incorporate DeepSpeech [1] into our lip movement model, which is a straightforward architecture consisting of five hidden layers. The first three layers are fully connected layers with relu activation, while the fourth layer is a bidirectional RNN. The last fully connected layer with relu activation takes the character distribution as input and output probabilities. We replace the fourth RNN layer with LSTM in practice and use the 26 MFCC audio features to speed up and improve the network's accuracy, rather than performing direct inference on the spectrogram.

The output of the DeepSpeech network is an array with dimensions $W \times D$, where W is the window size, and D is the number of characters in the alphabet, along with an additional blank label, blank space label, and repeat mark label. This means that, for the English language, D is equal to 29. This array passes through an encoder network (convolution layers) and decoder network L, generating a 5023×3 dimensional array of vertex displacements from T to integrate time information. As our lip movements are similar to those in [7], this array represents a 3D face in "zero poses".

3.4 Expression

Face Expression Representation. To enhance the realism of our face animation, we have developed an expression model branch that uses the MFCC features extracted from the audio as input to generate facial expressions. Our expression model assigns the vertices of a 3D mesh to the corresponding 3D facial expressions, as follows:

$$\mathbf{v}(\mathbf{x}) = \mathbf{b}_0 + \mathbf{B}\mathbf{x} \tag{1}$$

where b_0 is the neutral expression mesh, $\mathbf{B}$ defines the additive deviations from FACS-based expression mesh b_0 (blendshapes), and x is the blendshape coefficients vector. Our objective is to use the corresponding blendshape coefficients to transfer facial motion based on audio to the FLAME model. As this task involves regression, training a network using manually marked coefficients would be expensive and time-consuming. Instead, we estimate the blendshape coefficients dataset to audio using an extension of the method proposed in [11], then modify the generic blendshape model to match each facial expression. We first extract the MFCC features from the audio signal and the 3D facial expression coefficients of the FLAME model. Then, we design an architecture network relative to expression to establish the mapping between them.

Given the MFCC features of an audio sequence $\mathbf{S} = \{s^{(1)}, \ldots, s^{(T)}\}$, with its corresponding ground-truth expression coefficients $\boldsymbol{\psi} = \{\psi^{(1)}, \ldots, \psi^{(T)}\}$, and the predicted expression coefficients $\tilde{\boldsymbol{\psi}} = \{\tilde{\psi}^{(1)}, \ldots, \tilde{\psi}^{(T)}\}$, our audio-to-expression mapping can be formulated as:

$$\tilde{\psi}^{(t)} = U\left(E\left(s^{(t)}\right)\right) \tag{2}$$

where E denotes the emotion network and U denotes the decoder network in our expression model branch, as shown in Fig. 2.

Implementation. The objective of our expression model branch is to acquire the blendshape coefficients from audio signals to animate 3D facial expressions with speech. Firstly, we extract the MFCC features from the audio sequence, then we apply four 2D convolutional blocks separately on the frequency and time axes as the emotion network of our framework to avoid overfitting. To enhance the training and inference speed, we use a smaller kernel size of 3 for each convolutional block with a stride of 1, following the approaches in [15,22]. Moreover, we apply dropout to prevent overfitting and use the relu activation function. We integrate LSTM layers after the emotion networks to estimate the facial expression transformation in real time. Finally, the output of the LSTM is fed to another dense layer, called decoder network U, with a linear activation function to extract the coefficients $\psi \in \mathbb{R}^{50}$.

Expression Loss. We design a mean squared error (MSE) loss function for expression coefficients containing two loss terms to optimize our network as follows:

$$\mathcal{L}(U, E) = \mathbb{E}_{\psi}\left[(\psi - \phi(\mathbf{s}))^2\right]$$

$$+ \lambda \mathbb{E}_t\left[\sum_{t=0}^{T}\left(\phi(\mathbf{s})^{(t)} - \phi(\mathbf{s})^{(t-1)}\right)^2\right] \tag{3}$$

where $\phi(\mathbf{s}) = \widetilde{\psi}$ that is given in Eq. 2. The first term $\mathbb{E}_\psi$ measures the MSE loss between our emotion model's output and the ground-truth of expression blendshape coefficients, while the second term $\lambda \mathbb{E}_t$ is the inter-frame smooth loss computed by the squared L_2 norm, and λ is the weight of sequences information error. The loss function ensures the accuracy of results and temporal stability.

3.5 Fusion

The goal of fusion is to combine lip movements and expressions for a more realistic final facial animation. The lips movements are generated by the lower part of the face, while the expressions are audio-driven emotions that affect other parts of the face, such as the eyes, eyebrows, and nose. Both the lips-movement model branch and the expression model branch generate blend shape coefficients, which are fused to create the final face animation. The lips-movement model branch focuses on driving the lip's movements, while the expression model branch generates coefficients for other parts of the face. To generate the lips movements, our method is similar to VOCA [7], which learns the causal facial motions from speech and only applies to the lower face. Our facial expression can be altered using the blend weights, or expression blendshapes coefficients, which are learned from our audio-to-expression dataset based on our expression model branch (shown in Fig. 2). The expression blendshapes organization structure is the same as that provided by FLAME [17].

During inference, our ADLE generates a 3D facial model with the same mesh topology as the FLAME face mesh, which is compatible with FLAME, allowing for identity-dependent facial expression alteration by modifying the learned expression blendshapes coefficients and simultaneously fusing lips-movement.

4 Experiments

4.1 Constructing Our Dataset

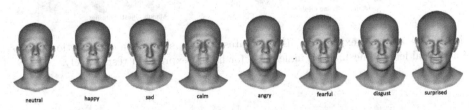

neutral   happy   sad   calm   angry   fearful   disgust   surprised

Fig. 3. Our dataset contains 8 different expressions of the 3D head as the basic expression of humans, and all the other expressions can be generated based on our ADLE architecture.

Our lips-movement dataset is constructed based on VOCASET [7], which comprises audio-4D scan pairs of 6 female and 6 male subjects. For each subject, we collect 40 English sentences of 3–5 s, capturing 3D meshes at 60fps. After processing, we register the raw 3D scans to the FLAME model, with all meshes in "zero poses" after removing global rotation, translation, and head rotation around the neck, as in [7]. To initialize the expression parameters ψ, we use DECA's algorithm [10] to establish a correspondence between the FLAME head template and audio sequences. While this initial expression basis does not satisfy our requirements for orthogonality and expression realism, it provides a useful starting point (Fig. 4).

Our objective is to reproduce people's expressions while ensuring that the lips move in sync with the audio. Since audio-to-lips movement mainly involves the lower part of the face, we avoid excessive interference with other parts of the face, such as the nose, eyes, and eyebrows, which primarily reflect non-lips expressions when speaking. Thus, we carefully adjust the initial meshes.

For our audio-to-expression 3D face dataset, we collect 6 female and 6 male subjects, The choice to incorporate a dataset comprising 8 distinct facial expressions primarily stemmed from the dataset's remarkable abundance and diversity. each displaying eight emotions, including neutral, happy, sad, calm, angry, fearful, disgust, and surprise, as shown in Fig. 3. Our dataset's scan speed is 50 fps, with 3-s-long mesh sequences accurately capturing audio-to-3D facial expressions, including blendshape coefficients $\psi \in \mathbb{R}^{50}$. Since VOCA requires the mouth to be in "zero poses", i.e. facial expression does not affect lips movement, we finetune our dataset to minimize the impact on lips movement with the help of an artist.

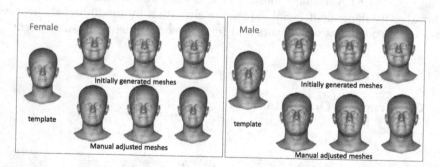

Fig. 4. Our audio-to-expression 3D face dataset. Here shows the construction results of a typical female mesh and a male mesh for happy expression respectively.

4.2   Training Details

We have divided our ADLE training into two tasks: training the lips-movement model branch and training the expression model branch. The training process for the lips-movement model branch is similar to that of [7] using the VOCASET. To train the expression model branch, we first ensure the accuracy of the emotion recognition network E on audio datasets, including RAVDESS [18]. Once we obtain the parameters for E, we proceed to train our expression model branch on our audio-to-expression 3D face dataset, using $\lambda = 0.1$ in Eq. 3. The input to the model is an audio feature vector processed by MFCCs, and the output is the coefficient vector $\psi \in \mathbb{R}^{50}$. We train our expression model for 500 epochs.

4.3 Evaluation

Quantitative evaluations such as forecast error and MES error are still being explored. Instead, we can make a perceptual assessment of the animation quality. Our trained model can be directly compared to the VOCA model [7], actor performance speech style, and different talking subjects. To ensure the validity and reliability of our visual evaluation, we carried out a comprehensive 3D face study involving a diverse panel of skilled artists and designers specializing in image processing and 3D animation. Additionally, we furnish a collection of audio-to-3D facial expressions to facilitate a comparative analysis against our network output outcomes.

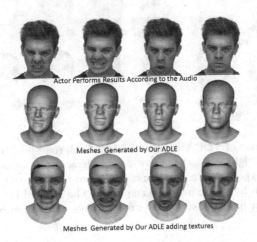

Fig. 5. The Comparison results of actor performs to our ADLE's according to the audio which expresses an 'angry' tone. Top: four frame renderings randomly intercepted from the video performed by the actor. Middle: our ADLE's output at the same frame using the same audio sequence. Bottom: adding the actor's face textures on the meshes in the middle row.

Comparison. We conduct a comparison between our ADLE and the state-of-the-art in realistic subject-specific audio-driven facial animation, VOCA [7]. To ensure a fair comparison, we align the FLAME topology and use 8 audio sequences containing different sequences of different actors to animate the static mesh with the same topology of the FLAME model. The results are shown in Fig. 6.

Comparison to the Actor Performance: We compared the testing results of our ADLE predictions with the effects produced by professional actors in the same audio sequences.

The texture's intricacies are delicately adjusted to capture the nuances of the upper half of the face, primarily focusing on the distinctions in eyebrows and eyes. Upon adding the texture, it influences the expression, resulting in noticeable changes. In the future, we plan to conduct quantitative experiments to assess the efficacy of our approach.

We compare processed testing results with our ADLE predictions and performed effects by professional actors in the same audio sequences as shown in Fig. 5. We can see that our ADLE's results in speech-driven 3D facial animation are similar to the actors as a whole. After adding the textures on the mesh shown in the third row of Fig. 5, the lip movements and expressions resemble the real actor's performance.

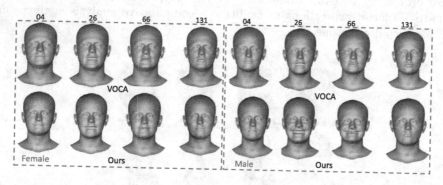

Fig. 6. The comparison of VOCA and our ADLE. Each row shows the initial states of a subject (left), and right is another three randomly selected animation frames drive by the audio which expresses a 'happy' tone. Note that both the outputs of VOCA and our ADLE are driven by the same audio sequence. The left red box shows the female meshes, and the right blue box shows are male meshes. (Color figure online)

5   Discussion

Our ADLE method can generate realistic facial animation for a wide range of adult faces based on audio sequences. For comparison, the state-of-the-art method VOCA only learns causal facial motions from speech, mostly present in the lower face. In contrast, our ADLE generates facial animation not only for the lips movements but also for the expressions learned from audio sequences. To ensure that the lips movements and expressions do not conflict with each other, we build an audio-to-expression dataset that does not include lips movement and a fusion algorithm that separates the two when necessary. However, we still need to address the issue of the mouth opening wider than usual when other facial units are relaxed, especially during very happy or angry speech.

One drawback of our method is that changes in expressions can only be detected through the eyes or face, which usually do not undergo significant geometric changes. This is because the 3D face mesh we use is not detailed enough, particularly for parts that undergo drastic changes during an expression, such as the eyebrows. Using more detailed meshes will improve the quality and realism of our ADLE method and surpass other state-of-the-art works.

6 Conclusion

We propose an innovative architecture, called Audio-Driven Lips and Expression' or ADLE', which enables the fast and precise generation of 3D human face animation with both lip movements and expressions using audio inputs only. Our ADLE learns lip animation and expression parameters from the audio sequence by leveraging a novel audio-expression-consistency strategy, while it can automatically generate accurate lip movements and vivid facial expressions on a 3D face from an audio sequence. Experiments validate that our ADLE outperforms other state-of-the-art methods.

Acknowledgements. This work was supported by the National Natural Science Foundation of China (Nos. 62376271, 62171321, 62162044, 62271074, 6226070885, and U22B2034).

References

1. Amodei, D., Ananthanarayanan, S., et al.: Deep speech 2: end-to-end speech recognition in English and mandarin. In: Proceedings of the 33rd International Conference on International Conference on Machine Learning, pp. 173–182 (2016)
2. Blanz, V., Vetter, T.: A morphable model for the synthesis of 3D faces. In: Proceedings of the 26th Annual Conference on Computer Graphics and Interactive Techniques, pp. 187–194 (1999)
3. Cao, C., Weng, Y., et al.: FaceWarehouse: a 3D facial expression database for visual computing. TVCG **20**(3), 413–425 (2014)
4. Cheng, S., Kotsia, I., et al.: 4DFAB: a large scale 4D database for facial expression analysis and biometric applications. In: CVPR (2018)
5. Cosker, D., Krumhuber, E., Hilton, A.: A FACS valid 3D dynamic action unit database with applications to 3D dynamic morphable facial modeling. In: ICCV, pp. 2296–2303 (2011)
6. Cosker, D.P., Marshall, A.D., et al.: Video realistic talking heads using hierarchical non-linear speech-appearance models. In: In MIRAGE (2003)
7. Cudeiro, D., Bolkart, T., et al.: Capture, learning, and synthesis of 3D speaking styles. In: CVPR (2019)
8. Ezzat, T., Geiger, G., Poggio, T.: Trainable videorealistic speech animation. In: Proceedings of the 29th Annual Conference on Computer Graphics and Interactive Techniques, pp. 388–398 (2002)
9. Fanelli, G., Gall, J., et al.: A 3-D audio-visual corpus of affective communication. IEEE Trans. Multimed. **12**(6), 591–598 (2010)

10. Feng, Y., Feng, H., Black, M.J., Bolkart, T.: Learning an animatable detailed 3D face model from in-the-wild images. ACM Trans. Graph. **40**(4), 1–13 (2021)

11. H. Li, J. Yu, Y.Y., Bregler, C.: Realtime facial animation with on-the-fly correctives. ACM Trans. Graph. **32**(4), 1–10 (2013). Article No. 42

12. Hussen Abdelaziz, A., Theobald, B.J., et al.: Modality dropout for improved performance-driven talking faces. In: Proceedings of the 2020 International Conference on Multimodal Interaction, pp. 378–386 (2020)

13. Xu, J., Liu, W., Xing, W., Wei, X.: MSPENet: multi-scale adaptive fusion and position enhancement network for human pose estimation. Vis. Comput. **39**, 1432–2315 (2023). https://doi.org/10.1007/s00371-022-02460-y

14. Kamel, A., Sheng, B., Li, P., Kim, J., Feng, D.D.: Hybrid refinement-correction heatmaps for human pose estimation. IEEE Trans. Multimed. **23**, 1330–1342 (2021). https://doi.org/10.1109/TMM.2020.2999181

15. Karras, T., Aila, T., et al.: Audio-driven facial animation by joint end-to-end learning of pose and emotion. ACM Trans. Graph. **36**(4), 1–12 (2017)

16. Konstantinos Vougioukas, S.P., Pantic, M.: Expressive speech-driven facial animation. ACM Trans. Graph. **24**, 1283–1302 (2005)

17. Li, T., Bolkart, T., et al.: Learning a model of facial shape and expression from 4D scans. ACM Trans. Graph. (Proc. SIGGRAPH Asia) **36**(6), 194:1–194:17 (2017)

18. Livingstone, S.R., Russo, F.A.: The Ryerson audio-visual database of emotional speech and song (RAVDESS): a dynamic, multimodal set of facial and vocal expressions in North American English. PLoS ONE **13**(5), 1–35 (2018)

19. Loper, M., Mahmood, N., et al.: SMPL: a skinned multi-person linear model. ACM Trans. Graph. (Proc. SIGGRAPH Asia) **34**(6), 248:1–248:16 (2015)

20. Paysan, P., Knothe, R., Amberg, B., Romdhani, S., Vetter, T.: A 3D face model for pose and illumination invariant face recognition (2009)

21. Pham, H.X., Wang, Y., Pavlovic, V.: End-to-end learning for 3D facial animation from speech. In: International Conference on Multimodal Interaction (2018)

22. Pham, H.X., Cheung, S., Pavlovic, V.: Speech-driven 3D facial animation with implicit emotional awareness: a deep learning approach. In: 2017 IEEE Conference on Computer Vision and Pattern Recognition Workshops (CVPRW), pp. 2328–2336 (2017)

23. Richard, A., Zollhöfer, M., Wen, Y., de la Torre, F., Sheikh, Y.: MeshTalk: 3D face animation from speech using cross-modality disentanglement. In: Proceedings of the IEEE/CVF International Conference on Computer Vision (ICCV), pp. 1173–1182 (2021)

24. Richardson, E., Sela, M., Or-El, R., Kimmel, R.: Learning detailed face reconstruction from a single image. In: CVPR (2017)

25. Yang, S., et al.: EnNeRFACE: improving the generalization of face reenactment with adaptive ensemble neural radiance fields. Vis. Comput. 1432–2315 (2022). https://doi.org/10.1007/s00371-022-02709-6

26. Simone Cammarasana, G.P.: Spatio-temporal analysis and comparison of 3D videos. Vis. Comput. **39**, 1432–2315 (2023). https://doi.org/10.1007/s00371-022-02409-1

27. Zhang, C., Zhao, Y., et al.: FACIAL: synthesizing dynamic talking face with implicit attribute learning. In: ICCV, pp. 3867–3876 (2021)

Multi-image 3D Face Reconstruction via an Adaptive Aggregation Network

Xiaoyu Chai[1,2], Jun Chen[1,2(✉)], Dongshu Xu[1,2], Hongdou Yao[1,2],
Zheng Wang[1,2], and Chia-Wen Lin[3]

[1] National Engineering Research Center for Multimedia Software,
School of Computer, Wuhan University, Wuhan, China
chenj.whu@gmail.com
[2] Hubei Key Laboratory of Multimedia and Network Communication Engineering,
Wuhan University, Wuhan, China
[3] Department of Electrical Engineering, National Tsinghua University,
Hsinchu 30013, Taiwan

Abstract. Image-based 3D face reconstruction suffers from inherent drawbacks of incomplete visible regions and interference from occlusion or lighting. One solution is to utilize multiple face images for collecting sufficient knowledges. Nevertheless, most existing methods typically do not make full use of information among different images since they roughly fuse the results of individual reconstructed face for multi-image 3D face modeling, thus may ignore the intrinsic relations within various images. To tackle this problem, we propose a framework named Adaptive Aggregation Network (ADANet) to investigate the subtle correlations among multiple images for 3D face reconstruction. Specifically, we devise an Aggregation Module that can adaptively establish both the in-face and cross-face relationships by exploiting the local- and long-range dependencies among visible facial regions of multiple images, thus can effectively extract complementary aggregation face features in the multi-image scenario. Furthermore, we incorporate contour-aware information to promote the boundary consistency of 3D face model. The seamless combination of these novel designs forms a more accurate and robust multi-image 3D face reconstruction scheme. Extensive experiments demonstrate the effectiveness of our proposed ADANet.

Keywords: 3D Face Reconstruction · Multiple Images · Adaptive Aggregation · Transformer

1 Introduction

In recent years, 3D-related studies have been a hot topic in computer vision and graphics communities, owing to the wide applications including [1, 8, 11, 16]. Particularly, reconstructing 3D face models from 2D images has attracted the interest of many researchers. Early approaches usually predict the parameters of 3D Morphable Model (3DMM) [17] for one facial image. Nevertheless, the

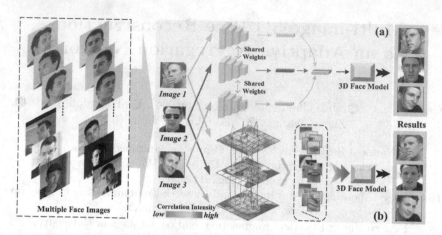

Fig. 1. For multi-image 3D face reconstruction, existing methods first extract image-wise features and then fuse them to predict the shared facial parameters. Such a 'simple-fusion' strategy not only underuses the information but is also susceptible to some factors in images, *e.g.* occlusions, as shown in (a). Our ADANet can adaptively aggregate information among multiple images by exploiting the local- and long-range correlations from in-face and cross-face aspects and prefer facial regions with higher correlation intensity to extract more complementary face features, as illustrated in (b). With this aggregation manner, we can obtain reconstructed 3D face with higher fidelity.

variations (*e.g.*, face rotation, occlusion, and illumination changes) in a single image often make only part of the face regions visible, thereby leading to many uncertainties. By contrast, multiple images of a subject (*e.g.*, image collections) provide more sufficient information of the face regions, which helps to eliminate ambiguity issues in a single-image scenario.

A variety of methods have been proposed to reconstruct high-fidelity 3D faces from multi-image data. A general way is to first employ the single-image based method, and then to fuse the results of each image to realize multi-image 3D face reconstruction, as shown in Fig. 1(a). For example, 3DMMCNN [25] first utilized Convolutional Neural Networks (CNN) to regress 3DMM parameters from one image, and then computed the weighted average of each parameter as a single identity vector of multi-image faces. Recent works try to exploit the geometric constraints among multiple images. MVFNet [26] designed a multi-view framework, in which view-consistency was maintained by a view alignment loss to generate consistent 3D face across views.

The aforementioned approaches have promoted multi-image 3D face reconstruction to reach a higher accuracy, but there still exist some drawbacks. On the one hand, most 3D face reconstructions with multiple images are based on conventional single-image methods but not fully considering the local- and long-range correlations, making them underuse the complementary information from multiple images, *e.g.* different facial parts may be presented in different images.

On the other hand, most current approaches often neglect or weaken the consistency between the boundaries of projected 3D models and input face silhouette by only using a pixel loss or landmark loss, which is usually insufficient to recover a high-fidelity face model. Very recently, attention-based architectures have been adopted to capture long-range correspondences among multiple inputs. Typically, for the current advanced transformer-based approaches such as ViT [9], the visible contents from distant regions can be aggregated with visual tokens. We propose a novel Adaptive Aggregation Network, namely ADANet, to address the above multi-image face reconstruction issues. Our ADANet can effectively establish contextual relations and capture complementary information within multiple facial images and aggregate them together by simultaneously exploiting the local- and long-range correlations from the in-face and cross-face in one or multiple images, as shown in Fig. 1(b). Besides, we incorporate contour-aware information to promote the facial geometric consistency of 3D models.

2   Proposed Method

The structure of our proposed method Adaptive Aggregation Network (ADANet) is illustrated in Fig. 2(a). The image encoder aims to extract face embedding of each image, as well as output multi-level features. Then the aggregation module, which consists of transformer blocks (TransBlk), learns to aggregate the complementary multi-image information by taking multi-level features and facial contour information into account. The renderer can project the 3D model to 2D plane for implementing a self-supervised end-to-end training scheme.

Specifically, ADANet takes $\mathbf{I} = \{I^1, I^2, \cdots, I^n\}$ with n different facial images as the inputs, each image $I \in \mathbb{R}^{H \times W \times 3}$ with height H and width W. Then, it produces a set of 3D models $\mathbf{M} = \{M^1, M^2, \cdots, M^n\}$ corresponding to each individual faces. The encoder $E_i(\cdot)$ outputs embeddings for each face $\mathbf{P} = \{P^1, P^2, \cdots, P^n\}$, containing pose, expression and lighting factors. It also extracts multi-level features $f_l \in \mathbb{R}^{h \times w \times c}$, where $h = H/2$, $w = W/2$ and $c = 385$, for generating visual tokens $\mathbf{T}$ across all regions. The contour information from $\mathbf{I}$ are integrated with $\mathbf{T}$, and then pass into the TransBlks to derive the shared face feature $f_s \in \mathbb{R}^{256}$. Finally, f_s and $\mathbf{P}$ are fed into a 3D reconstruction network $R_m(\cdot)$, as in [4,7], to produce 3D face models $\mathbf{M} = R_m(f_s, \mathbf{P})$, and the renderer $P_r(\cdot)$ generates the projected 2D face images $\mathbf{I}_r = P_r(\mathbf{M}, \mathbf{P})$.

2.1   Aggregation Module

Existing methods based on vision transformer such as [9] roughly take into account the whole images at one time, but neglect the differences and relations among individual images, thereby leading to redundant computation. To break these limitations, we devise an aggregation module which consists of stacked transformer blocks with two paths to aggregate multi-facial features from multiple images, as shown in Fig. 2(b). One is for image-wise processing, which

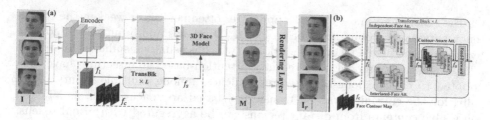

Fig. 2. Framework of our ADANet. (a) ADANet takes multiple face images of a subject as inputs, and then employs the encoder to extract image-wise features of each face image. Meanwhile, the multi-level features of each image are fused, guided by the facial contour-aware knowledge, and then fed into the TransBlk in aggregation module to obtain the complementary multi-image features for face modeling. (b) TransBlk contains the in-face and cross-face attentions to aggregate the most relevant contents from multiple images, and further utilizes contour information to enhance the 3D models. (Color figure online)

employs an in-face attention mechanism for all spatial positions, thus can effectively obtain representative facial features of each image. The other aims at multi-face data extraction, which is implemented by searching local facial regions with a cross-face attention mechanism at the same spatial correspondences of different images. Finally, these two kinds of features involving local- and long-range correlations from the two paths are aggregated to obtain complementary and robust features within multiple face images.

The image patches in the conventional Transformer only remain deteriorated structure information. To better preserve local spatial structures, we employ an encoder to extract multi-level features from the input image set $\mathbf{I}$. Thus, we fuse the features from the first three levels of encoder, in which five groups of convolutions are applied to consecutively down-sample the height and width of the feature map with a 0.5 scaling ratio to construct f_l. Then, all the f_l of n images are further concatenated to form multi-image feature $\mathbf{F}_l \in \mathbb{R}^{h \times w \times (nc)}$ with richer information.

Subsequently, we divide the multi-image face feature $\mathbf{F}_l$ along both the height and width dimensions into r parts for producing r^2 regions, in which every region is denoted as $\mathbf{F}_{pq}^i \in \mathbb{R}^{h/r \times w/r \times (nc)}$, where $i = 1, \ldots, n$, and $p, q = 1, 2, \ldots, r$. So there are $n \cdot r^2 \cdot (h/r) \cdot (w/r)$ tokens in total. We then deal with these tokens with two combination manners for estimating in-face and cross-face attentions. Firstly, we calculate spatial interactions of in-face tokens for each image, $i.e.$, $\mathbf{T}^i = \left\{ \mathbf{F}_{11}^i, \mathbf{F}_{12}^i, \ldots, \mathbf{F}_{rr}^i \right\}, i = 1, \ldots, n$, so that the Trans-Blk takes each $\mathbf{T}^i$ as an input and performs multi-head self-attention among the tokens. Secondly, we process the cross-face tokens among multiple images, just as $\mathbf{T}_{pq} = \left\{ \mathbf{F}_{pq}^1, \ldots, \mathbf{F}_{pq}^n \right\}, p, q = 1, \ldots, r$, so the relations and differences among local regions can be revealed and distinguished in each small spatial position. Two different ways are shown in Fig. 2(b) as the pink box and the green box respectively. The outputs of in-face and cross-face self-attention modules are fused together to form f_m, followed by a contour-aware fusion mechanism as described in Sect. 2.2 and a feed-forward network to output f_t with the same size as an input, formulated as:

$$f_m = Conv1\left(Cat(MSA(\mathbf{T}^i), MSA(\mathbf{T}_{pq}))\right) \oplus \mathbf{F}_l, \tag{1}$$

$$f_t = \text{FFN}\left(f_a\right) \oplus f_m, \tag{2}$$

where MSA is the multi-head self-attention as in [9]. Note that the mechanism for calculating in-face attention and cross-face attention are the same, and only their inputs vary in different combination ways. Cat means the concatenation operation along the channel dimension and $Conv1$ represents a 1×1 convolution to reduce the dimension as the inputs, and $\oplus$ means element-wise addition. In Eq. 2, f_a denotes the contour-aware feature from CFM, while FFN denotes the vanilla feed-forward network. The f_t is recursively used with L stacked blocks to repeat the aggregation process, which is followed by a Global Average Pooling layer to obtain the shared face feature f_s.

2.2 Contour-Aware Fusion Mechanism

For improving the ability to deal with 3D face modeling with ambiguous boundaries, we further incorporate facial silhouette into the TransBlk to ensure the structural information to be consistent with the original faces. To this end, we propose the Contour-Aware Fusion Mechanism (CFM) as the gray box shown in Fig. 2(b), which aims to fuse the facial contour information from the input face images to refine the transformed features.

There are two stages in CFM. First, the visible face regions are acquired by computing the segmentation mask of the face region as [18] to avoid interference of backgrounds or occlusions, and then applied an edge-aware detection method in [14] to obtain facial contours. This process denoted as $f_c = E_c(I^n) \in \mathbb{R}^{H \times W \times 1}$, where $E_c(\cdot)$ represents the operation of extracting face contour map. Second, we import f_c and f_m into contour-aware self-attention, in which the Query-Key-Value can well merge the contour map into the image features. Specifically, we transform f_c and f_m into Q, K and V with 1×1 convolutions, just as:

$$Q = C_q\left(f_c\right), K = C_k\left(f_m\right), V = C_v\left(f_m\right), \tag{3}$$

where Q, K and V preserved the original spatial sizes. Specifically, we employ 1×1 convolutions to transform f_c and f_m into Q, K and V with the original spatial sizes. We then flatten them along the spatial dimension to obtain the 2D embeddings $\mathcal{Q}$, $\mathcal{K}$ and $\mathcal{V} \in \mathbb{R}^{512 \times (nc)}$, and calculate the fused features as:

$$f_f = softmax\left(\frac{\mathcal{Q} \cdot \mathcal{K}^T}{\sqrt{H/4 \times W/4 \times C}}\right)\mathcal{V}. \tag{4}$$

In addition, we employ a residual connection by adding f_f and f_m, and then use a convolutional layer to obtain the output f_a:

$$f_a = CFM\left(f_c, f_m\right) \oplus f_m. \tag{5}$$

By this design, CFM facilitates the ADANet to acquire more richer structural information, which is of great significance to reconstruct 3D face models with explicit boundaries.

2.3 Loss Functions

For the entire pipeline of ADANet, we adopt the self-supervised learning scheme to train our network, which includes five loss functions as described below.

The reconstruction loss $\mathcal{L}_{rec}$ enforces the rendered face images $\mathbf{I}_r$ to be consistent with the original inputs $\mathbf{I}$ by minimizing the dense pixels discrepancies [4]:

$$\mathcal{L}_{rec} = \frac{1}{WHC} \sum \|\mathbf{I} - \mathbf{I}_r\|_2^2, \tag{6}$$

where W, H and C refer to the size of images.

In order to preserve high-frequency details in facial textures, we introduce adversarial loss $\mathcal{L}_{adv}$ based on a discriminator $D(\cdot)$ of patchGAN [21], which aims to distinguish between $\mathbf{I}$ and $\mathbf{I}_r$:

$$\mathcal{L}_{adv} = \log\left(1 - D\left(\mathbf{I}\right)\right) + \log D(\mathbf{I}_r). \tag{7}$$

The identity loss $\mathcal{L}_{id}$ facilitates the similarity of faces in $\mathbf{I}$ and $\mathbf{I}_r$ by calculating the cosine distance between their identity features extracted by a face recognition network $F_{id}(\cdot)$ [5]:

$$\mathcal{L}_{id} = 1 - \frac{F_{id}\left(\mathbf{I}\right) \cdot F_{id}\left(\mathbf{I}_r\right)}{\|F_{id}\left(\mathbf{I}\right)\|_2 \|F_{id}\left(\mathbf{I}_r\right)\|_2}. \tag{8}$$

We also employ the landmark loss $\mathcal{L}_{lmk}$ to help align the results by calculating the Euclidean distances between the detected landmark locations in $\mathbf{I}$ and $\mathbf{I}_r$:

$$\mathcal{L}_{lmk} = \frac{1}{K} \sum_{k=1}^{K} \|H(\mathbf{I}) - H(\mathbf{I}_r)\|_2, \tag{9}$$

where $H(\cdot)$ denotes the face alignment network [6], and k represents the number of landmarks.

Besides, to increase the accuracy of the reconstructed face boundaries, we design a facial contour consistency loss $\mathcal{L}_{con}$, in which two face contour maps are detected from $\mathbf{I}$ and $\mathbf{I}_r$ respectively:

$$\mathcal{L}_{con} = \|E_c(\mathbf{I}) - E_c(\mathbf{I}_r)\|_2^2, \tag{10}$$

where $E_c(\cdot)$ extracts the contour maps as described in Sect. 2.2.

To sum up, our final loss functions $\mathcal{L}$ can be expressed as:

$$\mathcal{L} = \lambda_1 \mathcal{L}_{rec} + \lambda_2 \mathcal{L}_{adv} + \lambda_3 \mathcal{L}_{id} + \lambda_4 \mathcal{L}_{lmk} + \lambda_5 \mathcal{L}_{con}, \tag{11}$$

where λ_1, λ_2, λ_3, λ_4 and λ_5 are the weights of different terms.

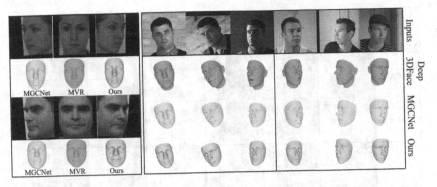

Fig. 3. Qualitative results on predicted facial geometry. We compare our method with MGCNet [20] and MVR [29] on Bosphorus [19] dataset shown in the left part. And we demonstrate our results with Deep3DFace [7] and MGCNet [20] on AFLW2000-3D [30] dataset in the right part.

3   Experiments

3.1   Datasets and Implementation

The training datasets include 300W-LP [30] and Multi-PIE [13], where the former contains over 60,000 images derived from 3,837 face images by varying synthesis poses, and the latter contains over 750,000 images collected from 337 subjects with different view angles and lighting conditions. The image size are 224×224, and the facial mesh topology is defined by Basel Face Model (BFM) [17], but exclude the ear and neck region, and contains 36K vertices. The encoder and renderer are adopted from [12]. To train ADANet, we adopt Adam optimizer with an initial learning rate of 0.0001, and the λ values of loss terms are empirically set as 2.0, 0.5, 1.0, 0.015 and 0.5 to bring losses with similar magnitudes. In our experiments, we set $n = 3$ images, $r^2 = 16$ regions, $L = 6$ blocks and 4 heads in each attention module. The number of facial landmark $k = 68$. Note that for the single-image methods adopted in our experiments, we refer to the formulation in [25] to fuse the weighted features of individual faces for multi-image reconstruction with the normalized facial confidence provided by MTCNN [28].

3.2   Results and Comparisons

1) Qualitative Comparison
We first perform qualitative comparisons to visualize the reconstructed facial geometries with representative methods as shown in Fig. 3. The MGCNet [20] utilizes multi-view geometry consistency to provide more reliable constraints on face pose. While MVR [29] proposes a Tri-UNet to concatenate features from each view and then extract the common facial features by a decoder. The Deep3DFace [7] learns a confidence net to produce element-wise scores for aggregating 3DMM coefficients from multiple images. In Fig. 3, the first two rows

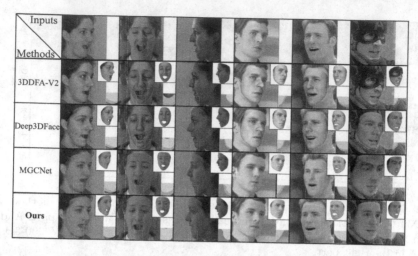

Fig. 4. Comparisons of face models with 3DDFA-V2 [15], Deep3DFace [7] and MGC-Net [20]. To better visualize their differences, we present the close-up views in different colors to indicate different meanings (Yellow: the overlap between the face model and face region, Green: the area of face model shrinks inside the face silhouette, Red: the area of face model exceeds the face region). (Color figure online)

presents the visual comparisons of several examples from Bosphorus [19] with neutral expression under different poses. In our method, the 3D face is reconstructed by shared face feature of each identity. Compared to the other methods, the visual results show that our 3D faces have better geometry consistency with the inputs. The last four rows in Fig. 3 illustrates the reconstruction results of samples from AFLW2000-3D [30] with different expressions, poses and illuminations. Compared with Deep3DFace [7] and MGCNet [20], our results present the face geometry with higher fidelity and more accurate expressions, which demonstrates our adaptive aggregation strategy can better capture complementary information and thus produce more realistic face models.

Then, in Fig. 4, we show some 3D reconstructions with our method and other state-of-the-arts, namely 3DDFA-V2 [15], Deep3DFace [7] and MGCNet [20], on the controlled and in-the-wild data. We can observe that, especially from the close-ups, our method can reconstruct face models with higher faithful shape and texture under multi-image scenarios. Specifically, the alignments of our face silhouette are more accurate than other methods, which reveals our face contour fusion mechanism can eliminate the ambiguity of boundaries and promote the face silhouette consistency with the inputs.

2) Quantitative Comparison

We evaluate the accuracy of reconstructed models on two datasets containing 3D scans, namely BU-3DFE [27] and MICC [3], in which the former contains seven different expressions, the latter provides neutral expression in 'cooperative', 'indoor' and 'outdoor' conditions.

Table 1. Geometric errors of multi-image face reconstruction on BU-3DFE dataset.

Method	MoFA [24]	MFM [23]	FML [22]	Deep3DFace [7]	MGCNet [20]	Ours
Mean	3.22	1.81	1.79	1.63	1.55	**1.50**
STD	0.77	0.47	0.45	0.33	0.31	**0.28**

We first evaluate the compared methods on BU-3DFE [27] following [22]. The reconstruction error is calculated by the point-to-point root mean squared error (RMSE) between the predictions and the ground-truth. From Table 1, our results have lower error than the other multi-image methods [7,20,22–24], which indicates that our adaptive aggregation strategy can better capture complementary information by simultaneously exploiting the local- and long-range correlations among different images and thus produce more accurate 3D models.

Table 2. Average and standard deviation of RMSE on MICC Dataset.

Method	Cooperative	Indoor	Outdoor
3DDFA-V1 [30]	2.69 ± 0.64	2.23 ± 0.40	2.22 ± 0.56
RPN [10]	2.30 ± 0.54	2.02 ± 0.50	2.10 ± 0.60
UR3D [12]	1.87 ± 0.61	1.86 ± 0.60	1.87 ± 0.57
3DDFA-V2 [15]	1.85 ± 0.54	1.82 ± 0.49	1.83 ± 0.56
Deep3DFace [7]	1.83 ± 0.59	1.78 ± 0.53	1.78 ± 0.59
MGCNet [20]	1.73 ± 0.48	1.78 ± 0.47	1.75 ± 0.47
Ours	$\mathbf{1.66 \pm 0.45}$	$\mathbf{1.61 \pm 0.42}$	$\mathbf{1.63 \pm 0.45}$

We further test the compared methods on MICC dataset [3], as shown in Table 2. Following [12], we crop the ground-truth mesh to 95 mm around the nose tip and run ICP algorithm [2] for rigid alignment, then calculate the point-to-plane RMSE [20]. The results show that our method outperforms the compared methods, such as [7,10,12,15,20,30], under different conditions in terms of the mean and variance of reconstruction error, which verifies the effectiveness of our adaptive aggregation manner for multiple face images. The visual comparisons of several examples with error maps are presented in Fig. 5, which indicates our method achieves higher accuracy over MVFNet [26] and MGCNet [20], especially around the face contours.

3.3   Ablation Study

We conduct ablation studies on MICC dataset [3] in 'cooperative' setting with the following variant structures of ADANet: 1) Only the vanilla transformer is utilized to predict shared feature of multiple images. 2) The transformer with

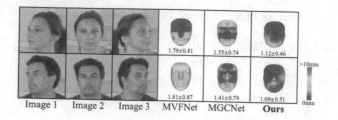

Fig. 5. Visualization of error maps on examples in MICC dataset.

only in-face attention module (IFA). 3) The transformer with only cross-face attention module (CFA). 4) The transformer with both in-face and cross-face attention modules but regardless of CFM. 5) The complete structure of ADANet. As shown in Table 3, the results of the aforementioned ablation studies demonstrate the effectiveness of our proposed ADANet to construct a more accurate model under multi-image scenarios.

Table 3. The ablation study of variant structures on MICC dataset.

Variants	T	T + IFA	T + CFA	T + IFA&CFA	ADANet
RMSE	1.77	1.74	1.73	1.69	**1.66**

We further conduct ablation studies on MICC dataset [3] in 'cooperative' setting to verify the effects of different loss terms. Among them, $\mathcal{L}_{rec}$ and $\mathcal{L}_{adv}$ are used as basic loss terms to achieve 3D face reconstruction. $\mathcal{L}_{id}$ helps reduce the root mean square error of the reconstruction model by promoting the identity similarity between I and I_r. $\mathcal{L}_{lmk}$ further reduces the root mean square error of the reconstruction results by aligning facial landmarks. $\mathcal{L}_{con}$ improves the accuracy of the reconstruction model by constraining the consistency of facial contours between I and I_r. The corresponding results are shown in Table 4. It indicates the importance of each loss term in achieving better reconstruction results for 3D face models.

Table 4. The ablation study of loss terms on MICC dataset.

$\mathcal{L}_{rec}$	$\mathcal{L}_{adv}$	$\mathcal{L}_{id}$	$\mathcal{L}_{lmk}$	$\mathcal{L}_{con}$	RMSE
✓	✓	−	−	−	1.78
✓	✓	✓	−	−	1.73
✓	✓	✓	✓	−	1.70
✓	✓	✓	✓	✓	1.66

4   Conclusion

In this paper, we propose a novel ADANet for multi-image 3D face reconstruction, in which the complementary information can be aggregated by adaptively exploiting the local- and long-range correlations among multiple images, as well as incorporating contour prior knowledge to promote the face geometric consistency. Extensive experiments demonstrate that our ADANet can effectively improve the ability in dealing with 3D face reconstructions from multiple images.

References

1. Ali, S.G., et al.: Cost-effective broad learning-based ultrasound biomicroscopy with 3D reconstruction for ocular anterior segmentation. Multimed. Tools Appl. **80**, 35105–35122 (2021)
2. Amberg, B., Romdhani, S., Vetter, T.: Optimal step nonrigid ICP algorithms for surface registration. In: Proceedings of the IEEE Conference on Computer Vision and Pattern Recognition, pp. 1–8 (2007)
3. Bagdanov, A.D., Del Bimbo, A., Masi, I.: The florence 2D/3D hybrid face dataset. In: Proceedings of the Joint ACM Workshop on Human Gesture and Behavior Understanding, pp. 79–80 (2011)
4. Chai, X., Chen, J., Liang, C., Xu, D., Lin, C.W.: Expression-aware face reconstruction via a dual-stream network. IEEE Trans. Multimed. **23**, 2998–3012 (2021)
5. Deng, J., Guo, J., Xue, N., Zafeiriou, S.: ArcFace: additive angular margin loss for deep face recognition. In: Proceedings of the IEEE Conference on Computer Vision and Pattern Recognition, pp. 4690–4699 (2019)
6. Deng, J., Zhou, Y., Cheng, S., Zaferiou, S.: Cascade multi-view hourglass model for robust 3D face alignment. In: Proceedings of the IEEE International Conference on Automatic Face & Gesture Recognition, pp. 399–403 (2018)
7. Deng, Y., Yang, J., Xu, S., Chen, D., Jia, Y., Tong, X.: Accurate 3D face reconstruction with weakly-supervised learning: from single image to image set. In: Proceedings of the IEEE Conference on Computer Vision and Pattern Recognition Workshops, pp. 285–295 (2019)
8. Dong, Y., Peng, C.: Multi-GPU multi-display rendering of extremely large 3D environments. Vis. Comput. 1–17 (2022)
9. Dosovitskiy, A., et al.: An image is worth 16×16 words: transformers for image recognition at scale. In: Proceedings of the International Conference on Learning Representation, pp. 1–22 (2020)
10. Feng, Y., Wu, F., Shao, X., Wang, Y., Zhou, X.: Joint 3D face reconstruction and dense alignment with position map regression network. In: Proceedings of the European Conference on Computer Vision, pp. 534–551 (2018)
11. Furuya, T., Liu, W., Ohbuchi, R., Kuang, Z.: Hyperplane patch mixing-and-folding decoder and weighted chamfer distance loss for 3D point set reconstruction. Vis. Comput. **39**, 1–18 (2022)
12. Genova, K., Cole, F., Maschinot, A., Sarna, A., Vlasic, D., Freeman, W.T.: Unsupervised training for 3D morphable model regression. In: Proceedings of the IEEE Conference on Computer Vision and Pattern Recognition, pp. 8377–8386 (2018)
13. Gross, R., Matthews, I., Cohn, J., Kanade, T., Baker, S.: Multi-pie. Image Vision Comput. **28**(5), 807–813 (2010)

14. Guan, W., Wang, T., Qi, J., Zhang, L., Lu, H.: Edge-aware convolution neural network based salient object detection. IEEE Signal Process. Lett. **26**(1), 114–118 (2018)
15. Guo, J., Zhu, X., Yang, Y., Yang, F., Lei, Z., Li, S.Z.: Towards fast, accurate and stable 3D dense face alignment. In: Vedaldi, A., Bischof, H., Brox, T., Frahm, J.-M. (eds.) ECCV 2020. LNCS, vol. 12364, pp. 152–168. Springer, Cham (2020). https://doi.org/10.1007/978-3-030-58529-7_10
16. Lukić, T., Balázs, P.: Limited-view binary tomography reconstruction assisted by shape centroid. Vis. Comput. **38**, 695–705 (2022)
17. Paysan, P., Knothe, R., Amberg, B., Romdhani, S., Vetter, T.: A 3D face model for pose and illumination invariant face recognition. In: Proceedings of the IEEE International Conference on Advanced Video and Signal Based Surveillance, pp. 296–301 (2009)
18. Saito, S., Li, T., Li, H.: Real-time facial segmentation and performance capture from RGB input. In: Leibe, B., Matas, J., Sebe, N., Welling, M. (eds.) ECCV 2016. LNCS, vol. 9912, pp. 244–261. Springer, Cham (2016). https://doi.org/10.1007/978-3-319-46484-8_15
19. Savran, A., et al.: Bosphorus database for 3D face analysis. In: Schouten, B., Juul, N.C., Drygajlo, A., Tistarelli, M. (eds.) BioID 2008. LNCS, vol. 5372, pp. 47–56. Springer, Heidelberg (2008). https://doi.org/10.1007/978-3-540-89991-4_6
20. Shang, J., et al.: Self-supervised monocular 3D face reconstruction by occlusion-aware multi-view geometry consistency. In: Vedaldi, A., Bischof, H., Brox, T., Frahm, J.-M. (eds.) ECCV 2020. LNCS, vol. 12360, pp. 53–70. Springer, Cham (2020). https://doi.org/10.1007/978-3-030-58555-6_4
21. Shrivastava, A., Pfister, T., Tuzel, O., Susskind, J., Wang, W., Webb, R.: Learning from simulated and unsupervised images through adversarial training. In: Proceedings of the IEEE Computer Vision and Pattern Recognition, pp. 2107–2116 (2017)
22. Tewari, A., et al.: FML: face model learning from videos. In: Proceedings of the IEEE Conference on Computer Vision and Pattern Recognition, pp. 10812–10822 (2019)
23. Tewari, A., et al.: Self-supervised multi-level face model learning for monocular reconstruction at over 250 Hz. In: Proceedings of the IEEE Conference on Computer Vision and Pattern Recognition, pp. 2549–2559 (2018)
24. Tewari, A., et al.: MoFA: model-based deep convolutional face autoencoder for unsupervised monocular reconstruction. In: Proceedings of the IEEE International Conference on Computer Vision Workshops, pp. 1274–1283 (2017)
25. Tuan Tran, A., Hassner, T., Masi, I., Medioni, G.: Regressing robust and discriminative 3D morphable models with a very deep neural network. In: Proceedings of the IEEE Conference on Computer Vision and Pattern Recognition, pp. 5163–5172 (2017)
26. Wu, F., et al.: MVF-Net: multi-view 3D face morphable model regression. In: Proceedings of the IEEE Conference on Computer Vision and Pattern Recognition, pp. 959–968 (2019)
27. Yin, L., Wei, X., Sun, Y., Wang, J., Rosato, M.J.: A 3D facial expression database for facial behavior research. In: Proceedings of the International Conference on Automatic Face and Gesture Recognition, pp. 211–216 (2006)
28. Zhang, K., Zhang, Z., Li, Z., Qiao, Y.: Joint face detection and alignment using multitask cascaded convolutional networks. IEEE Signal Process. Lett. **23**(10), 1499–1503 (2016)

29. Zhao, W., Yang, C., Ye, J., Yan, Y., Yang, X., Huang, K.: From 2D images to 3D model: weakly supervised multi-view face reconstruction with deep fusion. arXiv preprint arXiv:2204.03842 (2022)
30. Zhu, X., Lei, Z., Liu, X., Shi, H., Li, S.Z.: Face alignment across large poses: a 3D solution. In: Proceedings of the IEEE Conference on Computer Vision and Pattern Recognition, pp. 146–155 (2016)

METRO-X: Combining Vertex and Parameter Regressions for Recovering 3D Human Meshes with Full Motions

Guiqing Li[(✉)], Chenhao Yao, Huiqian Zhang, Juncheng Zeng, Yongwei Nie, and Chuhua Xian

South China University of Technology, Guangzhou 510006, China
ligq@scut.edu.cn

Abstract. It is well known that regressing the parametric representation of a human body from a single image suffers low accuracy due to sparse information use and error accumulation. Although being able to achieve higher accuracy by avoiding these issues, directly regressing vertices may result in vertex outliers. We present METRO-X, a novel method for reconstructing full-body human meshes with body pose, facial expression and hand gesture from a single image, which combines the advantages from the two disciplines so as to achieve higher accuracy than parameter regression while bear denser vertices and generate smoother shape than vertices regression. It first detects and extracts hands, head and the whole body parts from a given image, then regresses the vertices of three parts separately using METRO, and finally fits SMPL-X to the reconstructed meshes to obtain the complete parametric representation. Experimental results show that METRO-X outperforms the ExPose method, with a significant 23% improvement in body accuracy and a 35% improvement in gesture accuracy. These results demonstrate the potential of our approach in enabling various applications.

Keywords: Full-body model reconstruction · 3D from monocular images · Gestures and pose

1 Introduction

Recovery of 3D human meshes from a single image has attracted much attention because of its wide range of applications such as virtual reality. However, it remains a challenge due to the complex articulation of the human body.

Recent advances in attention mechanisms enable mesh regression approaches [4,19,20] to achieve promising performance in recovering 3D body shapes from a single image. METRO [19] is the first leveraging the mesh transformer architecture to learn both local and global range interactions among joints and mesh vertices, which achieves higher accuracy than those of parameter regression approaches. Unfortunately, vertex regression methods such as METRO usually suffer from noise, roughness, and distortion in predicting mesh vertices as shown

B. Sheng et al. (Eds.): CGI 2023, LNCS 14496, pp. 40–52, 2024.
https://doi.org/10.1007/978-3-031-50072-5_4

in Fig. 1. Furthermore, due to memory constraints of current hardware, this kind of methods often have to conduct the regression on a coarse mesh and therefore an upsampling step is required in order to obtain a dense mesh. Although being able to improve efficiency, it usually fails to recover fine details.

FastMETRO [4] can be viewed as an accelerated version of METRO. It also provides a regressor to predict the SMPL parameters [22] from the recovered dense mesh to address the issues of METRO. However, FastMETRO does not present any analysis on the parameter regressor. In addition, like METRO, it neither considers facial expressions and hand gestures.

Motivated by the above observations, we propose a simple yet effective architecture named METRO-X (METRO for eXpressive human recovery) that takes advantage of both vertices and parameter regression methods. METRO-X includes three part-specific modules to regress the body, hand, and face from the corresponding regions cropped from the original image. Following METRO [19], each part module consists of a vertex regressor and a parameter regressor. The vertex regressor predicts a coarse mesh from the cropped image. It employs a multi-layer mesh transformer to exploit the non-local relationship among 3D key-points (e.g., body joints, hands joint, and facial landmarks) and mesh vertices. The parameter regressor leverages multiple fully connected layers and residual blocks to predict SMPL-X parameters from the mesh vertices. The outputs of the three modules is then assembled together to obtain a complete SMPL-X [25] mesh. Experimental results demonstrate that METRO-X achieves high accuracy reconstruction and high efficiency regression of 3D full-body human mesh, while avoiding the distortion artifacts.

Our contributions can be summarized as follows:

- We present METRO-X, a METRO-based method for regressing parameters of SMPL-X from a single image. To capture more details, we exploit three part-specific modules to predict body, hands, and face respectively.
- We propose a simple yet effective architecture consisting of a coarse mesh regressor and a parameter regressor. The mesh regressor employs a Transformer encoder to capture non-local relation among 3D keypoints and vertices while the parameter regressor leverages pamatric human body models to avoid distortion artifacts.
- Experimental results demonstrate the effectiveness and plausibility of METRO-X in producing high-quality 3D human parametric representation.

2   Related Works

In this section, we first review approaches which only recover body meshes and then discuss those involving human body, face and hands.

2.1   Human Body Shape Recovery

We begin with a concise introduction to optimization-based approaches, followed by a primary focus on regression-based methods.

Optimization-based methods involve fitting parametric human models to pseudo labels, such as 2D keypoints [2,3]. They often demand extensive iterations. Consequently, current optimization-based techniques are frequently combined with regression methods to enhance their efficiency and effectiveness [3,17,31].

Regression-based approaches employ deep neural networks to directly process pixel-level data. These regression networks can be categorized into two types: parameter regression and non-parameter regression. Many methods employ parametric models to reconstruct human meshes and typically predict the parameters of these models from the images [11,14,18]. Nevertheless, an excessive reliance on the structure of parametric models can hinder advancements in this field. Rather than predicting the parameters of a human mesh template, some methods attempt to directly regress voxel occupancy information [29] or mesh vertex positions [4,20]. Recent state-of-the-art methods [4,19] demonstrate that non-parameter regression tend to outperform parameter regression approaches in accuracy due to their flexibility. However, the constraints of the latter are too relax to yield noise free and full detail results.

2.2 Human Body Shape Recovery with Full Motion

Compared to abundant solutions available for recovering the body-only [11, 14,30], hand-only [16], and face-only [7] meshes, full-body mesh recovery has received relatively less attention due to its challenging nature and the lack of annotated datasets. Research in the field of full-body mesh recovery begins with the proposal of full-body models, such as SMPL-X [26], along with their corresponding optimization-based methods. To overcome the slow and unnatural issues of optimization-based methods, several regression-based methods [5,6] have been proposed recently. ExPose [5] is a pioneering algorithm that introduces a framework comprising three specialized modules. These modules are designed to predict body, hand, and face meshes by utilizing part images extracted from the raw input. In this paper, we refer to the practice of ExPose.

3   Method

3.1   Preliminaries

SMPL-X [25] is a parametric human model controlled by pose $\theta \in \mathbb{R}^{165}$, shape $\beta \in \mathbb{R}^{10}$ and expression $\psi \in \mathbb{R}^{10}$ parameters. Given θ, β and ψ, the SMPL-X model outputs a posed mesh $M(\theta, \beta, \psi)$ with $N = 10475$ vertices and $K = 54$ joints. The 3D joints can be calculated by a linear regressor W_{reg}, i.e., $\mathcal{J}_{3D} \in \mathbb{R}^{K \times 3} = W_{reg}M$. In this paper, our final mesh is generated using SMPL-X, and the skeleton is based on it as well.

METRO introduces a novel progressive dimensionality reduction scheme [19]. As depicted in Fig. 2, it employs multiple encoder layers to alternate between self-attention and dimensionality reduction. METRO [19] receives body joints and mesh vertex queries as inputs. It perform concatenation of the image feature vector with 3D coordinates of every keypoint and vertex. This results in a set of input queries. Finally, the output is a coarse mesh with vertices aligned to the input image.

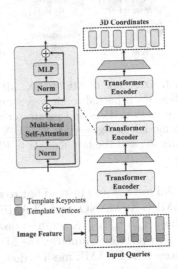

Fig. 1. Typical artifacts of vertex regression.

Fig. 2. Details of METRO [19].

3.2   Model Architecture

As depicted in Fig. 3, METRO-X employs separate predictions for body mesh, hand mesh, and face mesh. Using a single high-resolution image of an individual as input, we initially utilize established image segmentation tools (Detectron2 [33]) to extract the body, hand, and face segments from the image separately. Subsequently, these distinct segments are fed into separate CNN to capture their basic image features. Each partial body mesh is generated by a separate Transformer Encoder. Transformers output the vertices of coarse meshes. We use each of them and the corresponding parameter regressors to regress the body parameters, hand parameters and face parameters respectively. Finally, the integration stage consolidates all parts to generate a unified whole-body mesh.

3.3   Mesh Downsampling

Due to memory constraints, the Transformer structure is limited in its ability to handle a large number of inputs. Therefore, we avoid direct operation on

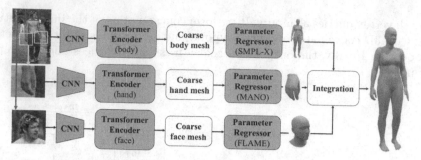

Fig. 3. Overview of METRO-X. METRO-X predicts separate body, hand, and face meshes. Each partial mesh is generated by a different Transformer Encoder. We use coarse mesh vertices and parameter regressors to regress each part's parameters. The body module is regressed to SMPL-X pose θ_b and shape β, the hand module to MANO gesture θ_h, and the face module to FLAME expression ψ and pose θ_f.

original meshes and instead opt to subsample them [28]. To obtain coarse meshes for SMPL-X, MANO, and FLAME, downsampling is applied to their respective meshes. The SMPL-X mesh is downsampled twice, resulting in a coarse mesh with 655 vertices. Similarly, the MANO mesh is downsampled once, yielding 195 vertices. The FLAME mesh is downsampled twice, resulting in 314 vertices. The resulting meshes after downsampling are presented in Fig. 4.

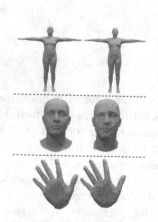

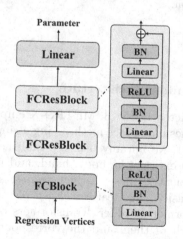

Fig. 4. Mesh pairs for body, head, hand. Each pair consists of a original mesh on the left, and a coarse mesh on the right.

Fig. 5. Details of our parameter regressor.

3.4   Transformer Encoder

After we extract a global feature vector X from the final layer of the CNN (typically with a dimension of 2048), we proceed to input this feature into the subsequent Transformer for further processing. Our Transformer encoder utilizes the METRO [19] structure. To reduce network calculation, the input of the Transformer encoder are simplified template mesh vertices provided in Sect. 3.3, and the output are also simplified vertices denoted as $\tilde{V}_{3D}$. The output simplified vertices $\tilde{V}_{3D}$ are then used as the input for the parameter regressor.

3.5   Parameter Regressor

The structure of regressor is shown in Fig. 5, which consists of one FCBlock, two FCResBlocks, and a linear layer sequentially. For the three modules of body, hand, and face, specific parameter models are used respectively, and coarse mesh vertices predicted in the previous stage are used as input. Regressors have the same structure, except for the dimensions of the input and output layers. To speed up the learning process, we combine the regressed coarse mesh vertices $\tilde{V}_{3D}$ with corresponding template mesh vertices in the input. The input size is $\tilde{N} \times 6$, where $\tilde{N}$ is the number of vertices of the rough mesh, and the output results are different model parameters. The body part is regressed to the pose parameters θ_b and shape parameters β of SMPL-X, the hand part is regressed to the pose parameters θ_h of MANO, and the face part is regressed to the first 10 expression parameters ψ and pose parameters θ_f of FLAME.

3.6   Integration

In the integration stage, we employ SMPL-X to unify the body, face, and hands. SMPL-X, a combination of SMPL, MANO, and FLAME, exhibits a specific correspondence between its components. Specifically, the facial expression parameters of SMPL-X directly align with FLAME, and we utilize ψ obtained from Sect. 3.5 without intermediary steps. As for the pose parameters, they represent the rotation of each joint, and $\theta_b, \theta_h, \theta_f$ from the previous stage seamlessly integrate into $\theta = \{\theta_b, \theta_h, \theta_f\}$. Lastly, for the body shape parameter, we can directly employ β that were regressed in Sect. 3.5 without further adjustments. Once we obtain these parameters $\{\theta, \beta, \psi\}$, we can generate the whole-body mesh $M(\theta, \beta, \psi)$ directly using the SMPL-X model.

3.7   Training Losses

Our training loss is split into two parts: Transformer encoder loss and parameter regressor loss. We have a dataset $D = \left\{ I^i, \hat{V}_{3D}^i, \hat{K}_{3D}^i, \hat{K}_{2D}^i \right\}_{i=1}^T$, with T samples. In each sample, I represents an RGB image, $\hat{V}_{3D}^i$ represents the annotated coarse meshes, and N represents the number of vertices. The ground truth for 3D and 2D keypoints, with M keypoints, is denoted as $\hat{K}_{3D}^i$ and $\hat{K}_{2D}^i$, respectively.

Transformer Encoder Loss. Let V_{3D} denote vertices after upsampling, K_{3D} be the 3D keypoints. We use L_1 loss to minimize the error. The vertex loss is $\mathcal{L}_V = \frac{1}{N} \sum_{i=1}^{N} \left\| V_{3D} - \hat{V}_{3D} \right\|_1$ and the 3D joint loss is $\mathcal{L}_K = \frac{1}{M} \sum_{i=1}^{M} \left\| K_{3D} - \hat{K}_{3D} \right\|_1$. The predicted camera parameter is used to project 3D keypoints onto 2D plane. The 2D projection loss is $\mathcal{L}_K^{proj} = \frac{1}{M} \sum_{i=1}^{M} \left\| K_{2D} - \hat{K}_{2D} \right\|_1$. We adopt a hybrid training strategy using different datasets, including datasets with 3D annotations and datasets without 3D annotations. The total loss function is as follows:

$$\mathcal{L} = \alpha \times (\mathcal{L}_V + \mathcal{L}_K) + \mathcal{L}_K^{proj} \tag{1}$$

where α is a binary flag, indicating the availability of 3D ground truths.

Parameter Regressor Loss. 3D keypoints can be computed from meshes [11]. The 3D keypoint and 2D keypoint losses of parametric regressors are defined as $\mathcal{L}_K^{reg3D} = \frac{1}{M} \sum_{i=1}^{M} \left\| K_{3D}^{reg} - \hat{K}_{3D} \right\|_1$ and $\mathcal{L}_K^{reg2D} = \frac{1}{M} \sum_{i=1}^{M} \left\| K_{2D}^{reg} - \hat{K}_{2D} \right\|_1$. We use $\mathcal{L}_{smplx}$, $\mathcal{L}_{mano}$, and $\mathcal{L}_{flame}$ to represent losses of SMPL-X, MANO and FLAME parameter regressor respectively. $\mathcal{L}_{\theta_b}$ and $\mathcal{L}_{\beta_b}$ are the L_2 loss of the pose and shape of SMPL-X. $\mathcal{L}_{\theta_h}$ is the L_2 loss of the gesture of MANO. And $\mathcal{L}_\psi$ is the L_2 loss of expression of FLAME.

$$\mathcal{L}_{smplx} = \alpha \times \mathcal{L}_K^{reg3D} + L_K^{reg2D} + \mathcal{L}_{\theta_b} + \mathcal{L}_{\beta_b} \tag{2}$$

$$\mathcal{L}_{mano} = \alpha \times \mathcal{L}_K^{reg3D} + L_K^{reg2D} + \mathcal{L}_{\theta_h} \tag{3}$$

$$\mathcal{L}_{flame} = \alpha \times \mathcal{L}_K^{reg3D} + L_K^{reg2D} + \mathcal{L}_\psi \tag{4}$$

4 Experiments

4.1 Implementation Details

We used Pytorch and Huggingface transformer library to implement METRO-X. Our model includes three branches for body, hand, and face reconstruction, which are trained individually with a learning rate of 1e-4 that decays by a factor of 10 at the 50th epoch. We trained our model on mini-batches of size 16 for 100 epochs on a machine with two NVIDIA V100 GPUs. To improve convergence and robustness, we assumed the training sets contained right-hand-only samples by reflecting left-hand samples. It takes 0.73 s to compute one sample during testing.

4.2 Datasets and Evaluation Metrics

Following the practices of previous work [2,5,19], we train and test METRO-X on several datasets, including Human3.6M [8], 3DPW [23], MPI-INF-3DHP [24],

COCO [21], MPII [1], FreiHAND [35], FFHQ [12], EHF [25], LSP [9] and LSP-Extended [10]. Four metrics are used to quantitatively evaluate the performance of METRO-X in our experiments: MPJPE [8], PA-MPJPE [34], PVE [27], and PA-PVE. These metrics evaluate the accuracy of 3D joint location and the error of the 3D surface. All metrics are computed in the same way as previous work [19]. The default unit is millimeters (mm).

Table 1. 3D joint location errors on 3DPW [23].

Method	MPJPE ↓	PA-MPJPE ↓
HMR [11]	99.3	81.3
GraphCMR [15]	96.5	70.3
SPIN [14]	87.1	59.2
VIBE [13]	82.0	51.9
MPS-Net [32]	89.6	56.4
MAED [30]	88.0	52.9
METRO w/ reg [19]	87.6	53.6
Mesh Graphormer w/ reg [20]	82.1	51.9
FastMETRO w/ reg [4]	–	51.0
METRO-X	**81.6**	**49.2**

4.3 Quantitative and Qualitative Evaluation

Evaluation on 3D Joint Location Estimation. Table 1 presents MPJPE [8] and PA-MPJPE [34] two indices of results by these approaches among which METRO-X performs best. For fair comparisons, we input only one image to MPS-Net [32] and MAED [30], which are video-based methods. It is worth noting that the main body of METRO [19], Mesh Graphormer [20] and FastMETRO [4] are non parameter regressors and they also provide a SMPL [22] parameter regressors denoted as reg.

Table 2. Full motion reconstruction errors on EHF [25].

Method	PVE ↓				PA-PVE ↓			
	Full-body	Body	Hands	Face	Full-body	Body	Hands	Face
SMPLify-X [2]	146.2	231.3	34.4	23.6	68.0	75.4	12.5	8.4
ExPose [5]	81.9	116.4	39.3	**19.5**	57.4	55.1	13.0	**5.6**
METRO-X	**76.7**	**89.3**	**25.2**	26.2	**57.1**	**53.1**	**11.3**	10.1

Evaluation on Full Motion Recovery. We evaluate the proposed approach on EHF [25] by recovering shapes with full-body motion using the PVE metric [27]. Table 2 summarizes the results. Note that the reconstructed results for SMPLify-X and ExPose are respectively generated by using the source codes and the pretrained network by the authors. Compared to SMPLify-X [2], METRO-X improves accuracy by 61% on PVE. For hands reconstruction, METRO-X brings improvement over ExPose [5] by 35.8% on PVE, and reduces the PA-PVE to 11.3 mm. Nevertheless, the accuracy of face reconstruction by METRO-X is not so good, and more discussion can be found in Subsect. 4.5.

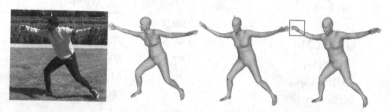

Fig. 6. Qualitative comparison of body and hands reconstruction on 3DPW. From left to right: the input image, ground-truth, results by METRO [19] and METRO-X.

Fig. 7. Qualitative comparison of full motion reconstruction. From left to right are results on GettyImage, LSP [9], and LSP-Extend [10], respectively displaying input image, predictions by METRO [19], ExPose [5] and METRO-X.

Qualitative Comparison. We present additional qualitative results for METRO-X in Fig. 6. We compare METRO-X with METRO [19] on body and hand mesh recovery, using three examples from the 3DPW dataset [23]. Our approach accurately captures the pose of the left hand. Additional results on the GettyImage, LSP [9] and LSP-Extend [10] benchmarks are shown in Fig. 7, which demonstrate that METRO-X is competitive. METRO [19] yields noisy results and cannot recover hand gestures and facial expressions, while ExPose [5] generates accurate body and face meshes but fails to capture good hand gestures, particularly for the left hand. Our approach generates smoother reconstructions and more accurate hand gestures, although it fails to generate expressions with an open mouth.

Table 3. Ablation study on Human3.6M.

Method	MPJPE ↓	PA-MPJPE ↓
merged	66.1	44.9
METRO-X	**54.6**	**39.1**

Fig. 8. An failure example with extreme facial expression.

4.4 Ablation Study

We conducted an ablation study by merging the three experts of METRO-X into a single architecture, denoted as merged. The results on Human3.6M [8] benchmark are reported on Table 3. Separating a single model into three branches can improve its performance of around 17% which indicate the necessity of partial-wise architecture of METOR-X.

4.5 Limitations

Though METRO-X improves performance under full-body mesh recovery, we found it challenging to handle facial expressions. Table 2 reveals that the face expert provides inaccurate results compared to other methods. Figure 8 visualizes the erroneous result of face expert, while body and hands are accurate. Since the Transformer encoder can not handle a large number of vertices, the face encoder and regressor of METRO-X heavily relies on the coarse face mesh. In our current implementation, we downsample FLAME meshes twice to obtain coarse ones with 314 vertices. The regression network can not capture enough meaningful features due to lack of details in the coarse face mesh, leading to inaccurate facial expression estimation.

5 Conclusions

We propose METRO-X to reconstruct a complete 3D human body model from a single RGB image. It leverages high accuracy of results by vertex regression to improve the parameter regression. The body pose and hand gesture in the reconstructed mesh by METRO-X is highly accurate, with good alignment to the image and natural poses. Nevertheless, capability of METRO-X to capture facial expressions should be strengthened in future work. We may consider simplifying the head mesh in a manner respecting face feature lines so that the vertex regressor is able to capture richer expressions.

References

1. Andriluka, M., Pishchulin, L., Gehler, P., Schiele, B.: 2D human pose estimation: new benchmark and state of the art analysis. In: Proceedings of the IEEE Conference on Computer Vision and Pattern Recognition, pp. 3686–3693 (2014)
2. Bogo, F., Kanazawa, A., Lassner, C., Gehler, P., Romero, J., Black, M.J.: Keep It SMPL: automatic estimation of 3D human pose and shape from a single image. In: Leibe, B., Matas, J., Sebe, N., Welling, M. (eds.) ECCV 2016. LNCS, vol. 9909, pp. 561–578. Springer, Cham (2016). https://doi.org/10.1007/978-3-319-46454-1_34
3. Chen, D., Song, Y., Liang, F., Ma, T., Zhu, X., Jia, T.: 3D human body reconstruction based on SMPL model. Vis. Comput. **39**(5), 1893–1906 (2022). https://doi.org/10.1007/s00371-022-02453-x
4. Cho, J., Youwang, K., Oh, T.H.: Cross-attention of disentangled modalities for 3D human mesh recovery with transformers. In: Avidan, S., Brostow, G., Cisse, M., Farinella, G.M., Hassner, T. (eds.) Computer Vision – ECCV 2022. ECCV 2022. LNCS, vol. 13661, pp. 342–359. Springer, Cham (2022). https://doi.org/10.1007/978-3-031-19769-7_20
5. Choutas, V., Pavlakos, G., Bolkart, T., Tzionas, D., Black, M.J.: Monocular expressive body regression through body-driven attention. In: Vedaldi, A., Bischof, H., Brox, T., Frahm, J.-M. (eds.) ECCV 2020. LNCS, vol. 12355, pp. 20–40. Springer, Cham (2020). https://doi.org/10.1007/978-3-030-58607-2_2
6. Feng, Y., Choutas, V., Bolkart, T., Tzionas, D., Black, M.J.: Collaborative regression of expressive bodies using moderation. In: 2021 International Conference on 3D Vision (3DV), pp. 792–804 (2021)
7. Feng, Y., Feng, H., Black, M.J., Bolkart, T.: Learning an animatable detailed 3D face model from in-the-wild images. ACM Trans. Graph. **40**(4), 1–13 (2021)
8. Ionescu, C., Papava, D., Olaru, V., Sminchisescu, C.: Human3. 6 m: large scale datasets and predictive methods for 3D human sensing in natural environments. IEEE Trans. Pattern Anal. Mach. Intell. **36**(7), 1325–1339 (2013)
9. Johnson, S., Everingham, M.: Clustered pose and nonlinear appearance models for human pose estimation. In: Proceedings of the British Machine Vision Conference, pp. 12.1–12.11 (2010)
10. Johnson, S., Everingham, M.: Learning effective human pose estimation from inaccurate annotation. In: Proceedings of the IEEE Conference on Computer Vision and Pattern Recognition, pp. 1465–1472 (2011)
11. Kanazawa, A., Black, M.J., Jacobs, D.W., Malik, J.: End-to-end recovery of human shape and pose. In: Proceedings of the IEEE Conference on Computer Vision and Pattern Recognition, pp. 7122–7131 (2018)
12. Karras, T., Laine, S., Aila, T.: A style-based generator architecture for generative adversarial networks. In: Proceedings of the IEEE Conference on Computer Vision and Pattern Recognition, pp. 4396–4405 (2019). https://doi.org/10.1109/CVPR.2019.00453
13. Kocabas, M., Athanasiou, N., Black, M.J.: VIBE: video inference for human body pose and shape estimation. In: Proceedings of the IEEE Conference on Computer Vision and Pattern Recognition, pp. 5253–5263 (2020)
14. Kolotouros, N., Pavlakos, G., Black, M.J., Daniilidis, K.: Learning to reconstruct 3D human pose and shape via model-fitting in the loop. In: Proceedings of the IEEE International Conference on Computer Vision, pp. 2252–2261 (2019)
15. Kolotouros, N., Pavlakos, G., Daniilidis, K.: Convolutional mesh regression for single-image human shape reconstruction. In: Proceedings of the IEEE Conference on Computer Vision and Pattern Recognition, pp. 4501–4510 (2019)

16. Li, M., et al.: Interacting attention graph for single image two-hand reconstruction. In: Proceedings of the IEEE Conference on Computer Vision and Pattern Recognition, pp. 2761–2770 (2022)

17. Li, X., Li, G., Li, T., Lv, J., Mitrouchev, P.: Remodeling of mannequins based on automatic binding of mesh to anthropometric parameters. Vis. Comput. 1–24 (2022)

18. Li, Z., Liu, J., Zhang, Z., Xu, S., Yan, Y.: CLIFF: carrying location information in full frames into human pose and shape estimation. arXiv preprint arXiv:2208.00571 (2022)

19. Lin, K., Wang, L., Liu, Z.: End-to-end human pose and mesh reconstruction with transformers. In: Proceedings of the IEEE Conference on Computer Vision and Pattern Recognition, pp. 1954–1963 (2021)

20. Lin, K., Wang, L., Liu, Z.: Mesh graphormer. In: Proceedings of the IEEE International Conference on Computer Vision, pp. 12939–12948 (2021)

21. Lin, T.Y., et al.: Microsoft coco: Common objects in context. In: Proceedings of the European Conference on Computer Vision, pp. 740–755 (2014)

22. Loper, M., Mahmood, N., Romero, J., Pons-Moll, G., Black, M.J.: SMPL: a skinned multi-person linear model. ACM Trans. Graph. 34(6), 1–16 (2015)

23. von Marcard, T., Henschel, R., Black, M., Rosenhahn, B., Pons-Moll, G.: Recovering accurate 3d human pose in the wild using IMUs and a moving camera. In: European Conference on Computer Vision (ECCV), September 2018

24. Mehta, D., et al.: Monocular 3D human pose estimation in the wild using improved CNN supervision. In: 2017 International Conference on 3D Vision (3DV), pp. 506–516 (2017). https://doi.org/10.1109/3DV.2017.00064

25. Pavlakos, G., et al.: Expressive body capture: 3D hands, face, and body from a single image. In: Proceedings IEEE Conference on Computer Vision and Pattern Recognition, pp. 10975–10985 (2019)

26. Pavlakos, G., et al.: Expressive body capture: 3D hands, face, and body from a single image. In: Proceedings of the IEEE Conference on Computer Vision and Pattern Recognition, pp. 10975–10985 (2019)

27. Pavlakos, G., Zhu, L., Zhou, X., Daniilidis, K.: Learning to estimate 3D human pose and shape from a single color image. In: Proceedings of the IEEE Conference on Computer Vision and Pattern Recognition, pp. 459–468 (2018)

28. Ranjan, A., Bolkart, T., Sanyal, S., Black, M.J.: Generating 3D faces using convolutional mesh autoencoders. In: Proceedings of the European Conference on Computer Vision, pp. 704–720 (2018)

29. Varol, G., et al.: Bodynet: volumetric inference of 3D human body shapes. In: Proceedings of the European Conference on Computer Vision, pp. 20–36 (2018)

30. Wan, Z., Li, Z., Tian, M., Liu, J., Yi, S., Li, H.: Encoder-decoder with multi-level attention for 3D human shape and pose estimation. In: Proceedings of the IEEE International Conference on Computer Vision, pp. 13033–13042 (2021)

31. Wang, K., Zhang, G., Yang, J., Bao, H.: Dynamic human body reconstruction and motion tracking with low-cost depth cameras. Vis. Comput. 37, 603–618 (2021)

32. Wei, W.L., Lin, J.C., Liu, T.L., Liao, H.Y.M.: Capturing humans in motion: temporal-attentive 3D human pose and shape estimation from monocular video. In: Proceedings of the IEEE Conference on Computer Vision and Pattern Recognition, pp. 13211–13220 (2022)

33. Wu, Y., Kirillov, A., Massa, F., Lo, W.Y., Girshick, R.: Detectron2 (2019). https://github.com/facebookresearch/detectron2

34. Zhou, X., Zhu, M., Pavlakos, G., Leonardos, S., Derpanis, K.G., Daniilidis, K.: MonoCap: monocular human motion capture using a CNN coupled with a geometric prior. IEEE Trans. Pattern Anal. Mach. Intell. **41**(4), 901–914 (2019). https://doi.org/10.1109/TPAMI.2018.2816031
35. Zimmermann, C., Ceylan, D., Yang, J., Russell, B., Argus, M., Brox, T.: FreiHAND: a dataset for markerless capture of hand pose and shape from single RGB images. In: Proceedings of the IEEE International Conference on Computer Vision, pp. 813–822 (2019)

Automatic Digitization and Orientation of Scanned Mesh Data for Floor Plan and 3D Model Generation

Ritesh Sharma[1]([✉])[iD], Eric Bier[2][iD], Lester Nelson[2][iD], Mahabir Bhandari[3][iD], and Niraj Kunwar[3][iD]

[1] University of California, Merced, USA
rsharma39@ucmerced.edu
[2] Palo Alto Research Center, Palo Alto, USA
{bier,lnelson}@parc.com
[3] Oak Ridge National Laboratory, Oak Ridge, USA
{bhandarims,kunwarn1}@ornl.gov

Abstract. This paper describes a novel approach for generating accurate floor plans and 3D models of building interiors using scanned mesh data. Unlike previous methods, which begin with a high resolution point cloud from a laser range-finder, our approach begins with triangle mesh data, as from a Microsoft HoloLens. It generates two types of floor plans, a "pen-and-ink" style that preserves details and a drafting-style that reduces clutter. It processes the 3D model for use in applications by aligning it with coordinate axes, annotating important objects, dividing it into stories, and removing the ceiling. Its performance is evaluated on commercial and residential buildings, with experiments to assess quality and dimensional accuracy. Our approach demonstrates promising potential for automatic digitization and orientation of scanned mesh data, enabling floor plan and 3D model generation in various applications such as navigation, interior design, furniture placement, facilities management, building construction, and HVAC design.

Keywords: Clustering based methods · Floor plans · Augmented Reality · 3D Models

1 Introduction

Floor plans are useful for many applications including navigating in building interiors; remodeling; efficient placement of furniture; placement of pipes; heating, ventilation, and air conditioning (HVAC) design; and preparing an emergency evacuation plan. Depending on the application, different kinds of floor plan are appropriate. For remodeling building interiors or designing HVAC systems, users

---

R. Sharma—Worked on this research work during his internship at Palo Alto Research Center.

Supplementary Information The online version contains supplementary material available at https://doi.org/10.1007/978-3-031-50072-5_5.

may prefer a drafting-style floor plan that focuses on planar walls and removes furniture and other clutter. For furniture placement, navigation, or evacuation planning, users may prefer a more detailed floor plan that shows the positions of furniture, cabinets, counter tops, etc. In either case, producing a floor plan can be time consuming, requiring expert skills, such as measuring distances and angles or entering data into a CAD program. Furthermore, it may need to be done more than once because a building changes when walls and furniture are moved, added, or removed. So it is valuable to be able to generate floor plans automatically with little or no training.

To generate floor plans, it helps to begin with accurate data that can be collected automatically. Laser range finders, smartphones, tablets, and augmented reality (AR) headsets are some of the devices that have made it easier to collect high-resolution building data in the form of RGBD images, point clouds, and triangle meshes. In this paper, we describe a method for generating drafting-style and pen-and-ink-style floor plans by leveraging incomplete and imperfect triangle mesh data. This approach efficiently generates both types of floor plans accurately, supporting a wide range of applications.

Main Contribution. We describe a new method for generating accurate floor plans using poorly captured triangle mesh data from the Microsoft HoloLens 2. The main contributions are:

- A modified Density-Based Spatial Clustering of Applications with Noise (DBSCAN) algorithm, using blocks to capture wall height and thickness.
- An orientation-based clustering method that finds walls at arbitrary angles.
- The use of k-means clustering to rotate the mesh to the principal axes and to identify the floor and ceiling.
- Generating two kinds of precise floor plans from incomplete mesh data.

2   Related Work

Floor plans are crucial for many applications. Software approaches to floor plan creation depend on data availability and data format. Our work builds on previous research on data collection and floor plan computation.

Data Collection. Indoor environments can be captured in many formats, including RGBD images, point clouds, and triangle meshes. Zhang et al. [29] uses panoramic RGBD images as input and reconstructs geometry using structure grammars, while [21] uses a 3D scan to extract plane primitives and generates models using heuristics. A single image is used in some deep learning methods [8,11,13,14,30] to generate cuboid-based layouts for a single room. Detailed semi-constrained floor plan computations for a complete house require processing a 3D scan of the house [15]; the complete scan increases accuracy, but increases computing requirements and time. Pintore and Gobbetti [23] proposed a technique to create floor plans and 3D models using an Android device camera, leveraging sensor data and statistical techniques. Chen et al. [7] introduced an augmented reality system utilizing the Microsoft Hololens for indoor layout assessment, addressing intuitive evaluation and efficiency challenges. In our approach, we begin with a triangle mesh from a HoloLens 2, using its Spatial Mapping software [18], which has been surveyed by Weinmann et al. [27].

Floor Plan Computations. Early methods [1,3,22,28] relied on image processing techniques, such as histograms and plane fitting, to create floor plans from 3D data. While [22] creates a floor plan by detecting vertical planes in a 3D point cloud, [3] uses planar structure extraction to create floor plans. These techniques rely on heuristics and were prone to failure due to noise in the data.

There has been much progress in floor plan computation using graphical models [4,9,12]. Such models [10] are also used to recover layouts and floor plans from crowd-sourced images and location data. One interactive tool [16] creates desirable floorplans by conforming to design constraints.

Pintore et al. [24] characterizes several available input sources (including the triangle meshes that we use) and output models and discusses the main elements of the reconstruction pipeline. It also identifies several systems for producing floor plans, including FloorNet [15], and Floor-SP [6].

Monszpart et al. [19] introduced an algorithm that exploits the observation that distant walls are generally parallel to identify dominant wall directions using k-means. Our approach also utilizes k-means, but does so to identify walls in all directions, not just the dominant ones.

Cai et al. [5] uses geometric priors, including point density, indoor area recognition, and normal information, to reconstruct floorplans from raw point clouds.

In contrast to Arikan et al. [2], which employed a greedy algorithm to find plane normal directions and fit planes to points with help from user interaction, our approach is automatic. It also differs from the work of [20], which focuses on removing clutter and partitioning the interior into a 3D cell complex; our method specifically divides the building into separate walls.

Our work is related to [22] and [26]. In [22], floor plan generation starts with a laser range data point cloud, followed by floor and ceiling detection using a height histogram. The remaining points are projected onto a ground plane, where a density histogram and Hough transform are applied to generate the line segments that form a floor plan. In projecting to 2D, their method risks losing information that may be useful for creating 3D models or detailed floor plans. Similarly, [26] utilizes a histogram-based approach to detect ceilings and floors. Their method involves identifying taller wall segments to create a 2D histogram, and then employing heuristics based on histogram point density to compute the floor plan. Our approach differs from [22] and [26] by aligning the mesh with global coordinate axes and not relying on laser data or a point cloud. Working primarily with 3D data throughout the pipeline, it benefits from enhanced information and generates both a 3D model and a floor plan.

3   Methodology

We compute floor plans in four main steps (see Algorithm 1). First, a user captures the interior of the building as a triangle mesh using an augmented reality headset. The mesh is oriented to align with primary axes, and the building is divided into stories. Floors and ceilings are removed, and flat walls are detected if desired. Finally, one of two floor plan styles is generated by slicing and projecting the resulting 3D model. Next we describe these steps in detail.

Data Collection. Indoor environments can be captured in various formats using different devices. We use a Microsoft HoloLens 2 headset to capture triangle mesh data, annotating the mesh using voice commands.

Capturing the Triangle Mesh. The HoloLens provides hardware and software to create a 3D representation of the indoor environment using triangles, as shown in Fig. 1-left. The headset overlays the triangles on the user's view of the building interior. Although the headset captures most of the walls, floors, and ceilings, data may be missing from some regions, as in the figure.

Algorithm 1. Methodology

1: $\mathcal{M} \leftarrow CaptureData(\mathcal{E})$;
2: $\mathcal{PM} \leftarrow MeshOrientation\ (\mathcal{M})$;
3: $\mathcal{RM} \leftarrow RemoveCeilingsAndFloors\ (\mathcal{PM})$;
4: $\mathcal{FP} \leftarrow ComputeFloorPlan\ (\mathcal{RM})$;
5: **return** $\mathcal{FP}$.

Fig. 1. Left: A triangle mesh is being computed by a HoloLens. Right: The yellow block marks a sensor position. The thick yellow line, known as the *probe*, shows the proposed position and orientation of a sensor or other annotation. (Color figure online)

Annotating the Mesh. To capture object positions such as sensors, thermostats, windows, and doors, we developed an augmented reality (AR) user interface. This interface uses eye gaze detection and voice commands to enable users to place synthetic objects at desired locations, as shown in Fig. 1-right where a synthetic sensor object is added to the immersive environment, superimposed on a physical sensor.

3.1   Mesh Orientation

After the annotated triangle mesh is captured, geometric processing is performed. Initially, the mesh's orientation is based on the user's starting position and gaze direction. To generate a floor plan, we must determine the floor's position and facing direction. The AR headset provides a rough estimation of gravity direction, but additional computation improves precision.

Orienting the Floor. To determine the mesh orientation, we tested two methods: (1) compute the shortest edges of the mesh bounding box, and (2) cluster the facing directions of mesh triangles using spherical k-means. Method (1) works for buildings with constant altitude and large floor area, but it fails on others, so we mainly use Method (2), described in Algorithm 2.

Algorithm 2 applies to a broad range of meshes, including multi-story buildings with vertical dominance. It uses the surface normal vector of each triangle Δ in the mesh $\mathcal{M}$ and filters out triangles deviating significantly from the positive y direction, preserving those likely to represent the floor (Δ').

We use a spherical coordinates k-means algorithm with $k = 1$ to find the dominant direction g_m of these triangles. We discard triangles that are more than an angle ϕ from the dominant direction and repeat the k-means algorithm until ϕ_{min} is reached (e.g., start with $\phi = 30$ degrees and end with $\phi_{min} = 3$). This gives an estimate of the true gravity direction g_t.

To orient the mesh, we compute the angle θ between g_t and the negative y-axis and determine the rotation axis $\mathcal{Y}$ by taking their cross product. We rotate the mesh by θ around the $\mathcal{Y}$ axis, ensuring a horizontal floor. Further details on this method for floor orientation are in Algorithm 2.

Figure 2 shows a model where the floor is not level, but tilts down from near to far and from right to left. After Algorithm 2, the floor is horizontal.

Finding the Height of the Floor. After orienting the mesh to have a horizontal floor, we find the altitude of the floor in the y direction: we take the centroid of each mesh triangle whose facing direction is within a small angle of the positive y axis. We create a histogram of the y coordinates of these centroids, with each bucket representing a vertical range, such as 2 in. We consider adjacent pairs of buckets and look for the pair with the highest number of points, such as $(0, 1)$, $(1, 2)$, etc. For a single-story building, we search for two large bucket pairs representing the floor (near the bottom) and the ceiling (near the top).

Algorithm 2. Orienting the floor using the Spherical k-means method

---

1: **for each** $\Delta \in \mathcal{M}$ **do**
2:      **if** N of Δ facing into the room **then**
3:          $\Delta' \leftarrow \Delta$;
4: **while** $\phi < \phi_{min}$ **do**
5:      $\phi, g_m \leftarrow SphericalKmeans(\Delta', 1)$;
6:      **for each** N of $\Delta \in \mathcal{M}$ **do**
7:          **if** $angle(N) < \phi$ **then**
8:              $\Delta' \leftarrow \Delta$;
9: $g_t \leftarrow -y$;
10: $\theta \leftarrow \arccos(g_t \cdot g_m)$;
11: $\mathcal{Y} \leftarrow g_t \times g_m$;
12: $\mathcal{M} \leftarrow rotateMesh(\theta, \mathcal{Y})$;

If the building has sunken floors or raised ceilings, the histogram will show spikes at similar but not identical altitudes. To ensure that we locate true ceilings

Fig. 2. A model where the floor is not level initially

and floors, we search for a gap of several feet (such as the expected floor-to-ceiling height of a room) between the low and high histogram spikes. The spikes below this gap are probably floors, and those above are probably ceilings.

To generate the floor plan, we choose the highest of the floor levels and the lowest of the ceiling levels as the computed floor and ceiling levels, respectively. Pairing the buckets rather than taking them individually ensures that we do not overlook spikes in the histogram if the mesh triangles are distributed evenly across two adjacent buckets.

Rotate Mesh and Associated Annotations. Our next goal is to align the mesh model's primary wall directions with the axes of Euclidean coordinates.

One optional step is to eliminate mesh triangles whose surface normals are within a small angle from the positive or negative y directions, as these are probably ceiling or floor triangles. This step is not mandatory, but decreases the number of triangles to be processed. Additionally, we eliminate all triangles below the computed floor altitude and all above the computed ceiling altitude.

We then examine the surface normals of the remaining triangles. We express each normal in spherical coordinates and use spherical k-means clustering to identify the dominant wall directions. Assuming the building has mainly perpendicular walls, there will be four primary wall directions, so we can set $k = 4$ for k-means clustering. If the model still has floor and ceiling triangles, we can set $k = 6$ to account for the two additional primary directions. Figure 3-left

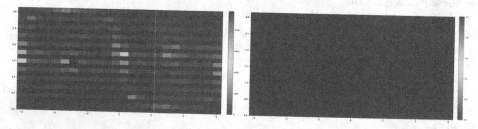

Fig. 3. Left: A heat map of triangle facing directions in spherical coordinates. The horizontal axis is the angle θ around the y-axis. The vertical axis is the angle ϕ from the south pole to the north pole. Warmer colors indicate more triangles per direction bucket. Right: The six cluster centers show the directions of the ceiling (top red dot), the floor (bottom red dot) and the four primary wall directions (dots running left to right at medium height). (Color figure online)

illustrates a heat map of surface normal directions in spherical coordinates from an office building mesh.

Figure 3-left contains many light blue rectangles that are far from any cluster center (e.g., far from the buckets that are red, orange, and white). These represent triangles whose facing directions do not line up with any of the primary walls, floors, or ceilings. Such triangles exist for two reasons: (1) Building interiors contain many objects that are not walls, floors, or ceilings, such as furniture, documents, office equipment, artwork, etc. These objects may be placed at any angle. (2) The AR headset generates triangles that bridge across multiple surfaces (e.g., that touch multiple walls) and hence point in an intermediate direction. To compensate, we use a modified version of spherical coordinates k-means clustering that ignores triangle directions that are outliers as follows:

After computing spherical k-means in the usual way, we look for all triangles in each cluster whose facing direction is more than a threshold θ_1 from the cluster center. We discard all such triangles. Then we run k-means again, computing updated cluster centers. Then we discard all triangles that are more than θ_2 from each cluster center where $\theta_2 < \theta_1$. We repeat this process several times until we achieve the desired accuracy. For example, in our current implementation, we use this sequence of angles θ_i in degrees: [50, 40, 30, 20, 10, 5, 3]. Once our modified k-means algorithm completes, we have 4 (or 6) cluster centers. Figure 3-right shows sample results for $k = 6$.

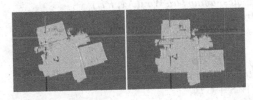

Fig. 4. The mesh model of building B1 (left) that is not aligned initially and the same after wall alignment (right). (Color figure online)

Once the primary wall directions are computed, we pick the cluster with the largest number of triangles, take its direction (cluster center), project that direction onto the $x - z$ plane, and call it θ_{wall}. We rotate the mesh by the angle between θ_{wall} and the x axis. Now the primary walls will be pointing along the x axis. Figure 4-left shows a building that is not aligned with the axes. Figure 4-right shows the same building after wall rotation. Adding in the x axis (in red) and z axis (in blue), we see that the walls are now well-aligned with the axes.

Dividing a Mesh into Separate Levels. The HoloLens can digitize multi-story buildings. Given a multi-story model, we can compute a floor plan for each story. The process is similar to the one used in Sect. 3.1 to find the height of the floor. First, our system computes a histogram, as shown in Fig. 5 and segments the building into multiple levels, as shown in Fig. 5-middle and right.

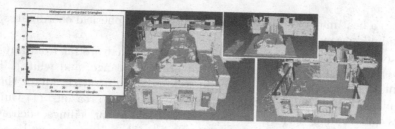

Fig. 5. Left: Using the triangles that face nearly straight up or straight down, plot a histogram of the centroid altitudes, weighted by triangle surface area. Histogram spikes are likely altitudes for floors and ceilings. Middle: A two-story building. Right: the two stories of that building.

3.2   Floor Plan Computation

Our floor plan computation depends on the type of floor plan desired and whether the mesh is oriented with respect to the global axes. If we desire a pen-and-ink style floor plan and the mesh is oriented, we can simply pass the mesh M to the *ComputeAndSuperimposeSlices*() function, as in line 14 of Algorithm 3.2.

Algorithm 3. Compute Floor Plan

1: $\Phi \leftarrow \emptyset$
2: **for each** $\Pi_i \in \Pi$ **do**
3:      $\Delta_i \leftarrow GetTrianglesFacingThisWay(\mathcal{M}, Pi_i)$
4:      $\mathcal{C}_i \leftarrow GetCentroids(\Delta_i)$
5:      $CL_i \leftarrow ModifiedDBSCAN(\mathcal{C}_i, l, w, h)$
6:      $WS \leftarrow \emptyset$
7:      **for each** $CL_{ij} \in CL_i$ **do**
8:          **if** CL_{ij} *extends floor to ceiling* **then**
9:              $WS \leftarrow WS + CL_{ij}$
10:     **for each** $WS_k \in WS$ **do**
11:         $\mathcal{R} \leftarrow ComputeRectangles(WS_k)$
12:     $\Phi_i \leftarrow \Phi_i + \mathcal{R}$
13: $M' \leftarrow AssembleWalls(\Phi)$
14: $\mathcal{FP} \leftarrow ComputeAndSuperimposeSlices(M')$
15: **return** $\mathcal{FP}$

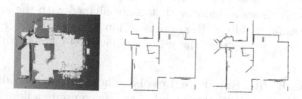

Fig. 6. Left: 3D model. Middle: floor plan obtained via spherical k-means with k = 6. Right: floor plan from a modified DBSCAN that supports more wall orientations.

However, if the mesh is not properly oriented, we align it with the global axes before computing the floor plan. If a drafting-style floor plan is desired, we utilize lines 2–13 of Algorithm 3.2 to compute flat walls. Then we slice the mesh to derive the floor plan using line 14 of the algorithm.

Computing Flat Walls. To generate a drafting-style floor plan, we compute flat walls and separate them from other building contents using these steps:

Wall Directions. Once the floor and ceiling are removed, the remaining walls consist of triangles having surface normals parallel to the xz plane assuming $-y$ is the gravity direction. We use these surface normals to divide the triangles into k sets based on their facing directions Π_i, which we call *wall directions*, denoted as Π. For our initial experiment, we consider $k = 4$ for the principal directions (North, East, South, and West). With these parameters, we are able to achieve precise floor plans in buildings where walls are along principal directions. However, this approach fails when the walls of the building face in arbitrary directions, as in Fig. 6. In such cases, we use spherical k-means to find all the wall directions and then pass them to our DBSCAN algorithm.

DBSCAN. For each wall direction, we perform a modified DBSCAN algorithm: We compute the centroid C of each triangle Δ_i. For each centroid point C_i during DBSCAN, we count the number of other centroid points that are near enough to be considered neighbors. However, instead of looking for neighbors in a sphere around each point as for traditional DBSCAN in 3D, we look for neighbors in a rectangular block of length l, width w and height h centered on the point. This block is tall enough to reach from floor to ceiling in the y direction, a little less wide than a door in the direction parallel to the proposed wall (e.g., 1.5 feet), and a few inches in the wall direction (to allow for walls that deviate slightly from being perfectly flat). Relying on the National Building Code, the wall's minimum height is set at 8 feet, with a thickness of 8 in. After DBSCAN, the mesh triangles are grouped into wall segments WS.

Filtering. We discard wall segments that are not good candidates, such as walls that are too small, that aren't near the floor, or that aren't near the ceiling.

Plane Fitting. For each wall segment, we find a plane that has the same facing direction as the wall direction and that is a good fit to the triangle centroids in that wall segment. Given that the points are tightly collected in this direction, simply having the plane go through any centroid works surprisingly well. However, it is also possible to choose a point more carefully, such as by finding a point at a median position in the wall direction.

Rectangle Construction. For each remaining wall segment, we construct rectangles $\mathcal{R}$ that lie in the fitted plane and are as wide as the wall segment triangles in width and as tall as the wall segment triangles in height.

Mesh Replacement. For floor plan construction, we discard the original mesh triangles and replace them with the new planar wall rectangles to serve as a de-cluttered mesh. If the subsequent steps use libraries that expect a triangle mesh, we use two adjacent right triangles in place of each rectangle.

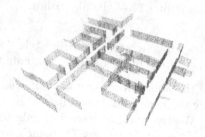

Fig. 7. A building mesh sliced at multiple altitudes.

Slicing the Mesh to Produce a Floor Plan. To produce a pen-and-ink style floor plan, we take our mesh after it has been rotated to have a level floor and to have walls aligned with the primary axes, and we slice that mesh at multiple altitudes. As described above, our histogram of y values allows us to identify the height of the floor or floors and the height of the ceiling or ceilings. We pick a floor height, such as the highest floor, call it y_{floor}. We pick a ceiling height, such as the lowest ceiling, call it $y_{ceiling}$. Then we choose a series of y values between y_{floor} and $y_{ceiling}$, such as an even spacing of y values:

$$y_i = y_{floor} + (y_{ceiling} - y_{floor}) * \left(\frac{i}{n}\right) \tag{1}$$

for each i such that $0 \leq i \leq n$. For each y_i, we compute the intersection of the mesh with the plane $y = y_i$. We end up with a stack of slices (see Fig. 7).

Fig. 8. Left: An oriented mesh from part of a building. Center: The results of DBSCAN. Each color represents a different wall segment. Right: The computed flat walls.

We can use the same method to produce a drafting-style floor plan. In this case, we begin with the flat wall model instead of the full mesh. This model has fewer details to capture by slicing at multiple altitudes, so we may choose to slice at a single intermediate altitude.

Drawing the Floor Plan. For either style of floor plan, we can project the slices to a plane by ignoring the y coordinates of the resulting line segments and plotting the resulting (x, z) coordinates as a two-dimensional image. We have also found it informative and aesthetically pleasing to draw the lines of each slice in a partially-transparent color, so that features that occur at multiple altitudes appear darker than features that occur only at a single altitude.

As an example, Fig. 8-left shows a mesh gathered from a commercial building. Figure 8-center shows the result of our DBSCAN on that data. Figure 8-right shows the flat walls that result after mesh replacement. Figure 9-right shows the drafting-style floor plan that results from slicing the flat walls. Figure 9-left shows the pen-and-ink floor plan made by slicing the oriented mesh at multiple altitudes.

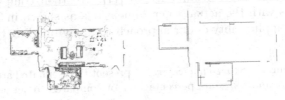

Fig. 9. Pen-and-ink floor plan (left) and drafting floor plan (right) from Fig. 8's model.

Drawing Synthetic Objects. Because our data comes from an AR headset, we can add synthetic objects to mark the positions of objects in a room, such as sensors and windows. We can display these objects in our 3D models and floor plans. For the steps of mesh processing described above, we note the geometric transformations applied to the mesh and apply the same transformations to the synthetic objects, which then appear in the correct places in the 3D views and in the floor plans. For example, the black objects in Fig. 8-left represent the objects placed by the user to show the positions of sensors and windows. Likewise, the red objects in the floor plan of Fig. 9-left are those same objects, projected onto the same plane as the mesh slices.

4   Experiments

We evaluated our approach to capturing 3D scans using AR headsets. We compared the floor plan dimensions with actual building dimensions and provided intermediate results: floor plans and 3D models. We also calculated the time taken for our algorithm steps. To demonstrate the approach robustness, we evaluated using multiple building types, including commercial buildings B1 and B2 and a residential building B3. Additionally, we validated our floor plan generation on the Matterport2D dataset [25].

Scanned Data Analysis. We evaluated the precision of floor plan generation by comparing the actual dimensions of the rooms with the computed floor plan.

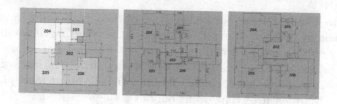

Fig. 10. (a): Building measurement. (b): Scan S1 of the building. (c): Scan S2.

Figure 10(a) illustrates the measurement of the building, which was scanned twice with our AR. We call these scans S1 and S2 (see Fig. 10(b) and Fig. 10(c)) For each scan, floor plans are computed and the dimensions are computed using geometric modeling software, Rhino [17]. We then compared the computed dimensions with the actual room dimensions as shown in Table 1. These results show the applicability of our approach to many building types.

Table 1. Scan Accuracy: $S1area$ and $S2area$ represent the estimated area of each room for two scans. $S1_{err}$ and $S2_{err}$ are percentage error compared to actual dimensions.

Room	Area	$S1_{area}$	$S1_{err}\%$	$S2_{area}$	$S2_{err}\%$
202	24.1243	24.037	0.4	32.7107	1.7
203	7.991	5.5332	30.8	6.9699	12.8
204	31.9608	31.9032	0.2	31.7484	0.7
205	32.5398	33.3375	−2.5	32.6814	−0.4
206	32.9304	32.6536	0.8	32.592	1.0

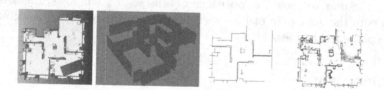

Fig. 11. First: 3D model of building B3. Second: computed flat walls. Third: drafting style floor plan. Fourth: pen-and-ink style floor plan.

Our method can compute a floor plan even from relatively incomplete mesh data. With a higher quality HoloLens scan, the resulting floor plan is more precise. Figure 11 displays S1 results: both types of floor plan and the 3D model.

Orienting Floor and Walls. We must orient the mesh properly. Spherical k-means is compute intensive so we optimize it to get good performance. In Fig. 4, we see the mesh of B1 before and after alignment, which took 12.4 s, of which 10.6 were spent aligning walls using spherical k-means.

Partitioning into Stories. We can detect a multi-story building and divide it into stories with an additional step. The algorithm projects triangles onto the positive y-axis and creates a histogram showing horizontal peaks. By analyzing the peaks in the histogram, we can determine the number of stories. Figures 5 and 12 show a 2-story residential building and a multi-story model from the Matterport3D dataset [25] that were partitioned into stories.

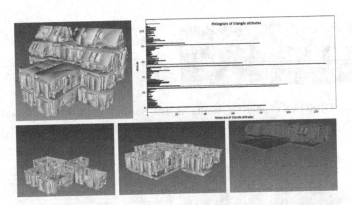

Fig. 12. A three-story model from Matterport3D (top-left) and its triangle altitude histogram (top-right). The bottom figure shows the building sliced into levels.

Finding Planar Walls. To generate a drafting-style floor plan, we eliminate details and identify planar walls. The modified DBSCAN algorithm is the most time-consuming step. In the model of Fig. 13, with 79,931 vertices and 134,235 faces, it took 27.4 s to prepare the data and run DBSCAN and an additional 3.79 s to construct flat walls from the generated clusters. For the residential building of Fig. 14, with 173,941 vertices and 285,840 faces, it took 76 s to prepare and run DBSCAN and 23.36 s to compute flat walls. The results for a Matterport3D model appear in Fig. 15.

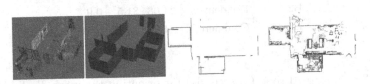

Fig. 13. First: DBSCAN clustering results for building B2. Second: plane-fitted flat walls. Third: drafting-style floor plan. Fourth: pen-and-ink style floor plan.

Generating the Floor Plan. The final step of our floor plan generation is to slice the mesh at different heights and superimpose the slices. Figures 13, 14, and 15 show floor plans generated using our approach.

We conducted experiments to evaluate the effects of changing graphical settings when rendering pen-and-ink floor plans. Each setting consists of a different combination of line segment opacity and slice count. We found that an opacity setting of 0.5 produced a floor plan that met our expectations. We also found that a floor plan with 100 slices provided a good balance between level of detail and clutter reduction. Optimal numbers will depend on use case.

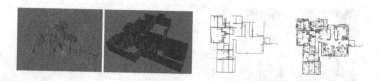

Fig. 14. First: DBSCAN clustering results for B2. Second: plane-fitted flat walls. Third: drafting-style floor plan. Fourth: (c) pen-and-ink style floor plan.

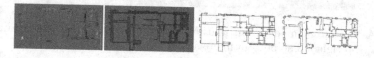

Fig. 15. First: DBSCAN clustering results for a model from Matterport3D. Second: plane-fitted flat walls. Third: drafting-style floor plan. Fourth: pen-and-ink floor plan.

Table 2. Computation (Seconds): T_o, T_p, T_{sd} are times for orienting the mesh, finding planar walls, and slicing/drawing.

Building	Type	T_o	T_p	T_{sd}
B1	Commercial	12.1	31.2	0.5
B2	Residential	24.08	81.5	0.9
B3	Commercial	4.63	15.17	0.51

Table 2 lists elapsed time (in seconds) for orienting the mesh T_o, finding flat walls T_p and slicing and drawing T_{sd} for buildings B1, B2 and B3.

5   Conclusion and Future Work

In summary, our new approach for generating floor plans from triangle mesh data collected by augmented reality (AR) headsets produces two styles: a detailed pen-and-ink style and a simplified drafting style. Our algorithms align the mesh data with primary coordinate axes to produce tidy floor plans with vertical and horizontal walls, while also allowing for the removal of ceilings and floors and the separation of multi-story buildings into individual stories. Our approach integrates with AR, supporting the addition of synthetic objects to physical geometry and providing a detailed 3D model and floor plan.

Potential applications include navigation, interior design, furniture placement, facility management, building construction, and HVAC design. Moving forward, we plan to enable support for sloping ceilings, automate wall and door detection, and integrate with other tools such as energy simulators. Finally, we plan to compare our approach with existing state-of-the-art methods in terms of accuracy and computational time. We also plan to explore the applicability of block-based DBScan for 3D reconstruction from incomplete scans. Our approach has the potential to revolutionize the way we generate and visualize floor plans.

References

1. Adan, A., Huber, D.: 3D reconstruction of interior wall surfaces under occlusion and clutter. In: 2011 International Conference on 3D Imaging, Modeling, Processing, Visualization and Transmission, pp. 275–281 (2011). https://doi.org/10.1109/3DIMPVT.2011.42
2. Arikan, M., Schwärzler, M., Flöry, S., Wimmer, M., Maierhofer, S.: O-snap: optimization-based snapping for modeling architecture. ACM Trans. Graph. **32**(1) (2013). https://doi.org/10.1145/2421636.2421642
3. Budroni, A., Boehm, J.: Automated 3D reconstruction of interiors from point clouds. Int. J. Archit. Comput. **8**(1), 55–73 (2010). https://doi.org/10.1260/1478-0771.8.1.55
4. Cabral, R.S., Furukawa, Y.: Piecewise planar and compact floorplan reconstruction from images. In: 2014 IEEE Conference on Computer Vision and Pattern Recognition, pp. 628–635 (2014)
5. Cai, R., Li, H., Xie, J., Jin, X.: Accurate floorplan reconstruction using geometric priors. Comput. Graph. **102**, 360369 (2022). https://doi.org/10.1016/j.cag.2021.10.011
6. Chen, J., Liu, C., Wu, J., Furukawa, Y.: Floor-SP: inverse cad for floorplans by sequential room-wise shortest path. In: The IEEE International Conference on Computer Vision (ICCV) (2019)
7. Chen, N., Lu, Z., Yu, X., Yang, L., Xu, P., Fan, Y.: Augmented reality-based home interaction layout and evaluation. In: Magnenat-Thalmann, N., et al. (eds.) Advances in Computer Graphics. CGI 2022. LNCS, vol. 13443, pp. 395–406. Springer, Cham (2022). https://doi.org/10.1007/978-3-031-23473-6_31

8. Dasgupta, S., Fang, K., Chen, K., Savarese, S.: Delay: robust spatial layout estimation for cluttered indoor scenes. In: 2016 IEEE Conference on Computer Vision and Pattern Recognition (CVPR), pp. 616–624 (2016). https://doi.org/10.1109/CVPR.2016.73

9. Furukawa, Y., Curless, B., Seitz, S.M., Szeliski, R.: Reconstructing building interiors from images. In: 2009 IEEE 12th International Conference on Computer Vision, pp. 80–87 (2009). https://doi.org/10.1109/ICCV.2009.5459145

10. Gao, R., et al.: Jigsaw: indoor floor plan reconstruction via mobile crowdsensing. In: Proceedings of the 20th Annual International Conference on Mobile Computing and Networking, pp. 249–260. MobiCom '14, Association for Computing Machinery, New York, NY, USA (2014). https://doi.org/10.1145/2639108.2639134

11. Hsiao, C.W., Sun, C., Sun, M., Chen, H.T.: Flat2layout: flat representation for estimating layout of general room types. ArXiv abs/1905.12571 (2019)

12. Ikehata, S., Yang, H., Furukawa, Y.: Structured indoor modeling. In: 2015 IEEE International Conference on Computer Vision (ICCV), pp. 1323–1331 (2015). https://doi.org/10.1109/ICCV.2015.156

13. Kruzhilov, I., Romanov, M., Babichev, D., Konushin, A.: Double refinement network for room layout estimation. In: Palaiahnakote, S., Sanniti di Baja, G., Wang, L., Yan, W.Q. (eds.) ACPR 2019. LNCS, vol. 12046, pp. 557–568. Springer, Cham (2020). https://doi.org/10.1007/978-3-030-41404-7_39

14. Lee, C.Y., Badrinarayanan, V., Malisiewicz, T., Rabinovich, A.: RoomNet: end-to-end room layout estimation. In: 2017 IEEE International Conference on Computer Vision (ICCV), pp. 4875–4884 (2017)

15. Liu, C., Wu, J., Furukawa, Y.: FloorNet: a unified framework for floorplan reconstruction from 3D scans. In: Ferrari, V., Hebert, M., Sminchisescu, C., Weiss, Y. (eds.) ECCV 2018. LNCS, vol. 11210, pp. 203–219. Springer, Cham (2018). https://doi.org/10.1007/978-3-030-01231-1_13

16. Liu, H., Yang, Y.L., AlHalawani, S., Mitra, N.J.: Constraint-aware interior layout exploration for precast concrete-based buildings. Vis. Comput. (CGI Special Issue) **29**, 663–673 (2013)

17. McNeel, R., et al.: Rhinoceros 3D, Version 6.0. Robert McNeel & Associates, Seattle, WA (2010)

18. Microsoft: Spatial mapping (2022). https://docs.microsoft.com/en-us/windows/mixed-reality/spatial-mapping

19. Monszpart, A., Mellado, N., Brostow, G.J., Mitra, N.J.: Rapter: rebuilding man-made scenes with regular arrangements of planes. ACM Trans. Graph. **34**(4) (2015). https://doi.org/10.1145/2766995

20. Mura, C., Mattausch, O., Pajarola, R.: Piecewise-planar reconstruction of multi-room interiors with arbitrary wall arrangements. Comput. Graph. Forum **35**(7), 179–188 (2016). https://doi.org/10.1111/cgf.13015

21. Murali, S., Speciale, P., Oswald, M.R., Pollefeys, M.: Indoor Scan2BIM: building information models of house interiors. In: 2017 IEEE/RSJ International Conference on Intelligent Robots and Systems (IROS), pp. 6126–6133 (2017). https://doi.org/10.1109/IROS.2017.8206513

22. Okorn, B., Xiong, X., Akinci, B.: Toward automated modeling of floor plans. In: Proceedings of the Symposium on 3D Data Processing, Visualization and Transmission, vol. 2 (2010)

23. Pintore, G., Gobbetti, E.: Effective mobile mapping of multi-room indoor structures. Vis. Comput. **30**(6–8), 707–716 (2014)

24. Pintore, G., Mura, C., Ganovelli, F., Fuentes-Perez, L.J., Pajarola, R., Gobbetti, E.: State-of-the-art in automatic 3D reconstruction of structured indoor environments. Comput. Graph. Forum (2020). https://doi.org/10.1111/cgf.14021
25. Ramakrishnan, S.K., et al.: Habitat-matterport 3D dataset (HM3d): 1000 large-scale 3D environments for embodied AI. In: Thirty-fifth Conference on Neural Information Processing Systems Datasets and Benchmarks Track (Round 2) (2021). https://openreview.net/forum?id=-v4OuqNs5P
26. Turner, E., Zakhor, A.: Watertight as-built architectural floor plans generated from laser range data. In: 2012 Second International Conference on 3D Imaging, Modeling, Processing, Visualization Transmission, pp. 316–323 (2012). https://doi.org/10.1109/3DIMPVT.2012.80
27. Weinmann, M., Wursthorn, S., Weinmann, M., Hübner, P.: Efficient 3D mapping and modelling of indoor scenes with the microsoft hololens: a survey. PFG-J. Photogramm. Remote Sens. Geoinf. Sci. **89**(4), 319–333 (2021)
28. Xiong, X., Adan, A., Akinci, B., Huber, D.: Automatic creation of semantically rich 3D building models from laser scanner data. Autom. Constr. **31**, 325–337 (2013). https://doi.org/10.1016/j.autcon.2012.10.006
29. Zhang, J., Kan, C., Schwing, A.G., Urtasun, R.: Estimating the 3D layout of indoor scenes and its clutter from depth sensors. In: 2013 IEEE International Conference on Computer Vision, pp. 1273–1280 (2013). https://doi.org/10.1109/ICCV.2013.161
30. Zou, C., Colburn, A., Shan, Q., Hoiem, D.: Layoutnet: reconstructing the 3D room layout from a single RGB image. In: 2018 IEEE/CVF Conference on Computer Vision and Pattern Recognition (CVPR), pp. 2051–2059. IEEE Computer Society, Los Alamitos, CA, USA, June 2018. https://doi.org/10.1109/CVPR.2018.00219

An Adaptive-Guidance GAN
for Accurate Face Reenactment

Xiaoyu Chai[1,2] , Jun Chen[1,2(✉)] , Dongshu Xu[1,2] , and Hongdou Yao[1,2]

[1] National Engineering Research Center for Multimedia Software,
School of Computer, Wuhan University, Wuhan, China
chenj.whu@gmail.com
[2] Hubei Key Laboratory of Multimedia and Network Communication Engineering,
Wuhan University, Wuhan, China

Abstract. Face reenactment has been widely used in face editing, augmentation and animation. However, it is still challenging to generate photo-realistic target face with accurate pose or expression as reference face, meanwhile retain the identity as the source face. To achieve this goal, we propose an Adaptive-Guidance Generative Adversarial Network (AD-GAN) for accurate face reenactment. Unlike previous methods that control GANs by either directly employing a simple set of vectors or sparse representations (*e.g.*, facial landmarks or boundaries), which ignore the correspondence between reference and source faces, thus leading to inaccurate reenactment or artifacts on target faces. We devise a Correlation Module (CM) that can adaptively establish dense correspondence between a 3D face model as the conditions and the latent features from sources to formulate an indicator map for implementing explicit control of target faces. Besides, the Texture Module (TM) and Guiding Blocks (GB) in generator can restore the facial appearance distorted by expression or pose changes, and progressively guide the generation process. Extensive experiments demonstrate the superiority of our AD-GAN in generating photo-realistic and accurately controllable images.

Keywords: Face Reenactment · Generative Adversarial Network · Accurate Control · Dense Correspondence

1 Introduction

Face reenactment aims at animating a source face by a reference face with arbitrary pose or expression as the reference face, while keep the original appearance and identity of the source face. Due to the wide applications of face reenactment such as augmented reality, telepresence and animation movies, it has long been a topic of great research interests. However, it is difficult to generate target face with accurate pose or expression as the references, as well as causing artifacts on target faces. Therefore, it is essential to develop effective methods to enhance the controllability for reenacted face generation.

B. Sheng et al. (Eds.): CGI 2023, LNCS 14496, pp. 70–82, 2024.
https://doi.org/10.1007/978-3-031-50072-5_6

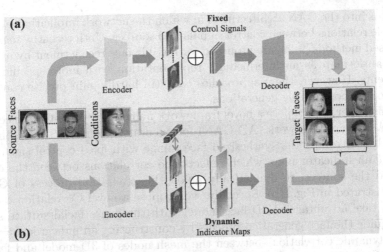

Fig. 1. (a) Conventional face reenactment pipeline, in which the encoder extracts feature maps from sources and directly combined with the conditions, *e.g.* condition vector or facial landmarks, in a fixed form, thus producing inaccurate target face. (b) Our proposed AD-GAN for accurate face reenactment, in which the conditions are adaptively interactive with facial features to produce dynamic indicator maps for implementing explicit control of target faces.

To deal with these issues, earlier works for controlled face reenactment primarily relied on a target vector [6] specifying the desired face expression or pose, to change the relative intensity of certain factors as the condition information in the generation process. These vector-conditioned methods [10,13] can produce coarsely manipulated target faces with globally consistent structures but result in vagueness in local regions. To improve the controllability of a model, subsequent studies [8,26] employ representations with more sufficient and explicit information to boost GANs, which have many applications including [2,18,19,25], to generate controllable and photorealistic faces. For example, the facial landmarks and even 3D face models are considered as the guidance for arbitrary face reenactment. Compared with the directly vector-conditioned methods, these manners incorporate more specific spatial information. However, we argue that current spatial-based approaches can still hardly construct explicitly controllable GANs. For the first reason, the control signals are usually in the sparse form, which inevitably brings about uncertainties. For example, the face landmarks or boundaries carry scant facial contour information as the guidance, whereas real faces have continuous spatial structures, thus leading to semantic ambiguity in generated local facial regions. Let alone the vector-conditioned methods only offer discrete and rough category labels. For the second reason, existing methods usually adopt the control signal with a fixed form, but rarely consider that the control signal has a dynamic influence on the sources since it should act on the activate regions of source faces with certain intensities to implement explicit control over the generative process. Most previous methods [20,24] directly inject conditions into the GAN architectures, in which the network implicitly learns the unreliable relations between control signals and sources. Until recently, semantic-level-based methods [9, 29] are proposed for flexible face reenactment by utilizing the semantic map as an intermediate representation with more specific facial components. However, these approaches can still hardly gain precise control of expression or pose during generations.

In this paper, we propose a novel framework named Adaptive-Guidance Generative Adversarial Network (AD-GAN) for accurate face reenactment. Instead of directly controlling the synthesized face image with fixed control signals, we construct an indicator map, which reflects the correlations between the conditions and the sources, to dynamically guide the generation process of GANs, as demonstrated in Fig. 1(b). Specially, we propose a novel Correlation Module (CM) to take advantage of 3D face model with the dense facial surface structure to guide the face generation process by constructing an indicator map that reflects dynamic correlations between the mesh nodes of 3D model and feature maps of input images. In addition, we introduce a Texture Module (TM) to restore the realistic face appearance that deteriorated by facial expression or pose changes during the learning process in GANs by harnessing the unwrapped facial texture map. With these novel design modules, our AD-GAN enables face reenactment with accurate control of target faces, as well as photo-realistic facial appearance generation.

The contributions of our work are as follows:

1) We propose a novel Adaptive-Guidance Generative Adversarial Network (AD-GAN) to realize face reenactment with accurate expression and pose, in which the CM utilizes 3D face model with sufficient spatial information to guide the face generation process with an indicator map that reflects dynamic correlations between the mesh nodes of 3D model and feature maps of source images.
2) We design a Texture Module (TM) to recover the facial appearance degradation when the facial spatial transformation in reenactment, and Guiding Block (GB) to progressively guide the generation process for producing photo-realistic target face images.
3) Qualitative and quantitative experimental results have demonstrated that our method is able to synthesize reenacted faces with high photo-realism while preserving accurate controllability of expression and pose.

2   Methodology

The overall framework of AD-GAN is illustrated in Fig. 2(a). The Mapping Network, $\mathcal{D}_m (\mathbf{I}_r) \rightarrow C_r$, is utilized for converting the reference $\mathbf{I}_r$ to the face mesh $C_r \in \mathbb{R}^{N \times D}$ as condition, which contains the explicit and dense 3D coordinates of a facial surface. The Correlation Module (CM), $\mathcal{G}_c (C_r, f_d, F_s) \rightarrow F_m$, takes the condition C_r, the deformation feature f_d from the Embedding Extractor and the source face feature F_s to estimate the indicator map F_m, which implies the distinct correspondence between C_r and F_s to guide the face generation process.

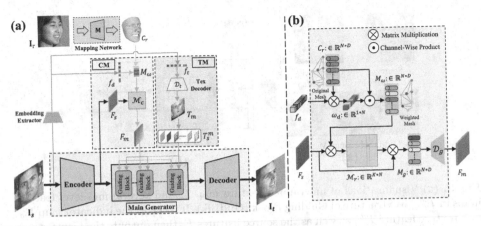

Fig. 2. (a) The framework of proposed AD-GAN. Given a source face $\mathbf{I}_s$ and a reference face $\mathbf{I}_r$, the Image Encoder extracts feature F_s from $\mathbf{I}_s$, and the Embedding Extractor produces the deformation feature f_d and the texture feature f_t. The CM receives the face mesh C_r corresponding to $\mathbf{I}_r$, F_s and f_d to produce an indicator map F_m. The TM utilizes f_t to generate the texture map T_m. Finally, F_m and T_m are injected into the Guiding Blocks of Main Generator to control the generation process. (b) The Correlation Module (CM), which aims to establish explicit and dense correspondences between the C_r from the Mapping Network and source features F_s from image encoder, thus producing an indicator map F_m.

The Texture Module (TM), $\mathcal{G}_t(f_t) \to T_m$, is devised to produce an unwrapped facial texture map by a Texture Decoder to refine the face appearance degradation caused by facial spatial transformation of expression or pose changes. The main generator architecture, $\mathcal{G}(\mathbf{I}_s, F_m, T_m) \to \mathbf{I}_t$, transforms the source face $\mathbf{I}_s$ to the target face $\mathbf{I}_t$, and we further design several Guiding Blocks within it to improve the performance. Note that the Mapping Network and the Texture Decoder in TM are pre-trained models similar with [27] and [17].

2.1 Correlation Module

Figure 2(b) illustrates the structure of Correlation Module (CM), which contains two stages: constructing the correlation matrix and producing the indicator map. The mapping network offers a spatial-aware condition C_r with sufficient geometric information, where each vertex in face mesh has a different deformation intensity, thus the CM should first emphasize high-related and surpass less-useful ones. In light of this, we take a deformation feature $f_d = \mathcal{E}_e(\mathbf{I}_s) \in \mathbb{R}^{1 \times M}$, where $\mathcal{E}_e$ is an Embedding Extractor to extract f_d and a texture feature f_t, to calculate the node-wise attention value: $\omega_d = softmax(f_d \mathbf{W}_d C_r^\top M_p)$, where $\mathbf{W}_d \in \mathbb{R}^{M \times D}$ denotes the weights of a fully-connected layer and $\omega_d \in \mathbb{R}^N$, $M_p \in \mathbb{R}^N$ used for further processing the C_r. Then, the weighted control signal can be solved by $M_\omega = \omega_g \odot C_r \in \mathbb{R}^{N \times D}$, where $\odot$ is the channel-wise product. With the guidance of C_r, the CM attempts to establish the explicit and dense

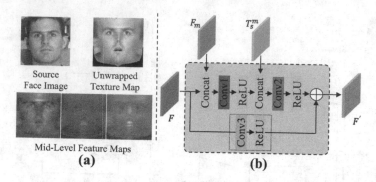

Fig. 3. (a) Visualizations of unwrapped texture map T_s and several mid-level feature maps in T_s^m. (b) Structure of Guiding Block (GudBlk). It receives the indicator map F_m and texture feature T_s^m, as well as the source features F, then outputs the transformed features F'.

relationship between M_ω and F_s by constructing a correlation matrix $\mathcal{M}_r$ in which each element indicates their spatial relationships. It can be formulated as:

$$\mathcal{M}_r(i,j) = \frac{\hat{f}_g(i)^\top \hat{f}_p(j)}{\left\|\hat{f}_g(i)\right\| \left\|\hat{f}_p(j)\right\|}, \tag{1}$$

where $\hat{f}_g(i)$ and $\hat{f}_p(j)$ represent the channel-wise centralized feature of $f_g(i)$ and $f_p(j)$ in position i and j, i.e., $\hat{f}_g(i) = f_g(i) - mean(f_g(i))$, and $\hat{f}_p(j) = f_p(j) - mean(f_g(j))$. The features $f_g = M_\omega\theta_g \in \mathbb{R}^{N \times D}$ and $f_p = F_s\theta_p \in \mathbb{R}^{K \times N}$ are transformed by the learnable parameters θ_g and θ_p for calculating their interactions.

Subsequently, we warp f_p in the formation of $M_g \in \mathbb{R}^{N \times D}$, by using the correlation matrix to select the most related feature pixels in f_p as

$$M_g(i) = \sum_j \underset{j}{softmax}(\boldsymbol{\alpha}\mathcal{M}_r(i,j)) \cdot f_p(j), \tag{2}$$

where $\underset{j}{softmax}$ means the softmax operator across j and $\boldsymbol{\alpha}$ is the coefficient that determines the intensity of the softmax. To obtain the final indicator map F_m, we feed M_g into a Guidance Decoder $\mathcal{D}_g$, which consists of several 2D convolutional up-sampling blocks to expand the spatial size of the feature maps. This can be described as $F_m = \mathcal{D}_g(M_g) \in \mathbb{R}^{W \times H \times C}$.

2.2 Texture Module

We devise the Texture Module (TM) to restore the distorted facial appearances which are caused by face geometry changes during reenactment. In TM, the source face $\mathbf{I}_s$ is first fed into the Embedding Extractor $\mathcal{E}_e$ to obtain the texture feature $f_t = \mathcal{E}_e(\mathbf{I}_s) \in \mathbb{R}^{1 \times T}$, followed by a pre-trained Texture Decoder $\mathcal{D}_t$ [17] to generate the unwrapped texture map T_s. This procedure can be formulated as follows:

$$T_s = \mathcal{D}_t(\mathcal{E}_e(\mathbf{I}_s)). \tag{3}$$

Instead of directly injecting the unwrapped texture map into the generation process, we employ several convolution operations to extract the mid-level feature as well as down-scale the feature size to match the source features, as shown in Fig. 3(a). The outputs of TM are formulated as $T_s^m = T_s \boldsymbol{W}_m$, where $\boldsymbol{W}_m$ are the weights of convolutions.

2.3 Main Generator

As shown in Fig. 2(a), the main generator $\mathcal{G}$ takes the indicator map F_m from $\mathbf{I}_s$ and texture feature T_m^s to synthesize the target face $\mathbf{I}_t$. $\mathcal{G}$ consists of an image encoder $\mathcal{G}_e$, n cascaded Guiding Blocks $\mathcal{G}_b$ and an image decoder $\mathcal{G}_d$. Specifically, each $\mathcal{G}_b$, shown in Fig. 3(b), first concatenates F_m and T_m^s with F to inject the spatial and texture information via several convolution and ReLU activation operations, then a residual connection is also added to maintain the original information. The whole face generation process with the main generator $\mathcal{G}$ can be formulated as:

$$\begin{aligned} \mathbf{I}_t &= \mathcal{G}\left(\mathbf{I}_s, F_m, T_m^s\right) \\ &= \mathcal{G}_d\left(\mathcal{G}_e\left(\mathbf{I}_s\right), \mathcal{G}_b\left(F_m, T_m^s\right)\right), \end{aligned} \tag{4}$$

where $\mathcal{G}_e$, $\mathcal{G}_b$ and $\mathcal{G}_d$ represent the encoder, the GudBlk and decoder, respectively.

2.4 Loss Functions

Since our method is a GAN-based framework, we first introduce an Adversarial Loss $\mathcal{L}_{adv}$ into the training stage to improve the realism of the generated target face image:

$$\mathcal{L}_{adv} = \mathbb{E}\left[\log \mathcal{D}\left(\mathbf{I}_s\right)\right] + \mathbb{E}\left[\log\left(1 - \mathcal{D}\left(\mathcal{G}\left(\mathbf{I}_s, \mathbf{I}_r\right)\right)\right)\right] \tag{5}$$

where $\mathcal{D}$ represents the discriminator similar with [28].

To encourage the target face $\mathbf{I}_t$ preserving the identity of the source $\mathbf{I}_s$, we employ an Identity-Preserving Loss $\mathcal{L}_{id}$ by calculating the cosine distance between the identity features from a pre-trained LightCNN [22] model $\mathcal{F}_{id}$ as follows:

$$\mathcal{L}_{id} = 1 - \frac{\mathcal{F}_{id}\left(\mathbf{I}_s\right) \cdot \mathcal{F}_{id}\left(\mathbf{I}_t\right)}{\left\|\mathcal{F}_{id}\left(\mathbf{I}_s\right)\right\|_2 \left\|\mathcal{F}_{id}\left(\mathbf{I}_t\right)\right\|_2}. \tag{6}$$

The output $\mathbf{I}_t$ should be consistent with the semantics of the ground-truth image $\mathbf{I}_{gt}$. We thereby penalize the Perceptual Loss $\mathcal{L}_{per}$ to minimize the semantic discrepancy:

$$\mathcal{L}_{per} = \left\|\psi_l\left(\mathbf{I}_{gt}\right) - \psi_l\left(\mathbf{I}_t\right)\right\|_1, \tag{7}$$

where ψ_l is the activation after the *relu* 4_2 layer in the VGG-19 network [16] since it mainly contains high-level semantics.

We employ Reconstruction Loss $\mathcal{L}_{rec}$ to measure the L1 distance between the ground-truth image $\mathbf{I}_{gt}$ and the generated target face $\mathbf{I}_t$ as:

$$\mathcal{L}_{rec} = \frac{1}{WH} \sum_{x=1}^{W} \sum_{y=1}^{H} \|\mathbf{I}_{gt} - \mathbf{I}_t\|_1 \odot \mathcal{M}_v, \tag{8}$$

where $\mathcal{M}_v$ is the visibility mask, $\odot$ is the Hadamard-product operation, W and H are the width and height of an image.

We utilize the Cycle Loss $\mathcal{L}_{cyc}$ to constrain the cycle consistency that the converted $\mathbf{I}_t$ is able to convert back again:

$$\mathcal{L}_{cyc} = \left\| \mathcal{G}\left(\mathcal{G}(\mathbf{I}_s, \mathbf{I}_r^t), \mathbf{I}_r^s \right) - \mathbf{I}_s \right\|_1, \tag{9}$$

where $\mathbf{I}_r^s$ and $\mathbf{I}_r^t$ are the corresponding control signal with respect to $\mathbf{I}_s$ and $\mathbf{I}_t$.
To sum, we optimize the following total objective:

$$\mathcal{L} = \lambda_1 \mathcal{L}_{adv} + \lambda_2 \mathcal{L}_{id} + \lambda_3 \mathcal{L}_{per} + \lambda_4 \mathcal{L}_{rec} + \lambda_5 \mathcal{L}_{cyc}, \tag{10}$$

where λ_i represents the weight parameters.

3 Experiments

3.1 Experimental Setup

Datasets. We utilize Multi-PIE [4] and VoxCeleb1 [11] datasets to train AD-GAN. Multi-PIE contains over $730,000$ images of 337 subjects with different poses, illuminations and expressions. VoxCeleb1 is extracted from YouTube videos, which includes over 100k utterances with $1,251$ different identities. The test split of VoxCeleb1 and CelebV [21] are adopted for evaluating face reenactment with same and different identities, respectively. There are $2,083$ images sampled from randomly selected 100 videos of VoxCeleb1 test split, and $2,000$ images are uniformly sampled from every identity of CelebV. All the images are cropped to 256×256. We run [1] to acquire the 3D meshes from references.

Implementations. The model is trained using PyTorch on Ubuntu 20.04 With 2 Titan V GPUs. We adopt Adam optimizer [7] with the learning rate of 2×10^{-4}. The batch size is set as 16. The weights for the loss terms are empirically set as 1, 1, 10, 10 and 5 with respect to λ_1, λ_2, λ_3, λ_4 and λ_5. The dimension of f_d and f_t are set as $M = T = 128$. We define the vertex number of the face mesh as $N = 53,215$. There are $D = 3$ channels of each vertex, which represent the value of x, y, and z coordinates, respectively. The $\mathcal{E}_e$ is a pre-trained model [22] for producing f_d and f_t.

Metrics. We adopt the following metrics to evaluate the quality of the results as in [5]. CSIM (the cosine similarity) is used to evaluate the quality of identity preservation according to the embedding vectors generated by a pre-trained face recognition network [3]. PRMSE (the root mean square error of the head pose angles) is utilized to inspect the capability of the model to properly reenact the pose and the expression of the reference. AUCON is the ratio of identical facial action unit values between the generated images and the reference images.

Source   Reference   w/o CM   w/o TM   Full

Fig. 4. Visual examples of ablation study on CelebV with different variants.

3.2   Experimental Results

Ablation Study. We conduct the ablation study on CelebV dataset to demonstrate the effectiveness of each component in AD-GAN with three different settings: (1) *w/o CM*: All the modules are reserved except for CM is removed, and replaced by directly concatenating the feature f_c with source features in GB. (2) *w/o TM*: All the modules are reserved except for TM is removed, thus unrefined texture features are injected into GB. (3) *Full*: Keep all modules.

Figure 4 shows the results of our model with different variants on CelebV. Several examples of source faces are reenacted by the reference faces with the corresponding 3D meshes. We can observe that the *Full* model produces the best results for both the photo-realistic and control ability of the target face. The CM can facilitate the expression and pose of reenacted faces that are more consistent with references, *e.g.* the angle of the head pose and the degree of opening mouth. And the TM can effectively improve image quality and reduce artifacts by producing the unwrapped texture map, *e.g.* the color of skin and black regions on the faces.

Table 1. Evaluation result of ablation study for reenactment faces on CelebV.

Model	CSIM ↑	PRMSE ↓	AUCON ↑
w/o CM	0.594	4.37	0.674
w/o TM	0.441	3.51	0.701
Full	**0.653**	**3.14**	**0.731**

Table 1 further demonstrates different variants of our model on CelebV. For identity preservation (*i.e.*, CSIM), both CM and TM have a certain impact on the target face identity, since the shape and texture of the targets are not well handled during the generation process for the lack of CM and TM. While the

Table 2. Evaluation result of face reenactment on VoxCeleb1.

Method	CSIM ↑	PRMSE ↓	AUCON ↑
X2Face [20]	0.689	3.26	0.813
Monkey-Net [14]	0.697	3.46	0.770
NeuralHead-FF [23]	0.229	3.76	0.791
FirstOrder [15]	0.693	3.59	0.847
PIRenderer [12]	0.761	3.09	0.842
Ours	**0.787**	**3.01**	**0.873**

CM can effectively enhance the network to control face pose and expression, therefore achieving better PRMSE and AUCON values. The results of the *Full* model reveal that the CM and TM are both beneficial for pose and expression control, as well as identity preserving for face reenactment.

Qualitative Results. We conduct and analyze a series of qualitative experiments on the VoxCeleb1 datasets to demonstrate the high performance of the generated images and the controllability of our proposed framework compared with other representative methods. As the results are shown in Fig. 5, Our *AD-GAN* can successfully reenact source face images to similar ones of expression and pose in reference faces, and also alleviate the identity preservation problem regardless of the condition faces are of the same identity or not. As for *X2Face* [20], which directly utilizes image warping by a 128-dimensional condition vector, the background of the generated image seems to affect the facial structure, thus producing a severe distortion in some regions. *NH-FF* [23] which exploits AdaIN layers and is controlled by facial landmarks, performs well in the case of intra-identity transferring. However, for different identities, it is prone to generating blur images as the insufficient landmark guidance. *DAE-GAN* [24], which feeds the face embedding into a conditional generator with pose vector, exhibits slightly better performance in terms of image quality and controllability, but the identity of the generated faces is not well preserved.

Quantitative Results. We quantitatively verify the performance of our method on VoxCeleb1 and CelebV datasets. First, we compute the results of different models for face reenactment by the same identity on VoxCeleb1, as listed in Table 2. It is worth noting that the *Monkey-Net* [14] adopts feature-level warping to implement face manipulation. *NH-FF* [23] utilizes AdaIN layers to import face landmark information. For *FirstOder* [15], we use the source image as the initial condition image to perform relative motion transfer. *PIRenderer* proposes to change 3DMM parameters to control target face generation. Notably, the highest score in CSIM demonstrates that our method achieves better identity consistency with the source face image than other methods. Besides, the results of PRMSE and AUCON show our method is competitive with other methods, especially for pose rotation, indicating our method with explicit control signals can synthesize targets that are more inclined to sustain the source pose and expression.

Fig. 5. Comparisons on the VoxCeleb1 test dataset. The first two columns shows the Intra-identity face reenactment, the last three columns display the Inter-identity face reenactment.

We then evaluate the results of different models for face manipulation by different identities on CelebV, as listed in Table 3. Our method outperforms all others in every metric. Specifically, the low CSIM score from *NH-FF* [23] is an indirect evidence of the lack of capacity in AdaIN-based methods. However, our proposed AD-GAN is capable of preserving target identity information, thus

Table 3. Evaluation result of face reenactment on CelebV.

Method	CSIM ↑	PRMSE ↓	AUCON ↑
X2Face [20]	0.450	3.62	0.679
Monkey-Net [14]	0.451	4.81	0.584
NeuralHead-FF [23]	0.108	3.30	0.722
FirstOrder [15]	0.462	3.90	0.667
PIRenderer [12]	0.533	3.39	0.714
Ours	**0.643**	**3.19**	**0.728**

outperforming other models in CSIM. As for PRMSE and AUCON, other methods adopt fixed control signals to guide the face generation, while our results surpass others demonstrating that the proposed dynamic indicator map can more faithfully manipulate the target pose and expression from condition faces.

4   Conclusion

We propose a novel Adaptive-Guidance GAN (AD-GAN) for accurate face reenactment, in which the Correlation Module (CM) can effectively utilize 3D face model to guide the face generation process with an indicator map that reflects dynamic correlations between the mesh nodes of 3D model and feature maps of sources, so that the reenacted face can be better consistent with the same pose and expression as the sources. Besides, we design a Texture Module (TM) to recover the degraded facial appearance during the generation procedure by yielding an unwrapped texture map. Compared with previous methods, our network can generate results with more natural looking while keeping accurate control ability.

References

1. Chai, X., Chen, J., Liang, C., Xu, D., Lin, C.: Expression-aware face reconstruction via a dual-stream network. IEEE Trans. Multimedia **23**, 2998–3012 (2021)
2. Cheema, M.N., et al.: Modified GAN-cAED to minimize risk of unintentional liver major vessels cutting by controlled segmentation using CTA/SPET-CT. IEEE Trans. Ind. Inform. **17**, 7991–8002 (2021)
3. Deng, J., Guo, J., Xue, N., Zafeiriou, S.: Arcface: additive angular margin loss for deep face recognition. In: Proceedings of the IEEE Conference on Computer Vision and Pattern Recognition, pp. 4690–4699 (2019)
4. Gross, R., Matthews, I., Cohn, J., Kanade, T., Baker, S.: Multi-pie. Image Vision Comput. **28**(5), 807–813 (2010)
5. Ha, S., Kersner, M., Kim, B., Seo, S., Kim, D.: Marionette: few-shot face reenactment preserving identity of unseen targets. In: Proceedings of the AAAI Conference on Artificial Intelligence, pp. 10893–10900 (2020)
6. He, Z., Zuo, W., Kan, M., Shan, S., Chen, X.: AttGAN: facial attribute editing by only changing what you want. IEEE Trans. Image Process. **28**(11), 5464–5478 (2019)
7. Kingma, D.P., Ba, J.: Adam: a method for stochastic optimization. In: International Conference on Learning Representations, pp. 1–15 (2015)
8. Kowalski, M., Garbin, S.J., Estellers, V., Baltrušaitis, T., Johnson, M., Shotton, J.: CONFIG: controllable neural face image generation. In: Vedaldi, A., Bischof, H., Brox, T., Frahm, J.-M. (eds.) ECCV 2020. LNCS, vol. 12356, pp. 299–315. Springer, Cham (2020). https://doi.org/10.1007/978-3-030-58621-8_18

9. Lee, C., Liu, Z., Wu, L., Luo, P.: MaskGAN: towards diverse and interactive facial image manipulation. In: Proceedings of the IEEE Conference on Computer Vision and Pattern Recognition, pp. 5549–5558 (2020)
10. Liu, M., et al.: STGAN: a unified selective transfer network for arbitrary image attribute editing. In: Proceedings of the IEEE Conference on Computer Vision and Pattern Recognition, pp. 3673–3682 (2019)
11. Nagrani, A., Chung, J.S., Zisserman, A.: VoxCeleb: a large-scale speaker identification dataset. In: Proceedings of the Annual Conference of the International Speech Communication Association, pp. 2616–2620 (2017)
12. Ren, Y., Li, G., Chen, Y., Li, T.H., Liu, S.: PIRenderer: controllable portrait image generation via semantic neural rendering. In: Proceedings of the IEEE International Conference on Computer Vision, pp. 13759–13768 (2021)
13. Shen, Y., Luo, P., Yan, J., Wang, X., Tang, X.: FaceID-GAN: learning a symmetry three-player GAN for identity-preserving face synthesis. In: Proceedings of the IEEE Conference on Computer Vision and Pattern Recognition, pp. 821–830 (2018)
14. Siarohin, A., Lathuilière, S., Tulyakov, S., Ricci, E., Sebe, N.: Animating arbitrary objects via deep motion transfer. In: Proceedings of the IEEE Conference on Computer Vision and Pattern Recognition, pp. 2377–2386 (2019)
15. Siarohin, A., Lathuilière, S., Tulyakov, S., Ricci, E., Sebe, N.: First order motion model for image animation. In: Advances in Neural Information Processing Systems 32, pp. 7137–7147 (2019)
16. Simonyan, K., Zisserman, A.: Very deep convolutional networks for large-scale image recognition. In: International Conference on Learning Representations, pp. 1–14 (2014)
17. Tran, L., Liu, X.: On learning 3D face morphable model from in-the-wild images. IEEE Trans. Pattern Anal. Mach. Intell. 43(1), 157–171 (2019)
18. Wang, L., Sun, Y., Wang, Z.: CCS-GAN: a semi-supervised generative adversarial network for image classification. Vis. Comput. 38, 2009–2021 (2022)
19. Wen, Y., et al.: Structure-aware motion deblurring using multi-adversarial optimized CycleGAN. IEEE Trans. Image Process. 30, 6142–6155 (2021)
20. Wiles, O., Koepke, A.S., Zisserman, A.: X2Face: a network for controlling face generation using images, audio, and pose codes. In: Ferrari, V., Hebert, M., Sminchisescu, C., Weiss, Y. (eds.) ECCV 2018. LNCS, vol. 11217, pp. 690–706. Springer, Cham (2018). https://doi.org/10.1007/978-3-030-01261-8_41
21. Wu, W., Zhang, Y., Li, C., Qian, C., Loy, C.C.: ReenactGAN: learning to reenact faces via boundary transfer. In: Ferrari, V., Hebert, M., Sminchisescu, C., Weiss, Y. (eds.) ECCV 2018. LNCS, vol. 11205, pp. 622–638. Springer, Cham (2018). https://doi.org/10.1007/978-3-030-01246-5_37
22. Wu, X., He, R., Sun, Z., Tan, T.: A light CNN for deep face representation with noisy labels. IEEE Trans. Inf. Foren. Secur. 13(11), 2884–2896 (2018)
23. Zakharov, E., Shysheya, A., Burkov, E., Lempitsky, V.: Few-shot adversarial learning of realistic neural talking head models. In: Proceedings of the IEEE Conference on Computer Vision and Pattern Recognition, pp. 9459–9468 (2019)
24. Zeng, X., Pan, Y., Wang, M., Zhang, J., Liu, Y.: Realistic face reenactment via self-supervised disentangling of identity and pose. In: Proceedings of the AAAI Conference on Artificial Intelligence, pp. 12757–12764 (2020)
25. Zhang, Y., Han, S., Zhang, Z., Wang, J., Bi, H.: CF-GAN: cross-domain feature fusion generative adversarial network for text-to-image synthesis. Vis. Comput. 39, 1283–1293 (2023)
26. Zhao, J., et al.: Dual-agent GANs for photorealistic and identity preserving profile face synthesis. In: Advances in Neural Information Processing Systems 30 (2017)

27. Zhou, Y., Deng, J., Kotsia, I., Zafeiriou, S.: Dense 3D face decoding over 2500fps: joint texture & shape convolutional mesh decoders. In: Proceedings of the IEEE Conference on Computer Vision and Pattern Recognition, pp. 1097–1106 (2019)
28. Zhu, J., Park, T., Isola, P., Efros, A.A.: Unpaired image-to-image translation using cycle-consistent adversarial networks. In: Proceedings of the IEEE International Conference on Computer Vision, pp. 2223–2232 (2017)
29. Zhu, P., Abdal, R., Qin, Y., Wonka, P.: SEAN: image synthesis with semantic region-adaptive normalization. In: Proceedings of the IEEE Conference on Computer Vision and Pattern Recognition, pp. 5104–5113 (2020)

Reconstructing Neutral Face Expressions with Disentangled Variational Autoencoder

Grina Wiem[1,2]($\boxtimes$) (ID) and Douik Ali[1] (ID)

[1] University of Sousse, Networked Objects Control and Communication Systems Laboratory, National School of Engineers of Sousse, Sousse Technology Center, Sahloul Belt Road, Sousse 4054, Tunisia
grinawiem@gmail.com, ali.douik@eniso.u-sousse.tn
[2] University of Monastir, National Engineering School of Monastir, Rue Ibn Jazzar, Monastir 5035, Tunisia

Abstract. This study tackles unsupervised learning for disentangled representations in facial expression generation. It introduces a novel deep architecture by combining FactorVAE and β-VAE concepts, incorporating the Ranger optimizer and Dropout layers. The goal is to learn disentangled representations that capture essential facial expression factors, like the neutral expression, while ensuring independence between different expression dimensions. This approach achieves faster convergence and improved optimization, striking a better balance between disentanglement and reconstruction quality. The method enables accurate and diverse facial expression generation and enhances model generalization through adaptive learning rate adjustments. The learned disentangled representations also facilitate the generation of realistic and interpretable facial expressions, making it a promising approach for various facial expression generation tasks.

Keywords: Face expression generation · Disentangled representation · Variational autoencoder · Ranger optimizer

1 Introduction

Representation learning is a fundamental aspect of machine learning research, where the quality of input representations significantly impacts the performance of algorithms [6,9,10]. Deep learning methods have gained popularity for implicitly learning representations, but they often suffer from overfitting and lack generalization beyond the training data distribution. To address these limitations, task-agnostic unsupervised learning has emerged as a promising approach, aiming to learn features that exhibit high performance across diverse tasks. Disentangled representations [7,8], characterized by individual latent units capturing specific generative factors, hold significant promise for achieving generalization and interpretability. This concept has been explored in the context of learning essential properties without requiring supervised knowledge of generative factors. While earlier attempts focused on supervised approaches, recent works [9] such as β-VAE [19] and FactorVAE [24], have shifted towards unsupervised methods. β-VAE extends the Variational Autoencoder (VAE) [10] with a hyperparameter β to encourage factorized latent representations. On the other hand, FactorVAE [24], a state-of-the-art approach, addresses unsupervised disentangled representation learning in data with independent generative factors [11]. Facial expression generation [11,21,23] is a crucial aspect of computer vision research, with profound implications for human-computer interaction, emotion analysis, virtual reality, and entertainment industries. However, achieving this task remains challenging due to the complexity and high-dimensional nature of facial expressions. To address this challenge, we propose a novel deep architecture that builds upon the principles of FactorVAE and β-VAE, two state-of-the-art unsupervised learning methods for disentangled representation learning. By integrating the Ranger optimizer with Dropout layers, our approach encourages a factorial distribution of facial expression representations, ensuring independence between different facial expression dimensions. This promotes faster convergence during the learning process and allows for more efficient optimization of model parameters.

The main objective of this paper is to achieve disentangled representations that effectively capture the essential generative factors responsible for facial expressions. We aim to strike a balance between the fidelity of facial expression reconstruction and the disentanglement of the underlying factors, thereby enabling accurate and diverse facial expression generation. The contributions of this paper lie in advancing the field of unsupervised learning for facial expression generation by incorporating cutting-edge techniques to disentangle facial expression representations. We experimentally validate our approach on the CelebA dataset, showcasing its superiority over existing methods in capturing facial expression variations while ensuring interpretability and generalization. In the following sections, we present the details of our proposed deep architecture, the methodology used to learn disentangled facial expression representations, and the experimental results demonstrating the effectiveness of our approach. Additionally, we discuss the implications of our findings and future directions for research in the domain of facial expression generation using unsupervised learning techniques.

2   Related Works

Several recent research works have emerged, concentrating on different facets of VAEs. Here we explore several existing works that have tackled the challenges posed by VAEs.

The β-VAE [19] incorporates a hyperparameter β to control the balance between reconstruction accuracy and the disentanglement of latent variables. By adjusting the value of β, the β-VAE allows for a trade-off between reconstruction accuracy and the disentanglement of the latent variables. By incorporating disentangled representations in β-VAE [9,10,19] entails formulating and training the model with an emphasis on fostering the acquisition of latent variables that are both independent and interpretable. Burgess et al. provided a detailed analysis of the disentanglement properties of β-VAE [19] by exploring the relationship between the β parameter and the resulting disentanglement and proposes a new metric for quantifying disentanglement. Kim and Mnih proposed the Factor-VAE model [1] which extends the VAE framework with a specific objective that encourages the independence of the latent factors. To achieve disentanglement, FactorVAE introduces a specific training objective that emphasizes independence between the latent factors. Additionally, Zhao, Kim, and Zhang presented another variant of the VAE framework known as Information Maximizing Variational Autoencoder (InfoVAE) [2].

Recent works in the field of VAEs [2,19] have made significant advancements, tackling issues like disentanglement, sample quality, information preservation, and integrating adversarial training. These contributions have led to more robust and interpretable representations of complex data, improving the learning and generation capabilities of VAEs. While the examples mentioned above demonstrate progress, it is essential to explore the latest research literature for additional advancements and refinements in this area.

This paper offers a comprehensive explanation of β-VAE and FactorVAE frameworks, along with insights into the Ranger optimizer and Dropout layers as regularization techniques. It highlights the benefits of using the Ranger optimizer within Dropout layers, leading to improved disentangled representations and preventing overfitting. These techniques demonstrate significant potential in applications like data generation, feature extraction, and anomaly detection, making this paper a valuable contribution in the field of VAEs.

3 Proposed Method

In this section, we describe the methodologies employed in this study, specifically focusing on the β-VAE and FactorVAE frameworks.

3.1 β Variational Autoencoder

β Variational Autoencoder [19] is an extension of the standard VAE framework that introduces an additional hyperparameter, β, to the objective function:

$$\mathcal{L}(\theta, \phi; x, z, \beta) = \mathbb{E}_{q_\phi(z|x)}[log p_\theta(x|z)] - \beta D_{KL}(q_\phi(z|x)p(z)) \qquad (1)$$

The method of β-VAE [19] aims to learn more disentangled and interpretable latent representations. By introducing a stronger constraint on the latent space, the model learns meaningful and independent factors of variation in the data, enhancing interpretability. The value of β determines the trade-off between reconstruction fidelity and disentanglement in the learned latent representations z. Higher values of β (usually $\beta > 1$) encourage more disentangled representations. When β equals 1, β-VAE is equivalent to the original VAE. The β-VAE objective applies additional pressure for the posterior $q_\phi(z|x)$ to match the factorized unit Gaussian prior $p(z)$, imposing constraints on the latent bottleneck z while ensuring data reconstruction. However, higher β values may lead to a trade-off between reconstruction accuracy and disentanglement, as information loss occurs when data passes through the limited capacity of z. Achieving better disentanglement with higher β may result in decreased reconstruction accuracy due to the compression of information in the latent space. However, β-VAE often faces a trade-off between achieving better disentanglement and maintaining high reconstruction fidelity. Higher values of β that encourage stronger disentanglement may lead to a decrease in reconstruction accuracy, as the model has to compress more information into the limited capacity of the latent space.

3.2   Factor Variational Autoencoder

FactorVAE aims to learn a latent representation capturing underlying variation in the data while ensuring accurate reconstruction. It promotes a factorial distribution of the latent representation, encouraging independence across dimensions. This is achieved through an additional regularization term based on the TC measure, quantifying statistical dependence among latent variables. The objective function of FactorVAE combines the standard VAE reconstruction loss with this regularization term, promoting disentanglement. It comprises three main components: the reconstruction loss, the Kullback-Leibler (KL) divergence term, and the TC term.

$$\mathcal{L}_{recon} = arg_{\phi,\theta}min - \mathbb{E}_{q\phi}(z|x) \left[log(p_\theta\left(x|z\right)) \right] \tag{2}$$

$$\mathcal{L}_{TC} = KL. \left[q(z) \parallel \prod_j q(z_j) \right] \tag{3}$$

$$\mathcal{L}_{KL} = \sum_j KL\left[q(z_i) \parallel p(z_i) \right] \tag{4}$$

$$\mathcal{L} = \alpha\mathcal{L}_{recon} + \beta \cdot \mathcal{L}_{KL} + \gamma \cdot \mathcal{L}_{TC} \tag{5}$$

where, $\mathcal{L}_{recon}$ represents the reconstruction loss, which measures the discrepancy between the input data and the output of the VAE decoder. $\mathcal{L}_{KL}$ designates the Kullback-Leibler (KL) divergence term, which regularizes the latent space by encouraging it to be close to the prior distribution. $\mathcal{L}_{TC}$ indicates the TC term, which promotes disentanglement by encouraging independence among the dimensions of the latent representation. β references the hyperparameter that controls the importance of the KL divergence term. γ denotes the hyperparameter that controls the importance of the TC term. FactorVAE's objective function consists of three main components: the reconstruction loss, KL divergence term, and TC term, with their specific forms varying depending on the implementation. In our case, we used the cross-entropy loss function to calculate the reconstruction loss. The relative weights of the three terms (L_{recon}, L_{KL}, and L_{TC}) are determined by hyperparameters α, β, and γ. Setting α and γ to 1 while allowing β to be greater than 1, we achieved precise calculations for each term using a closed-form solution. Estimating the TC term through a classifier and the density-ratio trick promotes the learning of disentangled representations.

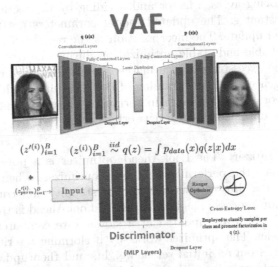

Fig. 1. Overview of the structure our proposed network which follows a carefully designed structure that combines various components Encoder, Decoder, Latent Space, Discriminator, Ranger Optimizer and Dropout Layers. The structure of the network provides a solid foundation for our research, allowing us to explore the potential benefits of employing these techniques within the VAE framework.

3.3 Ranger Optimizer

Ranger [16] is an optimizer that combines the techniques of Rectified Adam (RAdam) [18] and LookAhead [17]to provide improved performance in training deep neural networks. It aims to overcome some limitations of traditional optimization methods such as Adam and achieve faster convergence and better generalization. Ranger combines the benefits of RAdam, which addresses the convergence issues of Adam, and LookAhead, which introduces the concept of "slow weights" to stabilize the learning process. The key idea behind LookAhead is to create a "backup" of the weights at a slower update rate and use them to perform a lookahead step during training.

Rectified Adam. RAdam [18] aims to improve the stability and convergence of the adaptive learning rate used in Adam, especially during initial iterations. It introduces a dynamic rectification term to adjust the adaptive learning rate behavior. The RAdam update equation involves calculating the rectification term r_t, which stabilizes and adjusts the learning rate based on the magnitude of gradients. This term is derived from the ratio between the exponentially weighted moving average of the squared gradients $\hat{v}$ and the bias-corrected moving average of v. The rectified update $\hat{m}$ is obtained by adjusting the gradients using the bias-corrected moving average factor and dividing by the rectification term r_t plus a small constant ϵ. The updated model parameters are then computed using this rectified update. The incorporation of the rectification term, RAdam provides more reliable and stable optimization during the training process. It helps mitigate the excessive variance in the adaptive learning rate, leading to improved convergence and faster training of deep learning models. RAdam has demonstrated favorable performance in various applications and has become a popular choice for optimizing neural networks.

Lookahead Optimizer. The LookAhead optimizer is a powerful technique designed to enhance the performance of base optimizers when training deep neural networks. It addresses issues related to stability and convergence during the optimization process. The key feature of LookAhead is the introduction of "slow weights," which are updated at a slower rate compared to the main weights of the model. The optimizer works by performing a series of optimization steps, starting from an initial set of weights and then updating the "slow weights" through interpolation with the weights obtained after a certain number of steps. By incorporating the LookAhead step, the optimizer promotes smoother optimization trajectories and prevents the model from being trapped in suboptimal solutions. This leads to improved speed and stability in stochastic gradient descent algorithms. The technique has demonstrated its effectiveness in optimizing deep neural networks, ultimately resulting in better convergence during training.

3.4 Dropout Regularization

The Dropout layer is a regularization technique used in neural networks to prevent overfitting and improve generalization. It randomly deactivates a fraction of neurons during training, reducing reliance on specific connections and features and promoting the learning of more robust and generalized representations. In the proposed framework, the Dropout layer is integrated after the two fully connected layers of both the encoder and the decoder. During training, a Dropout rate of 0.2 is used, randomly setting 20% of units to zero in each iteration. This introduces stochasticity and reduces reliance on specific connections or features, helping the network learn more robust and generalizable representations. The Dropout process involves generating a binary mask for each training example, where each element indicates whether a corresponding unit should be dropped out or kept. The mask is then applied to the output of the previous layer, deactivating certain units and passing the modified output to the next layer for further processing. During inference or testing, the Dropout layer is turned off to make consistent and deterministic predictions. This ensures that the network's predictions are not influenced by randomness during training, allowing it to utilize the collective knowledge acquired and produce more reliable outputs.

4   Experiments

In this section, we present the experimental setup and results of our proposed deep architecture for facial expression generation, Fig. 1. We conduct a comprehensive evaluation to demonstrate the effectiveness of our approach in learning disentangled representations and generating realistic neutral facial expressions.

4.1   CelebA Dataset

The CelebA dataset [20] is a valuable resource with rich statistics, containing 10,177 unique identities and a vast collection of 202,599 face images, encompassing celebrities and individuals. Each image is annotated with 40 binary attribute labels, providing intricate facial attribute information like glasses, smile, oval face, narrow eyes, large lips, and more. The dataset exhibits variations in pose, background, and other factors, making it comprehensive for exploration and analysis. To optimize training, we resized the CelebA images in our study to 64 × 64 pixels, reducing memory requirements and computational intensity. Training on smaller images accelerated forward and backward propagation, ensuring faster training times while retaining essential details for the task. The CelebA dataset was thoughtfully split into three subsets: a training set (80% - 160,000 images), a validation set (10% - 20,000 images), and a test set (10% - 20,000 images). This balanced distribution enables the model to be trained on a substantial portion while having separate data for evaluation. The validation set is used for hyperparameter tuning and monitoring performance during training to prevent overfitting. Lastly, the test set allows unbiased evaluation of the model's generalization capability on unseen data

4.2   Experimental Details

In this study, we addressed unsupervised learning for disentangled representations using the CelebA dataset, incorporating ideas from FactorVAE and β-VAE. Our proposed approach leveraged the Ranger optimizer and Dropout layers, leading to significant improvements in the model. The method encouraged factorial representation distribution and ensured dimension independence, resulting in faster convergence. Dropout layers introduced regularization, making the model more robust and improving generalization to unseen data, outperforming FactorVAE and β-VAE networks. The approach achieved a superior balance between disentanglement and reconstruction quality, accurately capturing generative factors of facial expressions and enhancing image fidelity. The Ranger optimizer provided adaptive learning rate adjustments, improving optimization of model parameters. The study demonstrated enhanced convergence and generalization capabilities, validating the effectiveness of our approach. Overall, our work provides valuable insights into unsupervised learning and facial expression generation, paving the way for more interpretable and realistic models with broader applications.

4.3   Results and Discussion

When training our network with Dropout, the recognition loss curve in Fig. 2 shows slightly slower convergence due to random unit deactivation. However, this leads to improved generalization and better long-term performance. Dropout also promotes smoother convergence, acting as a regularization technique by introducing noise to prevent overfitting during training. The inclusion of Dropout layer with the Ranger optimizer in our model results in faster convergence, reduced overfitting, and better generalization. The Dropout encourages the learning of robust representations, leading to lower recognition loss on unseen data compared to a traditional VAE. The regularization helps the model handle input variations and noise, resulting in a more stable and reliable recognition loss curve. Our network with the Dropout layer allows for exploring diverse latent variable configurations, leading to a richer set of generated faces (Fig. 3). The Dropout layer introduces stochasticity and acts as a regularizer, encouraging the model to explore different paths during training. As a result, the model captures a wider range of facial expressions and features, generating more diverse and realistic facial expressions. In Fig. 3, the Dropout layer promotes smoother optimization, preventing co-adaptation among neurons and leading to smoother transitions between generated face images in the latent space. This results in more visually realistic and consistent attribute changes when traversing the latent space. The generated faces also exhibit enhanced clarity and visibility of facial features, indicating the model's improved ability to disentangle underlying factors and generate faithful representations of facial expressions compared to FactorVAE. The Dropout layer in the VAE network enhances regularization, feature learning, and reduces co-adaptation (Fig. 4). By introducing stochasticity during training, the Dropout layer promotes robustness and improved capture of essential facial characteristics. The Dropout layer enhances VAE robustness

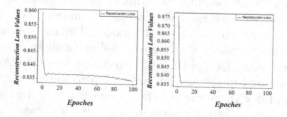

Fig. 2. Reconstruction loss of our enhanced network compared to the FactorVAE network after 100 epochs of training the model on CelebA dataset.

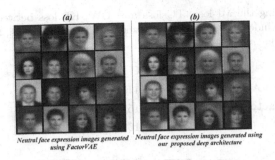

(a)   *(b)*

Neutral face expression images generated   *Neutral face expression images generated using*
using FactorVAE   *our proposed deep architecture*

Fig. 3. Comparing the neutral expression faces generated by our improved network with those generated by the FactorVAE.

Table 1. Comparing the reconstruction loss, total loss and KL loss between our enhanced network, which includes the Ranger optimizer and Dropout layers, and the original β-VAE and FactorVAE networks.

	Recon Loss	Total Loss	kl loss
β-**VAE**	0.7369	0.7214	9.5698
FactorVAE	0.8421	0.8350	6.2876
Our	0.8449	0.8369	0.4165

to input variations, resulting in visually appealing and realistic generated face images. It prevents co-adaptation among neurons, disentangling latent representations for distinct facial expressions. The generated faces exhibit clearer and defined facial features, crucial for accurate expression capture. As shown in Fig. 4, the histogram of generated face images demonstrates a more organized and distinguishable distribution, indicating that the model has effectively learned meaningful and disentangled representations. The Dropout layer's regularization effect ensures that the model does not overfit to specific details of the training data but generalizes well to unseen variations, resulting in a diverse and rich set of generated faces. Appealing and realistic outputs. We use an SVM classifier to quantitatively evaluate face identity preservation in learned disentangled representations. SVM is effective in high-dimensional spaces, making it suitable for face representation learning. By testing the classifier's accuracy in identifying individuals from the disentangled representations, we assess how well the model retains essential identity information while generating neutral facial expressions. The confusion matrix (Fig. 5) serves as a valuable tool for visualizing the classifier's performance in machine learning tasks. Our classification task involves identifying faces from a collection of randomly generated faces using our proposed deep architecture. The SVM classifier successfully predicts the person's identity from 1000 generated faces with 94% accuracy, with only 6% misclassified as different individuals. Our model outperforms β-VAE and FactorVAE networks, as shown in Fig. 5.

Table 2. Comparing the MI loss, TC loss and DW_KL loss between our enhanced network, which includes the Ranger optimizer and Dropout layers, and the original FactorVAE network.

	MI_Loss	TC_Loss	DW_KL_Loss
β-VAE	12.8569	−11.4528	5.1568
FactorVAE	16.9747	−15.8943	7.3283
Our	16.26621	−16.0552	0.9647

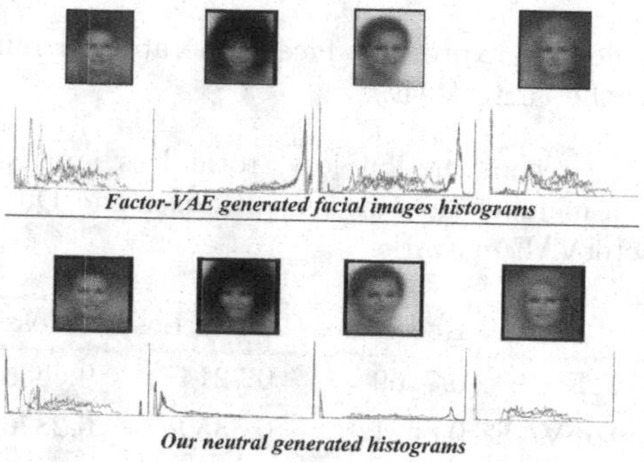

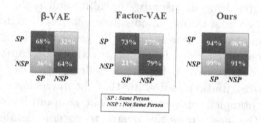

Fig. 4. Comparing the histogram of randomly selected neutral faces generated by our enhanced network with the histogram of neutral faces generated by the FactorVAE.

β-VAE		Factor-VAE		Ours	
SP	68% 32%	SP	73% 27%	SP	94% 06%
NSP	36% 64%	NSP	21% 79%	NSP	09% 91%
	SP NSP		SP NSP		SP NSP

SP : Same Person
NSP : Not Same Person

Fig. 5. The confusion matrix presents the results of the SVM classifier in predicting whether a person's face is the same or not from a dataset of 1000 resulting face images.

4.4   Conclusion

In this study, we addressed unsupervised learning for disentangled representations using the CelebA dataset, incorporating ideas from FactorVAE and β-VAE. Our proposed approach leveraged the Ranger optimizer and Dropout layers, leading to significant improvements in the model. The method encouraged factorial representation distribution and ensured dimension independence, resulting in faster convergence. Dropout layers introduced regularization, making the model more robust and improving generalization to unseen data, outperforming FactorVAE and β-VAE networks. The approach achieved a superior balance between disentanglement and reconstruction quality, accurately capturing generative factors of facial expressions and enhancing image fidelity. The Ranger optimizer provided adaptive learning rate adjustments, improving optimization of model parameters. The study demonstrated enhanced convergence and generalization capabilities, validating the effectiveness of our approach. Overall, our work provides valuable insights into unsupervised learning and facial expression generation, paving the way for more interpretable and realistic models with broader applications.

References

1. Kim, H., Mnih, A.: Disentangling by factorising. In: International Conference on Machine Learning (PMLR 2018), pp. 2649–2658 (2018)
2. Hao, X., Shafto, P.: Coupled variational autoencoder. arXiv preprint arXiv:2306.02565 (2023)
3. Xu, Z., Hao, G.-Y., He, H., et al.: Domain-Indexing Variational Bayes: Interpretable Domain Index for Domain Adaptation. arXiv preprint arXiv:2302.02561 (2023)
4. Gao, Haoxiang, Hua, K., Wei, L., et al.: Building a learnable universal coordinate system for single-cell atlas with a joint-VAE model. bioRxiv, p. 459281 (2021)
5. İskif, A.: Vector quantized variational autoencoder (VQ-VAE) in image compression (2021)
6. Latif, S., Rana, R., Khalifa, S., et al.: Survey of deep representation learning for speech emotion recognition. IEEE Trans. Affect. Comput. (2021)
7. Banerjee, S., Joshi, A., Turcot, J.: The universal face encoder: learning disentangled representations across different attributes. In: Proceedings of the IEEE/CVF Conference on Computer Vision and Pattern Recognition, pp. 1071–1080 (2023)
8. Fernandez-de-Cossio-Diaz, J., Cocco, S., Monasson, R.: Disentangling representations in restricted boltzmann machines without adversaries. Phys. Rev. X **13**(2), 021003 (2023)
9. Li, D., Pan, F., He, J., et al.: Style miner: find significant and stable explanatory factors in time series with constrained reinforcement learning. arXiv preprint arXiv:2303.11716 (2023)
10. Fontanini, T., Ferrari, C., Bertozzi, M., et al.: Automatic generation of semantic parts for face image synthesis. arXiv preprint arXiv:2307.05317 (2023)
11. Reddy, A.G., Balasubramanian, V.N., et al.: On causally disentangled representations. In: Proceedings of the AAAI Conference on Artificial Intelligence, pp. 8089–8097 (2022)
12. Kim, M., Wang, Y., Sahu, P., et al.: Bayes-FactorVAE: hierarchical Bayesian deep auto-encoder models for factor disentanglement. In: Proceedings of the IEEE/CVF International Conference on Computer Vision, pp. 2979–2987 (2019)
13. Yu, H., Li, H.: A conditional factor VAE model for pump degradation assessment under varying conditions. Appl. Soft Comput. **100**, 106992 (2021)
14. Rezende, D.J., Viola, F.: Taming vaes. arXiv preprint arXiv:1810.00597 (2018)
15. Fidon, L., Ourselin, S., Vercauteren, T.: Generalized wasserstein dice score, distributionally robust deep learning, and ranger for brain tumor segmentation: BraTS 2020 challenge. In: Crimi, A., Bakas, S. (eds.) BrainLes 2020. LNCS, vol. 12659, pp. 200–214. Springer, Cham (2021). https://doi.org/10.1007/978-3-030-72087-2_18
16. Wright, L., Demeure, N.: Ranger21: a synergistic deep learning optimizer. arXiv preprint arXiv:2106.13731 (2021)

17. Zhang, G., Niwa, K., Kleijn, W.B.: Lookahead diffusion probabilistic models for refining mean estimation. In: Proceedings of the IEEE/CVF Conference on Computer Vision and Pattern Recognition, pp. 1421–1429 (2023)
18. Wan, Z., Yuxiang, Z., Gong, X., et al.: DenseNet model with RAdam optimization algorithm for cancer image classification. In: 2021 IEEE International Conference on Consumer Electronics and Computer Engineering (ICCECE), pp. 771–775. IEEE (2021)
19. Cheng, T., Arguin, J.-F., Leissner-Martin, J., et al.: Variational autoencoders for anomalous jet tagging. Phys. Rev. D **107**(1), 016002 (2023)
20. Zhang, Y., et al.: CelebA-spoof: large-scale face anti-spoofing dataset with rich annotations. In: Vedaldi, A, Bischof, H., Brox, T., Frahm, J.-M. (eds.) ECCV 2020. LNCS, vol. 12357, pp. 70–85. Springer, Cham (2020). https://doi.org/10.1007/978-3-030-58610-2_5
21. Otberdout, N., Ferrari, C., Daoudi, M., et al.: Génération d'expressions faciales 3D dynamiques clairsemées à denses. Dans: actes de la conférence IEEE/CVF sur la vision par ordinateur et la reconnaissance de formes, pp. 20385–20394 (2022)
22. Otberdout, N., Daoudi, M., Kacem, A., et al.: Génération d'expressions faciales dynamiques sur l'hypersphère de hilbert avec des réseaux antagonistes génératifs conditionnels de Wasserstein. IEEE Trans. Pattern Anal. Mach. Intell. **44**(2), 848–863 (2020)
23. Zhang, J., Yu, H.: Améliorer la reconnaissance de l'expression faciale et son interprétabilité en générant une carte de motifs d'expression. Reconnais. Formes **129**, 108737 (2022)
24. Luo, Z., Zuo, R., Xiong, Y., et al.: Metallogenic-factor variational autoencoder for geochemical anomaly detection by ad-hoc and post-hoc interpretability algorithms. Nat. Resour. Res. 1–19 (2023)

CaSE-NeRF: Camera Settings Editing of Neural Radiance Fields

Ciliang Sun⬤, Yuqi Li(✉)⬤, Jiabao Li⬤, Chong Wang⬤, and Xinmiao Dai⬤

Faculty of Electrical Engineering and Computer Science, Ningbo University,
Ningbo, China
liyuqi1@nbu.edu.cn

Abstract. Neural Radiance Fields (NeRF) have shown excellent quality in three-dimensional (3D) reconstruction by synthesizing novel views from multi-view images. However, previous NeRF-based methods do not allow users to perform user-controlled camera setting editing in the scene. While existing works have proposed methods to modify the radiance field, these modifications are limited to camera settings within the training set. Hence, we present Camera Settings Editing of Neural Radiance Fields (CaSE-NeRF) to recover a radiance field from a set of views with different camera settings. In our approach, we allow users to perform controlled camera settings editing on the scene and synthesize the novel view images of the edited scene without re-training the network. The key to our method lies in modeling each camera parameter separately and rendering various 3D defocus effects based on thin lens imaging principles. By following the image processing of real cameras, we implicitly model it and learn gains that are continuous in the latent space and independent of the image. The control of color temperature and exposure is plug-and-play, and can be easily integrated into NeRF-based frameworks. As a result, our method allows for manual and free post-capture control of the viewpoint and camera settings of 3D scenes. Through our extensive experiments on two real-scene datasets, we have demonstrated the success of our approach in reconstructing a normal NeRF with consistent 3D geometry and appearance. Our related code and data is available at https://github.com/CPREgroup/CaSE-NeRF.

Keywords: neural radiance field · camera setting editing · novel view synthesis · image-based rendering

1 Introduction

Post-capture camera settings editing is a low-level task in computer vision that allows users to adjust camera settings, such as the viewpoint, exposure, and color temperature, after capturing images or videos with a digital camera. It has the potential to improve image and video quality, and enhance the overall user experience by providing control over the captured content. Many studies have

B. Sheng et al. (Eds.): CGI 2023, LNCS 14496, pp. 95–107, 2024.
https://doi.org/10.1007/978-3-031-50072-5_8

Fig. 1. We recover a neural radiance field from (a) multiple views with different exposure, color temperature, and focusing distance. Our method can render novel views with arbitrary (b) exposures, color temperatures and (c) focusing distance.

explored the editing of white balance [2], exposures [21], and focusing distance [18]. However, few works have extended camera settings editing to 3D scene.

The rapid advancement of the Neural Radiance Field (NeRF) [19] provides the possibility of photorealistic synthesis of new view images of complex 3D scenes, and has inspired a large amount of follow-up work [4,5,22,26]. However, it relies on consistent camera settings when capturing input views with a digital camera. And any deviation from these camera settings can greatly impact the quality of the reconstructed scene, leading to a significant decrease in the quality of NeRF. However, most of the existing NeRF editing works focus on editing the shapes and the styles of objects in the scene [11,27].

In this paper, we aim to expand NeRF to enable user-controlled camera settings editing of the scene and recover the radiance field from a set of views with varying camera settings. This method is particularly useful in situations where consistent camera settings were not maintained during the initial capture, as it enables users to make changes to the camera settings of previously captured content. We expand upon NeRFocus [25] and propose an effective framework, called *CaSE-NeRF*, that enables post-capture **C**amera **S**ettings **E**ditting of **N**eural **R**adiance **F**ield. The proposed framework can effectively handle the control of color temperature, exposure, and focusing distance, and recover the full-camera-settings NeRF in an end-to-end manner. It allows for manual and free post-capture control of the viewpoint and camera settings of 3D scenes (Fig. 1). Our main contributions can be summarized as follows:

- We propose a comprehensive approach, CaSE-NeRF, which enables the recovery of the neural radiance field from multiple views, each with varying exposure, color temperature, and focusing distance.
- We model the camera settings within a camera's image processing pipeline, which allows for the meticulous editing of individual settings. Our method is generalized as it can be seamlessly integrated as a plug-and-play module with various NeRF variants.
- We build a multi-view dataset consisting of images with varying camera settings. In comparison with existing methods, our method achieves the best performance on this dataset.

2 Related Work

2.1 Novel View Synthesis

New view synthesis is a classic and extensively studied problem in the fields of computer vision and graphics. Various existing methods include image-based rendering [9], as well as explicit geometric representations such as voxel grids [17], point clouds [1], triangle meshes [14], and multiplanar images [24]. Recently, some studies have employed signed distance functions (SDFs) [12] to model scenes. Another promising approach is the use of NeRF [19], which leverage hidden neural representations to achieve high-quality new-view reconstruction and rendering. The success of NeRF has inspired a great deal of follow-up work. For instance, certain studies employ diverse techniques to expedite the training or inference phases [6]. NeRF is being applied to dynamic scenes [8], relighting [23], Panoptic segmentation [15] and human avatars [28].

2.2 Post-capture Camera Settings Editing

Post-capture camera settings editing tasks are performed to achieve specific visual goals, such as enhancing image quality, adjusting color balance, adjusting exposure, or removing unwanted elements. Some works [21] have adopted the Retinex theory [16] to correct exposure, which posits that improperly exposed images can be expressed as a pixel-wise multiplication of target images captured with correct exposure settings and illumination maps. And some methods [2] have proposed using deep neural networks to correct the white balance settings of camera-rendered images. Inspired by image editing techniques, our method applies camera settings editing to 3D scenes.

Recently, there have been some works applying image editing to NeRF, enabling the editing of 3D scenes, such as HDR [10,13], color control [20], and depth of field effects [25]. However, these methods can only handle single camera settings editing, limiting the ability to render images with arbitrary camera settings. On the contrary, our approach reconstructs a normal NeRF with consistent 3D geometry and appearance, while modeling each component separately, enabling users to specify camera settings for rendering.

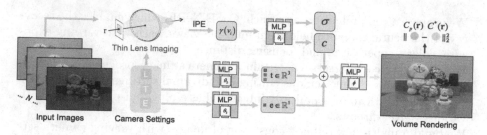

Fig. 2. An overview of our training framework. Given a set of images captured with different camera settings, first we based on a thin lens imaging model to achieve defocusing effects. Subsequently, we obtain the white balance gain t and exposure gain e. The operator $\oplus$ stands for an element-wise product. By integrating all gains, we obtain the pixel point $C_p(\mathbf{r})$. The radiance field is supervised using the input RGB $C^*(\mathbf{r})$.

3 Method

3.1 Preliminaries

The training pipeline is visualized in Fig. 2. To calculate the pixel's color, NeRF gives a ray $r(q) = o + qs$, where o and s are the origin and direction of the ray respectively, and q denotes distance along the ray. Traditional NeRFs use a pinhole imaging model and can only represent in-focus scenes. To simulate defocus effects, we replace rays by cones and build our thin lens imaging model upon NeRFocus [25]. The cones' radii are determined by the focal length of the corresponding ray and the pixel size on the image plane. We divide the conical frustum into N intervals $\delta_i = [q_i, q_{i+1})$ and compute the mean and covariance $(\boldsymbol{\mu}, \boldsymbol{\sigma}) = r(\delta_i)$ of the conical frustum for each interval. Then we apply an integrated positional encoding to featurize each interval:

$$\gamma(\boldsymbol{\mu}, \boldsymbol{\Sigma}) = \left\{ \begin{bmatrix} \sin\left(2^h \boldsymbol{\mu}\right) \exp\left(-2^{h-1} \operatorname{diag}(\boldsymbol{\Sigma})\right) \\ \cos\left(2^h \boldsymbol{\mu}\right) \exp\left(-2^{h-1} \operatorname{diag}(\boldsymbol{\Sigma})\right) \end{bmatrix} \right\}_{h=0}^{H-1} \tag{1}$$

where $\gamma(\cdot)$ is a mapping from two-dimentioanl space $\mathbb{R}^2$ into a higher dimensional space $\mathbb{R}^H$, and H is a hyperparameter which is set to 16.

These features serve as input to an MLP with weights θ_1, which produces a density σ and a color c. Finally, we use Eq. (3) to perform volume rendering and obtain the predicted colors for all frustums:

$$\forall \delta_i \in q, \quad (\sigma_i, c_i) = \operatorname{MLP}\left(\gamma\left(r\left(\delta_i\right)\right); \theta_1\right), \tag{2}$$

$$C(\mathbf{r}) = \sum_{i=1}^{N} K_i \left(1 - \exp\left(-\sigma_i(q_{i+1} - q_i)\right)\right) c_i, \tag{3}$$

where $K_i = \exp\left(-\sum_{j=1}^{i-1} \sigma_j (q_{j+1} - q_j)\right)$ denotes the accumulated transmittance.

3.2   Defocus Effect Control

In the proposed model, when a spatial point is not in focus on the focal plane, its projection onto the sensor plane becomes a blob shape instead of a pixel, which is referred to as the circle of confusion (CoC) and is responsible for defocus effects. The diameter of this CoC is denoted by d_e which is calculated based on the fundamental lens equation. We incorporate the advantage of Mip-NeRF [3], which extends the receptive field of a pixel to a blob rather than a pixel. And then we invert the imaging process of a thin lens and calculate the beam paths of each point within a circular area after inverse thin lens imaging. The diameter of the circular blob area is d_c. Finally, these beam paths and the circle of confusion form a composite cone that represents the path of a pixel's beam as shown in Fig. 2. The diameter d of the composite cone can be obtained as:

$$d = d_c + d_e = \frac{d_0 z_\alpha (f + L)}{fL} + \left| \frac{A (L - z_\alpha)}{L} \right|, \tag{4}$$

where d_0 denotes the diameter of the pixel's receptive field, A denotes the aperture size, f denotes the focal length, L denotes the focus distance, and z_α denotes a plane on the ray that is parallel to the sensor plane.

We divide the composite cone by placing the α plane at different distances intervals z_i, $i \in \{1, ..., N+1\}$ to create N conical frustums v_i, and use Eq. (2) and Eq. (3) to obtain the volume density σ and color c:

$$(\sigma_i, c_i) = \mathrm{MLP}_{\theta_1} (\gamma (v_i) ; \theta_1). \tag{5}$$

3.3   Color Temperature and Exposure Control

To reconstruct a 3D scene with new color temperature and exposure from input images, the critical issue lies in how to extract the original scene's colors and exposure values from the input images and account for the impact of various camera settings on the scene. From Sect. 3.2, we obtain color c, akin to RAW radiance without additional image processing. Subsequently, we apply the learned gains from the network to the scene, and these gains work directly to the actual digital processing in-camera imaging pipeline, handling the RAW image.

Our method is based on color consistency in multi-view images with the same camera settings, which dictates that the entire scene should exhibit consistent color characteristics before and after applying the same camera gain adjustments. By incorporating supervision from multiple viewpoints, we are able to implicitly separate the diverse camera gain factors involved in this process:

$$C_p (\mathbf{r}) = f (C (\mathbf{r}), t, e) \tag{6}$$

where $C (\mathbf{r})$ denotes the color at pixel point p, $f (\cdot)$ denotes the camera settings gain function, $C_p (\mathbf{r})$ is the color of the corresponding pixel point after the gain adjustment. In this paper, we only consider the color temperature and exposure settings in the camera setting. We don't parameterize a variable to represent all camera settings, but model each component to achieve controllable adjustment of all gains. We use two fully connected neural networks to learn the gains:

$$t = \text{MLP}_{\theta_2}(\text{T}) \tag{7}$$

$$e = \text{MLP}_{\theta_3}(\text{E}) \tag{8}$$

where parameter T and E represents the color temperature and Exposure Value in the input image. These parameters can be easily read from EXIF files that contain photo metadata. Here $t = [w_r, w_g, w_b]^T \in \mathbb{R}^3$ is the color temperature gains and $e \in \mathbb{R}^1$ is the exposure gain. These gains are decoupled from the image content, allowing us to manipulate the scene by simply providing the camera settings as inputs to the network. Our method eliminates the need for retraining and enables us to obtain gains beyond the training dataset.

Thus, given a pixel point and based on the actual white balance model. The calculation for $I(\mathbf{r})$ the pixel point after the color temperature gain is as follows:

$$I(\mathbf{r}) = C(\mathbf{r}) \cdot t = [c_r, c_g, c_b]^T \cdot [w_r, w_g, w_b]^T \tag{9}$$

where the operator $\cdot$ stands for an element-wise product. To make the color temperature gains physically correct, we use Sigmoid activation function to force t to be non-negative. Subsequently, we apply the obtained exposure gain e from the network to $I(\mathbf{r})$. In accordance with the nonparametric Camera Response Functions (CRF) calibration method [7], we apply a logarithmic radiance domain transformation to all the images as:

$$C_p(\mathbf{r}) = G_\phi(\ln(I(\mathbf{r}) * e)) \tag{10}$$

where G_ϕ denotes a non-linear CRF that maps scene irradiance to image intensity. The CRF is represented as an MLP and jointly optimized during training.

In general, we learn camera setting gains that are view-independent but continuous in the latent space. This enables us to reconstruct 3D scenes for arbitrary camera settings, including those not included in the training set.

3.4 Optimization

We use a two-step coarse-to-fine training strategy to train our model. In the initial coarse sampling phase, we uniformly sample 128 samples within the near and far bounds $[q_n, q_f]$ to divide frustums and compute the coarse rendered color $C_p^c(\mathbf{r})$. For the fine sampling, we calculate the importance weights $w_i = K_i(1 - \exp(-\sigma_i(q_{i+1} - q_i)))$ based on the coarse samples. Then, we employ inverse transform sampling to generate 128 samples and compute the fine rendered colors $C_p^f(\mathbf{r})$. We minimize coarse and fine reconstruction losses:

$$\mathcal{L} = \sum_{\mathbf{r} \in \mathcal{R}} \lambda \mathcal{L}_{mse}\left(C_p^c(\mathbf{r}), C^*(\mathbf{r})\right) + \mathcal{L}_{mse}\left(C_p^f(\mathbf{r}), C^*(\mathbf{r})\right) \tag{11}$$

where $\mathcal{R}$ denotes the set of rays in training data, $C^*(\mathbf{r})$ denotes the ground truth color corresponding to ray $\mathbf{r}$ taken from an input image, λ denotes a hyperparameter (we set $\lambda = 0.1$ in all experiments), and $\mathcal{L}_{mse}$ denotes mean squared error.

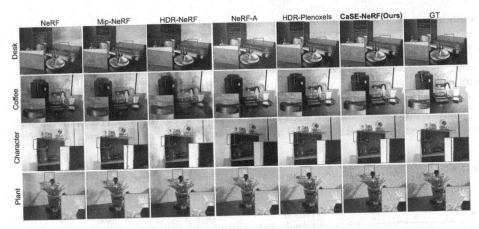

Fig. 3. Comparisons on novel views of real world scenes. The red-boxed regions exhibit our method's superior performance in intricate details. (Color figure online)

4 Experiment

Implementation Details. We employed the Adam optimizer with a logarithmically annealed learning rate that decays from 5×10^{-4} to 5×10^{-6}, and other hyperparameters $\beta_1 = 0.9$, $\beta_2 = 0.999$, $\epsilon = 10^{-6}$. The batch size of the composite cones is set as 2048 with 300K training steps on an RTX 3090 GPU.

Datasets. We evaluated the proposed method on the collected two datasets. One is the real-world dataset proposed in [13], which includes 30–50 views with varying exposure and white balance values at 3000K, 3500K, and 4000K for each scene. The other dataset comprises four real scenes captured using a Canon EOS 750D in manual mode with varying exposures, white balances, and focus distance. The exposure was set to $\pm$3EV at the basis image, and we used white balance values of 3200K, 5200K, and 7000K. Additionally, we captured images with varying levels of defocus. The dataset includes 40–60 views. Every set of five input views has two of them with different exposures and color temperatures applied, and each view also has a different focusing distance.

4.1 Novel View Synthesis of Real Scenes

We compare our CaSE-NeRF with NeRF [19], Mip-NeRF [3], HDR-NeRF [10], NeRF-A [20], and HDR-Plenoxels [13] in novel views on the dataset proposed in [13]. For quantitative evaluation, we use three metrics: PSNR, SSIM, and LPIPS.

It is worth noting that NeRF-A is a variant of NeRF-W [20] that uses only appearance embeddings without transient embeddings. It employs an optimized appearance embedding to explain image-dependent appearances in the input. HDR-NeRF [10] introduces a differentiable tone mapper to model the process that radiance becomes pixel values, and it omits white balance parameters. HDR-Plenoxel [13] simulates the physical process of in-camera image acquisition by modeling high dynamic range radiance. During the inference process, the appearance embedding of the NeRF-A is set to align with the appearance embeddings of scenes with the same camera settings in the training dataset. In instances where the training dataset lacks the matching camera settings, the appearance embedding is assigned a value of zero. For HDR-Plenoxels, during its inference, we use the same appearance gains as in the camera settings of the training set. If there are no scene images with the same camera settings in the training set, we use the gains initialized by HDR-Plenoxels for each scene image.

Table 1. Quantitative results of novel view synthesis on real scenes. We present the average results of the test sets for each dataset, the best results are shown in bold.

Method	Desk			Character			Coffee			Plant		
	PSNR($\uparrow$)	SSIM($\uparrow$)	LPIPS($\downarrow$)	PSNR($\uparrow$)	SSIM($\uparrow$)	LPIPS($\downarrow$)	PSNR($\uparrow$)	SSIM($\uparrow$)	LPIPS($\downarrow$)	PSNR($\uparrow$)	SSIM($\uparrow$)	LPIPS($\downarrow$)
NeRF [19]	11.419	0.550	0.506	14.911	0.838	0.455	13.919	0.769	0.473	19.794	0.708	0.515
Mip-NeRF [3]	12.517	0.556	0.493	17.725	0.864	0.402	14.539	0.794	0.446	21.731	0.733	0.438
HDR-NeRF [10]	17.442	0.606	0.404	14.115	0.721	0.408	15.710	0.777	0.362	20.684	0.507	0.560
NeRF-A [20]	19.987	0.833	0.384	22.445	0.905	0.312	20.366	0.711	0.352	22.314	0.742	0.470
HDR-Plenoxels [13]	25.880	0.859	0.336	29.680	0.949	0.280	20.232	0.895	0.311	24.016	0.768	0.386
CaSE-NeRF (Ours)	**27.178**	**0.920**	**0.223**	**31.430**	**0.979**	**0.222**	**23.677**	**0.953**	**0.276**	**26.243**	**0.874**	**0.236**

Table 2. Quantitative comparison of novel view synthesis on our proposed real-world datasets, the best results are shown in bold.

Model	Dolls			Medicine			Plane			Board		
	PSNR($\uparrow$)	SSIM($\uparrow$)	LPIPS($\downarrow$)	PSNR($\uparrow$)	SSIM($\uparrow$)	LPIPS($\downarrow$)	PSNR($\uparrow$)	SSIM($\uparrow$)	LPIPS($\downarrow$)	PSNR($\uparrow$)	SSIM($\uparrow$)	LPIPS($\downarrow$)
NeRF-A	29.940	0.950	0.310	30.451	0.935	0.305	30.065	0.957	0.312	28.066	0.920	0.326
HDR-Plenoxels	30.492	0.924	0.299	31.754	0.918	0.279	32.425	0.947	0.233	31.052	0.951	0.245
CaSE-NeRF (Ours)	**35.884**	**0.977**	**0.216**	**38.860**	**0.985**	**0.140**	**36.923**	**0.983**	**0.175**	**33.028**	**0.978**	**0.189**

Figure 3 presents the comparisons of the synthesis novel view of six methods on the four real-world scenes of the dataset [13]. We generate the result images using the camera settings present in the training set, ensuring a fair comparison. Observing the image patches with enlarged details, it is evident that our method demonstrates superior perceptual quality compared to other methods. Because NeRF-A employs an appearance embedding to capture the overall appearance of the entire scene, resulting in the entanglement of all camera settings within the embedding and it lacks the ability to decompose each camera settings, such as exposure and color temperature. HDR-Plenoxels use a Leaky Saturation Mask to suppress saturation regions during the optimization process. And it integrates all camera settings into a single parameter, enabling the representation of appearance. However, it still lacks the ability to accurately separate individual camera settings. As a result, both methods fail to effectively synthesize certain details.

Quantitative results are also summarized in Table 1. Our approach shows the best image quality in PSNR, SSIM, and LPIPS among the methods. Moreover, HDR-Plenoxels are limited in their ability to apply camera settings that were not present in the training set. NeRF-A's appearance embedding is viewpoint-dependent, even when applied with camera settings present in the training set, it cannot fully and accurately represent all camera settings. Therefore, it fails to apply camera settings that are outside the scope of the training set.

We also conduct a comparison between our CaSE-NeRF, NeRF-A [20], and HDR-Plenoxels [13] in novel views on our captured dataset, which includes variations in color temperature, exposure, and focusing distance. Other methods fail to reconstruct normal 3D scenes under diverse camera settings, which leads to exclusion from the comparison. Quantitative results are presented in Table 2.

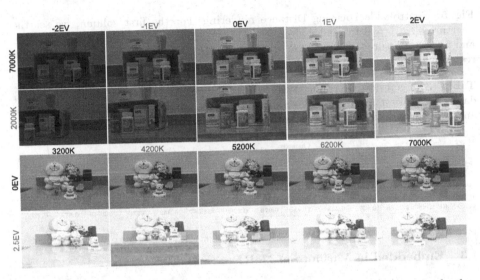

Fig. 4. Controllable Color Temperature and Exposure rendering. We can control color temperature and exposure to render images from a novel view. The first row of each dataset fixes the camera pose, while the second row varies the camera pose.

4.2   Controllable Rendering at Novel View Synthesis

Arbitrary Color Temperature and Exposure. We randomly vary the color temperature T and exposure E to render images with arbitrary settings and show some results in Fig. 4. The red camera settings represent configurations that are not present in the training set, while the black settings indicate those that exist. The results demonstrate that we can accurately render images with arbitrary color temperature and exposure, which is impossible in previous methods.

Arbitrary Focusing Distance. We conduct an experiment wherein we maintain a novel constant camera pose and vary the focusing distance L. By observing the resulting novel view images in Fig. 5, we observe that adjusting the focus distance caused a corresponding change in the focusing plane of the image. This serves as empirical evidence that our method is capable of manipulating L. Please refer to the supplemental video for more results.

Fig. 5. Controllable Focusing Distance rendering. For the first column, we set the aperture size $A = 0$ to render all-in-focus image. And we vary the focus distance L and fix the aperture size $A = 0.2$ in other figures. In each subsequent column, the clear region is displayed at the top-right, middle-right, and bottom-right, respectively.

Table 3. Quantitative comparison of different NeRF frameworks on real-world datasets, the best results are shown in bold. (w) denotes using the color temperature and exposure control module, while (w/o) denotes its absence.

Model	Desk			Character			Coffee			Plant		
	PSNR(↑)	SSIM(↑)	LPIPS(↓)	PSNR(↑)	SSIM(↑)	LPIPS(↓)	PSNR(↑)	SSIM(↑)	LPIPS(↓)	PSNR(↑)	SSIM(↑)	LPIPS(↓)
NeRF(w/o)	11.419	0.550	0.506	14.911	0.838	0.45	13.919	0.769	0.473	19.794	0.708	0.515
NeRF(w)	26.175	0.902	0.253	26.175	0.902	0.253	22.471	0.932	0.309	26.175	0.902	0.253
TensoRF(w/o)	11.905	0.517	0.466	16.430	0.768	0.528	14.501	0.712	0.522	19.384	0.619	0.527
TensoRF(w)	26.281	0.904	0.231	28.620	0.969	0.255	21.433	0.882	0.343	24.090	0.869	0.246
CaSE-NeRF (Ours)	**27.178**	**0.920**	**0.223**	**31.430**	**0.979**	**0.222**	**23.677**	**0.953**	**0.276**	**26.243**	**0.874**	**0.236**

4.3   Embedded in Variants of NeRF

Since our implicit color temperature and exposure control module generates gain on the rendered colors, it can work as a plug-and-play module on variants of the NeRF. To demonstrate this, we substitute two modern NeRF architectures(NeRF [19] and TensoRF [6]) with network architectures integrating the proposed modules and compare the performance of the original twos and the changed twos on the dataset proposed in [13]. The quantitative results are shown in Table 3. The modified networks can achieve close performance to ours.

4.4   Ablation Study

We conduct ablation experiments on the hyperparameter of integrated positional encoding. We experiment with different values of H with our full model and plot the PSNR and SSIM curves of reconstructed view images in Fig. 6. It should be noted that setting $H = 16$ yielded promising results for PSNR, SSIM in the test set for individual scenes. Increasing the value of H beyond this point did not lead to a significant improvement in performance.

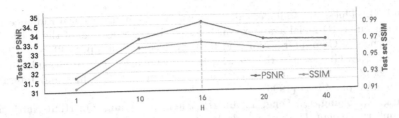

Fig. 6. The evaluation of the visual performances of the proposed model with varying numbers of H. Note that PSNR(blue) and SSIM(orange) are shown in the figure. (Color figure online)

5   Conclusion

This paper presents the CaSE-NeRF framework, which supports the reconstruction of post-capture editable 3D scenes from images acquired with different camera settings. The framework enables users to arbitrarily manipulate camera settings, such as color temperature, exposure, and focusing distance, and generate novel view images of 3D scenes. The control modules used in this framework can be seamlessly integrated with different NeRF variants. Results obtained from experiments of our method on various real-world scene datasets demonstrate its overall effectiveness and generalizability.

Acknowledgements. This work is supported by Key Research and Development Program of Ningbo (No. 2023Z225).

References

1. Achlioptas, P., Diamanti, O., Mitliagkas, I., Guibas, L.: Learning representations and generative models for 3D point clouds. In: International Conference on Machine Learning, pp. 40–49 (2018)
2. Afifi, M., Brubaker, M.A., Brown, M.S.: Auto white-balance correction for mixed-illuminant scenes. In: Proceedings of the IEEE/CVF Winter Conference on Applications of Computer Vision, pp. 1210–1219 (2022)
3. Barron, J.T., Mildenhall, B., Tancik, M., Hedman, P., Martin-Brualla, R., Srinivasan, P.P.: Mip-NeRF: a multiscale representation for anti-aliasing neural radiance fields. In: Proceedings of the IEEE/CVF International Conference on Computer Vision, pp. 5855–5864 (2021)
4. Bortolon, M., Del Bue, A., Poiesi, F.: VM-NeRF: tackling sparsity in NeRF with view morphing. In: International Conference on Image Analysis and Processing, pp. 63–74 (2023)
5. Chen, Z., Qiu, J., Sheng, B., Li, P., Wu, E.: GPSD: generative parking spot detection using multi-clue recovery model. Vis. Comput. **37**(9–11), 2657–2669 (2021)
6. Chen, A., Xu, Z., Geiger, A., Yu, J., Su, H.: TensoRF: tensorial radiance fields. In: Proceedings of the European Conference on Computer Vision, pp. 333–350 (2022)
7. Debevec, P.E., Malik, J.: Recovering high dynamic range radiance maps from photographs. In: ACM SIGGRAPH 2008 Classes, pp. 1–10 (2008)

8. Gafni, G., Thies, J., Zollhofer, M., Nießner, M.: Dynamic neural radiance fields for monocular 4D facial avatar reconstruction. In: Proceedings of the IEEE/CVF Conference on Computer Vision and Pattern Recognition, pp. 8649–8658 (2021)
9. Gortler, S.J., Grzeszczuk, R., Szeliski, R., Cohen, M.F.: The lumigraph. In: Proceedings of the 23rd Annual Conference on Computer Graphics and Interactive Techniques, pp. 43–54 (1996)
10. Huang, X., Zhang, Q., Feng, Y., Li, H., Wang, X., Wang, Q.: HDR-NeRF: high dynamic range neural radiance fields. In: Proceedings of the IEEE/CVF Conference on Computer Vision and Pattern Recognition, pp. 18398–18408 (2022)
11. Jambon, C., Kerbl, B., Kopanas, G., Diolatzis, S., Drettakis, G., Leimkühler, T.: NeRFshop: interactive editing of neural radiance fields. In: Proceedings of the ACM on Computer Graphics and Interactive Techniques, vol. 6, no. 1 (2023)
12. Jiang, C., Sud, A., Makadia, A., Huang, J., Nießner, M., Funkhouser, T.: Local implicit grid representations for 3D scenes. In: Proceedings of the IEEE/CVF Conference on Computer Vision and Pattern Recognition, pp. 6001–6010 (2020)
13. Jun-Seong, K., Yu-Ji, K., Ye-Bin, M., Oh, T.H.: HDR-Plenoxels: self-calibrating high dynamic range radiance fields. In: Avidan, S., Brostow, G., Cisse, M., Farinella, G.M., Hassner, T. (eds.) Computer Vision – ECCV 2022. ECCV 2022. LNCS, vol. 13692, pp. 384–401. Springer, Cham (2022). https://doi.org/10.1007/978-3-031-19824-3_23
14. Kanazawa, A., Tulsiani, S., Efros, A.A., Malik, J.: Learning category-specific mesh reconstruction from image collections. In: Ferrari, V., Hebert, M., Sminchisescu, C., Weiss, Y. (eds.) ECCV 2018. LNCS, vol. 11219, pp. 386–402. Springer, Cham (2018). https://doi.org/10.1007/978-3-030-01267-0_23
15. Kundu, A., et al.: Panoptic neural fields: a semantic object-aware neural scene representation. In: Proceedings of the IEEE/CVF Conference on Computer Vision and Pattern Recognition, pp. 12871–12881 (2022)
16. Land, E.H.: The retinex theory of color vision. Sci. Am. **237**(6), 108–129 (1977)
17. Liao, Y., Donne, S., Geiger, A.: Deep marching cubes: learning explicit surface representations. In: Proceedings of the IEEE Conference on Computer Vision and Pattern Recognition, pp. 2916–2925 (2018)
18. Lijun, W., Xiaohui, S., Jianming, Z., Oliver, W., Chih-Yao, H.: DeepLens: shallow depth of field from a single image. ACM Trans. Graph. **37**(6), 6 (2018)
19. Mildenhall, B., Srinivasan, P.P., Tancik, M., Barron, J.T., Ramamoorthi, R., Ng, R.: NeRF: representing scenes as neural radiance fields for view synthesis. In: Vedaldi, A., Bischof, H., Brox, T., Frahm, J.-M. (eds.) ECCV 2020. LNCS, vol. 12346, pp. 405–421. Springer, Cham (2020). https://doi.org/10.1007/978-3-030-58452-8_24
20. Martin-Brualla, R., Radwan, N., Sajjadi, M.S., Barron, J.T., Dosovitskiy, A., Duckworth, D.: NeRF in the wild: neural radiance fields for unconstrained photo collections. In: Proceedings of the IEEE/CVF Conference on Computer Vision and Pattern Recognition, pp. 7210–7219 (2021)
21. Moran, S., Marza, P., McDonagh, S., Parisot, S., Slabaugh, G.: DeepLPF: deep local parametric filters for image enhancement. In: Proceedings of the IEEE/CVF Conference on Computer Vision and Pattern Recognition, pp. 12826–12835 (2020)
22. Qiu, J., Zhu, Y., Jiang, P.T., Cheng, M.M., Ren, B.: RDNeRF: relative depth guided NeRF for dense free view synthesis. Vis. Comput. 1–13 (2023)
23. Rudnev, V., Elgharib, M., Smith, W., Liu, L., Golyanik, V., Theobalt, C.: NeRF for outdoor scene relighting. In: Proceedings of the European Conference on Computer Vision, pp. 615–631 (2022)

24. Tucker, R., Snavely, N.: Single-view view synthesis with multiplane images. In: Proceedings of the IEEE/CVF Conference on Computer Vision and Pattern Recognition, pp. 551–560 (2020)
25. Wang, Y., Yang, S., Hu, Y., Zhang, J.: NeRFocus: neural radiance field for 3D synthetic defocus. arXiv preprint arXiv:2203.05189 (2022)
26. Yang, G.W., Liu, Z.N,, Li, D.Y., et al.: JNeRF: an efficient heterogeneous NeRF model zoo based on Jittor[J]. Comput. Vis. Media 9(2), 401–404 (2023)
27. Yuan, Y.J., Sun, Y.T., Lai, Y.K., Ma, Y., Jia, R., Gao, L.: NeRF-editing: geometry editing of neural radiance fields. In: Proceedings of the IEEE/CVF Conference on Computer Vision and Pattern Recognition, pp. 18353–18364 (2022)
28. Zhao, F., Yang, W., Zhang, J., Lin, P., Zhang, Y., Yu, J.: HumanNeRF: efficiently generated human radiance field from sparse inputs. In: Proceedings of the IEEE/CVF Conference on Computer Vision and Pattern Recognition, pp. 7743–7753 (2022)

A Submodular-Based Autonomous Exploration for Multi-Room Indoor Scenes Reconstruction

Yongwei Miao[1,2]([✉]), Haipeng Wang[1], Ran Fan[2], and Fuchang Liu[2]([✉])

[1] College of Mechanical Engineering, Zhejiang Sci-Tech University, Hangzhou, China
[2] School of Information Science and Technology, Hangzhou Normal University, Hangzhou, China
{ywmiao,liufc}@hznu.edu.cn

Abstract. To autonomously explore and densely recover an unknown indoor scene is a nontrivial task in 3D scene reconstruction. It is challenging for scenes composed of compact and complicated interconnected rooms with no priors. To address this issue, we aim to use autonomous scanning, reconstruct multi-room scenes, and produce a complete reconstruction in as few scans as possible. With a progressive discrete motion planning module, we introduce submodular-based planning for automated scanning scenarios to efficiently guide the active scanning by Next-Best-View until marginal gains diminish. The submodular-based planning gives an approximately optimal solution of "Next-Best-View" which is NP-hard in case of no prior knowledge. Experiments show that our method can improve scanning efficiency significantly for multi-room scenes while maintaining reconstruction errors.

Keywords: Autonomous Exploration · Indoor Scenes Reconstruction · Submodular Function · Pose Graph Optimization

1 Introduction

Exploring unknown indoor scenes autonomously is an open problem and gives challenging for autonomous scene reconstruction [9]. Reconstructing indoor environments is the foundation of numerous applications, ranging from augmented and virtual reality [20] to domestic robot navigation [9]. Existing methods specialized in reconstruction always perform a *"navigation-by-reconstruction"* scanning strategy, relies on human observation for the current room environment and make the first scannable view for the robot at great randomness [1,10,12,17], which is supposed to be given the optimal scanning trajectory and outputs high-quality 3D models by fusing local geometric information from the visible surface [11,19]. We establish an progressively autonomous scanning framework for multiple rooms scene by driving a ground robot to scan rooms sequentially. In addition, compared with hand-held scanning [18], which requires continuous and careful sampling on regions with sufficient geometric and photometric features for robust tracking [3,4], we adopt the panoramic scanning scheme, where in-

B. Sheng et al. (Eds.): CGI 2023, LNCS 14496, pp. 108–119, 2024.
https://doi.org/10.1007/978-3-031-50072-5_9

place rotations are easier to be tracked, which becomes a practical alternative for industrial or commercial applications [13]. Our work makes the following contributions:

- We propose an autonomous scanning method for complex structure rooms without priors via submodular function optimization for "Next-Best-View" and marginal utility principle for stopping scanning automatically.
- We proposed the "1st View" selection method without any manual intervention to improve the scanning initialization and overcome the incomplete vertical coverage of scanning devices.
- We proposed an offline scene optimization framework for high coverage and high registration accuracy for multi-room indoor scenes with a hierarchical pose optimization method.

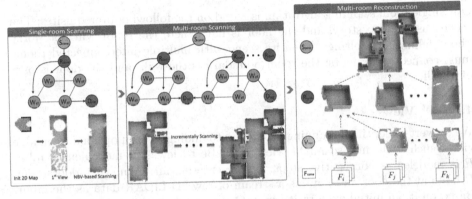

Fig. 1. Flow diagram of the proposed method. Left: our scanning method splits a room into elements in a Manhattan representation based on the divide-and-conquer principle and drives a ground robot to scan the room following the path given by a submodular-based optimization. Middle: we extend our scanning strategy to multi-room cases based on a "Scene–Room–Doors" based hierarchical scene structure graphs. Right: we accomplish multi-room reconstruction using incrementally indoor scene scanning process and reconstruction based on fusion of frames from different views.

2   Related Work

Known Indoor Structural Reconstruction. Following the popularity of hierarchical representation in games, some researchers use this representation in large-scale indoor reconstruction to come up with a more feasible reconstruction. Ikehata *et al.* [8] devises a structure grammar that drives the dense reconstruction algorithm and sequentially applies it to recover a structured model. Mura *et al.* [13] lifts the restrictive Manhattan-World assumptions as the only priors on the indoor environment, which can reconstruct indoor scene robustly.

Unknown Structural Scene Scanning. Existing methods with high-coverage and high-efficiency mainly divided into three types: object-driven, structure-driven, and hybrid object-structure-driven. Object-driven methods utilize the abundant semantic objects in a scene and traverse them one by one in a greedy way [11]. Structure-driven methods are specifically for the large-scale indoor scene [10]. Hybrid structure-object-driven methods merge structure and object properties into a scene topological representation [7, 16].

3   Overview

We introduce a novel scanning approach allowing to optimize the 1st View and Next-Best-View and a hierarchical semantic graph based reconstruction for multi-room scenes. An overview of the proposed approach is illustrated in Fig. 1.

4   Single-Room Scanning and Reconstruction

Our single-room scanning algorithm is based on the following prerequisites: The scene has a single story, and the floor is flat, where the robot will not worry about falling and jolting; an entire scene with multiple interconnected rooms must connect with doors; the room boundary is the wall, and the door is part of a wall.

4.1   1st View

We convert the optimal scanning problem into finding a set of optimal scannable views, such as the first scannable view, Next-Best-View. The movement of robot R is modeled as consecutive steps. Before entering an unknown indoor room, R halts at the door and obtains a stream of raw 2D LiDAR data as the input. Based on it, an initial exploration map Ω is generated. R is unable to scan any information from blind areas since mounted scanners have limited vertical views. Thus, we should move R to the 1st View, where R starts scanning and keeps updating Ω incrementally. This searching process mainly depends on maximizing D_{Blind}.

Blind Area. One in-place rotation scanning in a valid scannable view will produce consecutive RGB-D frames. Because of the limited vertical scanning view, a closed-loop should be considered to ensure registration and tracking quality robustness. We compute the blind area and exclude it from the exploration area. $D_{\text{Blind}} = h_R * \tan\left(\frac{\pi}{2} - \frac{\gamma_v}{2}\right) - \frac{w_R}{2}$, where h_R is the height of R's scanner, w_R is the width of R, D_{Blind} is the width of the blind area.

1st View Metric. We assign a pixel block a different score according to its label, where **FREE** is $+1$, **OBSTACLE** is -1, and **UNDERLYING** is $+0$. With such a labeled grid map, we define a scannable score using its neighboring labels and distance from the current view, $F_M(V) = \left(1 - \frac{1}{8}\sum_{i=1}^{8} L_{V_i}\right) + D_{V_R \to V}$, where L_{V_i} represents the label type of the pixel block occupied by V_i. $D_{V_R \to V}$ represents the A^* path length between the current view V_R and a candidate view V. The smaller F_M is, the higher scannable possibility is.

4.2 Submodular-Based Next-Best-View

The high-level goal is to find an optimized subset of viewpoints iteratively from a more extensive set of candidate views that maximize the information gained about the 3D surface of the current scene. We have developed a simple method built on a mathematical optimization framework that maximizes information about uncertain occluded space. At the core of our method lies a submodular objective function based on the total occluded information gained by the collection of viewpoints. After selecting Next-Best-View sequentially via a submodular-based greedy strategy, the robot samples panorama-style data in place and updates room-level global volume incrementally. The robot stops room scanning based on the marginal utility principle. The goal of the method is to predict the Next-Best-View for the ground robot that yields complete scanning and good reconstruction quality. Let $VC = \{\tau_1, \ldots, \tau_n\}$ be the scanned view. We want to solve a optimization problem: $VC^* = \underset{VC \in PC}{\arg\max} \, IG(VC)$, where PC denotes the power set of the view and VC^* is our objective function measuring the amount of occluded information observed by all the scanned views.

Definition 1. *The accumulated occluded information gained from* VC *is the sum of voxels' occluded evidence:* $IG(VC) = \sum_{i}^{NV} VI(v_i, VC)$.

Search Next-Best-View via Approximately Submodular Optimization. Submodularity provides us to approximate the optimal solution with guarantees via a greedy algorithm.

Theorem 1. $IG(VC)$ *is a submodular function.*

Proof. Let $A, B \subset VC$, where $A \subset B$. Let c is a candidate and $c \notin A$, $c \notin B$. Obviously, in terms of the occluded information, more views can never reduce the occluded information. So to incorporate the occluded information gained by the candidate view c into the objective function $IG(VC)$, we have $IG(\{c\} | VC) \geqslant IG(VC)$. Moreover, let v_i be an occluded voxel. The variation $\Delta(v_i, \{c\} | VC)$ is $\Delta(v_i, \{c\} | VC) = VI(v_i, \{c\} \cup VC) - VI(v_i, VC) = \min(o(v_i, c), 1 - VI(v_i, VC))$. Since $VC_A \subseteq VC_B$, we have $\Delta(\{c\} | A) \geq \Delta(\{c\} | B)$. The function $IG(VC)$ becomes *monotone* and *submodular*, which namely is a submodular function.

By utilizing the submodular function-based greedy strategy, the room scanning will reach high coverage after sparsely-sampled views. After T times scanning, we can compute the total occluded information gain $IG(VC)$, and then, the average information is $\overline{IG} = \frac{IG(VC)}{T}$, the increasing information gain $IG_t(vp_t) = \sum_{j}^{NV} VI(v_j, \{vp_t\})$. Using Marginal Utility, a principle derived from submodular function theory, we could stop room scanning when the occluded information gained tends to saturate. Algorithm 1 summarizes the entire process.

Ω^{OE} represents the **OCCLUDED Evidence Volume**. $\overline{IG}$ and IG_t indicate the average information gain and the real-time information gain respectively. D_t indicates scanned RGB-D data.

Algorithm 1: Greedy Next-Best-View Search.

    Input : 1st view V_0, the exploration Map Ω;
    Output: Next-Best-Views $VP = \{vp_1, \ldots, vp_n\}$;
1   $\Omega^{OE} \leftarrow \phi;\ \overline{IG} \leftarrow \emptyset;\ IG_0 \leftarrow \emptyset;\ D_0 \leftarrow \emptyset$;
2 **repeat**
3   Local 3D Scanning $D = \{D_i\} \cup D;\ \Omega^{OE},\ \Omega \leftarrow$ IncreUpdateFrom(D);
4     $VC \leftarrow$ FindCandidats($\Omega^{OE},\ \Omega$);
5     $IG_i \leftarrow \sum\limits_{i}^{NV} VI\left(v_i, \{c\}\right)$;
6     $c \leftarrow argmax\ IG_i;\ VP = \{c\} \cup VP;\ \overline{IG} = IG\left(VP\right)/T$;
7   MoveTo (c);
8 **until** $IG_i < \overline{IG}$;

In this paper, we assign **POINT Evidence** to measure the intensity of semantics information in a voxel and **OCCLUDED Evidence** to measure the occluded information of a voxel. **Point Evidence** quantifies the statistical intensity of points inside the voxel. It is mainly expressed proportionally to the number of points in each voxel $pe_i = \frac{(1-\alpha)ns_i + (1+\alpha)no_i}{ns_i + no_i} = 1 - \alpha\frac{ns_i - no_i}{ns_i + no_i}$, where pe_i represents the point evidence value of voxel v_i. ns_i is the number of plane-type points, while no_i is non-plane-type. We introduce a penalization term α, which encourages non-plane points and penalizes plane points. We adopt volume fusion to improve robustness which will perform weighted integration between incrementally updated global evidence volume and current volume. **Occluded Evidence** encodes the occluded information of a voxel. The expected occluded information for one candidate depends on all the past and other candidates. To make the computation of candidate views feasible, we assume that a single view v can provide occluded information about the 3D surface. For a single voxel τ the occluded information measured by the camera is given by $o(v, \tau)$. The measurement of occluded information can be denoted as the equation: $o\left(v_i, \tau_j\right) = \sum\limits_{PV_{ij}^k \in PV_{ij} \backslash PV_{ij}^{free}} \prod\limits_{l=1}^{k-1} e^{-\rho_l}\left(1 - e^{-\rho_k}\right) pe_{ij}^k$, where $PV_{ij}^{free} = \{v_k \in PV_{ij}; fe_k = \text{TRUE}\}$ is the **FREE** voxel, which should be removed from the voxel path between the view and the voxel. The formulation denotes the 3D radiative scattering of the voxel τ_j alone the camera ray between v_i and the voxel. The density $\rho_i = \frac{np_i}{\max\{np_i\}_i^{Nv}}$ can be denoted as the density of matter in the voxel, where np_i is the number of points in a voxel, and Nv is the number of voxels in current global volume.

The above mathematical model approximate realistic scenes. However, it indeed allow us to re-formulate our Next-Best-View selection problem in a way that exploits submodularity as an approximate solution of the problem.

5 Multi-Room Scanning and Reconstruction

To drive the robot to the room sequentially, we should extract essential structural elements from all the existing rooms. Room structure extraction could effectively regularize noise sensor data and preserve some geometrical features from sharp parts. To improve the efficiency of the multi-room indoor scene exploration, we also utilize the greedy strategy in rooms traversal. The robot starts from a random door and ends at some place inside the room. After the room structure extraction, the robot will move to the nearest unvisited door connected to an unknown room and start a new scanning. For large building-scale environments [14,15], it is difficult to integrate the method [21] which processes RGB-D frames all at once to generate a globally consistent model. Due to the accumulated drift and noise, the poses need to be optimized to achieve global consistency. However, to handle a building-scale scene in one shot is infeasible since many variables should be optimized. Our method provides a kind of practical solution based on divide-and-conquer strategy. After autonomous scanning guided by our strategy, we utilize a hierarchical scene structure to realize efficient and globally consistent offline reconstruction. According to the scanning order, the frames are divided into room-level and view-level. Every frame in the view-level will be registrated frame-by-frame and then a view-level local pose graph will be computed. Subsequently, we perform a local optimization [4] inside a view-level pose graph to maintain local consistency. Finally, we register the room-level pose graph among each other to generate a globally consistent model.

6 Results and Analysis

Setup. The simulation is implemented by using OpenGL on a virtual environment. We simulate a groud robot equipped with 2 virtual RGB-D cameras simulating the Azure Kinect sensor for separately capturing 720p RGB-D streams at 30 Hz. We assume the sensor has a depth range of $[0.5, 5.0]$ m and a hight of 1.75 m. These sensors are mounted with $30°$ difference in the inclination angle, and reach $90°$ vertical Field-of-View. In our experiments, we perform a panorama-style in-place scanning. It took the robot about 24 s to rotate by $360°$ in-place an produce about 24×2 frames. We add depth noise according to the sampled RGB-D frame proposed by Handa et al. [6]. The simulation runs on a computer with Intel Core i5-10400, 20 GB RAM, and an NVIDIA GeForce RTX 3060. The 2D pixel map Ω is constructed with a resolution of 0.4 m. We set the upper limit of linear and angular speed of the robot is 1.2 m/s and $15°$/s. Our benchmark dataset is built upon the virtual scene dataset Matterport3D [2]. We select 5 representative scenes which contain at least six compact interconnected rooms, as Fig. 3 shows.

6.1 Comparison and Evaluation

In this section, we conduct a series of comparisons by evaluating our method with related existing methods in terms of scanning coverage, efficiency, and reconstruction quality. Take the scanning manner and path planning strategy into account, we choose our baselines from several relevant state-of-the-art panorama-style greedy techniques: Bayesian optimization-based exploration method (BO) [1], adaptive **hierar**chical method (HIE) [12]. Up to our knowledge, our 1st view searching method is the first work to consider the starting view position in autonomous room scanning. From this perspective, it is inappropriate to compare our results to other existing algorithms. To make fair comparison, we reimplement these two methods [1,12] integrating with our 1st view searching module.

Table 1. Evaluation of different methods in terms of scanning efficiency

Method	OURS				HIE [12]				BO [1]			
	$\overline{T}$	$\overline{\varphi}$	$\overline{V}$	$\overline{ot}$	$\overline{T}$	$\overline{\varphi}$	$\overline{V}$	$\overline{ot}$	$\overline{T}$	$\overline{\varphi}$	$\overline{V}$	$\overline{ot}$
Scene 1	**17**	**97%**	**6%**	**634 s**	34	99%	3%	1303 s	30	98%	3%	1030 s
Scene 2	**19**	**97%**	**5%**	**709 s**	50	98%	2%	1926s	30	97%	3%	1047 s
Scene 3	**26**	**96%**	**4%**	**1000 s**	34	98%	2%	1328 s	33	97%	3%	1141 s
Scene 4	**20**	**98%**	**4%**	**774 s**	39	99%	2%	1504 s	37	99%	2%	1287 s
Scene 5	**27**	**94%**	**3%**	**1019 s**	30	95%	3%	1159 s	29	94%	3%	1021 s

Metric. We design three of evaluation metrics to quantitatively evaluate both reconstruction quality and scanning efficiency. Since our reconstruction results are dense model with large number of triangles than those of virtual models in public datasets. It is not reasonable to compare the difference in terms of triangle meshes. We utilize the generated point cloud instead of triangle meshes. **Scan times.** The times T for a robot to accomplish scanning a room. **Running time.** The whole running ot time includes scanning time, program running time, and motion time. Typically for a scanning task, it takes approximately 24 s for our simulated platform to perform stable in-place rotation panoramic sampling and 5 s for program running time. **Coverage.** Given our reconstruction result S, and the corresponding ground truth T. Two clouds is considered geometrically identical if and only if their (symmetric) Hausdorff [5] distance is zero. We utilize $\varphi_{T \to S} = \frac{100}{\sum A(t)} \sum_{t \in T} A(t) \min_{s \in S} \|s - t\|_2^0$ to indicate the coverage between our result and the ground truth. And we set $A(t) = 1$. **RMS Error.** Similar to the definition of Hausdorff distance in coverage comparison. We denote $\varphi_{S \to T} = \frac{1}{\sum A(s)} \sum_{s \in S} A(s) \min_{t \in T} \|t - s\|_2$ as RMS Error. **Time utilization rate.** We observe that rotation in-place for robots consumes most of time during the room scanning. The proportion of moving time takes less percentages, which reflects the efficiency of finding a Next-Best-View. Therefore, we compute the ratio of moving times and entire scanning time to indicate the time utilization $V(\varphi, T) = \frac{\varphi_{T \to S}}{\overline{T}} \times 100\%$. To measure scanning efficiency, we design four metrics: average of scan times $\overline{T}$, average of coverage $\overline{\varphi}$, average of time utilization rate $\overline{V}$, and average whole running time $\overline{ot}$ to evaluate different methods' scanning efficiency at different scenes (Fig. 2).

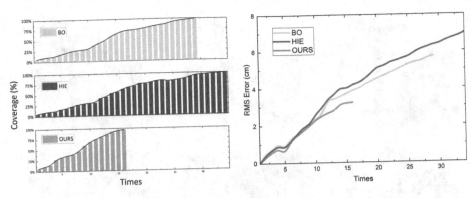

Fig. 2. Left: Coverage is increasing along with scan times. Our method achieves high coverage more quickly than the other two methods.Right: RMS Error is increasing along with scan times. Our method achieves lower incremental RMS Error than the other two methods.

Table 1 reports that our method achieves highest scanning efficiency in terms of $\overline{T}$. Our method use less scanning times to finish scanning a room. Despite slight dropping on average coverage $\overline{\varphi}$, our method is superior to quickly searching Next-Best-Views for large-scale rooms. Bigger value in $\overline{V}$ shows higher time utilization. HIE [12] outperforms in terms of coverage due to it represents the scene as octree, and divides the invisible information according to different scales, and adjusts the stopping scanning threshold according to the density of different positions in the voxel model. Our method can integrate these advanced techniques for improvements in future. We observe HIE [12] keeps in scanning unknown area overlooking the information gains diminishing. That is why HIE [12] can achieve the highest scanning coverage. It is not suitable for autonomous scanning of multi-room scenes. On the contrary, BO [1] pays excessive attention to information gain, which decays with distance from robot. To maximize information gain, BO [1] is inclined to select a view as close as possible, which leads to small exploration range for Next-Best-View. As the results about $\overline{V}$ and $\overline{t}$ show, it can be seen that the increase in the number of samples significantly increases the overall time consumption due to the excessive proportion of data sampling time during each scan. Compared with other methods, we make balance of partial and whole, and the greedy strategy based on submodular function can take account of coverage and speed.

6.2   Reconstruction Results

We show the reconstruction result and scanning path on different scenes in Fig. 3. It is clearly that our method gives a simple path and guarantees the completeness of indoor scenes. Especially, our method achieves fast and complete scanning in open spaces. Thanks to the marginal effect principle, the robot stops at the right time instead of keeping scanning captiously.

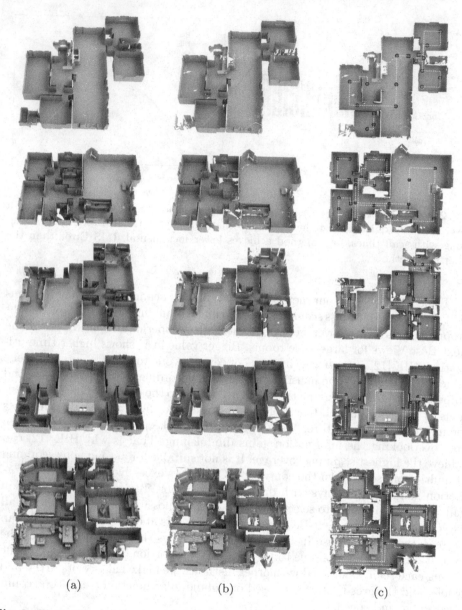

(a)   (b)   (c)

Fig. 3. Illustration of the Reconstruction Result. 3(a) shows the Ground Truth 3D models; 3(b) shows the reconstructed 3D models; 3(c) shows the reconstructed 3D models with scanning paths, where the dotted line represents the robot scanning path, the rectangles represent the robot initial position in this room, and the circles represent real scanned views.

It is worth noting that the last scene shows some areas with sparse reconstruction due to the limited scannable area. The panorama-style scanning may suffer significant overlaps, leading to some inevitable unscanned areas. We can deal with this issue by adjusting the vertical view to a larger angle for scanning the small room with a compact layout. We investigate the effects of vertical view in Fig. 4. Here, we take $90°, 100°, 110°, 120°$ as examples, with the increasing vertical view, the holes are filled in reconstruction results, which means higher scanning completeness can be obtained by increasing the vertical view of scanning devices. In addition, we also discussed the effect of the vertical view on 1st view selection. At the rightmost of Fig. 4, we can notice that as the vertical view angle gradually increases, the blind area decreases, and the starting scanning view of the room scanning, i.e., the 1st view, gets closer to the door of the room.

6.3   Ablation Study

Table 2. Ablation study on "1st View" and marginal utility

3D Model	OURS	w/o 1st View	w/o Mar Uti	OURS	w/o 1st View	w/o Mar Uti
		$\overline{T}$			$\overline{V}$	
Scene 1	7	8	10	14.24%	12.27%	9.83%
Scene 2	11	12	15	9.05%	8.16%	6.73%
Scene 3	6	7	9	16.63%	14.13%	11.78%
Scene 4	4	5	5	24.83%	19.86%	20.13%
Scene 5	6	7	8	15.21%	13.08%	11.69%

To further illustrate the effectiveness of the proposed scanning method, the ablation experiments are performed on four scenarios with regard to three options affecting scanning speed and coverage of scenes. **w/o 1st View selection:** From Table 2, we can see that the average scan times increases without using 1st Views, which demonstrates that the 1st View selection is important for initialization of scanning. **w/o marginal utility principle:** We tried to scan multi-room scenes without the marginal utility instead of the rate of scene coverage updating $\Delta\varphi < 0.05$. Table 2 shows that the average scan times increases without using the marginal utility principle for stopping scanning. These two ablation experiments show that these two strategies proposed in this paper can significantly speed up scanning speed. **w/o hierarchical pose estimation:** Based on the method [21], the 3D model of the indoor scene is reconstructed offline. We conduct an ablation experiment of whether to optimize registration raw data via the hierarchical optimization method. As shown in Fig. 4, there is an increasing trend of RMS Error without using pose map optimization. The reason is that the registration error will be accumulate incrementally without global pose optimization. The increasing trend of error accumulation is very small after the room level pose graph optimization. This ablation experiment shows that in a large-scale unknown indoor scene composed of multiple rooms, hierarchical pose optimization greatly reduces the cumulative error of registration between scanning views.

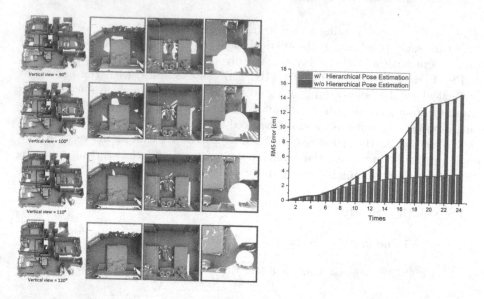

Fig. 4. Left: The study on vertical view. With the increase of vertical view, the holes are filled in reconstruction results, and the 1st view gets closer to the door. Right: Ablation study on hierarchical pose graph optimization. The growth of RMS errors have a big gap with and without hierarchical pose estimation.

7   Conclusions

We propose an indoor scene scanning method based on the greedy strategy of the submodular function. We select Next-Best-View based on submodular optimization greedy strategy until the marginal gains diminish. The whole scenes are organized by hierarchical structure and recovered incrementally. The experiments demonstrate that our submodular-based scanning works effectively for large-scale unknown scenes containing multiple rooms. In the future, we will continue improving the selection strategy by using reinforcement learning and some neural rendering methods.

Acknowledgments. This work was partially supported by the National Natural Science Foundation of China under Grant No. 61972458, and the Zhejiang Provincial Natural Science Foundation of China under Grant No. LZ23F020002. The authors would like to thank the anonymous reviewers for their helpful and valuable comments and suggestions.

References

1. Bai, S., Wang, J., Chen, F., Englot, B.: Information-theoretic exploration with Bayesian optimization. In: 2016 IEEE/RSJ International Conference on Intelligent Robots and Systems (IROS), pp. 1816–1822. IEEE (2016)
2. Chang, A., et al.: Matterport3D: learning from RGB-D data in indoor environments. arXiv preprint arXiv:1709.06158 (2017)

3. Chen, Z., Qiu, J., Sheng, B., Li, P., Wu, E.: GPSD: generative parking spot detection using multi-clue recovery model. Vis. Comput. **37**(9–11), 2657–2669 (2021)
4. Choi, S., Zhou, Q.Y., Koltun, V.: Robust reconstruction of indoor scenes. In: Proceedings of the IEEE Conference on Computer Vision and Pattern Recognition, pp. 5556–5565 (2015)
5. Cignoni, P., Rocchini, C., Scopigno, R.: Metro: measuring error on simplified surfaces. In: Computer Graphics Forum, vol. 17, pp. 167–174. Wiley Online Library (1998)
6. Handa, A., Whelan, T., McDonald, J., Davison, A.J.: A benchmark for RGB-D visual odometry, 3D reconstruction and slam. In: 2014 IEEE International Conference on Robotics and Automation (ICRA), pp. 1524–1531 (2014). https://doi.org/10.1109/ICRA.2014.6907054
7. Hepp, B., Nießner, M., Hilliges, O.: Plan3D: viewpoint and trajectory optimization for aerial multi-view stereo reconstruction. ACM Trans. Graph. (TOG) **38**(1), 1–17 (2018)
8. Ikehata, S., Yang, H., Furukawa, Y.: Structured indoor modeling. In: Proceedings of the IEEE International Conference on Computer Vision, pp. 1323–1331 (2015)
9. Kehoe, B., Patil, S., Abbeel, P., Goldberg, K.: A survey of research on cloud robotics and automation. IEEE Trans. Autom. Sci. Eng. **12**(2), 398–409 (2015)
10. Li, L., et al.: Improving autonomous exploration using reduced approximated generalized voronoi graphs. J. Intell. Robot. Syst. **99**, 91–113 (2020)
11. Liu, L., et al.: Object-aware guidance for autonomous scene reconstruction. ACM Trans. Graph. (TOG) **37**(4), 1–12 (2018)
12. Low, K.L., Lastra, A.: An adaptive hierarchical next-best-view algorithm for 3D reconstruction of indoor scenes. In: Proceedings of 14th Pacific Conference on Computer Graphics and Applications (Pacific Graphics 2006), pp. 1–8. Citeseer (2006)
13. Mura, C., Mattausch, O., Pajarola, R.: Piecewise-planar reconstruction of multi room interiors with arbitrary wall arrangements. In: Computer Graphics Forum, vol. 35, pp. 179–188. Wiley Online Library (2016)
14. Qin, Y., Chi, X., Sheng, B., Lau, R.W.: Guiderender: large-scale scene navigation based on multi-modal view frustum movement prediction. Vis. Comput. **39**, 1–11 (2023). https://doi.org/10.1007/s00371-023-02922-x
15. Qiu, J., Yin, Z.X., Cheng, M.M., Ren, B.: Rendering real-world unbounded scenes with cars by learning positional bias. Vis. Comput. **39**, 1–14 (2023). https://doi.org/10.1007/s00371-023-03070-y
16. Quintana, B., Prieto, S., Adán, A., Vázquez, A.S.: Semantic scan planning for indoor structural elements of buildings. Adv. Eng. Inform. **30**(4), 643–659 (2016)
17. Selin, M., Tiger, M., Duberg, D., Heintz, F., Jensfelt, P.: Efficient autonomous exploration planning of large-scale 3-d environments. IEEE Robot. Autom. Lett. **4**(2), 1699–1706 (2019)
18. Wang, L., Yi, L., Zhang, Y., Wang, X., Wang, W., Wang, X.: 3D reconstruction method based on N-step phase unwrapping. Vis. Comput. **39**, 1–13 (2023). https://doi.org/10.1007/s00371-023-03054-y
19. Xu, K., et al.: Autonomous reconstruction of unknown indoor scenes guided by time-varying tensor fields. ACM Trans. Graph. (TOG) **36**(6), 1–15 (2017)
20. Zhang, J., Zhu, C., Zheng, L., Xu, K.: Rosefusion: random optimization for online dense reconstruction under fast camera motion. ACM Trans. Graph. (TOG) **40**(4), 1–17 (2021)
21. Zhou, Q.Y., Miller, S., Koltun, V.: Elastic fragments for dense scene reconstruction. In: Proceedings of the IEEE International Conference on Computer Vision, pp. 473–480 (2013)

Learning Degradation for Real-World Face Super-Resolution

Jin Chen[1,2], Jun Chen[1,2(✉)], Xiaofen Wang[1,2], Dongshu Xu[1,2], Chao Liang[1,2], and Zhen Han[1,2]

[1] National Engineering Research Center for Multimedia Software, School of Computer, Wuhan University, Wuhan, China
{chenjin_2046,wxiaofen,xudongshu,cliang}@whu.edu.cn, chenj.whu@gmail.com
[2] Hubei Key Laboratory of Multimedia and Network Communication Engineering, Wuhan University, Wuhan, China

Abstract. Acquiring degraded faces with corresponding high-resolution (HR) faces is critical for real-world face super-resolution (SR) applications. To generate low-resolution (LR) faces with degradation similar to those in real-world scenarios, most approaches learn a deterministic mapping from HR faces to LR faces. However, these deterministic models fail to model the various degradation of real-world LR faces, which limits the performance of the following face SR models. In this work, we learn a degradation model based on conditional generative adversarial networks (cGANs). Specifically, we propose a simple and effective weight-aware content loss that adaptively assigns different content losses to LR faces generated from the same HR face under different noise vector inputs. It significantly improves the diversity of the generated LR faces while having similar degradation to real-world LR faces. Compared with previous degradation models, the proposed degradation model can generate HR-LR pairs, which can better cover various degradation cases of real-world LR faces and further improve the performance of face SR models in real-world applications. Experiments on four datasets demonstrate that the proposed degradation model can help the face SR model achieve better performance in both quantitative and qualitative results.

Keywords: Learning degradation · Weight-aware content loss · Face super-resolution

1 Introduction

Individuals stay away from cameras, resulting in rather small faces captured in the wild. It poses a great challenge to the following face-related tasks [1,2]. Face SR can restore HR faces from LR observations and achieve significant performance by mining priors [3–8] or optimizing network designs [9,10]. However, most methods are performed on LR faces with predefined settings (*e.g.*, bicubic

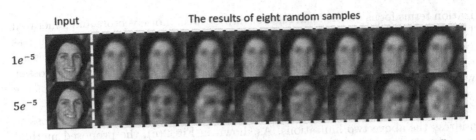

Fig. 1. Comparison of the LR faces generated by the degradation model under different weights of the regularization term in MSGAN [21]. The resolution of input and output are 64×64 pixels and 16×16 pixels, respectively.

downsampling). The gap between predefined LR faces and real-world LR faces leads to degraded performance of face SR models in real-world applications.

Recently, some methods [11–13] simultaneously consider more degradation factors and further set broader parameters or randomly shuffle different degradation factors to simulate the complex degradation of real-world LR images, but the degradation modes of many generated LR images are inconsistent with that in real-world scenarios. Some other methods [14–17] adaptively learn deterministic mappings through adversarial learning but may fail to simulate the diverse degradation of real-world LR images. To better simulate the diverse degradation of real-world LR images, in DeFlow [18], a flow-based degradation model is proposed, but its parameters are often too large. In PDM [19], a linear degradation model that jointly learns blur kernel distribution and noise distribution is proposed, but it cannot simulate the nonlinear degradation in real scenarios. In UsrDU [20], the authors propose to learn the uncertainty of image degradation and simulate diverse degradation by a posteriori sampling. In SCGAN [24], a degradation model based on cGANs is proposed. As shown in Fig. 2(a), it uses noise vectors sampled from a distribution to simulate varies degradation modes of real-world LR faces that are supervised by the same content loss l_c. Due to the mode collapse issue [26] of cGANs, it can only generate a few degradation modes, which limits the performance of the following face SR models.

Motivated by the success of cGANs-based methods with regularization terms in diversity image synthesis tasks [21–23], we rethink the degradation model based on cGANs. As shown in Fig. 2(b), in MSGAN, a regularization term l_{div} is proposed to maximize the ratio of distances between two noise vectors and the generated results to keep them away from each other. When using it directly to generate LR faces with diversity degradation, we find that it is sensitive to weights. As shown in Fig. 1, when the weight of the regularization term is set to $1e^{-5}$, the generated LR faces have limited diversity (top row), but when the weight is set to $5e^{-5}$, the generated LR faces show structural distortion (bottom row). In DivCo [23], a latent-augmented contrastive loss is proposed to constrain both 'positive' and 'negative' relations between the generated images in the latent space, but it is only a slight improvement. There are two limitations of using those regularization terms for learning degradation. First, these regularization terms focus on the local relationship between noise vectors and generated LR faces, leading to slow convergence of the network; Second, these regularization terms are usually optimized with content loss. However, these two losses are optimized in opposite directions, so the network must balance these two losses, which causes the network to struggle between the diversity and fidelity of the generated LR faces.

In this work, we propose a simple yet effective weight-aware content loss to address the above two limitations. As shown in Fig. 2(c), the proposed method can adaptively assign different weights of content loss $w_i l_c$ to different generated faces from a global perspective. It makes the generated LR faces from the same HR face under different noise vector inputs guided by different content losses, effectively alleviating the mode collapse issue and improving the diversity of the generated LR faces. Meanwhile, it does not need to jointly optimize two losses in opposite directions and alleviates the distortion of the generated LR faces. In summary, the main contributions can be summarized as follows: (i) We propose a weight-aware content loss to improve the diversity of the generated LR faces while having similar degradation as the real LR faces. (ii) Qualitative and quantitative experimental results on four datasets demonstrate the superiority of the proposed method for improving the performance of the face SR model.

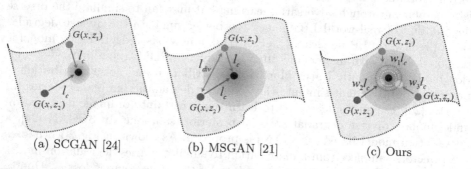

(a) SCGAN [24]   (b) MSGAN [21]   (c) Ours

Fig. 2. Comparison of different strategies for enhancing the diversity of the generated LR faces.

2   Proposed Method

2.1   Preliminaries

To learn a degradation model based on cGANs to generate diverse LR faces. The objective of the degradation model $\mathcal{L}_T$ usually consists of two terms, the GAN loss $\mathcal{L}_G$ and the content loss $\mathcal{L}_C$.

$$\mathcal{L}_T = \mathcal{L}_G + \lambda \mathcal{L}_C, \tag{1}$$

where the $\mathcal{L}_G$ aims to narrow the gap between the generated LR faces and the real-world LR faces, while the $\mathcal{L}_C$ aims to maintain some content information between the output and the input.

For the $\mathcal{L}_G$, the training scheme often jointly learns the discriminator D and the conditional generator G by optimizing the following adversarial objective:

$$\min_G \max_D \mathcal{L}_{cGAN}(G, D) = \mathbb{E}_{x,y}[\log D(x, y)] \\ + \mathbb{E}_{x,z}[\log(1 - D(x, G(x, z)))], \tag{2}$$

where x is an HR input, y is a generated LR face, and z is a noise vector sampled from a distribution that is expected to perturb the output.

For the $\mathcal{L}_C$, it is usually a regression loss and we use the $\mathcal{L}_1$ loss here.

$$\mathcal{L}_C(G) = \|G(x, z) - B(x)\|_1, \tag{3}$$

where $B(\cdot)$ denotes a degradation operation.

To generate diverse LR faces, the degradation model is expected to generate LR faces with different degradation modes under different noise vectors. But in the training, the degradation model is likely to observe only a sample of the input. From Eq. 3, we know that the content loss of generated LR faces from the same HR face under different noise vector inputs is the same. On the other hand, the GAN loss $\mathcal{L}_G$ focuses on generating LR faces that are indistinguishable from real-world LR faces, and has only a limited ability to distinguish small differences between the generated LR faces corresponding to different noise vectors. So, it causes the conditional generator G to produce only a few degradation modes close to the center of the distribution and ignore other degradation modes far from the center of the distribution.

2.2   Regularization via Weight-Aware Content Loss

Through the above analysis, we can see that the generated LR faces under different noise vectors have the same content loss, which leads to the lack of diversity in the generated LR faces to some extent. To relax this constraint, an intuitive solution is to provide different real-world LR faces with different degradation modes to guide the generated LR faces from the same HR face under different noise vector inputs. However, it is difficult to collect different degraded faces of an HR face in real scenarios. To address this issue, we propose a simple yet effective weight-aware content loss, where the weight only depends on the noise vector. By this soft constraint, the generated LR faces from the same HR face under different noise vector inputs can be guided by different content losses, which alleviates the model collapse issue and further improves the diversity of the generated LR faces.

To design this weighting function, the following criteria need to be considered: (i) it is related to the noise vector z; (ii) it needs to maintain the similarity of different generated LR faces. Based on the above considerations, we design a weighting function $w(z)$ as follows:

$$w(z) = (1 - \alpha) \cdot Mean[\exp(-\frac{z^2}{2})] + \alpha, \tag{4}$$

where the first term is used to represent the aggregation degree of degraded LR faces in the degradation space, and we design it according to the Gaussian distribution density function. $Mean[\cdot]$ denotes the mean operator to transform a multidimensional tensor into a scalar value. The second term is a lower bound to constrain the similarity between different LR faces and the setting of the parameter α will be discussed further in Sect. 3.3. Using this weighting function, different weights can be adaptively assigned based on the distance of the sampled noise from the center of the distribution. It also guides the degradation model to learn to generate LR faces with different degrees of content information, thus increasing the diversity of the generated LR faces.

Total Loss. The final full objective loss $\mathcal{L}_{T,new}$ of our degradation model is:

$$\mathcal{L}_{T,new} = \mathcal{L}_G + \lambda w(z)\mathcal{L}_C, \tag{5}$$

where λ is used to balance the contribution of different losses, which we empirically set to 0.02 in the experiments.

2.3   The Network Architecture

The proposed degradation network consists of two modules: a conditional degradation generation network G_{deg} and the discriminator network D_{deg}. The input of the G_{deg} contains an HR face I_{hr} and a noise vector z ($z \in R^{16}$), which is sampled from a distribution. z is first passed through a fully connected layer, and the output is reshaped and concatenated with I_{hr}. Then the concatenated maps are sequentially passed through a convolution layer, two DResBlock [24], two RRDB blocks [12], another convolution layer, and a Tanh layer to output the result. All convolutions in the G_{deg} are 3×3 kernel size with 64 channels. And we use the LR discriminator in SCGAN as D_{deg}. To demonstrate the superiority of the proposed degradation model for improving the performance of the face SR model, we adopt the architecture used in ESRGAN [12] as the face SR model.

3   Experiments

3.1   Implementation Details

Datasets and Metrics. Following the experimental setup in SCGAN, we conduct experiments mainly on four datasets. For training, we randomly select 20,000 high-quality faces from the FFHQ [27] dataset and 4,000 low-quality faces from the Widerface [28] dataset to construct the unpaired training set. In the test stage, we randomly select 1,000 faces from the LS3D-W_balanced [29] dataset and perform bilinear downsampling to evaluate the SR performance of LR faces with simple degradation. We randomly select another 2,500 faces from the FFHQ dataset and perform random degradation to evaluate the SR performance of LR faces with complex degradation. We use the Widerface and

WebFace datasets, which contain 2,000 and 1,028 real-world LR faces to evaluate the SR performance of LR faces with unknown degradation. The detailed description and setting of the four datasets can be found in Section IV-A in SCGAN. In the experiment, HR faces and LR faces are resized to 64 × 64 pixels and 16 × 16 pixels, respectively. For two synthetic datasets, we evaluate the SR performance with PSNR, SSIM [31] and LPIPS [32] metrics since the corresponding HR faces are available. For two real-world datasets, we evaluate the quality of SR images with two no-reference evaluation metrics, FID [33] and NIQE [34].

Training Details. The whole training is conducted in two stages: the learning degradation stage and the face SR stage. In the learning degradation stage, we optimize the proposed degradation model on the unpaired training set via Adam [30] solver with $\beta_1 = 0.9$ and $\beta_2 = 0.999$. The learning rate is initialized as $1e^{-4}$ and is decayed to $5e^{-6}$ linearly for 200 epochs with a batch size of 128. In the face SR stage, we first use the degradation model to produce degraded LR faces similar to real-world LR faces, and then use the constructed pseudo HR-LR pairs to train the face SR model. We optimize the face SR model via Adam solver with $\beta_1 = 0.9$ and $\beta_2 = 0.999$. The learning rate is initialized as $1e^{-4}$ and is decayed to $1e^{-5}$ linearly for 200 epochs with a batch size of 48. For a fair comparison, the proposed method and other comparison methods in the experiments are retrained on the training set. We implement our method in PyTorch and run on two NVIDIA TiTan V GPUs.

3.2 Comparison with Other Methods

We compare our methods with state-of-the-art degenerate learning methods and some regularization methods, including High2Low [25], DASR [17], MSGAN [21], DivCo [23], UsrDU [20], PDM [19], SCGAN [24].

Evaluation of Two Synthetic Datasets. Here, we evaluate the performance of different methods on two synthetic datasets with different degradation. As shown in Table 1, we can see that our method obtains higher PSNR and SSIM scores than the other methods, while the LPIPS scores are lower than the other methods. As shown in Fig. 3 (the top four rows), the results produced by MSGAN, DivCo, DASR, PDM, and UsrDU are blurred and lack texture details, especially the results produced by UsrDU show a color shift. Both High2Low and SCGAN produce texture-rich faces, but there are many pseudo-textures and even structural distortions in the images. For example, as shown in the ninth column and the fourth row in Fig. 3, the result generated by SCGAN shows a structural distortion in the left cheek region. On the contrary, our method generates realistic faces in ensuring the structure consistent with the ground-truth HR faces.

Evaluation of Two Real-World Datasets. Now, we evaluate the performance of different methods on two real-world datasets with unknown degradation. As shown in Table 2, we can see that our method achieves lower FID and NIQE

Table 1. Quantitative results of the proposed method with other comparison methods on two synthetic datasets, LS3D-W_balanced and FFHQ.

Method	LS3D-W_balanced ×4			FFHQ ×4		
	PSNR ↑	SSIM ↑	LPIPS ↓	PSNR ↑	SSIM ↑	LPIPS ↓
Bicubic	21.82	0.6625	0.4134	18.70	0.5914	0.4265
High2Low [25]	22.29	0.7296	0.0763	20.50	0.6919	0.0858
MSGAN [21]	24.79	0.8027	0.1015	20.13	0.7329	0.1383
DivCo [23]	24.77	0.8033	0.1016	20.13	0.7322	0.1384
DASR [17]	24.74	**0.8111**	0.0777	19.79	0.7248	0.1094
PDM [19]	23.68	0.7508	0.0822	19.55	0.6788	0.1048
UsrDU [20]	21.69	0.6412	0.1444	18.42	0.5778	0.1689
SCGAN [24]	22.89	0.7513	0.0737	19.92	0.7008	0.0833
Ours+z_0	**25.16**	0.8104	0.0599	19.87	0.7113	0.0878
Ours	25.09	0.8069	**0.0569**	**20.56**	**0.7283**	**0.0783**

Table 2. Quantitative results of the proposed method with other comparison methods on two real-world datasets, Widerface and WebFace.

Method	Widerface ×4		WebFace ×4	
	FID ↓	NIQE ↓	FID ↓	NIQE ↓
Bicubic	180.42	18.8702	189.38	18.2949
High2Low [25]	39.76	14.7429	56.01	14.3752
MSGAN [21]	63.15	15.6043	78.46	15.0072
DivCo [23]	62.88	15.1619	77.93	15.4286
DASR [17]	65.78	15.4347	81.88	15.0325
PDM [19]	42.29	15.1521	60.02	14.9288
UsrDU [20]	49.43	16.0346	63.47	16.5864
SCGAN [24]	39.02	14.8413	55.18	14.2971
Ours+z_0	40.77	14.8822	60.53	13.7207
Ours	**38.85**	**14.3251**	**54.69**	**13.7069**

scores than the other methods on two real-world datasets. As shown in Fig. 3 (the bottom four rows), MSGAN is prone to produce blurry faces, similar to DivCo and DASR. The faces produced by PDM contain many random pseudo textures because it does not simulate the complex degradation of real-world LR faces. The faces generated by UsrDU still have a color shift. High2Low and SCGAN produce texture-rich faces, but there are many pseudo-textures in the images. On the contrary, our proposed method still produces realistic faces and contains fewer pseudo-textures. The faces reconstructed with our method look more natural.

3.3   Ablation Study

Effect of parameter α. In Eq. 4, the parameter α is a lower bound used to constrain the similarity between different LR faces, which controls the degree of diversity of the generated LR faces to some extent. Here, we will further discuss the effect of parameter α on the SR performance at different settings. As shown in Fig. 4 (a) and (c), when the parameter α is set large (*e.g.*, 0.7), the generated faces are not sufficiently diverse, which limits the performance of the face SR model. As the parameter α decreases, the degradation model can generate LR faces with more diversity, thus further decreasing the LPIPS and FID scores. And when the parameter α is 0.3, the lowest LPIPS scores are obtained on two synthetic datasets, 0.0783 and 0.0569, and the lowest FID scores are achieved on two real-world datasets, 54.69 and 38.85, respectively. When the parameter α is further reduced (*e.g.*, 0.1), the LPIPS and FID metrics do not improve further. It may be that when the parameter α is too small, the diversity of the generated LR faces further increases, but many generated LR faces do not match the degradation modes of the test faces, which interferes with the learning of the face SR model to some extent. As shown in Fig. 4(b) and (d), the PSNR and NIQE metrics also show a consistent trend. Since the proposed degradation

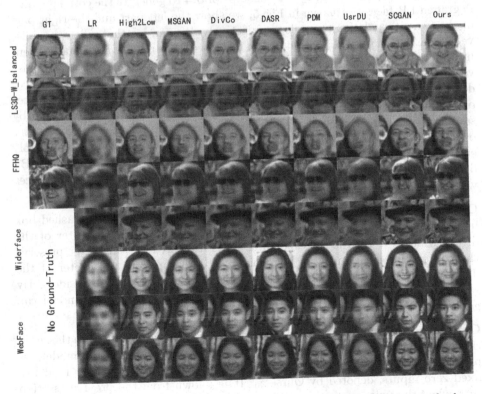

Fig. 3. Comparison of visual quality by our method and other comparison methods on LS3d-W_balanced, FFHQ, Widerface, and WebFace datasets (from top to bottom).

model is based on adversarial learning, we focus on LPIPS and FID metrics, while PSNR and NIQE are auxiliary metrics. Therefore, the parameter α is set to 0.3 in the following experiments.

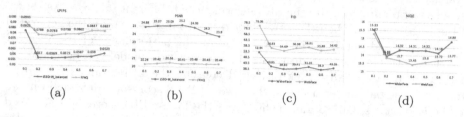

(a)   (b)   (c)   (d)

Fig. 4. Quantitative results for parameter α at different settings on four datasets. (a) and (b) show the LPIPS and PSNR results on LS3D-W_balanced and FFHQ, (c) and (d) show the FID and NIQE results on Widerface and WebFace.

We also show the visualization results of the generated samples with different parameters α. Specifically, we perform linear interpolation between two noise vectors z_1 and z_2 ($z_1 = -2$, $z_2 = 2$) in steps of **0.4** to generate the corresponding degraded LR faces. As shown in Fig. 5, we show the left part and the right part of the two interpolation examples, respectively. We can see that when the noise vectors are set to **0**, the generated LR faces are keep almost the same content information under different parameters α (red dotted box), and when the noise vectors are set to -2 or **2**, the content similarity of the generated LR faces decreases (green dotted box). Meanwhile, we can also see that as the parameter α decreases, the content similarity corresponding to the LR faces generated by sampling at different intervals also decreases. For example, when the parameter α is 0.3 (yellow dotted box), the generated LR faces are more distinguishable each other than those generated with a parameter of 0.7 (cyan dotted box). By decreasing the parameter α, the degradation model can generate more LR faces with different content information.

One-to-Many Degradation Examples. As shown in the yellow dashed box in Fig. 5, we can see that when the noise vector is close to the center of the distribution ($z = 0$), the corresponding generated LR face can better preserve the content information, while the noise vector is far from the center of the distribution, the corresponding generated LR face is more blurred (sides). By sampling in different intervals of the distribution, the degradation model can generate LR faces with different degradation modes.

Compared with the Deterministic Model. To better demonstrate the superiority of our degradation model over the deterministic degradation model, we perform comparative experiments by substituting z in the degradation model to fixed zero inputs, denoted by Ours+z_0. It is known from the previous section that when the noise vector is equal to 0, the corresponding generated LR face can better preserve the content information. As shown in Table 1 and Table 2

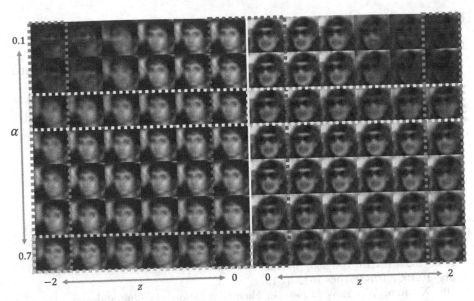

Fig. 5. Qualitative generation results of the proposed degradation model under different noise vectors and different parameter α.

(bottom two rows), the Ours+z_0 can better handle simple degraded LR faces on the LS3D-W_balanced dataset, with slightly better PSNR and SSIM scores than ours. With the proposed weight-aware content loss, the degradation model can learn to generate the LR faces with different degradation modes to better cover different degradation cases in real scenes. Thus, the SR performance of the proposed degradation model consistently outperforms Ours+z_0 on the other three datasets with complex or unknown degradation, which indicates that the proposed degradation model can better improve the SR performance of the face SR model in real-world applications.

4   Conclusion

In this work, we learn a degradation model based on cGANs architecture. Specifically, we propose a simple and effective weight-aware content loss to assign different content losses to the generated LR faces from the same HR face under different noise vector inputs. It alleviates the model collapse issue of cGAN-based methods and improves the diversity of the generated LR faces. Extensive experiments on four datasets demonstrate that the proposed degradation model can help the face SR model achieve better performance in the wild.

Acknowledgements. This research was supported partially by National Nature Science Foundation of China (62072347, U1903214, 62071338, 61876135), in part by the Nature Science Foundation of Hubei under Grant (2018CFA024, 2019CFB472), in part by Hubei Province Technological Innovation Major Project (No. 2018AAA062).

References

1. Deng, J., Guo, J., Ververas, E., et al.: RetinaFace: single-shot multi-level face localisation in the wild. In: Proceedings of the IEEE/CVF Conference on Computer Vision and Pattern Recognition, pp. 5203–5212 (2020)
2. Wang, H., Wang, S., Fang, L.: Two-stage multi-scale resolution-adaptive network for low-resolution face recognition. In: Proceedings of the 30th ACM International Conference on Multimedia, pp. 4053–4062 (2022)
3. Ying, L., Dinghua, S., Fuping, W., et al.: Learning wavelet coefficients for face super-resolution. Vis. Comput. **37**, 1613–1622 (2021)
4. Wen, Y., Chen, J., Sheng, B., et al.: Structure-aware motion deblurring using multi-adversarial optimized CycleGAN. IEEE Trans. Image Process. **30**, 6142–6155 (2021)
5. Li, H., Sheng, B., Li, P., et al.: Globally and locally semantic colorization via exemplar-based broad-GAN. IEEE Trans. Image Process. **30**, 8526–8539 (2021)
6. Kalanke, N.S., Tomar, A.S., et al.: Face super resolution through face semantic and structural prior. In: Arya, K.V., Tripathi, V.K., Rodriguez, C., Yusuf, E. (eds.) ICIT 2022. LNNS, vol. 685, pp. 159–166. Springer, Singapore (2023). https://doi.org/10.1007/978-981-99-1912-3_15
7. Hu, X., Ren, W., Yang, J., et al.: Face restoration via plug-and-play 3D facial priors. IEEE Trans. Pattern Anal. Mach. Intell. **44**(12), 8910–8926 (2021)
8. Lu, T., Wang, Y., Zhang, Y., et al.: Rethinking prior-guided face super-resolution: a new paradigm with facial component prior. IEEE Trans. Neural Netw. Learn. Syst. 10–15 (2022)
9. Chen, C., Gong, D., Wang, H., et al.: Learning spatial attention for face super-resolution. IEEE Trans. Image Process. **30**, 1219–1231 (2020)
10. Shi, J., Wang, Y., Dong, S., et al.: IDPT: interconnected dual pyramid transformer for face super-resolution. In: International Joint Conference on Artificial Intelligence, pp. 1306–1312 (2022)
11. Zhang, K., Liang, J., Van, Gool, L., et al.: Designing a practical degradation model for deep blind image super-resolution. In: Proceedings of the IEEE/CVF International Conference on Computer Vision, pp. 4791–4800 (2021)
12. Wang, X., Xie, L., Dong, C., et al.: Real-ESRGAN: training real-world blind super-resolution with pure synthetic data. In: Proceedings of the IEEE/CVF International Conference on Computer Vision, pp. 1905–1914 (2021)
13. Zhang, W., et al.: A closer look at blind super-resolution: degradation models, baselines, and performance upper bounds. In: Proceedings of the IEEE/CVF Conference on Computer Vision and Pattern Recognition, pp. 527–536 (2022)
14. Yuan, Y., Liu, S., Zhang, J., et al.: Unsupervised image super-resolution using cycle-in-cycle generative adversarial networks. In: Proceedings of the IEEE Conference on Computer Vision and Pattern Recognition Workshops, pp. 701–710 (2018)
15. Fritsche, M., et al.: Frequency separation for real-world super-resolution. In: 2019 IEEE/CVF International Conference on Computer Vision Workshop, pp. 3599–3608 (2019)
16. Chen, S., Han, Z., Dai, E., et al.: Unsupervised image super-resolution with an indirect supervised path. In: Proceedings of the IEEE/CVF Conference on Computer Vision and Pattern Recognition Workshops, pp. 468–469 (2020)
17. Wang, L., Wang, Y., Dong, X., et al.: Unsupervised degradation representation learning for blind super-resolution. In: Proceedings of the IEEE/CVF Conference on Computer Vision and Pattern Recognition, pp. 10581–10590 (2021)

18. Wolf, V., et al.: DeFlow: learning complex image degradations from unpaired data with conditional flows. In: Proceedings of the IEEE/CVF Conference on Computer Vision and Pattern Recognition, pp. 94–103 (2021)

19. Luo, Z., Huang, Y., Li, S., et al.: Learning the degradation distribution for blind image super-resolution. In: Proceedings of the IEEE/CVF Conference on Computer Vision and Pattern Recognition, pp. 6063–6072 (2022)

20. Ning, Q., Tang, J., Wu, F., et al.: Learning degradation uncertainty for unsupervised real-world image super-resolution. In: Proceedings of the 31st International Joint Conferences on Artificial Intelligence, pp. 1261–1267 (2022)

21. Mao, Q., Lee, H.Y., Tseng, H.Y., et al.: Mode seeking generative adversarial networks for diverse image synthesis. In: Proceedings of the IEEE/CVF Conference on Computer Vision and Pattern Recognition, pp. 1429–1437 (2019)

22. Yang, D., Hong, S., Jang, Y., et al.: Diversity-sensitive conditional generative adversarial networks. arXiv preprint arXiv:1901.09024 (2019)

23. Liu, R., Ge, Y., Choi, C.L., et al.: DivCo: diverse conditional image synthesis via contrastive generative adversarial network. In: Proceedings of the IEEE/CVF Conference on Computer Vision and Pattern Recognition, pp. 16377–16386 (2021)

24. Hou, H., Xu, J., Hou, Y., et al.: Semi-cycled generative adversarial networks for real-world face super-resolution. IEEE Trans. Image Process. **32**, 1184–1199 (2023)

25. Bulat, A., Yang, J., Tzimiropoulos, G.: To learn image super-resolution, use a GAN to learn how to do image degradation first. In: Proceedings of the European Conference on Computer Vision, pp. 185–200 (2018)

26. Arjovsky, M., Bottou, L.: Towards principled methods for training generative adversarial networks. arXiv preprint arXiv:1701.04862 (2017)

27. Karras, T., Laine, S., Aila, T.: A style-based generator architecture for generative adversarial networks. In: Proceedings of the IEEE/CVF Conference on Computer Vision and Pattern Recognition, pp. 4401–4410 (2019)

28. Yang, S., Luo, P., Loy, C.C., et al.: Wider face: a face detection benchmark. In: Proceedings of the IEEE Conference on Computer Vision and Pattern Recognition, pp. 5525–5533 (2016)

29. Bulat, A., Tzimiropoulos, G.: How far are we from solving the 2D & 3D face alignment problem? (and a dataset of 230,000 3D facial landmarks). In: Proceedings of the IEEE International Conference on Computer Vision, pp. 1021–1030 (2017)

30. Kingma, D.P., Ba, J.: Adam: a method for stochastic optimization. arXiv preprint arXiv:1412.6980 (2014)

31. Wang, Z., Bovik, A.C., Sheikh, H.R., et al.: Image quality assessment: from error visibility to structural similarity. IEEE Trans. Image Process. **13**(4), 600–612 (2004)

32. Zhang, R., Isola, P., Efros, A.A., et al.: The unreasonable effectiveness of deep features as a perceptual metric. In: Proceedings of the IEEE Conference on Computer Vision and Pattern Recognition, pp. 586–595 (2018)

33. Heusel, M., Ramsauer, H., Unterthiner, T., et al.: GANs trained by a two timescale update rule converge to a local nash equilibrium. In: Advances in Neural Information Processing Systems, vol. 30 (2017)

34. Mittal, A., Soundararajan, R., Bovik, A.C.: Making a "completely blind" image quality analyzer. IEEE Signal Process. Lett. **20**(3), 209–212 (2012)

Rendering and Animation

Visualization of Irregular Tree Canopy Centerline Data from a Depth Camera Based on an Optimized Spatial Straight-Line Fitting

Hairong Gu[✉], Jiale Wang, Yanhui Hu, Jixiang Wang, Lishun Sun, and Mostak Ahamed

Chang'an University, Xi'an, Shaanxi, China
guhairong@chd.edu.cn

Abstract. We propose a new method to visualize the centerline of a single tree canopy based on a depth camera. Firstly, the depth camera captures the image of the target tree to obtain the 3D point cloud data, which is filtered and denoised. Then, we used the Poisson surface reconstruction method to reconstruct the 3D spatial surface of the point cloud data to restore the real scene accurately. In addition, we used Random Sampling Consensus (RANSAC) and Least Square Circle (LSC) in MATLAB software to fit circles to the 3D point cloud. We proposed a new spatial straight-line fitting method to visualize the centerline of the tree crown. The method has the advantage of no error in the spatial scattering Z-coordinate, and the fitted straight line is perpendicular to the xoy plane. The new method produces a smaller root mean square error (RMSE) than the traditional spatial straight line fitting method. This method can be effectively applied to practical applications such as tree crown pruning, providing accurate positional information for the positioning of tools during the pruning process. Ultimately, the pruning time can be shortened, and the accuracy of the pruning process can be improved.

Keywords: 3D reconstruction · Point cloud · Poisson surface reconstruction · Circle fitting · Spatial straight-line fitting

1 Introduction

The green belt is an important part of the expressway, and it must be trimmed regularly to ensure that the height and width of the hedge meet safety standards. However, the traditional vehicle-mounted hedge trimmer often trims the hedge by manually operating the mechanical arm to move the trimming tool near the hedge. This trimming method is complicated to operate and has low positioning

This work was supported by the Key Research and Development Program of Shaanxi Province (2023-YBSF-104) and the Open Fund of Key Laboratory (219925230289).

ⓒ The Author(s), under exclusive license to Springer Nature Switzerland AG 2024
B. Sheng et al. (Eds.): CGI 2023, LNCS 14496, pp. 135–146, 2024.
https://doi.org/10.1007/978-3-031-50072-5_11

accuracy. With machine vision technology's continuous development and pop-ularization, mechanical informatization has accelerated. This paper proposes a depth camera to scan the tree to obtain point cloud information. Through pro-cessing point cloud data, three-dimensional modeling is carried out, and the canopy centerline of the tree is visualized.

Many scholars have recently focused on 3D reconstruction using depth sen-sors. Some scholars have proposed a new background and foreground segmenta-tion method that can improve the background subtraction accuracy of related algorithms by considering color and depth data together [1]. Yang et al. pro-posed a new blind image motion deblurring method [2]. Some scholars have studied the Algorithm of 3D model construction of depth cameras, such as an improved classical Kinect Fusion algorithm, which can reconstruct indoor scenes with high precision [3]. Ail et al. proposed a 3D reconstruction method by Ultra-sound Biomicroscopy [4]. Liu et al. proposed an automatic reconstruction of a building piping system using LiDAR scanning point cloud data and can predict piping centerline points [5]. In addition, some scholars have proposed to utilize deep learning models for target detection [6,7]. The research object of this paper is outdoor trees. However, most of the above reconstruction methods are based on indoor scenes, and their reconstruction effect in a strong light environment is not ideal. To solve this problem, we adopt a depth camera based on binocular stereo vision [8], which is less affected by illumination conditions. Inspired by [9–11], this paper adopts mean filtering and a Poisson surface reconstruction algorithm based on the general process of 3D modeling [12].

Visualization of the tree's centerline fitting is the focus of this paper. For circle fitting methods, least squares (LS) [13] is the most widely used algorithm for both planar and spatial circles [14,15]. In addition, the optimized circle fit-ting algorithm [16–18] greatly improves the accuracy and speed of circle fitting. The fitting of spatial straight lines cannot directly adopt the LS method or the total least squares (TLS) method as the plane straight line fitting because the 3D straight line has six parameters and is not a simple linear relationship. To solve this problem, some scholars simplified six parameters to four by transform-ing the standard equation of a spatial straight line and obtained the geometric parameters of a spatial straight line based on the TLS method [19]. Xi et al. assume that there is no error in the coordinate component of the Z direction in three-dimensional space [20]. As a central axis perpendicular to the ground is needed when pruning trees, the above fitting methods can not be actually applied to fitting the canopy centerline. Therefore, this paper proposes a new fitting space straight line fitting method to visualize the canopy centerline. This method is suitable for determining the canopy centerline position when pruning trees because there is no error in the Z coordinates of scattered points in space, and the fitted straight line is perpendicular to the xoy plane. Inspired by [15,16], this paper proposes using a hybrid RANSAC and LSC algorithm to fit the tree canopy point cloud data.

As a whole, we propose a communication system consisting of a computer, a depth camera, and a rack. We first collect the point cloud information of the target and then build a three-dimensional model by computer. Secondly, the key information points are extracted from the three-dimensional model, and RANSAC and LSC hybrid algorithm fits the center points of sections with different heights. Finally, according to the data fit in the global domain, the centerline line is obtained, which is the centerline of the target tree canopy.

2 Method

2.1 Image Feature Extraction and Matching

This paper selects the Intel RealSense D435i depth camera. The flow of 3D reconstruction based on a depth camera is shown in Fig. 1. Image matching is a common method used in computer vision, which involves comparing two or more images and finding the common features between them. Based on these features, various transformations can be found between the images. Common image matching methods include methods that rely on image gray-scale information and methods that rely on features. The method that relies on image gray-scale information analyzes the entire image pixel by pixel and calculates the gray-scale value of each pixel. However, the gray-scale value is highly affected by lighting, distortion, and the material of the object, causing it to vary greatly between images, making it less stable. Therefore, we have chosen the feature-based matching method, and we have used the OpenCV (Open Source Computer Vision Library) feature algorithm interface to compare the commonly used SIFT [21], SURF [22], and ORB [23] methods for feature point detection, as shown in Fig. 2.The number of features extracted by each method and the time required to perform the extraction are shown in Table 1.

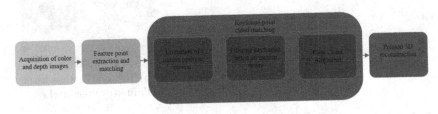

Fig. 1. 3D model reconstruction process with depth camera

(a) SIFT　　　　　　　(b) SURF　　　　　　　(c) ORB

Fig. 2. Image feature extraction by different methods

Table 1. Calculation results of three methods.

METHOD	Number of image features	Detection time/(ms)
SIFT	6083	756.509
SURF	4552	725.533
ROB	534	51.375

Feature extraction is performed on 100 frames of randomly collected image data, and the comparison of the number of feature points extracted is shown in Fig. 3. The time required for tree feature extraction using the ORB algorithm is the shortest, but the number of feature points extracted is relatively small. Since the object of this experiment is a tree in an outdoor environment with apparent texture features, selecting the ORB algorithm can ensure that enough feature points are extracted while reducing the matching time.Next, we use the Brute-Force Matcher method for feature matching and adopt the RANSAC algorithm to eliminate the wrong matching points between two frames to improve the matching accuracy, as shown in Fig. 4.

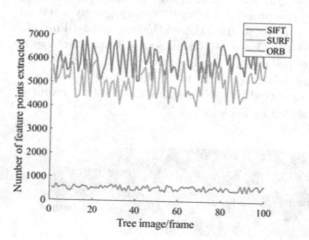

(a) Brute-Force Matcher method

(b) RANSAC algorithm eliminates mismatches

Fig. 3. Number of matched features with different methods

Fig. 4. Image feature point matching

2.2   Keyframe-Based Point Cloud Alignment

The Iterative Closest Point (ICP) algorithm is a classical method commonly used for solving 3D-3D point-to-point pose estimation problems proposed by Besl et al. [24]. Wang et al. [25] proposed a new 3D alignment algorithm based on improved ICP. The corresponding points in the point cloud is weighted to reduce the number of iterations of the ICP algorithm. Hu et al. [26] proposed a 3D point cloud stitching algorithm based on matching scores, which removes the point cloud with low matching scores and minimizes the cumulative matching error. Since the solution of the transformation matrix has errors, when multiple frames of information are fused, the errors will accumulate and lead to significant errors in point cloud alignment. Therefore, it is crucial to select images reasonably to improve the reconstruction accuracy of the model, and these selected images are usually called keyframes.

In this paper, the first image is selected as the first keyframe, and the coordinate system of the first keyframe is used as the global coordinate system. The keyframe selection process is shown in Fig. 5, which compares the current frame image with the current key frame image and calculates the rotation matrix and translation matrix between the two frames based on the matching points to find out the motion error between the two frames and determine whether the motion error threshold is satisfied. If it is satisfied, set this frame as the current keyframe. Otherwise, select the next frame and continuously repeat the above process to select keyframes. The error threshold range is as in Eq. 1,

$$norms = |min(\|R\|, 2\pi - \|R\| + \|T\|)| \tag{1}$$

where R and T are the rotation matrix, translation matrix between the two frames of the image respectively.

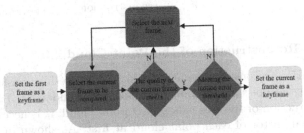

Fig. 5. Keyframe selection process

According to the above process, eight keyframes are selected (Fig. 6), and the stitched point cloud image is shown in Fig. 7. As shown in Fig. 7a, many "floating points" (noise points) and unnecessary background point cloud is in the cloud image before filtering. PCL's point cloud filtering module provides many flexible and practical filtering processing algorithms [27]. We use straight-through filtering and radius filtering to filter the point cloud and display it in the MeshLab software interface, as shown in Fig. 7b.

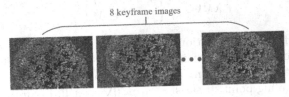

Fig. 6. Filtered keyframes

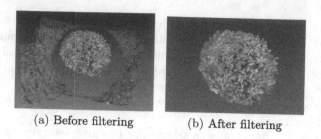

(a) Before filtering   (b) After filtering

Fig. 7. Point cloud of tree canopy

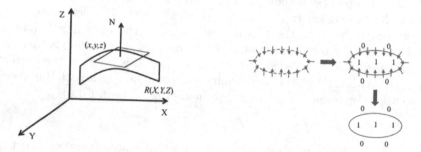

Fig. 8. Schematic diagram of point cloud normal

Fig. 9. Schematic diagram of Poisson reconstruction

2.3   Poisson Reconstruction of the Point Cloud

The Poisson surface reconstruction algorithm is a 3D mesh reconstruction algorithm based on the Poisson equation proposed by Kazhdan M [12]. In the 3D surface reconstruction of the tree canopy 3D point cloud, it is necessary to estimate the normal vector of each point cloud at first. As shown in Fig. 8, there is a three-dimensional point cloud data in the three-dimensional space, where a certain point (x, y, z) and the fitting surface of the three-dimensional point cloud is $R\ (X, Y, Z)$. The normal vector N of the tangent plane of the point is the normal vector of the surface at that point.

In point cloud space, 0 and 1 represent the inner and outer surfaces of an unknown surface. If an element belongs to this set, it is 1; If an element does not belong to this set, it is recorded as 0. Assuming that the surface of an object is M, its indicator function χ_M is

$$\chi_M(x) = \begin{cases} 0, & x \notin M \\ 1, & x \in M \end{cases} \tag{2}$$

The Poisson surface reconstruction process is to find the indicator function of the model according to the sampling point cloud containing normals. It makes the gradient of the indicator function approximate the vector domain defined by the given sampling point. It satisfies $min_x \|\nabla x - V\|$. Figure 9 is a schematic diagram of Poisson reconstruction.

Poisson Reconstruction Process. Firstly, indicator function χ_M is smoothed by a smoothing filter function $\tilde{F}$, and for the input point cloud data that arbitrarily satisfies $p \in \partial M$. The indicator function χ_M is approximately solved by using the derivative of the convolution of $\chi_M * F$ functions, and each normal vector is transformed into a gradient space,

$$\nabla\left(\chi_M * \tilde{F}\right)(q_0) = \nabla \int_M \tilde{F}(q-p)dp = \int_{\partial M} \tilde{F}(q_0 - p)\, \vec{N}_{\partial M}(p)dp \qquad (3)$$

where $N_{\partial M}(p)$ is the normal vector inside each point direction. The $\tilde{F}(q)$ is the smoothing filter. The $\tilde{F}(q-p)$ indicates that $\tilde{F}$ moves along the p direction.

Due to the discreteness of sampling points in the 3D point cloud, the normal vector N of each point q in the point cloud is not necessarily known, so $N_{\partial M}(p)$ distribution is unknown. This paper uses piecewise approximation to solve it. Model surface ∂M is divided into different disjoint surface areas ∂S according to space, $\partial S \subset \partial M$. s is the point in the segmented area. Transform Eq. 3 into integral summation, and replace it with the integral of the function corresponding to $s.p$ and the area of ∂S.

$$\nabla\left(\chi_M * \tilde{F}\right)(q_0) = \sum_{s \in S} \int_{\partial S} \tilde{F}(q-p)\vec{N}_{\partial M}(p)dp \approx \sum_{s \in S} ||\tilde{F}(q\ s.p)s.\vec{N} = \vec{V}(q) \qquad (4)$$

The vector space $\vec{V}(q)$ can be obtained from Eq. 4.

According to Laplace transformation, the indicator function χ in the function space is solved according to the vector space $\vec{V}(q)$, so that the gradient $\nabla\chi$ of the function χ is similar to $\vec{V}(q)$ and can be transformed into the Poisson equation.

$$\Delta\tilde{\chi} = \nabla \cdot \vec{V} = \nabla \cdot \nabla\chi \qquad (5)$$

Δ is Laplace operator, ∇ is divergence operator. The above formula is the Poisson equation, and $\tilde{\chi}$ is the function to be solved.

Finally, the scattered point cloud is triangulated, and then the surface of each triangular mesh is generated. An optimal threshold is selected for obtaining the reconstructed model surface ∂M, sampling points estimate the indicator function, and the isosurface is obtained, as shown in Fig. 10. The tree canopy's three-dimensional point cloud model is subjected to Poisson reconstruction, isosurface drawing, and triangular meshing, as shown in Fig. 11.

2.4 Visualization of Tree Canopy Centerline

Fitting Circles Based on RANSAC and LSC Algorithms. For circle fitting, the RANSAC algorithm has the advantage of being faster but is susceptible to noise interference and can be more problematic when three points are not selected appropriately. The LSC algorithm has the advantage of taking all edge points into account to give a globally balanced solution but is heavily disturbed by noise. As a result, we have combined the advantages of both

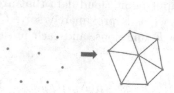
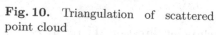

Fig. 10. Triangulation of scattered point cloud

Fig. 11. 3D reconstruction of the tree canopy

and developed the algorithm process shown in Fig. 12. Firstly, we employed the RANSAC algorithm to randomly select three points from the point cloud set. These points were used to calculate the center and radius of the circle. Secondly, for each data point, the distance to the estimated circle was calculated. If the distance was less than a given threshold D, the point was considered as an inner point. Otherwise, it was considered as an outer point. Finally, the interior points were fitted using LSC, and the final fit to the circle was output.

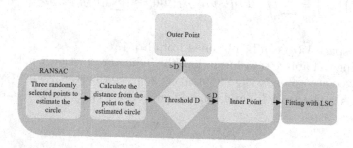

Fig. 12. Hybrid algorithm for circle fitting process

To sample a cross-section of the 3D point cloud model of trees, we can intercept the point cloud at a specific range, such as −0.86 m to −0.85 m, as shown in Fig. 13. After projecting the 3D points onto a 2D plane, and we can perform LSC fitting to analyze the roundness error, which is approximately 0.025 m.

Centerline Fitting of Tree Canopy We fit the entire model layer by layer. For example, models with heights from −0.95 m to −0.60 m were sampled and fitted at 0.02 m intervals, as shown in Fig. 14. In this way, we can obtain the centerline coordinates of each circle in different cross-sections. After obtaining the center points of the circles of each section, we fit them with both the traditional spatial straight-line method (Method A) and the novel proper method proposed in this paper (Method B). Method B uses a fitting approach that involves projecting scattered points onto a 2D plane (xoy plane). The process begins by calculating

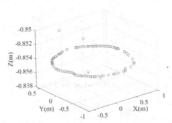

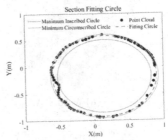

(a) Point cloud selected at -0.86m ∼ -0.85m   (b) Fitting effect diagram

Fig. 13. Analysis of point cloud at −0.9 m–0.85 m section

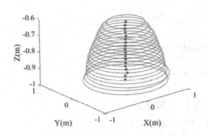

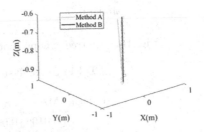

Fig. 14. Circle center point fitting diagram

Fig. 15. Comparison of two different spatial straight-line fits

the average values of the scattered points in the X and Y directions, represented by Xmean and Ymean. These values serve as the coordinates of the fitted straight line in the X and Y directions, respectively. The results of these two methods are compared in Table 2, and the corresponding plots are presented in Fig. 15.

Table 2. Calculation results of two methods.

METHOD	ME	SSE	MSE	RMSE
A	0.0533	0.0153	0.0008	0.0247
B	0.0196	0.0038	0.0002	0.0108

According to Table 2, the errors of Method B are more miniature than Method A's, which shows that the fitting effect of Method B is ideal.

3 Experiments

We chose four trees as experimental subjects, and the step-by-step procedure is as follows.

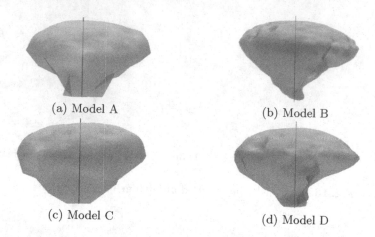

(a) Model A   (b) Model B

(c) Model C   (d) Model D

Fig. 16. The tree canopy centerline fitting effect diagram

Table 3. Analysis of fitting errors.

MODEL	ME	SSE	MSE	RMSE
A	0.0196	0.0038	0.0002	0.0108
B	0.0303	0.0106	0.0005	0.0230
C	0.0153	0.0034	0.0002	0.0139
D	0.0223	0.0056	0.0003	0.0172

1) Using a Realsense D435i depth camera, we scan the area in front of the tree and obtain its depth data, keyframe images, and point cloud through vision software running on a PC.
2) To reconstruct the 3D model, we first denoise the point cloud data obtained in step 1 and perform point cloud registration based on keyframe images to obtain a point cloud file in Ply format. Then the 3D model is established by the Poisson reconstruction Algorithm.
3) The centerline of the tree is visualized by a hybrid RANSAC and LSC algorithm. Then, the centerline of the tree is visualized using the spatial linear fitting method proposed in this paper, as shown in Fig. 16. After analysis, the error in fitting the centerline is shown in Table 3.

According to Table 3, the RMSE of all four models is within 0.025. This accuracy can meet the requirements for fitting the centerline of the tree canopy.

4   Conclusion

This paper proposes a novel method to study the visualization of the tree crown centerline. Firstly, the depth camera and PC perform a 3D reconstruction of the target. Subsequently, we use a hybrid RANSAC and LSC algorithm to fit a circle to the scattering cloud, find the circle's center point, and propose a new algorithm for fitting the centerline of the canopy. The advantage of this method is that there is no error in the spatial scattering Z-coordinate, and the fitted line is perpendicular to the xoy plane. In future work, we plan to investigate how to integrate these functions to develop a one-click function that generates a canopy centerline immediately after scanning a target tree. This proposed approach could provide a convenient and efficient method for capturing the 3D structure of tree canopies, which is critical for a range of green pruning applications.

Acknowledgement. This work was supported by the Key Research and Development Program of Shaanxi Province (2023-YBSF-104) and the Open Fund of Key Laboratory (219925230289).

References

1. Camplani, M., Salgado, L.: Background foreground segmentation with RGB-D kinect data: an efficient combination of classifiers. J. Vis. Commun. Image Represent. **25**(1), 122–136 (2014)
2. Tang, S.J., Zhu, Q., Chen, W., Darwish, W., Wu, B.: Structure-aware motion deblurring using multi-adversarial optimized CycleGAN. IEEE Trans. Image Process.: Publ. IEEE Signal Process. Soc. **30**, 6142–6155 (2021)
3. Choi, S., Zhou, Q.Y., Koltun, V.: Robust reconstruction of indoor scenes. In: IEEE Conference on Computer Vision & Pattern Recognition, pp. 5556–5565. IEEE (2015)
4. Ali, S.G., et al.: Cost-effective broad learning-based ultrasound biomicroscopy with 3D reconstruction for ocular anterior segmentation. Multimed. Tools Appl. **80**(6), 1–8 (2020)
5. Xie, Y., Li, S., Liu, T., Cai, Y.: As-built BIM reconstruction of piping systems using PipeNet. Autom. Constr. **147**, 104735 (2023)
6. Zeng, L., Duan, X., Pan, Y., Deng, M.: Research on the algorithm of helmet-wearing detection based on the optimized YOLOv4. Vis. Comput. **39**(5), 2165–2175 (2022)
7. An, F.P., Liu, J.E., Bai, L.: Object recognition algorithm based on optimized non-linear activation function-global convolutional neural network. Vis. Comput. **38**(2), 1–13 (2022)
8. Zheng, T.X., Huang, S., Li, Y.F., Feng, M.C.: Review on key technologies of 3D reconstruction based on vision. Acta Autom. Sinica **46**(4), 22 (2020)
9. Tong, S., Xu, X.G., Yi, C.T., Shao, C.Y.: Overview of 3D reconstruction technology based on vision. Comput. Appl. Res. **28**(07), 17–23 (2011)
10. Zhang, Z.H.: Point cloud data processing of three-dimensional reconstruction model of object by 3D laser scanning. Nonlinear Opt. Quantum Opt. **52**(3a4) (2020)
11. Ma, D.: Precise processing of point cloud data in omni-directional scanning based on three-dimensional laser sensor. J. Nanoelectron. Optoelectron. **12**(9), 940–944 (2017)
12. Kazhdan, M.M., Bolitho, M., Hoppe, H.: Poisson surface reconstruction. In: Eurographics Symposium on Geometry Processing, pp. 61–70 (2006)
13. Gillard, J.: Circular and linear regression: fitting circles and lines by least squares. J. Roy. Stat. Soc. **174**(3), 843 (2011)

14. Wu, H.: Least squares spatial circle fitting method for straightness measurement of single pile foundations for offshore wind power. Waterway Ports **43**(5), 683–688 (2022)
15. Huang, L.F., Wang, W., Wu, N.X.: Research on circle fitting and error evaluation algorithm based on least square principle. Mech. Eng. Autom. (2), 3 (2020)
16. Qin, F., Wang, T., Zhang, Z.H.: A new method of spatial linear fitting. Geospa. Inf. **21**(3), 21–24 (2023)
17. Qin, F., Lu, S., Zhang, Z.H.: A spatial circle fitting method based on BFGS algorithm. Urban Surv. **6**, 164–167 (2022)
18. Guo, J.F., Yang, J.M.: An iterative procedure for robust circle fitting. Commun. Stat. - Simul. Comput. **48**(6), 1872–1879 (2018)
19. Yao, Y.B., Huang, S.H., Kong, J., He, J.Q.: Total least squares algorithm for spatial line fitting. Geom. Inf. Sci. Wuhan Univ. **39**(05), 571–574 (2014)
20. Yang, X.I.: A method for fitting of a space straight line. J. Qiqihar Univ. **25**(2), 5 (2009)
21. Lowe, D.: Distinctive image features from scaleinvariant keypoints. Int. J. Comput. Vision **60**(2), 91–100 (2004)
22. Allaberdiev, S., Yakhyoev, S., Fatkhullayev, R., Chen, J.: Speeded-up robust feature matching algorithm based on image improvement technology. J. Comput. Commun. **7**, 1–10 (2019)
23. Rublee, E., Rabaud, V., Konolige, K., Bradski, G.R.: ORB: an efficient alternative to SIFT or SURF. In: IEEE International Conference on Computer Vision, ICCV 2011, Barcelona, Spain, pp. 2564–2571. IEEE (2011)
24. Liang, B., Zhang, J.Y., Tang, D.K.: Fast iterative closest point-simultaneous localization and mapping (ICP-SLAM) with rough alignment and narrowing-scale nearby searching. J. Donghua Univ. (Engl. Edn.) **34**(4), 583–590 (2017)
25. Wang, X., Zhao, Z.L., Capps, A.G., Hamann, B.: An iterative closest point approach for the registration of volumetric human retina image data obtained by optical coherence tomography. Multimed. Tools Appl. **76**(5), 6843–6857 (2017)
26. Hu, F.C., Li, Y.G., Feng, M.C.: Continuous point cloud stitch based on image feature matching constraint and score. IEEE Trans. Intell. Veh. **4**(3), 363–374 (2019)
27. Li, R.X., Zou, J.W.: Research on point cloud filtering algorithm based on PCL library. Satell. Telev. Broadband Multimed. **13**, 82–84 (2020)

Finernet: A Coarse-to-Fine Approach to Learning High-Quality Implicit Surface Reconstruction

Dan Mei and Xiaogang Wang[✉]

College of Computer and Information Science, Southwest University, Chongqing, China
wangxiaogang@swu.edu.cn

Abstract. Recent studies have shown that implicit neural representation can be effectively applied to geometric surface reconstruction. Existing methods have achieved impressive results. However, they often struggle to recover geometric details, or require normal vectors as supervisory information for surface points, which is often unavailable in actual scanned data. In this paper, we propose a coarse-to-fine approach to enhance the geometric details of the reconstructed results without relying on normal vectors as supervision, and able to fill holes caused by missing scanned data. In the coarse stage, a local spatial normal consistent term is presented to estimate a stable but coarse implicit neural representation. In the fine stage, a local fitting penalty is proposed to locally modify the reconstruction results obtained in the previous stage to better fit the original input data and recover more geometric details. Experimental results on three widely used datasets (ShapeNet, SRB and ABC) indicate that our method is very competitive when compared with current state-of-the-art methods, especially for restoring the geometric details.

Keywords: Implicit surface reconstruction · Signed distance field (SDF) · High-quality reconstruction · Deep learning

1 Introduction

The problem of reconstructing 3D surfaces from point clouds is a crucial and widely applied field in computer graphics and computer vision. In recent years, with the development of deep learning, implicit neural representation with flexible expressive capabilities have been employed in surface reconstruction tasks [1–6]. So far, most previous works directly regressing implicit surfaces. However, without accurate ground truth data, networks are prone to falling into local optima [7], leading most methods to require normal vectors [4,6] or signed distance functions (SDF) [5] as supervision to guide the network towards favorable solutions. Nonetheless, raw scanned point clouds typically lack normal

© The Author(s), under exclusive license to Springer Nature Switzerland AG 2024
B. Sheng et al. (Eds.): CGI 2023, LNCS 14496, pp. 147–158, 2024.
https://doi.org/10.1007/978-3-031-50072-5_12

vectors, which poses significant challenges for reconstruction. Although existing methods, such as SAL [1] and DiGS [2], can reconstruct geometric surfaces from unorganized point clouds, they struggle to generate surfaces with rich details and complex topology. Thus, reconstructing high-fidelity geometric surfaces from point clouds without additional supervision (i.g., SDF and normal vectors) remains an exceedingly difficult task.

In this work, we propose a coarse-to-fine approach Finernet for generating geometric surfaces with rich details based on SIREN [6] without normal vectors as supervision, taking into account the missing scan point cloud data, unavailability of normal vectors and the tendency of neural networks to learn low-frequency signal. The entire training process is divided into two parts: the coarse stage and the fine stage. During the coarse stage, a local smoothness regularization is applied to eliminate artifacts caused by the lack of supervised normal vectors, which results in a low-frequency geometric surface. Then in the fine stage, an approximate SDF supervised penalty is applied to add details to the coarse geometry, thereby generating a high-frequency geometric surface. In summary, the main contributions of this paper are summarized as follows:

1) We introduce a local normal smoothing regularization (L_{smooth}) to eliminate undesirable artifacts caused by the lack of normal supervision and fill the holes caused by missing scan point clouds.
2) We provide an approximate SDF supervision regularization ($L_{sdf'}$) for adding rich geometric details to smooth surfaces.
3) To obtain shapes with high-frequency signal from point clouds directly, we employ a coarse-to-fine approach to maximize the role of L_{smooth} and $L_{sdf'}$.
4) Our approach exhibits strong competitiveness compared to current state-of-the-art methods on the task of surface reconstruction from point clouds directly, in both qualitative and quantitative.

2   Related Work

2.1   Surface Reconstruction

Classical methods for surface reconstruction from point clouds, including both explicit and implicit methods [8–10], suffer from the limitation of handling complex point cloud data and generating high-quality surfaces. Recently, learning-based methods [1,2,4,5,11–15] using neural networks has been proposed for surface reconstruction, more relevant to our work. The implicit neural network generally generates shapes by fitting SDF directly with or without extra 3D supervision (e.g., ground truth SDF and normal vectors) and get the final explicit geometry using isosurface extraction algorithms [16,17].

2.2   High-Frequency Representation in Neural Networks

Nerf [18] has shown that traditional multilayer perceptron (MLP) tends to produce low-frequency results. Therefore, SIREN [6] and IDF [19] achieved

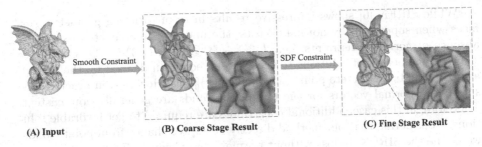

(A) Input   **(B) Coarse Stage Result**   **(C) Fine Stage Result**

Fig. 1. The reconstruction results at different stages of the process.

impressive reconstruction results in detail representation by replacing the ReLU activation layer of the network with the sin function. Similarly, FFN [20] processes low-dimensional data spaces with Fourier functions before being fed into the network to learn high-frequency functions. And 3D-Former [21] uses a spatially coarse-to-fine method to obtain fine monocular scene reconstruction results. Contrastingly, we propose a progressive training method to obtain a detailed geometric surface from unorganized point clouds from coarse-to-fine.

3 Formulation

3.1 Review of SIREN

Our method for shape representation using SDF is based on SIREN [6], which generates high-quality shapes by fitting SDF directly on *oriented point clouds*. And the neural network architecture employs the sine as an activation function. Specifically, a SIREN can be represented as:

$$\Phi(x) = W_n(\phi_{n-1} \circ \phi_{n-2} \circ ... \circ \phi_0)(x) + b_n, \phi_i(x_i) = sin(W_i x_i + b_i), \quad (1)$$

where $\phi_i : R^{M_i} \mapsto R^{N_i}$ is the ith layer of an MLP. It consists of the affine transform defined by the weight matrix W_i and the biases $b_i \in R^{N_i}$ applied on the input $x_i \in R^{M_i}$, followed by the sine nonlinearity applied to each component of the resulting vector. To learn SDF directly from oriented point clouds, SIREN [6] introduced the loss function by solving the eikonal equation with a boundary constraint. Denoting the input domain as Ω (including on-surface points and off-surface points set to $[-1,1]^3$) and the on-surface points as Ω_0, the loss function given in Eq. 2:

$$L_{SIREN} = \lambda_0 \int_{\Omega} |\|\nabla_x \Phi(x)\|_2 - 1| \, dx + \lambda_1 \int_{\Omega_0} \|\Phi(x)\|_2 \, dx$$
$$+ \lambda_2 \int_{\Omega_0} (1 - \langle \nabla_x \Phi(x), n(x) \rangle) dx + \lambda_3 \int_{\Omega \backslash \Omega_0} exp(-\alpha |\Phi(x)|) dx, \quad (2)$$

where $\alpha >> 1$ and $(\lambda_0, \lambda_1, \lambda_2, \lambda_3) = (50, 3000, 100, 100)$.

While SIREN [6] shows impressive results in reconstructing geometric surfaces when supervised by normal vectors, the undesirable artifacts arise in the absence of normal constraints, i.e., $\int_{\Omega_0}(1 - \langle\nabla_x\Phi(x), n(x)\rangle)dx$. This is due to the non-uniqueness of solutions to the Eikonal equation defined by the boundary constraints at discrete points, i.e., $\int_{\Omega_0}\|\Phi(x)\|_2\,dx$. However, in practice, the supervised normal vectors for the raw point clouds are generally non-existent. Therefore, in this case, additional constraints are required to get favorable solutions. Considering that our method directly generates shapes from point clouds, we define the SIREN [6] loss without normal supervision as Eq. 3:

$$L_{SIREN\_wo\_n} = \lambda_0 \int_{\Omega} \left|\|\nabla_x\Phi(x)\|_2 - 1\right| dx + \lambda_1 \int_{\Omega_0} \|\Phi(x)\|_2\,dx$$
$$+ \lambda_3 \int_{\Omega\setminus\Omega_0} exp(-\alpha|\Phi(x)|)dx, \tag{3}$$

And we set hyperparameters $(\lambda_0, \lambda_1, \lambda_3) = (50, 3000, 100)$, same with SIREN [6].

3.2   Coarse Geometry Generator

Suppose two data points are sufficiently close geometrically, ideally, the corresponding normal vectors are nearly equal [22]. Therefore, when normal vector supervision is unavailable, minimizing the predicted normal vector differences between geometrically close points can be used as a penalty term to alleviate artifacts caused by the absence of normal supervision. However, directly applying this regularization term to on-surface points tends to generate a very low-frequency surface. Thus, we apply the regularization term to off-surface points. Note that the off-surface points $(\Omega\setminus\Omega_0)$ are randomly sampled points generated within the $[-1,1]^3$, following a uniform distribution, which is consistent with SIREN [6].

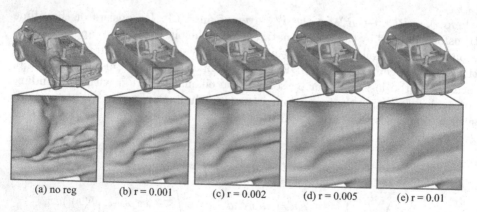

(a) no reg   (b) r = 0.001   (c) r = 0.002   (d) r = 0.005   (e) r = 0.01

Fig. 2. The impact of different radius r on the reconstruction results. Note that we have only incorporated the smooth regularization based on our baseline.

Specifically, for each off-surface point x (i.e., $\Omega \setminus \Omega_0$), the sufficiently proximal neighboring points x' are generated by unit direction vectors v randomly generated along directions within the tangent plane of radius r around x (i.e., $x' = x + v * radius$). Thus, the smoothing regularization term can be defined as follows:

$$L_{smooth} = \int_{\Omega \setminus \Omega_0} \|\nabla\phi(x) - \nabla\phi(x + v \cdot r)\|_2 \, dx. \tag{4}$$

Experimental results show that, for the normalized point clouds, selecting a radius r within the range of 0.002 to 0.005 achieves smooth coarse geometry surfaces while preserving as many details as possible (see Fig. 2).

3.3   Fine Geometry Generator

While smooth regularization partially addresses the issue of artifacts mainly arising from the lack of ground truth normal vectors as supervision, its reconstruction results tend to exhibit low-frequency geometric surfaces, as shown in Fig. 1(b). However, in the absence of accurate ground truth data (e.g., SDF or normal vectors) as supervision, the optimization process is prone to get stuck in local minima [7]. Therefore, simply increasing the frequency values of our baseline's activation function does not improve reconstruction results. In order to achieve high-frequency surface reconstruction results, we additionally provide an approximate SDF supervision ($L_{sdf'}$). This is inspired by dynamic base surfaces (DBS) [23], which are continuously adjusted to fit the three-dimensional shape suggested by the point clouds (Fig. 3).

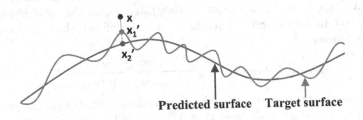

Fig. 3. Illustration of approximate SDF supervision in 2D space.

For our model, a better network means the ability to accurately estimate the SDF values of given points in space. Therefore, for a given point x in space, the objective of the network is to minimize the distance between the projection point on the surface represented by the input points (x_1') and on the surface predicted by the network (x_2'). Furthermore, since $L_{sdf'}$ is employed during the surface geometry refinement stage, we desire even subtle variations in position to lead to more significant penalization. Thus, we generate random sampling points x around the surface represented by the input point cloud. Note that here we perform an approximation calculation, which means under the condition that the on-surface normalized points Ω_0 is dense, ideally, the projection point of x onto the ground truth surface to be the closest point x_1' in Ω_0.

Denoting the set of x is Ω_1, we described $L_{sdf'}$ as follows:

$$L_{sdf'} = \int_{\Omega_1} \left\| (x - \Phi(x) \cdot \overrightarrow{n_x}) - x_1' \right\|_2^2 dx, \tag{5}$$

where $\Phi(x)$ and $\overrightarrow{n_x}$ respectively represent the predicted SDF and normal vector values of x by the neural network, i.e., $x_2' = x - \Phi(x) \cdot \overrightarrow{n_x}$.

3.4   Progressive Training

Due to the disparate optimization objectives of the two regularization terms mentioned in Sect. 3.2 and Sect. 3.3, simply overlaying them to fit the surface does not generate the expected shapes with rich details (see Fig. 6(d)). Therefore, we train the network using a progressive training approach, i.e., we divide the entire training process into two stages, the coarse stage and the fine stage. Meanwhile, the network parameters obtained at the end of the coarse stage serve as the initial values for the fine stage network parameters. Specifically, the details of the entire training process can be obtained from the following context.

In the coarse stage, *i.e., the first* 70% *of the entire training process*, L_{smooth} is employed with a constant weight, and the loss for the coarse stage can be defined as follows:

$$L_{coarse} = L_{SIREN\_wo\_n} + \lambda_{smooth} L_{smooth}, \tag{6}$$

where $\lambda_{smooth} = 1000$, represents the weight of L_{smooth}.

Then, at 70% to 80% of the training process, the non-linear decay function decreases λ_{smooth} from λ_{smooth_0} (set to 1000) at 70% of the total iterations to min_{smooth} (set to 100) at 80%. Therefore, we can definite the non-linear decay function as follows:

$$\lambda_{smooth} = \lambda_{smooth_0} - \frac{1 - cos(prog \cdot \pi)}{2 \cdot (\lambda_{smooth_0} - min_{smooth})}, \tag{7}$$

where *prog* represents the current iteration percentage relative to the percentage of the entire descent interval. Note that λ_{smooth} will remain constant at 100 in the subsequent training.

In the fine stage, *i.e., when the training percentage reaches* 70% *to* 100%, the corresponding loss function is defined as follows:

$$L_{fine} = L_{SIREN\_wo\_n} + \lambda_{sdf'} L_{sdf'}, \tag{8}$$

where $\lambda_{sdf'}$ represents the weight of $L_{sdf'}$. And $\lambda_{sdf'}$ increases non-linearly from $\lambda_{sdf_0'}$ (set to 800) to $max_{sdf'}$ (set to 1000) using the non-linear increasing function as follows:

$$\lambda_{sdf'} = \lambda_{sdf_0'} + \frac{1 - cos(prog \cdot \pi)}{2 \cdot (max_{sdf'} - \lambda_{sdf_0'})}, \tag{9}$$

where *prog* represents the current iteration percentage, the same as defined earlier. Note that $\lambda_{sdf'}$ is set to 0 during the coarse stage (Fig. 4).

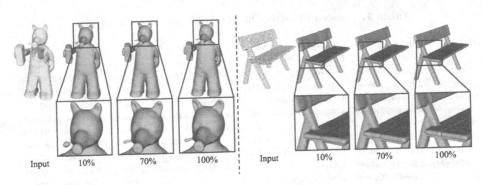

Fig. 4. The visualization of the reconstruction results as the training progresses on non-CAD (left) and CAD (right).

4   Experiments Results

4.1   Datasets, Implementation Details and Evaluation Metrics

Datasets. We evaluate our reconstruction quality on the surface reconstruction benchmark (SRB) [14], ShapeNet dataset which preprocessing and split of Williams et al. [15] and ABC dataset [24].

Implementation Details. We run our reconstruction method on a desktop PC with a 3.30GHz Intel i9-7900K CPU and an NVIDIA RTX-3090Ti GPU. Our method is implemented in Pytorch using the ADAM optimizer with a learning rate of $1e^{-4}$ for MLP decoders. For our baseline, we employ the same network architecture (i.e., 3 hidden layers with 256 units and a sine activation function with a frequency of 30) and hyperparameters (i.e., we use $(\lambda_0, \lambda_1, \lambda_3) = (50, 3000, 100)$ in $L_{SIREN\_wo\_n}$) as SIREN. Furthermore, we set the loss weights to $\lambda_{smooth} = 1000$ at the beginning of the coarse stage, and $\lambda_{sdf'} = 800$ at the beginning of the fine stage. In addition, for all our experiments, we extract the mesh representing the zero level set of the shape using the marching cubes algorithm [17], which uses a grid whose shortest axis is 512 elements.

Evaluation Metrics. In order to quantify the reconstruction quality, the Chamfer (d_C), squared Chamfer (d_C^{sq}) and Hausdorff (d_H) distances are used. Given two sets of points χ_1 and χ_2 in 3D space to be compared, the definitions of d_C, d_C^{sq} and d_H are as follows:

$$d_C(\chi_1, \chi_2) = \frac{1}{2}(d_{\overrightarrow{C}}(\chi_1, \chi_2) + d_{\overrightarrow{C}}(\chi_2, \chi_1)), \tag{10}$$

$$d_C^{sq}(\chi_1, \chi_2) = \frac{1}{2}(d_{\overrightarrow{C}}^{sq}(\chi_1, \chi_2) + d_{\overrightarrow{C}}^{sq}(\chi_2, \chi_1)), \tag{11}$$

$$d_H(\chi_1, \chi_2) = max(d_{\overrightarrow{H}}(\chi_1, \chi_2), d_{\overrightarrow{H}}(\chi_2, \chi_1)), \tag{12}$$

Table 1. Squared Chamfer Distance (d_C^{sq}) on ShapeNet [15].

Class	IGR [4]		SIREN [6]		SAL [1]		DiGS [2]		Ours	
	mean↓	median↓	mean↓	median↓	mean↓	median↓	mean↓	median↓	mean↓	median↓
airplane	6.81e-03	6.28e-03	1.88e-04	3.43e-05	1.07e-05	8.34e-06	**3.69e-06**	3.65e-06	5.44e-06	**3.37e-06**
bench	2.26e-03	1.36e-03	1.82e-05	1.12e-05	3.73e-05	1.43e-05	7.56e-06	**6.13e-06**	6.13e-06	6.37e-06
cabinet	2.33e-04	2.52e-04	1.05e-04	1.19e-04	3.28e-04	4.48e-04	**1.42e-05**	1.34e-05	1.46e-05	1.27e-05
car	8.43e-05	2.82e-05	4.39e-04	3.82e-04	2.94e-04	8.89e-05	4.15e-05	**1.97e-05**	3.49e-05	2.77e-05
chair	2.85e-03	2.35e-03	4.17e-05	4.07e-05	1.12e-03	7.93e-05	1.12e-04	7.10e-06	9.08e-06	6.81e-06
display	3.32e-03	3.80e-03	1.71e-04	1.52e-04	8.73e-05	2.15e-05	1.12e-04	7.10e-06	**9.13e-06**	6.81e-06
lamp	1.69e-03	3.56e-04	1.02e-04	7.23e-05	6.68e-04	1.51e-04	1.94e-04	1.28e-05	**9.13e-06**	8.88e-06
loudspeaker	1.50e-04	2.47e-05	8.92e-04	6.77e-04	1.15e-03	5.55e-04	5.09e-04	5.33e-04	1.86e-05	1.05e-05
rifle	3.19e-03	3.12e-03	1.79e-04	7.28e-05	2.53e-05	1.75e-05	**2.26e-06**	2.22e-06	2.26e-06	2.43e-05
sofa	4.73e-04	1.87e-04	3.25e-04	2.70e-04	5.49e-04	2.05e-04	5.11e-05	2.33e-05	2.26e-06	1.92e-06
table	6.46e-03	5.80e-03	4.44e-04	3.71e-04	1.85e-04	1.77e-04	2.79e-04	1.74e-04	1.53e-05	1.63e-05
telephone	1.41e-03	1.41e-03	1.64e-04	1.64e-04	9.89e-06	9.89e-06	5.80e-06	5.80e-06	1.16e-05	1.19e-05
watercraft	4.40e-04	4.40e-04	1.67e-04	1.93e-04	2.73e-05	1.42e-05	6.80e-06	6.85e-06	**4.82e-06**	**4.82e-06**
All Classes	2.55e-03	1.30e-03	2.01e-04	8.69e-05	3.56e-04	2.36e-05	7.63e-05	7.78e-06	**6.33e-06**	**5.78e-06**
									1.18e-05	**7.44e-06**

Table 2. Hausdorff Distance (d_H) on ShapeNet [15].

Class	IGR [4]		SIREN [6]		SAL [1]		DiGS [2]		Ours	
	mean↓	median↓	mean↓	median↓	mean↓	median↓	mean↓	median↓	mean↓	median↓
airplane	2.68e-01	2.44e-01	1.69e-01	4.47e-02	2.21e-02	1.49e-02	**1.07e-02**	9.48e-03	1.40e-02	**7.93e-03**
bench	1.51e-01	1.26e-01	2.99e-02	2.39e-02	2.61e-02	2.05e-02	2.28e-02	8.04e-03	**8.70e-03**	**7.85e-03**
cabinet	9.63e-02	1.18e-01	1.06e-01	9.80e-02	7.80e-02	8.44e-02	3.71e-02	2.24e-02	**1.49e-02**	**1.04e-02**
car	5.83e-02	5.22e-02	1.25e-01	1.31e-01	7.29e-02	7.84e-02	5.41e-02	4.87e-02	4.92e-02	4.51e-02
chair	1.99e-01	2.53e-01	7.15e-02	4.18e-02	1.22e-01	7.21e-02	2.99e-02	8.46e-03	**1.00e-02**	**7.66e-03**
display	1.65e-01	1.90e-01	1.89e-01	1.33e-01	4.26e-02	2.79e-02	1.09e-02	**9.47e-03**	9.86e-03	9.51e-03
lamp	1.15e-01	1.19e-01	1.31e-01	6.62e-02	1.16e-01	9.80e-02	5.36e-02	2.01e-02	**2.53e-02**	**1.02e-02**
loudspeaker	6.78e-02	4.17e-02	1.67e-01	1.60e-01	1.40e-01	1.62e-01	2.06e-01	2.05e-01	**2.28e-02**	**1.49e-02**
rifle	1.64e-01	1.69e-01	6.84e-02	3.54e-02	2.44e-02	1.82e-02	5.77e-03	5.23e-03	**4.19e-03**	**4.15e-03**
sofa	1.26e-01	1.13e-01	1.42e-01	1.36e-01	9.59e-02	9.03e-02	7.44e-02	5.70e-02	**3.61e-02**	**3.35e-02**
table	3.19e-01	3.52e-01	1.81e-01	1.66e-01	3.30e-02	2.78e-02	1.03e-01	7.38e-02	**1.16e-02**	**1.04e-02**
telephone	1.18e-01	1.18e-01	1.75e-01	1.75e-01	2.54e-02	2.54e-02	3.81e-02	3.81e-02	**2.25e-02**	**2.25e-02**
watercraft	1.41e-01	1.56e-01	8.04e-02	9.13e-02	3.63e-02	3.47e-02	1.41e-02	1.20e-02	**1.06e-02**	**1.01e-02**
All Classes	1.59e-01	1.51e-01	1.10e-01	6.88e-02	6.33e-02	3.75e-02	3.98e-02	1.03e-02	**1.72e-02**	**9.20e-03**

where

$$d_{\vec{C}}(\chi_1, \chi_2) = \frac{1}{|\chi_1|} \sum_{x_1 \in \chi_1} (\min_{x_2 \in \chi_2} \|x_1 - x_2\|_2), \tag{13}$$

$$d_{\vec{C}}^{sq}(\chi_1, \chi_2) = \frac{1}{|\chi_1|} \sum_{x_1 \in \chi_1} (\min_{x_2 \in \chi_2} \|x_1 - x_2\|_2^2), \tag{14}$$

$$d_{\vec{H}}(\chi_1, \chi_2) = \max_{x_1 \in \chi_1} \min_{x_2 \in \chi_2} \|x_1 - x_2\|_2 . \tag{15}$$

Table 3. Chamfer (d_C) and Hausdorff (d_H) distances of SRB [14]. The *Scans* column serve as a measure of the reconstruction's overfit to the simulation scans.

Method	Anchor GT $d_c \downarrow$	$d_h \downarrow$	Scans d_c	d_h	Lord Quas GT $d_c \downarrow$	$d_h \downarrow$	Scans d_c	d_h	Dc GT $d_c \downarrow$	$d_h \downarrow$	Scans d_c	d_h	Gargoyle GT $d_c \downarrow$	$d_h \downarrow$	Scans d_c	d_h	Daratech GT $d_c \downarrow$	$d_h \downarrow$	Scans d_c	d_h
IGR [4]	1.26	20.45	**0.13**	**1.19**	0.81	13.09	**0.08**	1.42	0.17	3.56	**0.08**	<u>2.72</u>	0.78	18.61	**0.10**	1.26	0.39	7.81	0.13	1.96
SIREN [6]	0.80	35.57	<u>0.14</u>	2.15	0.40	8.79	**0.08**	**0.64**	0.43	7.40	0.09	2.76	0.52	27.76	**0.10**	0.98	0.23	15.09	**0.10**	**1.71**
SAL [1]	0.66	14.76	0.30	14.66	0.20	3.04	0.19	1.59	0.30	5.60	0.20	3.28	0.27	<u>4.34</u>	0.24	3.99	0.59	8.99	0.32	7.07
DiGS [2]	<u>0.33</u>	<u>6.85</u>	0.19	1.39	<u>0.13</u>	<u>1.46</u>	0.09	0.75	<u>0.16</u>	1.46	0.09	**2.68**	**0.18**	**4.22**	0.14	0.92	<u>0.22</u>	3.22	0.12	<u>1.76</u>
Ours	**0.29**	**6.65**	<u>0.14</u>	<u>1.21</u>	**0.12**	**0.87**	**0.08**	<u>0.74</u>	**0.15**	<u>2.37</u>	**0.08**	2.74	**0.18**	4.58	<u>0.11</u>	<u>0.93</u>	<u>0.22</u>	3.72	0.12	<u>1.76</u>

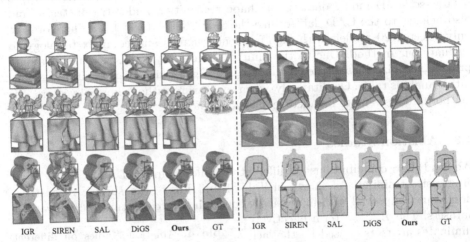

IGR   SIREN   SAL   DiGS   **Ours**   GT | IGR   SIREN   SAL   DiGS   **Ours**   GT

Fig. 5. Surface reconstruction results on ShapeNet [15] (top), SRB [14] (middle) and ABC [24] (bottom). Note that the ground truth of SRB [14] is provided as point clouds, and here we present the visualization results of the input simulated scanned data.

4.2 Reconstruction Quality

Surface Reconstruction on ShapeNet Dataset [15]. We evaluate our method on a subset of the ShapeNet dataset provided by Williams et al. [15] which has 13 classes. And 100 models were selected from these 13 object categories, encompassing a diverse range of objects while excluding models with simple topologies. The quantitative and qualitative results are reported in Table 1, Table 2 and Fig. 5. As can be read from the table and inspected in the figure, in the absence of normal vectors as supervised data, IGR [4] and SIREN [6] tend to produce artifacts. Furthermore, when dealing with shapes that possess complex topological structures (e.g., the base of the lamp) and intricate details (e.g., the sight for the rifle), SAL [1] and DiGS [2] fail to generate shapes with rich details. However, our Finernet tends to generate high-fidelity geometric surfaces.

Surface Reconstruction on SRB Dataset [14]. We also evaluate our method on the simulated scan and ground truth data provided in Williams et al. [14]. The dataset presented comprises a set of five shapes, each possessing complex topological structures and high-level details, in addition to missing data. The quantitative and qualitative results are reported in Table 3 and Fig. 5. Although our reconstruction results surpass the majority of the state-of-the-art methods we compared against, there are instances where our method does not exhibit the best performance. That is primarily due to the presence of extensive missing point cloud data, which introduces a certain degree of error when identifying the nearest point on the ground truth surface to serve as the projected point. The optimization of reconstructing the results will be discussed in Sect. 5.

Surface Reconstruction on ABC Dataset [24]. The ABC dataset [24] is a large-scale 3D model dataset for shape recognition and retrieval tasks, and also belongs to the CAD dataset like the ShapeNet dataset [25]. Therefore, we only selected 20 models with high-frequency signals and complex topology to evaluate our method. Due to the limited number of models selected, we only provide visualizations of the submodels (see Fig. 5) without presenting a qualitative analysis table. Qualitatively, when comparing without normal vectors, our method produces more detailed geometric surfaces.

4.3   Ablation Studies

We study the contributions of different modules, namely L_{smooth}, $L_{sdf'}$, and progressive training. As shown in Table 4 and Fig. 6, the surface reconstruction results improved with increasingly constrained architectures across various datasets. The L_{smooth} term effectively eliminates artifacts caused by the lack of normal vectors as supervision. Then, the $L_{sdf'}$ term further enhanced the reconstruction details of the surfaces. Finally, the progressive training approach maximized the effectiveness of the two aforementioned regularization terms.

Table 4. Ablation studies on different datasets (average d_c).

Baseline	L_{smooth}	$L_{sdf'}$	prog training	ShapeNet [15]	SRB [14]	ABC [24]
✓				3.46e-03	4.76e-01	5.28e-01
✓	✓			1.86e-03	2.12e-01	4.13e-01
✓	✓	✓		1.84e-03	2.06e-01	4.10e-01
✓	✓	✓	✓	1.73e-03	1.92e-01	3.93e-01

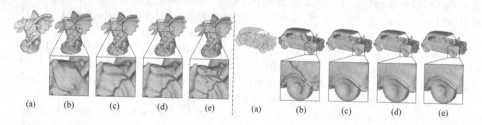

Fig. 6. Ablation studies of our method on non-CAD(left) and CAD(right). (a) Input (unorganized point clouds); (b) Baseline; (c) Using L_{smooth}; (d) Using L_{smooth} and $L_{sdf'}$ directly; (e) Using L_{smooth} and $L_{sdf'}$ with progressive training.

5 Conclusions

In this paper, we propose a progressive network that generates high-quality implicit geometric surfaces from raw point clouds without any pre-processing in a coarse-to-fine manner. Compared with the state-of-the-art methods, experimental results show the high competitiveness of our approach in enhancing the performance of reconstructed results with rich details.

Limitation and Future Work. Although impressive reconstruction results on many models have been achieved with our method, there is still room for improvement in reconstructing models with missing scan data. This is because the approximate SDF supervision penalty can introduce computational errors when there is a large region of data missing. To address this issue, we plan to optimize our method from two aspects in the future. On the one hand, we plan to discard points that are located beyond a certain distance when computing the approximate projected points of randomly sampled points around the surface, considering these randomly sampled points are likely to fall within regions with missing point cloud data in this case. On the other hand, we will consider the self-similarity and symmetry of the model to improve the reconstruction quality of missing point cloud positions.

Acknowledgements. We thank the anonymous reviewers for their valuable comments. This work was supported in part by Natural Science Foundation of China (No. 62102328), in part by the Fundamental Research Funds for the Central Universities (No. SWU120076) and in part by the Open Project Program of State Key Laboratory of Virtual Reality Technology and Systems, Beihang University (No. VRLAB2023C01).

References

1. Atzmon, M., Lipman, Y.: SAL: sign agnostic learning of shapes from raw data. In: Proceedings of the IEEE/CVF Conference on Computer Vision and Pattern Recognition, pp. 2565–2574 (2020)
2. Ben-Shabat, Y., Koneputugodage, C.H., Gould, S.: DiGS: divergence guided shape implicit neural representation for unoriented point clouds. In: Proceedings of the IEEE/CVF Conference on Computer Vision and Pattern Recognition, pp. 19323–19332 (2022)
3. Chen, Z., Zhang, H.: Learning implicit fields for generative shape modeling. In: Proceedings of the IEEE/CVF Conference on Computer Vision and Pattern Recognition, pp. 5939–5948 (2019)
4. Gropp, A., Yariv, L., Haim, N., Atzmon, M., Lipman, Y.: Implicit geometric regularization for learning shapes. arXiv preprint arXiv:2002.10099 (2020)
5. Park, J.J., Florence, P., Straub, J., Newcombe, R., Lovegrove, S.: DeepSDF: learning continuous signed distance functions for shape representation. In: Proceedings of the IEEE/CVF Conference on Computer Vision and Pattern Recognition, pp. 165–174 (2019)
6. Sitzmann, V., Martel, J., Bergman, A., Lindell, D., Wetzstein, G.: Implicit neural representations with periodic activation functions. Adv. Neural. Inf. Process. Syst. **33**, 7462–7473 (2020)

7. Park, K., et al.: Nerfies: deformable neural radiance fields. In: Proceedings of the IEEE/CVF International Conference on Computer Vision, pp. 5865–5874 (2021)
8. Kazhdan, M., Bolitho, M., Hoppe, H.: Poisson surface reconstruction. In: Proceedings of the Fourth Eurographics Symposium on Geometry Processing, vol. 7 (2006)
9. Liu, S., Liu, T., Hu, L., Shang, Y., Liu, X.: Variational progressive-iterative approximation for RBF-based surface reconstruction. Vis. Comput. **37**, 2485–2497 (2021)
10. Yang, Z., Deng, J., Chen, F.: Fitting unorganized point clouds with active implicit b-spline curves. Vis. Comput. **21**, 831–839 (2005)
11. Ali, S.G., et al.: Cost-effective broad learning-based ultrasound biomicroscopy with 3D reconstruction for ocular anterior segmentation. Multimedia Tools Appl. **80**, 35105–35122 (2021)
12. Huang, X., Tang, L., Liu, Y., Qi, S., Zhang, J., Liao, Q.: NIST: learning neural implicit surfaces and textures for multi-view reconstruction. In: Ni, S., Wu, T.Y., Geng, J., Chu, S.C., Tsihrintzis, G.A. (eds.) Advances in Smart Vehicular Technology, Transportation, Communication and Applications, pp. 385–395. Springer, Cham (2023). https://doi.org/10.1007/978-981-99-0848-6_30
13. Morreale, L., Aigerman, N., Guerrero, P., Kim, V.G., Mitra, N.J.: Neural convolutional surfaces. In: Proceedings of the IEEE/CVF Conference on Computer Vision and Pattern Recognition, pp. 19333–19342 (2022)
14. Williams, F., Schneider, T., Silva, C., Zorin, D., Bruna, J., Panozzo, D.: Deep geometric prior for surface reconstruction. In: Proceedings of the IEEE/CVF Conference on Computer Vision and Pattern Recognition, pp. 10130–10139 (2019)
15. Williams, F., Trager, M., Bruna, J., Zorin, D.: Neural splines: fitting 3D surfaces with infinitely-wide neural networks. In: Proceedings of the IEEE/CVF Conference on Computer Vision and Pattern Recognition, pp. 9949–9958 (2021)
16. Bai, C., Liu, G., Li, X., Li, R., Sun, S.: Orienting unorganized points and extracting isosurface for implicit surface reconstruction. Vis. Comput. **38**(6), 1945–1956 (2022)
17. Lorensen, W.E., Cline, H.E.: Marching cubes: a high resolution 3D surface construction algorithm. ACM Siggraph Comput. Graph. **21**(4), 163–169 (1987)
18. Mildenhall, B., Srinivasan, P.P., Tancik, M., Barron, J.T., Ramamoorthi, R., Ng, R.: NeRF: representing scenes as neural radiance fields for view synthesis. Commun. ACM **65**(1), 99–106 (2021)
19. Yifan, W., Rahmann, L., Sorkine-Hornung, O.: Geometry-consistent neural shape representation with implicit displacement fields. arXiv preprint arXiv:2106.05187 (2021)
20. Tancik, M., et al.: Fourier features let networks learn high frequency functions in low dimensional domains. Adv. Neural. Inf. Process. Syst. **33**, 7537–7547 (2020)
21. Yuan, W., Gu, X., Li, H., Dong, Z., Zhu, S.: Monocular scene reconstruction with 3D SDF transformers. arXiv preprint arXiv:2301.13510 (2023)
22. Hoppe, H., DeRose, T., Duchamp, T., McDonald, J., Stuetzle, W.: Surface reconstruction from unorganized points. In: Proceedings of the 19th Annual Conference on Computer Graphics and Interactive Techniques, pp. 71–78 (1992)
23. Azariadis, P.N.: Parameterization of clouds of unorganized points using dynamic base surfaces. Comput. Aided Des. **36**(7), 607–623 (2004)
24. Koch, S., et al.: ABC: a big cad model dataset for geometric deep learning. In: Proceedings of the IEEE/CVF Conference on Computer Vision and Pattern Recognition, pp. 9601–9611 (2019)
25. Chang, A.X., et al.: Shapenet: an information-rich 3D model repository. arXiv preprint arXiv:1512.03012 (2015)

Fine-Grained Web3D
Culling-Transmitting-Rendering Pipeline

Anning Huang[1] , Zhicheng Liu[1], Qian Zhang[1], Feng Tian[2(✉)],
and Jinyuan Jia[1(✉)]

[1] Tongji University, Shanghai, China
jyjia@tongji.edu.cn
[2] Duke Kunshan University, Kunshan, China
feng.tian978@dukekunshan.edu.cn

Abstract. Web3D has gradually become the mainstream online 3D technology to support Metaverse. However, massive multiplayer online Web3D still faces challenges such as slow culling of potentially visible set at servers, networking congestion and sluggish online rendering at web browsers. To address the challenges, in this paper we propose a novel Web3D pipeline that coordinates PVS culling, networking transmitting, and Web3D rendering in a fine-grained way. The pipeline integrates three key steps: establishment of a granularity-aware voxelization scene graph, fine-grained PVS culling and transmitting scheduling, and incremental instanced rendering. Our experiments on a massive 3D plant have demonstrated that the proposed pipeline outperforms existing Web3D approaches in terms of transmitting and rendering.

Keywords: Web3D · Potential visible set culling · Fine-grained transmitting · Lightweight rendering · Pipeline

1 Introduction

Web3D technology greatly enriches the information expression and presentation, increasing user interactivity and immersive experiences. It has a wide range of application prospects in the field of virtual reality. At the same time, the metaverse has received high market attention, with many believing it to be the next generation of the internet [22]. Web3D technology provides powerful technical means and more detailed data supplementation for the realization of the metaverse, and the emergence of the Web3D metaverse is imminent. However, the online display of massive-scale scene applications on the Web3D side still faces a few challenges [4].

The online presentation of Web3D massive-scale scenes is constrained by the calculating and rendering capabilities of the web browser. It also needs to consider various factors such as network transmitting, data parsing, and caching, which differ significantly from local graphics rendering.

To address these challenges, in this paper we propose a pipeline for massive-scale Web3D scenes that integrates culling, transmitting, and rendering. The main contributions can be summarized as follows:

B. Sheng et al. (Eds.): CGI 2023, LNCS 14496, pp. 159–170, 2024.
https://doi.org/10.1007/978-3-031-50072-5_13

(1) Granularity-aware Voxelization Scene Graph: Developing a granularity-aware voxelization scene graph for massive-scale Web3D preprocessing at server, which is used for scene management and quick culling operations.
(2) Fine-grained progressive culling and transmitting: Proposing a fine-grained culling of potentially visible set (PVS) and progressive online transmitting scheduling method to achieve low latency response in Web3D.
(3) Incrementally Scheduling of Instanced Rendering: Proposing an incremental scheduling method of instanced rendering and caching for real time accessing of massive Web3D scenes.

2 Related Work

To our best knowledge, there is no existing systematic solution specifically tailored for Web3D massive-scale scenes. In the following we review related works on the PVS culling, online transmitting, and web rendering.

2.1 Potential Visible Set Culling

To reduce or alleviate the latency and stuttering caused by online loading of large-scale 3D scenes, it is essential to compute PVS of the large-scale 3D scene. The earliest proposed interest domain was the circular interest domain [1]. However, this method resulted in a large number of components to be picked up. Lau and Jia et al. [11,13] introduced more loading priorities, making the loading schedule more flexible. Liu et al. [17] proposed a three-dimensional incremental frustum of interests (FOI). Wang et al. [25] extracted reliable dominant planes to infer the complete large-scale scene structures. However, these methods are unable to handle massive-scale scenes.

Lin [18] proposed a PVS calculation method based on Voronoi diagrams, but it still lacks practical application experience in large-scale scenes. Hladky, Xue and Robles et al. [9,21,29] optimized the visibility calculation from different perspectives. However, they only implemented an accurate visibility culling algorithm for large-scale scenes composed of 2.5D.

Thomas et al. [12] proposed an active region visibility technique that uses ray casting to determine potential visible triangle groups in space. Corbalan et al. [5] proposed a new microstructure technique that avoids rendering invisible surfaces and reduces memory and GPU computational costs. However, these solutions are not suitable for online real-time roaming due to their long processing time when dealing with massive-scale scenes.

2.2 Online Transmitting

Due to the enormous data size of large-scale 3D scenes and the widespread lack of network bandwidth, various lightweight loading modes have been adopted.

Relying solely on deduplication for lightweight methods has limitations in terms of scene scale and repetition rate. Therefore, lightweight streaming and incremental transmitting methods have been proposed. The Progressive Meshes (PM) method proposed by Hoppe et al. [10] overcame the weaknesses of discrete LoD in network transmitting. Wen et al. [26,27] first applied lightweight instantiation processing to the 3D scene, achieving lightweight streaming and progressive transmitting scheduling. Englert [7] and Zhou [28] et al. improved lightweight methods and reduced the data size of instantiated 3D scenes. However, these component partitioning methods are not suitable for all types of scenes and components with varying complexity.

To address the pain points of online loading of 3D scenes, further granular processing is needed. Liu et al. [15,16] divided massive buildings into exterior and interior parts and segmented the interior space into subspaces, effectively alleviating the online loading and rendering pressure of large-scale Web3D building scenes. Wang et al. [24] proposed interest-driven transmission method. Li et al. [14] proposed a multi-level granularity loading scheduling mechanism based on interest levels. They further improved the online loading speed of 3D architectural scenes based on the interest level of components.

However, these methods suffer from the issue of prolonged culling and transmitting time when handling massive-scale scenes. This paper addresses this issue by developing granularity-aware voxelization scene graph and proposing fine-grained culling and transmitting for massive-scale scenes.

2.3 Online Rendering

Rendering for massive-scale online visualization requires reducing the load on applications, networks, and devices from various aspects [20]. Chuang and Chen [2,3] have utilized powerful cloud computing capabilities to perform visualization calculations on BIM spaces and then transmit the rendering results to web clients for display. However, this approach overly relies on the hardware capabilities of the cloud, and suffers from significant rendering and transmitting delays.

Many studies have proposed rendering schemes from the perspective of model simplification. Sun and Trani [23] proposed using pre-generated level of detail (LoD) representations for building data, allowing the data to be displayed using lower-precision LoD models. Cohen-Or and Mattausch [19] emphasized data culling to reduce rendering data. Hildebrandt et al. [8] addressed reducing network transmitting and frontend caching pressure by replacing 3D model data with pre-projected 2D images during client interactions. Dong et al. [6] proposed a fine-grained parallel rendering approach for extremely large scenes. However, none of them have developed a comprehensive transmitting and rendering solution. In this paper we propose an incrementally rendering scheduling approach.

3 Pipeline

This paper proposes an integrated fine-grained pipeline for culling, transmitting and rendering, which includes three key technologies: fine-grained voxelization preprocessing, fine-grained transmitting scheduling, and fine-grained instanced rendering. The key technologies are illustrated in Fig. 1.

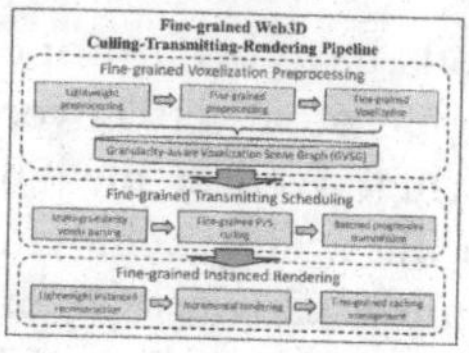

Fig. 1. Fine-grained Web3D Pipeline for Integrated Culling-Transmitting-Rendering

(1) Fine-grained Voxelization Preprocessing: We develop a granularity-aware voxelization scene graph for massive-scale scenes. The components are assigned to corresponding levels based on their visual importance. To measure the visual importance, we propose the concept of voxelizing density.

(2) Fine-grained Transmitting Scheduling: We achieve batched rapid retrieval of visible components from coarse-grained to fine-grained, from rough visibility to accurate visibility, in a progressive manner. Simultaneously, the visible components are transmitted to the browser side.

(3) Fine-grained Instanced Rendering: We incrementally load the multi-batch visible component set and preload the potentially visible component set within a certain range, and dynamically monitor and manage the browser-side data cache.

4   Scene Preprocessing

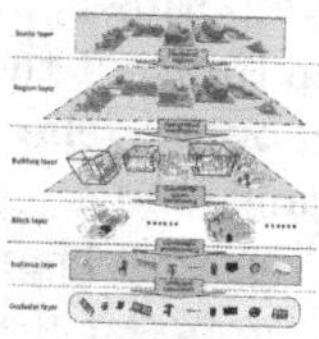

Fig. 2. Voxelization Scene Graph

As shown in Fig. 2, the scene graph proposed in this paper has multi-granularity. The most important one is the block layer where the voxels are divided into multiple granularities, and the voxelizing density of instanced components within each granularity is within the corresponding voxel range.

4.1   Fine-Grained Voxelization

Constructing the scene graph requires a multi-level voxelization preprocessing of the scene. The entire massive-large-scale 3D scene undergoes instantiation checks and bounding box calculation. Divide space equally with a plane perpendicular to the longest axis. The first, second, and third level voxels were obtained through N, $N + 3$, and $N + 6$ calculations.

4.2 Granularity-Aware Partitioning

To fulfill the users' demand for visual richness during scene navigation, the scene components need to be allocated to the first-, second-, and third-level voxels according to certain rules. To measure the significance of instanced components in the scene, our paper proposes the definition of voxelizing density. The voxelizing density VD_i of component i is defined as follows:

$$VD_i = \frac{(r_i^2 Num_{instance})}{V_{scene}} \tag{1}$$

Where r_i is the bounding sphere radius of component i, $Num_{instance}$ is the instantiation count of the component, and V_{scene} is the volume of the scene's bounding box.

Components are sorted based on the voxelizing density. The component's instantiated bounding box is used to determine the voxels it occupies. The components with high voxelizing density are placed in the first-level voxels, those with medium voxelizing density are placed in the second-level voxels, and those with low voxelizing density are placed in the third-level voxels.

4.3 Subregion Division

After the scene space division and component voxelizing are completed, the scene is further divided into subregions based on the voxels. The center point of the voxel's bounding box is considered its coordinate, and K-means clustering is performed. The number of subregions equals the number of buildings in the scene's building layer, which is determined through manual selection. Based on the clustering results, the entire 3D scene is divided into several subregions.

Through this method, the massive-scale 3D scene is divided into multiple subregions, each containing a number of voxels that store fine-grained component information.

5 Fine-Grained Progressive Culling and Transmitting

Through scene graph, the current visible component set is quickly calculated based on user roaming information during real-time roaming. The process of batched progressive fine-grained transmitting scheduling is shown in Fig. 3.

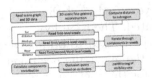

Fig. 3. Batched progressive fine-grained transmitting scheduling

5.1   Voxelizing Density and Projected Area

Due to the limited perception of image richness by the human eye, objects with too small a projection area on the screen cannot be noticed. At this point, these objects can be removed from the rendering.

The instanced components with voxelizing density within a certain range have projected areas on the screen within a proportional range. Therefore, components are divided into multi-granularity of voxels based on the voxelizing density and implements granularity-aware voxelization, which facilitates fast calculation during the culling process.

5.2   FVS Culling and Transmitting Scheduling

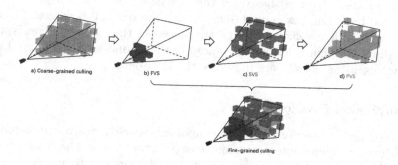

Fig. 4. Fine-grained culling based on scene graph

As shown in Fig. 4, the first step, calculate the voxel set within the field of view by frustum culling. The weights of all voxels are sorted to obtain a list of voxels to be loaded. The voxels are sorted based on their distance from the field of view. The parts that are closer to the viewpoint and contribute more are selected and represented as the First Visible Set (FVS).

To avoid excessive time spent on occlusion culling, the FVS is immediately transmitted to the browser side and loaded after frustum culling.

The calculation of component contribution is done using the maximum occlusion replacement. The maximum occlusion replacement is the maximum occluding face of a mesh model in a certain direction. In this paper, the maximum occlusion replacement is calculated for the x-axis, y-axis, and z-axis directions. Firstly, the mesh model is voxelized, and the maximum sampling area in the sampling direction is calculated. The edge loops are connected and simplified, and finally, triangulation is performed to obtain several triangles. The sum of the triangle areas represents the maximum occlusion in that direction.

The calculation formula for the contribution C_i of component i within the field of view is:

$$C_i = \frac{\sum_{dir} \sum_k^n s_{dir,k}}{|viewPoint - center_i|^2} \quad (2)$$

where **dir** represents the x-axis, y-axis, and z-axis directions, $s_{dir,k}$ represents the area of the triangle in that direction, $viewPoint$ represents the coordinates of the viewpoint, and $center_i$ represents the coordinates of the center of the component.

After completing the FVS calculation, the visible set is transmitted to the web end. Since this part belongs to the clearly visible set, set its status as visible.

5.3   SVS and PVS Culling and Transmitting Scheduling

After the calculation and transmitting of the First Visible Set (FVS) is completed, the calculation of the Second Visible Set (SVS) and the PVS continues. Rasterize the component occlusion replacement in the backend and calculate the occlusion to obtain an accurate visible set, which is SVS. The SVS is transmitted to the browser side.

After the calculation and transmitting of SVS, an estimation is made for PVS in the current field of view. A certain distance is extended forward from the current field of view, and frustum culling calculations are performed based on the scene graph. Components that contribute above a certain threshold are considered as components that may be loaded in the future, which is PVS.

After the completion of SVS and PVS calculations, continuously monitor the status of FVS data transmitting in real-time. Once the FVS transmitting is completed, transmit SVS and PVS data to the web end sequentially.

6   Incrementally Scheduling of Instanced Rendering

This paper proposes a component-based distributed loading and rendering method based on visibility status. The scheduling process is shown in Fig. 5.

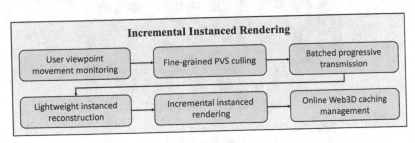

Fig. 5. Incremental instanced rendering

6.1   Incremental Instanced Web3D Rendering

As shown in Fig. 6, when the user roams the scene in the browser, the browser monitors the user's real-time viewpoint. The server progressively calculates and transmits FVS, SVS and PVS.

Apply instanced rendering to components and find similar components in the scene, and then the spatial transformation relationship between similar components is calculated to obtain the transformation matrix. During loading, the base component mesh model is used along with the transformation matrix to generate the instanced models.

After the browser loads the component data, if the component belongs to the PVS, it is temporarily set as invisible.

6.2   Online Scheduling of Caching Web3D

Based on the results of visibility calculation and considering factors such as component retention time and instantiation, caching scheduling is performed for the components in the web. For invisible components, the resource exceeding the capacity of the webpage node cache is converted to the "to be cleaned" state, until these components data are cleaned up and removed.

This Web3D caching management algorithm divides components based on culling results, distinguishing the resources that need to be cleaned, thus reducing computational overhead during the cleaning process. Through these methods, lightweight, fast, and accurate Web3D cache management is achieved.

7   Experimental Results and Performance Analysis

We conducted tests on the fine-grained pipeline for Web3D massive-scale scene.

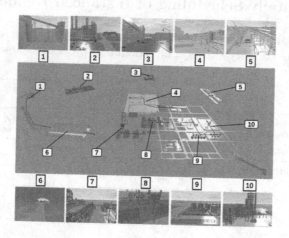

Fig. 6. Snap shots of Massive Scene of the Plant

A massive-scale plant was chosen to test our culling-transmitting-rendering pipeline. This scene has approximately 2,500,000 3D components and 400,000,000 triangles. The data size is 106 GB. The scene is shown in Fig. 6 and the numbers indicate 10 subregions.

7.1   Web3D Data Transmitting

We selected 20*5*20 viewpoints in the scene. The camera is oriented towards the positive and negative directions of the x-axis, y-axis, and z-axis. The voxel count within the field of view, average data size are recorded. The results are shown in Fig. 7 where "One-time culling and transmitting" refers to merge the culling and transmitting, without fine-grained processing proposed in this paper.

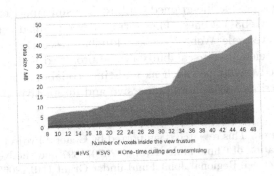

Fig. 7. Transmitting data size testing

From Fig. 7, it can be observed that, to achieve the same visual effect, the transmitting data size of the fine-grained progressive transmitting algorithm is significantly smaller than that of the one-time transmitting algorithm.

7.2   Comparison Testing

As reviewed earlier, Li proposed CEBOW [14]. To compare our proposed pipeline with CEBOW, we conducted tests by recording the number of triangles from 20*5*20 viewpoints and measuring rendering frame rates and transmitting delays. The results are shown in Fig. 8.

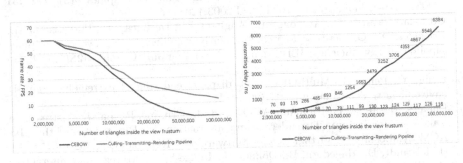

Fig. 8. Rendering frame rate and transmitting delay comparison

From the figure, it can be seen that our pipeline has advantages in terms of frame rates and transmitting delays for massive-scale scenes. As the number of computed triangles increases, CEBOW experiences rendering stutters, excessive transmitting delays, thus is unable to support online real-time transmission and rendering.

The URL for our paper is http://smartweb3d.com/CTR-pipeline/.

8   Conclusion

In this paper we propose a fine-grained Culling-Transmitting-Rendering pipeline for massive-scale Web3D scenes. This forms a fine-grained online scheduling solution for massive-scale Web3D scenes. Further research can be conducted to enhance the efficiency and scalability of the proposed method. Additionally, exploring advanced techniques such as real-time collaboration and interactive features may contribute to a more immersive and interactive metaverse experience.

Acknowledgements. This research is supported by General Project of National Natural Science Foundation of China under Grant 6207071897 and the Key Project of the National Natural Science Regional Joint Fund under Grant U19A2063.

References

1. Airey, J.M.: Increasing update rates in the building walkthrough system with automatic model-space subdivision and potentially visible set calculations. The University of North Carolina at Chapel Hill (1990)
2. Chen, H.M., Chang, K.C., Lin, T.H.: A cloud-based system framework for performing online viewing, storage, and analysis on big data of massive BIMs. Autom. Constr. **71**, 34–48 (2016)
3. Chuang, T.H., Lee, B.C., Wu, I.C.: Applying cloud computing technology to BIM visualization and manipulation. In: 28th International Symposium on Automation and Robotics in Construction, vol. 201, pp. 144–149 (2011)
4. Cohen-Or, D., Chrysanthou, Y., Silva, C., Durand, F.: A survey of visibility for walkthrough applications. IEEE Trans. Visual Comput. Graphics **9**(3), 412–431 (2003). https://doi.org/10.1109/TVCG.2003.1207447
5. Corbalan-Navarro, D., Aragón, J.L., Anglada, M., De Lucas, E., Parcerisa, J.M., Gonzalez, A.: Omega-test: a predictive early-z culling to improve the graphics pipeline energy-efficiency. IEEE Trans. Visual Comput. Graphics **28**(12), 4375–4388 (2021)
6. Dong, Y., Peng, C.: Multi-GPU multi-display rendering of extremely large 3D environments. Vis. Comput. 1–17 (2022)
7. Englert, M., Jung, Y., Klomann, M., Etzold, J., Grimmy, P., Jia, J.: A streaming framework for instant 3D rendering and interaction. In: Proceedings of the 21st ACM Symposium on Virtual Reality Software and Technology, p. 192 (2015)
8. Hildebrandt, D., Hagedorn, B., Döllner, J.: Image-based strategies for interactive visualisation of complex 3D geovirtual environments on lightweight devices. J. Location Based Serv. **5**(2), 100–120 (2011)
9. Hladky, J., Seidel, H.P., Steinberger, M.: The camera offset space: real-time potentially visible set computations for streaming rendering. ACM Trans. Graph. (TOG) **38**(6), 1–14 (2019)

10. Hoppe, H.: Progressive meshes. In: Proceedings of the 23rd Annual Conference on Computer Graphics and Interactive Techniques, pp. 99–108 (1996)
11. Jia, J., Wang, W., Hei, X.: An efficient caching algorithm for peer-to-peer 3D streaming in distributed virtual environments. J. Netw. Comput. Appl. **42**, 1–11 (2014)
12. Koch, T., Wimmer, M.: Guided visibility sampling++. Proc. ACM Comput. Graph. Interact. Tech. **4**(1), 1–16 (2021)
13. Li, F.W., Lau, R.W., Kilis, D.: Gameod: an internet based game-on-demand framework. In: Proceedings of the ACM Symposium on Virtual Reality Software and Technology, pp. 129–136 (2004)
14. Li, K., Zhao, H., Zhang, Q., Jia, J.: CEBOW: a cloud-edge-browser online Web3D approach for visualizing large BIM scenes. Comput. Animat. Virtual Worlds **33**(2), e2039 (2022)
15. Liu, X., He, C., Zhao, H., Jia, J., Liu, C.: Building information modeling indoor path planning: a lightweight approach for complex BIM building. Comput. Animat. Virtual Worlds **32**(3–4), e2014 (2021)
16. Liu, X., He, C., Zhao, H., Jia, J., Liu, C.: Exteriortag: automatic semantic annotation of BIM building exterior via voxel index analysis. IEEE Comput. Graphics Appl. **41**(3), 48–58 (2021)
17. Liu, X., Xie, N., Tang, K., Jia, J.: Lightweighting for Web3D visualization of large-scale BIM scenes in real-time. Graph. Models **88**, 40–56 (2016)
18. Lu, L., Yang, C., Wang, W., Zhang, J.: Voronoi-based potentially visible set and visibility query algorithms. In: 2011 Eighth International Symposium on Voronoi Diagrams in Science and Engineering, pp. 234–240. IEEE (2011)
19. Mattausch, O., Bittner, J., Wimmer, M.: CHC++: coherent hierarchical culling revisited. In: Computer Graphics Forum, vol. 27, pp. 221–230. Wiley Online Library (2008)
20. Mwalongo, F., Krone, M., Reina, G., Ertl, T.: State-of-the-art report in web-based visualization. In: Computer Graphics Forum, vol. 35, pp. 553–575. Wiley Online Library (2016)
21. Robles-Ortega, M.D., Ortega, L., Feito, F.R.: Efficient visibility determination in urban scenes considering terrain information. ACM Trans. Spat. Algorithms Syst. (TSAS) **3**(3), 1–24 (2017)
22. Thalmann, N.M., Kim, J., Papagiannakis, G., Thalmann, D., Sheng, B.: Computer graphics for metaverse. Virtual Reality Intell. Hardware **4**(5), ii–iv (2022). https://doi.org/10.1016/j.vrih.2022.10.001. https://www.sciencedirect.com/science/article/pii/S2096579622000997
23. Trani, M.L., Cassano, M., Todaro, D., Bossi, B.: BIM level of detail for construction site design. Procedia Eng. **123**, 581–589 (2015)
24. Wang, M., Jia, J., Xie, N., Zhang, C.: Interest-driven avatar neighbor-organizing for P2P transmission in distributed virtual worlds. Comput. Animat. Virtual Worlds **27**(6), 519–531 (2016)
25. Wang, W., Gao, W.: Efficient multi-plane extraction from massive 3D points for modeling large-scale urban scenes. Vis. Comput. **35**, 625–638 (2019)
26. Wen, L., Jia, J., Liang, S.: LPM: lightweight progressive meshes towards smooth transmission of Web3D media over internet. In: Proceedings of the 13th ACM SIGGRAPH International Conference on Virtual-Reality Continuum and its Applications in Industry, pp. 95–103 (2014)
27. Wen, Laixiang, Xie, Ning, Jia, Jinyuan: Client-driven strategy of large-scale scene streaming. In: Tian, Qi., Sebe, Nicu, Qi, Guo-Jun., Huet, Benoit, Hong, Richang,

Liu, Xueliang (eds.) MMM 2016. LNCS, vol. 9517, pp. 93–103. Springer, Cham (2016). https://doi.org/10.1007/978-3-319-27674-8_9

28. Zhou, W., Tang, K., Jia, J.: S-LPM: segmentation augmented light-weighting and progressive meshing for the interactive visualization of large man-made web3d models. World Wide Web J. **21**, 1425–1448 (2018)

29. Xue, J., Zhai, X., Qu, H.: Efficient rendering of large-scale cad models on a GPU virtualization architecture with model geometry metrics. In: 2019 IEEE International Conference on Service-Oriented System Engineering (SOSE), pp. 251–2515. IEEE (2019)

The Chemical Engine Algorithm and Realization Based on Unreal Engine-4

Xu Lu[1], Shuo Xiong[2(✉)], Tao Wu[1], Ke Zhang[2], Yue Zhang[2], Yachang Wang[3], and Qilong Kou[3]

[1] School of Software, Huazhong University of Science and Technology, Wuhan, China

[2] School of Journalism and Information Communication, PSS Lab of Big Data and National Communication Strategy, MOE, Huazhong University of Science and Technology, Wuhan, China
xiongshuo@hust.edu.cn

[3] Shenzhen City Tencent Computer System Co. Ltd., Shenzhen, China

Abstract. The Chemical Engine is a new concept introduced by Nintendo company as a counterpart to the traditional physics engine in game development. However, Nintendo has not released any details of the Chemical Engine, also Nintendo blurred the definition between "chemical" and "physical". Therefore, this paper clarifies the concept of physical engine and chemical engine in game development, then based on the definition, two chemical engine algorithms are proposed. One is called the "elemental energy" algorithm, which is based on Nintendo's philosophy and optimized for future scalability, "elemental energy" can be widely used in general game scenarios. The second one is called the "factorization and properties" algorithm, which is more in line with the definition of chemistry in academics, this method can realistically render chemical reactions, but the realization is more difficult and too costly to use in game development. Therefore, this paper provides a specific means of implementation in the Unreal Engine 4 engine based on the elemental energy algorithm Through the analysis of the achievement and experiment, the cost and method of the "elemental energy" algorithm are reasonable. Therefore, the scheme is more practical in this scenario, and it could be widely used in commercial game development.

Keywords: Chemical Engine · Unreal Engine-4 · Graphic Algorithm · Plugin Design

1 Introduction

Attributed to the accessibility, powerful interactive simulations, and realistic physical environment, computer graphics engines (also called "game engines") are playing the important role in game development. Through code or blueprints,

Supported by Tencent computer system Co. Ltd.

game developers could create their opuses with highly realistic physical rules [1]. For example, while the player throws a ball at a standing high point with a certain initial speed, the ball will follow a parabolic trajectory. In fact, during the game development process, the game designer or programmer do not need to write extra coding resource to describe or create the parabolic trajectory function, therefore, we call it "Physical Game Engine" (abbreviated as physics engine). No matter the "Unity 3D" or "Unreal Engine 4" (abbreviated as UE4), they are all the best Physical Game Engine in the commercial area, and widely used all over the world.

While the word "Physics" existed, of course, we have the corresponding vocabulary "Chemistry". If the concept of physics in-game means "the calculation of movement based on certain rules", then the concept of chemistry in-game implies "the calculation of state based on certain rules". In other words, the physical engine is the simulation of collision detection and scene destruction in the game scene, and the chemical engine is a simulation of chemical changes in the interaction of elements and substances. The research achievements and commercial applications of the physical engines are extra mature, even the children could build a real physical game script although they know nothing about physics theory. Therefore, the literature review on physical engines is outside the scope of this paper. In contrast, we have to clarify the development history and definition of the chemical engine. Actually, the chemical engine will not perform the chemical reactions 100 percent by chemistry theory, it is a game engineering concept that was created by the famous game company– Nintendo.

The chemical engine originated mainly from Nintendo's game "*The Legend of Zelda: Breath of the Wild*" (abbreviated as *Breath of the Wild*) [2], which is an algorithm for calculating state changes, which can be understood as a kind of state counter built into all objects, recording their states and values in real-time. It is affected by the player's actions and various external events, and when the quantitative changes accumulate to a certain value, a qualitative change occurs. The reason for calling it a "chemical engine" is the desire to create "chemical-like reactions" in the game. However, following the definition by Nintendo, some physical reactions are categorized as "chemical", for example, the water change into ice (because it is common in the game when you use the icy magic, etc.), also Nintendo just show some basic idea without any detail of algorithm or technique publicly [3], however this technology is very important for metaverse in future [4]. In order to solve the issue, some existing work was referred to, for example the large-scale scene navigation method GuideRender can fuse features of different domains with attention. [5]. Through the Unreal Engine 4, a team has tested the usability of this method and has created 3D reactive models and physical models that run based the systems [6]. Therefore, in this paper, we will introduce Nintendo's philosophy about the chemical engine in Sect. 2, then based on the original idea, we propose two methods to try to achieve the chemical engine design in Sect. 3. Later, the elemental energy algorithm which is the easiest to implement in the engineering process was chosen and performed the implementation of the chemical engine effect in the UE4 environment, the technical details were introduced in Sect. 4. Finally, the conclusion was given.

2   Current Chemical Engine

2.1   Original Chemical Engine of Nintendo

At the Game Developers Conference (GDC) in the 2017 year, the creators of *Breath of the Wild* Aonuma Eiji shared their design philosophy, introducing the concept of "multiplicative" gameplay and chemical engine for the first time in front of the world.

The engine that was used for creating Breath of the Wild is Havok Game Dynamics SDK, which is used to simulate realistic physics effects, introduce the laws of physics into virtual scenarios, and increase the interactivity of the project. Also, the built-in physics collision detection functions help designers facilitate game development. The core concept of the physical engine was combined by *Collision* and *Movement*.

However, the Breath of the Wild development team designed a different set of physics laws in the game different from our real world. They call it as the concept of "Telling clever lies", which means lie more as much as possible based on the correct physics laws. On this basis, the *Breath of the Wild* team created the Chemical Engine in Havok, and the two-pronged approach of the physical Engine and the Chemical Engine has made the development of the entire open world very clear.

According to Nintendo's public information. The rules in the game should be managed by the unity of physics and chemistry, intuitively understood while creating infinite possibilities through the "*Player Action* multiply *Field*". In *Breath of the Wild*, states are defined in detail as following concept: *Element* (e.g. fire, water, wind, electricity) and *Material* (e.g. wood, iron, role). The chemical engine of the game treats elements and materials based on three rules:

1 The element can change the state of the material: just like fire can turn a green tree into a bare branch.
2 An element can change the state of another element: just like water can extinguish a fire.
3 Materials and materials cannot influence each other: just like wood cannot change the iron to another material or elements.

These three rules seem to be quite simple, but they form various interesting events in the game world. The combination of physics and chemistry further enhances the richness of game-play, also this idea expanded the freedom of the Open world/Sandbox game. Nintendo proposes the core and key model to realizing the "multiplicative" game-play as Fig. 1 shows. Based on the philosophy of "Action x Field x Object", different permutations of player behavior and game scenes form can create thousands of interaction effects. For example, in *Breath of the Wild* the player could put a live bass in a different environment, such as

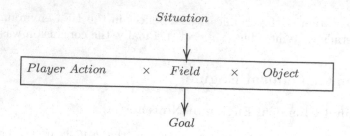

Fig. 1. The chemical engine idea of Nintendo

beside lava or in the snow, then the player will get a corresponding grilled or frozen bass. That is where the chemical engine comes into play, as the player picks up an item as a 'material', and under the influence of the temperature as an 'element', the 'material' changes state and becomes A new 'material' is created, as in Fig. 2.

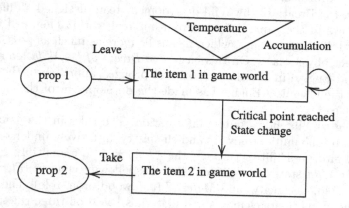

Fig. 2. Specific applications of the chemical engine

2.2   The Chemical Engine in Genshin

"*Genshin*" is an open-world Action Role Play Game (ARPG) developed by Chinese game company Mihoyo, which shares some similarities with *Breath of the Wild* in terms of its design core, therefore, *Genshin* inherits to some extent from the chemical engine. However, *Genshin* has a clear bias towards the chemical engine design: it places more emphasis on the impact of the chemical engine on the battle experience than on exploration. In *Genshin*, the chemical engine places more emphasis on the concept of elemental attachment (for example "element + character"), and a weaker influence of elements on the state of items in the open world.

In addition, *Genshin* features a chemical engine designed with reaction mechanisms between elements in mind, which differs from previous RPGs. The chemical engine of *Genshin* also includes interactions between scenes, and natural elements or objects, such as a thunderstorm that causes the water or lightning element to be attached to the characters in the scene. However, Mihoyo did not release any technical details of the chemical engine design as Nintendo did (although Nintendo also only display a basic framework).

2.3   Research Questions

Both Nintendo and Mihoyo show that the concept of the "chemical engine" in the game is not the same as chemistry in the real world. Typical examples are water turning into ice and water putting out a fire, which is the realm of thermodynamic physics; metal conducting electricity, which is the realm of electricity; even the mechanics involved, such as the road becoming wet and slippery, which is a change in friction and has nothing to do with chemistry totally. These physical changes are all defined by Nintendo as "chemistry", which might come from a random naming by Nintendo technical supervisor Takuhiro Dohta, or it could be a marketing concept by Nintendo in conjunction with *Breath of the Wild*.

But at least we can confirm that the physical engines like Unity or UE4 are only the "mechanical engine". In the fields of electricity, optics, and thermodynamics, the current game development engine has not been able to realize it. Therefore, the physical engine is also a kind of commercial concept.

In any case, it is important to clarify the meaning of the chemical engine in the game world and agree with Nintendo's naming concept in order to facilitate subsequent research and engineering, the definition is as below:

Definition 1. *The game development engine involves physical changes except for mechanical engines, as well as chemical reactions in the true sense of the world, which are all referred to in the game world as chemical engines.*

According to the definition and Nintendo's previous concept, we propose two chemical engine algorithms, then choose the first one for achievement.

3   Two Algorithms for Chemical Engine Design

This section specifies two chemical engine algorithms, the first of which draws on Nintendo's philosophy of treating all objects commonly found in games as elements (not in the real concept of chemistry) and grouping them into broad classifications where certain reactions can occur between elements to make states change, a model suitable for the development of games like Zelda. The second algorithm is built on a real chemical engine, expressing molecular formulae in the form of factorisation, confirming that each number in the database corresponds to a unique substance as far as possible, and using physical properties to describe the properties of that substance; this model is suitable for real chemical engine development and implementation to break the Nintendo vocabulary definition problem while being able to be removed from the game development scenario and being able to be truly applied to chemistry related education, exploration and research. However, the second algorithm is far more difficult than the first, both in terms of engineering and workload, and therefore only the 'elemental energy' part of the paper has been completed at the implementation level. The whole structure of the algorithm is as the Fig. 3 shows.

3.1   Elemental Energy

Basic Concept. The elemental energy is similar to the Nintendo philosophy, however, we create some new content and simplified the algorithm. For example, in our elemental energy method, both elements and materials were combined as the "Elemental category" in Fig. 3. There is a big defect in Nintendo's idea, *"The element can change the state of the material, the element can change the state of another element, materials, and materials cannot influence each other"*– however, how to define the targets belong to "element" or "material"? Is the "wind" belongs to "element"? If "water" belongs to "element", so how about "ice"? Above all these questions, Nintendo had not given any explanation. Therefore, we set all the targets in the "Elemental category", while expanding the target types in the future such as "poison" or "soul", it will be very convenient. In the current algorithm, we list 10 types of element categories that are commonly used in games, they are *Fire, Water, Electric, Plant, Wind, Magnet, Ice, Iron, Earth,* and *Air.*

Based on the elemental category, the concept of energy relationship and decision condition were proposed. The previous concept decides the interaction possible between each element, for example, fire can burn the plant, iron can conduct electricity, wind cannot change the magnet, etc. The subsequent concept decides the interaction threshold. For example, water can put out fire, but drops of water cannot put out a campfire; ice can change water into ice, but enough freezing time is needed.

Algorithm Mechanism. For all the elemental categories, we set 4 relationships to process them. They are *"assimilation, alienation, Increment and Decrement".* The detailed concept as Eq. 1 to 4 shows.

$$b + a-> b(with\ property\ of\ a) + a \tag{1}$$

$$b + a-> c + a \tag{2}$$

$$b + a-> B \tag{3}$$

$$B + a-> b \tag{4}$$

– **Assimilation.** As Eq. 1 shows. It means when "element b" touches "element a", "element b" acquires the properties of "element a", the properties will change during this process, but the total amount will not. For example, the element electronic can make water or iron electrically charged.

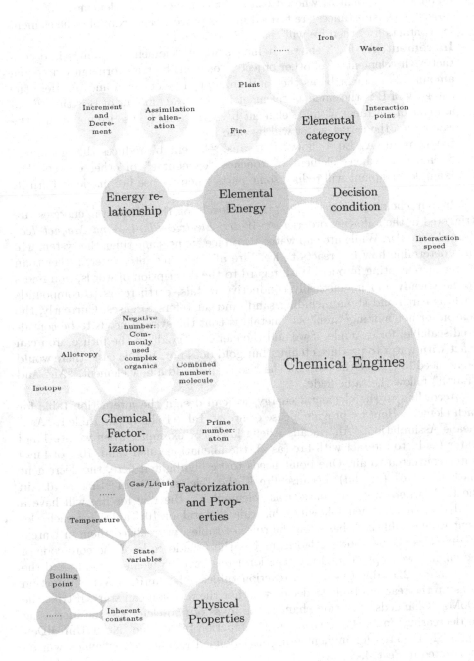

Fig. 3. The structure of two chemical engine algorithms

- **Alienation**. As Eq. 2 shows. It means "element b" is converted to an equal amount of "element c" when it comes into contact with "element a" of other objects, new substances are formed in this process. For example, the element ice contacts fire, then ice will change into water.
- **Increment**. As Eq. 3 shows. It means when "element b" comes into contact with "element a" of other objects, "element b" transforms into an equal amount of "element b" as the total amount of "element a and b". Here the category of B is the same as "element b", but the amount of B is the sum of amount of "element a" and "element b". For example, use ice magic into the water then the target water will become ice.
- **Decrement**. As Eq. 4 shows. It means "element b" reduces the amount of "element a" when "element b" touches "element a" of other objects. For example, the plant will reduce some parts when we use fire magic to burn it.

In our chemical engine, the priority levels of the elemental energies are triggered in the following order: *Fire–Water–Electric–Plant–Wind–Magnet–Ice–Iron–Earth–Air*. While fire and water act on ice at the same time, the system will first determine how fire reacts to ice. Fire alienates ice into water, rather than water incrementing into ice. With regard to the description of words, iron refers to electrically and magnetically conductive metals, earth refers to compounds such as earth and stone including sand, and air refers to gases. Currently, the reason for not naming "iron" as "metal" is that the system needs to be considered scalable; for example, if we add the element "gold" in the future, iron can react with water to produce etching, but gold does not. In this case, there would be no need to change the name of the "iron", just add a new element. "Air" and "Earth" follow the same logic.

According to the elemental energy, we can design the interaction table for each element. Here we provide a case of fire as Table 1 shows (In Table 1, "Ass" means Assimilation; "Ali" means Alienation). For example, when we use 1 mol water (as b) to interact with fire (as a), the alienation ruled valid, 10% of 1 mol water converted to air. One point needs to be highlighted here, the decrement marked as "0" (invalid), because fire is the "element a". In other words, in the table where water is marked as "element a", the row for fire will have a valid decrement. Then following this rule, a total of 10 Tables for each element were established, based on the rules of tables, we realized them in Unreal Engine 4 as Sect. 4 shows. Algorithm 1 is the pseudo code of the core code of the engine, we implemented the reaction rules for each element and stored the them into a 2D table that called reaction table, the "CanReactWith" function looks up the reaction table to decide whether the reaction can start. If true, the "DoMassChangeds" function changes the mass of two elements, the increasing (or decreasing) mass is also stored in the reaction table. The "NotifyUnrealDelegates" function is for implementing user-defined reaction effect which will be interpreted in Sect. 4.

Algorithm 1. Element reaction algorithm

Require: Two entities with elemental energy(One is called trigger the other is called reactant)

Ensure: The trigger tries to react with the reactant

   if CanReactWith(trigger, reactant) **then**

      DoMassChanges(trigger, reactant)

      NotifyUnrealDelegates(trigger, reactant)

   end if

Table 1. Elemental energy interaction relationship of "element fire"

Fire (as a)	Ass	Ali	Alienation Element 1	Alienation Element 2	Increment	Decrement	Interaction point (mol)	Interaction Speed(s)
Water	0	0.1	Air	0	0	0	1	1
Electric	0	0	0	0	0	0	0	0
Plant	0	0	0	0	0	1	0.5	2
Wind	1	0	0	0	0	0	2	3
Magnet	0	0	0	0	0	0	0	0
Ice	0	1	Water	0	0	0	1	1
Iron	1	0	0	0	0	0	5	10
Earth	0	0	0	0	0	0	0	0
Air	0	0	0	0	0	0	0	0

3.2 Factorization and Properties

The Elemental Energy method is easy to realize and easy for expanding in the future, however, this concept follows the Nintendo's philosophy, not the real chemical reaction. Therefore, we proposed another algorithm which was called "factorization" to patch it. In contrast, the factorization method, although providing a realistic representation of the chemical reactions, from a computer engineering point of view, relies on huge database construction and is difficult to implement in a short time. Consequently, in this paper, only the algorithm was given.

For any composite number C, it is necessarily possible to decompose the composite number into the product of several prime numbers by a unique factorization as $C = \prod_{i=1}^{n} P_i$. Similarly, any substance or molecule is necessarily capable of being decomposed into a number of certain atomic compositions, what could be described as $Molecule = \prod_{i=1}^{n} Atom_i$. In this case, each atom can be marked by a unique corresponding prime number, and in most cases, a specific composite number can refer to a unique chemical molecule. For example in Table 2, we use 1st prime number "2" to represent Hydrogen, the 6th prime number "13" to represent Carbon, and so on. Then, the water can be marked by $76 = 2^2 * 19 = H_2O$, similarly the carbon dioxide can be marked by $4693 = 13 * 19^2 = CO_2$. For each positive integer other than 1, it can correspond to at most one molecular compound, even in the face of isotopes or allotropy issues, we could use 4 and 8 to represent Deuterium and Tritium, or use 13 and 169 to represent Graphite and Diamond. According to this idea, we could establish a database to save the information (physical properties) for commonly used atoms and molecules. The physical properties contain state variables such as temperature or gas/liquid state, and inherent constants such as electrical conductivity or melting point.

Table 2. Prime Number and Corresponding Atom

No.	1	2	...	6	7	8	...
Atom	H	He		C	N	O	...
Prime	2	3	...	13	17	19	...

Compared with the elemental energy algorithm, it is very clear to notice that the factorization and properties method has three defects as below:

1 It cannot distinguish Isomer, for example the n-Pentane and Isopentane.
2 For organic matter, the numbering would be astronomical.
3 For the whole system, the database needs a huge amount of work.

These issues almost existed in organic chemistry, therefore, we could express the common organic substances in the game as negative numbers, such as "−1" represent alcohol, "−2" represent fibre and "−3" represent meat etc. Overall, the factorization approach allows for a more accurate description of chemical reactions and creates a realistic chemical engine. However, it is more applicable to inorganic chemistry and appears to be inappropriate in terms of cost for the game due to the amount of engineering involved. Therefore, a full realization based on this algorithm has not been done in this paper.

4   The Chemical Realization Technique of Elemental Energy Method

4.1   Brief Introduction of the Elemental Energy Chemistry Engine

The Elemental Energy Chemistry Engine is implemented as a plugin of Unreal Engine 4 (can be easily migrated to Unreal Engine 5 as needed), so we called it Chemistry Plugin in the following paragraph. [7] The Chemistry Plugin is mainly composed of two components, Trigger and Reactant. Each component has an attribute called Chemical Element (e.g. fire, water etc.) and can be attached to any entity. Once an entity is attached to the Fire Reactant component, we deem that the property of the entity is Fire, and thus the entity can interact with other entities attached to the Trigger component.

4.2   Detailed Implementation of Chemistry Engine

The architecture of the game is an Entity-Component System (abbreviated as ECS), which means the game world consists of various entities and each entity can own some components. Entities and components are a one-to-many relationship, and what kind of capabilities an entity has depends entirely on which components it has, and by dynamically adding or removing components, you can change the behavior of the entity at runtime. [8] In Chemistry Plugin, trigger and reactant are two specific components inherited from Unreal Engine build-in class USceneComponent.

We define three bases enumerate variables, chemistry element, reaction state, and reaction code. Chemistry element is the attribute of trigger and component, the values of chemistry element are none, iron, plant, water, fire, earth, wind, magnet, electric, air, and ice (the initial base element in the chemical engine). The reaction state is the state of trigger and reactant, the values of it are none, started, successfully, failed, and interrupted. Reaction code is the description of reaction type, the values of it are none, assimilation, alienation, increment, and decrement. Whether the trigger and the reactant can react and the type of reaction is stored in the reaction lookup table. The reaction lookup table is a two-dimensional table, and each element is a node that stores the type of reaction.

One of the key questions for implementing Chemistry Plugin is how to handle the communication between the trigger component and reactant component, in other words, how can we start a reaction in the game. In Chemistry Plugin, we use two methods to start the reaction, collision detection, and line trace.

Collision Detection. Unreal Engine provides a delegate for us to bind a user-defined function to the component overlap signature, and when the component collides with another component or entity, the user-defined function will be called. [9] The user-defined function judges whether the external conditions (e.g. temperature) and the internal conditions (e.g. the relationship between trigger and reactant) are met the reaction requirements if true the reaction is started.

Line Trace. In this method, we define a line collision line trace function to detect the entity or component in front of the trigger owner. The specific implementation is to first obtain the position and angle of the owner of the trigger's eyes viewpoint. This position is the start position of the line trace. Then, the end position of the line trace is calculated based on the trigger reach length property. The line trace algorithm is shown as Algorithm 2.

By performing a line trace on the start position and end position, it is determined whether there is a collision with an object. If true, the reaction process is entered.

The process of starting a reaction through the collision detection method and line trace method is shown in Fig. 4.

Another issue is how to achieve the reaction effect in the game, in other words, after we start a reaction through collision detection or line trace, how

Algorithm 2. Line trace
_____

Owner = Triggger.GetOwner()
StartLoc, Rotator = Owner.GetActorEyesViewPoint()
EndLoc = StartLoc + ReachLength · Rotator.Vector
IsHit = LineTraceSingleByChannel(HitComp, StartLoc, EndLoc)
if IsHit **then**
    Reactant = HitComp
    Try start reaction
end if
_____

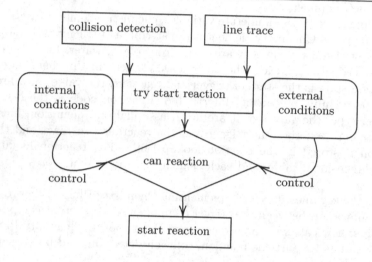

Fig. 4. Collision detection and line trace to start reaction

do we achieve corresponding reaction effects based on different interactions or objects. In Unreal Engine we use the blueprint to achieve this functionality. Blueprint is a visual programming tool that allows for the creation and control of game objects and logic in the Unreal Engine without the need to write code. [10] It is a powerful feature of the Unreal Engine that enables people without programming knowledge to create complex interactive experiences and games.

We create two delegates called on trigger state changed and on reactant state changed for the blueprint to call. When the trigger and reactant start the reaction and all reaction condition is satisfied, the state of the two delegates are changed (e.g. from none to successful). In the blueprint event graph we just assign the delegates and bind our reaction effect functions to these two delegates as Fig. 6, when the state of the trigger or reactant is changed, the corresponding reaction effect function will be called. In the reaction effect function, we can define different reaction effects for different elements. In Fig. 5(a), the character can use ice magic to shoot ice magic ball and when ice magic ball collides with the river attached with water reactant component, the ice is spawned as the consequence of the reaction between the ice trigger component and the water

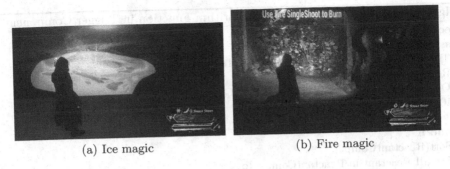

(a) Ice magic   (b) Fire magic

Fig. 5. Reaction effect demonstration in Unreal Engine

reactant component. Also as shown in Fig. 5(b), for a tree, we can add burning particle effects to the reaction effect with the fire element in the reaction function and cause the tree to be destroyed after a few seconds of delay.

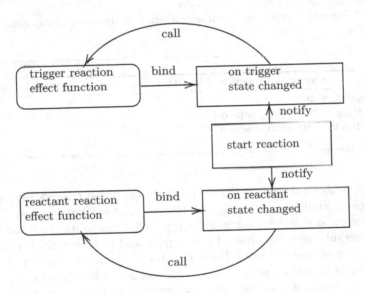

Fig. 6. Bind reaction effect functions to delegates

The final key problem is the reaction sequence and inter-trigger/reactant communication for an entity with multiple triggers or reactants when using the collision detection method to start a reaction. The trigger component has its own collision component, thus the collision between the trigger and reactants may follow a specific sequence due to the collision volumes. However, the reaction sequence should be determined by the implementation-defined rules rather than the order of the collision events. To solve this problem, when the first trigger component collides with another entity, we get the owner of the trigger component, then by using the get components by the class method we can get all

---

Algorithm 3. Sequential reaction Algorithm Function in Trigger Component

---

Require: OtherActor(Collision Actor)
Ensure: Reactant.TriggerNumCnt = 0
  TriggerComps = this.GetCompByClass(Trigger Class)
  ReactantComps =
  OtherActor.GetCompByClass(Reactant Class)
  if ReactantComps is empty **then**
    End reaction
  end if
  Sort(ReactantComps)
  for all Reactant in ReactantComps **do**
    if this Trigger uses Collision Detection **then**
      Reactant.TriggerNumCnt
      $\leftarrow$ Reactant.TriggerNumCnt+1
    end if
  end for
  if Reactant.TriggerNumCnt = Trigger **then**
    for all Reactant in ReactantComps **do**
      Call Sequential reaction Algorithm Function in Reactant Component
    end for
  end if

Algorithm 4. Sequential reaction Algorithm Function in Reactant Component

---

Sort(TriggerComps)
  for all Trigger in TriggerComps **do**
    This Reactant try start reaction
  end for

---

the trigger methods owned by the owner and store these triggers into an array called triggers. Similarly, we can get all the reactant components owned by the reactant owner and store them in an array called reactants. Sort the triggers and the reactants, now the order of the triggers and the reactants is correspond with the order of reactant rules. Use a counter to count the number of triggers that are already colliding with reactant components, when the counter is equal to the size of reactants, we can start the reaction from the first trigger in the triggers array. The algorithm is shown in Algorithm 3 and 4.

4.3 Additional Work

In order to facilitate people other than developers to add elements and reaction rules to the chemical engine, we represent the reaction rule table in a JSON file format and visualize it through a web page. By simply modifying the definition of the enumerated variable Chemistry Element and modifying the reaction rule in JSON file, a new element or reaction rule can be added. Through the webpage, we can also manage the reaction rule. Since the reaction lookup table is loaded at runtime, there is no need to recompile the code after modifying the reaction rules. Simply restart the project to apply the changes. Adding a new element to the chemistry engine requires recompiling the project because it modifies the underlying code.

5 Conclusion

We have implemented an elemental energy chemistry engine based on the philosophy of Nintendo, and applied this chemistry engine to a specific scenario, creating a set of concrete blueprint event graphs that allow for the interaction and reaction of elements. The chemistry engine provides a framework within which the reaction effects can be implemented in the blueprint, allowing for the realization of almost any reaction effect. Furthermore, we have displayed the reaction rules in two formats - JSON files and web pages - to facilitate the customization of reaction rules by non-developers. However, due to the excessive number of external conditions associated with the chemistry engine, this paper has only hard-coded a portion of the external conditions and has not provided an interface for easily adding external conditions. This aspect could be considered a key improvement point, enabling developers to easily add external conditions to the chemistry engine framework implemented in this paper without having to modify the core code of the reaction process. Looking towards the future, we hope to provide an elemental energy chemistry engine that allows for the free definition of element properties and reaction rules (internal conditions) as well as external conditions, with the implementation of reaction effects separated from the engine core code.

Acknowledgment. The authors would like to thank the fund support by Tencent computer system Co. Ltd.

References

1. Szirmay-Kalos, L., Magdics, M.: Adapting game engines to curved spaces. Vis. Comput. **38**(12), 4383–4395 (2022)
2. Vidqvist, J.: Open-world game design: case study: the legend of zelda: breath of the wild (2019)
3. Giakalaras, M.: 3D technologies for cultural heritage. gaming engines. Department of Cultural Technology and Communication, University of Aegean, Lesvos, 81100
4. Thalmann, N.M., Kim, J., Papagiannakis, G., Thalmann, D., Sheng, B.: Computer graphics for metaverse, George Papagiannakis (2022)
5. Qin, Y., Chi, X., Sheng, B., Lau, R.W.H.: Guiderender: large-scale scene navigation based on multi-modal view frustum movement prediction. Vis. Comput. 1–11 (2023)
6. Day, S., Smallwood, W.K., Kuhn, J.: Simulating industrial control systems using node-red and unreal engine 4. In: Choo, K.-K.R., Morris, T., Peterson, G., Imsand, E. (eds.) NCS 2021. LNNS, vol. 310, pp. 13–21. Springer, Cham (2022). https://doi.org/10.1007/978-3-030-84614-5_2
7. Lee, J.: Learning unreal engine game development. Packt Publishing Ltd (2016)

8. Härkönen, T.: Advantages and implementation of entity-component-systems (2019)
9. Zhang, J.: Implementation of common interaction modes based on UE4. In: 2022 IEEE International Conference on Artificial Intelligence and Computer Applications (ICAICA), pp. 436–439. IEEE (2022)
10. Shah, R.: Mastering the art of unreal engine 4-blueprints. Lulu.com (2014)

Enhanced Direct Lighting Using Visibility-Aware Light Sampling

Geonu Noh⬤, Hajin Choi⬤, and Bochang Moon(✉)⬤

Gwangju Institute of Science and Technology, Gwangju 61005, South Korea
bmoon@gist.ac.kr

Abstract. Next event estimation has been widely applied to Monte Carlo rendering methods such as path tracing since estimating direct and indirect lighting separately often enables finding light paths from the eye to the lights effectively. Its success heavily relies on light sampling for direct lighting when a scene contains multiple light sources since each light can contribute differently to the reflected radiance on a surface point. We present a light sampling technique that can guide such a light selection to improve direct lighting. We estimate a spatially-varying function that approximates the contribution of each light on surface points within a discretized local area (i.e., a voxel in an adaptive octree) while considering the visibility between lights and surface points. We then construct a probability distribution function for sampling lights per voxel, which is proportional to our estimated function. We demonstrate that our light sampling technique can significantly improve rendering quality thanks to improved direct lighting with our light sampling.

Keywords: light sampling · direct lighting · next event estimation

1 Introduction

Global illumination methods such as path tracing [16] and bidirectional path tracing [31] have been widely adopted in production rendering scenarios [5,9, 10], where simulating accurate light propagation between lights and 3D virtual models should be conducted. While such Monte Carlo (MC) integration-based algorithms can reduce errors in their rendering images by increasing the number of samples, it often requires non-trivial rendering times to generate a visually acceptable rendering output without noticeable noise.

A commonly adopted technique for reducing the variance in the rendered images is to split the light transport equation into direct and indirect illumination parts and then attempt to connect the eye subpaths, determined by ray tracing from the eye, to lights by casting shadow rays from a surface point (i.e., direct lighting). This simple but effective strategy is commonly referred to as next event estimation (NEE) and has been widely employed in rendering frameworks [15,25] since it often reduces the MC variance drastically.

© The Author(s), under exclusive license to Springer Nature Switzerland AG 2024
B. Sheng et al. (Eds.): CGI 2023, LNCS 14496, pp. 187–198, 2024.
https://doi.org/10.1007/978-3-031-50072-5_15

While this direct lighting is conceptually simple and can be easily implemented, it technically requires determining a sampling probability for selecting a light source when multiple light sources exist in a scene. A straightforward light selection approach is uniform sampling (i.e., allocating the equal probability for each light), but it can be ineffective since the contribution of light sources can vary significantly per light and surface point.

A natural extension to uniform sampling is to assume that all light sources are visible from surface points and to adjust the light selection probability of being proportional to a potential contribution (e.g., light power) of each light source, referred to as spatial sampling [29]. This simple light selection strategy, spatial sampling, can be effective when all light sources are unoccluded from surface points. However, it is often suboptimal when selected light sources are invisible from the points. Unfortunately, exact visibility information between two points (e.g., a surface point and a point on a light) cannot be pre-determined since it requires tracing a shadow ray that is typically computationally expensive. As a result, a computationally efficient process that closely approximates the visibility information is a technical requirement for an ideal light selection process.

As a recent example of guiding light sampling using visibility information, Guo et al. [12] discretized the scene space, i.e., a space determined by the axis-aligned bounding box of a scene, into a 3D regular grid and estimated the visibility between two voxels using uniformly generated but with a small number of visibility samples. Then the stored visibility was used as the light selection probability so that the lights with high probability, which can be likely visible from a surface point, could be more selected than the other lights with low probability. It enables avoiding unnecessary sample allocations to invisible lights, but it can also be sub-optimal when the contributions of multiple visible lights are significantly different. One may extend this method to consider the potential contributions of lights together with their estimated visibility via multiple importance sampling [28,30], but its performance improvement can still be restricted due to the sparse visibility approximation with a uniform grid structure.

This paper also addresses the light sampling problem (i.e., selecting a light for direct lighting at a surface point). However, we approximate more comprehensive information, a potential light contribution (e.g., light power) together with visibility, so that we can guide the light selection more effectively by forming a light sampling probability of being proportional to the contribution of light sources to a surface point. To this end, we estimate a spatially-varying function that approximates the contribution of each light source per local region using an adaptively constructed octree.

We demonstrate that our approach can produce more accurate rendering results (e.g., up to 7× lower errors) than the existing approaches (e.g., spatial sampling and [12]) given equal-time budgets, thanks to improved direct lighting with our light selection for various rendering scenes where multiple lights exist.

2   Related Work

To solve the direct illumination integral, one typically applies a Monte Carlo (MC) integration (i.e., a numerical approximation of the integral), and its approximation quality (i.e., the difference between the approximate value and the unknown ground truth), mainly depends on the randomly chosen light samples. One of the most popular approaches is to reduce the approximation error (i.e., the variance of the MC integration) using carefully selected light samples by adjusting the probability of generating such samples [29]. Such techniques often constructed their sampling probability by taking terms in the direct light transport equation into account (e.g., the emissive light energy [1,23], the bidirectional reflectance distribution function (BRDF) [19], and both the light energy and BRDF [4,6]). Ghosh and Heidrich [11] presented a two-stage sampling method where they applied a Monte Carlo sampling using the BRDF and lights at the first stage and then used a mutation strategy to allocate more samples to partially-occluded regions in the later stage.

Importance sampling for direct lighting has also received attention for rendering scenarios where many lights exist. A well-known approach to making the sampling scalable against many lights (e.g., hundreds of thousands of lights) is to use light clusters maintained in an acceleration structure (e.g., a light tree) and select a light according to their importance (i.e., the radiance contribution at a surface point) [7,17,20,35,36]. Additionally, progressively refining the sample distribution was recently explored [18,24,33] so that the sample distribution for direct lighting can have a similar shape to the unknown radiance contribution as collecting more samples in rendering.

The sophisticated importance sampling aforementioned can be necessary when rendering a scene with environment lights or thousands of lights. Nonetheless, it can be preferable in practice to choose a simpler alternative that does not require an expensive data structure (e.g., light trees) for typical scenes with moderate numbers of small lights. For example, one can select a light according to the light power, the area, and the distance to a surface point, and then sample a point on the selected light [29]. A variant of this technique was implemented, referred to as spatial sampling, in a well-known rendering framework [25]. While this simple approach can behave well when all lights are visible to the shading point, its efficiency gain over the most straightforward approach (i.e., uniform light selection) can disappear when the visibilities between shading points and lights vary significantly. Guo et al. [12] employed a computationally efficient data structure (i.e., a uniform grid), to contain estimated visibility between two voxels, and showed that this estimated visibility could be exploited for selecting a visible light. However, this approach did not consider the relative importance of unoccluded light sources (e.g., light power). Like these simple methods, we focus on rendering scenarios where the number of lights is moderate and propose an improved light sampling using a more comprehensive estimation of light contributions while maintaining a low computational overhead so that our technique can be a practical choice for rendering scenarios where multiple lights exist.

Path Guiding. Importance sampling for indirect lighting also has been actively explored. A widely adopted strategy is to adjust the sampling density of secondary rays to be proportional to the incoming radiance from the rays per surface point [30], often called path guiding. Well-known approaches include

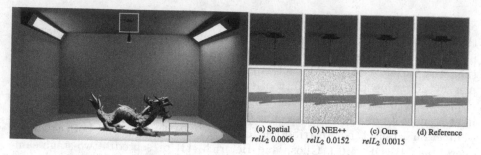

(a) Spatial   (b) NEE++   (c) Ours   (d) Reference
$relL_2$ 0.0066 $relL_2$ 0.0152 $relL_2$ 0.0015

Fig. 1. Equal-time comparisons (in twenty secs) of light sampling techniques for a scene with three lights. We render the scene without indirect illumination to show the visual differences among the tested methods clearly. We measured the numerical accuracy of rendered images using a relative L_2 error ($relL_2$) [27].

approximating the contribution of indirect light radiance with the Gaussian mixture model [13,34] and a spatial-directional tree [8,21]. Rath et al. [26] recently showed that considering the variance of the pixel estimator can make path guiding effective. A popular alternative to such approaches is to devise a deep neural network that can guide the sampling of indirect light paths [2,14,22,37–39]. The path guiding techniques are orthogonal to importance sampling for direct lighting, including ours, and can be used together for more effective rendering.

3 Problem Statement and Motivation

This paper aims to reduce the variance of direct lighting by carefully choosing lights to be sampled according to their estimated contribution. This section provides a background on direct lighting and present a light selection problem for direct lighting, followed by a motivation for our light selection approach. The computation of the direct illumination can be formulated into an area form [29]:

$$L_d(x, \omega) = \int_A L_e(x, x')\rho(x, x', \omega)V(x, x')G(x, x')\mathrm{d}x', \tag{1}$$

which produces the outgoing radiance $L_d(x, \omega)$ on a surface point x with direction ω by integrating the emitted radiance $L_e(x, x')$ from the points x' on the surface A of light sources. $\rho(x, x', \omega)$ is the bidirectional reflectance distribution function (BRDF), $V(x, x')$ is the visibility (one if x and x' are mutually visible and zero otherwise), and the geometric term $G(x, x') = \frac{\cos\theta_x \cos\theta_{x'}}{\|x-x'\|^2}$. A Monte Carlo (MC) estimator for the direct lighting (Eq. 1) can be written by

$$\langle L_d(x, \omega) \rangle = \frac{L_e(x, x')\rho(x, x', \omega)V(x, x')G(x, x')}{p(x'|x)}, \tag{2}$$

which provides an unbiased estimate of the ground truth radiance $L_d(x, \omega)$ by randomly selecting a light sample x' given the surface point x. This sampling process is controlled by the selection probability, probability density function (PDF) $p(x'|x)$. Note that one can simply take an averaged value of the estimates when selecting multiple light samples.

The PDF $p(x'|x)$ can be decomposed into two terms, one for selecting a light and the other for sampling a point on the chosen light, i.e., $p(x'|x) = p(E_l|x)p(x'|E_l)$ where E_l is a l-th light ($l \in [1, L]$) given L lights in the scene.

A common choice of choosing E_l (i.e., $p(E_l|x)$) is to consider the contribution of the light into the outgoing radiance $L_d(x, \omega)$. For example, a well-known renderer, PBRT [25], exploits the spatial sampling strategy that varies the PDF of selecting a light per a discretized scene region. Specifically, it divides a scene space into M voxels, each of which contains a PDF (e.g., $p(E_l|x)$ for surface points x in the m-th voxel V_m). The spatial sampling constructs the probability $p(E_l|x)$ for selecting the l-th light E_l to be proportional to the following function:

$$f(x, E_l|x \in V_m) = \frac{1}{N_m} \sum_{i=1}^{N_m} \frac{L_e(x_i, x_i')G(x_i, x_i')}{p(x_i'|E_l)}, \tag{3}$$

which is computed using N_m number of randomly generated points x_i inside the voxel and light samples x_i' on the l-th light. The function $f(\cdot)$ varies per voxel and light, and thus the function should be evaluated for each voxel and light using the randomly selected points x_i and x_i'. Then, the PDF $p(E_l|x)$ at a surface point x in the m-th voxel is determined to be proportional to the $f(\cdot)$, i.e., $p(E_l|x) \propto f(\cdot)$.

The PDF $p(x'|E_l)$ of selecting a specific point x' on the l-th light depends on the properties of the light (e.g., the shape) and was well-established in an early method [29]. We employ the existing technique for the PDF $p(x'|E_l)$ and refer to PBRT [25] for more details on this sampling.

Our Motivation for the Light Selection $p(E_l|x)$. The estimated direct illumination term ($\langle L_d(x, \omega) \rangle$ in Eq. 2) is an unbiased estimate of the ground truth $L_d(x, \omega)$. Still, it typically suffers from non-trivial variance (thus a noisy estimate) unless many samples are used. As a result, a careful light selection strategy, whose PDF varies per surface point x, is required to minimize the variance of the estimate.

Spatial sampling offers a simple means that builds a spatially-varying PDF using a discretized data structure (i.e., voxels), but it does not consider the visibility $V(x, x')$ between two points x and x' (see Eq. 3). Similarly, Guo et al. [12] proposed NEE++ that is an improved direct light sampling considering voxel-to-voxel visibility. Then, given a surface point, it tries to choose only visible lights that can contribute to the radiance but does not consider relative importance among visible lights introduced by the other terms such as $L_e(x_i, x_i')$ in Eq. 2.

To make the direct lighting more effective, we extend the spatial sampling into a more comprehensive one that includes the visibility term additionally while considering the original terms ($L_e(x_i, x_i')$ and $G(x_i, x_i')$). Figure 1 shows an example result where the existing techniques (spatial sampling [25] and NEE++ [12]) do not effectively reduce the noise from the direct illumination due to their incomplete consideration. On the other hand, our technique shows a rendering

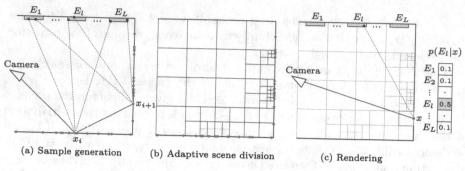

Fig. 2. As a pre-processing step, we determine the surface points through path tracing with one sample per pixel (a) and split the space adaptively according to the density of vertices to estimate the contribution of each local region from each light (b). Then, we perform the original path tracing with direct lighting whose light selection probability is proportional to our target function stored in the octree (c).

result with much-reduced noise thanks to a more effective light sampling, which will be presented in the following section.

4   Visibility-Aware Light Sampling with an Adaptive Octree

This section presents a simple but effective light sampling by estimating spatially-varying light contributions. Analogously in the existing sampling strategy (e.g., spatial sampling), we discretize the scene space into multiple voxels, each of which contains a localized target function:

$$g(x, E_l | x \in V_m) = \sum_{i=1}^{N_m} \frac{L_e(x_i, x_i')G(x_i, x_i')V(x_i, x_i')}{N_m p(x_i'|E_l)}, \tag{4}$$

which approximates the l-th light contribution to the points within a local space (i.e., the m-th voxel V_m). The major modification to the existing one (Eq. 3) is that we incorporate the visibility term $V(x_i, x_i')$ so that visible lights can have more chance to be selected for direct lighting.

Our next task is to compute the localized function per voxel for each light using N_m samples so that the light selection PDF $p(E_l|x)$ (i.e., a probability of selecting l-th light at the surface point x within m-th voxel) can be constructed to be proportional to the target function (i.e., $p(E_l|x) \propto g(\cdot)$). Figure 2 illustrates our framework where we estimate our localized target function as a pre-processing (Sect. 4.1) and perform the rendering using direct lighting with our light sampling.

4.1   Estimation of Our Localized Target Function

We estimate the localized target function $g(x, E_l | x \in V_m)$ (Eq. 4) to locally vary the light selection probability $p(E_l|x)$ for direct lighting in the original rendering. Analogously in spatial sampling (in Sect. 3), we discretize the scene space into disjoint voxels where each voxel contains L light contributions, i.e., $g(x, E_1 | x \in V_m), ..., g(x, E_L | x \in V_m)$. Note that all the points x within a voxel V_m share the same target function, $g(x, E_l | x \in V_m)$, and thus we can reduce its approximation errors by creating more voxels. Unfortunately, estimation of the target function requires non-trivial computational efforts since each voxel should evaluate N_m samples (see Eq. 4). As a result, we should employ a simple but compact data structure that approximates the light contributions appropriately without forming a large number of voxels.

To this end, we present an octree-based estimation where each leaf node (a voxel) estimates L light contributions. Specifically, we perform path tracing to collect samples (L-dimensional vectors) for constructing the octree. We generate one sample per pixel to make the computational overhead of this process small and set the maximum ray depth of the path tracing to three to approximate light contributions for scene areas where direct lighting can be potentially performed, i.e., not just the region intersected by the camera rays. Whenever we find an intersection point x_i, we cast a shadow ray towards a light sample x_i' for each light and evaluate

$$g(x_i, E_l) = \frac{L_e(x_i, x_i') G(x_i, x_i') V(x_i, x_i')}{p(x_i' | E_l)}. \tag{5}$$

Note that the $g(x_i, E_l)$ is computed for each light (i.e., for $E_1, ..., E_L$) per a surface point x_i and thus we have an L-dimensional value at a surface point x_i. We treat the $\mathbf{g}(x_i) = \{g(x_i, E_1), ..., g(x_i, E_L)\}$ as a sample in $\mathbb{R}^L$ for our octree construction.

Once the samples are generated, we construct an adaptive octree whose leaf node contains roughly the same number of samples $\mathbf{g}(x_i)$. Note that the density of surface points x_i is typically non-uniform, and thus the voxel size of each leaf node needs to be adaptively determined by the density of the points. To control this adaptive process, we take an input parameter that controls the number of leaf nodes, which will be detailed in the subsequent paragraph.

After collecting N_m samples for each voxel (i.e., a leaf node in the tree), we compute our localized target function $g(x, E_l | x \in V_m)$ (Eq. 4) using the N_m samples (i.e., $\mathbf{g}(x_i)$ whose $x_i \in V_m$). Note that once the tree is generated (i.e., evaluating the target function per each leaf node), we do not need to store the individual samples. Once this tree-building process is completed, we perform the original rendering, i.e., a standard path tracing with direct lighting. For direct lighting in the rendering process, we select a light according to the light selection probability $p(E_l | x)$ that is proportional to our target function.

Implementation Details. We initially divide the bounding box of the scene space into $4 \times 4 \times 4$ equal-sized voxels (i.e., a uniform octree with depth two). Then, we recursively divide the voxels by limiting the number of samples inside the voxels. Specifically, we split a voxel only if the number of samples within the voxel is larger than $\frac{4N}{T}$ where N and T are the total sample count and a user-specified parameter that controls the number of leaf nodes, respectively. We observed that

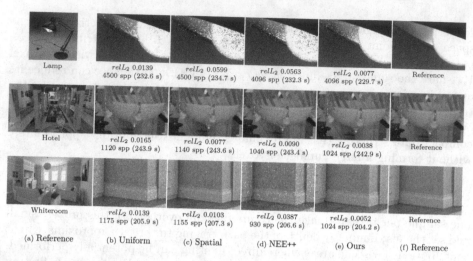

Fig. 3. Equal-time comparisons of light sampling techniques. We vary the samples per pixel (spp) per each method for the same-time test. The Lamp scene has two lights (in the bulb and on the ceiling), the Hotel has nine area lights, and the Whiteroom has eight area lights. The times in the parenthesis are the total rendering times, including the overheads of tested methods.

the number of leaf nodes increases roughly proportional to the parameter T with this setting. We set the T to 4096 unless otherwise specified. We integrated our light selection into a well-known rendering framework, PBRT [25]. The original implementation of PBRT treats each primitive of a mesh light as an individual light source, increasing the number of lights L unnecessarily. We modified the existing implementation to treat a mesh light as a single light source.

5 Results and Discussion

We compare our method with existing light sampling techniques, spatial sampling [25] and NEE++ [12]. As a baseline, we also test the most straightforward choice, uniform sampling, which assigns the same probability for all lights. We use path tracing while varying the light sampling strategy for direct lighting. All tests have been done on a PC with an AMD Ryzen 3990X CPU.

Comparisons of Light Sampling Methods. Figure 3 shows equal-time comparisons of our method and existing light sampling techniques. Spatial sampling and NEE++ produce higher errors than the uniform sampling method for the Lamp and Whiteroom scene. It indicates that considering a partial term (e.g., light sampling without visibility consideration or only using visibility estimation) is not robust. Ours, however, consistently generates lower errors than the baseline and the existing methods, thanks to our more accurate estimation of light contribution. In addition, NEE++ fails to capture the spatially varying visibility due to their use of sparse uniform structure, worsening the results even than the

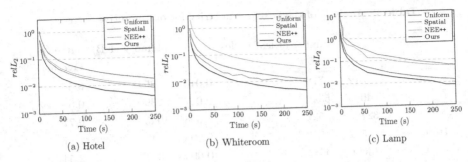

Fig. 4. Numerical convergences of path tracing with different light selection strategies.

Table 1. Breakdowns of our total rendering times (in secs) for the results in Fig. 3.

Scene	spp	Sample generation	Octree building	Rendering	Total
Lamp	4096	0.12	0.47	229.1	229.7
Hotel	1024	0.74	1.78	240.4	242.9
Whiteroom	1024	0.63	1.21	202.3	204.2

uniform sampling method even in the relatively simple scene with respect to the visibility (i.e., the Lamp). On the other hand, our selection using an adaptive octree structure makes a much-improved result than the existing methods, e.g., more than 7× lower errors than NEE++. We also test the numerical convergence of the tested methods over time in Fig. 4. As shown in the figure, the benefit of our technique for path tracing is consistently maintained over time.

Our Computational Overhead. Table 1 shows a breakdown of the total rendering times reported in Fig. 3. Note that our pre-processing is decomposed into two stages, the sample generation and the octree construction (see Fig. 2). As seen in the table, our computational overhead is minor (e.g., 0.257% to 1.046%) in the total times, given the offline settings.

Analysis of Our Voxel Granularity. Our method controls the voxel granularity of the octree by a user-specified parameter T (discussed in Sect. 4). Table 2 shows our computational and memory overheads with rendering accuracy by varying the T. Using a large T (and thus many voxels) does not necessarily improve the rendering quality since the number of samples, $g(x_i)$ used to construct the localized target function within a voxel, decreases and thus leads to noisy estimates of the light contributions. Also, with a small T, the rendering quality degrades as our light selection strategy cannot appropriately capture the locally varying light contributions due to a high discretization error. Consequently, we set the T to the chosen number, 4096, for all tested scenes.

Limitations and Future Work. The main limitation of the proposed method is that, like the other light selection methods, it cannot drastically improve the rendering quality for the scenes where most of the scene regions are lit by indirect

Table 2. Analysis of the voxel granularity for our adaptive octree.

Scene	T	Number of leaf nodes	relL$_2$	Memory (KB)	Time (s) Overhead
Lamp	512	778	0.0102	35	0.50
	4096	5349	0.0077	239	0.59
	32768	43527	0.0081	1945	0.77
Hotel	512	596	0.0051	43	1.97
	4096	4789	0.0038	345	2.54
	32768	38914	0.0037	2801	2.99
Whiteroom	512	505	0.0073	34	1.47
	4096	4537	0.0052	309	1.90
	32768	39250	0.0089	2672	2.21

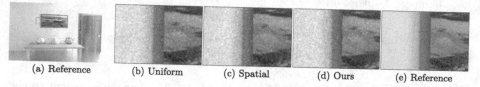

(a) Reference   (b) Uniform   (c) Spatial   (d) Ours   (e) Reference

Fig. 5. Failure cases of the light sampling techniques for the Veach-Ajar scene with 4K spp. The spatial sampling ($relL_2$: 0.104) and ours ($relL_2$: 0.103) become ineffective and do not improve the uniform sampling ($relL_2$: 0.106).

lighting. Figure 5 shows a clear example where our method does not improve the rendering quality compared to the baseline (i.e., uniform sampling). Given the specific scene setting, light sources are located behind the door, and thus our light selection for direct lighting cannot be effective. Note that this is also a counter-example of the use of direct lighting.

In addition, our target function (Eq. 4) does not fully consider the direct lighting integrand (Eq. 2) since we do not consider the BRDF. Note that our method is unbiased, like the other light selection methods, and this partial consideration does not indicate that one cannot use general materials. Nevertheless, it is desirable to extend our method to a more comprehensive one with BRDF for further improving direct lighting. Also, we test our light sampling with unidirectional path tracing, but it would also be interesting to integrate our sampling into other light transport techniques (e.g., bidirectional path tracing [31] and metropolis light transport [32]) and path-reusing techniques (e.g., [3]). We leave such extensions to future work.

Acknowledgements. We thank the anonymous reviewers for feedback on our paper and the following authors and artists for the 3D models or scenes: Asian Dragon (the Stanford Computer Graphics Laboratory), Lamp (UP3D), Whiteroom (Jay-Artist), and Veach-Ajar (Benedikt Bitterli). The Hotel scene was bought from TurboSquid.

This work was supported in part by Ministry of Culture, Sports and Tourism and Korea Creative Content Agency (No. R2021080001) and by the National Research Foundation of Korea (NRF) grant funded by the Korea government (MSIT) (No. RS-2023-00207939).

References

1. Agarwal, S., Ramamoorthi, R., Belongie, S., Jensen, H.W.: Structured importance sampling of environment maps. ACM Trans. Graph. **22**(3), 605–612 (2003)
2. Bako, S., Meyer, M., DeRose, T., Sen, P.: Offline deep importance sampling for Monte Carlo path tracing. Comput. Graph. Forum **38**(7), 527–542 (2019)
3. Bitterli, B., Wyman, C., Pharr, M., Shirley, P., Lefohn, A., Jarosz, W.: Spatiotemporal reservoir resampling for real-time ray tracing with dynamic direct lighting. ACM Trans. Graph. **39**(4), 1–17 (2020)
4. Burke, D., Ghosh, A., Heidrich, W.: Bidirectional importance sampling for direct illumination. In: Proceedings of the 16th Eurographics Conference on Rendering Techniques, pp. 147–156 (2005)
5. Burley, B., et al.: The design and evolution of Disney's Hyperion renderer. ACM Trans. Graph. **37**(3), 1–22 (2018)
6. Clarberg, P., Akenine-Möllery, T.: Practical product importance sampling for direct illumination. Comput. Graph. Forum **27**(2), 681–690 (2008)
7. Conty Estevez, A., Kulla, C.: Importance sampling of many lights with adaptive tree splitting. Proc. ACM Comput. Graph. Interact. Tech. **1**(2), 1–17 (2018)
8. Diolatzis, S., Gruson, A., Jakob, W., Nowrouzezahrai, D., Drettakis, G.: Practical product path guiding using linearly transformed cosines. Comput. Graph. Forum **39**(4), 23–33 (2020)
9. Fascione, L., et al.: Manuka: a batch-shading architecture for spectral path tracing in movie production. ACM Trans. Graph. **37**(3), 1–18 (2018)
10. Georgiev, I., et al.: Arnold: a brute-force production path tracer. ACM Trans. Graph. **37**(3), 1–12 (2018)
11. Ghosh, A., Heidrich, W.: Correlated visibility sampling for direct illumination. Vis. Comput. **22**(9), 693–701 (2006)
12. Guo, J.J., Eisemann, M., Eisemann, E.: Next event estimation++: visibility mapping for efficient light transport simulation. Comput. Graph. Forum **39**(7), 205–217 (2020)
13. Herholz, S., Elek, O., Vorba, J., Lensch, H., Křivánek, J.: Product importance sampling for light transport path guiding. Comput. Graph. Forum **35**(4), 67–77 (2016)
14. Huo, Y., Wang, R., Zheng, R., Xu, H., Bao, H., Yoon, S.E.: Adaptive incident radiance field sampling and reconstruction using deep reinforcement learning. ACM Trans. Graph. **39**(1), 1–17 (2020)
15. Jakob, W.: Mitsuba renderer (2010). http://www.mitsuba-renderer.org
16. Kajiya, J.T.: The rendering equation. SIGGRAPH Comput. Graph. **20**(4), 143–150 (1986)
17. Ki, H., Oh, K.: A GPU-based light hierarchy for real-time approximate illumination. Vis. Comput. **24**(7), 649–658 (2008)
18. Lai, Y.C., Chou, H.T., Chen, K.W., Fan, S.: Robust and efficient adaptive direct lighting estimation. Vis. Comput. **31**(1), 83–91 (2015)
19. Lawrence, J., Rusinkiewicz, S., Ramamoorthi, R.: Efficient BRDF importance sampling using a factored representation. ACM Trans. Graph. **23**(3), 496–505 (2004)

20. Liu, Y., Xu, K., Yan, L.Q.: Adaptive BRDF-oriented multiple importance sampling of many lights. Comput. Graph. Forum **38**(4), 123–133 (2019)
21. Müller, T., Gross, M., Novák, J.: Practical path guiding for efficient light-transport simulation. Comput. Graph. Forum **36**(4), 91–100 (2017)
22. Müller, T., Mcwilliams, B., Rousselle, F., Gross, M., Novák, J.: Neural importance sampling. ACM Trans. Graph. **38**(5), 1–19 (2019)
23. Ostromoukhov, V., Donohue, C., Jodoin, P.M.: Fast hierarchical importance sampling with blue noise properties. ACM Trans. Graph. **23**(3), 488–495 (2004)
24. Pantaleoni, J.: Importance sampling of many lights with reinforcement lightcuts learning. arXiv preprint arXiv:1911.10217 (2019)
25. Pharr, M., Jakob, W., Humphreys, G.: Physically Based Rendering: From Theory to Implementation, 3rd edn. Morgan Kaufmann Publishers Inc., Burlington (2016)
26. Rath, A., Grittmann, P., Herholz, S., Vévoda, P., Slusallek, P., Křivánek, J.: Variance-aware path guiding. ACM Trans. Graph. **39**(4), 1–12 (2020)
27. Rousselle, F., Knaus, C., Zwicker, M.: Adaptive sampling and reconstruction using greedy error minimization. ACM Trans. Graph. **30**(6), 1–12 (2011)
28. Sbert, M., Havran, V.: Adaptive multiple importance sampling for general functions. Vis. Comput. **33**(6), 845–855 (2017)
29. Shirley, P., Wang, C., Zimmerman, K.: Monte Carlo techniques for direct lighting calculations. ACM Trans. Graph. **15**(1), 1–36 (1996)
30. Veach, E.: Robust Monte Carlo methods for light transport simulation. Stanford University (1998)
31. Veach, E., Guibas, L.: Bidirectional estimators for light transport. In: Sakas, G., Müller, S., Shirley, P. (eds.) Photorealistic Rendering Techniques, pp. 145–167. Springer, Heidelberg (1995). https://doi.org/10.1007/978-3-642-87825-1_11
32. Veach, E., Guibas, L.J.: Metropolis light transport. In: Proceedings of the 24th Annual Conference on Computer Graphics and Interactive Techniques, SIG-GRAPH 1997, pp. 65–76. ACM Press/Addison-Wesley Publishing Co. (1997)
33. Vévoda, P., Kondapaneni, I., Křivánek, J.: Bayesian online regression for adaptive direct illumination sampling. ACM Trans. Graph. **37**(4), 1–12 (2018)
34. Vorba, J., Karlík, O., Šik, M., Ritschel, T., Křivánek, J.: On-line learning of parametric mixture models for light transport simulation. ACM Trans. Graph. **33**(4), 1–11 (2014)
35. Walter, B., Fernandez, S., Arbree, A., Bala, K., Donikian, M., Greenberg, D.P.: Lightcuts: a scalable approach to illumination. ACM Trans. Graph. **24**(3), 1098–1107 (2005)
36. Wang, Y.C., Wu, Y.T., Li, T.M., Chuang, Y.Y.: Learning to cluster for rendering with many lights. ACM Trans. Graph. **40**(6), 1–10 (2021)
37. Zheng, Q., Zwicker, M.: Learning to importance sample in primary sample space. Comput. Graph. Forum **38**(2), 169–179 (2019)
38. Zhu, S., et al.: Hierarchical neural reconstruction for path guiding using hybrid path and photon samples. ACM Trans. Graph. **40**(4), 1–16 (2021)
39. Zhu, S., et al.: Photon-driven neural reconstruction for path guiding. ACM Trans. Graph. **41**(1), 1–15 (2021)

Point Cloud Rendering via Multi-plane NeRF

Dongmei Ma[1], Juan Cao[2], and Zhonggui Chen[1(✉)] [iD]

[1] School of Informatics, Xiamen University, Xiamen, China
chenzhonggui@xmu.edu.cn
[2] School of Mathematical Sciences, Xiamen University, Xiamen, China

Abstract. We propose a new neural point cloud rendering method by combining point cloud multi-plane projection and NeRF [12]. Existing point-based rendering methods often rely on the high-quality geometry of point clouds. Meanwhile, NeRF and its extensions usually query the RGB and volume density of each point through neural networks, thus leading to a low inference efficiency. In this paper, we project point features to multiple random depth planes and feed them into a 3D convolutional neural network to predict the RGB and volume density maps. Then we synthesize a novel view through volume rendering. Projecting point features to multiple planes reduces the impact of geometry error and improves the rendering efficiency. Experimental results on the DTU and ScanNet dataset show that our approach achieves state-of-the-art results. Our source code is available at https://github.com/Mayxmu/PCMP-NeRF.

Keywords: Point cloud rendering · Neural radiance fields · Novel view synthesis

1 Introduction

Novel view synthesis (NVS) creates an immersive experience by synthesizing photo-realistic images from different viewpoints in a 3D scene, which is the technical base for the metaverse to become a kind of concrete expression in the future [18]. Image-based rendering (IBR) methods synthesize a novel view through view warping and image inpainting [9] from given images and an approximate geometric model. They require less computational cost than physically based rendering but usually only work well for novel views close to the original.

Recently, NeRF [12] and its extensions [14,15,24] train multi-layer perceptions (MLPs) to map the coordinates in the entire 3D space to the corresponding RGB and volume density, then synthesize photo-realistic images through volume rendering. However, due to unnecessary point sampling in blank space and neural point querying, these methods usually lead to long training and inference time unless carefully optimize all core components like Instant-ngp [13].

Representing 3D scenes as point clouds is an effective way to avoid sampling in blank space. However, previous point rendering methods usually ignore the complex occlusion relationships between 3D objects and tend to display artifacts.

B. Sheng et al. (Eds.): CGI 2023, LNCS 14496, pp. 199–210, 2024.
https://doi.org/10.1007/978-3-031-50072-5_16

To alleviate this problem, Point-NeRF [22] and Point2NeRF [26] directly generate NeRFs from 3D point clouds and made it a success. Unfortunately, their training and inference efficiency is still limited by the neural point querying. In this paper, we present a new NVS system via point multi-plane projection and volume rendering. We learn the features of every point and project them onto random depth planes to form feature maps. The feature maps are fed into a 3D CNN to produce their RGB and volume density maps, then we render them by volume rendering. Before feeding the feature maps into the network, we employ a positional encoding on them, which enables the 3D CNN to represent higher-frequency functions.

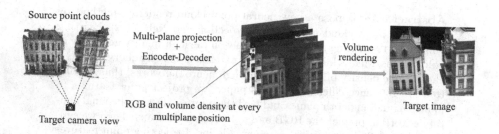

Fig. 1. Overview of our proposed method.

The overview of our method is shown in Fig. 1. By avoiding the point query, we achieve more efficient rendering than NeRF-based methods. Further, since we check the visibility of points, our approach is less susceptible to the geometric accuracy of point clouds than point-based rendering. We evaluate our method on the DTU dataset and ScanNet dataset, and the results show that our method performs better than prior works.

To summarize, our technical contributions are:

- A new approach for synthesizing novel views by projecting point features to hierarchical randomly sampled depth planes, which proves robust to geometry noise and performs relatively high inference efficiency.
- By introducing volume rendering, high-quality rendering can also be achieved on sparse point clouds.
- Our method presents more texture details of 3D scenes by transforming point features with positional encoding.

2   Related Work

We classify point-based view synthesis methods into two categories, one directly renders point clouds and the other combines with NeRF.

Point-Based Novel View Synthesis. The traditional point cloud rendering method assigns a disk to each point and estimates their normal vector and radius, then rasterizes and combines the disk pieces to render a complete surface. Bui et al. [3] leveraged a CNN to learn the mapping of disk fragments to the surface. To reduce the reliance on the geometry of point clouds, Wang et al. [20] and Zhang et al. [25] optimized point clouds using a differentiable renderer to match the target rendering.

NPBG [2] rasterizes the featured point clouds and uses a 3D CNN to render the image without the step of splatting. Subsequently, a series of similar methods [11,17] were proposed to rasterize and render point clouds with different neural networks. Dai et al. [6] projected the point features to multiple planes and directly synthesized the image through a 3D CNN. SynSin [21] projects a single-view image to 3D space and leverages a generative adversarial network (GAN) to generate the featured point cloud, then uses a neural renderer to synthesize a novel view. NPBG++ [16] directly utilizes the multiple views to predict the point features, which makes the model generalizable and improves the rendering efficiency. Although these methods eliminate the step of splatting, they still expect an accurate point cloud geometry.

Point Cloud Rendering with NeRF. Point-NeRF [22] is the first approach to combine NeRF and point representation, which reconstructs 3D point clouds through the multi-view stereo technique [23] and adopts an MLP to regress the point feature to RGB and volume density. To reduce the number of parameters that need to be trained, Point2NeRF [26] introduces Hypernetwork [7] into the pipeline. Recently, Huang et al. [8] simplified the modeling of NeRF to the location of intersections of rays and point clouds. Since they only sampled one point when rendering one pixel, they achieved more efficient rendering, but it requires a high-quality point cloud geometry.

3   Method

Our approach projects a featured point cloud to multi-plane feature maps and predicts their RGB and σ maps, then renders a photo-realistic image by using volume rendering. The pipeline of our method is shown in Fig. 2.

3.1   3D Representation

Learnable Point Feature. We assign each point a feature vector $\mathbf{F}$, which is initialized with its 3D coordinates $\mathbf{p}$ and 3D RGB $\mathbf{c}$. In addition, we use a 5D vector $\mathbf{a}$ to represent the appearance characteristics such as reflection of the points. When training the neural network, we backpropagate the gradient to the point features $\mathbf{F}$, which means that our point feature is learnable.

Since the appearance of a point is usually view-dependent, we concatenate the point feature with the 3D normalized view direction $\mathbf{v}$ of each point, so that the neural network can accurately predict the color of the point at different viewpoints. Finally, the dimension of the point feature $\mathbf{F}$ is 14 (3+3+5+3).

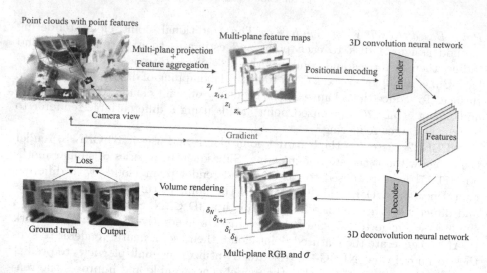

Fig. 2. The pipeline of our approach.

Multi-planar Neural Radiance Field

Multi-plane Hierarchical Sampling Strategy. Supposing the resolution for rendering is $H \times W$, we project the points within the minimum depth z_n and maximum depth z_f of the point cloud to N planes with the size of $H \times W$ according to the known camera poses. As Fig. 3 shows, we divide the camera frustum in depth $[z_n, z_f]$ evenly into N small frustums. In the p-th frustum, we sample a plane at a random depth $z_p \in [z_{pn}, z_{pf}]$, whose size corresponds to the rendering resolution. In fact, we sample uniformly at random from within each small frustum:

$$z_p \sim \mathcal{U}\left[z_n + \frac{p-1}{N}(z_f - z_n), z_n + \frac{p}{N}(z_f - z_n)\right]. \qquad (1)$$

Point Feature Projection. When projecting the point features onto the feature plane, in order to reduce the dependence on the quality of the point clouds, we consider all points in the small frustum. Assuming that the coordinates of a pixel on the feature plane are (x, y, z), n is the total number of points in the small frustum and i represents the index of a point. The feature $\mathbf{F}_{(x,y,z)}$ of this pixel is calculated by the equation:

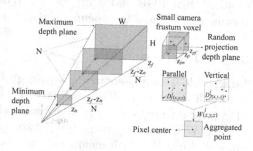

Fig. 3. Point projection and aggregation.

$$\mathbf{F}_{(x,y,z)} = \frac{\sum_{i=1}^{n} w^i_{(x,y,z)} \times \mathbf{F}^i_{(x,y,z)}}{\sum_{i=1}^{n} w^i_{(x,y,z)}}, \tag{2}$$

$$w^i_{(x,y,z)} = (1 - D^i_{1(x,y,z)})^\alpha \times (\frac{1}{1 + D^i_{2(x,y,z)}})^\beta, \tag{3}$$

where $\mathbf{F}^i_{(x,y,z)}$ is the feature of the i-th point, and $w^i_{(x,y,z)}$ is the weight of the i-th point aggregated to this pixel. As shown in Fig. 3, $w^i_{(x,y,z)}$ is calculated based on two distances: $D^i_{1(x,y,z)}$ is the Euclidean distance in the parallel direction between the pixel center and the coordinates that the i-th point projected to the feature plane. $D^i_{2(x,y,z)}$ is the depth distance between the i-th point and the feature plane. The parameters α and β control the blending weight of these two distances.

3.2 Volume Rendering

We feed the feature maps of all planes to a 3D CNN to predict a 3-channel RGB map $\mathbf{c}$ and a 1-channel volume density map σ. Then we render the $\mathbf{c}$ and σ maps following the principles introduced by classic volume rendering [12]:

$$\hat{\mathbf{C}} = \sum_{i=1}^{N} T_i(1 - \exp(-\sigma_{z_i}\delta_{z_i}))\mathbf{c}_{z_i}, \quad T_i = \exp(-\sum_{j=1}^{i-1} \sigma_{z_i}\delta_{z_i}) : \mathbb{R}^2 \rightarrow \mathbb{R}^+ \tag{4}$$

where T_i represents the accumulated transmittance map from the first plane to the i-th plane. $T_i(x, y)$ can be considered as the probability of a ray that travels from the camera to a pixel (x, y, z_i) on the i-th plane without being occluded. δ_{z_i} is the depth distance between plane $i-1$ and plane i.

3.3 Network and Training Design

Network Architecture. We adopt a 3D UNet as the backbone, and the network architecture is shown in Fig. 4. The network receives multi-plane feature maps as inputs, and outputs a set of RGB maps $\{\mathbf{c}_{z_i} \mid i = 1, \cdots, N\}$ and volume density maps $\{\sigma_{z_i} \mid i = 1, \cdots, N\}$.

The advantage of using a 3D CNN is that the network can automatically learn the information of adjacent pixels and depths in the perceptive field, thereby reducing the impact of geometry errors.

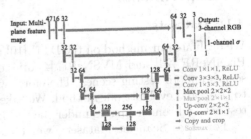

Fig. 4. The 3D UNet architecture.

Positional Encoding. We apply a function $\gamma : \mathbb{R}^3 \rightarrow \mathbb{R}^{3 \times 2 \times L}$ on the feature of each pixel in the feature maps, where L is a hyperparameter. In order to use as low-dimensional feature vectors as possible to learn higher frequent features of the point cloud, we encode $\mathbf{c}$, $\mathbf{p}$, and $\mathbf{v}$ separately. We lift the dimension of $\mathbf{c}$ and $\mathbf{p}$ to $3 \times 2 \times L_1$, then add $\gamma(\mathbf{c})$ and $\gamma(\mathbf{p})$ similar to [19]. In terms of $\mathbf{v}$, we lift its dimension to $3 \times 2 \times L_2$. The encoding function γ we use is:

$$\gamma(\mathbf{p}) = [\sin 2^0 \pi \mathbf{p}, \cos 2^0 \pi \mathbf{p}, \cdots, \sin 2^{L-1} \pi \mathbf{p}, \cos 2^{L-1} \pi \mathbf{p}] \tag{5}$$

Loss Function. There are two terms in the loss function: RGB L1 loss and perceptual loss. Specifically, we extract features of the output images and ground truths through 'conv1-2', 'conv2-2', 'conv3-2', 'conv4-2', and 'conv5-2' layers from a VGG-19 network. The perceptual loss is computed as a weighted sum of the L1 loss on each extracted feature. The total loss is calculated as:

$$\mathcal{L} = \lambda_c \|\mathbf{C}_{gt} - \hat{\mathbf{C}}\|_1 + \sum_{i=1}^{5} \lambda_i \|\phi_i(\mathbf{C}_{gt}) - \phi_i(\hat{\mathbf{C}})\|_1, \tag{6}$$

where $\mathbf{C}_{gt}$ and $\hat{\mathbf{C}}$ are the RGB of ground truth and output. $\{\phi_i \mid i = 1, \cdots, 5\}$ are layers of VGG-19 network. λ_c is the weight of RGB L1 loss, and $\{\lambda_i \mid i = 1, \cdots, 5\}$ are hyperparameters to balance the respective perceptive loss term.

Feature Optimization. We update the feature $\mathbf{F}$ according to the weight by which it is aggregated to the pixel on the feature plane. Note that we do not update the view direction $\mathbf{v}$ of each point. In the light of the chain rule, we update the point feature $\mathbf{F}$ as:

$$\mathbf{F} = \mathbf{F} - l_{pr} \times w^i_{(x,y,z)} \times \mathbf{g}_{(x,y,z)}, \tag{7}$$

where l_{pr} indicates the learning rate for the point feature, and $\mathbf{g}_{(x,y,z)}$ is the gradient derived from the loss function to the features of each pixel (x, y, z) on the feature map. $w^i_{(x,y,z)}$ represents the aggregated weight of the i-th point to the pixel (x, y, z).

4 Experiments

4.1 Datasets

We evaluate our method on the DTU [10] and ScanNet [5] datasets respectively. PixelNeRF [24] and MVSNeRF [4] divided the DTU dataset into 88 training scenes and 16 testing scenes. Therefore, we select 10 scenes from their test set to train and evaluate our method. We take 1/8 of the views in each scene as the test set and render images under the resolution of 512×640.

For the ScanNet dataset, we train and evaluate our approach on 'scene0000_00', 'scene0010_00', 'scene0101_00', and 'scene0241_00'. We select 12.5% of all views as the test set. To avoid views too similar to the test set in the training set, we delete the adjacent frames of the test set in the training set. The resolution we use for ScanNet is 480×640.

Table 1. Quantitative comparisons on the DTU and the ScanNet dataset.

Method	DTU				ScanNet			
	Ours	NeRF	MVSNeRF	PixelNeRF	Ours	BPCR	NPBG++	NeRF
PSNR (dB) ↑	26.91	**27.01**	26.63	19.31	25.38	**25.88**	25.27	25.74
SSIM ↑	**0.944**	0.826	0.930	0.789	**0.815**	0.794	0.772	0.780
LPIPS ↓	**0.116**	0.253	0.168	0.382	**0.208**	0.414	0.448	0.537
Inference(s)↓	**0.76**	21.22	9.43	66.75	**0.54**	8.41	1.99	19.78

4.2 Implementation Details

Point Projection and Positional Encoding. We project the point clouds onto $N = 32$ feature planes. Both α and β in Eq. 3 are set to 1. For $\mathbf{c}$ and $\mathbf{p}$, we set the positional encoding hyperparameter $L_1 = 4$, and we choose $L_2 = 3$ for $\mathbf{v}$. Including a 5-dimensional appearance feature $\mathbf{a}$, the dimension of the feature we feed into the network is 47 (24+18+5).

Training Details. We use the Adam optimizer to train our network with an initial learning rate $l_r = 2e^{-4}$. The learning rate for point feature l_{pr} is initialized as 0.01, which will be decreased by 0.005 every 10 epochs and finally set to 0.001. We train 30 epochs for each scene on a single NVIDIA TITAN Xp GPU, which takes about two days.

4.3 View Synthesis on DTU

We present our results on the DTU dataset and compare them with NeRF-based methods including NeRF, MVSNeRF, and PixelNeRF. We train NeRF and our network on the training views and evaluate them on the test set. For PixelNeRF and MVSNeRF, we evaluate their models pre-trained on the DTU dataset. We evaluated the rendering results using the PSNR, SSIM and LPIPS. The results in Table 1 show that our method achieves the best SSIM and LPIPS, and NeRF produces the highest PSNR. As for the inference time, we compute all pixels in parallel rather than rendering only a pixel at a time, which greatly increases the inference speed as shown in the last row in Table 1.

Qualitative comparisons in Fig. 5 prove that our method presents the best visual quality. We render more highlight and texture details such as highlight and cracks on the surface of the sculpture in Fig. 5(b). The patterns on the fruit surface are severely blurred by NeRF in Fig. 5(c). Moreover, even if MVSNeRF is able to render highlight and texture details, it generates artifacts at the edges of the green pepper in Fig. 5(d). Obviously, the results of PixelNeRF are over-smoothed and lack sufficient texture details.

4.4 View Synthesis on ScanNet

We compare our method with the NeRF-based method NeRF and the point cloud-based method BPCR [8] and NPBG++. We test our network, BPCR,

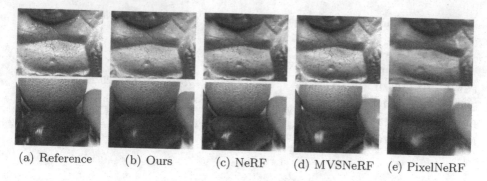

(a) Reference   (b) Ours   (c) NeRF   (d) MVSNeRF   (e) PixelNeRF

Fig. 5. Comparisons with NeRF, MVSNeRF, and PixelNeRF on the DTU dataset.

and NeRF on the test set and evaluate the model of NPBG++ pre-trained on the ScanNet dataset. For a fair comparison, we test BPCR, NPBG++, and our method on point clouds reconstructed by the same system. Table 1 shows that while BPCR achieves a slightly better PSNR, our approach gets the best SSIM and LPIPS.

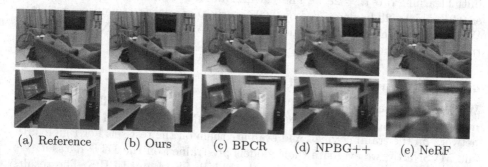

(a) Reference   (b) Ours   (c) BPCR   (d) NPBG++   (e) NeRF

Fig. 6. Comparisons with BPCR, NPBG++, and NeRF on the ScanNet dataset.

As shown in Fig. 6, we notice that BPCR and NPBG++ produce artifacts at the edges of the chair, which is caused by geometry noise. The performance of NeRF in Fig. 6(e) is also not that ideal in general, and dense training views are required to render better results. Our method is proven to achieve the best visual quality in Fig. 6(b).

4.5 Robustness to Sparse Point Clouds

To save the memory and computational cost for point projection, we hope the model learns and renders from a relatively sparse point cloud. Unfortunately, sparse point clouds may exhibit false occlusion relationships, causing backgrounds that should be occluded to appear in the image during rendering. While both NPBG++ and our approach are point-based rendering methods, we

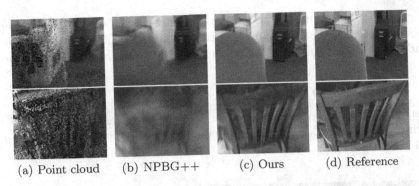

(a) Point cloud   (b) NPBG++   (c) Ours   (d) Reference

Fig. 7. Comparison with NPBG++ processing sparse point clouds.

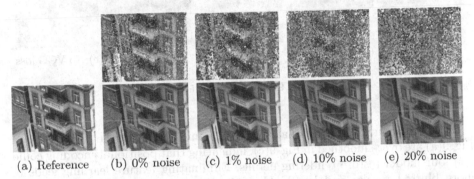

(a) Reference   (b) 0% noise   (c) 1% noise   (d) 10% noise   (e) 20% noise

Fig. 8. Results of our approach processing point clouds with geometry noise. The first row shows the point clouds without and with geometry noise, and the second row displays the results of our method.

observe that NPBG++ cannot avoid occlusion errors dealing with sparse point clouds of 'scene0010_00' and 'scene0020_00' (800,000 points on average) in the ScanNet as shown in Fig. 7. By projecting the features of the points to feature planes and adopting volume rendering, our approach reduces the dependence on geometric accuracy, so that the correct occlusion relationships could be recovered in the rendering results even at a low point density.

4.6   Robustness to Geometry Noise

Point clouds reconstructed by multi-view stereo techniques [23] or RGBD scanners often contain noise, so we expect our method to be robust to geometry noise. To verify the ability against noise, we add geometry noise to the point clouds in the DTU dataset, then feed them into our pipeline to train and test. For the point cloud of scene 'scan21', we move all the points along a random direction for a Gaussian distributed distance. We set the mean of the Gaussian distribution to 0 and set the variances to 1%, 10%, and 20% of the diagonal length of the bounding box, respectively. Figure 8 displays the visualization of point clouds with geometry noise and the test results on these point clouds. Experimental results demonstrate that our approach still synthesizes high-quality views in the second row in Fig. 8 even when the geometry of the point clouds is visually noisy.

4.7 Ablation Study

To verify the effect of positional encoding (P.E.), point feature learning (F.L.), and the VGG loss in $\mathcal{L}$, we ablate these modules respectively when training on the DTU dataset.

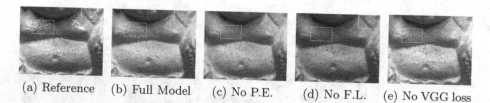

(a) Reference   (b) Full Model   (c) No P.E.   (d) No F.L.   (e) No VGG loss

Fig. 9. Ablation studies.

After removing the positional encoding, some cracks in the yellow box in Fig. 9(a) are over-smoothed in Fig. 9(c), indicating that positional encoding could help our model restore rendering details. Eliminating feature learning leads to more blurred results and less highlight in the green box in Fig. 9(d), which demonstrates that the model has learned the appearance of the points in addition to color. When only the RGB L1 loss is included in the loss function $\mathcal{L}$, since it is sensitive to the error of individual pixels, the overall visual quality in Fig. 9(e) is slightly worse than that of the complete model in Fig. 9(b). In Table 2, the complete model outperforms other models on PSNR, SSIM, and LPIPS.

Table 2. Quantitative results of ablation studies.

	Full model	No P.E.	No feature learning	No VGG loss
PSNR (dB) ↑	**26.97**	25.43	26.15	26.92
SSIM ↑	**0.834**	0.782	0.812	0.783
LPIPS ↓	**0.112**	0.152	0.142	0.233

5   Conclusion

In this study, we propose a new method for neural point rendering by combining point multi-plane projection and volume rendering. The projection of point features reduces the dependence on the geometric accuracy of the point clouds, and the correct occlusion relationships between points can be recovered by volume rendering. In addition, the application of positional encoding enables our network to render more texture details. Experimental results on the DTU dataset and ScanNet dataset indicate that our method outperforms state-of-the-art novel view synthesis approaches on visual quality. In the future, we will try to introduce pre-trained point cloud encoders into our pipeline to improve the generalization ability of our approach. Besides, we will also investigate effective network architectures such as BLS proposed in [1] to achieve similar performance but with a much faster speed.

Acknowledgements. The research was supported by the National Natural Science Foundation of China (Nos. 61972327, 62272402, 62372389), the Natural Science Foundation of Fujian Province (No. 2022J01001), and the Fundamental Research Funds for the Central Universities (No. 20720220037).

References

1. Ali, S.G., et al.: Cost-effective broad learning-based ultrasound biomicroscopy with 3D reconstruction for ocular anterior segmentation. Multimed. Tools Appl. **80**, 35105–35122 (2021)
2. Aliev, K.-A., Sevastopolsky, A., Kolos, M., Ulyanov, D., Lempitsky, V.: Neural point-based graphics. In: Vedaldi, A., Bischof, H., Brox, T., Frahm, J.-M. (eds.) ECCV 2020, Part XXII. LNCS, vol. 12367, pp. 696–712. Springer, Cham (2020). https://doi.org/10.1007/978-3-030-58542-6_42
3. Bui, G., Le, T., Morago, B., Duan, Y.: Point-based rendering enhancement via deep learning. Vis. Comput. **34**, 829–841 (2018)
4. Chen, A., et al.: MVSNeRF: fast generalizable radiance field reconstruction from multi-view stereo. In: Proceedings of the IEEE/CVF International Conference on Computer Vision, pp. 14124–14133 (2021)
5. Dai, A., Chang, A.X., Savva, M., Halber, M., Funkhouser, T., Nießner, M.: ScanNet: richly-annotated 3D reconstructions of indoor scenes. In: Proceedings of the IEEE Conference on Computer Vision and Pattern Recognition, pp. 5828–5839 (2017)
6. Dai, P., Zhang, Y., Li, Z., Liu, S., Zeng, B.: Neural point cloud rendering via multi-plane projection. In: Proceedings of the IEEE/CVF Conference on Computer Vision and Pattern Recognition, pp. 7830–7839 (2020)
7. Ha, D., Dai, A., Le, Q.V.: Hypernetworks. arXiv preprint arXiv:1609.09106 (2016)
8. Huang, X., Zhang, Y., Ni, B., Li, T., Chen, K., Zhang, W.: Boosting point clouds rendering via radiance mapping. arXiv preprint arXiv:2210.15107 (2022)
9. Iizuka, S., Simo-Serra, E., Ishikawa, H.: Globally and locally consistent image completion. ACM Trans. Graph. (TOG) **36**(4), 1–14 (2017)
10. Jensen, R., Dahl, A., Vogiatzis, G., Tola, E., Aanæs, H.: Large scale multi-view stereopsis evaluation. In: Proceedings of the IEEE Conference on Computer Vision and Pattern Recognition, pp. 406–413 (2014)
11. Kopanas, G., Philip, J., Leimkühler, T., Drettakis, G.: Point-based neural rendering with per-view optimization. In: Computer Graphics Forum, vol. 40, pp. 29–43. Wiley Online Library (2021)

12. Mildenhall, B., Srinivasan, P.P., Tancik, M., Barron, J.T., Ramamoorthi, R., Ng, R.: NeRF: representing scenes as neural radiance fields for view synthesis. Commun. ACM **65**(1), 99–106 (2021)
13. Müller, T., Evans, A., Schied, C., Keller, A.: Instant neural graphics primitives with a multiresolution hash encoding. ACM Trans. Graph. **41**(4), 102:1–102:15 (2022)
14. Qiu, J., Yin, Z.X., Cheng, M.M., Ren, B.: Rendering real-world unbounded scenes with cars by learning positional bias. Vis. Comput. 1–14 (2023)
15. Qiu, J., Zhu, Y., Jiang, P.T., Cheng, M.M., Ren, B.: RdNeRF: relative depth guided nerf for dense free view synthesis. Vis. Comput. 1–13 (2023)
16. Rakhimov, R., Ardelean, A.T., Lempitsky, V., Burnaev, E.: NPBG++: accelerating neural point-based graphics. In: Proceedings of the IEEE/CVF Conference on Computer Vision and Pattern Recognition, pp. 15969–15979 (2022)
17. Rückert, D., Franke, L., Stamminger, M.: ADOP: approximate differentiable one-pixel point rendering. ACM Trans. Graph. (TOG) **41**(4), 1–14 (2022)
18. Thalmann, N., Kim, J., Papagiannakis, G., Thalmann, D., Sheng, B.: Computer graphics for metaverse. Virtual Reality Intell. Hardw. **4**, ii–iv (10 2022)
19. Vaswani, A., et al.: Attention is all you need. In: Advances in Neural Information Processing Systems, vol. 30 (2017)
20. Wang, Y., Serena, F., Wu, S., Öztireli, C., Sorkine-Hornung, O.: Differentiable surface splatting for point-based geometry processing. ACM Trans. Graph. **38**(6), 1–14 (2019)
21. Wiles, O., Gkioxari, G., Szeliski, R., Johnson, J.: SynSin: end-to-end view synthesis from a single image. In: Proceedings of the IEEE/CVF Conference on Computer Vision and Pattern Recognition, pp. 7467–7477 (2020)
22. Xu, Q., et al.: Point-NeRF: point-based neural radiance fields. In: Proceedings of the IEEE/CVF Conference on Computer Vision and Pattern Recognition, pp. 5438–5448 (2022)
23. Yao, Y., Luo, Z., Li, S., Fang, T., Quan, L.: MVSNet: depth inference for unstructured multi-view stereo. In: Proceedings of the European Conference on Computer Vision (ECCV), pp. 767–783 (2018)
24. Yu, A., Ye, V., Tancik, M., Kanazawa, A.: pixelNeRF: neural radiance fields from one or few images. In: Proceedings of the IEEE/CVF Conference on Computer Vision and Pattern Recognition, pp. 4578–4587 (2021)
25. Zhang, Q., Baek, S.H., Rusinkiewicz, S., Heide, F.: Differentiable point-based radiance fields for efficient view synthesis. arXiv preprint arXiv:2205.14330 (2022)
26. Zimny, D., Trzciński, T., Spurek, P.: Points2NeRF: generating neural radiance fields from 3D point cloud. arXiv preprint arXiv:2206.01290 (2022)

Fast Geometric Sampling for Phong-Like Reflection

Shuzhan Yang[1,2] and Han Su[1,2(✉)]

[1] School of Computer Science, Sichuan Normal University, Chengdu, China
jkxy_sh@sicnu.edu.cn
[2] Visual Computing and Virtual Reality Key Laboratory of Sichuan Province,
Chengdu 610066, China

Abstract. Importance sampling is a critical technique for reducing the variance of Monte Carlo samples. However, the classical importance sampling based on the Bidirectional Reflectance Distribution Function (BRDF) is often complex and challenging to implement. In this work, we present a simple yet efficient sampling method inspired by Phong's reflectance model. Our method generates samples of rays using geometric vector operations, replacing the need for BRDF. We explain our implementation of this method on WebGL and demonstrate how we obtain per-pixel random numbers in GLSL. We also conduct experiments to compare our method's speed and patterns to the Phong distribution. The results show that our sampling process can simulate reflections similar to Phong, but is about three times faster than traditional Phong or other BRDF importance sampling methods. Our sampling method is applicable to both real-time and offline rendering, making it a useful tool for computer graphics applications.

Keywords: Sampling · BRDF · Monte Carlo

1 Introduction

Importance sampling is a critical sampling strategy used in Monte Carlo integration to improve the efficiency of ray tracing. Importance sampling usually involves generating samples according to the Bidirectional Reflectance Distribution Function (BRDF). Ideally, The sampling distribution should be consistent with the BRDF curve to ensure that important proportions are sampled more. However, conventional methods of BRDF importance sampling can be complex and slow. Meanwhile, several accurate reflectance models have been proposed, but some lack simplicity. For instance, GGX is a popular model requiring a complex process to properly sample the Visible Normals Distribution Function (VNDF). Heitz [6,7] described this process, which involves projecting the hemispherical surface along the ray, uniformly sampling it on the projection surface, calculating the coordinates of the point on the hemispherical surface, transforming the hemispherical surface into a semi-ellipsoidal surface, calculating the normals, and finally transforming the normals to world space. Generally, this

B. Sheng et al. (Eds.): CGI 2023, LNCS 14496, pp. 211–222, 2024.
https://doi.org/10.1007/978-3-031-50072-5_17

process requires several coordinate transformations, which add to the complexity and computational overhead of the importance sampling.

In addition to Monte Carlo sampling, there exist various techniques that aim to produce real-time glossy reflections. One such technique involves the use of precomputed blurred mipmaps, as demonstrated by Ashikhmin et al. [1] and McGuire et al. [10] to simulate Phong or Blin-Phong reflections. However, these techniques are limited in their ability to handle dynamic lighting or occluded objects, leading to decreased accuracy and versatility in certain scenarios.

To improve the efficiency of Monte Carlo ray tracing, we propose a new method for sampling that can bring a significant increase in performance by simplifying the sampling process. Specifically, we aim to skip coordinate transformations and obtain vectors directly in world space. In Sect. 5 of this paper, we demonstrate the effectiveness of our approach, showing that it can result in a steady increase in rendering performance. While the improvements achieved may seem small, given the large number of times that sampling is performed per frame, even a small gain in efficiency can be observed and is worth pursuing.

Given the complexities of BRDF importance sampling, we seek an efficient reflectance model or an approximation that simplifies the sampling process. In this paper, we focus on Phong [11], a widely used BRDF model [8] that is simple and fast, but has some limitations. Phong BRDF is simple and fast though it clearly has some limitations as compared to other modern BRDFs: non-energy conserving, non-reciprocal. We propose a method to generate samples similar to Phong but faster, while also making up for some of its shortcomings. In Sect. 2, we introduce some details of Phong, and in Sect. 3 about its sampling routine.

In this paper, we introduce a simple geometric sampling routine for simulating Phong-like isotropic specular reflections. We review the BRDF importance sampling procedure and identify slow parts of sampling process, and then compare with traditional importance sampling in terms of efficiency and similarity. Finally, we implement on a WebGL application and discuss how to extend for fast refraction.

2   Related Work

2.1   Phong-Like Distribution

In 1975, Phong proposed a simple shading model [11] that has since been widely used in various graphics applications, particularly in the rasterization pipeline, owing to its simplicity. However, this model is not suitable for ray tracing. Even though the Phong model seems straightforward, it still requires rotating vectors to generate random rays around a given light direction. On the other hand, more precise models were favored in ray tracing, and accuracy was given more importance than speed. Taking inspiration from Phong's work, we devised a method for generating samples without the need for rotation.

The limitations of the Phong model are evident when compared to other modern distributions. It is a rough model and cannot accurately represent rays that form an obtuse angle against the perfect specular reflective direction. Additionally, compensating for energy loss is required when ray samples are below the surface. Despite these limitations, the Phong model is still widely used in the industry, particularly in cases where a perfectly photo-realistic result is not required. For instance, Gooch et al. [5] used the Phong lighting model as a basis for approximating human-drawn technical illustrations. Nowadays, the Phong shading model is available in almost every graphics library.

Inspired by the Phong model, we want to find a sampling framework that accommodates such reflections that are similar to Phong. We define Phong-like reflection as the reflectance distribution of rays that are symmetric with respect to the perfect specular reflective direction. These reflections are generally simple because they are irrelevant to the normal(though we still have to deal with cosine weight and fresnel).

3   Importance Sampling for Phong

Considering the direct light from a light source, the original Phong model for specular reflection is:

$$L_s = f_s E = k_s \cos^n \alpha E \qquad (1)$$

where L_s is the reflected specular radiance, f_s the BRDF, E the incidence irradiance from the light, k_s the specular reflectivity, n the exponent defining surface smoothness, $\alpha \in [0, \frac{\pi}{2}]$ the angle between the perfect specular reflective direction and the outgoing direction.

But it is difficult to sample the Phong distribution while maintaining energy conservation. Lafortune et al. [9] proposed a modified model to keep energy conservation approximately. This way of doing importance sampling for BRDF includes these steps:

1. First, get the direction of the incoming ray which is usually in world space. If the ray starts from the camera, the camera location minus the point location(interpolated from the vertex shader) gets the incoming ray direction which is in world space. In other cases like path tracing, the incoming ray might be a reflection ray of another point, but this ray also has to be in world space.
2. Set up a local coordinate system usually based on the normal (Phong uses the ray direction as the base). Tom Duff summarised several ways of building an orthonormal basis [4]. But this process is not without cost, and according to their survey, this takes 8–20 ns.
3. Then, use the probability density function (pdf) to generate one or more samples of rays. Take Phong, for example. The specular part of modified Phong BRDF [9] is:

$$f_s = k_s \frac{n+2}{2\pi} \cos^n \alpha, \alpha \in [0, \frac{\pi}{2}] \qquad (2)$$

where $\alpha \in [0, \frac{\pi}{2}]$ the angle between the perfect specular reflective direction and the outgoing direction, k_s the specular reflectivity, n the factor in defining how smooth the surface is, x the normalization factor.

But BRDF measures the viewing brightness of the surface rather than light density in space. So ideally, in order to do a complete importance sampling, we want to take into account the $\cos \theta$ factor and generate samples according to cosine weighted BRDF like:

$$x \cos^n \alpha \cos \theta \tag{3}$$

where θ is the angle between the normal and the outgoing ray direction. And the pdf should integrate to 1.

$$\iint_\Omega x \cos^n \alpha \cos \theta \sin \theta d\theta d\varphi = 1 \tag{4}$$

Calculating the analytical value of x is challenging due to the coherence between α and θ, as highlighted in [2]. As a compromise, a common approach is to omit $\cos \theta$, as suggested by Lafortune et al. [9], and use the following pdf:

$$pdf = \frac{n+1}{2\pi} \cos^n \alpha, \alpha \in [0, \frac{\pi}{2}] \tag{5}$$

4. Transform the resulting vector from local space to world space by rotation. This process can be done with vector operations or a matrix.

It is apparent that classical importance sampling is not straightforward. In Sect. 3 we are going to describe how to get rid of steps 2 and 4 and generate samples just in world space.

4   Geometric Sampling

The reason we call it geometric sampling is that we see the resulting samples as vectors and use vector operations to manipulate them. Our task is to generate a couple of rays given an incoming ray direction. In a nutshell, our approach consists of these steps:

1. Generate a random vector.
2. Move it up a little bit.
3. Add (blend) it to the ray.
4. Normalize(optional).

4.1   Intuition

Inspired by Phong distribution, first we can assume the surfaces is perfectly smooth and calculate the reflection ray r (which has been normalized), then generate samples r_i based on r. In other words, we want a function f:

$$r_i = f(r, V_{rand}) \tag{6}$$

where V_{rand} is a vector $(x_1, x_2, x_3...x_n)$ that is generated by random numbers $(\xi_1, \xi_2, \xi_3...)$. This way, we are able to generate multiple samples of rays followed by a single reflection operation by varying the random numbers. By comparison, the conventional methods of sampling the normals generate one sample for a reflection operation. Notice that, although glsl has a built-in "reflect()" function, it can be relatively slow. According to Khronos Group's document, it is calculated as I - 2.0 * dot(N, I) * N, where I is the incoming ray and N the normal.

The intuition of Phong is to generate random rays by rotating the direction of the reflected ray, but we want to do it in another way. If a normalized vector p rotates around another normaliz vector p_0 by an angle θ, we can get the resulting p' that has the same length as p using the following formula:

$$p' = p\cos\theta + (1 - \cos\theta)(p_0 \cdot p)p_0 + \sin\theta(p_0 \times p) \tag{7}$$

Basic arithmetic operations such as addition and subtraction are computationally efficient, requiring only one CPU cycle to execute. However, more complex operations such as sine and cosine functions are considerably slower and can be a power-intensive process. Although some operations can be parallelized, the computational cost of such operations can still be high. The above rotation process can also be done using a transform matrix, but not necessarily faster.

4.2   Add(blend) with the Ray

Since vector rotation is so costly, the original thought is to replace it with vector addition. First, we generate a random vector V_{rand} from the position of one pixel in world space. Then we add it to the reflection direction r. Now that we have the result ray r_i, we can intersect it with the area light and do Monte Carlo integration. That seems nice and clean, but another problem occurs. Considering a very rough surface like Lambertian, the reflection rays are completely random, which means we need the coherence of the original ray to be zero otherwise the added vector should be infinite. In our practice (3), r needs to be blended with R_s (short for roughness), which can limit the vector length to a finite value.

$$r_i = f(r, V_{rand}) = r(1 - R_s) + V_{rand}R_s \tag{8}$$

We can transform the reflection ray r to obtain samples r_i, as shown in Eq. 8. If maintaining the length of r_i is necessary, it can be further normalized. This step can be performed using GLSL's built-in function "mix()", which is one of the fastest built-in functions in GLSL.

4.3   Generate Desired V_{rand}

The real question is how to find a V_{rand} distribution to make r_i satisfy the reflection that we want. In theory, we can simulate any BRDF using (3), as long as we figure out the V_{rand} distribution in 3D space. For Phong-like distribution, we consider its V_{rand} as a form of symmetric distribution inside a sphere, and this distribution can be broken down into two parts: one is uniform distribution on a sphere, the other is a factor that controls the distance of samples to the sphere center. We generate a 3d random vector using three uniform random numbers ξ_1, ξ_2, ξ.

$$\begin{cases} V_x = 2\xi_1 - 1, \\ V_y = \sqrt{1 - V_x^2}\sin(2\pi\xi_2), \\ V_z = \sqrt{1 - V_x^2}\cos(2\pi\xi_2), \end{cases} \tag{9}$$

Now that we have the uniform sphere distribution, we add $N \cdot R_s$ to avoid energy loss (discussed in Sect. 4.4), and then multiply it with another factor $D(\xi)$ to get the distribution of V_{rand}. $D(\xi)$ is a critical parameter that actually controls the size and shape of highlights. In Sect. 4.6, we will discuss various values of $D(\xi)$ in more detail.

$$V_{rand} = (V_{xyz} + N * R_s)D(\xi) \tag{10}$$

where $D(\xi)$ is used to control the radius of distribution, Rs the roughness. $D(\xi)$ also can be precalculated. Equation 8, 9, 10 are the core formulas of our method, and we leave lines of glsl codes of how they are implemented in the appendix.

4.4   Avoid Energy Loss

Sometimes rays are intercepted by the surface (Fig. 9), which will cause energy loss. For energy conservation, it is possible to check these situations first and then invert those intercepted rays. That is the same issue that Heitz mentioned [6], the difference between NDF and VNDF. Traditional reject sampling of NDF is inefficient, and causes fireflies. And we use a simpler and faster solution in Eq. 10.

Another thing that should be considered is the cosine weight factor. In the previous description, we generate uniform samples on a sphere and scale it using $D(\xi)$. This is a very quick approximation when the light direction is not close to the surface. But when the roughness is close to 1, we must take into consideration the $\cos\theta$ between N and r_i. We know that for Lambertian reflection, the probability density forms a sphere on the surface. Notice that we blend r with R_s to get r_i.

Our solution for these two problems is to move all the samples up a little bit. In formula 10 we add $R_s * N$ to r_i, not only making an approximation of $\cos\theta$ weighted integral, but also moving all the invisible rays to be exactly above the surface, which means we don't need an extra calculation to decide if a ray is intercepted by the ground.

It is feasible because $\cos\theta$ has little impact when R_s is small. On the other hand, the precision of Phong itself is not high, especially when R_s increases, whereas our model blends into Lambertian, so it is not inappropriate to simulate $\cos\theta$ roughly. We measured the precision in our experiments in Fig. 10.

4.5   Monte Carlo Integration

In the previous section, we generated samples, and the next step is to complete the Monte Carlo integration. Since it is often difficult to obtain a closed-form expression for BRDF, we will represent it as $f(r, r_i)$ for convenience. Assuming that our generated samples r_i follow a probability density function of $p(r_i)$, we can calculate the radiance of a point x as seen from direction r_0 using the following equation:

$$L(x, r_0) = \int_\Omega L(r_i) f(r, r_i) \cos(\theta) \mathrm{d}r_i$$

$$= \int_\Omega L(r_i) \frac{f(r, r_i)}{p(r, r_i)} p(r, r_i) \cos(\theta) \mathrm{d}r_i$$

where $\rho(r, r_i)$ is BRDF, θ the angle between normal and r_i. According to importance sampling, we have Monte Carlo integral at point x:

$$L(x, r_0) = \lim_{n \to +\infty} \frac{1}{n} \sum_{i=1}^{n} L(r_i) \frac{f(r, r_i)}{p(r_i)} \cos(\theta) \tag{11}$$

This equation is the common form of importance sampling. And in Sect. 4.4 we have tried additional processes to fit $p(r_i)$ to approximate $f(r, r_i) \cos(\theta)$, but we still have not considered the Fresnel effect, so the Frenel coefficient $F(r_i)$ is left in the integral.

$$L(x, r_0) \approx \lim_{n \to +\infty} \frac{1}{n} \sum_{i=1}^{n} L(r_i) F(r_i) \tag{12}$$

in which $L(r_i)$ is the radiance received by r_i, N the normal, $F(r_i)$ is Fresnel coefficient.

4.6 Distribution

The form of distribution is not fixed but mainly depends on three factors: $D(\xi)$, which we use to control the shape of the highlight; Rs, the roughness which determines how $\cos \alpha$ weight influence the distribution; View angle as compared to normal, which affect the accuracy of our approximation towards the microfacet model. But if we only take $D(\xi)$ for consideration and ignore the 3.3 step, it is actually percentile point function (PPF), we can inverse it to get the following cumulative distribution function (CDF):

$$cdf(\xi) = D^{-1}(\xi), \xi \in [0, 1] \tag{13}$$

where ξ measures the deviation from the original ray r. $D(\xi) = \frac{1}{R_s} \| r_i - r + r \cdot R_s \|$. The probability density function is the derivative of cdf:

$$pdf(\xi) = \frac{\mathrm{d}D^{-1}(\xi)}{\mathrm{d}\xi}, \xi \in [0, 1] \tag{14}$$

First, let us consider when roughness = 1. It can be proved that the distribution is equal to the Lambert distribution.

When the roughness is not 1, we simulate it and draw the probability density in Fig. 1. These samples are observed from the r direction, and the maximum radius is equal to R_s. Definitely, we want it to look close to a normal distribution while keeping it as simple as possible. Also, we compute the pdfs with respect to ξ and draw them in Fig. 2. We test a few examples, and $\sqrt{\xi}$ is supreme for its simplicity while $1 - \sqrt{1 - \sqrt{\xi}}$ has a smooth edge.

For instance, let's consider the function $D(\xi) = -\log(1 - \sqrt{\xi})$, which can map the ξ values from the interval $(0, 1)$ to $(0, \text{infinity})$, thus providing a long tail distribution similar to the GGX model. However, this type of function can cause rays to cross the surface, which disrupts our procedure and requires us to detect whether a ray is intercepted, and compensate for the resulting energy loss. Moreover, this can also lead to visible noise, making it an inefficient choice for practical implementations.

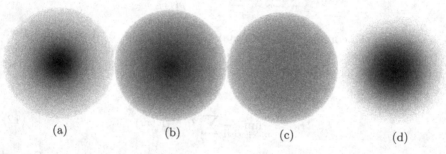

(a)   (b)   (c)   (d)

Fig. 1. Comparing different distribution for different D(ξ). (a): $D(\xi) = \xi$, (b): $D(\xi) = \sqrt{\xi}$, (c): $D(\xi) = \sqrt[3]{\xi}$, (d): $D(\xi) = 1 - \sqrt{1 - \sqrt{\xi}}$. Viewing from the r direction(the reflection ray of a smooth surface), we record the position of the samples. The maximum radius of each distribution is R_s. In the first picture, the samples are too close to the center, whereas the second and third have a sharp edge.

4.7   Compared to Phong

The modified Phong BRDF for specular reflection [9] can be written as $k_s \frac{n+2}{2\pi} \cos^n \alpha$. One limitation is that θ must be clamped to $[0, \frac{\pi}{2}]$ [9], while in our method, rays of $[\frac{\pi}{2}, \pi]$ are also included, which means we can handle well the transition between roughness 0 to roughness 1.0. Figure 4 shows the variance for metallic materials at different roughness.

In Fig. 5, we render a glossy surface under an area light for a few commonly used BRDFs. The results show that the result of ours2 is pretty close to Phong. In the first picture, the highlight of ours1 is darker with a sharper edge as expected. The result fits the pdf curves in Fig. 3, since the distribution of ours1 is scattered from the center. Note that GGX appears to be much rougher at the same roughness as ours. Therefore we use 0.1 for GGX and 0.3 for ours, but still, GGX has a wider gradient around the highlight than the others.

In Fig. 6, we add environment to our scene, and as expected, the difference is small in general. In the first row, they all seem very similar at a low roughness.

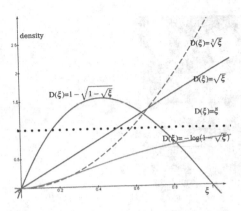

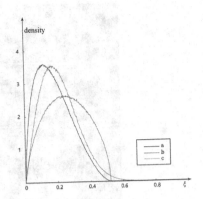

Fig. 2. Pdfs for different $D(\xi)$. Normally, ξ should be restricted to $[0, 1]$, otherwise the operation in 3.3 to prevent energy loss is invalid.

Fig. 3. $pdf(\alpha)$ for different distribution. (a): $D(\xi) = 1 - \sqrt{1 - \sqrt{\xi}}$, (b): Phong, (c): $D(\xi) = \sqrt{\xi}$.

While in the second row, ours1 seems a bit rougher, although its R_s is 0.5, equal to ours2. But we can also notice that the Phong model becomes inaccurate for its sharpest highlight in the second row. As we mentioned, α is clamped to $[0, \frac{\pi}{2}]$.

Regarding other advantages: We can save the major computation of random numbers generation and reuse it every frame from a texture; No need to convert between world space and tangent space. All the samples of rays are on the same side as normal, not intercepted; We can do the reflection operation once and generate multiple rays.

Blinn [3] pointed out that the experimental results generally match the Phong model, except when the view direction is almost parallel to the surface. Phong doesn't actually sample according to a particular normal distribution, so the actual distribution is not as accurate as Torrance-Sparrow's [12] model. However, in actual production, the tiny difference would not be as obvious as it is in the experiment if we use a normal map or bump map for the material and the normals constructed from NDF will likely be hidden by the normal map.

5   Performance

It is actually hard to measure the accurate time of GPU drawing a frame. To estimate the efficiency of our method, we make a simple quad filling up the screen of 1880 * 1812, and use a triangle light on it. Then we switch to different BRDFs and record their rendering time. The frequency of our GPU rx580 is restricted to 300 mhz to make the result noticeable. With our approach, the time spent on sampling per frame is within 0.1 ms, which is much shorter than the traditional ways.

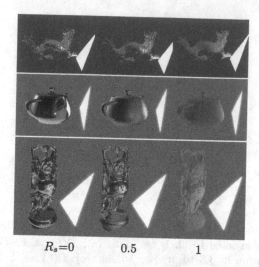

$R_s=0$ 0.5   1

Fig. 4. Unlike Phong, our method is able to handle well the transition between smooth and rough surfaces.

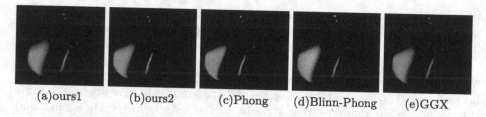

(a)ours1   (b)ours2   (c)Phong   (d)Blinn-Phong   (e)GGX

Fig. 5. Shape of highlights comparing different BRDFs. ours1: $D(\xi) = \sqrt{\xi}$, ours2: $D(\xi) = 1 - \sqrt{1 - \sqrt{\xi}}$

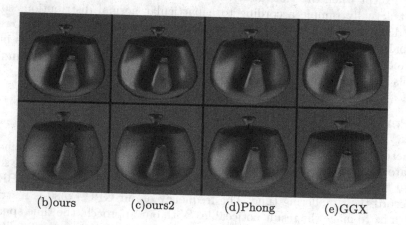

(b)ours   (c)ours2   (d)Phong   (e)GGX

Fig. 6. Teapot under the environmental light compared to other BRDFs. ours1: $D(\xi) = \sqrt{\xi}$, ours2: $D(\xi) = 1 - \sqrt{1 - \sqrt{\xi}}$

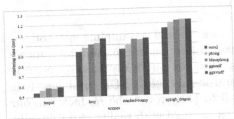

	1sample(without raytracing and base drawing)	100samples (without raytracing)	Drawing latency
phong	0.256	27.3	42.7
blinn-phong	0.289	30.6	46.0
GGX	0.388	40.5	56.8
ours	0.067	8.36	23.2
Base drawing time	1.71	1.71	1.71
Raytracing time (including base draw)	0.178	19.5	19.5

Fig. 7. Performance comparison across different scenes. The result shows that our method gains a steady performance increase across different scene. Note that as the polygonal faces increases, more time is spent on other process.

Fig. 8. performance comparison. We tested rendering a simple glossy quad, and the results show the remaining sampling time after subtracting the ray tracing time.

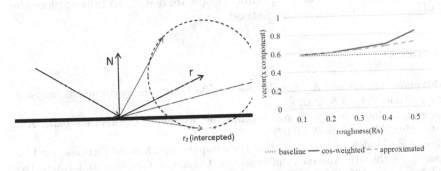

Fig. 9. Offset samples along the normal direction. Some rays are intercepted before we add $N * Rs$.

Fig. 10. Adding $N * R_s$ to approximate $\cos \theta$. We measured a ray reflected on surfaces with different roughness, which is acceptable.

Figure 8 shows that our method is three times faster than traditional sampling. With our method, the major time is left on ray-triangle interception. Note that the drawing latency does not equal the ray tracing time plus the sampling time because some operations are possibly parallel on GPU.

In Fig. 7, we measure the performance comparison across different scenes. The result shows that our method gains a steady performance increase across different scenes. Note that as the polygonal faces increase, more time is spent on rasterization or vertex interpolation.

6   Conclusion and Future Work

This paper introduces a novel reflectance model and a sampling method for Phong-like reflection that offers significant acceleration in the sampling process while retaining precision. Our method is ideal for physically based rendering because it doesn't result in energy loss and avoids the 'VNDF' problem. It is also flexible across roughness values from 0 to 1. However, the R_s factor in our model needs further experimentation to better align with reality. Additionally, the BRDF is currently unavailable in closed form, and our approach is currently only available as a fast sampling method.

Overall, our method provides a fast and accurate approach for sampling Phong-like reflections in physically based rendering. It has the potential to improve the efficiency and realism of ray tracing in various lighting scenarios. However, there are still limitations and areas for improvement, such as the fitting of the R_s factor to real-world materials and the extension to anisotropic reflection. Further research and experimentation are needed to fully explore the capabilities and limitations of our method.

References

1. Ashikhmin, M., Ghosh, A.: Simple blurry reflections with environment maps. J. Graph. Tools **7**(4), 3–8 (2002)
2. Baker, J.A.: Integration over spheres and the divergence theorem for balls. Am. Math. Mon. **104**(1), 36–47 (1997)
3. Blinn, J.F.: Models of light reflection for computer synthesized pictures. In: Proceedings of the 4th Annual Conference on Computer Graphics and Interactive Techniques, pp. 192–198 (1977)
4. Duff, T., et al.: Building an orthonormal basis, revisited. J. Comput. Graph. Tech. (JCGT) **6**(1) (2017)
5. Gooch, A., Gooch, B., Shirley, P., Cohen, E.: A non-photorealistic lighting model for automatic technical illustration. In: Proceedings of the 25th Annual Conference on Computer Graphics and Interactive Techniques, pp. 447–452 (1998)
6. Heitz, E.: Sampling the GGX distribution of visible normals. J. Comput. Graph. Tech. **7**(4), 1–13 (2018)
7. Heitz, E., d'Eon, E.: Importance sampling microfacet-based BSDFs using the distribution of visible normals. In: Computer Graphics Forum, vol. 33, pp. 103–112. Wiley Online Library (2014)
8. Kurt, M.: Real-time shading with Phong BRDF model. J. Sci. Eng. **21**(63), 859–867 (2019)
9. Lafortune, E.P., Willems, Y.D.: Using the modified Phong reflectance model for physically based rendering (1994)
10. McGuire, M., Evangelakos, D., Wilcox, J., Donow, S., Mara, M.: Plausible Blinn-Phong reflection of standard cube MIP-maps. Technical report, Citeseer (2013)
11. Phong, B.T.: Illumination for computer generated pictures. Commun. ACM **18**(6), 311–317 (1975)
12. Torrance, K.E., Sparrow, E.M.: Theory for off-specular reflection from roughened surfaces. Josa **57**(9), 1105–1114 (1967)

Multi-GPU Parallel Pipeline Rendering with Splitting Frame

Haitang Zhang[1,2] , Junchao Ma[1]([⊠]) , Zixia Qiu[1,2] , Junmei Yao[3] ,
Mustafa A. Al Sibahee[4] , Zaid Ameen Abduljabbar[5,6,7] ,
and Vincent Omollo Nyangaresi[8]

[1] College of Big Data and Internet, Shenzhen Technology University,
Shenzhen, China
majunchao@sztu.edu.cn
[2] College of Applied Technology, Shenzhen University, Shenzhen, China
[3] College of Computer Science and Software Engineering,
Shenzhen University, Shenzhen, China
[4] National Engineering Laboratory for Big Data System Computing Technology,
Shenzhen University, Shenzhen, China
[5] Department of Computer Science, College of Education for Pure Sciences,
University of Basrah, Basrah, Iraq
[6] Computer Engineering Department, Al-Kunooze University College, Basrah, Iraq
[7] Huazhong University of Science and Technology,
Shenzhen Institute, Shenzhen, China
[8] Faculty of Biological and Physical Sciences,
Tom Mboya University, Homabay, Kenya

Abstract. In order to achieve real-time rendering of cloud gaming, a
large amount of computing resources of graphics processing units (GPU)
are required. In this paper, we propose a multi-GPU parallel pipeline
rendering approach that makes full use the computing power of multiple GPUs to accelerate real-time ray tracing rendering effectively. This
approach enables heterogeneous GPUs to render the same frame coop-
eratively through a dynamic splitting frame load balancing scheme, and
ensures that each GPU is assigned with the suitable size of splitting frame
based on its rendering ability. A fine-grained parallel pipeline method
divides the process of rendering into more detailed steps that enable multiple frames to be rendered in parallel, which improves the utilization of
each step and speeds up the output of frames. With the experiments on
various dynamic scenes, the results show that the number of frames per
second (FPS) of the multi-GPU system composed of two GPUs is 2.2
times higher than that of the single GPU system, while the multi-GPU
system composed of three GPUs has increased to 3.3 times.

Keywords: Multi-GPU · Ray tracing · Split frame rendering ·
Parallel pipeline · 3D render

B. Sheng et al. (Eds.): CGI 2023, LNCS 14496, pp. 223–235, 2024.
https://doi.org/10.1007/978-3-031-50072-5_18

1   Introduction

Cloud gaming is an emerging form of gaming in the computer game industry. Cloud gaming systems render the game scenes on cloud servers and stream the encoded game scenes to thin clients over broadband networks [10]. On the client side, users can enjoy a high-quality video game experience without requiring any high-end processors or graphics cards [5]. Image quality and interaction latency can affect the gaming experience of cloud gaming players [23]. Ray tracing makes images more realistic [2], real-time rendering enables images output rapidly, and combining them together in cloud gaming has a significant benefit. In order to achieve real-time ray tracing rendering, a large amount of computing and storage resources are required [14,30]. Multiple GPUs can provide stronger computing and rendering abilities [11], thereby improving the performance, operational efficiency, and stability of cloud gaming. However, the collaborative work of multiple GPUs faces many challenges such as heterogeneous GPU synchronization, task partitioning and scheduling.

A lot of research efforts have been devoted to multi-GPU systems in recent years. Tolo et al. [25] propose multi-GPU rendering with the sort-first and sort-last approaches in the light of Vulkan, which divides image equally and assigns to different GPUs for rendering, then composes the results of each GPU into a full image. While the researchers' work improves system performance and decreases the rendering time, it may run into problems with imbalanced loads between diverse GPUs. Ren and Lis [21] use a split frame rendering scheme (SFR) for multi-GPU systems in rasterization pipeline and address load imbalance problem by a draw command scheduler. Dong and Peng [8] reveal a parallel rendering approach with multiple GPUs in rasterization pipeline using OpenGL and CUDA, which fully utilizes distributed GPU memory and integrates seamlessly with inter-GPU load balancing. There is a lot of research work around rasterization pipeline, and there is also some research work on ray tracing. Budge et al. [4] present a software system that exploits hybrid computational resources to accelerate path-traced rendering of complex scenes and its path tracer scales well with CPUs, GPUs and memory. Shane et al. [22] outline the methods of implementing multiple GPUs accelerated the calculation process of ray tracing in CUDA and use binary stereolithography file-type format within the CUDA-based ray tracing codes to decline the time overhead.

From the aforementioned research, we can find that taking multi-GPU into consideration is the most common way to enhance the system computing power at the hardware layer. In addition, there is a lot of work that improves specific ray tracing algorithms and accelerates them with multiple GPUs. However, by properly scheduling the workflow of multiple GPUs in the rendering pipeline and optimizing the system architecture, the rendering speed of ray tracing can also be improved. In this paper, we present a parallel pipeline rendering approach using the multi-GPU architecture, which can coordinate heterogeneous GPUs to accelerate ray tracing rendering efficiently. The contributions of our work are summarized as follows:

- Combining the computing power of different GPUs, we realize a multi-GPU parallel rendering system with SFR under ray tracing pipeline.
- We propose a fine-grained parallel pipeline rendering scheme, which divides the whole process of rendering into more detailed steps and enables multiple frames to be rendered in different stages concurrently.
- Due to the bottleneck of the uniform image segmentation strategy in SFR, we provide a load balancing method called dynamic splitting frame scheme, which splits frame based on computing power of each GPU and enables heterogeneous GPUs from different manufacturers to work together.

The rest of the paper is organized as follows: Sect. 2 introduces the related work. Section 3 illustrates and analyzes the proposed methods and system. Section 4 discusses the experimental environment and the results of the system evaluation. Section 5 shows the conclusion and future work.

2 Related Work

Many studies have been devoted to improving rendering pipelines. Soler et al. [24] introduce a real-time indirect lighting rendering technique that uses a deferred rendering pipeline and G-Buffer to compute indirect illumination in the scene. Wihlidal [28] proposes a novel technique for optimizing the graphics pipeline using compute shaders and a new approach to execute vertex shading and post-processing in the graphics pipeline. Deng et al. [7] propose a render-based factorization, which utilize GPU's high parallel rendering pipeline to build the bidirectional relationship between light fields and display layers. Wang et al. [26] propose a dedicated rendering pipeline for computing polygon-based holograms, which is able to render realistic holograms with smooth shading at a high speed. The previous work focuses on the optimization of the rendering process for a single image, but the process of multiple images from the rendering stage to the presenting stage can be further optimized by rational scheduling of rendering tasks and parallel processing.

Parallel processing is a critical issue for multiple GPUs to work together. Molnar et al. [16] describe three parallel rendering methods of subdividing rendering into sub-tasks which can be parallelly processed in different processors: sort-first, sort-middle and sort-last. Based on the concepts and theories of sort-first and sort-last, some research work on high-performance parallel rendering systems has been published. For sort-first method, Scalable Link Interface (SLI) [17] and CrossFire [1] both have multi-GPU configurations that automatically control two and more graphics cards to render in parallel by their graphics drivers without application programming. These configurations make multiple GPUs appear as a single logical entity to the user and do not support for independent execution on each GPU [15]. SFR and alternate frame rendering (AFR) are primary parallel rendering modes based on sort-first method offered by both manufacturers. SFR splits the image into different parts and assigns all parts to each GPU for parallel rendering, then composes the results to a complete image before presenting. AFR assigns consecutive images to different GPUs for parallel rendering, then present the results alternately. Qin et al. [19] propose a multi-modal prediction network that utilizes previous frames, user inputs and object information to predict the future orientation and position of the view frustum. As for sort-last method, Liu et al. [13] describe a decoupled parallel rendering approach in shared memory multi-GPU system with sort-last parallel rendering method which enables the rendering and compositing stages to execute in parallel. Tolo et al. [25] propose a multi-GPU rendering with Vulkan which can both perform well with the sort-first and sort-last approaches. Previous studies investigate the multi-GPU parallel rendering problem under rasterization rendering pipeline, without considering the parallel improvement of the system under ray tracing rendering pipeline. Besides, previous studies mainly consider multi-GPU systems which is composed of homogeneous GPU, and may face the problem that heterogeneous GPUs can not be performed well. The collaboration of GPUs from different manufactures presents considerable challenges.

Our work, specially, studies multi-GPU parallel rendering under the ray tracing rendering pipeline. We adopt SFR as the parallel collaboration scheme and consider load balancing between GPUs with different performance. Meanwhile, we take a deep dive into the ray tracing rendering process and propose a parallel pipeline rendering scheme which further improves the system's parallelism.

3   Implementation of Our Multi-GPU System

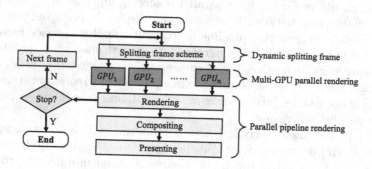

Fig. 1. The overview of our multi-GPU system.

In order to fully utilize the rendering ability of multi-GPU, the system should maximize the usage of GPU and central processing unit (CPU) [13]. As for our multi-GPU system, both GPU and CPU are taken into account, and we balance the relationship between them, so as to achieve high performance.

The overview of our multi-GPU system is shown in Fig. 1, which describes the life cycle of each frame from input to output. Firstly, with the frame inputting, we split them into multiple sub-tasks by our dynamic splitting frame scheme and assign each sub-task to different GPUs. All GPUs parallelly render the sub-tasks in the rendering stage and output all the results to the compositing stage.

With the completion of each rendering, the system will call the next frame for processing without receiving the stop instruction. In the compositing stage, all the fragmented results processed separately are composed into a complete frame. Finally, in the presenting stage, the system presents the complete frame to the screen. Our system optimizes the rendering process from different aspects to improve the rendering speed of frames without sacrificing rendering quality. The main idea of our multi-GPU system consists of three parts: multi-GPU parallel rendering, parallel pipeline rendering scheme and dynamic splitting frame scheme. We will describe and analyze them in detail in the following subsections.

3.1   Multi-GPU Parallel Rendering

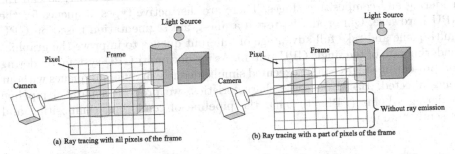

(a) Ray tracing with all pixels of the frame   (b) Ray tracing with a part of pixels of the frame

Fig. 2. Implementation of frame splitting in ray tracing rendering pipeline.

Ray tracing rendering pipeline is adopted in our multi-GPU system. As shown in Fig. 2(a), the camera shoots ray to all pixels and each pixel is colored after the ray intersects the model and the light source [6,27]. We update shader codes to accurately control ray emission [18]. As shown in Fig. 2(b), ray tracing with a part of pixels of the frame while the other pixels without any ray emission, thus realizing frame splitting. Since each pixel is shaded independently of the others, ray tracing, by contrast, is more suitable for SFR than rasterization.

In SFR, a single frame needs to be divided into multiple parts and assigned to each GPU. After rendering the allocated task, each GPU outputs the rendered data to the compositing stage. All data are transferred from GPU to CPU for compositing a complete frame, then the data are copied and synthesized in memory through the main process in the CPU [3]. Finally, the complete frame is transferred from CPU to one GPU for presenting [25]. We describe the multi-GPU system implemented in this way as the multi-GPU system of SFR with one copying thread, abbreviated as MGSOT. Compared to a single GPU system, it adds a compositing stage and brings more rendering lag. Despite the high transfer latency, using multithreaded programming in the CPU can effectively accelerate the data parallel transfer and control the latency at a low level. In the actual experiments of CPU data copying, using *memcpy* as the replication function, the transmission delay is increased by 21 milliseconds (ms) at the viewport of 1280×720. After using 240 threads to execute *memcpy* function in parallel, the time overhead of copying is steadily reduced to less than 1 ms. MGSOT can be improved by the multi-GPU system of SFR with multiple copying threads (MGSMT). The methods describe in the following subsections can be further improved on this basis.

3.2   Parallel Pipeline Rendering Scheme

Consider the overall life cycle of a frame consisting of three stages: rendering, compositing and presenting. We can find that the rendering stage occurs in the GPU, the compositing stage is more related to the CPU, and the presenting stage takes place in the GPU, but does not involve the use of GPU cores. The GPU and CPU can work simultaneously without interfering with each other, so can the rendering and compositing stages. There are distinctive types of queues for the GPU hardware, Qiu et al. [20] reveal a fine-grain segmentation based on GPU multi-queue and take full advantage of different queues to improve the graphics rendering rate of the single GPU system. As for our multi-GPU system, rendering and presenting stages can be executed simultaneously in different queues without being affected. Based on these characteristics, we propose a parallel pipeline rendering scheme (PPR) to build the pipeline of rendering, compositing and presenting stages.

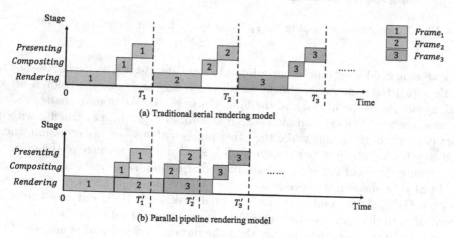

Fig. 3. The rendering time variation under different rendering models.

We visualize the optimization effect of PPR. As shown in Fig. 3, it depicts the total rendering time variation for the same number of frames with different rendering models. The horizontal axis of each figure is time. T_1, T_2 and T_3 in Fig. 3(a) denote the rendering time of different frames, similar to T_1', T_2' and T_3' in Fig. 3(b). The vertical axis is the executed stage of frames, from the beginning of rendering to the end of presenting. As shown in the legend in the upper right corner, the numbers in the rectangle indicate which frame is currently being executed. Traditional serial rendering model is shown in Fig. 3(a), in which after the previous frame completes the presenting stage, the next frame begins to render, resulting in low utilization. PPR model is shown in Fig. 3(b), the next frame begins rendering only after the previous frame completes the rendering stage. It has the advantage of processing multiple frames in different stages parallelly, which can overlap the time spent in different stages and thus output more frames in a period of time.

3.3 Dynamic Splitting Frame Scheme

Dividing the frame and distributing the parts to multiple GPUs is the main idea of SFR in multi-GPU systems. By observing the parallel rendering of multiple GPUs in the rendering stage, the slowest rendering GPU determines the final rendering time. Therefore, the frame splitting strategy determines how much work each GPU needs to do, which in turn affects the rendering time [9, 12]. The traditional strategy of splitting frame is uniform segmentation, which can achieve an excellent performance in multi-GPU systems with the same kind of GPU. When there is a large performance gap between multiple GPUs, it will raise the rendering time, which will bring a great waste of resources. Dynamic splitting frame scheme (DS) is proposed to overcome this problem.

In DS, each frame is split and allocated based on the rendering ability of each GPU, enabling stronger GPU to render more work and weaker GPU to render less work. By using DS, the rendering work is properly distributed to each GPU, so that the total rendering time is minimized.

We will describe and analyze DS further. We adopt FPS (the number of frames per second) as the performance metric of GPU and assume that the number of GPUs in our multi-GPU system is m. To render a frame, the cost of the GPU_i $(i \leq m)$ during the rendering stage is $time_i$. According to the definition of FPS, fps_i can be calculated by the reciprocal of $time_i$, and then we calculate the FPS matrix:

$$FPS = \begin{bmatrix} fps_1 \; fps_2 \cdots fps_m \end{bmatrix}$$

The current frame splitting rate can be represented by $Rate_{old}$ matrix, which consists of:

$$Rate_{old} = \begin{bmatrix} rate_1 \; rate_2 \cdots rate_m \end{bmatrix}$$

Each element of $Rate_{old}$ matrix is not more than 1, and the sum of all elements is 1. Meanwhile, we define the new frame splitting rate matrix as $Rate_{new}$, which can be calculated by $Rate_{old}$ and FPS, specifically as the Hadamard product of $Rate_{old}$ and FPS divided by the Inner product of $Rate_{old}$ and transposed FPS:

$$Rate_{new} = \frac{Rate_{old} \circ FPS}{Rate_{old} \cdot FPS^T}$$

$Rate_{new}$ will replace $Rate_{old}$ as the latest frame splitting rate to split subsequent frames, so as to allocate different proportion of the frame to each GPU to achieve the minimum overall rendering time.

4   Experimental Results

In the experiments, we utilize four relatively powerful GPUs to build our multi-GPU systems. The single GPU system (SGS) used for comparison in the experiments is derived from Willems' ray tracing reflection model [29], and we use ray tracing algorithms to simulate the specular reflection effect. FPS is used as a performance metric to evaluate multi-GPU systems. To evaluate our multi-GPU system, referred to as multi-GPU system with multiple copying threads, parallel pipeline rendering scheme and dynamic splitting frame scheme (MGSMT+PPR+DS), we conduct two sets of experiments:

1. Vertical experiment. We drill vertically inside our multi-GPU system to experiment and evaluate the effectiveness of our proposed schemes.
2. Horizontal experiment. We horizontally extend and scale out to experiment and evaluate the performance changes of our multi-GPU system (MGSMT+PPR+DS) on different numbers of GPUs.

Table 1. Homogeneous hardware.

Hardware	Descriptions
CPU	Intel (R) Xeon (R) Gold 6248R
RAM	256 GB
GPU$_1$	NVIDIA Quadro RTX 4000 8G
GPU$_2$	NVIDIA Quadro RTX 4000 8G
GPU$_3$	NVIDIA Quadro RTX 4000 8G

Table 2. Heterogeneous hardware.

Hardware	Descriptions
CPU	Intel (R) Xeon (R) Gold 6248R
RAM	256 GB
GPU$_1$	NVIDIA Quadro RTX 4000 8G
GPU$_2$	NVIDIA Quadro RTX 4000 8G
GPU$_3$	NVIDIA GeForce RTX 3080Ti 12G

4.1   Vertical Experiment

Table 3. Description of the various methods employed for the experiments.

Methods	Descriptions
SGS	Single GPU system
MGSOT	Multi-GPU system of SFR with one copying thread
MGSMT	Multi-GPU system of SFR with multiple copying threads
MGSMT+PPR	MGSMT with parallel pipeline rendering scheme
MGSMT+PPR+DS	MGSMT+PPR with dynamic splitting frame scheme

In order to better demonstrate the advantages of our proposed methods, we test the performance of various methods in our multi-GPU systems, as shown in Table 3. We conduct experiments using homogeneous and heterogeneous multi-GPU environments as shown in Tables 1 and 2, respectively. The experimental

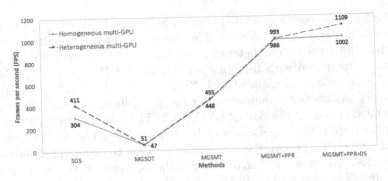

Fig. 4. Experimental results with using various methods.

results are shown in Fig. 4. The horizontal axis represents the five different methods used. The vertical axis represents the FPS of rendering. The blue straight line located at the bottom of the figure shows the experimental results of homogeneous multi-GPU system, while the red dashed line located at the top shows the experimental results of heterogeneous multi-GPU system.

As for homogeneous multi-GPU system, compared with SGS, MGSOT has two additional identical GPUs, which makes the use of multi-GPU parallel rendering with an additional CPU compositing stage. The benefit generated by the multi-GPU parallel rendering is less than the time cost of the compositing stage, which brings more time overhead. MGSMT is an improvement of MGSOT and its multithreaded parallel copy greatly shortens the time spent on the composition, so that the advantages of the multi-GPU parallel rendering exceed the disadvantages brought by the compositing stage. The combination of MGSMT and PPR further reduces the impact of the additional compositing stage. It optimizes the execution of serial rendering at different stages for parallel execution, so that each stage can overlap with each other over time and reduce the execution time. MGSMT combined with PPR and DS schemes has the best performance. From the experimental result of MGSMT with PPR and DS, the performance of multiple GPUs is further optimized by DS.

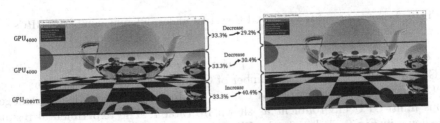

Fig. 5. Optimization of rendering regions in heterogeneous multi-GPU system using DS scheme.

As for heterogeneous multi-GPU system, SGS uses $RTX3080Ti$, which performs much better than $RTX4000$. Through experimental results, it can be found that the FPS of the heterogeneous multi-GPU system has a similar performance compared with the homogeneous multi-GPU system in MGSOT, MGSMT, and MGSMT combined with PPR schemes. That is because, though $RTX3080Ti$ renders faster than the other two $RTX4000$, the final FPS depends on the rendering time of the slowest GPU. MGSMT combined with PPR and DS schemes has improved the performance by dynamically adjusting the rendering region of each GPU through the DS scheme, so that the overall rendering time is the shortest. As shown in Fig. 5, through the DS scheme, the rendering area of $RTX3080Ti$ is increased to 40.4%, while the other two GPUs are decreased to 29.2% and 30.4% respectively, and the final FPS is increased from 558 to 590. Compared to homogeneous multi-GPU system, DS scheme provides better performance in heterogeneous multi-GPU systems.

The vertical experiment indicates that the multithreaded programming, PPR and DS schemes proposed in this paper can enhance the utilization of system resources, thereby improving the FPS. And our final multi-GPU system (MGSMT+PPR+DS), builds on SFR and combines the advantages of PPR and DS. It overcomes the problem of uneven allocation of resources, improves the speed of data flow, makes full use of the computing power of the system, and further improves the overall performance of the system.

4.2 Horizontal Experiment

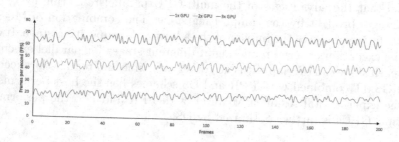

Fig. 6. Performance of the multi-GPU system under different number of GPUs.

To better estimate the overall performance of our multi-GPU system (MGSMT+PPR+DS), various number of GPUs are set up in the system: single GPU, double GPUs and triple GPUs. We conduct experiments using homogeneous multi-GPU environment as shown in Table 1. The experimental results are shown in Fig. 6, it depicts the FPS of our multi-GPU system under different number of GPUs for the case of rendering 200 frames with 3840×1377 viewport. The three curves represent one to three GPUs from bottom to top, respectively. The average FPS for single GPU is 20, the average FPS for double GPUs is 44, and the average FPS for triple GPUs is 66. Double-GPU system and triple-GPU system achieve 2.2 and 3.3 times improvement in FPS compared to the single GPU system, respectively. The improvement is mainly brought by multiple GPUs rendering ability and PPR. In terms of the multi-GPU rendering ability, multiple GPUs can linearly diminish the rendering time, which means a two times speedup for the double GPUs system and a three times speedup for the triple GPUs system. From the perspective of PPR, the rendering time is much larger than the accumulation of the compositing and presenting time for particularly complex scenes, thus the boost is slightly more than 1. From the DS perspective, the minor performance difference caused by the system consisting of multiple homogeneous GPUs, yielding a smaller performance improvement.

The horizontal experiment indicates that our multi-GPU system with PPR and DS effectively elevating the processing speed of ray tracing. As the number of GPUs increase, the acceleration effect is more obvious, and the speedup ratio is 1.1 times the number of GPUs.

5   Conclusion and Future Work

In this paper, in order to enhance the system 3D rendering ability and effectively accelerate the ray tracing graphics rendering process, we propose a multi-GPU parallel pipeline rendering approach based on SFR. In our multi-GPU system, each frame is split into multiple parts, which are assigned to different GPUs for rendering. All rendering results are merged to a whole frame rapidly through multi-threads in the compositing stage. Finally, we present the whole frame on the screen without sacrificing rendering quality. A novel parallel pipeline rendering scheme is applied in the system and multiple frames can be parallelly rendered in various stages, which can overlap the processing time of different stages and speed up the FPS effectively. Additionally, a load balancing method called dynamic splitting frame is proposed, which measures the rendering ability of each GPU and allocates the appropriate splitting size of frame to minimize rendering time, and the method performs well in heterogeneous multi-GPU systems. The experimental results illustrate that our multi-GPU rendering system attains $1.1 \times Number\ of\ GPU$ times speedup comparing with a single GPU system and effectively improves the graphics rendering ability. Our system has a potential application prospect in the field of computer game. Combining the proposed system and the computer game is the direction of our future efforts.

Acknowledgements. This work is supported by the university-enterprise cooperative R&D project of SZTU (grant no. 20221061030001) and the National Natural Science Foundation of China (grant no. 62072317).

References

1. AMD. ATI CrossFire Pro User Guide. Tech. rep. (2009)
2. Bikker, J.: Real-time ray tracing through the eyes of a game developer. In: 2007 IEEE Symposium on Interactive Ray Tracing, pp. 1–10 (2007)

3. Brodtkorb, A.R., Hagen, T.R., Sætra, M.L.: Graphics processing unit (GPU) programming strategies and trends in GPU computing. J. Parall. Distrib. Comput. **73**(1), 4–13 (2013)
4. Budge, B., Bernardin, T., Stuart, J.A., Sengupta, S., Joy, K.I., Owens, J.D.: Out-of-core data management for path tracing on hybrid resources. Comput. Graph. Forum (2009). https://doi.org/10.1111/j.1467-8659.2009.01378.x
5. Cai, W., et al.: A survey on cloud gaming: Future of computer games. IEEE Access **4** (2016)
6. Carr, N.A., Hall, J.D., Hart, J.C.: The ray engine. In: Proceedings of the ACM SIGGRAPH/EUROGRAPHICS Conference on Graphics Hardware, pp. 37–46 (2002)
7. Deng, N., He, Z., Yang, X.: Render-based factorization for additive light field display. Comput. Animat. Virt. Worlds **32**(3–4), e2010 (2021)
8. Dong, Y., Peng, C.: Multi-GPU multi-display rendering of extremely large 3d environments. Vis. Comput. 1–17 (2022)
9. Eilemann, S., Makhinya, M., Pajarola, R.: Equalizer: a scalable parallel rendering framework. IEEE Trans. Visual Comput. Graph. **15**(3), 436–452 (2009). https://doi.org/10.1109/TVCG.2008.104
10. Huang, C.Y., Hsu, C.H., Chang, Y.C., Chen, K.T.: Gaminganywhere: an open cloud gaming system. In: Proceedings of the 4th ACM Multimedia Systems Conference (MMSys 2013), pp. 36–47. Association for Computing Machinery (2013)
11. Igehy, H., Stoll, G., Hanrahan, P.: The design of a parallel graphics interface. In: Proceedings of the 25th Annual Conference on Computer Graphics and Interactive Techniques, pp. 141–150 (1998). https://doi.org/10.1145/280814.280837
12. Jia, S., Zhang, W., Wang, G., Pan, Z., Yu, X.: A real-time deformable cutting method using two levels of linked voxels for improved decoupling between collision and rendering. Vis. Comput. **39**(2), 765–783 (2023)
13. Liu, H., Wang, P., Wang, K., Cai, X., Zeng, L., Li, S.: Scalable multi-GPU decoupled parallel rendering approach in shared memory architecture. In: 2011 International Conference on Virtual Reality and Visualization, pp. 172–178. IEEE (2011)
14. de Macedo, D.V., Rodrigues, M.A.F.: Real-time dynamic reflections for realistic rendering of 3d scenes. Vis. Comput. **34**, 337–346 (2018)
15. Moerschell, A., Owens, J.D.: Distributed texture memory in a multi-GPU environment. Comput. Graph. Forum **27**, 130–151 (2008)
16. Molnar, S., Cox, M., Ellsworth, D., Fuchs, H.: A sorting classification of parallel rendering. IEEE Comput. Graph. Appl. **14**(4), 23–32 (1994)
17. NVIDIA. SLI Best Practices. Tech. rep. (2011)
18. Purcell, T.J., Buck, I., Mark, W.R., Hanrahan, P.: Ray tracing on programmable graphics hardware. In: ACM SIGGRAPH 2005 Courses (SIGGRAPH 2005), p. 268-es. Association for Computing Machinery (2005)
19. Qin, Y., Chi, X., Sheng, B., Lau, R.W.: Guiderender: large-scale scene navigation based on multi-modal view frustum movement prediction. Vis. Comput. 1–11 (2023). https://doi.org/10.1007/s00371-023-02922-x
20. Qiu, Z., Ma, J., Zhang, H., Al Sibahee, M.A., Abduljabbar, Z.A., Nyangaresi, V.O.: Concurrent pipeline rendering scheme based on GPU multi-queue and partitioning images. In: International Conference on Optics and Machine Vision (ICOMV) (2023)
21. Ren, X., Lis, M.: Chopin: scalable graphics rendering in multi-GPU systems via parallel image composition. In: 2021 IEEE International Symposium on High-Performance Computer Architecture (HPCA), pp. 709–722. IEEE (2021)
22. Riley, S., Diefes, L., Bechtold, L., Barry, M.: Multi-GPU accelerated ray tracing using cuda, pp. 676-686 (2022). https://scholar.sun.ac.za/

23. Shea, R., Liu, J., Ngai, E.C.H., Cui, Y.: Cloud gaming: architecture and performance. IEEE Network **27**(4), 16–21 (2013)
24. Soler, C., Hoel, O., Rochet, F.: A deferred shading pipeline for real-time indirect illumination. In: ACM SIGGRAPH 2010 Talks. Association for Computing Machinery (2010). https://doi.org/10.1145/1837026.1837049
25. Tolo, L.O., Viola, I., Geitung, A., Soleim, H., Patel, D.: Multi-GPU rendering with the open Vulkan API. In: Norsk IKT-konferanse for forskning og utdanning (2018)
26. Wang, F., Ito, T., Shimobaba, T.: High-speed rendering pipeline for polygon-based holograms. Photon. Res. **11**(2), 313–328 (2023)
27. Whitted, T.: An improved illumination model for shaded display. In: ACM Siggraph 2005 Courses, p. 4-es (2005)
28. Wihlidal, G.: Optimizing the graphics pipeline with compute. In: Game Developers Conference, vol. 2 (2016)
29. Willems, S.: Examples and demos for the new Vulkan API (2018). https://github.com/SaschaWillems/Vulkan
30. Zhang, B., Sheng, B., Li, P., Lee, T.Y.: Depth of field rendering using multilayer-neighborhood optimization. IEEE Trans. Vis. Comput. Graph. **26**(8), 2546–2559 (2019)

Molecular Surface Mesh Smoothing with Subdivision

Dawar Khan[1] , Sheng Gui[2,3] , and Zhanglin Cheng[1](✉)

[1] Shenzhen VisuCA Key Lab, Shenzhen Institute of Advanced Technology, Chinese Academy of Sciences, Shenzhen, China
zl.cheng@siat.ac.cn
[2] LSEC, NCMIS, Key Laboratory of Systems and Control, Institute of Systems Science, Academy of Mathematics and Systems Science, Chinese Academy of Sciences, Beijing, China
[3] School of Mathematical Sciences, University of Chinese Academy of Sciences, Beijing, China

Abstract. Smoothing with subdivision has several popular techniques. However, these techniques have several limitations including mesh deformation, no care of mesh quality, and increasing mesh complexity. Molecular meshes having a distinct surface with abrupt changes from concave to convex and vice versa are further challenging for these techniques. In this paper, we formulated a smoothing algorithm for molecular surface meshes. This algorithm integrates the advantages of three well-known algorithms including Catmull-Clarck, Loop, and Centroidal Voronoi tessellation (CVT) with an error control module. CVT is used for pre-processing, and the remaining two for smoothing. We find new vertices like Catmull-Clarck and connect them like Loop. Unlike Catmull-Clark, which is generating a quad mesh, we establish a new connection making it triangular. We control the geometric loss by backward translation of the vertices toward the input mesh. We compared the results with previous methods and tested the algorithm with different numerical analysis and modeling applications. We found our results with significant improvements and always robust for downstream applications.

Keywords: Molecular Graphics · Surface mesh · Mesh smoothing

1 Introduction

Molecular modeling is an exciting research field at the intersection of many disciplines, including computer graphics, mathematics, molecular biology, biophysics, and chemistry [1,2]. Surface meshes play a vital role in various fields to represent 3D structures and volumetric data. Surfaces of bio-molecules are important pieces of information in molecular science [3–6]. Molecular surface meshes can help to get information about various functionalities including structure prediction, docking and implicit-solvent modeling, protein folding, molecular interactions, and calculation of their areas and volumes [2,7]. Unfortunately, raw meshes are generated with several issues including self-intersections, lower triangle quality, redundancies, and a non-smooth surface. Therefore, further refinement and smoothing is required to improve the quality of the generated mesh for applicability in the downstream applications [7–9]. Protein Data

Bank (PDB) (https://www.rcsb.org/) provides various PDB files (i.e. the textual file formats for 3D structures of proteins) to the molecular science community. TMSmesh [2] or any other alternative tool can be used to generate surface mesh from PDB files. These meshes need further processing to improve their quality and representation. Recently, several molecular surface remeshing methods have been proposed for mesh quality improvement. Unfortunately, there is no particular interest toward the smoothing of molecular surface meshes.

Smoothing with sub-division is a standard methodology with a number of well-known algorithms. For example, the Catmull-Clark algorithm [10] is famous for tessellation of B-spline surfaces. However, since it generates a quad mesh instead of typical triangular meshes, therefore it is not directly applicable to molecular meshes. Loop [11] is an alternative of the Catmull-Clark [10] which subdivides the triangles into four triangles and calculates new positions for the points to achieve a smoother surface. Similarly, least square surface smoothing (LS3) [12], Butterfly smoothing and midpoint algorithm are also used for smoothing. However, most of these methods are effective for surfaces with continuous curvature surfaces. Molecular surface with its unique curvature variation with abrupt changes from concave to convex and vice versa is challenging for smoothing. However, there is no specific method for smoothing molecular surface meshes. Similarly, there is no comparative study to compare the effect of the existing smoothing method on molecular surface meshes. Smoothing algorithms and especially subdivision based smoothing are typically found with two main issues. First, they failed due to the geometric errors and in-ward deformation of the concave surfaces. Second, they are typically skipping the extraordinary vertices for edge split.

In this paper, we handle these two issues and proposed a molecular surface smoothing algorithm. The algorithm starts with CVT [13] initialization and proceeds with extraordinary vertices removal followed by triangles splitting for mesh smoothing. The geometric error is controlled via backward translation where the vertices are mapped back toward the input surface. In the following, we have listed our key contributions.

1. We proposed a smoothing algorithm that starts with CVT, and proceeds with triangles subdivision and error minimization. The error driven smoothing approach controls the possible geometric loss (i.e., deformation) during the smoothing.
2. We evaluated the results on different aspects including visual perception, geometric error, and success in the downstream applications (i.e., PBE analysis [14], TetGen, FEM analysis, and AFMPB).
3. We conducted a comparative study of the state-of-the-art methods for molecular surface meshes. We also examined the smoothing results of each method with and without the use of pre-processing using CVT [13]. We compared our results with previous methods and found significant improvements.

2   Related Work

Molecular surfaces follow different molecular structures and thereby give different surface definitions. This section briefly reviews mesh generation and mesh improvements in the context of molecular surfaces. The recent surveys [1,15,16] are suggested for further reading. Mesh simplification-based methods [17], Delaunay triangulation [18],

CVT [13,19] and many more methods [20] are widely used for general surface remeshing. Error control and topology preservation is a key challenge in any remeshing method [21]. Typical angle improvement has also gained key attention, where small and large angles are eliminated [22].

Mesh generation from the protein files is an important first phase of molecular surface meshing. TMSmesh [2,23] is a well-known tool for triangular surface mesh generation of the Gaussian surface from an input PQR file (i.e. a primary input format for biomolecular structure). Ray-casting method [24] is another method for surface triangulation of complex bio molecules. These meshes are used in implicit solvent modeling, simulations using the boundary element method (BEM) and the finite element method (FEM) [24]. The mesh generated from the proteins is further refined for quality enhancement. This process is called molecular surface remeshing. In this context, SMOPT [25] is a tool that eliminates all redundant elements and intersecting triangles from the raw mesh. Similarly, Khan *et al.* [7] used real-time adaptive remeshing (RAR) [26] as initialization followed by cutting low-quality triangles and re-filling the holes to reach a good quality mesh. Mesh smoothing [27] is important for various applications. This method [27] robustly works on different types of meshes, including molecular meshes, imaging data, and industrial models. Cheng and Shi [28] also improved the quality of molecular surface meshes using their method of restricted union of balls. Similarly, other molecular surface remeshing methods [29] are also available. However, there is no work on smoothing molecular surface meshes. Some well-known smoothing methods are summarized below.

Centroidal Voronoi Tessellation (CVT): CVT is widely used in mesh processing and other related applications in its two well-known implementations (Lloyd algorithm [19] and quasi-Newton optimization [13]). It is a unique tessellation of Voronoi diagrams which each seed is moved to the center of mass of the corresponding Voronoi cell.

Catmull-Clarck Subdivision: Catmull-Clarck method [10] is used to generate or tessellate the B-spline surface by subdivision [30]. For any polygonal input mesh, it generates a final mesh as a quad mesh. It skips the subdivision near the extraordinary (irregular) vertices. Doo and Sabin method [31] is another subdivision for bi-quadratic uniform B-splines.

Loop Subdivision: Unlike, Catmull-Clark, the Loop subdivision method [11] is for triangular meshes. Inspired by the B-spline curves properties, Loop method smooths surface mesh using an iterative subdivision of the triangles.

LS3 Method: LS3 [12] first simply splits the triangles to an increased number of triangles, then applies mesh regularization followed by a projection to local least-squares approximation patch. It provides better results than Loop (standard subdivision), especially near the extraordinary vertices.

Butterfly Method: Butterfly [32] is also based on the subdivision of each triangle into four triangles by adding new vertices into the edges. The position of newly added vertices is calculated from an affine combination of the neighboring vertices whereas the original vertices are kept in their original position.

Midpoint Method: Midpoint algorithm connects the points from the middle of the edges with each other to form a smoother yet denser mesh [33]. Similarly, another similar approach used a four-directional box spline cube from the mid-edge to form a new mesh [34]. Catmull-Clarck, Loop, Doo, and Sabin method are actually giving the mid-point subdivisions of different degrees [35].

2.1 Comparative Study

One of our main objectives is to see the effect of mesh smoothing on molecular surfaces and to control their limitations with additional operators. In this regard, we first conducted a comparative analysis of different methods to evaluate their results. Then, we propose an optimal smoothing method that integrates existing methods yielding a composite method of mesh smoothing (Sect. 3). We observed that some minor preprocessing can significantly increase the smoothing results. Therefore, we studied the result of pre-processing on different methods (Sect. 3.1). In addition to pre-processing, we noticed that there is a considerable geometric loss during the smoothing process. To preserve the input shape, we apply a backward translation (Sect. 3.4) which controls the geometric error. The literature review (Sect. 2) shows that there are no specific smoothing techniques for molecular surface meshes. In fact, there exist a number of well-known techniques for smoothing general meshing models. However, there is no study to show their effect on molecular surface meshes. In this study, we first conduct a comparative analysis of four well-known smoothing methods including LS3, Catmull-Clark method, Loop subdivision, butterfly, and midpoint method.

3 Our Method

Algorithm 1 represents our method of molecular mesh smoothing. The algorithm takes an input mesh M_i and returns a smoother output mesh M_f. A step-by-step explanation of the proposed algorithm is given below.

Algorithm 1. Molecular Mesh Smoothing(M_0)

1: $M_f \leftarrow \text{Repair}(M_i)$
2: $M_f \leftarrow \text{CVT}(M_f, 3, 30)$
3: $M_f \leftarrow \text{Regularize}(M_f)$
4: $P_{\text{List}} \leftarrow \text{MidPointofedges}(M_f)$
5: $P_{\text{List}} \leftarrow \text{NewPositions}(P_{\text{List}})$
6: $M_f \leftarrow \text{Triangulate}(P_{\text{List}})$
7: $M_f \leftarrow \text{Repair}(M_i)$
8: $M_f \leftarrow \text{MinimizeError}(M_f)$
9: *Return* M_f
10: *End*

Mesh repair (step-1): We removed the major defects including self-intersections, redundant elements, holes, and isolated vertices.

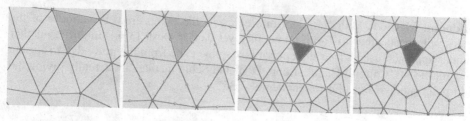

Fig. 1. Triangulation process with subdivision. From left to right: the input mesh (CVT-initialized), next is the new points (green) insertion at the mid-points of the edges. Next is the connection establishment among these points to make it a triangular mesh. The positions of these points have been calculated like the Catmull-Clark method. The far right is the Catmull-Clarck subdivision of triangular mesh where each input triangle is divided into three quads. (Color figure online)

CVT initialization (step-2): We apply CVT method with 5 iterations of the Lloyd [19] and 30 iterations of the quasi-Newton optimization [13].

Regularization (step-3): This step improves the mesh regularity by removing the irregular (extraordinary) vertices.

Creating new vertices/points (step-4): For each edge we added a new vertex in the middle of it.

Updating positions of new vertices (step-5): The positions of new vertices are calculated in a similar way to the Catmull-Clarck method.

Connecting the vertices (step-6): Unlike Catmull-Clarck, we connect the vertices for triangular mesh instead of quad mesh (see Fig. 1).

Mesh repair (step-7): Apply mesh repair (same as step-1).

Error Control (step-8): One of the main limitations of the smoothing algorithm is the geometric error. We used d_H for calculating the geometric error. We control this error by projecting the final mesh in the direction toward the input mesh. In the following subsection, we briefly explain the key modules of our algorithms.

3.1 CVT-Initialization

CVT [13] has significant contributions to surface remeshing. It has been either extended or used as initialization to a surface remeshing algorithm. A recent survey [16] has a comprehensive chapter on the CVT-based surface remeshing. Inspired by these methods, we also used CVT as initialization. Since, the input molecular surface meshes are found with major defects. In pre-processing, we cleaned all the meshes and eliminate their major defects including self-intersections, redundant elements, holes and isolated vertices. The input meshes for all the methods in our comparison are refined with these defects eliminations. We also used CVT for these methods, and we analyzed the results with and without CVT pre-processing. Considering the significant improvement of the CVT, we keep CVT as a mandatory initialization step in our smoothing algorithm.

3.2   Elimination of Extraordinary Vertices

Most of the subdivision methods including the Catmull-Clarck and Loop method skips the splitting in extraordinary vertices (i.e., vertices with *valence* ≥ 7. To address this issue, we improve the regularity of the vertices by applying valence optimization and local remeshing operators including edge split and collapse [8]. We then apply edge splitting on all edges without any consideration of the extraordinary vertices.

3.3   Sub-division Strategy

We create new vertices in the middle of edges in a similar way to the Catmull-Clarck method. However, since we deal with triangular mesh while the Catmull-Clarck method is for quad meshes. We store these vertices and connect them as a triangular mesh instead of a quad mesh (see Fig. 1). We keep the original vertices' positions (the input mesh and the newly created vertices) for backward translation (Sect. 3.4).

3.4   Error Control and Backward Translation

Mesh smoothing algorithms in general have one common limitation of the deformation. The concave surface move inward during smoothing. For example, in Figure 2 (left), the back is the original surface whereas the blue line is after smoothing. The molecular surfaces have amazing patterns in surface with abrupt changes from concave to convex and vice versa. Therefore, in some parts of the surface, the mesh deforms inward while in others it deforms outward depending upon the concavity/convexity of the part. To control this deviation, we used Hausdorff distance d_H and calculated the geometric error for each vertex. Inspired by error-driven remeshing [21] which prevents the remeshing operator if it creates a geometric error greater than a given threshold, we first apply smoothing but later each vertex is translated toward the original mesh in a magnitude of average d_H of the vertex and its neighborhood. For this purpose, we previously store the original mesh coordinates including new (created with subdivision) and old vertices.

The Hausdorff distance d_H between an input surface mesh M_i and an output surface mesh M_f is calculated as

$$d_H = \max\{d_H(M_i, M_f), d_H(M_f, M_i)\}, \quad (1)$$

where

$$d_H(M_i, M_f) = \max_{v_i \in M_i}\{d(v_i, M_f)\}, \quad (2)$$

and

$$d_H(M_f, M_i) = \max_{v_f \in M_f}\{d(v_f, M_i)\}, \quad (3)$$

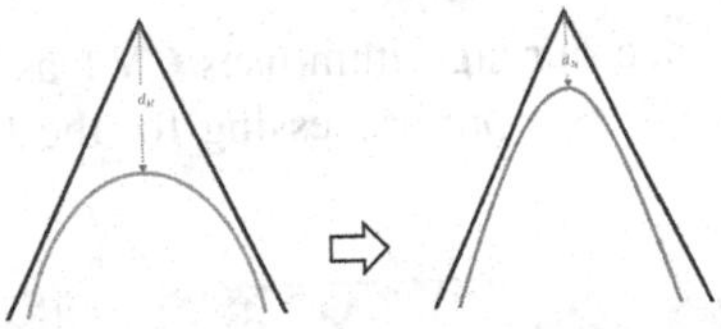

Fig. 2. Geometric error control. Left: Before applying the backward translation. Right: After applying backward translation.

The Hausdorff distance is asymmetric, i.e., Eqs. 2 and 3 are not (necessarily) yielding same value [16]. However, in our case, we calculated d_H in one direction, as follows. For each vertex $v_i \in M_i$ we found its nearest vertex $v_f \in M_f$ and label v_i as the original position of v_f. Then each vertex $v_f \in M_f$ is translated back toward its original position $v_i \in M_i$, in a calculated distance. Since there is a change from concave to convex and vice versa, the direction of vertex translation also changes. Each vertex is translated along its normal toward the original position. The magnitude of translation is calculated as the average of the calculated distances for local vertices i.e. the vertices having their original vertex (v_i) on the same side of the v_f. In other words, the concave region and convex region have translations in opposite directions. Finally, we calculated the exact magnitude of translation dt_{v_f} for each vertex $v_f \in M_f$ as

$$dt_{v_f} = \min\left[d_H(v_i, v_f), \frac{1}{2}\{\text{Mean}(dt), d_H(v_i, v_f)\}\right], \tag{4}$$

where $d_H(v_i, v_f)$ is the Hausdorff distance between v_f and v_i, and $\text{Mean}(dt)$ is the local mean of the translations.

4   Experimental Results

This section presents our experimental results on different models. We have a comparative analysis of our method with existing methods including Loop [11], Midpoint method, LS3 [12], Butterfly, and CVT. Our method is in two types including Our_d which is a direct method without CVT and Our_c is our method with CVT initialization. We also show a few results of the Catmul-Clarck method [10], however, since the Catmul-Clarck method generates quad mesh, we excluded it from our comparison. We apply each method and observe its effect on topology preservation, area, and volume and also see their visual results. Most importantly, we observed their effect on the downstream applications including TetGen, Salvation energy, and solving the Poisson-Boltzmann Equation (PBE). Inspired by the PBE analysis [14], we analyzed the effect of smoothing on the PBE.

4.1   The Effect of CVT Initialization

Since our algorithm uses CVT as initialization, therefore, we first check the effect of CVT as a pre-processing for the Loop and our method. Figure 3 shows the results of

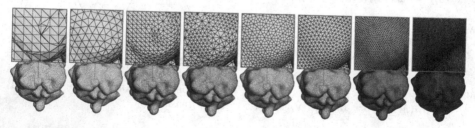

Fig. 3. Results of CVT-based and direct smoothing using Loop and our method. From left to right: Input, CVT, direct Loop, CVT-based Loop, Catmull-Clarck, and our results with 1, 2, and 3 iterations.

CVT-based Loop, direct Loop (without CVT pre-processing), Catmull-Clarck, and our results. We noticed that for small molecules the CVT pre-processing has no significant improvement, however, for large-scale molecules (see Fig. 6), the CVT pre-processing can improve the results significantly.

4.2 Comparative Analysis

We used 6 different molecular models having different levels of complexity (number of atoms in a molecule and different number of vertices in surface mesh). Two models have lower complexity (ADP and 1WO0), two have middle (6BST and AChE) and two are with higher complexity (CONNEXIN and nAChR). CVT pre-processing is mandatory for our method (although we also show our results without CVT i.e., Our_d). For the remaining methods, we only used CVT pre-processing for the large molecules. The lower and middle complexity models were directly smoothed. Similarly, each method was executed with 3 iterations. For our method, although more iterations can give better results, however, since the complexity is increased drastically, we found only one or two iterations are optimal for the large molecules.

Figure 4 shows the smoothing results of the aforementioned methods and our method. For these small molecules, we used our method without CVT i.e., our direct (Our_d), and our with CVT (i.e., Our_c). We see that Our_c results are smoother than others. Therefore, we keep CVT pre-processing as a mandatory step for our method in the remaining four models (middle and large size molecules). Table 1 shows the statistical results and effect on the downstream applications. We see although the geometric error (d_H is relatively higher, our method succeeds (except for more iterations on complex models). Figure 5 shows results of AChE and 6BST and Figure 5 shows results of CONNEXIN and nAChR using our method and with the other methods.

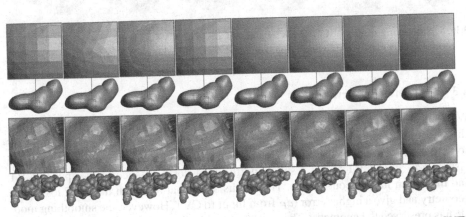

Fig. 4. Smoothing results of ADP (top) and 1WO0 (bottom). From left to right: Input, CVT, Butterfly, Midpoint, Loop, LS3, Our_d (without CVT), and Our_c.

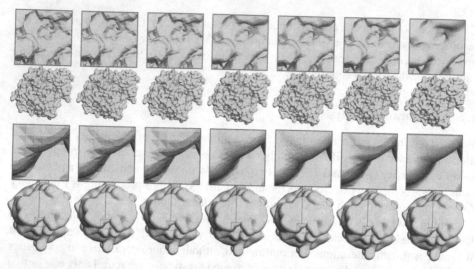

Fig. 5. Smoothing results of AChE (top) and 6BST (bottom). From Left to right: Input, Butterfly, Midpoint, Loop, LS3, Our_d and Our_c.

Fig. 6. Smoothing results of CONNEXIN and nAChR with CVT as a pre-processing. From left to right: CVT, Butterfly, Midpoint, Loop, LS3, and Our_c (all taking CVT as input mesh).

4.3   Geometry Preservation

We control the geometric error by backward vertex translation (see Sect. 3.4). Table 1 shows results of area, volume, and geometry preservation as well as the applicability of some downstream applications (TetGen and AFMPB). Table 2 presents the Hausdorff distance d_H from CVT to our results, and the Hausdorff distance from input to CVT and then from input to our results. The results show that although the CVT losses the geometry and give a higher error (d_H from Input to CVT. However, the smoothing module has preserved the geometry. The two-stage processing (CVT followed by smoothing with subdivision) has caused a higher d_H, which needs careful handling and has been minimized with backward translation. The two values of d_H separated by "/" in Tables 2 and 1 (from left to right) indicate maximum and mean values, respectively.

Table 1. Statistical results including number of vertices #v, number of facets #f, surface's area (unit: Å^2) and its volume (unit: Å^3) and success in the downstream applications including AFMPB (unit: $kcal/mol$) and TetGen. The PDB IDs/molecular names are mentioned as model names. Our results are in two classes. Our_d results are directly generated from input whereas Our_c results are generated with a pre-processing step using CVT. The d_H is calculated from the relevant model (input or CVT) using the percent Bounding box (%bb).

Model	#Atoms	Method	#v	#f	Area	Volume	Genus	d_H (max/mean)	Time (Sec.)	Tet-Gen	AFMPB (solv. energy)
ADP	39	Input	2130	4256	363.860	457.635	0	/	/	√	−2.29526e+02
		Butterfly	26084	52164	365.624	459.624	0	0.1970/0.0336	0.03	×	−2.26376e+02
		Midpoint	25376	50748	363.860	457.635	0	0.0000/0.0000	0.03	√	−2.27584e+02
		Loop	24850	49696	360.537	454.821	0	0.2640/0.0388	0.02	√	−2.28770e+02
		LS3	24953	49902	364.464	460.333	0	0.2307/0.0438	0.02	√	−2.26708e+02
		Our_d	136194	272384	361.435	455.890	0	0.2130/0.0236	0.02	√	−2.27528e+02
		Our_c (1 itr)	8514	17024	359.541	453.509	0	0.0988/0.0179	2.09+0.02	√	−2.30190e+02
		Our_c (2 itr)	34050	68096	359.235	453.251	0	0.1058/0.0202	2.09+0.05	√	−2.29304e+02
		Our_c (3 itr)	136194	272384	359.154	453.154	0	0.0946/0.0201	2.09+0.08	√	−2.28675e+02
1WO0	312	Input	21306	42608	1773.888	2760.472	0	/	/	√	failed
		Butterfly	37113	74222	1779.841	2764.196	0	0.1798/0.0090	0.04	×	failed
		Midpoint	37052	74100	1773.888	2760.472	0	0.0000/0.0000	0.04	√	failed
		Loop	36437	72870	1758.801	2766.101	0	0.2589/0.0239	0.03	√	−4.49081e+02
		LS3	36437	72870	1758.801	2766.101	0	0.2453/0.0240	0.03	√	−4.49073e+02
		Our_d	1363458	2726912	1748.431	2755.170	0	0.1454/0.0097	0.06	√	failed
		Our_c (1 itr)	812674	170080	1735.769	2752.042	1	0.0553/0.0065	2.43+0.04	√	−4.50371e+02
		Our_c (2 itr)	340160	680320	1733.642	2751.525	1	0.0573/0.0071	2.43+0.23	√	−4.48495e+02
		Our_c (3 itr)	1360640	2721280	1733.088	2751.396	1	0.0583/0.0074	2.43+1.00	√	−4.50371e+02
6BST	478	Input	12700	25396	2122.797	5093.473	0	/	/	√	−9.18690e+02
		Butterfly	40116	80228	2127.801	5099.284	0	0.1697/0.0149	0.02	×	−9.1527e+02
		Midpoint	39776	79548	2122.797	5093.473	0	0.0000/0.0000	0.03	√	−9.17070e+02
		Loop	36836	73668	2068.379	5072.094	0	0.3989/0.0461	0.02	√	−9.19471e+02
		LS3	39859	79714	2119.474	5099.629	0	0.2461/0.0245	0.03	√	−9.16328e+02
		Our_c (1 itr)	50794	101584	2087.300	5080.822	0	0.1236/0.0095	2.45+0.03	√	−9.1861e+02
		Our_c (2 itr)	203170	406336	2084.852	5080.040	0	0.1443/0.0104	2.45+0.11	√	−9.17219e+02
		Our_c (3 itr)	812674	1625344	2100.717	5087.460	0	0.1481/0.0108	2.45+0.42	√	−9.14112e+02
AChE	8280	Input	158088	317072	37653.082	69064.279	225	/	/	√	failed
		Butterfly	159064	319024	37655.945	69064.279	225	0.1058/0.0002	0.05	×	failed
		Midpoint	159064	319024	37653.082	69058.967	225	0.0000/0.0000	0.06	√	failed
		Loop	159074	319044	34127.752	68257.394	225	0.2589/0.0409	0.05	√	failed
		LS3	159093	319082	36258.819	68795.525	225	0.1900/0.0223	0.05	√	failed
		Our_c (1 itr)	119280	239780	32888.514	67245.736	306	0.1598/0.0227	9.54+0.06	√	−2.59951e+03
		Our_c (2 itr)	478949	959118	32554.118	67163.592	306	0.1893/0.0240	9.54+0.25	√	−2.67480e+03
		Our_c (3 itr)	1917192	3836792	36103.478	67143.454	243	0.1988/0.0251	9.54+1.01	√	−2.67756e+03
CONNEXIN	19883	Input	107500	215120	55604.892	209415.593	31	/	/	√	failed
		CVT	20037	40271	50894.068	206516.428	50	/	6.25	×	−1.04021e+04
		Butterfly	61193	122583	51210.284	207549.057	50	0.1755/0.0289	0.03	√	−1.05693e+04
		Midpoint	61185	122567	50894.068	206516.428	50	0.0000/0.0000	0.04	√	−1.07020e+04
		Loop	61893	123983	46680.495	205282.695	50	0.3173/0.0692	0.03	√	−1.12228e+04
		LS3	62385	124967	49698.680	207245.189	50	0.2756/0.0412	0.03	√	−1.07329e+04
		Our_c (1 itr)	78624	157584	48957.611	205874.022	85	0.1529/0.0256	6.25+0.04	√	−1.08945e+04
		Our_c (2 itr)	315000	630336	48501.469	205720.178	85	0.1913/0.0279	6.25+0.92	√	−1.08687e+04
		Our_c (3 itr)	1260504	2521344	48380.646	205682.147	85	0.2010/0.0292	6.25+3.72	√	−1.07691e+04
nAChR	30385	Input	1723785	3448430	132771.753	279403.254	216	/	/	√	−1.50568e+04
		CVT	131553	265496	124082.347	272327.492	598	/	24.56	×	−1.48978e+04
		Butterfly	144054	290498	124108.127	272588.264	598	0.0940/0.0017	0.10	√	−1.49459e+04
		Midpoint	144054	290498	124082.347	272327.492	598	0.0000/0.0000	0.10	√	−1.86603e+04
		Loop	144160	290710	112087.567	262082.910	598	0.2782/0.0462	0.11	√	−1.60666e+04
		LS3	144194	290778	119214.424	271155.990	598	0.1451/0.0208	0.11	√	−1.64064e+04
		Our_c (1 itr)	528589	1059714	120288.268	270700.959	635	0.0928/0.0090	24.56+0.23	√	failed
		Our_c (2 itr)	2118157	4238850	119310.696	270306.343	635	0.1123/0.0103	24.56+1.19	√	failed
		Our_c (3 itr)	8476432	16955400	119046.284	270207.420	451	0.1238/0.0111	24.56+5.23	√	failed

Table 2. Geometry preservation: The Hausdorff distance d_H from the input, d_H from CVT and d_H between input and CVT (calculated in bounding box i.e., %bb). Our_c presents results of our method with 3 iterations.

Model	$d_H(\text{Input}, \text{CVT})$ max/mean	$d_H(\text{CVT}, Our_c)$ max/mean	$d_H(\text{Input}, Our_c)$ max/mean
ADP	0.1287/0.0208	0.1401/0.0209	0.3337/0.0665
1WO0	0.1175/0.0097	0.0597/0.0074	0.1636/0.0249
6BST	0.1539/0.0119	0.0917/0.0107	0.2335/0.0336
AChE	0.2265/0.0330	0.1911/0.0250	0.4344/0.0806
CONNEXIN	0.2410/ 0.0346	0.1788/0.0289	0.3887/ 0.0930
nAChR	0.7290/0.0147	0.1124/0.0111	0.3450/ 0.0406

5   Discussion and Conclusion

A simple approach of smoothing molecular meshes is proposed. CVT initialization plays an important role in smoothing, however, it takes a relatively long time. Another factor is the complexity of the mesh. The 1 iteration results are always successful for downstream applications, but 3 iterations fail in AFMPB for large models. In visual perception, the 3 iterations give smoother result. In a comparative analysis, our method gives better visual results than all existing methods. Some of the existing methods often fail in downstream applications. The running time and the complexity are drastically increased with a number of iterations. This is the reason that the large models fail for AFMPB. There is no significant difference for small models in running times. However, for large models, our method has a longer time caused by CVT initialization. If we look at the time complexity, the 2nd and 3rd iterations took longer time than the first iterations as the complexity of the mesh (number of vertices) increases with the number of iterations. The geometric error is controlled by backward translation. The study will help the molecular science community who are interested in molecular surface analysis and molecular surface meshes.

Limitations and Future Work. We do not have some mathematical proof and did not consider the efficiency of the algorithm. The geometric error still needs further control. In the future, we plan to control the complexity of the mesh and study the mathematical trade-off between mesh complexity and accuracy.

Acknowledgements. This work was supported in part by NSFC (No. 62150410433, 61972388), Shenzhen Science and Technology Program (GJHZ20210705141402008), and CAS-PIFI (No. 2020PT0013).

References

1. Gui, S., Khan, D., Wang, Q., Yan, D.-M., Lu, B.-Z.: Frontiers in biomolecular mesh generation and molecular visualization systems. Vis. Comput. Ind. Biomed. Art **1**, 7:1–7:13 (2018)
2. Chen, M., Tu, B., Lu, B.: Triangulated manifold meshing method preserving molecular surface topology. J. Mol. Graph. Model. **38**, 411–418 (2012)

3. Mazala, D., Esperança, C., Marroquim, R.: Laplacian face blending. Comput. Animat. Virtual Worlds **34**(2), e2044 (2023)
4. Dai, J., Fan, R., Song, Y., Guo, Q., He, F.: Mean: an attention-based approach for 3D mesh shape classification. Vis. Comput. 1–14 (2023)
5. Bukenberger, D.R., Lensch, H.P.: Be water my friend: mesh assimilation. Vis. Comput. **37**(9–11), 2725–2739 (2021)
6. Xu, R., et al.: A variational approach for feature-aware b-spline curve design on surface meshes. Vis. Comput. **39**, 1–15 (2023)
7. Khan, D., Yan, D.-M., Gui, S., Lu, B., Zhang, X.: Molecular surface remeshing with local region refinement. Int. J. Mol. Sci. **19**(5), 1383:1–1383:20 (2018)
8. Khan, D., Plopski, A., Fujimoto, Y., Kanbara, M., Cheng, Z., Kato, H.: Valence optimization and angle improvement for molecular surface remeshing. Vis. Comput. **36**(10), 2355–2368 (2020)
9. Ströter, D., Mueller-Roemer, J.S., Weber, D., Fellner, D.: Fast harmonic tetrahedral mesh optimization. Vis. Comput. **38**(9–10), 3419–3433 (2022)
10. Catmull, E., Clark, J.: Recursively generated b-spline surfaces on arbitrary topological meshes. Comput. Aided Des. **10**(6), 350–355 (1978)
11. Loop, C.: Smooth subdivision surfaces based on triangles. Master thesis, Department of Mathematics, The University of Utah (1987)
12. Boyé, S., Guennebaud, G., Schlick, C.: Least squares subdivision surfaces. In: Computer Graphics Forum, vol. 29, pp. 2021–2028. Wiley Online Library (2010)
13. Liu, Y., et al.: On centroidal Voronoi tessellation - energy smoothness and fast computation. ACM Trans. Graph. **28**(4), 101:1–101:11 (2009)
14. Pan, Q., Xu, G., Xu, G., Zhang, Y.: Isogeometric analysis based on extended loop's subdivision. J. Comput. Phys. **299**, 731–746 (2015)
15. Chen, M., Lu, B.: Advances in biomolecular surface meshing and its applications to mathematical modeling. Chin. Sci. Bull. **58**, 1843–1849 (2013)
16. Khan, D., et al.: Surface remeshing: a systematic literature review of methods and research directions. IEEE Trans. Visual Comput. Graphics **28**(3), 1680–1713 (2022)
17. Liu, Y.-J., Xu, C., Fan, D., He, Y.: Efficient construction and simplification of Delaunay meshes. ACM Trans. Graph. **34**(6), 174:1–174:13 (2015)
18. Cheng, S.-W., Dey, T.K., Shewchuk, J.R.: Delaunay Mesh Generation. CRC Press, Boca Raton (2012)
19. Lloyd, S.: Least squares quantization in PCM. IEEE Trans. Inf. Theory **28**, 129–137 (1982)
20. Schreiner, J., Scheidegger, C.E., Fleishman, S., Silva, C.T.: Direct (re)meshing for efficient surface processing. In: Computer Graphics Forum (Proc. EUROGRAPHICS), vol. 25, no. 3, pp. 527–536 (2006)
21. Hu, K., Yan, D.M., Bommes, D., Alliez, P., Benes, B.: Error-bounded and feature preserving surface remeshing with minimal angle improvement. IEEE Trans. Vis. Comput. Graph. **23**(12), 2560–2573 (2017)
22. Wang, Y., et al.: Isotropic surface remeshing without large and small angles. IEEE Trans. Vis. Comput. Graph. **25**, 2430–2442 (2019)
23. Liu, T., Chen, M., Lu, B.: Efficient and qualified mesh generation for Gaussian molecular surface using adaptive partition and piecewise polynomial approximation. SIAM J. Sci. Comput. **40**(2), B507–B527 (2018)
24. Decherchi, S., Rocchia, W.: A general and robust ray-casting-based algorithm for triangulating surfaces at the nanoscale. PLoS ONE **8**, 1–15 (2013)
25. Liu, T., Chen, M., Song, Y., Li, H., Lu, B.: Quality improvement of surface triangular mesh using a modified laplacian smoothing approach avoiding intersection. PLoS ONE **12**, 1–16 (2017)

26. Dunyach, M., Vanderhaeghe, D., Barthe, L., Botsch, M.: Adaptive remeshing for real-time mesh deformation. In: Eurographics 2013 - Short Papers, pp. 29–32 (2013)
27. Wang, J., Yu, Z.: A novel method for surface mesh smoothing: applications in biomedical modeling. In: Clark, B.W. (ed.) Proceedings of the 18th International Meshing Roundtable, pp. 195–210. Springer, Heidelberg (2009). https://doi.org/10.1007/978-3-642-04319-2_12
28. Cheng, H.-L., Shi, X.: Quality mesh generation for molecular skin surfaces using restricted union of balls. Comput. Geom. **42**(3), 196–206 (2009)
29. Quan, C., Stamm, B.: Meshing molecular surfaces based on analytical implicit representation. J. Mol. Graph. Model. **71**, 200–210 (2017)
30. Loop, C., Schaefer, S.: Approximating Catmull-Clark subdivision surfaces with bicubic patches. ACM Trans. Graph. **27**, 1–11 (2008)
31. Doo, D., Sabin, M.: Behaviour of recursive division surfaces near extraordinary points. Comput. Aided Des. **10**(6), 356–360 (1978)
32. Dyn, N., Levine, D., Gregory, J.A.: A butterfly subdivision scheme for surface interpolation with tension control. ACM Trans. Graph. **9**, 160–169 (1990)
33. Peters, J., Reif, U.: The simplest subdivision scheme for smoothing polyhedra. ACM Trans. Graph. **16**, 420–431 (1997)
34. Habib, A., Warren, J.: Edge and vertex insertion for a class of C1 subdivision surfaces. Comput. Aided Geom. Des. **16**(4), 223–247 (1999)
35. Prautzsch, H., Chen, Q.: Analyzing midpoint subdivision. Comput. Aided Geom. Des. **28**(7), 407–419 (2011)

Photorealistic Aquatic Plants Rendering with Cellular Structure

Jianping Su, Ning Xie$^{(\boxtimes)}$, and Xin Lou

Center for Future Media, University of Electronic Science and Technology,
Chengdu, China
cfm@uestc.edu.cn
https://cfm.uestc.edu.cn/index

Abstract. This paper presents a realistic real-time rendering method for aquatic plants, which considers their unique optical characteristics. While many render models has been proposed in real-time rendering of plant leaves, the rendering of aquatic plants is often inaccurate due to reliance on the botanical parameters and optical statistical characteristics of terrestrial plants. Through a qualitative analysis of the differences in optical properties between the cell structures of aquatic and terrestrial plants, we propose a rendering method for aquatic plants. The experimental results show that our method is effective in expressing the rendering appearance of aquatic plants. We also provide a solution for the construction of virtual reality underwater environments. Our contributions include a realistic real-time rendering model for aquatic plants, a real-time underwater roaming platform, and experimental evidence demonstrating our method's effectiveness in expressing the appearance of aquatic plants while balancing model efficiency and accuracy.

Keywords: Real-time rendering · Appearance modeling · Plant optics · Virtual reality · Physically based rendering

1 Introduction

Realistic Aquatic plants rendering is an interesting and important research topic with practical applications in underwater environment simulation, plant simulation, and digital art (Fig. 2).

Supported by organization Chengdu city Key R&D Support Plan (ID: 2019-FY08-00285-GX), the National key R&D program of China (Grant No.2022YFB3104600), Medical Science and Technology Project of Sichuan Health Committee (21PJ119), and Sichuan Science and Technology Program (2022NSFSC0640), the National Natural Science Foundation of China under Grant NO.61976156 and Educational Neuroscience Smart Learning (JGJX2022B38).

Supplementary Information The online version contains supplementary material available at https://doi.org/10.1007/978-3-031-50072-5_20.

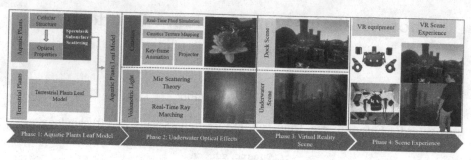

Fig. 1. Overview of our technical route. We analyzes the cell structure and optical characteristics of aquatic plants, and proposes a rendering model for such plants based on the rendering model of terrestrial plants. Given the complex lighting conditions underwater, we first simulate the underwater caustics and volumetric light effects. We then construct a water dock and underwater scene, and finally realize a real-time underwater roaming system based on the collaboration of virtual reality hardware.

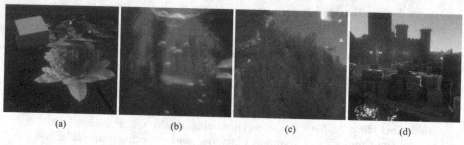

Fig. 2. Rendering Results. (a) water caustics, (b) underwater roaming perspective, (c) looking up in the water, (d) dock scene

In recent years, significant progress has been made in real-time rendering of plant with high photorealism through the development of various models and techniques. Research on plant rendering models mainly focuses on two aspects: first, abstract modeling of plant optical statistical characteristics to obtain a physically-based leaf illumination model, and second, combining the rendering model with botanical parameters to expand the types and states of plants that can be rendered from a parameter perspective. However, the rendering of plant leaves often relies on the botanical parameters and optical statistical characteristics of terrestrial plants, and the final rendering model is not accurate in expressing aquatic plants.

Therefore, to achieve realistic rendering of aquatic plants, it is necessary to develop a rendering method that considers the unique optical properties of aquatic plants. Based on the rendering method of terrestrial plants, we analyze the differences in refractive index, scattering, and absorption spectra of aquatic plant tissues and propose and experiment with a rendering method for aquatic plants. The experimental results show that our rendering method effectively expresses the appearance of aquatic plants.

In practical, we demonstrate our method in virtual reality. This provides a guiding solution for the construction of virtual reality underwater environments. Figure 1 shows the technical route of our research.

The main contributions of this paper are as follows:

1. Through the analysis of the cell structure and optical characteristics of aquatic plants, we propose a realistic real-time rendering model that can express the leaves of aquatic plants.
2. By combining virtual reality technology and realistic rendering of underwater plants and lighting environments, we have built a real-time realistic underwater roaming platform, which provides guidance for the construction of underwater environments in virtual reality solutions.
3. The experimental results demonstrate that our method is effective in expressing the rendering appearance of aquatic plants, striking a balance between model efficiency and accuracy.

2   Related Works

Leaf Models: The research on real-time plant leaf rendering began with plant optics. Gladimir et al. [1] proposed a Leaf Scattering Model (FSM) by assuming a homogeneous material inside the leaf and an isotropic material on the leaf surface. Vogelmann et al. [17] modeled plant leaves and proposed a leaf model with four layers of different optical properties. Govaerts et al. [5] successfully rendered the simplified three-layer blade model offline through Monte Carlo ray tracing. Jensen et al. [9] later proposed a simplified subsurface light transport model, which promoted the development of photorealistic plant rendering. On the basis of Govaerts, Franzke et al. [4] proposed a model for rendering plant leaves with a sense of transparency. This model has three layers of leaf tissue and two layers of boundaries inside and outside. Based on the actual blade measurement data, Wang et al. [19] combined the precomputed light transfer (PRT) [15] method, and proposed a parameterized three-layer blade model. The rendering speed of this rendering model can be Meet the requirements of real-time rendering. Based on the PROSPECT model [7], Miao et al. [13] proposed a more detailed model by parameterizing the effects of plant monocotyledonous properties, chlorophyll, carotenoids, water and dry matter on plant optical properties. However, the above research on plant rendering only focuses on terrestrial plants, and aquatic plants have different optical properties.

Real-Time Volumetric Lighting Rendering: When the light travels in the water, a beam will be observed due to the scattering of light, which is volumetric lighting, also known as "God rays". The method of accumulating light intensity [6], the Billboard patch method [11] and the radial blur post-processing method [8] are often used to simulate real-time volumetric light. Nathan proposed a method combining Ray Marching [16] and post-processing [18] to simulate real-time volumetric lighting and achieved good results.

Real-Time Water Caustics Rendering: Water caustics refers to the phenomenon in which light is refracted and reflected on water waves, forming a mottled pattern of light and shadow. The rendering of real-time water caustics effect includes caustics mapping [14], VOBPBT method based on photon mapping, sampling water caustics texture map [3,20] and other methods. Since caustics are caused by the transport light the water, it can be approximated as the result of a caustic texture projected downward. Therefore, the projection method can be used to simulate this complex physical process in video games.

Therefore, combining the rendering method of terrestrial plants with the cell characteristics of aquatic plants, so as to propose a rendering method suitable for aquatic plants and build a realistic virtual reality underwater scene is research focus.

3 Photorealistic Rendering Method of Aquatic Plants

3.1 Analysis of Aquatic Plant Cell Structure and Optical Properties

The cells of aquatic plants and terrestrial plants have similar structure. When light transporting trough cells, the change of radiance also follows the pattern described by Wang et al [19]. This also means: the radiative transfer of light in terrestrial plant cells is similar to that of aquatic plant cells. It is reasonable that using the rendering equation of terrestrial plants as the basis of the rendering equation of aquatic plants [12]. (More details about the rendering model of plant leaves can be found in our supplementary material Sect. 1.)

The traits of plant cells are determined by their growth environment, which varies significantly between aquatic and terrestrial plants. Terrestrial plants are more susceptible to water loss through transpiration compared to aquatic plants. As a result, the cell walls of terrestrial plants tend to be thicker and the epidermal cells more round. Additionally, many terrestrial plants have a wax layer on the surface to better retain water. In contrast, The leaves of aquatic plants are usually thin and not waxy. Aquatic plants, especially submerged plants, grow in water environments where their intercellular spaces are relatively large. To cope with this environment, aquatic plants have developed ventilatory tissues, such as air cavities, air sacs, and airways, which work together to help them absorb, transport, and utilize air more efficiently.

As the growth environment of plants determines their traits, the traits of plants also affect their optical characteristics. The outer structure of the leaf is collectively referred to as the cuticle. The wax structure of the cuticle is disorganized, amorphous, crystalline, or translucent, which causes it to mainly reflect and refract incident light. The cuticle is a tissue layer located outside the densely packed epidermal cells, which determines the high reflectance and refraction characteristics of the epidermal cells to light. According to the research conducted by Xiao et al. [21], the oblateness parameter can be used to measure whether the cell is round or flattened. The greater the oblateness, the flatter the cells. Experimental measurements of light transmission with different oblateness values were conducted, as well as the effect of epidermal cell oblateness on light curves and absorption under direct color light. We simplified the fitting of the data curve and obtained the enhancement term of oblateness to specular reflection, referring to the method of Miao et al [13]. This improvement introduces the oblateness parameter into the rendering equation, which expands the results that the rendering equation can express.

According to the above analysis, Aquatic plant BRDF is as follows:

$$f_r(X, \theta_i, \phi_i; \theta_r, \phi_r) = \frac{A}{2\pi} \frac{\sigma_s}{\sigma_a + \sigma_s} \gamma(X)$$
$$+ \frac{\rho_s(X) 1.7^{\frac{1}{1-\text{oblateness}}}}{\cos\theta_i \cos\theta_r \cos^4\alpha} \cdot \frac{\exp\left(-\frac{\tan^2\alpha}{m(X)^2}\right)}{4\pi m(X)^2} \tag{1}$$

where, controllable parameter *oblateness* represents how flat the cell is, and is in range (0,1).

3.2   Aquatic Plant Rendering Equation

For aquatic plants, the rendering follows the general physics-based rendering process. Let f_r refers to the BRDF term, which describes the reflection after the light interacts with the surface of the blade. f_t refers to the BTDF term, which describes the exit of the light penetrating the interior of the blade. f_t determines the permeability of the aquatic plant's appearance. For the BRDF item, it need to be processed separately according to different lighting information. Depending on the light frequency, f_r^d represents the BRDF term of direct lighting, and f_r^i represents the BRDF term of indirect lighting. The BRDF term of direct lighting is composed of two parts: the diffuse reflection of direct lighting and the specular reflection of direct lighting; and the BRDF term of indirect lighting can be also divided into two parts: the diffuse reflection of indirect lighting and the specular reflection of indirect lighting.

The diffuse reflection term of direct lighting is the macroscopic representation of the light emitted after multiple scattering inside the blade, so the Wrapped Lighting operation [2] can be performed on the direct light diffuse reflection to enhance the subsurface scattering. According to the formula, the final rendering equation as follows (more details in our supplementary material Sect. 2):

$$R_w = R \frac{(N, l) + w}{(1 + w)^2} \tag{2}$$

$$L_o = \left(f_{r_{\text{diffuse}}}^d \ R_w + \left(f_{r_{\text{specular}}}^d + f_{r_{\text{diffuse}}}^i + f_{r_{\text{specular}}}^i \right) R \right)(1 - P)$$
$$+ (f_t + c_{add}) R_i P \tag{3}$$

where L_o represents the outgoing radiance, R_w represents the incident radiance after Wrapped Lighting, and R represents the incident radiance without Wrapped Lighting. N represents the normal direction, L represents the lighting direction and w is an adjustable parameter in range (0,1) that can control the intensity of the subsurface scattering of the object. In the actual implementation, in order for the artists to quickly adjust the permeability of the rendered appearance of aquatic plants, a permeability parameter P in range $(0,1)$ can be introduced. R_i is the incident radiance that is multiplied by the opposite direction of the normal and the light direction. c_{add} is used to simulate the correction of the difference in color between the back of the blade and the front of the blade due to the different absorption rates of light of different wavelengths inside the blade after the light source penetrates the blade.

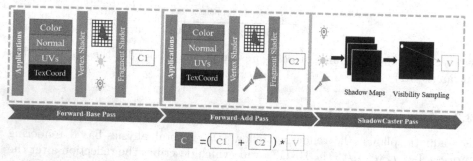

Fig. 3. Overview of three-pass shader Structure. The ForwardBase Pass handles the brightest parallel light and several vertex lights of high importance. The remaining pixel lights are handled by the ForwardAdd Pass. The ShadowCaster Pass is used for shadow casting.

4 Real-Time Rendering System of Aquatic Plants in Virtual Reality

4.1 Shader Design and Optimization for Aquatic Plant Rendering

In order to achieve the rendering effect of aquatic plants, this article proposes a vertex-fragment shader with three passes. To meet the requirements of different art resources, two shaders have been prepared, one for rendering aquatic plants with textures using transparent channels, and one for those without. The complete aquatic plant shader framework is shown in Fig. 3. (The descriptions of shader parameters can be found in our supplementary material Sect. 4)

4.2 Lighting Information Reconstruction

To achieve real-time rendering, we divide illumination into direct and indirect terms. The high-frequency direct lighting information can be obtained from main light source in the scene. For other light sources, their lighting information can be projected onto low-order spherical harmonic basis functions and then reconstructed by spherical harmonic functions when needed.

Image-based lighting method (IBL) [10] can provide indirect diffuse lighting. The skybox is used as a cubemap that provides ambient diffuse lighting information. The cubemap is then projected onto the spherical harmonic basis function for storage, where the basis function is the first three orders of the spherical harmonic function basis function. The specular term for indirect lighting can be implemented using the Split Sum Approximation method [10]. Reflection probes can be added to obtain a pre-filtered environment map. The final ambient light specular result is obtained by multiplying the sampling result of the pre-filtered environment map and the sampling result of the BRDF integral map.

The final lighting reconstruction is achieved by combining the direct lighting results, indirect lighting diffuse results, and indirect lighting specular results.

4.3 Real-Time Volumetric Light Implementation Based on Ray Marching

Real-time volumetric lighting based on ray marching technology can achieve high-quality volumetric lighting effects while ensuring real-time rendering frame rates. We defined several parameters for the ray marching algorithm to control the final result. At the beginning of the algorithm, we determined light stepping range based on the light source type. In the ray marching stage, every time the light advances one step, the light attenuation and the medium density change caused by the fog effect and noise texture are calculated based on the current position. Then, the phase function is calculated based on the angle between the current position and the light source, as well as the type of scattering. Finally, a ray marching operation is completed by accumulating the lighting results. The render result of volumetric light is shown in Fig. 4.

Fig. 4. Underwater volumetric light

4.4   Real-Time Water Caustics Implementation Based on Texture Mapping

The implementation of small-scale interactive water caustics is based on water wave simulation on subdivided water surface grids. When an object comes into contact with the water surface, a water surface mesh with a relatively high degree of subdivision is used to add an offset to the vertices of the water surface in the vertical direction according to the movement law of the fluid to simulate the water wave generated after the water surface contacts the object. When the water surface grid is deformed, we can calculate the area of each triangle on the grid and write the result of dividing the area of each triangle by the corresponding original area into a texture. This generates a real-time caustic texture that conforms to the movement of the water surface, as shown in Fig. 5(a).

In large-scale water areas, We pre-prepared a total of 256 underwater caustic images to implement a set of continuous frame animations that simulate the movement of water caustics. We added projectors to the large-scale water surfaces. This projector can project the material it mounts onto the object below according to the set parameters. The final effect is shown in Fig. 5(b).

(a)   (b)

Fig. 5. Water caustics

5   Analysis of Experimental Results

5.1   Experimental Platform Construction

The underwater roaming scene in the virtual reality of this paper uses the Unity3D game engine to build the basic roaming scene. Use SteamVR (version: 1.17.7) to build a virtual reality hardware-driven platform. Virtual reality experience with HTC Vive Pro device. The scenario runs on the PC side, the operating system is Windows 10 Professional Edition, and the version number is 20H2. Graphics hardware is NVIDIA GeForce RTX 3080.

The theme of the underwater roaming scene is a European-style wooden dock and an open water surface. The user can enter the water from the dock, and the underwater scene consists of several water plants, shells, sunken ships, old anchors, and other landscapes.

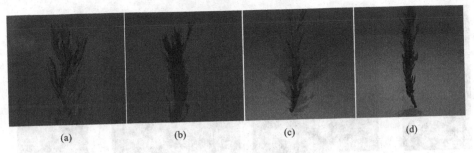

(a)   (b)   (c)   (d)

Fig. 6. The rendering result of a seaweed under the opposite direction of light source

5.2   Experiments

Rendering Result. Figure 6 shows the rendering results for two viewpoints relative to the light source. The results indicate that acceptable rendering results can be obtained under the same parameters, regardless of whether the light source is on the same side or the opposite side of the viewing angle. Notably, when the viewing angle is opposite to the light source, the surface scattering effect can still be observed behind the plants, despite the light source being blocked by them. In addition, adjusting the Intensity Multiplier can modify the intensity of the ambient light, which directly affects the encoding of the spherical harmonic function to the ambient diffuse reflection. Figure 7 shows that increasing this parameter brightens the overall rendering of the plant, and the change is visually acceptable.

Experimental Analysis. Firstly, the rendering results under different material parameter conditions were compared, as shown in Fig. 8: (a) and (b) experimental results show that by increasing the value of the Transmittance parameter, the leaf rendering results are more transparent. This parameter has the correct effect on changing the subsurface scattering and diffuse reflection intensity of the leaves as a whole; (c) and (d) express the reflection and scattering of light on aquatic plants with different chlorophyll content by adjusting the absorption coefficient and scattering coefficient the result of. For dark plants, the absorption coefficient is large, the scattering coefficient is small, and the final rendering effect is darker. Otherwise, the rendering result will be brighter. The control of these two parameters can express the change of the outgoing radiance of the same plant at different water depths; (e) and (f) Cell Oblateness has been modified. When the Oblateness of plant cells is reduced, the specular reflection of the plant itself is more obvious, which meets the expected rendering effect of our rendering model based on plant cell structure and optical characteristics; (g) and (h) experimental results show that our rendering model has acceptable effects on aquatic plants with different color parameters.

Then, we also compared the rendering results with mainstream real-time rendering shaders. Figure 9 shows the rendering effects of standard PBR shader, Speed Tree shader, Advanced Foliage shader and our method respectively. Our

(a) Intensity Multiplier = 1   (b) Intensity Multiplier = 1.5

Fig. 7. Rendering result of a seagrass under the different Intensity Multiplier

rendering effects have obvious effects in terms of plant transparency and specular reflection effects. (More experiment about rendering speed is in our supplementary material Sect. 3)

(a) Transmittance=0.2   (b) Transmittance=0.4   (c) Absorption Coefficient=0.9, Scattering Coefficient=0.1   (d) Absorption Coefficient=0.1, Scattering Coefficient=0.9

(e) Oblateness = 0.7   (f) Oblateness = 0.3   (g)   (h)

Fig. 8. Aquatic plant shader rendering results under different material parameters

(a) Standard PBR Shader   (b) Speed Tree Shader   (c) Advanced Foliage Shader   (d) Ours

Fig. 9. Rendering results of laminaria japonica using different shaders

6   Conclusion

We proposed a rendering model for aquatic plants based on their cell structure and optical characteristics. We optimized the shader and compared the rendering results with mainstream real-time rendering shaders. We also explored the effect of various material parameters on the rendering results of aquatic plants. Our results show that our rendering model has acceptable effects on aquatic plants with different color parameters, and it has advantages in terms of plant transparency and specular reflection effects compared with other shaders.

Future work can be done in several directions, such as adding more factors that affect the appearance of aquatic plants to the shader to achieve more realistic rendering, evaluating the computation time for the same quality of images, adding fully physically-based dynamic effects to simulate real-world fluid interactions underwater, and optimizing for VR devices to make real-time rendering faster. Furthermore, data-driven parameter optimization and random movement can be added to achieve more dynamic effects of aquatic plants.

References

1. Baranoski, G.V., Rokne, J.G.: Efficiently simulating scattering of light by leaves. Vis. Comput. **17**, 491–505 (2001)
2. Bredow, R., Imageworks, S.P.: Renderman on film. SIGGRAPH 2002 Course 16 notes, RenderMan in Production (2002)
3. Chang, D., Conover, A., Gustafson, S.: Finding particulate in finding dory. In: ACM SIGGRAPH 2016 Talks, pp. 1–2 (2016)
4. Franzke, O., Deussen, O.: Rendering plant leaves faithfully. In: ACM SIGGRAPH 2003 Sketches & Applications, p. 1 (2003)
5. Govaerts, Y.M., Jacquemoud, S., Verstraete, M.M., Ustin, S.L.: Three-dimensional radiation transfer modeling in a dicotyledon leaf. Appl. Opt. **35**(33), 6585–6598 (1996)
6. Iwasaki, K., Dobashi, Y., Nishita, T.: An efficient method for rendering underwater optical effects using graphics hardware. In: Computer Graphics Forum, vol. 21, pp. 701–711. Wiley Online Library (2002)
7. Jacquemoud, S., Baret, F.: Prospect: a model of leaf optical properties spectra. Remote Sens. Environ. **34**(2), 75–91 (1990)
8. Jambusaria, U., Katwala, N., Deulkar, K.: God rays in modern gaming. Int. J. Comput. Appl. **108**(11) (2014)
9. Jensen, H.W., Marschner, S.R., Levoy, M., Hanrahan, P.: A practical model for subsurface light transport. In: Proceedings of the 28th Annual Conference on Computer Graphics and Interactive Techniques, pp. 511–518 (2001)
10. Karis, B., Games, E.: Real shading in unreal engine 4. In: Proceedings of Physically Based Shading Theory Practice, vol. 4, no. 3, p. 1 (2013)
11. Li, R., et al.: Procedural generation and real-time rendering of a marine ecosystem. J. Zhejiang Univ. Sci. C **15**(7), 514–524 (2014)
12. Miao, T., Guo, X., Wen, W., Wang, C., Xiao, B.: 3D appearance modeling and visualization of maize leaf with agronomic parameters. Trans. Chin. Soc. Agric. Eng. **33**(19), 187–195 (2017)

13. Miao, T., Zhao, C., Guo, X., Lu, S.: A framework for plant leaf modeling and shading. Math. Comput. Model. **58**(3–4), 710–718 (2013)
14. Shah, M.A., Konttinen, J., Pattanaik, S.: Caustics mapping: an image-space technique for real-time caustics. IEEE Trans. Visual Comput. Graph. **13**(2), 272–280 (2007)
15. Sloan, P.P., Kautz, J., Snyder, J.: Precomputed radiance transfer for real-time rendering in dynamic, low-frequency lighting environments. In: Proceedings of the 29th Annual Conference on Computer Graphics and Interactive Techniques, pp. 527–536 (2002)
16. Tomczak, L.J.: GPU ray marching of distance fields. Technical University of Denmark, vol. 8 (2012)
17. Vogelmann, T.C.: Plant tissue optics. Annu. Rev. Plant Biol. **44**(1), 231–251 (1993)
18. Vos, N.: Volumetric light effects in killzone: shadow fall. In: GPU Pro 5, pp. 145–166. AK Peters/CRC Press (2014)
19. Wang, L., Wang, W., Dorsey, J., Yang, X., Guo, B., Shum, H.Y.: Real-time rendering of plant leaves. ACM Trans. Graph. **24**(3), 712–719 (2005). https://doi.org/10.1145/1073204.1073252
20. Wang, X., Zhang, R.: Rendering transparent objects with caustics using real-time ray tracing. Comput. Graph. **96**, 36–47 (2021)
21. Xiao, Y., Tholen, D., Zhu, X.G.: The influence of leaf anatomy on the internal light environment and photosynthetic electron transport rate: exploration with a new leaf ray tracing model. J. Exp. Bot. **67**(21), 6021–6035 (2016)

Colors, Painting and Layout

Staged Transformer Network with Color Harmonization for Image Outpainting

Bing Yu[✉], Wangyidai Lv, Dongjin Huang, and Youdong Ding

Shanghai University, Shanghai 200072, China
yubing1989@163.com

Abstract. Image outpainting aims at generating new looking-realistic content beyond the original boundaries for a given image patch. Existing image outpainting methods tend to generate images with erroneous structures and unnatural colors when extrapolating the sub-image all-side. To solve this problem, we propose a Transformer-based staged image outpainting network. Specifically, we restructure the encoder-decoder architecture by adding hierarchical cross attention to the connection in each layer. We propose a staged expanding module that splits the extrapolation into vertical and horizontal steps so that the generated images can have consistent contextual information and similar texture. A color harmonization module that adjusts both local and global color information is also presented to make color transitions more natural. Our experiments prove that the proposed method outperforms the advanced methods on multiple datasets.

Keywords: Image outpainting · Transformer · Color harmonization

1 Introduction

Image outpainting (a.k.a. image extrapolation or image extension) is an important task in computer vision and image processing, which focuses on how to extend image boundaries with reasonable structures and details. High-quality image extrapolation can benefit extensive applications, such as image editing [19], virtual reality [22], face recognition [6], and so on. In image editing, for example, it is often necessary to extend the field of view of travel photos to obtain desired backgrounds. Similarly, the extrapolation technique is one of the most efficient ways to create more immersive experiences for virtual reality viewers. Besides, image outpainting can be used to reconstruct visually plausible contents for occluded images with large or edge-missing areas, thereby improving the accuracy of face recognition.

Image outpainting is challenging because it requires completing a looking-realistic image from a small image patch. In addition, the result of image outpainting must maintain consistent contextual information and similar texture

Supplementary Information The online version contains supplementary material available at https://doi.org/10.1007/978-3-031-50072-5_21.

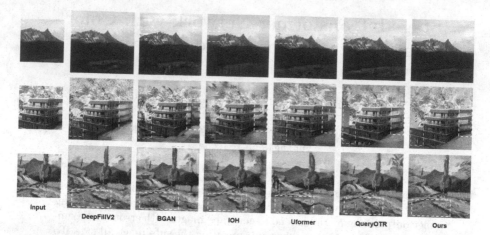

Fig. 1. Compared with DeepFillV2 [28], BGAN [22], IOH [23], Uformer [5], Query-OTR [27], our model can generate higher quality images on different datasets.

structure with the original image to ensure that the result is not overly distorted. Most of the current image outpainting methods [18,24,25] are mainly based on convolutional architectures, which have fast convergence and high generalization ability due to the inductive biases. However, for image outpainting, convolution may refer to relatively little information about neighboring pixels and has insufficient perception of global interaction, which affects the extrapolation results.

Recently, several Transformer-based methods [2,5,14,27] have been introduced to achieve image extrapolation. As shown in Fig. 1, although these models have the strong ability to complete an image from an image patch compared to previous methods, they still have issues that cannot be solved well, including appearance artifacts, distorted structures, blurry textures, and so on. Furthermore, the color transition between the generated part and the original image during staged extrapolation is very abrupt.

To solve the above problems, we propose a staged image outpainting network based on Transformer. We restructure the encoder-decoder architecture of the Vision Transformer (ViT) [4]. Following QueryOTR [27], we use a pre-trained ViT as our encoder to improve the accuracy of the network.

We divide the image extrapolation task into two stages. In the first stage, we expand the image vertically, and in the second stage, we expand the output of the first stage horizontally.

Moreover, we develop a color harmonization module (CHM) to solve color change problem. Specifically, the module is spilt into two main parts, with the first part focusing on the color harmonization of the generated part only, whereas another part emphasizes the color harmonization of the entire image.

Our contribution can be summarized in the following four parts:

- We propose a Transformer-based framework for image outpainting. It explores the staged expanding strategy and aims at achieving a looking-realistic image extension. Experiment on Scenery Dataset [26], Building Facades [5] and WikiArt [21] illustrate the superiority of our method.
- We propose an improved hierarchical cross attention to better learn global representation, which is conducive to preserving the shallow features.
- We propose a staged expanding module (SEM), which can pay attention to more directional information in each extrapolation stage, to make the results more consistent with semantic coherence in the specified direction.
- We propose a color harmonization module (CHM) by applying global and local color loss on generated image patches. With this approach, not only does the color of the parts outside the boundaries appear more realistic, but the color of the entire image is made uniform.

2   Related Work

2.1   Image Outpainting

Previous outpainting methods are patch-based methods [1,19] that perform content retrieval in a pre-prepared database and then stitch the matching patches onto the original image. These methods work well for simple images with repeating motifs. But for more complex images, if the dataset does not contain patches that correspond to the target image, they may cause a context mismatch. The advent of Generative Adversarial Networks (GANs) [7] has greatly promoted the development of image outpainting. Sabini et al. [18] first utilized generative adversarial networks to solve the image outpainting problem while adding a local discriminator to improve the quality of image outpainting. Wang et al. [24] proposed a semantic regeneration network, which used an encoder-decoder structure and contained two sub-networks, namely a feature expansion network and a context prediction network. Teterwak et al. [22] took advantage of the semantic conditions in the discriminator to tune the discriminator based on the semantic information of the pre-trained neural network. Guo et al. [9] proposed a novel spiral generative network that generates images in each direction in steps along a spiral curve, exploiting the correlation between the generated content and the extrapolation direction. Cheng et al. [3] solved the problem from the perspective of GANs inversion, extending the generator of Style-GAN2 [12] to generate spatially consistent micro-patches that create diverse pictures. These methods often lose the correlation between the generated content in the extrapolation direction due to the simultaneous extension of boundaries in both horizontal and vertical directions, resulting in peripheral blurring of the generated image.

2.2   Vision Transformer

Vision Transformer (ViT) [4] achieves higher image classification accuracy than traditional CNN networks, and also shows its outstanding performance on image outpainting tasks. Gao et al. [5] first applied the Transformer architecture in the image outpainting domain by adopting the U-shaped Structure [17] and replacing the CNN network in it with the Swin Transformer [16]. It uses shifted-window-based multi-head self-attention to encode the input image, making it easier to obtain global features of the image. Yao et al. [27] recast the image outpainting problem as a sequence-to-sequence autoregression problem, by using the global modeling capability of Vision Transformer to infer contextual information. Kong et al. [13] used Transformer to predict the image patches attached to image boundaries as hints, and then exploit an inpainting network to fill internal regions.

3   Methodology

Given an input image $x \in \mathbb{R}^{h \times w \times c}$ and filling margin m, our goal intends to extrapolate outside contents beyond the four boundaries of the input. Finally we can get a natural-looking extended image $X \in \mathbb{R}^{(h+2m) \times (w+2m) \times c}$. Our overall framework, as shown in the Fig. 2, is designed based on the GANs consisting of a Transformer-based generator and a PatchGAN discriminator [20].

3.1   Hierarchical Cross Attention

We utilize a pre-trained ViT encoder [10], which can leverage the strong overall perceptual capability of the transformer architecture. The decoder consists of L layers, Z_{sem} is the output feature of SEM Module and the position embedding E_{pos} is used before the first layer, which can be described as follows:

$$Z_0 = Z_{sem} + E_{pos} \tag{1}$$

where $E_{pos} \in \mathbb{R}^{R \times D}$, R is the sequence length and D is the vector size.

Each layer of encoder and decoder is connected by hierarchical cross attention, which is similar to skip connection. Skip connections use concat operation, but we employ hierarchical cross attention due to the transformer structure so that deep and shallow semantic information can be better combined. Each decoder block first includes a multi-headed self-attention layer. To facilitate information fusion, the decoder adds hierarchical cross attention to the original architecture to pass the shallow information. The encoder output of each layer is used as the key and value of the corresponding decoder layer, which aids the decoder in obtaining low-level features and generating higher-quality images. This process can be represented as:

$$Z_i' = MSA\left(LN\left(Z_{i-1}\right)\right) + Z_{i-1} \tag{2}$$

$$Z_i'' = HCA\left(LN\left(Z_i'\right), Z_{enc}^{L-i}\right) + Z_i' \tag{3}$$

where $i = 1, 2, \ldots, L$, LN represents the layer normalization, MSA means the multi-headed self-attention, HCA is the hierarchical cross attention, the Z_{enc}^{L-i} denotes the feature at $(L - i)$-th layer of the encoder.

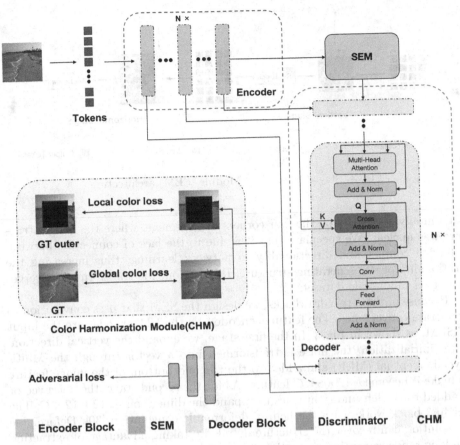

Fig. 2. Overview of our network architecture, which consists of a ViT encoder, decoder, staged expanding module and color harmonization module. We add the hierarchical cross attention between the Encoder and Decoder like skip connection.

Motivated by Conformer [8], a convolution module is applied after the cross attention layer to capture the relative-offset-based local correlations, which can be formulated as:

$$Z_i''' = Conv\left(Z_i''\right) + Z_i'' \tag{4}$$

$$Z_i = FFN\left(LN\left(Z_i'''\right)\right) + Z_i''' \tag{5}$$

where $Conv$ represents the convolution module and FFN is a feed forward network.

3.2 Staged Expanding Module

We found that many previous classical methods tend to expand images only horizontally, and the results when expanding all-side are significantly worse than

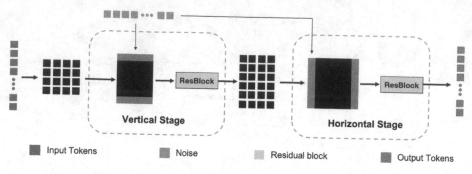

Fig. 3. Staged Expanding Module (SEM) architecture.

horizontally, especially on the four corners of the image, where the image structure was unclear. We speculate that it is due to the lack of connection between extended content and directionality in network learning, thus increasing the irrationality of the generating structure. In addition, the transformer converges slower on small-scale datasets.

Because of these two drawbacks, we design the SEM that uses convolution to accelerate convergence. The features encoded by the ViT encoder are the input of SEM, as shown in Fig. 3. In the first stage, we expand the vertical direction. After initialization, the noise is transformed into a vector through the Multilayer Perceptual (MLP) and added to the top and bottom of the image feature to make it become a $12 \times 8 \times C$ feature. As for the second stage, the noise vector is added to the left and right sides to expand the dimension to $12 \times 12 \times C$. The residual block works with the help of deformable convolution [30]. Deformable convolution can recover the structure details by taking advantage of extracting the long-range semantic information.

3.3 Color Harmonization Module

During the image outpainting process, the color transition may appear unnatural. Hue is an important part of color [15,29]. To further improve the image quality, following the design of hue-color loss [9], we propose a color harmonization module (CHM) to make the generated image X converge to the ground truth Y. The color loss is divided into two parts, the global color loss and local color loss. The global part pays attention to the color information of the whole image in order to balance the generated part and sub-image, which appears more harmonious. The local part focuses only on the outer part $\tilde{X}$ of the image to make it appear more colorful. The global and local color loss are defined as:

$$\mathcal{L}_{gc} = \frac{1}{N} \sum_{i,j} \left\{ 1 - \min\left(\cos\left(X_{i,j}, Y_{i,j}\right), \cos\left(1 - X_{i,j}, 1 - Y_{i,j}\right) \right) + \epsilon \right\}^{\gamma} \quad (6)$$

$$\mathcal{L}_{lc} = \frac{1}{N} \sum_{i,j} \left\{ 1 - \min\left(\cos\left(\tilde{X}_{i,j}, \tilde{Y}_{i,j}\right), \cos\left(1 - \tilde{X}_{i,j}, 1 - \tilde{Y}_{i,j}\right) \right) + \epsilon \right\}^{\gamma} \quad (7)$$

where ϵ and γ are the optimization parameter and N is the number of pixels. We set $\epsilon = 0.001$ and $\gamma = 0.4$ in our experiments.

Our color loss $\mathcal{L}_{color}$ is defined as the sum of above two loss functions:

$$\mathcal{L}_{color} = \lambda_{gc}\mathcal{L}_{gc} + \lambda_{lc}\mathcal{L}_{lc} \tag{8}$$

where both λ_{gc} and λ_{lc} are set to 0.5.

3.4 Loss Functions

We use four types of losses in the training process: the adversarial loss [7], the L1 loss, the perceptual loss [11], and the color loss.

Adversarial Loss. We optimize the generator and discriminator using the adversarial loss. The inputs of discriminator D are generated images X and real images Y. The adversarial loss is defined as:

$$\mathcal{L}_{adv} = E_{(Y)}\left[1 + \log D\left(Y\right)\right] + \mathbb{E}_{(X)}\left[1 - \log\left(D\left(X\right)\right)\right] \tag{9}$$

L1 Loss. We minimize the L1 distance between X and Y, which is defined as:

$$\mathcal{L}_{L1} = \|Y - X\|_1 \tag{10}$$

Perceptual Loss. Consistent with previous work, we leverage the pre-trained VGG-19 [20] network to extract image features. It is defined as:

$$\mathcal{L}_{perc} = E\left[\sum_i \lambda_i \|\phi_i\left(Y\right) - \phi_i\left(X\right)\|_1\right] \tag{11}$$

where ϕ_i means the i-th layer activation map of VGG and λ_i denotes the balancing weight of ith layer.

Total Loss. The total loss of our model can be defined as follows:

$$\mathcal{L}_{total} = \min_G \max_D \mathcal{L}_{adv} + \lambda_{L1}\mathcal{L}_{L1} + \lambda_{perc}\mathcal{L}_{perc} + \lambda_{color}\mathcal{L}_{color} \tag{12}$$

where λ_{L1}, λ_{perc} and λ_{color} are the trade-off weights. We set $\lambda_{L1} = 5$, $\lambda_{perc} = 10$ and $\lambda_{color} = 100$ in our experiments.

4 Experiments

4.1 Experimental Setup

We train and evaluate our model on three datasets: Scenery Dataset [26], Building Facades [5] and WikiArt [21]. Our model is trained on a single NVIDIA GeForce RTX 3090 GPU with PyTorch 1.13 and Cuda 11.6. We used the Adam optimizer and set the learning rate to 0.001. The batch size is set to 32.

We compare the proposed method with five image inpainting or outpainting approaches. DeepFillV2 [28] is an advanced image inpainting approach. BGAN [22], IOH [23] are two GAN-based outpainting methods. Uformer [5] and Query-OTR [27] are the most recent transformer-based image extrapolation approach.

Table 1. Quantitative results of different methods on the Scenery Dataset, the Building Facades and the WikiArt.

Method	Scenery				Building				WikiArt			
	FID↓	IS↑	PSNR↑	SSIM↑	FID↓	IS↑	PSNR↑	SSIM↑	FID↓	IS↑	PSNR↑	SSIM↑
DeepFillV2 [28]	31.365	3.943	21.612	0.753	29.852	4.933	17.762	0.704	22.921	7.541	18.700	0.665
BGAN [22]	48.022	3.541	18.714	0.650	47.569	4.430	15.773	0.613	37.653	5.514	16.229	0.573
IOH [23]	69.925	3.597	21.106	0.729	48.825	4.432	17.088	0.666	30.276	6.769	18.419	0.655
Uformer [5]	30.680	3.450	21.118	0.717	32.024	4.398	17.388	0.661	27.350	6.432	17.714	0.618
QueryOTR [27]	20.330	3.912	21.960	0.726	22.370	4.998	18.136	0.680	14.188	8.174	18.896	0.653
Ours	**19.787**	**4.013**	**22.389**	**0.757**	**21.665**	**5.127**	**18.415**	**0.707**	**12.547**	**8.969**	**19.241**	**0.668**

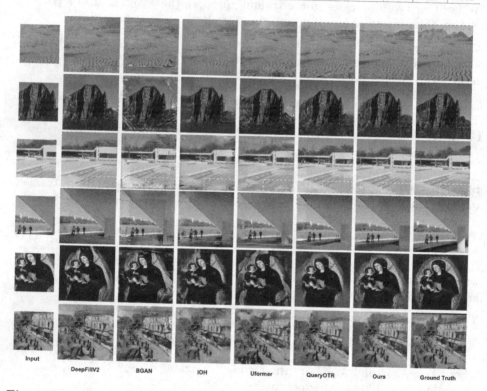

Input   DeepFillV2   BGAN   IOH   Uformer   QueryOTR   Ours   Ground Truth

Fig. 4. Qualitative results of different methods on Scenery Dataset, Building Dataset and WikiArt Dataset. From left to right: input images, DeepFillV2 [28], BGAN [22], IOH [23], Uformer [5], QueryOTR [27], the proposed method, and ground truth images.

4.2   Quantitative Comparison

We choose Frechet Inception Distance (FID), Inception Score (IS), peak signal-to-noise ratio (PSNR) and structural similarity index measure (SSIM) as our evaluation metrics. As shown in Table 1, the proposed method performs better than other approaches in terms of all metrics. With lower FID and higher IS, indicating that our method can generate images with higher quality and more visually plausible content. The improvements of PSNR and SSIM lead to less

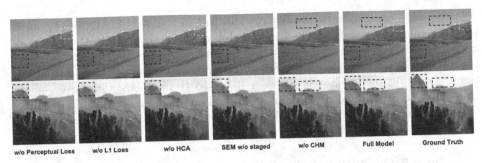

w/o Perceptual Loss   w/o L1 Loss   w/o HCA   SEM w/o staged   w/o CHM   Full Model   Ground Truth

Fig. 5. Qualitative results of ablation study on the Scenery Dataset.

Fig. 6. Failed Results in mixed scenarios.

image distortion. SSIM denotes structural similarity, and this significant increase indicates that our approach generates highly structured images.

4.3 Qualitative Comparison

The visual results on natural, building, and art datasets are shown in Fig. 4. Compared with the previous methods, our method can generate more structured images. It can be seen that the edges of the mountains can be shown more clearly in the red boxes. Our method performs better at filling damaged structures on more complex building dataset. The last two rows show that our method can also produce more realistic images for imaginative art paintings. For example, the character's headdress may be well-restored in the 5th row. Furthermore, our method can produce images with improved color transitions. For instance, from the 1st and 3rd rows, it can be clearly seen that compared to other methods, the generated outer parts have the most similar color to the sub-images.

4.4 Ablation Study

We conduct ablation experiments on Scenery Dataset. From the Table 2, it can be seen that deleting any of the modules leads to worse results. The experimental results are also visualized, as seen in Fig. 5. We train separately with no L1 loss or perceptual loss that will cause artifacts in the picture. CHM module also plays a crucial role. Removal of the CHM module will lead to worse results, particularly with PSNR and SSIM. As can be seen from Fig. 5, the difference in color between the two parts is more obvious in the yellow box. We also verified that the color loss only uses the local or global. Predictably, both the FID and SSIM will be reduced significantly. Once hierarchical cross attention is deleted, IS drops to 3.844 and the results fail to generate good detail. The addition of the convolution module to the decoder can also tremendously improve the IS to 4.013. The SEM module without staged expanding strategy results in poor performance. As illustrated in Fig. 5, the edge of the beach is not clearly depicted in 1st row. And in the 2nd row the outline of the mountains will become blurred.

Table 2. Quantitative results of ablation study on the Scenery Dataset.

	FID↓	IS↑	PSNR↑	SSIM↑
w/o $\mathcal{L}_{perc}$	24.589	3.889	22.320	0.751
w/o $\mathcal{L}_{L1}$	19.902	3.857	21.868	0.747
w/o HCA	20.068	3.844	22.002	0.749
decoder w/o conv	**19.743**	3.951	22.357	0.757
SEM w/o staged	19.828	3.899	22.232	0.750
CHM w/o global	21.134	3.954	22.246	0.751
CHM w/o local	21.119	3.903	22.085	0.746
w/o CHM	20.171	3.917	21.890	0.717
Full Model	19.787	**4.013**	**22.389**	**0.757**

4.5 Limitations

As shown in Fig. 6, it still has some cases that could not be solved well, such as mixed scenes of architecture, people and natural landscape. This may be due to chaotic structures that prevent networks from understanding clear structural features, resulting in poor images. It can be considered to combine semantic segmentation with image outpainting to solve this problem in the future.

5 Conclusion

In this paper, we propose a Transformer-based staged image outpainting network. The hierarchical cross attention is added to connect each layer of ViT encoder and decoder to propagate shallow features. The staged expanding module divides the extrapolation process into vertical and horizontal stages, which can produce images with consistent contextual information and structures. A color harmonization module is also designed to solve the problem of inconsistent color between the generated image and the original image. Experiments on natural, building and art datasets demonstrate the superiority of our method.

Acknowledgements. This work was supported by the Shanghai Natural Science Foundation of China under Grant No. 19ZR1419100.

References

1. Ballester, C., Bertalmio, M., Caselles, V., Sapiro, G., Verdera, J.: Filling-in by joint interpolation of vector fields and gray levels. IEEE Trans. Image Process. **10**(8), 1200–1211 (2001)
2. Chen, J., Fu, Z., Huang, J., Hu, X., Peng, T.: Boosting vision transformer for low-resolution borehole image stitching through algebraic multigrid. Vis. Comput. **38**(9–10), 3191–3203 (2022)
3. Cheng, Y.C., Lin, C.H., Lee, H.Y., Ren, J., Tulyakov, S., Yang, M.H.: InOut: diverse image outpainting via GAN inversion. In: Proceedings of the IEEE/CVF Conference on Computer Vision and Pattern Recognition, pp. 11431–11440 (2022)
4. Dosovitskiy, A., et al.: An image is worth 16x16 words: transformers for image recognition at scale. In: 9th International Conference on Learning Representations, ICLR 2021, Virtual Event, Austria, 3–7 May 2021 (2021)
5. Gao, P., et al.: Generalized image outpainting with U-transformer. Neural Netw. **162**, 1–10 (2023)
6. Ge, S., Li, C., Zhao, S., Zeng, D.: Occluded face recognition in the wild by identity-diversity inpainting. IEEE Trans. Circuits Syst. Video Technol. **30**(10), 3387–3397 (2020)
7. Goodfellow, I., et al.: Generative adversarial nets. In: Neural Information Processing Systems (2014)
8. Gulati, A., et al.: Conformer: convolution-augmented transformer for speech recognition. In: Interspeech 2020, 21st Annual Conference of the International Speech Communication Association, Virtual Event, Shanghai, China, 25–29 October 2020, pp. 5036–5040. ISCA (2020)
9. Guo, D., et al.: Spiral generative network for image extrapolation. In: Vedaldi, A., Bischof, H., Brox, T., Frahm, J.-M. (eds.) ECCV 2020. LNCS, vol. 12364, pp. 701–717. Springer, Cham (2020). https://doi.org/10.1007/978-3-030-58529-7_41
10. He, K., Chen, X., Xie, S., Li, Y., Dollár, P., Girshick, R.: Masked autoencoders are scalable vision learners. In: Proceedings of the IEEE/CVF Conference on Computer Vision and Pattern Recognition, pp. 16000–16009 (2022)
11. Johnson, J., Alahi, A., Fei-Fei, L.: Perceptual losses for real-time style transfer and super-resolution. In: Leibe, B., Matas, J., Sebe, N., Welling, M. (eds.) ECCV 2016. LNCS, vol. 9906, pp. 694–711. Springer, Cham (2016). https://doi.org/10.1007/978-3-319-46475-6_43
12. Karras, T., Laine, S., Aittala, M., Hellsten, J., Lehtinen, J., Aila, T.: Analyzing and improving the image quality of StyleGAN. In: Proceedings of the IEEE/CVF Conference on Computer Vision and Pattern Recognition, pp. 8110–8119 (2020)
13. Kong, D., Kong, K., Kim, K., Min, S.J., Kang, S.J.: Image-adaptive hint generation via vision transformer for outpainting. In: Proceedings of the IEEE/CVF Winter Conference on Applications of Computer Vision, pp. 3572–3581 (2022)
14. Lin, X., Sun, S., Huang, W., Sheng, B., Li, P., Feng, D.D.: EAPT: efficient attention pyramid transformer for image processing. IEEE Trans. Multimedia (2021)
15. Liu, Y., Guo, Z., Guo, H., Xiao, H.: Zoom-GAN: learn to colorize multi-scale targets. Vis. Comput., 1–12 (2023)
16. Liu, Z., et al.: Swin transformer: hierarchical vision transformer using shifted windows. In: Proceedings of the IEEE/CVF International Conference on Computer Vision, pp. 10012–10022 (2021)
17. Ronneberger, O., Fischer, P., Brox, T.: U-Net: convolutional networks for biomedical image segmentation. In: Navab, N., Hornegger, J., Wells, W.M., Frangi, A.F.

(eds.) MICCAI 2015. LNCS, vol. 9351, pp. 234–241. Springer, Cham (2015). https://doi.org/10.1007/978-3-319-24574-4_28

18. Sabini, M., Rusak, G.: Painting outside the box: image outpainting with GANs. arXiv preprint arXiv:1808.08483 (2018)

19. Shan, Q., Curless, B., Furukawa, Y., Hernandez, C., Seitz, S.M.: Photo Uncrop. In: Fleet, D., Pajdla, T., Schiele, B., Tuytelaars, T. (eds.) ECCV 2014. LNCS, vol. 8694, pp. 16–31. Springer, Cham (2014). https://doi.org/10.1007/978-3-319-10599-4_2

20. Simonyan, K., Zisserman, A.: Very deep convolutional networks for large-scale image recognition. In: 3rd International Conference on Learning Representations, ICLR 2015, San Diego, CA, USA, 7–9 May 2015, Conference Track Proceedings (2015)

21. Tan, W.R., Chan, C.S., Aguirre, H.E., Tanaka, K.: Ceci n'est pas une pipe: a deep convolutional network for fine-art paintings classification. In: 2016 IEEE International Conference on Image Processing (ICIP), pp. 3703–3707. IEEE (2016)

22. Teterwak, P., et al.: Boundless: generative adversarial networks for image extension. In: Proceedings of the IEEE/CVF International Conference on Computer Vision, pp. 10521–10530 (2019)

23. Van Hoorick, B.: Image outpainting and harmonization using generative adversarial networks. arXiv preprint arXiv:1912.10960 (2019)

24. Wang, Y., Tao, X., Shen, X., Jia, J.: Wide-context semantic image extrapolation. In: Proceedings of the IEEE/CVF Conference on Computer Vision and Pattern Recognition, pp. 1399–1408 (2019)

25. Wu, X., et al.: Deep portrait image completion and extrapolation. IEEE Trans. Image Process. **29**, 2344–2355 (2020)

26. Yang, Z., Dong, J., Liu, P., Yang, Y., Yan, S.: Very long natural scenery image prediction by outpainting. In: Proceedings of the IEEE/CVF International Conference on Computer Vision, pp. 10561–10570 (2019)

27. Yao, K., Gao, P., Yang, X., Sun, J., Zhang, R., Huang, K.: Outpainting by queries. In: Avidan, S., Brostow, G., Cissé, M., Farinella, G.M., Hassner, T. (eds.) Computer Vision-ECCV 2022: 17th European Conference, Tel Aviv, Israel, 23–27 October 2022, Proceedings, Part XXIII. pp. 153–169. Springer, Cham (2022). https://doi.org/10.1007/978-3-031-20050-2_10

28. Yu, J., Lin, Z., Yang, J., Shen, X., Lu, X., Huang, T.S.: Free-form image inpainting with gated convolution. In: Proceedings of the IEEE/CVF International Conference on Computer Vision, pp. 4471–4480 (2019)

29. Yu, X., Li, H., Yang, H.: Two-stage image decomposition and color regulator for low-light image enhancement. Vis. Comput. **39**(9), 4165–4175 (2023)

30. Zhu, X., Hu, H., Lin, S., Dai, J.: Deformable ConvNets V2: more deformable, better results. In: IEEE Conference on Computer Vision and Pattern Recognition, CVPR 2019, Long Beach, CA, USA, 16–20 June 2019 (2019)

SemiRefiner: Learning to Refine Semi-realistic Paintings

Keyue Fan and Shiguang Liu[✉]

College of Intelligence and Computing, Tianjin University, Tianjin 300350, China
lsg@tju.edu.cn

Abstract. The previous image optimization methods cannot complete the automatic refinement of semi-realistic paintings. Aiming at improving the efficiency of refinement manually, we propose an automatic refinement method for semi-realistic figure paintings guided by the line art. In order to enable the framework to adjust the draft color in the refinement process like a real painter, we design a color correction module, which automatically fixes the inappropriate color in the draft. In order to reduce artifacts and generate high-quality results, we use the line art to guide the refinement. We further devise a line art optimization module in the framework to ensure generation of high quality results by improving the quality of the line art. The experimental results and user surveys demonstrate the effectiveness of the proposed method.

Keywords: Image refinement · Line drawings · Semi-realistic paintings

1 Introduction

In animation, video games, and films, the creation of 2D paintings such as illustration and game concept art is a very important work. The semi-realistic painting is a style between flat color painting and realistic painting. In recent years, semi-realistic painting is a very popular 2D painting way, however, it is very difficult for non-professionals.

Refinement, a process of slowly reducing strokes, shaping volume, and painting fine results from the paved large color blocks, is a common vocabulary in the field of semi-realistic painting. Painters often adjust and correct the color of the screen at this stage. Refinement can transform a rough and fuzzy color draft into a final fine and clear high-quality semi-realistic painting. As shown in Fig. 1, the image on the left is a color draft, and the right one is the refined result. It can be seen that after refinement, the whole picture becomes clean, the scribbles and wrong strokes are corrected, the image has more details, and the color of the picture is richer and more harmonious. However, the process from the refinement of draft with basic color and shape to the preparation of draft that can be

This work was partly supported by the Natural Science Foundation of China under grant no. 62072328.

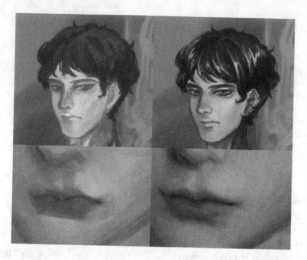

Fig. 1. The refinement of Semi-Realistic paintings is mainly achieved by continuously reducing strokes and depicting details. At the same time, painters often adjust and optimize the color of the screen at this stage.

used commercially is very mechanized and cumbersome, which must be realized manually at present, leading to a high cost of semi-realistic illustration drawing.

There are two important goals in the refinement task. One is to correct the strokes that exceed or deviate from the correct area in the draft, and generate rich details from the scrawled draft. The second is to modify and correct the colors in the draft. This task can be understood as a kind of work similar to image optimization, but the work on image optimization in the image processing field, including image super-resolution, image denoising, and image restoration, cannot achieve the above two goals.

To this end, this paper proposes an automatic refinement framework of semi-realistic paintings based on deep learning. In order to correct the wrong strokes in the color draft, this paper uses line draft constraint refinement. In view of the fact that the given line draft is also a draft, and the strokes may contain burrs and discontinuities, we design a line optimization framework, which first optimizes low-quality line draft into high-quality line draft. Then, the line draft is used to assist the refinement of the color draft, which improves the generation quality of the refinement framework. At the same time, adjusting the color of the draft, such as tone, light and shade, is also an important part of the refinement work. The framework should be able to adjust the color of the input draft to generate harmonious color results. In order to achieve this goal, this paper devises a color correction module. The experimental results and user surveys show that the color correction module can better adjust the colors in the draft and generate coordinated refinement results. Experiments show that the refinement framework can effectively realize automatic refinement of semi-realistic paintings. We summarize our contributions as follows:

- We propose SemiRefiner, an automatic refinement method for semi-realistic paintings guided by line draft.
- We design a color correction module to automatically correct the color problem in the draft by training through perceptual loss.
- We exploit the line draft to guide the refinement, and add a line optimization module to reduce structural distortion and generate high-quality results.

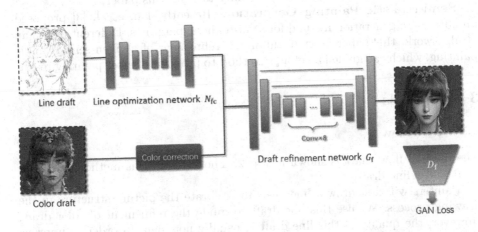

Fig. 2. Our method consists of three branches, of which each convolution block contains a 4×4 convolution layer and a ReLU layer. Note that, in addition to the decoder of the colorization net, other blocks also include a normalization layer. Shadows and lines are single-channel grayscale images, and color tips are 4-channel images with a mask.

2 Related Work

Refinement can be regarded as a type of image optimization task [9,11,13]. There have been many works on improving image quality, including image super-resolution, image restoration, and image denoising.

Image Super-Resolution. Dong et al. [2] proposed a deep learning method for super-resolution of a single image. Kim et al. [7] added the residual block to the super-differential network, learned the residual and achieved high learning rate through adjustable gradient clipping. Liu et al. [1] summarized and analyzed the deep learning based image super-resolution in detail. The super-resolution task can only make the blurred image clear, with the image semantics unadjusted. Therefore, it cannot be used to correct the scrawled and misplaced strokes in the thick paint draft, nor can it build a thin thick paint illustration from simple strokes.

Image Denoising. Zhang et al. [15] proposed a feedforward denoising convolution neural network. Guo et al. [4] trained a convolution blind denoising network, which achieved better results in the task of denoising the naturally distorted image. However, image denoising can only remove fine grain errors in the image, which cannot be used to correct large grain messy strokes.

Line Draft Guided Image Restoration. Some work uses the line draft to guide the image restoration task. Nazeri et al. [10] proposed a two-stage model, which divides the repair problem into two parts: structure prediction and image completion. Xu et al. [14] also proposed an edge guided image repair method. Hu et al. [5] introduced a decoder based on dual parallel network to generate images and edges simultaneously. Although this kind of online draft guidance method cannot be used to refine tasks, its idea of relying on online draft guidance provides inspiration for high-quality refining tasks in this paper.

Semi-realistic Painting Generation. Recently, Fan et al. [3] proposed an automatic generation method for semi-realistic paintings. Different from Fan et al.'s work, this paper aims at automatic refinement of a given semi-realistic painting, which can guide Fan et al.'s method to produce a better painting result.

3 Methods

3.1 Overview

The method flow chart is shown in Fig. 2. The input of this method is a color draft and a line draft.

Painters will first draw a line draft to calibrate the picture structure in the drawing process. We use this line draft to guide the refinement of color draft. However, the quality of this line draft is usually not high. In order to improve the quality of the final result, we first send the line draft to a line optimization network (Nfc), namely the orange network in the figure. The network aims to complete the missing parts of the original line draft and generate continuous and clear line draft. In order to adjust the overall color and fix the overall color problems such as low saturation and low contrast, the color draft will be fed to the color correction module (blue part).

Then, the optimization results of the line optimization network and the vector from the color correction module are input to the draft refinement network (green part) and refined, finally a high-quality semi-realistic figure paintings is generated.

3.2 Color Correction Module

We add a color correction module before the draft refinement network in the framework. The structure of the color correction module includes mirror filling layer with a convolution core size of 7×7, a convolution layer with step 1, and a PReLU active layer. This module extracts a 3-channel color image into a 64-channel vector. Because we add a reflection padding layer in the module, the width and height of the vector obtained are the same as those of the original image.

In order to make the optimization module effective, we have taken two measures. Firstly, in the process of skip connection to transfer the original vector, instead of using the shallow vector of the original image, we add the vector extracted from the color optimization block to the last of the upper sampling layer, so that the initial color can guide less color synthesis in the final generation process, and the optimized color will guide more color synthesis. Secondly, in the training process, we add structural loss and perceptual loss to the loss function. This allows the model to learn the color distribution of the entire dataset without overly depending on the color of the input image. Meanwhile, some pixel level losses are still used in the loss function to improve the convergence speed.

3.3 Draft Refinement Network

The main part of the refinement framework in this paper is a generation network with the U-Net structure (green part in Fig. 2). This part of the network is equipped with a Patch Discriminator, which provides a GAN loss for training draft refinement network G_f. The input of the network is the optimized color vector and a line sketch, and the final result is the high-quality semi-realistic paintings after refinement.

Line Optimization Module. In order not to add more input constraints and ensure the practicability of the method, this framework only uses a rough line sketch drawn by the painter in the drafting stage. High quality line drawings can improve the quality of the final results, but the quality of the line drawings drawn by painters in the draft stage is generally not high. In order to improve the quality of the line drawings, this paper designs a line optimization module. The line optimization module is shown in Fig. 2 (the orange part), which is composed of a lightweight U-Net network. The network performs 2 down-sampling, feature transformation through 4 convolutional blocks, and finally 2 up-sampling to obtain the optimized line draft. We have produced a low-quality, high-quality line draft pair dataset to train the network. The specific production method will be described in detail in Sect. 4. The network is trained with supervision, and the loss function is the smooth $L1$ loss. The line optimization network is N_{fc}, x_l is low quality line draft, y_l is continuous high quality line draft, and the loss function of the network is shown in Eq. 1.

$$L_{fc}(N_{fc}) = \mathbb{E}_{x_l, y_l}[\text{smooth}L_1(N_{fc}(x_l), y_l)] \tag{1}$$

Draft Refinement Network. The backbone network of the refinement framework is the draft refinement network G_f, which contains 3 down-sampling blocks and 8 feature transformation convolution blocks. The structure of the down-sampling and feature transformation convolution block includes a 3×3, a batch normalization (BN) layer and a PReLU layer. The 2D convolution step in the down sampled block is 2, and the 2D convolution step in the feature transformation block is 1. In the upsampling block, the convolution layer is replaced by a deconvolution layer with a step size of 2. In order to generate a result with higher saturation and brighter picture, we removed the normalized layer in the three upper sampling blocks.

At the same time, Karras et al. [6] believe that hair, clothes, and some fine textures can be considered random during the generation process, and adding noise in the image reconstruction process will improve the quality of the generated results. Inspired by this suggestion, we add a single channel Gaussian noise to the tail of the vector processed by each upsampling block to generate more details and avoid the generated image being too smooth. In order to standardize the final generation result between 0 and 1, in the output layer of generating RGB three channel images, we replace the ReLU layer with the Sigmoid function. Because the color correction module is added and the data set is not made to simulate low quality colors, the tone of the refinement network may be different from the color of the real image. Therefore, we incorporate the perceptual loss and SSIM (Structural Similarity) loss to the loss function, and reduce the weight of pixel level loss to ensure that the color correction module can be trained together with the generator.

The G_f is the generator of the draft refinement network, D_f is its corresponding discriminator, $\hat{y}_l$ is the result of $N_{fc}(y_l)$, x_f is the color draft, y_f is the real semi-realistic figure paintings, $\hat{y}_f$ is the result of $G_f(x_f, \hat{y}_l)$. The loss function of the network is as follows:

$$
\begin{aligned}
L_f(G_f, D_f) = \mathbb{E}_{x_f, \hat{y}_l, y_f} [& \delta_1 \mathrm{smooth} L_1(y_f - \hat{y}_f) \\
& + \delta_2 L_{SSIM}(y_f, \hat{y}_f) + \delta_3 L_{percp}(y_f, \hat{y}_f) \\
& - \lambda_3 \log(D_f(y_f)) - \lambda_3 \log(1 - D_f(\hat{y}_f))]
\end{aligned}
\tag{2}
$$

where $L_{percp}(\cdot)$ is the perceptual loss, $L_{SSIM}(\cdot)$ is the SSIM loss, $\mathrm{smooth} L_1(\cdot)$ is the smooth L_1 loss, δ_1, δ_2, δ_3, λ_3 are the weights of each loss item. In the training stage, δ_2, δ_3 are set to 10 and δ_1, λ_3 are set to 5.

4   Datasets and Training

4.1   Dataset for Draft Refinement Network

In order to train the draft refinement network, we collected 2,400 high-quality semi-realistic figure paintings from the open creation platform and the Danboo-image dataset. 49 pictures were randomly selected as the test set, and the rest of the data were used as the training set. For the training set and test set, we first select the characters in the illustration. First, we detect the face in the illustration, and then expand the location of the face to generate an illustration with a high proportion of people. Note that we cut out the characters in some images that cannot be detected normally.

We use the Sketchkeras [16] method to detect and extract the line draft, and adopt the PaintTransformer [17] to simulate the color draft. The Paint-Transformer is intended to transform a picture into oil painting at the stroke level rather than the pixel level. It gradually reduces the stroke size from rough strokes to finally generate oil painting works. Because the rendering process is coarse to fine, the intermediate result is a color draft, which is highly consistent with the color draft required in this paper. This method is very similar to the way painters draw drafts. Therefore, we use the intermediate results of this method to simulate the color draft, forming a color draft refinement image data pair.

The paired data enables us to conduct supervised training, reduce the difficulty of network training, and improve the quality of generation.

4.2 Line Draft Optimization

In order to train the line optimization network, we make data pairs of low-quality and high-quality line drafts. Low-quality line draft is the previously generated line draft. Because this method is more suitable for extracting flat color illustration, the image processing result with 3D structure is not ideal, and it can just simulate low quality line draft. For high-quality line draft, we adopt the Canny edge detection and adaptive threshold binarization to extract line draft, and use Eq. 3 to fuse these line drafts.

$$p = \max(0, p_1 + p_2 - 255) \tag{3}$$

where p_1 and p_2 are the pixels in the line draft obtained by the Canny edge detection and adaptive threshold binary edge extraction respectively, and p is the final high-quality line draft, with the value range of $[0, 255]$. These two line draft extraction methods respectively complete the missing lines in the other method, so that the line structure is clearer and a group of high quality line arts can be simulated.

5 Result and Evaluation

In this section, we show the results. We compared the proposed method with the state-of-the-art image optimization methods. The results show that our method can complete the automatic refinement of semi-realistic paintings. We also conducted ablation experiments to demonstrate the effectiveness of the color correction module and the line guidance and optimization network.

5.1 Results

Refined Results on the Test Set. This group of experiments shows the results of a group of models running on the test set. This test set is selected randomly from the data set. It contains 49 test pictures in the same format as the training set, including line draft, simulation draft, and real illustration. The test results are shown in Fig. 3. The leftmost column is the line draft extracted from the real thick painting works, the second column is the simulated color draft, the second column from the right is the real data, and the rightmost column is the final result of this method. It can be seen that our method has completed the task of automatic refinement of color draft, and the resulting visual effect is also good, with little blurry, distorted and wrong color blocks. Moreover, the color correction module has also taken effect, making certain optimization for the draft color.

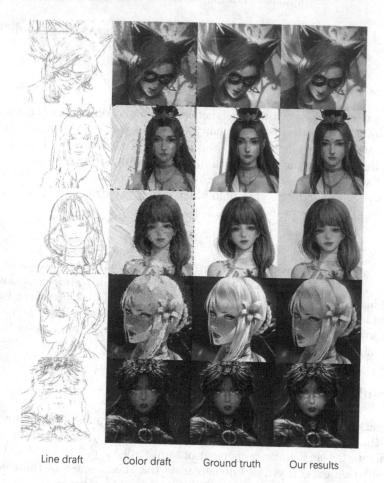

Line draft   Color draft   Ground truth   Our results

Fig. 3. The refined results on the test set.

Comparison with State-of-the-Art Image Optimization Methods.
Previous image optimization work included image denoising, image super resolution, and image restoration. In order to illustrate that it cannot be used for automatic refinement of semi-realistic paintings, we compare our method with a classical deep learning method for image denoising, image super resolution, and image restoration. The image denoising method for comparison is MemNet [12], the image superresolution method is SRGAN [8], and the image repair method is EdgeConnect [10]. The experimental results are shown in Fig. 4. Compared with real data, the proposed method in this paper corrects the wrong strokes and produces thick, high-quality illustrations.

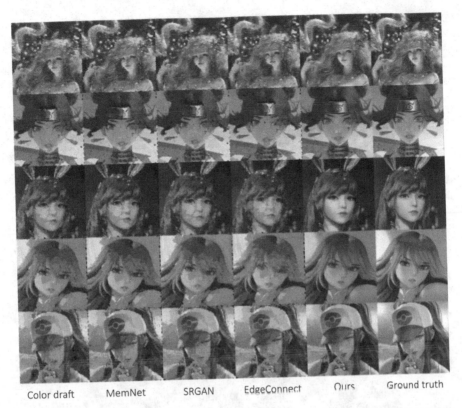

Color draft   MemNet   SRGAN   EdgeConnect   Ours   Ground truth

Fig. 4. A comparison of the results generated by MemNet [12], SRGAN [8], EdgeConnect [10], and our results.

5.2 Ablative Study

Validation of the Color Correction Module. The function of the color correction module is to adjust and correct many color problems in the draft, such as low contrast, low saturation, too dark color, etc. When the draft color is good, the color correction module will hardly work. When the draft color is poor, the module can correct these problems in time. Figure 5 shows an example of a set of color correction module correction problem color drafts, and the result of removing the module from the network.

Validation of the Line Optimization Module. The second group of experiments is about the ablation of line draft processing, and the results are shown in Fig. 6. From the graph, we can see that the result without line guidance contains a lot of structural errors and artifacts, which is especially obvious when refinement face with line optimization network. Line continuity and details are improved. It can be seen that blurring and artifacts are significantly reduced, indicating that it can assist the generation of sharper thinned images.

Color draft   w/o color   With color
                     correction   correction

Fig. 5. Verification of the color correction module.

6   Conclusion and Future Work

We proposed a method for automatic refinement of semi-realistic figure paintings. This work uses a line draft to guide the refinement of the draft, and a GAN
network architecture to generate high-quality semi-realistic figure paintings from
the color draft. In order to improve the quality of the results, a line optimization
model is added to the overall framework, which can repair scratched and dis-
continuous lines in the draft, so that the draft can better guide the refinement
work. At the same time, in the actual work of illustration refinement, the painter
will constantly modify the colors in the optimized draft. In order to achieve this
process, correct the errors or poor color matching in the draft, we propose a
color correction module, which enables the frame to eventually generate thick
painted figure illustrations with beautiful colors and correct structure.

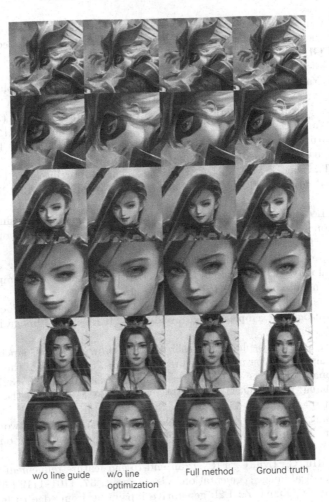

w/o line guide   w/o line   Full method   Ground truth
                   optimization

Fig. 6. Verification of the line optimization module.

However, the color optimization module in this paper cannot process some color drafts with single hue but good color matching results. This may be due to the loss of perception calculated based on the VGG-19 network using realistic image training. Training some pre-training networks for non-photorealistic images such as illustrations may contribute to the development of this field.

References

1. AL-Mekhlafi, H., Liu, S.: Single image super-resolution: a comprehensive review and recent insight. Frontiers Comput. Sci. **17**, 1–27 (2023)
2. Dong, C., Loy, C.C., He, K., Tang, X.: Image super-resolution using deep convolutional networks. IEEE Trans. Pattern Anal. Mach. Intell. **38**(2), 295–307 (2016)

3. Fan, K., Liu, S., Lu, W.: Learning to draw semi-realistic paintings from the manga line drawings and flat shadow. In: Magnenat-Thalmann, N., et al. (eds.) Proceedings of CGI, vol. 13443, pp. 305–317. Springer, Cham (2022). https://doi.org/10.1007/978-3-031-23473-6_24

4. Guo, S., Yan, Z., Zhang, K., Zuo, W., Zhang, L.: Toward convolutional blind denoising of real photographs. In: Proceedings of the IEEE/CVF Conference on Computer Vision and Pattern Recognition (CVPR), pp. 1712–1722 (2019)

5. Hu, J., Wang, C., Zhang, Y., Liu, L., Yin, Y., Zimmermann, R.: Parallel edge-image learning for image inpainting. In: Proceedings of the IEEE International Conference on Multimedia and Expo (ICME), pp. 1–6 (2022)

6. Karras, T., Laine, S., Aila, T.: A style-based generator architecture for generative adversarial networks. IEEE Trans. Pattern Anal. Mach. Intell. **43**(12), 4217–4228 (2021)

7. Kim, J., Lee, J.K., Lee, K.M.: Accurate image super-resolution using very deep convolutional networks. In: Proceedings of the IEEE Conference on Computer Vision and Pattern Recognition (CVPR), pp. 1646–1654 (2016)

8. Ledig, C., et al.: Photo-realistic single image super-resolution using a generative adversarial network. In: Proceedings of the IEEE Conference on Computer Vision and Pattern Recognition (CVPR), pp. 105–114 (2017)

9. Li, H., Sheng, B., Li, P., Ali, R.A., Chen, C.L.P.: Globally and locally semantic colorization via exemplar-based broad-GAN. IEEE Trans. Image Process. **30**, 8526–8539 (2021)

10. Nazeri, K., Ng, E., Joseph, T., Qureshi, F., Ebrahimi, M.: EdgeConnect: structure guided image inpainting using edge prediction. In: Proceedings of the IEEE/CVF International Conference on Computer Vision Workshop, pp. 3265–3274 (2019)

11. Qi, Y., Zhang, A., Wang, H., Li, X.: An efficient FCM-based method for image refinement segmentation. Vis. Comput. **38**, 2499–2514 (2022)

12. Tai, Y., Yang, J., Liu, X., Xu, C.: MemNet: a persistent memory network for image restoration. In: Proceedings of the IEEE International Conference on Computer Vision (ICCV), pp. 4549–4557 (2017)

13. Wang, D., Hu, G., Lyu, C.: FRNet: an end-to-end feature refinement neural network for medical image segmentation. Vis. Comput. **37**, 1101–1112 (2021)

14. Xu, S., Liu, D., Xiong, Z.: E2I: generative inpainting from edge to image. IEEE Trans. Circuits Syst. Video Technol. **31**(4), 1308–1322 (2021)

15. Zhang, K., Zuo, W., Chen, Y., Meng, D., Zhang, L.: Beyond a Gaussian denoiser: residual learning of deep CNN for image denoising. IEEE Trans. Image Process. **26**(7), 3142–3155 (2017)

16. Zhang, L.: Sketchkeras (2017). https://github.com/lllyasviel/sket-chKeras. https://github.com/lllyasviel/sketchKeras

17. Zou, Z., Shi, T., Qiu, S., Yuan, Y., Shi, Z.: Stylized neural painting. In: Proceedings of the IEEE/CVF Conference on Computer Vision and Pattern Recognition (CVPR), pp. 15684–15693 (2021)

MagicMirror: A 3-D Real-Time Virtual Try-On System Through Cloth Simulation

Zhanyi Huang[1], Wenqing Zhao[1], Tangsheng Guo[1], Jin Huang[1(✉)], Ping Li[2], and Bin Sheng[3]

[1] Wuhan Textile University, Wuhan, China
derick0320@foxmail.com
[2] Hong Kong Polytechnic University, Kowloon, Hong Kong
[3] Shanghai Jiao Tong University, Shanghai, China

Abstract. Nowadays, with the increasing development of online shopping, there exists a huge latent benefit area in clothing e-commerce. It has been leading the application of emerging technologies to this field. However, online shopping can not intuitively feel the material of clothes fabric and the dynamic effect of trying on clothes. Methodologies based on cloth simulation and human-computer interaction can be used to solve this challenge. In this paper, we proposed a virtual try-on system based cloth simulation technique to tackle the realism of cloth, using physical law in garment to strengthen the realism of virtual try-on and integrated markless motion capture technique realized by common RGB-D camera to synchronize movement of models and people. We also adopt a GPU acceleration solution to ensure real-time simulation. We realized the system based Unity3D using TaiChi Programming Language to control and stimulate the garment. And we verify the significance of GPU acceleration and conduct several experiments to prove the real-time performance of the simulation-based virtual try-on system. We compared the simulation time on CPU and GPU and validated the accuracy of motion capture satisfying virtual try-on task. In the end we conducted a user study to find out if the average consumer was satisfied with our proposed virtual try-on system.

Keywords: Virtual Try On · Real-time · Cloth Simulation · Garment Modeling · Motion Capture

1 Introduction

Virtual try-on, which is aimed at achieving the target of the remote try-on and personalize tailoring with garment factories. It is a vital practical application in the garment market. Using virtual try-on technique, consumers can try on a wide variety of clothes without the restrictions of location and time. Virtual try-on technology also can reduce the rate of clothing returns and exchange, saving consumers and manufacturers time and shipping costs. Furthermore, obtaining real-time speed in cloth animation has important applications not just in video

© The Author(s), under exclusive license to Springer Nature Switzerland AG 2024
B. Sheng et al. (Eds.): CGI 2023, LNCS 14496, pp. 287–299, 2024.
https://doi.org/10.1007/978-3-031-50072-5_23

Fig. 1. Our virtual try-on system scene effect display, we use RGBD camera to scan human body continually, and bind the action to the model and perform real-time fabric simulation to achieve virtual try-on.

games or movies but also in many interactive graphics applications. Limiting in hardware accuracy and speed, real-time cloth simulation has been big challenges even if we use GPU acceleration solution owing its huge amount of computing (Fig. 1).

Previous virtual try-on research is mainly focused on how to pair clothes with body pictures to synthesize fitting results. Image based virtual try on methods [10, 14, 30] are focused on transforming the garment pictures to suit body specific posture pictures, and dedicated to solving the problem of clothing and body coverage. To realize three-dimensional try sense, research begins to put clothes on 3D mannequins [3, 4, 23]. To achieve the goal of real-time virtual try-on, Stefan and Matthias et al. [15] began to use motion capture technique bind human and model movement. Manfredi and Capece et al. [20] use UDraper supported by Unreal Engine designed a virtual dressing room and use Onepose [32] to detect human movement.

Our research work is aimed at focusing on the idea of using TaiChi and Unity3D to build a real-time virtual try-on system overcoming the limitations through simulation techniques, called MagicMirror. We realized motion capture module through a single RGBD camera supporting MagicMirror with tracking customer's movements in real-time and anthropomorphic measurements to help create a customer's 3D virtual image model.

In this paper, we make the following contributions:

- We design a novel virtual try-on system with clothing simulation. With novel GPU-accelerated algorithms, our system can simulate clothes in real time. Our system shows the complete details of the clothes and the dynamic effect of interaction with all solids.
- We use the latest motion capture solutions. Comparing to previous similar virtual try-on systems, our system is able to capture human motion more accurately, Furthermore, we did a comparison experiment with other motion capture based virtual try-on systems and invited 50 participants for a user study.

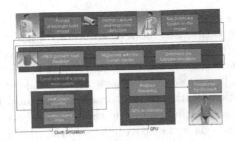

Fig. 2. The architecture of virtual try on system. It shows the whole system working pipeline. Consumers standing in front of machine, take some photos. Then computer compares with database library and finally generates a virtual digit human. Computer synchronizes two resources and simulate try on result.

2 Related Work

Relevant prior work of virtual try on includes studies of 2D virtual try on, 3D virtual try on, cloth simulation and motion capture.

2.1 Image Based Virtual Try on

In previous work, there already exist quantities classic methods about 2D virtual try-on tasks [10] and so on are based on Generative Adversarial Networks (GANs) [13]. To solve single posture try-on issue, some researchers have commenced expanding single pose on multi-pose virtual try-on. Research workers have made efforts to transfer the original image to appointed pose target [6]. However, the critical challenge that details of garment is still waiting to be solved. Du et al. [11] design a multi-stage framework to attempt to address the issue. Due to the limitations about 2D virtual try-on tasks, researchers have been exploring to present try-on result by 3D perspective, one is physical-based methods and the other is scan-based methods [24,27]. Then these two categories approaches tend to move towards learning-based 3D try-on methods [21]. However, the majority of these learning methods [21,23] rely on a preset digital wardrobe [3] and are built on the parametric SMPL [4] model, which restricts their practical usefulness. Zhao et al. [34] focused on generating more detailed depth estimation, but it only can represent one view perspective.

2.2 Cloth Simulation

The methods based on physical cloth simulation have been unique and attractive for researchers in computer graphics and developers in the fashion industry. Numerous elastic models have been experimented with to apply cloth simulation since the groundbreaking work of Terzopoulos et al. [28] in 1987. David and Andrew's work [2] and Narain et al. [17]'s introduction of finite element models into cloth simulation have also contributed to the development of these models.

Choi and Ko [8], Liu et al. [19] tried mass-spring models. Kaldor et al. [16], Cirio et al. [9] explore yarn-based models. In order for a simulator to take large time steps with numerical stability, early research focused on using implicit time integrators. Narain et al. [17], Volino et al. [29] rather than explicit ones Bridson et al. [5], Selle et al. [26]. Researchers have also looked into the possibility of replacing textile elasticity with position-based approaches, like position-based dynamics [22]and strain limiting [25]. The relationship between cloth elasticity and position-based methods was discovered by Liu et al. [19]

2.3   Virtual Try on System

Existing virtual try-on systems based video or augment reality usually are expressing a part of body such as eyeglasses [33] and shoes [1]. Pattern-based techniques are challenging for non-experts and need a specialist understanding of garment design. Zhou et al. [35] produced virtual outfits from a single photograph to solve the issue of digitising clothing. Using a depth camera to record genuine clothing, Chen et al. [7] constructed a coarse shape from the RGBD sequence of the obtained clothing. Gilda et al. [20] design an immersive and realistic try-on experience by integrating a high level of photorealism.

3   Method

3.1   Architecture of System

The virtual try-on system is shown as Fig. 2, which is divided into two types of functions. Physical clothing simulation and real-time virtual try-on animation. After parameters are finished, the system makes appropriate adjustments to the generated virtual image. The model is also used in the motion capture part. The motion capture module and clothing simulation module is based on this model.

3.2   Create Virtual Image

We use the Euclidean distance to compare with the Human dimensions of Chinese adults. The programming calculates the Euclidean distance between the current data and each standard data value, and selects the model with the smallest calculated value as the basic clothing size. The result can be computed by the following formula:

$$R = D(l_i, i) \tag{1}$$

where, l_i are n-dimensional vectors,i represents the $i-th$ measured feature data, and n is the number of contour feature points after principal component. The feature vector of the current frame is represented by i, while the current picture in the database is represented by l_i. The Euclidean distance between i and l_i is $D(l_i, i)$. Let's express i and l_i as follows:

$$i = [i_1, i_2, \ldots, i_n] \tag{2}$$

$$l_i = [l_{i1}, l_{i2,...,}l_{in}] \tag{3}$$

the Euclidean distance of the two is:

$$distance = \min(\|l_{l1} - i_1\|_2 + \|l_{l2} - i_2\|_2 + \dots \|l_{ln} - i_n\|_2)$$

$$= \min \sum_{j=1}^{n} \|l_{ij} - X_j\|_2 \tag{4}$$

The contour feature picture is referred to as Fig. 3. We estimate the actual length using the RGB-D camera, which includes arm length, upper body length, shoulder breadth, chest breadth, waist breadth, hip breadth, leg length, thigh width (single leg) and use 1 formula select consumer's virtual image.

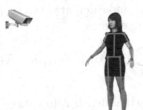

Fig. 3. The bone skeleton using camera estimating schematic diagram

3.3 Body Tracking

In order to make the virtual model's movements follow the consumer's movements in real time and without requiring the consumer to wear specific sensor devices, our system integrates a common RGBD camera. We have selected the key points when we build the virtual image before.

We built an image graph for each frame by extracting the RGB feature and then examining the connection between all potential picture pairs. We use Scale-Invariant Feature Transform. From each picture in the source image S_i, our algorithm extracts visual features V_i. Letting $S = \{S_i \mid i = 1, 2, \dots, N_S\}$.

$$V_i = \{(x_j, d_j \mid j = 1, 2, \dots, N_V)\} \tag{5}$$

where x_j is the $j - th$ pair feature point coordinate $x_j = (x, y)$ and d_j stands for a descriptor of the feature x_j

In matching correspond key points stage, the system identifies the point of correlation between every combination of images. For each image I_i, system matching module work to find feature correspondence for each feature which locates in every image S_j. The following definition describes the matching outcome between images S_i and S_j:

$$M_{i,j} = \{(S_i, S_j \mid 0 < i, j < N_S)\} \tag{6}$$

After matching correspond key points from each image, our system determines the connectedness among every pair of images to create an image graph. Each image I_i is represented by a node N_i in an image graph, and each node has connectivity C and local feature position x_j as shown below:

$$N_i = \{(x_j, C \mid j = 1, 2, \ldots, N_V), i = 1, 2, \ldots, N_S\} \tag{7}$$

Using two attributes, the connectivity $C = \{Cor, V\}$ denotes relational information with other nodes. The starting picture pair is chosen using Cor. The definition of the edge $E_{i,j}$ between nodes N_i and N_j is as follows:

$$E_{i,j} = \{N_i, N_j, M_{i,j} \mid S_i, Sj \in S_{input}, M_{i,j} > M_{th}\} \tag{8}$$

The virtual depth map(S_v^{dep}) is using the camera's sensor calculated. The system takes every ten images and calculates the average depth of the customer's image to restore depth information:

$$S_v^{dep} = \sum_{S_i \in S_{reg}} w(X_W)D(X_W^i), \quad X_W^i \quad in \quad S_i \tag{9}$$

where $D(X_W^i)$ denotes the virtual depth value of the X_W^i and $w(X_W)$ is average weight per every ten images.

3.4 Garment Modeling

The clothes' virtual models are downloaded from Internet free 3D Garment Models and edited in Marvelous Designer Garment Modeling Software. The former offers the latest clothing sets designed by fashion designers. And the latter can be designed by customers themselves. We designed some garments and Implemented an interface to simplify the production process of clothing. Both above two methods generated garments are saved to the object storage system through the database (Fig. 4).

(a) garment   (b) sewing   (c) try on result

Fig. 4. Motion capture results skeletal structure drawing display

3.5   Physical Cloth Simulation

The physical cloth simulation module is based on Unity3D and the control script we use Taichi programming language to implement simulation. At the beginning of simulation, the model is placed in a T-pose for easy correspondence between the arm and the point on the sleeve. We use Taichi to rewrite the physics laws and rendering part of the control script to faster simulation solving and render the result in time by Unity3D. The stitching force between fabric pieces is calculated as a linear function of the distance between the corresponding stitching points; the closer the stitching points are, the lower the stitching force is. Since cloth is a highly nonlinear body, to represent this property of the fabric, we adopt the FGM method proposed by Wang et al. [31] to solve the mesh deformation as well as the global smoothing problem, and use adaptive smoother to avoid smoothing if the residual has fallen below a certain threshold. We use Improved Euler Integration to determine the position of each particle. In the simulation process, Our system uses AABB bounding box method to detect collisions. Although in some aspects not as high as other bracketing accuracy, the AABB bracketing box has a short response time and high computational efficiency.

3.6   GPU Acceleration

To accelerate the simulation process, we need to accelerate the PBD simulation algorithm. We partially group of constraints using Jacobi Iterative Method and Gauss-Seidel Iterative Method based Fartarcangeli and Pellacini [12] to accelerate the constraints of Position based Dynamics and retain a portion of the serial iterations. The method breakdown the interdependence of the original constraint and finally maximize the parallel computation of each grouping constraint on the GPU and reduce the number of GPU core calls. We use Bron-kerbosch searching to find it. The algorithm can be described as follows:

Algorithm 1. Bron-Kerbosch maximum complete subgraph search algorithm

---

Require: The set of all nodes in the graph in $P.R = \varnothing X = \varnothing$. The adjacency of nodes is obtained by $N(v)$ mapping

Ensure: Maximum subgraph K in topology graph

    Bron-Kerbosch (R, P, X)

    if $P = \varnothing AND X = \varnothing$ **then**

        ADD R TO K

    end if

    for All nodes v in P **do**

        BronKerboSch($R \cup \{v\}, P \cap N(v), X \cap N(v)$)

        DELETE v FROM P

        ADD v TO X

    end for

Where R denotes the node set already in subgraph, P denotes node set probable in subgraph, X denotes node set already used and $N(v)$ denotes adjacency of nodes from v (Fig. 5).

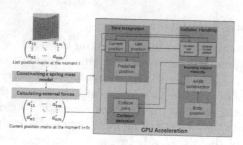

Fig. 5. The pipeline of simulation, using mass spring system to calculate the internal force between cloths, giving external force and updating clothing status by GPU acceleration algorithm.

4   Experiment

4.1   Simulation Experiment

Our experiment runs in an AMD Ryzen 5600G 3.9 GHz CPU and an NVIDIA GeForce RTX 3060 GPU. We have selected the 5 most common types of clothing for simulation, including T-shirt, skirt and so on. The runtime results of our cases both on CPU and GPU are shown in Table 1 and some results are shown as Fig. 6. We record average rates the result shows that compared with CPU simulation, The GPU acceleration is remarkable, and the frame rate meets the requirements of real-time virtual try-on.

We set the same cloth simulation parameter on all samples represented in this paper. We set the stiffness constants $K_{stretch} = 800$, $k_{shear} = 200$, $k_{bend} = 10^{-6}$ and set the damping stiffness constants for stretch, shear and bend constrains $k_{d,stretch} = 100$, $k_{d,sheer} = 1$ and $k_{d,bend}$. Above 6 parameters we cited in Baraff and Witkin [2] the simulation time step we set as $t = 0.002$.

4.2   Motion Capture Experiment

Then we tested the motion capture module alone on the PC mentioned above. And the method runs at an average of 30 fps. We use Kocabas et-al. [18] dataset to compare the model reconstruction quality and speed. We also compare our method with the reflective optical motion capture to evaluate the accuracy of single RGBD image pose. The results are shown as Fig. 7. And we tried to test this method on some difficult actions, the accuracy is not good as well as the smoothing movements. But we consider the accuracy is enough for real-time virtual try-on task.

To evaluate the markless motion capture actual working accuracy, we invited a coworker wear tights with reflective stickers and shot the same video for key point detection. We prepared 8 vicon motion analysis system to obtain motion data. The RGB-D camera is fixed on a tripod 1.5 m high and 2 m away from the coworker. A total of 30 sets of data were collected. We use Coefficient of Multiple Correlations, CMC and Root Mean Square Error, RMSE to measure

Table 1. The table records system performance for simulation mentioned above. Actual frame rate on CPU and GPU, average over the simulation, and four tasks percentage of simulation running time: EVAL: Forming a linear equation solution; CG: Solving equation; C/C: Collision detection between cloth; C/S: Collision detection between cloth and solids

	Name	#Verts/,#Tri.		CPU Frame	GPU Frame	task breakdown percentage			
				fps	fps	EAVL	CG	C/C	C/S
1	Single Cloth	5284	10742	3.09	60.83	70.3	94.7	/	/
2	T-shirt	52K	101K	0.72	40.05	33.4	58.2	45.9	2.3
3	caftan	56K	112K	0.63	33.56	31.7	47.3	28.4	4.6
4	skirt	52K	103K	0.56	32.47	28.3	42.6	48.2	6.7
5	shorts	50K	99K	0.81	34.74	32.6	59.7	42.6	2.1
6	trousers	56K	112K	0.72	31.61	30.3	54.9	43.5	3.9

(a) Dress Dresses   (b) Shorts   (c) Long skirt

(d) Pants   (e) T-shirt   (f) Skirt

Fig. 6. Some virtual common clothes simulation and rendering effects

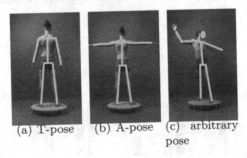

(a) T-pose   (b) A-pose   (c) arbitrary pose

Fig. 7. Field verification of motion capture results skeleton structure display

them. The results are shown as Table 2. We believe that our module can run in real time and without excessive errors.

Table 2. Comparison of our system and Kinect V2 with marker motion capture in terms of performance metrics

Joints movements	Root Mean Square Error RMSE		Multiple Correlations Coefficient CMC	
	with mark	our module	kinect v2	our module
shoulder	7.69	8.43	0.55	0.69
elbow	8.76	9.42	0.69	0.78
hip	8.48	8.86	0.48	0.5
knee	11.29	12.34	0.79	0.83
foot	26.18	28.04	0.52	0.56

4.3   User Study

To evaluate the perceived realism of the virtual try-on results created using our method, we conducted a user study. We invited 10 students from campus to experience the virtual try-on system and recorded the try-on results as videos. Then we dispatched these videos randomly to another 40 students.

We first showed the video of just clothes and ask them for the feel after watching the video. Each loop we show the different type of video twice. We summarize the answers to these questions with statistics and analyze it, then rank each question with five scores, the best-ranked was assigned 5, and the worst-ranked was assigned 1. For scores greater than 3 we consider that participants feel that the effect of the simulation is realistic. From the analysis of the data obtained as shown in Fig. 8. The results are shown as Table 3.

4.4   Ablation Experiment

To validate the collision detection and collision solving module performance, we set the ablation experiment. We disabled the collision module and regenerate the garments above, the generated pictures as Fig. 9 shows that clothes are sunk into model skeleton.

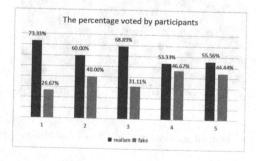

Fig. 8. Results of participant voting statistics, we combined the statistical scores for each question and calculated the final percentages

Table 3. Participants rate the virtual and real results, including the realism of clothing simulation, whether the clothing fits the virtual model and the real time of clothing simulation.

	T-shirt 1	T-shirt 2	caftan 1	caftan 2	skirt 1	skirt 2	shorts 1	shorts 2
realistic	82.56%	79.34%	77.82%	82.43%	43.54%	38.75%	63.59%	68.45%
Fitted models	78.25%	71.57%	83.42%	85.47%	60.32%	62.38%	75.64%	78.58%
Real-time availability	82.37%	87.63%	70.59%	72.68%	30.85%	34.72%	75.54%	73.06%

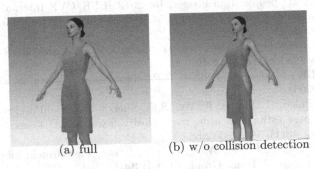

(a) full   (b) w/o collision detection

Fig. 9. The comparison with collision detection module removed

5   Limitations

Although we have achieved virtual try-on based cloth simulation based cloth simulation and can follow consumer movement to achieve virtual try on in real-time. The hand gesture recognition and face expression recognition we have neglected. Hand gesture recognition and face expression recognition are also resolved by motion capture technique based on the RGB-D camera. However, it may more key points detection and need train extra deep network to track them. Furthermore, hair simulation is also a difficult problem in computer graphics and computer simulation studies. So we also neglect it and just use the assets provided by Unity3D. Moreover, the cloth anisotropy we failed to implement due to time limitations, and we will implement it in the future work.

6   Conclusion

In this paper, we described our virtual try-on system solution. This approach integrates motion capture body tracking solution and real-time physical clothing simulation based TaiChi. The realistic virtual try-on experience consumers get with our system is our main advantage over other virtual try-on system solutions. In a manner akin to genuine cloth, the user's 3D virtual image and the surrounding surroundings interact in real-time with 3D clothing. Despite the great level of realistics, our system also has the benefit of being computationally inexpensive. This functionality would enable the creation of a smart mirror-enabled in-store shopping solution as well as a mobile and desktop-compatible online purchasing solution.

References

1. An, S., et al.: ARShoe: real-time augmented reality shoe try-on system on smart-phones. In: Proceedings of the 29th ACM International Conference on Multimedia, pp. 1111–1119 (2021)
2. Baraff, D.: Large steps in cloth simulation. In: Proc. SIGGRAPH '98, pp. 43–54 (1998)
3. Bhatnagar, B., Tiwari, G., Theobalt, C., Pons-Moll, G.: Multi-garment net: Learning to dress 3D people from images. In: 2019 IEEE/CVF International Conference on Computer Vision (ICCV), pp. 5419–5429 (2019). https://doi.org/10.1109/ICCV.2019.00552
4. Black, M.J., Matthew, L., Naureen, M., Gerard, P.M., Javier, R.: Skinned multi-person linear model. ACM (2015)
5. Bridson, R.E., Marino, S., Fedkiw, R.P.: Simulation of clothing with folds and wrinkles (2005)
6. Cao, Z., Hidalgo, G., Simon, T., Wei, S.E., Sheikh, Y.: OpenPose: realtime multi-person 2D pose estimation using part affinity fields. IEEE Trans. Pattern Anal. Mach. Intell. **43**(1), 172–186 (2021)
7. Chen, X., Zhou, B., Lu, F., Wang, L., Bi, L., Tan, P.: Garment modeling with a depth camera. ACM Trans. Graph. (TOG) **34**(6), 1–12 (2015)
8. Choi, K.J., Ko, H.S.: Stable but responsive cloth. In: ACM SIGGRAPH 2005 Courses, pp. 1-es (2005)
9. Cirio, G., Lopez-Moreno, J., Miraut, D., Otaduy, M.A.: Yarn-level simulation of woven cloth. ACM Trans. Graph. (TOG) **33**(6), 1–11 (2014)
10. Du, C., et al.: VTON-SCFA: a virtual try-on network based on the semantic constraints and flow alignment. IEEE Trans. Multimedia **25**, 777–791 (2022)
11. Du, C., Yu, F., Jiang, M., Wei, X., Peng, T., Hu, X.: Multi-pose virtual try-on via self-adaptive feature filtering. In: ICASSP 2022–2022 IEEE International Conference on Acoustics, Speech and Signal Processing (ICASSP), pp. 2544–2548 (2022). https://doi.org/10.1109/ICASSP43922.2022.9747847
12. Fratarcangeli, M., Pellacini, F.: Scalable partitioning for parallel position based dynamics. In: Computer Graphics Forum. vol. 34, pp. 405–413. Wiley Online Library (2015)
13. Goodfellow, I., et al.: Generative adversarial networks. Commun. ACM **63**(11), 139–144 (2020)
14. Han, X., Wu, Z., Wu, Z., Yu, R., Davis, L.S.: VITON: an image-based virtual try-on network. In: 2018 IEEE/CVF Conference on Computer Vision and Pattern Recognition, pp. 7543–7552 (2018). https://doi.org/10.1109/CVPR.2018.00787
15. Hauswiesner, S., Straka, M., Reitmayr, G.: Virtual try-on through image-based rendering. IEEE Trans. Visual Comput. Graph. **19**(9), 1552–1565 (2013)
16. Kaldor, J.M., James, D.L., Marschner, S.: Efficient yarn-based cloth with adaptive contact linearization. In: ACM SIGGRAPH 2010 Papers, pp. 1–10 (2010)
17. Kim, D., Koh, W., Narain, R., Fatahalian, K., Treuille, A., O'Brien, J.F.: Near-exhaustive precomputation of secondary cloth effects. ACM Trans. Graph. (TOG) **32**(4), 1–8 (2013)
18. Kocabas, M., Athanasiou, N., Black, M.J.: Vibe: video inference for human body pose and shape estimation. In: 2020 IEEE/CVF Conference on Computer Vision and Pattern Recognition (CVPR), pp. 5252–5262 (2020). https://doi.org/10.1109/CVPR42600.2020.00530

19. Liu, T., Bargteil, A.W., O'Brien, J.F., Kavan, L.: Fast simulation of mass-spring systems. ACM Trans. Graph. (TOG) **32**(6), 1–7 (2013)
20. Manfredi, G., Capece, N., Erra, U., Gilio, G., Baldi, V., Di Domenico, S.G.: TryItOn: a virtual dressing room with motion tracking and physically based garment simulation. In: De Paolis, L.T., Arpaia, P., Sacco, M. (eds.) XR Salento 2022. LNCS, vol. 13445, pp. 63–76. Springer, Cham (2022). https://doi.org/10.1007/978-3-031-15546-8_5
21. Mir, A., Alldieck, T., Pons-Moll, G.: Learning to transfer texture from clothing images to 3D humans. In: 2020 IEEE/CVF Conference on Computer Vision and Pattern Recognition (CVPR), pp. 7021–7032 (2020). https://doi.org/10.1109/CVPR42600.2020.00705
22. Müller, M.: Hierarchical position based dynamics. DBLP (2008)
23. Patel, C., Liao, Z., Pons-Moll, G.: TailorNet: predicting clothing in 3D as a function of human pose, shape and garment style. In: 2020 IEEE/CVF Conference on Computer Vision and Pattern Recognition (CVPR), pp. 7363–7373 (2020). https://doi.org/10.1109/CVPR42600.2020.00739
24. Pons-Moll, G., Pujades, S., Sonny, H.U., Black, M.J.: ClothCap: seamless 4D clothing capture and retargeting. ACM Trans. Graph. **36**(4CD), 1–15 (2017)
25. Provot, X.: Deformation constraints in a mass-spring model to describe rigid cloth behavior (2001)
26. Selle, A., Su, J., Irving, G., Fedkiw, R.: Robust high-resolution cloth using parallelism, history-based collisions, and accurate friction. IEEE Trans. Visual Comput. Graph. **15**(2), 339–350 (2009). https://doi.org/10.1109/TVCG.2008.79
27. Stoll, C., Gall, J., de Aguiar, E., Thrun, S., Theobalt, C.: Video-based reconstruction of animatable human characters. ACM Trans. Graph. **29**(6), 1–10 (2010). https://doi.org/10.1145/1882261.1866161
28. Terzopoulos, D., Platt, J., Barr, A., Fleischer, K.: Elastically deformable models. In: Proceedings of the 14th Annual Conference on Computer Graphics and Interactive Techniques, pp. 205–214 (1987)
29. Volino, P., Magnenat-Thalmann, N., Faure, F.: A simple approach to nonlinear tensile stiffness for accurate cloth simulation. ACM Trans. Graph. **28**(4), Article No (2009)
30. Wang, B., Zheng, H., Liang, X., Chen, Y., Lin, L., Yang, M.: Toward characteristic-preserving image-based virtual try-on network. In: Proceedings of the European Conference on Computer Vision (ECCV) (2018)
31. Wang, Z., Wu, L., Fratarcangeli, M., Tang, M., Wang, H.: Parallel multigrid for nonlinear cloth simulation. In: Computer Graphics Forum, vol. 37, pp. 131-141 (2018). https://doi.org/10.1111/cgf.13554
32. Wu, Y.L.: One pose fits all: a novel kinematic approach to 3D human pose estimation (2021)
33. Yamamoto, H., Moriya, T., Takahashi, T.: Development of a virtual try-on system for eyeglasses considering lens distortion. In: International Workshop on Advanced Imaging Technology (IWAIT) 2021, vol. 11766, pp. 409–414. SPIE (2021)
34. Zhao, F., et al.: M3D-VTON: a monocular-to-3D virtual try-on network. In: Proceedings of the IEEE/CVF International Conference on Computer Vision, pp. 13239–13249 (2021)
35. Zhou, B., Chen, X., Fu, Q., Guo, K., Tan, P.: Garment modeling from a single image. In: Computer Graphics Forum, vol. 32, pp. 85–91. Wiley Online Library (2013)

An Ancient Murals Inpainting Method Based on Bidirectional Feature Adaptation and Adversarial Generative Networks

Xingquan Cai, Qingtao Lu, Jiali Yao, Yao Liu, and Yan Hu[✉]

North China University of Technology, Beijing 100144, China
huyan0413@126.com

Abstract. To address the issue of varying degrees of damage in ancient Chinese murals due to their age and human-induced destruction, we propose a mural image restoration method based on bidirectional feature adaptation and adversarial generative networks. Firstly, we size and format the mural image. Subsequently, we construct an improved generator model that captures bidirectional semantic information, while introducing a spatial attention mechanism for adaptive feature enhancement for missing. Additionally, a spatial attention mechanism is introduced to adaptively enhance the features of known regions in the mural images. Furthermore, a discriminator model is constructed to discriminate between the restored mural images and real images, outputting a binary classification matrix. Finally, the network model is constrained by loss functions to generate mural images with rich textures. The experimental results show that the method realizes the restoration of mural images with different degrees of damage, and the restored mural images have finer texture information, which can contribute to the protection and inheritance of Chinese traditional culture.

Keywords: Mural Inpainting · Feature Adaptation · Generative Adversarial Network

1 Introduction

As one of China's ancient art forms, murals were extensively carved and painted in temples, palaces, and other occasions, preserving China's deep culture from ancient times [1]. They remain an important material for studying ancient history, culture, and art, with high cultural value.

However, due to the ancient age of murals and the continuous changes in natural environment and some human activities, many murals have suffered various degrees of damage [2]. Digital mural image protection has emerged as a solution, where murals are captured non-invasively, and computer digital and image processing technologies are used to repair damaged mural images digitally [3]. This is achieved by using the known image data information of the mural's known areas to estimate and fill the missing areas by a specific method

B. Sheng et al. (Eds.): CGI 2023, LNCS 14496, pp. 300–311, 2024.
https://doi.org/10.1007/978-3-031-50072-5_24

[4]. High-quality restoration of damaged mural images to realize the preservation and transmission of cultural heritage.

2   Related Work

Existing image inpainting methods can mainly be divided into two categories, traditional image inpainting and deep learning-based inpainting.

Traditional image inpainting techniques are mainly based on mathematical and physical methods, using different inpainting methods based on the degree of damage to the image, according to texture consistency and content similarity. In 2009, Barnes et al. [5] proposed an interactive image editing tool based on randomization algorithm, which is to find the best quality patch matching through random sampling, and this matching can be quickly propagated to surrounding areas based on the natural consistency of the image. In 2014, Huang et al. [6] proposed a method for using intermediate structure hints to automatically guide patch-based image completion [7]. The plane projection parameters are estimated to divide the known area into multiple planes, then returned to the baseline parallel image completion algorithm.

With the rapid development of deep learning technology in recent years, the advantages of deep learning in image processing are increasingly evident. In 2015, Ronneberger et al. [8,11] proposed the U-Net model. It has been widely used in the medical field [9]. The encoder and decoder structure can fuse low-level and high-level information features. In 2016, Pathak et al. [12] first applied GAN to image inpainting with the Context Encoders, which combines the encoder-decoder network structure and GAN. To address the shortcomings of Context Encoders, Iizuka et al. [10] introduced the Context Local Discriminator to generate image inpainting that is globally and locally semantically consistent. At the same time, the model introduced dilated convolution layers to increase the feature receptive field. Liao et al. [13] proposed the Edge-Aware Context Encoders based on Context Encoders to predict image edge structures, and used a fully convolutional network to complete image edge information. Then, the repaired edge image and damaged image were input to an improved Context Encoders to achieve image completion. In 2019, Nazeri et al. [14] proposed EdgeConnect. The edge generator first constructs edges for the missing regions, and then the completion network fills in the missing color information. Xie et al. [15] proposed a learnable attention map module in their work, which is used for end-to-end feature renormalization and mask updating learning. However, this method performs poorly in restoring images with a lot of texture information, and may produce artifacts [17].

Mural images often contain complex texture information, deep learning algorithms can also face challenges when trained directly on mural datasets, as the difficulty of training increases exponentially and the global structure of restored images may be discordant [18,19]. To overcome these challenges, this paper proposes a mural image inpainting algorithm based on bidirectional feature adaptation and adversarial generative networks. This algorithm prioritizes the overall structure of the restored image while also exhibiting a delicate approach to detail handling [20].

3   The Proposed Method

The existing inpainting methods perform well on small missing areas of mural images, but are not effective for large missing areas, often resulting in artifacts and blurring. To address these issues, this paper proposes a mural image inpainting method based on a bi-directional feature adaptation and adversarial generation network.

3.1   Constructing Repair Generation Networks

In this paper, we use a generator and a discriminator. The generator is mainly based on the U-Net network with improvements, and the discriminator uses a dual optimization discriminator to judge the generated repaired images. The model is shown in Fig. 1.

The generator network adopts an encoder-decoder structure, where the damaged wall painting image and the mask image are input into the generator network. The multi-layer encoder performs pooling on the input image to extract its feature in-formation, where the deep convolution focuses on the essential features while the shallow network focuses on the texture features. Multiple branch feature extraction is used to enhance the expression ability of different features, achieving a progressive repair of the wall painting image.

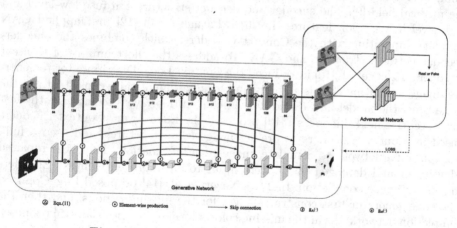

Fig. 1. Our generative adversarial network model.

Improved Partial Convolution Layer. PConv performs well in repairing irregular holes, and is used to operate on the image with the wall painting image feature map F^{in} and the binary mask M^{in} as input. Let W be the weight of the convolution filter, b be the corresponding bias, M^c be the convolution mask, and M be the corresponding 0-1 mask. We define the convolution mask M^{conv} as:

$$M^c = M^{in} \otimes k_m \tag{1}$$

where $\otimes$ denotes the convolution operator. PConv layers are mainly divided into the following steps:

Step 1. Mask convolution.

Given an input image and a binary mask image, the mask image is transformed into a masked image of the same size through a reverse convolution operation, representing the masked area. When the bias is 0, the mask convolution is defined as:

$$F^{conv} = W^T F^{in} \tag{2}$$

Step 2. Feature re-normalization.

Each pixel value binary mask or 0 and 1 in the mask image is divided by the number of pixels in the non-masked region. Then, Eqn. (3) can be used to calculate feature Map.

$$F^{out} = F^{conv} \odot g_A (M^c) \tag{3}$$

where $g_A(M^c)$ is an asymmetric Gaussian-shaped activation function. We further define the activation function of the attention map as:

$$g_A(M^c) = \begin{cases} a \exp(-\gamma_l M^c - \mu_2), & \text{if } M^c < \mu \\ 1 + (a-1)\exp(-\gamma_r M^c - \mu_2) & \text{otherwise} \end{cases} \tag{4}$$

where α, μ, γ and ϕ are learnable parameters, initialized to $\alpha = 1.1$, $\mu = 2.0$, $\gamma = 1.0$, $\phi = 1.0$.

Step 3. Mask update.

The activation function for updating the mask is defined as:

$$M' = g_M (M^c) \tag{5}$$

Capture Bidirectional Semantic Information Combining PConv and U-Net networks for image inpainting, where PConv is used to fill in the missing parts of the image, while the U-Net network is mainly used for feature extraction and reconstruction. The model not only concatenates forward but also concatenates backward after negating the pixels in the missing area of the image. Let M_e^c represent the convolution mask of the encoder feature F_e^{in}, and the decoder feature F_d^{in} is defined as:

$$M_d^c = M_d \otimes k_{M_d} \tag{6}$$

The steps for learning the reversible attention are as follows:

Step 1. Convolve the encoder feature F_e^{in} with the learnable weight matrix W_e^T, and apply the sigmoid function to the element-wise product of the result with the attention map $g_A(M^c)$.

$$F_e' = \left(W_c^T F_e^{in} \right) \odot g_A (M_e^c) \tag{7}$$

Step 2. Convolve the decoder feature F_d^{in} with the learnable weight matrix W_d^T, and multiply the result by the sigmoid function to apply element-wise multiplication to the attention map $g_A(M_d^c)$.

$$F_d' = \left(w_d^T F_d^{in} \right) \odot g_A (M_d^c) \tag{8}$$

Step 3. Add two attention maps to generate the output feature map F_d^{out}.

$$F_d^{out} = F_e{}' + F_d'$$ (9)

W_e and W_d are convolution filters. We define $g_A(M_d^c)$ as the reverse attention map. Then, the mask M_d^c is updated and deployed to the previous decoder layer.

$$M_d' = g_M\left(M_d^c\right)$$ (10)

Adaptive Feature Enhancement. We propose to introduce the SENet module into the generator structure based on attention-based normalization. This can weight the feature maps of each channel, so that the network can pay more attention to the most critical features. Additionally, the module has the advantage of lightweight computation and can adaptively adjust the importance of each feature information during the inpainting process of mural images. Therefore, it can be applied to mural inpainting networks to improve the inpainting quality. The SENet consists of three parts, and its structure is shown in Fig. 2.

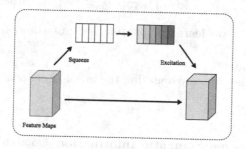

Fig. 2. The framework of SENet.

Step 1. Squeeze operation. The mural image feature map P with the size of $H \times W \times C$ is transformed into a feature vector of size $1 \times 1 \times C$ through the global average pooling operation.

$$F_{sq}\left(u_c\right) = \frac{1}{W \times H} \sum_{i=1}^{W} \sum_{j=1}^{H} u_c\left(i, j\right)$$ (11)

where $F_{sq}(\cdot)$ represents the squeeze operation, $U_c(i, j)$ denotes the element value located at (i, j) in the c-th channel of U_c, and W and H are the height and width of the feature map before squeezing operation.

Step 2. Excitation operation. This operation utilizes the ReLU activation function, the nonlinear sigmoid function, and two fully connected layers to cross-generate normalized weights ranging from 0 to 1, as shown in Eqn. (12).

$$F_{ex}\left(z, W\right) = \sigma\left(g\left(z, W\right)\right) = \sigma\left(W_2 \delta\left(W_1 z\right)\right)$$ (12)

where $F_{ex}(\cdot)$ represents the Excitation operation, $W2$ and $W1$ are fully connected layers, $\delta(\cdot)$ denotes the ReLu activation function, and $\sigma(\cdot)$ represents the sigmoid function.

SENet enhances the features by connecting channels, and the feature dimension of $H \times W \times C$ is the same for input and output, allowing seamless integration into the U-Net network model. During the training process, the weights of the SENet module can be automatically optimized through backpropagation algorithm, leading to further performance improvements on image inpainting tasks.

3.2 Constructing Repair Discrimination Networks

To improve the quality of restored paintings and maintain their global structural consistency, this paper introduces a dual discriminator in the model. It consists of a PatchGan and a contextual discriminator. The structure of the dual discriminator is shown in Fig. 3.

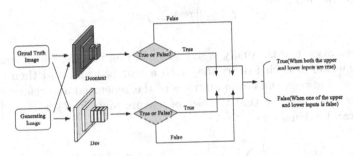

Fig. 3. The structure of the dual discriminator network.

The dual discriminator will input the repaired wall painting image generated by the generator and its real wall painting image into two discriminators, respectively, to judge and evaluate whether the repaired wall painting image is true. If either of the discriminators judges the image to be unsatisfactory, the output is false. Only when both discriminators achieve the expected effect, the output is true.

3.3 Calculate the Network Loss Function

In order to objectively evaluate the proposed method in this paper, we train our network by combining adversarial loss, pixel reconstruction loss, style loss, and perceptual loss.

Adversarial Loss Function. Adversarial loss is widely used in the fields of image generation and image inpainting. We can express adversarial loss as:

$$
L_{\text{adv}} = \min_{\Theta} \max_{D} \left(E_{I^{gt} \sim P_{\text{data}}(I^{gt})} D(I^{gt}) \right.
$$
$$
- E_{I^{\text{out}} \sim P_{\text{data}}(I^{\text{out}})} D(I^{\text{out}}) +
$$
$$
\left. \lambda E_{\hat{I} \sim P_{\hat{I}}} \left(\left(\left\| \nabla_{\hat{I}} D(\hat{I}) \right\| \right)^2 - 1 \right)^2 \right)
\tag{13}
$$

where $D(\cdot)$ represents the discriminator, we set λ to 10, randomly select factors from I_{gt} and I_{out}, and obtain I by linear interpolation.

Pixel Reconstruction Loss. Using I^{in} to represent the input image with holes, M^{in} as the binary mask region, and I^{gt} as the ground-truth image. The output can be defined as $I^{out} = \delta(I^{in}, M^{in}; \omega)$, where ω represents the model parameters to be learned. We use the $\ell 1$ norm error of the output image as the pixel reconstruction loss.

$$
L_{l_1} = \left\| I^{\text{out}} - I^{gt} \right\|_1
\tag{14}
$$

Style Loss. Style loss is usually based on the Gram matrix, which converts the style information of each feature map into a matrix form, and then calculates the difference between the Gram matrices of the generated and reference images as the style loss. Suppose that the size of feature map $P^i(I)$ is $Hi \times Wi \times Ci$. Style loss can be defined as:

$$
L_{\text{style}} = \frac{1}{N} \sum_{i=1}^{N} \frac{1}{C_i \times C_i} \times \left\| P^i \left(I^{gt} \right) \left(P^i \left(I^{gt} \right) \right)^T \right.
$$
$$
\left. - P^i \left(I^{\text{out}} \right) \left(P^i \left(I^{\text{out}} \right) \right)^T \right\|^2
\tag{15}
$$

Perceived Loss. The perceptual loss is achieved by measuring the similarity between the generated image and the original image, thus achieving the inpainting of the input image. The perceptual loss of the image patching network is defined as:

$$
L_{perc} = E \left[\sum_i \frac{1}{N_i} \left\| \varphi_i \left(I_{gt} \right) - \varphi_i \left(I_{pred} \right) \right\|_1 \right]
\tag{16}
$$

where $\varphi_i(\cdot)$ denote the i-th pooling layer.

Total Variation Loss. Combining the aforementioned four loss functions, our model loss function can be represented as:

$$
L_G = \alpha \, L_{adv} + \alpha_p L_{perc} + \alpha_s L_{style} + \alpha_{l1} L_{l1}
\tag{17}
$$

where α, α_p, α_s and α_{l1} are hyperparameters. In this experiment, we set $\alpha = 0.1$, $\alpha_p = 1$, $\alpha_s = 250$, and $\alpha_{l1} = 1$.

4   Experiments and Results Analysis

In order to verify the feasibility and effectiveness of the proposed method in this paper, we designed and implemented the mural image repair method.

In the experimental verification, the computer hardware environment used was Intel(R) Xeon(R) Silver 4110 CPU @ 2.10 GHz, 48 GB memory, NVIDIA GeForce RTX 6000 graphics card. The software environment was Windows 10 operating system. The running environment was Python 3.6, PyTorch 1.2, and Anaconda 3, and the comparative experiments were conducted under the same configuration.

4.1   Constructing the Dataset

In this paper, we used a self-made dataset of ancient Chinese murals. In our experiment, all images in the dataset were randomly cropped to 256×256 mural images and to form 13,000 mural images as the experimental dataset, of which 10,400 were used as the training set and the remaining 2,600 were used as the test set.

4.2   Comparison of Mural Inpainting Effects

In this paper, we compare the inpainting results of our method with those of existing methods.

Evaluation of Random Masking Inpainting Effectiveness. In the experiment, we set the mask ratio to 25%, contrast model is the mainstream method in the field of restoration. Figure 4(a) shows the original mural image, Fig. 4(b) shows the masked mural image, and Fig. 4(c) shows the restored image using the PConv [8] method. It can be seen that there are texture disorder and inpainting errors. Figure 4(d) shows the restored image using the CA [16] method. There are local gradient block effects in the restored mural images, and the inpainting effect is incomplete. Figure 4(e) shows the repaired image using the EC [14] method. It can be seen that there are inpainting errors and content blur.

In order to further objectively evaluate the inpainting results of the images in Fig. 4, this paper compares the results using PSNR and SSIM. The results are shown in Table. 1. Usually, a higher PSNR value indicates a higher quality of restored mural images. Structural similarity index is an indicator that measures the structural similarity between the restored mural images and the original images. The range of SSIM values is between 0 and 1, and the larger the SSIM value, the smaller the difference between the two compared images.

Evaluation of Repair Effects with Different Proportions of Masked Patches. We selected 10 images from each proportion of the masked wall painting images, the remaining values were averaged. The PSNR and SSIM values of each proportion of the mask under different algorithms are shown in Fig. 5, which were used to compare the objective quantitative evaluation of the inpainting effects under different proportions of masking.

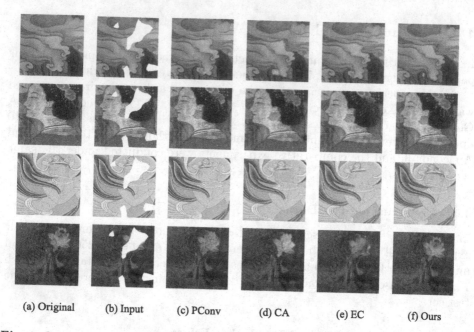

(a) Original   (b) Input   (c) PConv   (d) CA   (e) EC   (f) Ours

Fig. 4. Comparison of Random Masking Inpainting results by PConv [8], CA [16], EC [14] and Ours.

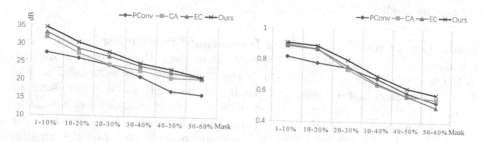

Fig. 5. PSNR and SSIM values of each masking ratio under different algorithms.

Real Mural Damage Repair Effect Evaluation. To further verify the effectiveness of the algorithm proposed in this paper, we conducted a repair experiment using 4 groups of real damaged mural images. Figure 6(a) is the initial mural image, Fig. 6(b) is the masked mural image, Fig. 6(c) is the repair image output by the PConv [8] method. Mural repaired by this method has incomplete problems. Figure 6(d) is the repair image output by the CA [16] method, mural repaired by CA has local gradient block effects. Figure 6(e) is the repair image output by the EC [14] method, this method repaired content of the mural image is blurred.

Table 1. PSNR values of each method under different algorithms.

Mural	PConv		CA		EC		Ours	
	PSNR	SSIM	PSNR	SSIM	PSNR	SSIM	PSNR	SSIM
1	23.61	0.79	26.25	0.81	23.77	0.78	29.93	0.84
2	21.45	0.80	25.29	0.73	20.63	0.71	26.37	0.85
3	23.71	0.79	24.38	0.76	26.42	0.71	28.55	0.83
4	24.33	0.74	23.16	0.72	21.41	0.71	25.03	0.81
5	20.69	0.78	21.06	0.78	22.36	0.72	25.69	0.82

User Study. In addition to the subjective evaluation, we invited 50 student volunteers to rate the repaired mural images. Table. 2 shows the average scores about real mural damage repair given by volunteers for the restored mural images. It can be seen that our method achieved better results in terms of overall structure and detail processing compared to other existing methods.

Table 2. Evaluation of inpainting quality scores for each algorithm.

	GL	EC	PConv	Ours
Overall structural	0.66	0.79	0.72	0.81
Quality of detail	0.69	0.80	0.71	0.83

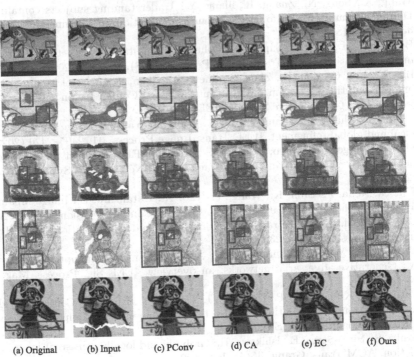

(a) Original   (b) Input   (c) PConv   (d) CA   (e) EC   (f) Ours

Fig. 6. Comparison of real inpainting results by PConv [8], CA [16], EC [14] and Ours.

5   Conclusion and Future Work

Aiming at the problem of varying degrees of damage to ancient mural images, this paper proposes a mural image restoration method based on bidirectional feature adaptive and adversarial generative networks. The experimental results prove the effectiveness of the method in this paper, and generate more realistic structures and details when repairing mural images. Both quantitative and qualitative results show the superiority of the method in this paper compared with existing methods.

In the future, we plan to extend this method to other mural image tasks, such as denoising of mural images. In addition, we will study the influence of prior information, especially structural knowledge, on image repair.

Acknowledgements. This work was supported by the Funding Project of Humanities and Social Sciences of the Ministry of Education in China (No. 22YJAZH002).

References

1. Wang, H., Li, Q., Jia, S.: A global and local feature weighted method for ancient murals inpainting. Int. J. Mach. Learn. Cybern. **11**(6), 1197–1216 (2020)
2. Wang, H., Li, Q., Zou, Q.: Inpainting of Dunhuang murals by sparsely modeling the texture similarity and structure continuity. ACM J. Comput. Cult. Heritage **12**(3), 1–21 (2019)
3. Wang, X., Song, N., Zhang, L., Jiang, Y.: Understanding subjects contained in Dunhuang mural images for deep semantic annotation. J. Documentation **74**(2), 333–353 (2018)
4. Bertalmio, M., Vese, L., Sapiro, G., Osher, S.: Simultaneous structure and texture image inpainting. IEEE Trans. Image Process. **12**(8), 882–889 (2003)
5. Liu, Y., Liu, C., Zou, H., Zhou, S., Shen, Q., Chen, T.: A novel exemplar-based image inpainting algorithm. In: 2015 International Conference on Intelligent Networking and Collaborative Systems. IEEE (2015)
6. Quan, W., Zhang, R., Zhang, Y., Li, Z., Wang, J., Yan, D.: Image inpainting with local and global refinement. IEEE Trans. Image Process. **31**, 2405–2420 (2022)
7. Shin, Y., Sagong, M., Yeo, Y., Kim, S., Ko, S.: PEPSI++: fast and lightweight network for image inpainting. IEEE Trans. Neural Netw. Learn. Syst. **32**, 252–265 (2020)
8. Liu, G., Reda, F., Shih, K., Wang, T., Tao, A., Catanzaro, B.: Image inpainting for irregular holes using partial convolutions. In: Computer Vision. ECCV (2018)
9. Wu, X., et al.: Deep portrait image completion and extrapolation. IEEE Trans. Image Process. **29**, 2344–2355 (2019)
10. Creswell, A., White, T., Dumoulin, V., Arulkumaran, K., Sengupta, B., Bharath, A.: Generative adversarial networks: an overview. IEEE Sig. Process. Mag. **35**, 53–65 (2018)
11. Pathak, D., Krahenbuhl, P., Donahue, J., Darrell, T., Efros, A.: Context encoders: feature learning by inpainting. In: 2016 IEEE Conference on Computer Vision and Pattern Recognition. IEEE (2016)
12. Iizuka, S., Simo-Serra, E., Ishikawa, H.: Globally and locally consistent image completion. ACM Trans. Graph. **36**(4), 1–14 (2017)

13. Liao, L., Hu, R., Xiao, J., Wang, Z.: Edge-aware context encoder for image inpainting. In: 2018 IEEE International Conference on Acoustics, Speech and Signal Processing. IEEE (2018)
14. Nazeri, K., Ng, E., Joseph, T., Qureshi, F.: Ebrahimi, M.: EdgeConnect: generative image inpainting with adversarial edge learning. CoRR (2019)
15. Xie, C., et al.: Image inpainting with learnable bidirectional attention maps. In: 2019 IEEE/CVF International Conference on Computer Vision. IEEE (2019)
16. Li, Y., Lu, H.: Natural image matting via guided contextual attention. In: The Thirty-Fourth AAAI Conference on Artificial Intelligence. AAAI (2020)
17. Sun, Q., et al.: A GAN-based approach toward architectural line drawing colorization prototyping. Vis. Comput. **38**(4), 1283–1300 (2022)
18. Li, H., Sheng, B., Li, P., Ali, R., Philip Chen, C.: Globally and locally semantic colorization via exemplar-based broad-GAN. IEEE Trans. Image Process. **30**, 8526–8539 (2021)
19. Liang, M., et al.: Multi-scale self-attention generative adversarial network for pathology image restoration. Vis. Comput. **39**(9), 4305–4321 (2023)
20. Jiang, Z., Zhang, W., Wang, W.: Fusiform multi-scale pixel self-attention network for hyperspectral images reconstruction from a single RGB image. Vis. Comput. **39**(8), 3573–3584 (2023)

An Image Extraction Method
for Traditional Dress Pattern Line
Drawings Based on Improved CycleGAN

Xingquan Cai, Sichen Jia, Jiali Yao, Yijie Wu, and Haiyan Sun[✉]

North China University of Technology, Beijing 100144, China
haiyansun22@126.com

Abstract. To address the problem of missing details in the general dress pattern line extraction method, we propose a traditional dress pattern line extraction method based on the improved CycleGAN. First, we input the traditional dress pattern image and extract the outline edge image by using a bi-directional cascade network. Afterwards, we construct an improved CycleGAN network model, input the traditional dress pattern image and its outline edge image into the generator model for line drawing extraction, use the discriminator model to discriminate between the generated image and the real image, and output the binary classification matrix. Finally, we construct the adversarial loss, cycle consistency loss and contour consistency loss functions to constrain the network model, output a detail rich line drawing image. Experiments show that the proposed method achieves the extraction of traditional dress pattern line images with perfect details, and the generated traditional dress pattern line images have more realistic and natural lines compared with other dress pattern line extraction methods. The method can accurately extract traditional costume pattern line images and contribute to the preservation and transmission of Chinese traditional costume culture.

Keywords: Traditional dress pattern · Improved CycleGAN · Contour consistency loss · Line drawing image extraction

1 Introduction

Clothing, as one of the essential material needs of human beings, represents a symbol of different times and cultures. Since ancient times, China has been known as the Land of Clothes for its unique dress culture. Traditional costume patterns are colourful and carry auspicious symbolic meanings, representing people's aspirations for a happy and beautiful life, and are an integral part of traditional Chinese culture. However, the rapid production and consumption patterns of modern society have led to the neglect of traditional costume patterns, and people have gradually forgotten the cultural connotations and beauty of traditional costume patterns. Therefore, it is important to preserve and pass on traditional costume culture.

B. Sheng et al. (Eds.): CGI 2023, LNCS 14496, pp. 312–323, 2024.
https://doi.org/10.1007/978-3-031-50072-5_25

By combining modern technology and information technology to preserve and pass on the cultural heritage of costume, and by establishing a library of materials for researchers to create creative designs, traditional costume patterns can be given a new lease of life. Therefore, this paper investigates a traditional dress pattern line image extraction method based on CycleGAN to promote the heritage and development of Chinese traditional dress culture.

2   Related Work

Costume pattern line extraction can be categorised as an image edge detection problem, which is a hot research problem in the field of image processing technology. The techniques related to image edge detection are mainly divided into three categories, traditional edge detection algorithms, manually set feature learning algorithms and deep learning algorithms [1,2].

The traditional edge detection algorithm [3] is mainly based on gradient information such as colour, texture and luminance to extract the line drawing information of the image, which has certain limitations. The main common are Sobel edge detection operator [4] and Canny edge detection operator [5,6]. The traditional edge detection algorithms only consider the gradient characteristics of the image, susceptible by noise interference occurs line drawing extraction incoherent problem.

Manual design feature learning algorithms [7,8] detect the edge information of an image by manually designing and extracting some specific image features. Konishi et al. [9] proposed to use statistical and learning methods to adaptively learn the probability distribution of edge filters. Felzenszwalb et al. [10] proposed the probability of boundary (Pb) algorithm, which effectively reduces the effect of noise on edge detection. The manually set feature learning algorithm is able to adaptively learn features with higher accuracy compared to traditional algorithms, but its training is complex and computationally slow.

Deep learning algorithms are currently categorised into two main algorithms based on convolutional neural networks (CNN) and generative adversarial network (GAN) edge detection [11]. Among the neural network-based edge detection methods, Xie et al. [12] proposed an end-to-end edge detection model based on HED. Ming et al. [13] proposed an RCF model for edge detection by cascading convolutional neural networks at different levels and scales. He et al. [14] proposed a bi-directional cascade network BDCN and introduced a scale enhancement module, which enables layer-specific supervision and is able to extract complete and clear image edge contour information. Current models based on generative adversarial networks [15,16] have shown excellent performance in style migration, photo restoration, and image denoising. Isola et al. [17] proposed CGAN to implement the conversion between different types of images, and proposed a training strategy based on the perceptual loss function-based training strategy makes the generated images more realistic. Zhu et al. [18] proposed a CycleGAN model for image style conversion without pairwise data, which solves the problem of restricted training dataset and also provides a new idea for line extraction research. Li et al. [19] proposed to use PLDGAN to extract portrait line drawings, which can generate high-quality portrait line drawings.

Therefore, inspired by these literatures, this paper investigates an improved CycleGAN method for extracting images of traditional dress pattern line drawings.

3 The Proposed Method

To preserve the existing traditional costume patterns and to facilitate researchers to automatically obtain the line drawings of the patterns, we focus on an improved CycleGAN method for extracting the line drawings of traditional costume patterns. Firstly, we input the traditional dress pattern image, extract the outline edge image of the traditional dress pattern using a bidirectional cascade network. Then, we construct an improved CycleGAN network model, input the traditional dress pattern image and its outline edge image into the generator model for line drawing extraction, use the discriminator model to discriminate between the generated image and the real image, and output the binary classification matrix. Finally, we construct loss functions to constrain the network model, output a detail rich line drawing image.

3.1 Construction of Bi-directional Cascade Network

In this paper, we construct a bi-directional cascade network (BDCN) to extract the contour edge map of the traditional costume. The lightweight network BDCN can fully extract multi-scale features and reduce the computational effort through the scale enhancement module, and the schematic diagram of this network structure is shown in Fig. 1. The network divides the 13 convolutional layers in VGG16 into five Incremental Detection (ID) blocks, each ID block is connected to a pooling layer to progressively expand the perceptual field of the next block and to achieve layer-specific supervision through a bidirectional cascade structure. Each ID block consists of multiple convolutional layers and a Scale Enhancement Module (SEM).

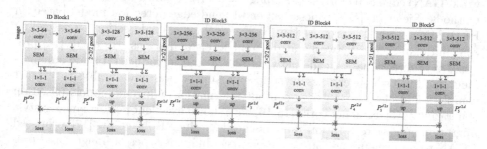

Fig. 1. Schematic diagram of the BDCN network structure.

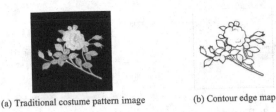

(a) Traditional costume pattern image   (b) Contour edge map

Fig. 2. Outline of a traditional costume pattern.

Each SEM consists of K dilation convolutions with different dilation rates. The dilation rate of the kth dilation convolution is r_k, which is calculated as shown in Eq. (1):

$$r_k = \max\left(1, r_0 \times k\right) \tag{1}$$

where r_k represents the expansion rate of the kth expansion convolution and r_0 represents the expansion rate factor. Next, the model fuses the SEM outputs from each ID block and feeds them into two 1×1 convolution layers to obtain two edge prediction maps p^{d2s} and p^{s2d} respectively. Finally, the edge prediction maps at different scales are fused to obtain the extracted traditional dress pattern contour edge map as shown in Fig. 2.

3.2 Construction of Improved CycleGAN Network

The generator network of the original CycleGAN is based on the UNet model, which is a deep convolutional residual network consisting of downsampled regions, residual blocks, and upsampled regions. During the downsampling convolution process, the image size gradually decreases and the extracted feature information becomes more and more high-level, while the low-level feature information such as texture and contour is gradually lost, resulting in low quality and incoherent lines in the extracted line art image.

We improve the generator on the basis of the original CycleGAN and use UNet++ as the generator of the line artwork images. The structure of UNet++ consists of a series of encoders and decoders connected by nested dense convolutional blocks, which can take better advantage of the light and deep layer features. The contour consistency loss function is used in addition to the cycle consistency loss function and the adversarial loss function to constrain the generated line-draft images, further ensuring the structural consistency between the input traditional dress pattern image and the output line-draft image.

The overall architecture of the CycleGAN is shown in Fig. 3, with p representing an image in the traditional dress pattern image domain and l representing an image in the traditional dress pattern line drawing domain. The original image of the traditional dress pattern p is passed through the generator G_l to obtain the corresponding line drawing image $\hat{l}$, and the line drawing image l is passed through the generator G_p to obtain the corresponding coloured traditional dress pattern image $\hat{p}$. Discriminator D_l determines whether the input line drawing image is a real image, and similarly discriminator D_p determines whether the input colour traditional dress pattern image is a real image.

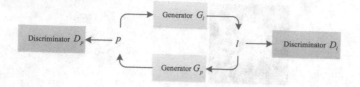

Fig. 3. The overall structure of the CycleGAN network.

Construction of Generator Model. In CycleGAN, generators G_l and G_p have the same structure. In this paper, we build the generator based on UNet++. The network structure of generator G_l is shown in Fig. 4 and consists of a series of nested dense convolutional blocks connected together. Four different depths of U-Net are used in the model, stacked in order from shallow to deep. The most important feature of UNet++ is that all the convolutional blocks are connected to each other by jump connections, which can effectively achieve feature reuse at different scales and thus improve the clarity and completeness of the generated line-drawn images. Taking node $X^{0,4}$ as an example, there is only one node $X^{0,0}$ connected to it in the generator of the original CycleGAN. In contrast, the jump path is redesigned in UNet++ so that node $X^{0,4}$ can receive jump connections from multiple nodes, namely nodes $X^{0,0}$, $X^{0,1}$, $X^{0,2}$ and $X^{0,3}$.

The network consists of a number of convolutional blocks. Firstly, the input image of the traditional dress pattern p and its corresponding contour edge map b are input. Then, the input image is encoded by downsampling to extract the feature map. Finally, the feature map is fused by upsampling and the extracted line image is output.

Construction of Discriminator Model. Compared with traditional discriminators, PatchGAN uses a discriminative strategy based on local regions of the image, which can discriminate the detailed parts of the image in a more detailed way. Therefore, this paper constructs two discriminators D_l and D_p based on PatchGAN with the same structure, as shown in Fig. 5. The discriminators receive the image generated by the generator or the real image, and then partition the input image into several matrices of size $n \times n$. Each matrix is

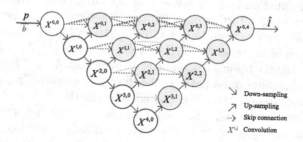

Fig. 4. Structure of the generator network.

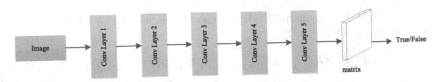

Fig. 5. Structure of the discriminator network.

discriminated as true or false, and finally the discriminated mean value of all matrices is taken as the discriminated value of the whole image.

The discriminator is mainly composed of the convolutional layers and the activation function layers. The first four convolutional layers use the Leaky ReLU activation function to enhance the performance of the network, and the output convolutional layer does not have the Leaky ReLU activation function. The specific calculation of this activation function is shown in Eq. (2), where λ takes the value 0.01, which can effectively avoid the problem of gradient sawtooth and enable the model to learn rich non-linear properties.

$$f(x) = \begin{cases} x, x > 0 \\ \lambda x, x \leq 0 \end{cases} \tag{2}$$

3.3 Loss Function

This paper uses three loss functions of adversarial loss, cycle consistency loss and contour consistency loss to bound the improved CycleGAN network model.

Adversarial Loss. The adversarial loss function is a binary cross-entropy loss function that is used to calculate the difference between the labels output by the discriminator network and the true labels. The loss calculation from the traditional dress pattern image to the generated black and white line art image is shown in Eq. (3).

$$\mathcal{L}_{\text{GAN}}(G_l, D_l, P, L) = \mathbb{E}_{l \sim p_{data}(l)}[\log D_l(l)] + \\ \mathbb{E}_{p \sim p_{data}(p)}[\log(1 - D_l(G_l(p)))] \tag{3}$$

$\mathbb{E}_{l \sim p_{data}(l)}[\log D_l(l)]$ in Equation (3) represents the error of the discriminator network on the real image, $\mathbb{E}_{p \sim p_{data}(p)}[\log(1 - D_l(G_l(p)))]$ represents the error of the discriminator network on the generated image, and $p_{data}(l)$ and $p_{data}(p)$ represent the distribution of the real image. Similarly, the adversarial loss function from the image domain of a black and white line drawing to the image domain of a traditional dress pattern is $\mathcal{L}_{\text{GAN}}(G_p, D_p, L, P)$.

Cycle Consistency Loss. In order to make the difference between the image and the original image as small as possible after the image has been mapped back to the original domain again through the generator in both directions, a cycle consistency loss is introduced and calculated using the L1 loss function. The calculation is shown in Eq. (4).

$$\mathcal{L}_{\text{CYC}}(G_p, G_l) = \mathbb{E}_{p \sim p_{data}(p)}[||G_p(G_l(p)) - p||_1)] + \\ \mathbb{E}_{l \sim p_{data}(l)}[||G_l(G_p(l)) - l||_1)] \tag{4}$$

Contour Consistency Loss. In order to further constrain the boundary of the generated image to be consistent with the original image, a contour consistency loss function $\mathcal{L}_b$ is introduced in this paper and is calculated as shown in Eq. (5).

$$\mathcal{L}_{\text{b}}(G_l) = \sum_{i,j} (\hat{l}_{i,j} - b_{i,j})^2 \tag{5}$$

$\hat{l}$ represents the generated traditional dress pattern image and b represents the corresponding outline edge of the input traditional dress pattern image. $\mathcal{L}_b$ is used to improve the quality of the generated line image by constraining the difference between the generated line image $\hat{l}$ and the contour edge map of the input traditional dress pattern image. Similarly, using the contour consistency loss constraint generator G_p, the calculation is shown in Eq. (6).

$$\mathcal{L}_{\text{b}}(G_p) = \sum_{i,j} (\hat{p}_{i,j} - b_{i,j})^2 \tag{6}$$

After the above analysis, the loss function of the network model in this paper can be expressed as $\mathcal{L}_{sum}$, which is calculated as shown in Eq. (7).

$$\mathcal{L}_{sum} = \mathcal{L}_{\text{GAN}}(G_l, D_l, P, L) + \mathcal{L}_{\text{GAN}}(G_p, D_p, L, P) \\ + \lambda \mathcal{L}_{\text{CYC}}(G_p, G_l) + \mu(\mathcal{L}_{\text{b}}(G_p) + \mathcal{L}_{\text{b}}(G_l)) \tag{7}$$

In Eq. (7), λ and μ represent the weights of the cycle consistency and contour consistency loss functions, respectively.

4   Experimental Results

The traditional dress pattern line extraction method is designed and implemented to verify the feasibility and the efficiency of the proposed method. For the experimental validation, the computer hardware environment used is Intel(R) Xeon(R) Silver 4110 CPU @ 2.10 GHz, 64 GB RAM, NVIDIA Quadro RTX 6000 graphics card. The software environment is Windows 10 operating system, while the running environment is Python 3.6, PyTorch 1.6 and Anaconda 3.

4.1   Construction of the Dataset

In order to achieve a better extraction of traditional costume patterns, the traditional costume pattern images and their corresponding line artwork images need to be collected. Considering the scarcity of existing datasets and the incomplete classification of data, this paper constructs a dataset containing 3010 images of traditional costume patterns and 937 images of line drawings, a total of 3947 images, through manual photography, web search and data crawling. Based on the pattern style and composition characteristics of traditional costume patterns, the collected traditional costume patterns were divided into three categories, geometric patterns, plant and flower patterns and animal patterns. Firstly, the cv2.bilateralFilter function was used to bilaterally filter the original dataset images to remove the noise in the images. Secondly, some of the images were data enhanced to further expand the dataset and remove low quality images. Finally, all images were set to 512×512 pixels. After constructing the dataset, the dataset was divided according to 8:2 to obtain the training set and the test set.

4.2 Experiment of the Extraction of Traditional Dress Pattern Lines Extraction

In order to verify the feasibility of extracting traditional dress pattern lines, this paper uses the PyTorch deep learning framework to design and implement an improved CycleGAN-based image extraction method for traditional dress pattern linework.

In the training process of the CycleGAN network model, firstly, the structures of generators G_l and G_p and the corresponding discriminators D_l and D_p are initialised. Then, the corresponding images are generated using the generators by inputting the traditional dress pattern image domain p and the line artwork image domain l. After that, the gradients of the generators and discriminators are calculated and the weight parameters of the network model are updated respectively. Finally, the current model is saved as a pt file every 5000 times according to the saving frequency.

In order to verify the feasibility of the method in this paper, the CycleGAN network model needs to be tested. The test results are shown in Fig. 6. Figure 6(a) represents the three types of pattern images to be tested. Figure 6(b) represents the line drawing images extracted by the method in this paper, and Fig. 6(c) represents the real labels. From Fig. 6, it can be seen that the line images generated by the method in this paper have realistic and natural line strokes, clear and complete, and meet the expected standard.

4.3 Ablation Experiment of Traditional Costume Pattern Lines Extraction

In order to validate the effectiveness of the traditional dress pattern line extraction method proposed in this paper, the experiments were first conducted by replacing the structure or adding part of the structure to the original CycleGAN, followed by testing and evaluating the improved network on the pre-processed dataset, and the test results are shown in Table 1.

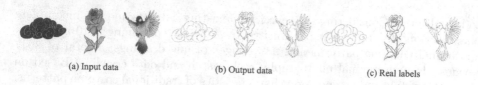

(a) Input data   (b) Output data   (c) Real labels

Fig. 6. Test results.

Table 1. Results of the evaluation of the objective indicators of the modules of the model.

Model	SSIM	MSE
CycleGAN	0.62	0.23
CycleGAN-U	0.68	0.18
CycleGAN-U-b	0.69	0.16

In Table 1, CycleGAN-U indicates the replacement of the generator structure of the original CycleGAN with UNet++, and CycleGAN-U-b is the addition of contour consistency constraints on top of the replacement generators. In this paper, the generated line images are evaluated quantitatively by two evaluation metrics, SSIM and MSE.

As can be seen in Table 1, both structures proposed in this paper improve the effect of line extraction to some extent. The base CycleGAN has an SSIM of only 0.62 and an MSE of only 0.23 for the traditional dress pattern line extraction. When the generator structure was replaced with UNet++, the model performance improved, with an increase in SSIM of 0.06 and a decrease in MSE of 0.05, proving that the structure is effective. Afterwards, adding the contour consistency constraint on top of this, SSIM rose to 0.69 and MSE decreased to 0.16. Both SSIM and MSE metrics improved compared to the original CycleGAN model, proving the effectiveness of the algorithm in this paper.

4.4 Comparative Experiment of Traditional Dress Pattern Lines Extraction

In order to further demonstrate the validity and stability of the method in this paper, a comparison experiment of traditional dress pattern line extraction was designed. The HED method [12], the RCF method [13] and the proposed method were compared and analysed under the same hardware environment. Figure 7 shows the results of the extraction of traditional dress patterns.

It is clear from the results that the HED method is blurred when extracting the geometric patterns, and the RCF method has serious loss of internal details. The HED and RCF methods lose leaf texture information when extracting plant and flower patterns. The HED and RCF methods also lost a large amount of internal detail information when extracting the animal pattern sketches. In contrast, when extracting the traditional dress pattern line drawing image, the lines

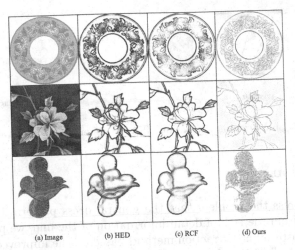

(a) Image   (b) HED   (c) RCF   (d) Ours

Fig. 7. Comparison of the results of the extraction of the traditional dress pattern line.

are clearer, more complete and more effective. This further demonstrates the effectiveness and stability of the algorithm in this paper.

Furthermore, the method of this paper is quantitatively evaluated with the traditional dress pattern line drawing images generated by other methods. The SSIM of HED, RCF and this paper's method are 0.58, 0.55, 0.69, and the MSE are 0.27, 0.33, 0.16, respectively. From the data, it can be seen that this paper's method obtains the optimal value in both SSIM and MSE, which proves the effectiveness of this paper's method.

At the same time, the images generated by each of the above methods were given to 100 respondents in the form of a questionnaire for evaluation and scoring out of 10. The questionnaire includes 15 groups of comparison images, and each respondent scores based on whether the lines of the extracted traditional dress pattern line drawing images are clear and complete, and whether there is any noise situation. The obtained data is taken as the mean value, and the final score situation is 8.9 points for HED method, 7.5 points for RCF method and 9.5 points for our method. As can be seen from the scores, the line drawing image extracted using this method has the highest score among all methods, which indicates that this paper's method produces the highest quality image and the extracted lines are clearer and more complete.

4.5 Experiments for Testing Other Types of Pictures

The method in this paper is not only suitable for extracting traditional dress pattern line drawing images, but also can be used for line drawing extraction of other types of images. Using the method of this paper for hand-drawn, cartoon, icon images for line drawing extraction, the extraction effect is shown in Fig. 8.

(a) Image (b) Line drawing

Fig. 8. Line drawing extraction effect of other types of pictures.

5 Conclusion

In order to address the problem that the general dress pattern line extraction method suffers from the lack of detail information of the line, we propose a traditional dress pattern line extraction method based on the improved CycleGAN. First, we input the traditional dress pattern image, and use the BDCN to extract features at different scales and fuse the edge prediction maps at different scales to output the outline edge image of the traditional dress pattern. Then, we construct the improved CycleGAN network, build two generators based on UNet++ network, and the mapping from the traditional dress pattern image domain to the line-draft domain and from the line-draft domain to the traditional dress pattern image domain is achieved by using the two generators respectively. Two discriminators are built based on the PatchGAN network. The discriminator takes the image generated by the generator or the real image, divides it into a number of matrices to discriminate between true and false, and takes the discriminative mean of all matrices as the discriminative value of the whole image. Next, a contour consistency loss function is introduced on top of the adversarial loss and cycle consistency loss to improve the quality of the generated line-drawing images by constraining the boundaries of the generated images with contour edge maps. Finally, the generator and discriminator of the model are trained until the loss function converges and the performance of the generator and discriminator is optimal, and the extracted line art images are output. The final design and implementation of this improved CycleGAN method for extracting traditional dress pattern images.

The next stage of research includes continuing to expand the traditional costume pattern dataset to further improve the accuracy and generalisation of the model.

Acknowledgements. This work was supported by the Funding Project of Beijing Social Science Foundation (No. 20YTB011).

References

1. Li, L., Tang, J., Ye, Z., et al.: Unsupervised face super-resolution via gradient enhancement and semantic guidance. Vis. Comput. **37**(9), 2855–2867 (2021)

2. Jiang, N., Sheng, B., Li, P., et al.: PhotoHelper: portrait photographing guidance via deep feature retrieval and fusion. IEEE Trans. Multimed. **25**, 2226–2238 (2023)
3. Li, C.-J., Qu, Z.: A review of deep learning based image edge detection algorithms. Comput. Appl. **40**(11), 3280–3288 (2020)
4. Kittler, J.: On the accuracy of the Sobel edge detector. Image Vis. Comput. **1**(1), 37–42 (1983)
5. Canny, J.: A computational approach to edge detection. IEEE Trans. Pattern Anal. Mach. Intell. **8**(6), 679–698 (1986)
6. Mei, Y., Zhuang, J.: Image pre-processing optimization algorithm based on Canny edge detection. Inf. Technol. **1**, 75–79 (2022)
7. Xiao, Y., Zhou, J.: Overview of image edge detection. Comput. Eng. Appl. **59**(5), 40–54 (2023)
8. Wang, N.-Y., Wang, W.-L., Hu, W.-J.: Thangka mural line drawing based on cross dense residual architecture and hard pixel balancing. IEEE Access **9**, 48841–48850 (2021)
9. Konishi, S., Yuille, A.-L., Coughlan, J.-M., et al.: Statistical edge detection: learning and evaluating edge cues. IEEE Trans. Pattern Anal. Mach. Intell. **25**(1), 57–74 (2003)
10. Felzenszwalb, P.-F., Huttenlocher, D.-P.: Efficient graph-based image segmentation. Int. J. Comput. Vision **59**(2), 167–181 (2004)
11. Saranya, M., Geetha, P.: A deep learning-based feature extraction of cloth data using modified grab cut segmentation. Vis. Comput. **39**, 4195–4211 (2023)
12. Xie, S.-N., Tu, Z.-W.: Holistically-Nested edge detection. In: Proceedings of the IEEE International Conference on Computer Vision, pp. 1395–1403. IEEE, Santiago (2015)
13. Liang, M., Hu, X.-L.: Recurrent convolutional neural network for object recognition. In: Proceedings of the IEEE Conference on Computer Vision and Pattern Recognition, pp. 3367–3375. IEEE, Boston (2015)
14. He, J.-Z., Zhang, S.-L., Yang, M., et al.: BDCN: bi-directional cascade network for perceptual edge detection. IEEE Trans. Pattern Anal. Mach. Intell. **44**(1), 100–113 (2020)
15. Ma, K.-Y., Wang, X.-H.: Research on cartoon face generation based on Cycle-GAN assisted with facial landmarks. In: Proceedings of International Conference on Cyber-Physical Social Intelligence, pp. 356–361. IEEE, Shenzhen (2022)
16. Liu, J.-S., Zhang, S., Ma, X., et al.: CycleGAN -based cloud2painting translation. In: Proceedings of IEEE International Conference on Computer Science, Artificial Intelligence and Electronic Engineering, pp. 5–8. IEEE, Hangzhou (2021)
17. Isola, P., Zhu, J.-Y., Zhou, T.-H., et al.: Image-to-Image translation with conditional adversarial networks. In: Proceedings of IEEE Conference on Computer Vision and Pattern Recognition, pp. 5967–5976. IEEE, Honolulu (2017)
18. Zhu, J.-Y., Park, T., Isola, P., et al.: Unpaired image-to-image translation using cycle-consistent adversarial networks. In: Proceedings of the IEEE International Conference on Computer Vision, pp. 2242–2251. IEEE, Venice (2017)
19. Li, S., Wu, F., Fan, Y., et al.: PLDGAN: portrait line drawing generation with prior knowledge and conditioning target. Vis. Comput. **39**, 3507–3518 (2023)

Parametrization of Measured BRDF
for Flexible Material Editing

Alexis Benamira$^{(\boxtimes)}$, Sachin Shah, and Sumanta Pattanaik

University of Central Florida, Orlando, USA
`alexis.benamira@knights.ucf.edu`

Abstract. Finding a low dimensional parametric representation of measured BRDF remains challenging. Currently available solutions are either not usable for editing, or rely on limited analytical solutions, or require expensive test subject based investigations. In this work, we strive to establish a parametrization space that affords the data-driven representation variance of measured BRDF models while still offering some of the artistic control of parametric analytical BRDFs. We present a machine learning approach that generates a parameter space relying on a compressed representation of the measured BRDF data. Our solution allows more flexible and controllable material editing possibilities than current machine learning solutions. Finally, we provide a rendering interface, for interactive material editing and interpolation based on the presented new parametrization system.

Keywords: Reflectance modeling and editing · Learning latent representations

1 Introduction

Natural material appearance is rich and varies over a large set of dimensions. This wide range of possible variations makes material appearance a hard function to represent and developing a corresponding parameter space is just as challenging. A function that is commonly used to represent material appearance is the Bidirectional Reflection Distribution Function (BRDF) and it falls into two main categories: analytical or measured. Analytical BRDFs have been successful at describing a variety of material appearances and several works have developed flexible parametrizations [2,13]. Unfortunately, analytical models are restricted in the range of appearances they can represent, thus triggering the idea of using measured BRDF. Indeed, with the increasing efficiency and accuracy of BRDF measurements as well as the decreasing cost of storage, datasets keep expanding and data-based reflection models have attracted a lot of attention [4,6,17]. However, in contrast to analytical models, parametrization of measured BRDF models remains challenging.

Supplementary Information The online version contains supplementary material available at https://doi.org/10.1007/978-3-031-50072-5_26.

In this work, we leverage a Deep Neural Network (DNN) to learn a new parameter space for measured materials. We rely on a β-Variational AutoEncoder (β-VAE), a specific network architecture which tries to enforce the creation of a disentangled latent space. The latent space is the space in which the compressed data lives. Disentangled means that each variable of the latent space is responsible for representing a specific generative factor and is insensitive to the factors represented by the other variables. Instead of using perceptual analysis through a cumbersome user study to define a control space, our set of variables is generated by the DNN through the training process. Then, in a second step, we explore the newly established parametrization space and we exert our visual perception to interpret the generative factors learned by the network.

Expanding on an unsupervised DNN training, our method enjoys the precise fitting and appearance richness of machine learning approaches while offering some flexible control over the material appearance like analytical models without requiring crowd-sourced experiments. The created parametrization space allows more flexible interpolation between materials than random manifold exploring or linear interpolation between compressed vectors. Indeed, our method allows control over which appearance characteristics are being interpolated and which are not while retaining a high reconstruction accuracy of the measured data.

The organization of the rest of the paper is as follows. First, we offer an overview of the state of the art in measured BRDF parametrization and other relevant current research. Then, we describe our method followed by our results before concluding.

2   Related Work

2.1   Measured BRDF Parametrization

Measured BRDF Datasets. Because analytical modeling of material appearance is complex, measured BRDF models have always attracted a lot of attention. Measurement techniques have become more accurate and simpler [16,20,26] as well as evaluation [25]. Various datasets of BRDF measurements are available [4,6]. In this work, we decided to use the MERL dataset [17] as it offers a wide set of material measurement data. Finding a parametrization for measured BRDF models has been achieved using three main approaches. The first by fitting an analytical model to the measurements. The goal of those efforts are twofold, first to improve the accuracy of the analytical model by comparing them to measured data [9,19]. Second is the possibility to edit measured BRDF by editing the fitted analytical model [3,28]. The primary challenge of this approach is to develop an analytical model complex enough to represent the richness of the measured data, yet simple enough so that the fitting process remains stable. A second method to parametrize measured BRDF calls for user studies and perceptual data gathering. This approach has the inherent advantage of offering a parametrization that is constitutively identifiable. It has been reported for a subset of appearance characteristics: by [30] on glossy reflections or [7] for translucency or in

[24] for metals. In a pioneering work, [23] offered an editing parametrization for all measured BRDF of the MERL dataset for all appearance characteristics. A third method is based on Machine Learning. It has been used to find manifold representations of measured BRDF data [17]. By analyzing where groups of similar materials are located on the manifold, they can find paths between those groups to edit the material appearance. The approach to find the manifold as well as the interpolation between material has been refined in [27] by relying on a Gaussian Process. However the editing is performed with pseudo-random manifold exploration. It is pseudo-random because the material clustering obtained on the manifold allows general control over the interpolation editing but does not allow precise control over specific appearance characteristics. We illustrate this lack of precise control in Sect. 4.3. In recent works, deep learning approaches oriented toward compressing the input measurements have been presented for BRDF [10,29,32] or other fields [5]. Their approaches offer some editing possibilities but do not allow the creation of a parametrization over the measured BRDF space. Indeed, the natural editing capabilities of those techniques is the linear interpolation of the compressed representation of the data. But as we illustrate Fig. 4, it is limited compared to our current method. Current machine learning and deep learning approaches lack control over the editing of the material appearance.

2.2 Disentangled Deep Neural Networks

One major drawback of Deep Neural Networks is their behavioral opacity. To offer some interpretability on the learning process a growing amount of AI research tries to develop models offering a disentangled and compressed representation of the input data [11,22]. Indeed, disentangled representations of data usually have good human interpretability. Simply put, each variable encodes a generative factor that is perceptually meaningful. Several different architectures have been described to find such a disentangled representation [8,14]. We picked the β-VAE architecture [8] for this work as it is the most studied one.

3   Method

3.1   Data Pre-processing

The MERL dataset [17] is composed of the measured BRDF of 100 isotropic materials. The raw data is stored in a 3-dimensional table shaped $(90, 90, 180)$ with high dynamic range RGB values for each entry. These high magnitude inputs can pose challenges for a DNN, so the following normalization scheme is adopted:

$$\hat{\rho} = \frac{\log\left(\rho * S + \varepsilon\right) - \log\left(\varepsilon\right)}{\log\left(1 + \varepsilon\right) - \log\left(\varepsilon\right)} \qquad (1)$$

where ρ is a single BRDF measurement, $\varepsilon = 0.01$ is a small constant and S is a scalar value used to render the MERL BRDF. S is $\frac{1.0}{1500}$ for the red channel,

$\frac{1.5}{1500}$ for the green channel, and $\frac{1.66}{1500}$ for the blue channel. To reduce the amount of data at the entry of our network, we discard 8/9 of the original slices at regular intervals. This ratio is chosen following [10]. We now have 21 RGB image slices, producing $63 \times 90 \times 90$ input size. The reconstruction of a full BRDF is obtained through linear interpolation between image slices.

3.2 Network Architecture

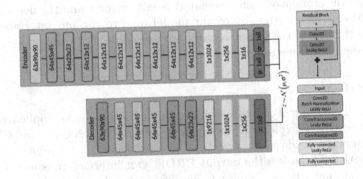

Fig. 1. Our β-VAE architecture.

We expand on the autoencoder introduced by [10] to create a new β-VAE to learn a latent space representation. The proposed β-VAE architecture is illustrated in Fig. 1. We choose a normal distribution $\mathcal{N}(0,1)$ as a prior.

3.3 Implementation Details

Our β-VAE network is trained in an unsupervised way and implemented using PyTorch [21]. The network is trained with the Adam optimizer [15], a learning rate of 3×10^{-5}, and batch size of 2 for 1000 epochs.

The loss function is formulated as:

$$\mathcal{L}_{KL}^{(i)} = -\frac{1}{2} \sum_{j=1}^{M} \left(1 + \log\left(\sigma_j^{(i)}\right)^2 - \left(\mu_j^{(i)}\right)^2 - \left(\sigma_j^{(i)}\right)^2 \right) \tag{2}$$

$$\mathcal{L} = \frac{1}{N} \sum_{i=1}^{N} \left(\| mask(\tilde{x}^{(i)}) - mask(x^{(i)}) \| + \beta_{norm} \mathcal{L}_{KL}^{(i)} \right) \tag{3}$$

where M is the dimensionality of the latent space, N is the mini-batch size, x is an input BRDF, $\tilde{x}$ is the reconstruction. $\|\cdot\|$ denotes the L_2 norm. The function $mask$ returns the set of all valid BRDF entries. $\beta_{norm} = \beta \frac{M}{N}$ where $\beta = 12$, $M = 8$ is the latent space size and $N = 63 \times 90 \times 90$ is the input size.

With regards to the dimension of the latent space, we trained a DNN with $M = 8$ and $M = 16$. When $M = 16$, the reconstruction accuracy of the network did not improve and we faced the same poor reconstruction with green materials. Furthermore, the latent parameters seemed less identifiable and did not seem to have control over a specific appearance characteristic. Hence, we decided to use $M = 8$ to further constrain the latent representation. It can be noted that by construction, the β-VAE architecture enables the compression-decompression of the input data. In our case, the $63 \times 90 \times 90$ input is compressed into an 8 elements vector. The storage of each material of the MERL dataset can be replaced by the storage of each associated latent vector z and the decoder of our β-VAE. After training, the size of our model used to run our interfaces is 78.9 MB while the size of the latent vectors are negligible. For comparison, the size of one of the MERL measurements is 35 MB.

3.4 Interfaces

For practical handling of our parametrization, we developed an applicative interface based on BRDFExplorer [2] to which we added Pytorch C++ and CPython. Our new interface loads a latent vector z and propagates it through the decoder of our β-VAE and renders the output BRDF. Our interface runs at an interactive framerate and allows the user to modify each value of the latent vector z, leveraging the full strength of our parametrization.

In addition, we put forward a second interface which relies on manifold exploration for editing z. This interface is created for comparison sake with the previous related techniques [17, 27, 32]. The latent vector z is mapped to a 2D embedding using Uniform Manifold Approximation and Projection (UMAP) [18]. UMAP is particularly useful because the algorithm preserves the global data structure and is invertible. A 2D point can be dragged over the manifold and mapped back to an 8-dimensions latent vector that is then passed through the decoder before rendering. We observe that this interface has limited editing control over generated material appearance as illustrated in another demonstration video available in the supplementary material.

4 Results

In this section, we illustrate the applicability of our approach and detail the outcomes. First, we demonstrate that we have successfully learned a parametrization space from the measured MERL BRDF dataset for flexible material editing. Second, we illustrate that our flexible parametrization affords the introduction of new generative parameters to the β-VAE learned set to expand the richness of possible material produced. Third, we show that our parametrization space allows flexible interpolation between materials as well as new material creation. Last, we display the high reconstruction accuracy of our parametrization and compare our results to analytical fitting and deep learning methods. We used Mitsuba renderer [12] to render our images and we obtained some of the scenes used to illustrate our work from [1].

4.1   Learned Parametrization over the Measured BRDF Space

Our goal is to learn a parametrization for measured BRDF model. To evaluate our parametrization, we perform a latent traversal of each of the 8 dimensions of our latent space. In other words, we modify the value of one of the latent parameters while leaving the others unchanged and render an image for each new value. In a second step, we exert our visual perception to express what we believe is the generative parameter being controlled by the latent variable. We exercise our perception only as a mean of identification of the parameters learned by our DNN. The learning process is unsupervised and does not require any human intervention.

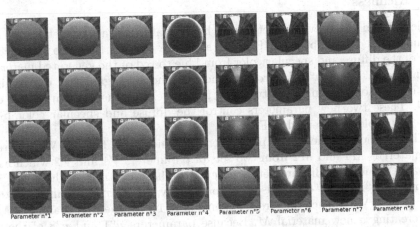

Fig. 2. Latent traversal of each variable of the latent space. We observe that each variable controls a distinct generative parameter. The names associated with each parameter are listed in Table 1. For metallic materials unchanged values are set to the values obtained for the aluminium BRDF measurement. For diffuse materials, only Parameter $n°5$ is changed in the aluminium set for illustration purposes.

Table 1. Using the same terminology as in [2], we associate a name to the generative factor controlled by each parameter. The association is achieved through visual perception.

Parameter $n°$	Controlled generative factor
1	Diffuse color from blue to red
2	Sheen
3	Subsurface
4	Clear coat from blue to red
5	Specular to Diffuse
6	Haziness
7	Color lightness
8	Specular color from red to blue

The results of the latent traversal are presented in Fig. 2. We observe that each parameter controls its own generative factor. By relying on our visual perception and using the same terminology as in [2], we associate a name to each individual parameter. The naming association is detailed in Table 1. The nomenclature presented in Table 1 is obtained only through our own perception. Some parameters are easily identifiable (e.g. $n°5$ and $n°6$) while others (e.g. $n°2$ and $n°3$) are harder and are amendable to interpretation. Therefore the interface that is demonstrated in the companion video will be made public for anyone to arbitrate according to its own perception.

4.2 New Parameters Creation for Expanded Material Appearance Richness

As detailed in the previous section, we have established a parametrization for the measured BRDF of the MERL dataset. We can see that two parameters control the diffuse and specular color from blue to red of the generated material: parameters $n°1$ and $n°8$. In order to increase the color gamut of our original parametrization, we included two new parameters to the set learned by our DNN. These two new parameters control the diffuse and specular color from green to purple as observed in Fig. 3.

The creation of these new parameters is achieved as follows. We generate two materials $M1$ and $M2$ from two sets of parameters $V1$ and $V2$ which have the same values for all parameters except for those controlling the color, i.e. parameters $n°1$ and $n°8$. As discussed previously, the two materials follow the RGB format. We replace the Green channel of $M1$ with the Red channel of $M2$, thus creating a new material M. Because parameters $n°1$ and $n°8$ of the set $V2$ initially controlled the red diffuse and specular color of $M2$, through this replacement, they now control the green diffuse and specular color of the new material M. Next, we add the parameters $n°1$ and $n°8$ of $V2$ to the set $V1$ creating a new set V parametrizing material M. Those two parameters, now numbered 9 and 10 are responsible for controlling the green color for diffuse and specular reflections as illustrated in Fig. 3.

Fig. 3. Manual enrichment of DNN-learned parameter set. New manually-created parameters control respectively the green specular and green diffuse color. When the green values are low, only red and blue remain thus creating purple. (Color figure online)

This post-processing manual addition of parameters is only possible because the initial parametrization learned by our DNN is flexible. Indeed, the color features are controlled by a limited number of parameters which allows us to modify the original purpose of the parameters. The two newly created parameters allow us to broaden the range of generated material appearances.

4.3   Flexible Material Editing

Previously available machine learning approaches relied on finding a path on a projected low dimensional manifold for editing the measured materials [17,27]. For comparison purposes we did project the latent space learned by our β-VAE onto a 2D manifold using the UMAP technique [18]. The results can be visualized in the companion video. We can identify some general appearance areas on the manifold. For example, the upper part is more diffuse and the bottom part is more specular. Navigating between the points allows some editing options. However, it proves quite challenging to interpolate between materials that are far apart on the manifold as it requires discovering a long path on the manifold. Moreover, it appears that on some paths, small steps on the manifold can create abrupt changes on the material appearance as illustrated in the companion video demonstrating the UMAP interface.

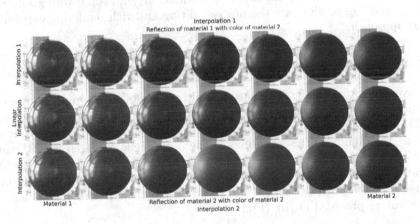

Fig. 4. A flexible interpolation between two very different looking materials. For interpolation 1, we set the parameters controlling the color ($n°1, 7, 8, 9, 10$) to the value of material 2 (here blue-metallic-paint) while setting the one representing the shape of the BRDF ($n°2, 3, 4, 5, 6$) to material 1 (here gold-metallic-paint3). We do the opposite for interpolation 2. For linear interpolation, all parameters are set to the mean value between parameters of material 1 and material 2. We can see that our parametrization offers more control and flexibility in the interpolation than current deep learning methods which only allow linear interpolation.

In contrast, our new parametrization provides much more flexibility and precise control over the interpolation of the materials as illustrated in Fig. 5. Instead of finding a path on a manifold for which we cannot precisely know which generative factor will be modified, our parametrization allows direct and precise control over specific generative factors.

Fig. 5. Material editing from hazy green specular (top left) to red diffuse (bottom right). First row: we change the color from green to blue by modifying parameters $n°9$ and $n°10$ (decrease the green contribution) and parameters $n°1$ and $n°8$ (increase blue contribution), then we reduce the haziness by changing parameter $n°6$. Second row: we transition from specular to diffuse using parameter $n°5$, then we modify the diffuse color from blue to red using parameters $n°1$ and $n°9$. (Color figure online)

Deep learning approaches allow the editing of the appearance by interpolation of the latent vector of different materials (as illustrated in the tool provided by [32]). We show in Fig. 4, that our approach enables a more detailed interpolation. Indeed, since each parameter of our latent vector controls an appearance characteristic, interpolating some parameters and not others allows greater interpolation capabilities than linear interpolation of all parameters. Thus our solution offers more flexible editing capabilities than current deep learning solutions. Figure 4 and Fig. 5, illustrate the precise editing and rich rendering capabilities of our approach.

4.4 High Fidelity Representation of Measured Materials

We have illustrated the flexible material editing capabilities of our parametrization and we will now demonstrate its accurate reconstruction of the original MERL materials. To do so, we render the reconstructed MERL materials and compare the quality of the renderings to the same scene rendered with the original MERL measurements. Using the Relative Absolute Error Metric (RelAE) metric, we compare our results against the following baseline methods: [3,10,29]. We use the code provided by [29] and [3] to obtain their RelAE results and the RelAE values provided in [10] (Fig. 6).

Table 2. Comparison of reconstruction performances between our method and previous work. We present the mean RelAE, the standard deviation and the number of materials with a RelAE above 5%.

Method	Mean RelAE	Std	Above 5% RelAE
Ours	0.032	0.0096	4
Hu et al. [10]	0.040	0.0099	9
Sztrajman et al. [29]	0.023	0.0235	11
Tabulated [3]	0.086	0.0457	84
GGX fitting [3]	0.11	0.0495	95

Table 2 sums up the results. We can observe that our method has the lowest standard deviation, the least number of materials with an error above 5% and gives the second best average reconstruction.

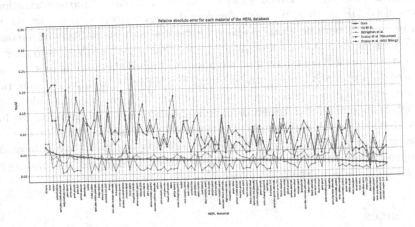

Fig. 6. Relative absolute error between rendered images (matpreview scene) using the reconstructed and the original MERL BRDF measurements. The lower the better. The deep learning methods (blue, green, orange) have better reconstruction performances than fitting methods (red and purple). (Color figure online)

We believe that our parametrization is a sensible solution toward closing the gap between analytical and measured BRDF models. It offers both good control over editing distinct generative appearance factors while retaining high reconstruction accuracy and offering a great range in the possible producible appearances.

5   Limitations and Future Work

We have identified two issues with the current representation of our latent space which require further investigations, namely the modularity and explicitness of the parametrization. For the modularity, we identified leaks of some parameters through others. For example, we noticed that the color control is slightly leaking on to parameters $n°7$ and $n°2$. The latter can be observed in Fig. 2. In future work we would like to prevent those leaks by improving our latent space representation like in [31]. The other limitation of our network is its explicitness. For example, our DNN cannot reproduce green by itself. Explicitness is not an issue specific to our DNN. Indeed, we can see that [10,29] have respectively 9 and 11 materials above 5% RelAE. Nonetheless, in future work, we would like to improve the natural explicitness of our network. In another direction, to further validate the nomenclature derived Table 1, we would like to perform a user study. Finally, this work is focused on the MERL dataset. Among many opportunities to consider for future developments, extending the approach to other material databases [4,6] would be an interesting option.

6   Conclusion

In an effort to combine the best of both worlds between the large range of appearances of measured BRDF models and the high control parametrization of analytical BRDF models, we have developed a novel deep learning-based approach to create a parametrization space for flexible material editing of measured BRDF. Our method relies on the unsupervised training of a β-VAE and does not require a test-subject investigation. We have illustrated the flexible editing capabilities of our approach for material editing. Furthermore, we have demonstrated that our set of learned parameters could be enriched with manual addition of parameters to extend the range of conceivable appearances. Finally, we have shown that our method parametrization enables a reconstruction of the data that is as good or better than current deep learning solutions. We believe that our approach leverages the great capacities of deep learning while removing one of its major drawback, the lack of control.

References

1. Bitterli, B.: Rendering resources (2016). https://benedikt-bitterli.me/resources/
2. Burley, B., Studios, W.D.A.: Physically-based shading at disney. In: ACM Siggraph, vol. 2012, pp. 1–7 (2012)
3. Dupuy, J., Heitz, E., Iehl, J.C., Poulin, P., Ostromoukhov, V.: Extracting microfacet-based BRDF parameters from arbitrary materials with power iterations. Comput. Graph. Forum **34**(4), 21–30 (2015)
4. Dupuy, J., Jakob, W.: An adaptive parameterization for efficient material acquisition and rendering. ACM Trans. Graph. **37**(6), 274:1–274:18 (2018)
5. Fan, X., Jiang, W., Luo, H., Mao, W.: Modality-transfer generative adversarial network and dual-level unified latent representation for visible thermal person re-identification. Vis. Comput., 1–16 (2022)
6. Filip, J., Vávra, R.: Template-based sampling of anisotropic BRDFs. Comput. Graph. Forum **33**(7), 91–99 (2014)
7. Gkioulekas, I., Xiao, B., Zhao, S., Adelson, E.H., Zickler, T., Bala, K.: Understanding the role of phase function in translucent appearance. ACM Trans. Graph. **32**(5), 147:1–147:19 (2013)
8. Higgins, I., et al.: beta-vae: learning basic visual concepts with a constrained variational framework. In: 5th International Conference on Learning Representations, ICLR (2017)
9. Holzschuch, N., Pacanowski, R.: A two-scale microfacet reflectance model combining reflection and diffraction. ACM Trans. Graph. **36**(4), 1–12 (2017)
10. Hu, B., Guo, J., Chen, Y., Li, M., Guo, Y.: DeepBRDF: a deep representation for manipulating measured BRDF. Comput. Graph. Forum **39**(2), 157–166 (2020)

11. Hu, J., et al.: Architecture disentanglement for deep neural networks. In: Proceedings of the IEEE/CVF International Conference on Computer Vision, pp. 672–681 (2021)
12. Jakob, W.: Mitsuba renderer (2010). http://www.mitsuba-renderer.org
13. Karis, B., Games, E.: Real shading in unreal engine 4. Proc. Physically Based Shading Theory Pract. **4**(3), 1 (2013)
14. Kim, H., Mnih, A.: Disentangling by factorising. In: International Conference on Machine Learning, pp. 2649–2658. PMLR (2018)
15. Kingma, D.P., Ba, J.: Adam: a method for stochastic optimization. In: 3rd International Conference on Learning Representations, ICLR (2015)
16. Li, Z., Shen, X., Hu, Y., Zhou, X.: High-resolution SVBRDF estimation based on deep inverse rendering from two-shot images. Vis. Comput., 1–14 (2022)
17. Matusik, W., Pfister, H., Brand, M., McMillan, L.: A data-driven reflectance model. ACM Trans. Graph. **22**(3), 759–769 (2003)
18. McInnes, L., Healy, J., Saul, N., Grossberger, L.: UMAP: Uniform manifold approximation and projection. J. Open Source Softw. **3**(29), 861 (2018)
19. Ngan, A., Durand, F., Matusik, W.: Experimental analysis of BRDF models. In: Proceedings of the Eurographics Symposium on Rendering, pp. 117–226 (2005)
20. Nielsen, J.B., Jensen, H.W., Ramamoorthi, R.: On optimal, minimal BRDF sampling for reflectance acquisition. ACM Trans. Graph. **34**(6), 1–11 (2015)
21. Paszke, A., et al.: Pytorch: an imperative style, high-performance deep learning library. In: Advances in Neural Information Processing Systems, vol. 32, pp. 8024–8035 (2019)
22. Ren, J., Li, M., Liu, Z., Zhang, Q.: Interpreting and disentangling feature components of various complexity from DNNs. In: International Conference on Machine Learning, pp. 8971–8981. PMLR (2021)
23. Serrano, A., Gutierrez, D., Myszkowski, K., Seidel, H.P., Masia, B.: An intuitive control space for material appearance. ACM Trans. Graph. **35**(6) (2016)
24. Shi, W., Wang, Z., Soler, C., Rushmeier, H.: A low-dimensional perceptual space for intuitive BRDF editing. In: EGSR 2021 - Eurographics Symposium on Rendering - DL-only Track, pp. 1–13. Saarbrücken, Germany (2021)
25. da Silva Nunes, M., Melo Nascimento, F., Florêncio Miranda Jr, G., Trinchão Andrade, B.: Techniques for BRDF evaluation. Vis. Comput. **38**(2), 573–589 (2022)
26. Sole, A., Guarnera, G.C., Farup, I., Nussbaum, P.: Measurement and rendering of complex non-diffuse and goniochromatic packaging materials. Vis. Comput. **37**(8), 2207–2220 (2021)
27. Soler, C., Subr, K., Nowrouzezahrai, D.: A versatile parameterization for measured material manifolds. Comput. Graph. Forum **37**(2), 135–144 (2018)
28. Sun, T., Jensen, H.W., Ramamoorthi, R.: Connecting measured BRDFS to analytic BRDFS by data-driven diffuse-specular separation. ACM Trans. Graph. **37**(6) (2018)
29. Sztrajman, A., Rainer, G., Ritschel, T., Weyrich, T.: Neural BRDF representation and importance sampling. Comput. Graph. Forum (2021)
30. Wills, J., Agarwal, S., Kriegman, D., Belongie, S.: Toward a perceptual space for gloss. ACM Trans. Graph. **28**(4) (2009)

31. Xiang, S., et al.: Disunknown: distilling unknown factors for disentanglement learning. In: Proceedings of the IEEE/CVF International Conference on Computer Vision, pp. 14810–14819 (2021)
32. Zheng, C., Zheng, R., Wang, R., Zhao, S., Bao, H.: A compact representation of measured BRDFs using neural processes. ACM Trans. Graph. **41**(2) (2021)

cGAN-Based Garment Line Draft Colorization Using a Garment-Line Dataset

Ruhan He[1,2], Xuelian Yang[1,2(✉)], and Jin Huang[1,2]

[1] School of Computer Science and Artificial Intelligence, Wuhan Textile University, Wuhan 430200, China
[2] Hubei Provincial Engineering Research Center for Intelligent Textile and Fashion, Wuhan 430200, China
1965267847@qq.com

Abstract. Garment line draft is the basis of clothing design. Automatic or semi-automatic colorization of garment line draft will improve the efficiency of fashion designers and reduce the drawing cost. In this paper, we present a garment line draft colorization method based on cGAN, which can support user interaction by adding scribbles to guide the colorization process. Due to the inadequacy of the garment line drafts, we construct a paired garment-line image dataset for training our colorization model. While existing methods for line art colorization are able to generate plausible colorized results, they tend to suffer from the color bleeding issue. We introduce a region segmentation fusion mechanism to aid colorization frameworks in avoiding color bleeding. The experimental results show that each module in the method can contribute to the final result. In addition, the comparison with the classical methods that our method can avoid large areas of leakage in the background and have cleaner garment details.

Keywords: Garment line draft · Interactive Colorization · cGAN · Garment-line image dataset

1 Introduction

In recent years, with the rapid development of deep learning techniques in image processing, The high quality performance of Generative Adversarial Networks(GANs) [1] are nowadays widely used for image-to-image conversion tasks. For example, image denoising [12,13], image superresolution [14,15], image coloring [16–18],etc. In order to better control the generation of images. conditional Generative Adversarial Network (cGAN) [2] was proposed. For example, during training, input image as condition [19], or category label as edge information [18,20]. Isola et al. [3] proved that cGAN is a general solution to the problem of image-to-image conversion, including line art colorization. Nevertheless, there is no automatic colorization pipelines for garment line art colorization (Fig. 1).

© The Author(s), under exclusive license to Springer Nature Switzerland AG 2024
B. Sheng et al. (Eds.): CGI 2023, LNCS 14496, pp. 337–348, 2024.
https://doi.org/10.1007/978-3-031-50072-5_27

Fig. 1. Colorization results. The garment line drafts from the constructed dataset

Several recent methods have explored approaches for guided image colorization [4–11]. Some works are mainly focused on images containing greyscale information [5,6,11]. A user can colorize a greyscale image by color points or color histograms [11], or colorize a manga based on reference images [6] with color points [5]. These methods can achieve impressive results but can neither handle sparse input like sketch. To address these issues, researchers have also explored more data-driven colorization methods [4,7,9]. Nevertheless, the results often contains unrealistic colorization and artifacts.

To address the above issues, the key contributions of this paper are summarized as follows.

- The paired garment-liner image dataset was constructed, specifically for the task of coloring garment line drafts.
- We introduce a region segmentation fusion mechanism to help mitigate colour bleeding artefacts during the colorization of garment line drafts.
- We introduce a new local feature network into the cGAN architecture to enhance the generalization ability of the network trained with synthetic data.

2   Related Work

2.1   Line Drafts Colorization

Automatic colorization method can generate diversified images with reasonable colors. For some special types of images, the user-guided approach allows precise control of the coloring process. AlacGAN [21] inserts the scribble image into the down-sampling layer of the generator encoder at a size of 1/16 of the input line art. This reduces the accuracy of the graffiti information and leads to color leakage. Style2Paints-V3 [22] proposes a two-stage method that allows users to manually repair incorrect colors. It solves the problem of color leakage through user interaction.

Another type of user-guided information is the reference image. style2Paints-V1 [23] and SCFT [24] transfer the color information from the reference image to the sketch, so that the coloring sketch shares similar color content with the reference image. MUNIT [25] and CoCosNet [26] can also be used to color the line art using the reference image.

Language or text markers can also be used as a form of user instruction. Sketch scene colorization [27] uses several long sentences describing different objects and different colors to color a scene sketch step by step. Tag2pix [28] uses two types of text markers as user instructions for line art coloring. However, the color bleeding problem cannot be overcome very well. Therefore, we introduce a region segmentation fusion mechanism that allows the colouring model to colour each region as correctly as possible.

2.2 Line Drafts Region Segmentation

Semantic segmentation methods are commonly used in image segmentation tasks. However, this method may fail for garment line draft images with dense lines and high complexity. Regional segmentation is different from semantic segmentation. It is an important part of this method, but few works pay attention to this direction SketchParse [29] is a data-driven, region-based framework for semantic segmentation of sketches. It mainly deals with simple sketches and is difficult to adapt to complex line arts, such as illustrations, line drafts, etc. It is very cumbersome to manually create regional semantic annotation for it.

The DanbooRegion [30] dataset provides paired illustrations and regional maps. DanbooRegion aims to extract regions from illustrations and cartoon images. Region maps can be converted to skeleton maps, which store semantically meaningless region segmentation information. Skeleton maps can be used as an auxiliary guide to provide segmentation information to the colouring network, so we employ it in our approach to mitigate the color leakage problem.

2.3 Related Datasets

Eitz et al. [6] collected 20000 sketches, including 250 categories of daily objects. However, its line structure is simple and there is no one-to-one corresponding real image. Sangkloy et al. [4] presented the first large-scale collection of sketch-photograph pairs. Its line structure is relatively simple, which is made by the staff by hand, and is greatly affected by the staff's drawing skills. Qian et al. [8] produced a 716 pairs of sketch-photo pair data set, including only shoes and chairs. However, the sketches had simple lines and could not fully depict the detailed information of real photographs.

The existing open source dataset has a simple line structure, which is far from the real photos. Therefore, it cannot be used as a dataset for colorization model. We propose a method to generate clothing simulation line draft one-to-one inverse for real clothing images based on the existing and relatively effective edge detection algorithm. Ultimately, a new garment-line dataset is constructed to solve the problem of lack of dataset in this experiment.

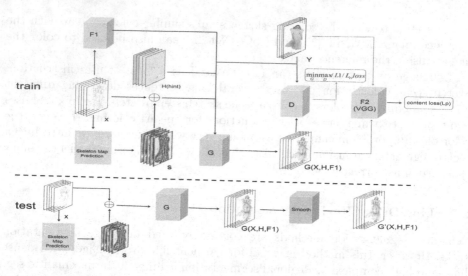

Fig. 2. Network architecture.The overall consists of two parts: training and testing.

3   Method

3.1   Overall Model Structure

We propose a new network model of image synthesis architecture based on cGAN, as shown in Fig. 2. The generator model is conditionally dependent not only on the output of the local feature network, but also on the line draft image H with simulated user color point strokes. The discriminator model is only conditional on the output of the local feature network. The network model is trained in an end-to-end manner by combining the extracted line draft image with the simulated user color dot stroke image. In the test phase, colorized images are output based on real garment line draft and user-given color point strokes. During the training process, random blocks of paint from the blurred original colour image are superimposed onto the corresponding positions in the extracted line art image. A simulated user coloured dot stroke is generated.

3.2   Generator Model and Discriminator Model

The generator(G)model is shown in Fig. 3. Based on the ideas of [5] and [6], we added a pre-trained model Sketch-a-Net [7] to the G as the local feature extraction network F1. We also use the local features as conditional input to the discriminator(D), as shown in Fig. 3. This effectively alleviates the problem of overfitting of the extracted line art image by the generator model. F1 network consists of 5 convolution layers and corresponding excitation layers. The sixth layer stacks the high-level semantic features extracted by the feature extraction network and the local features extracted by the local feature network on the channel dimension as input. It plays the role of fusing features.

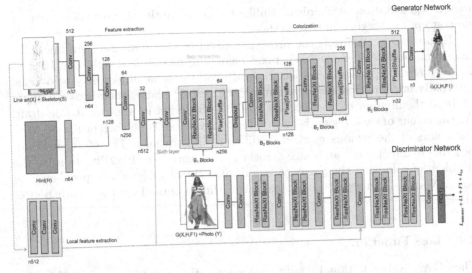

Fig. 3. Architecture of Generator and Discriminator Network with corresponding number of feature maps (n) and stride (s) indicated for each convolutional block.

The colorization network consists of 4 sub-network modules with a similar structure. The sub-network module consists of a convolution layer, a number of ResNeXt modules and an upsampling layer. Inspired by literature [9] and [10], the normalization layer is not used in the network model structure. This makes the coloring more accurate and the color distribution of the generated color image more flexible.

The D model is shown in Fig. 3. It is mainly composed of convolution layer, excitation layer, ResNeXt module and full connection layer. The convolution core size of the first convolution layer is 7, the moving step is 1, and the zero-filling is 3. The convolution kernel size of the second convolution layer is 4, the step size is 2, and the zero-filling is 1. Two ResNeXt modules are used as a base unit, with the base set to 8 and no null convolution added. The first step is set to 1, and the second step is set to 2 to perform a down-sampling operation. Then a convolutional layer with a kernel size of 1, a step size of 1 and a zero-fill of 0. It is added to increase the number of feature map channels. In the middle convolution layer of the discriminator model network, the local features obtained from the local feature network are fused. The convolution layers all use LeakyReLU with a slope of 0.2 as the excitation function.

3.3   Region Segmentation Algorithms

In order to alleviate the problem of edge color overflow during coloring, researchers often use the method of image semantic segmentation. Each pixel in the image is classified and each pixel has only one category. However, The garment line drafts are generally quite complex. To sum up, we introduce the region segmentation mechanism. Unlike image semantic segmentation, there is no concept of category in this method.

Region segmentation is the process of dividing the input garment line draft into a number of Regions, each pixel belonging to one and only one Region. Regions are independent of object category and the same object may be divided internally into multiple regions. During the testing phase, there was no upper limit to the number of regions that could be included in a garment line draft. As the colour of each region is chosen randomly, there is no correlation between the colors of the regions marked in different illustrations. Therefore, it is not possible to directly use an image translation network (e.g. Pix2Pix) to solve the problem of colouring the garment line drafts. To solve the above problems, we use a Normal-from-region conversion algorithm proposed by DanbooRegion et al.

3.4   Loss Function

The cGAN adds additional conditional information y, which needs to be combined with x and z. As shown in Eq. 1.

$$\min_{G} \max_{D} V(D,G) = E_{x \sim p_{data}(x)}[log D(x|y)] + E_{z \sim p_z(z)}[log(1 - D(G(z|y)))]$$

$$(1)$$

x is the real sample, and z is the generated sample, and y is the condition input to G, D to constrain the output.

Isola et al. [3] proposed that it is beneficial to mix the loss function of GANs with traditional losses such as L1 and L2 losses. L1 loss is more beneficial than L2 loss to reduce blur. As shown in Eq. 2.

$$L1 = \sum_{i=1}^{N} |x_i - G(z_i)|$$

$$(2)$$

The F1 model generates more noise when performing local feature extraction. Therefore, we use a total variance loss function (TV loss) to smooth the output. The L_{tv} shown in Eq. 3.

$$L_{tv} = \sum_{i,j} ((x_{i,j-1} - x_{x,j})^2 + (x_{i+1,j} - x_{x,j})^2)^{\beta/2}$$

$$(3)$$

As shown in formula 3, where $x_{i,j}$ represents a pixel point in the input image, and $x_{i,j-1}$ represents the pixel point in the horizontal direction of the current pixel, and $x_{i+1,j}$ represents the pixel point in the vertical direction of the current pixel.

We use the VGG19 network model for a global feature extraction network, using L_p as the loss function. As shown in Eq. 4.

$$L_p = \sum_{i} ||\phi((\hat{x}_i) - \phi(x_i)||^2$$

$$(4)$$

The final total loss function is defined as shown in Eq. 5.

$$L = W_{\min_G \max_D V(D,G)} * \min_G \max_D V(D,G) + \\ W_{L_1} * L_1 + W_{L_{tv}} * L_{tv} + W_{L_p} * L_p$$

(5)

Our output still encounters some noise and lack of smoothness. We perform post-processing using a joint bilateral filter. The formula is shown in Eq. 6.

$$J_p = 1/k_p \sum_{q \in \Omega} I_q f(||p - q||)g(||\tilde{I}_p - \tilde{I}_q||)$$

(6)

4   Experiments

All colorization models were retrained on the dataset constructed in this paper.

4.1   Construction of the Garment-Line Dataset

To avoid copyright disputes and to ensure the quality of the garment line drafts. We obtained a total of 150 pairs of data through online purchase and offline collection. After comparison and screening, 75 pairs of data were finally obtained. It takes time and effort. The number of images is limited and the quality is uneven.

We use the Web Driver library to crawl the fashion show pictures of the four major fashion weeks from 2020 to 2022 released by the EEFF.NET. Finally, we got 853 pairs of garment-line datas and 550 individual images of real garment. We used the PhotoShop tool to decolorize them and extract the lines. Finally got 800 pairs of data after screening.

Fig. 4. Data set display diagram

The garment line drafts extracted using the PhotoShop tool have a lot of missing information and do not convey enough details. We tried four edge detection algorithms, Canny, SketchKeras, HED and U²-Net, for inverse generation of one-to-one images of garment line drafts.

The edges of the garment line drafts extracted by the Canny algorithm are clear but incoherent. SketchKeras algorithm extracts garment line drafts with clear edges but blurred internal lines. HED algorithm can extract the garment line drafts with clear edges (thick edges), but it loses a lot of internal details. U^2-Net extracts garment lines with clear and coherent edges. It contains a lot of interior details of garment and is less noise. The line thickness is consistent, and the overall effect is very close to the hand-drawn garment line draft. Finally, the dataset was constructed using U^2-Net. A portion of the dataset is shown in Fig. 4.

4.2   The Experimental Results

By adding each module one by one, the effect of each module in the proposed method is studied. The results of each stage are shown in Fig. 5.

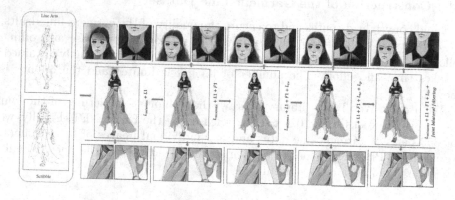

Fig. 5. Results by Stage

We can see that the original result ($L_{mm} + L_1$) is generally good. Blending and overflow can be seen around the edges. We added a Sketch-a-Net network model to the network for local feature extraction. The results ($L_{mm} + L_1 + F_1$) show that blending is reduced (see neck), color spillover is reduced (see head, hands, legs) and blurring is alleviated a little. But Sketch-a-Net model brings more noise to the results, so we use the L_{tv} to smooth. In addition, L_p is added to the feature space to refine the output. The output is now better. Finally, the joint bilateral filter makes the image clearer.

4.3   Comparison Experiments

Petalica Paint is a commercial colorization website. Three coloring styles are available: Tanpopo, Satsuki and Canna. Style2Paints is a powerful automatic coloring software for AI comic strips. Figure 6 shows how our results compare with Petalica Paint and Style2Paints.

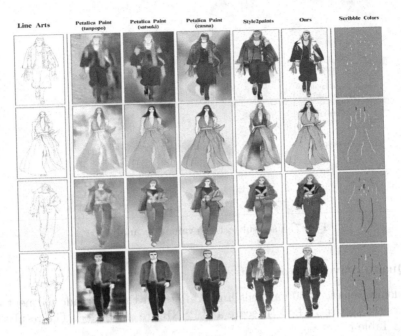

Fig. 6. Comparison with Petalica Paint(Tanpopo, Satsuki, Canna) and Style2paints

Through experiments, it is found that Petalica Paint has higher saturation, but the mixing overflow of background and face is serious, and the boundary is not obvious. Style2Paints tends to cause the color of the figure's skin to blend with the borders of the garment. Our method can avoid large-scale leakage and create a cleaner picture on the whole, especially on the face and skin of the people.

4.4 Qualitative Comparisons

The characteristics of image colorization task determine that its final coloring effect cannot be accurately measured by hard indicators. Visual effect is the more important evaluation standard.

16 pieces of garment-line drafts images are randomly selected from the constructed dataset(8 images of women's and 8 images of men's). A total of 50 users aged 22–30 were invited. From the above 5 colorization methods, choose their favorite color results and the image with less edge color overflow. For the subjective user evaluation, we showed 50 users with image of the real fashion garments, the relative garment line drafts and the output colored garment line drafts. Users were required to complete the voting independently. The statistical results are shown in the Boxplot shown in Fig. 7.

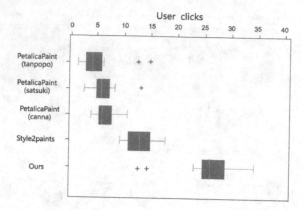

Fig. 7. User subjective evaluation analysis

4.5 Quantitative Comparisons

We randomly selected 500 garment line drafts from the self-made garment-line dataset as the test set. The FID score and PSNR are calculated. The results are shown in Table 1.

Table 1. Quantitative comparison of coloring methods based on FID, PSNR scores

Training Configuration	FID(↓)	PSNR(↑)
Petalica Paint(canna)	108.28	19.04
Petalica Paint(tanpopo)	91.14	21.51
Petalica Paint(satsuki)	86.28	22.78
Style2paints	65.73	31.73
Ours(No local feature extraction)	65.28	32.47
Ours	64.36	33.29

According to Table 1, our method has a lower FID score and a higher PSNR score. This indicates that our results have a better overall quality compared to the results from the three Petalica Paint frameworks. Compared to the Style2paints method, there is some improvement in the indicator values. In addition, removing local features from the network during training causes the FID value to rise. This suggests that the method in this paper produces higher quality colourisation results.

5 Conclusions

In this paper, we propose a colorization method of garment line draft based on cGAN. A region segmentation fusion mechanism is introduced to produce clean and aesthetically pleasing colouring sketches. In addition, the loss function is specially designed to reduce the mixing and overflow of results. Finally, we use the joint bilateral filter to smooth the results and output a clearer and vivid colored image. In some cases, when two adjacent regions have the same semantic concept, our model may still be unable to connect the two regions and depict them in different colors. In order to enable the model to understand the semantic content of the segmented area of the garment line draft, we can combine the transfer learning on the human body analysis data set to form a further expansion of our work.

References

1. Goodfellow, I., Pouget-Abadie, J., Mirza, M., et al.: Generative adversarial nets. In: Neural Information Processing Systems. MIT Press, Cambridge (2014)
2. Mirza, M., Osindero, S.: Conditional generative adversarial nets. In: Computer Science, pp. 2672–2680 (2014)
3. Isola, P., et al.: Image-to-Image translation with conditional adversarial networks. In: The IEEE Conference on Computer Vision and Pattern Recognition (CVPR), pp. 1125–1134 (2017)
4. Sangkloy, P., Burnell, N., Ham, C., et al.: The sketchy database: learning to retrieve badly drawn bunnies. ACM Trans. Graph. 35(4), 119 (2016)
5. Furusawa, C., Hiroshiba, K., Ogaki, K., Odagiri, Y.: Comicolorization: semi-automatic manga colorization. In: SIGGRAPH Asia 2017 Technical Briefs, vol. 12. ACM (2017)
6. Hensman, P., Aizawa, K.: cGAN-based manga colorization using a single training image. arXiv preprint arXiv:1706.06918 (2017)
7. Yu, Q., et al.: Sketch-a-Net: a deep neural network that beats humans. Int. J. Comput. Vision 122(3), 411–425 (2017)
8. Qian, Y., Feng, L., Song, Y.Z., et al.: Sketch me that shoe. In: 2016 IEEE Conference on Computer Vision and Pattern Recognition(CVPR), pp. 799–807. IEEE, Piscataway (2016)
9. Xie, S., Girshick, R,, Dollár, P., et al.: Aggregated residual transformations for deep neural networks. IEEE (2016)
10. Hu, J., Shen, L., Albanie, S., et al.: Squeeze-and-excitation networks. arXiv preprint arXiv:1704.04861 (2017)
11. Liu, X., Wu, W., Li, C., Li, Y., Wu, H.: Reference-guided structure-aware deep sketch colorization for cartoons. Comput. Vis. Media 8(1), 135–148 (2022)
12. Liu, G., Dang, M., Liu, J., Xiang, R., Tian, Y., Luo, N.: True wide convolutional neural network for image denoising. Inf. Sci. 610, 171–184 (2022)
13. Li, P., Li, Z., Pang, X., Wang, H., Lin, W., Wentai, W.: Multi-scale residual denoising GAN model for producing super-resolution CTA images. Ambient Intell. Humaniz. Comput. 13(3), 1515–1524 (2022)
14. Xinyue, W., Chen, Z., Peng, C., Ye, X.: MMSRNet: pathological image super-resolution by multi-task and multi-scale learning. Biomed. Signal Process. Control 81, 104428 (2023)
15. Li, W., Zhou, K., Qi, L., Lu, L., Lu, J.: Best-buddy GANs for highly detailed image super-resolution. In: AAAI, pp. 1412–1420 (2022)

16. Lu, P., Yu, J., Peng, X., Zhao, Z., Wang, X.: Gray2colornet: transfer more colors from reference image. In: Proceedings of the 28th ACM International Conference on Multimedia, pp. 3210–3218 (2020)
17. Vitoria, P., Raad, L., Ballester, C.: Chromagan: adversarial picture colorization with semantic class distribution. In: Proceedings of the IEEE/CVF Winter Conference on Applications of Computer Vision, pp. 2445–2454 (2020)
18. Li, Z., Geng, Z., Kang, Z., Chen, W., Yang, Y.: Eliminating gradient conflict in reference-based line-art colorization. In: ECCV 17, pp. 579–596 (2022)
19. Shu-Yu Chen, Jia-Qi Zhang, Lin Gao, Yue He, Shihong Xia, Min Shi, Fang-Lue Zhang.: Active Colorization for Cartoon Line Drawings. In: IEEE Trans. Vis. Comput. Graph. 28(2), 1198–1208 (2022)
20. Chen, W., Hays, J.: Sketchygan: towards diverse and realistic sketch to image synthesis. In: Proceedings of the IEEE Conference on Computer Vision and Pattern Recognition, pp. 9416–9425 (2018)
21. Ci, Y., Ma, X., Wang, Z., Li, H., Luo, Z.: User-guided deep anime line art colorization with conditional adversarial networks. In: Proceedings of the 26th ACM International Conference on Multimedia, pp. 1536–1544 (2018)
22. Zhang, L., Li, C., Wong, T.-T., Ji, Y., Liu, C.: Two-stage sketch colorization. ACM Trans. Graph. (TOG) 37(6), 1–14 (2018)
23. Zhang, L., Ji, Y., Lin, X., Liu, C.: Style transfer for anime sketches with enhanced residual u-net and auxiliary classifier gan. In: 2017 4th IAPR Asian Conference on Pattern Recognition (ACPR), pp. 506–511. IEEE (2017)
24. Lee, J., Kim, E., Lee, Y., Kim, D., Chang, J., Choo, J.: Reference-based sketch image colorization using augmented-self reference and dense semantic correspondence. In: Proceedings of the IEEE/CVF Conference on Computer Vision and Pattern Recognition, pp. 5801–5810(2020)
25. Huang, X., Liu, M.-Y., Belongie, S., Kautz, J.: Multi-modal unsupervised image-to-image translation. In: Proceedings of the European conference on computer vision (ECCV), pp. 172–189 (2018)
26. Zhang, P., Zhang, B., Chen, D., Yuan, L., Wen, F.: Cross-domain correspondence learning for exemplar-based image translation. In: Proceedings of the IEEE/CVF Conference on Computer Vision and Pattern Recognition, pp. 5143–5153 (2020)
27. Zou, C., Mo, H., Gao, C., Du, R., Fu, H.: Language-based colorization of scene sketches. ACM Trans. Graph. (TOG) 38(6), 1–16 (2019)
28. Kim, H., Jhoo, H. Y., Park, E., Yoo, S.: Tag2pix: line art colorization using text tag with secat and changing loss. In: Proceedings of the IEEE/CVF International Conference on Computer Vision, pp. 9056–9065 (2019)
29. Sarvadevabhatla, R.K., Dwivedi, I., Biswas, A., Manocha, S.: Sketchparse: towards rich descriptions for poorly drawn sketches using multi-task hierarchical deep networks. In: Proceedings of the 25th ACM international conference on Multimedia, pp. 10–18 (2017)
30. Zhang, L., Ji, Y., Liu, C.: DanbooRegion: an illustration region dataset. In: Vedaldi, A., Bischof, H., Brox, T., Frahm, J.-M. (eds.) ECCV 2020. LNCS, vol. 12358, pp. 137–154. Springer, Cham (2020). https://doi.org/10.1007/978-3-030-58601-0_9

PCCNet: A Few-Shot Patch-Wise Contrastive Colorization Network

Xiaying Liu[1], Ping Yang[1], Alexandru C. Telea[2], Jiří Kosinka[3], and Zizhao Wu[1(✉)]

[1] Hangzhou Dianzi University, Hangzhou, China
{xiayingliu,wuzizhao}@hdu.edu.cn
[2] Utrecht University, Utrecht, The Netherlands
a.c.telea@uu.nl
[3] University of Groningen, Groningen, The Netherlands
j.kosinka@rug.nl

Abstract. Few-shot colorization aims to learn a model to colorize images with little training data. Yet, existing models often fail to keep color consistency due to ignored patch correlations of the images. In this paper, we propose PCCNet, a novel Patch-wise Contrastive Colorization Network to learn color synthesis by measuring the similarities and variations of image patches in two different aspects: inter-image and intra-image. Specifically, for inter-image, we investigate a patch-wise contrastive learning mechanism with positive and negative samples constraint to distinguish color features between patches across images. For intra-image, we explore a new intra-image correlation loss function to measure the similarity distribution which reveals structural relations between patches within an image. Furthermore, we propose a novel color memory loss that improves the accuracy of the memory module to store and retrieve data. Experiments show that our method allows the correctly saturated color to spread naturally over objects and also achieves higher scores in quantitative comparisons with related methods.

Keywords: Colorization · Contrastive Learning · Memory Networks

1 Introduction

Image colorization aims to create color images from grayscale ones in the most natural manner possible. Existing methods [12,30] typically build models that allow coloring any kind of grayscale images by training them on large, generic, image datasets such as ImageNet [1] or COCO [14]. However, such models tend to output an average, desaturated result, where the specific hues one would ideally get can be lost. Other artifacts include the inability to consider rare exemplars.

Supplementary Information The online version contains supplementary material available at https://doi.org/10.1007/978-3-031-50072-5_28.

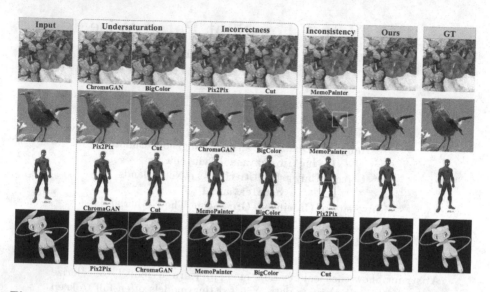

Fig. 1. Compared with existing colorization methods (ChromaGAN [24], BigColor [11], Pix2Pix [6], Cut [19] and MemoPainter [28]), PCCNet has distinctive superiority in ensuring color saturation, color correctness and color consistence.

For instance, flowers are often colorized red, while in reality they can have a wide spectrum of hues. Few-shot colorization aims to address this by enabling the model to remember what color an object should be with limited training data (few images of a few specific classes). In this category, Yoo *et al* . [28] proposed the MemoPainter colorization model, which can generate compelling results. However, the color propagation *within* an image can appear unnatural due to the lack of attention to the image patches.

Three main challenges exist when performing few-shot colorization: Colors should be (1) *consistent*, *i.e.*, they should appear visually natural and the image should avoid mottled (mixed) hues and color bleeding artifacts. Also, colors should be (2) *correct*, meaning that the generated colors should match the ground-truth ones, even if the model was trained with only a few examples exhibiting some specific type of imagery and colors. Finally, colors should be (3) *saturated*, which means the colors should be bright rather than slightly gray.

In this work, we propose a novel patch-wise contrastive colorization network, dubbed PCCNet, to address the above three challenges; see Fig. 1. Specifically, to make sure the produced colors are *consistent* and also visually natural, our method investigates a patch-wise contrastive learning mechanism to learn the patch correlations *across* images. Further, our method explores a correlation loss function in order to learn the patch correlations *within* an image. More concretely, we measure intra-image patches correlations from the perspective of patch data distribution similarity. Additionally, the color information stored in the memory module guides the coloring process to remember the *correct* colors and ensure the generation of *saturated* colors.

To summarize, our main contributions are:

- We first apply patch-wise contrastive learning to image colorization with stronger supervision achieved by using a self-supervised approach.
- We investigate a patch-wise contrastive loss and an intra-image correlation loss to learn patch correlations in two aspects: inter-image and intra-image.
- We use a memory module with a new training strategy to remember the colors of rare objects, allowing for few-shot or one-shot learning.

2   Related Work

Many works have been proposed on learning automatic colorization models using large numbers of image pairs (grayscale or color). Zhang et al . [30] treated the regression colorization problem as a classification one to generate saturated results. Subsequent improvements included using two-branch dual-task structures [24,29] and three-branch triple-task structures [8,9] to add classification, fine-grained semantic parsing, or both, to the colorization process. Su et al . [21] applied object-level colorization to clearly separate objects and background. MemoPainter [28] used a memory network to help remember the color of objects. Hong et al . [4] proposed an iterative generative model to attain diversity and possible colorization. Recent methods [11,26] used the rich color prior encapsulated in a GAN to guide the colorization network to generate diverse color images. Transformer-based architectures [7,12] improved colorization by focusing on global information. In addition, the exemplar-based image colorization [13] and the line drawing with colorization [22] had also attracted the attention of scholars. In this context, our proposed PCCNet is an automatic colorization model which makes better use of the patch correlations focusing on solving a few-shot learning problem.

3   Proposed Method

Image colorization aims to recover the channels $(a, b) \in \mathbb{R}^{H \times W \times 2}$ from the channel $L \in \mathbb{R}^{H \times W \times 1}$, where (L, a, b) is specified in the CIE Lab color space. Our PCCNet consists of three main modules: patch sampling (P), color memory (M), and colorization (C), see Fig. 2.

3.1   Patch Sampling Module

The patch sampling module P consists of an encoder and an F sub-net (see Fig. 2). The encoder is identical to the one used by the colorization module (see Sect. 3.3) and also shares the latter's weights. Multi-scale features are obtained from the encoder and then fed to the F sub-net. We pass the (a, b) channels through P to obtain the embedding vectors $\mathbf{w}_k$ and $\mathbf{z}_k$ which represent image patches. The index k, $1 \leq k \leq 256$, indicates the location of the patches in the image. For each patch of the output image, there is a corresponding patch

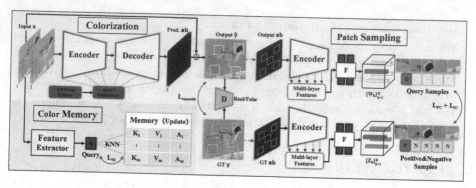

Fig. 2. Overview of the PCCNet framework. C (colorization) synthesizes a colorized image $\hat{y}$ form the grayscale input x in collaboration with P (patch sampling) and M (color memory). During training, our model continuously updates the memory while modulating C with the color feature of the ground truth, and also extracts patches from P to calculate two patch-wise losses. During testing, our model retrieves the nearest color feature from M as a condition to guide C.

of the ground-truth image as its positive example, labeled as the positive pair $(\mathbf{w}, \mathbf{z}^+) \sim p_{\mathbf{wz}^+}$. For negative examples, the remaining $\mathbf{z}_k$ except for $\mathbf{z}^+$ are all negatives $\mathbf{z}^- \sim p_Z$.

We improve the performance in terms of optimizing the negative sampling strategy and removing negative-positive coupling (NPC) effects [27] of InfoNCE. There are some easy negatives, such as $\mathbf{z}_4$ in Fig. 3a, that do not contribute significantly to the comparison mechanism. To avoid being overly influenced by those easy-negatives, we use the method of hard-negative sampling modeled by the von Mises-Fisher distribution [20]. The distribution q_{Z^-} is defined as

$$q_{Z^-}(\mathbf{z}^-) \propto e^{\beta \mathbf{z}^+ \cdot \mathbf{z}^-} p_Z(\mathbf{z}^-), \tag{1}$$

where $\cdot$ denotes dot product and the *concentration parameter* β [16] controls the hardness of negative sampling.

Patch-wise Contrastive Loss L_{PC}. The NPC effect refers to the diminishing gradient of InfoNCE by easy negative and positive samples, which in turn makes training harder. To prevent the NPC effect, we formulate this loss, called L_{PC}, by using a decoupled InfoNCE loss, measuring the correlation between image patches, as

$$L_{PC} = E_{(\mathbf{w}, \mathbf{z}^+) \sim p_{\mathbf{wz}^+}} \left[-\log \frac{e^{\mathbf{w} \cdot \mathbf{z}^+ / \tau}}{N E_{\mathbf{z}^- \sim q_{\mathbf{z}^-}} \left[e^{\mathbf{w} \cdot \mathbf{z}_i^- / \tau} \right]} \right], \tag{2}$$

where N denotes the number of negative examples and the *temperature parameter* τ is set to 0.07. In terms of implementation, we use

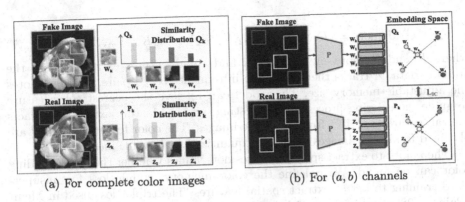

(a) For complete color images   (b) For (a, b) channels

Fig. 3. Patch correlation through similarity distribution.

$$E_{\mathbf{z}^- \sim q_{\mathbf{z}^-}}\left[e^{\mathbf{w}\cdot\mathbf{z}^-/\tau}\right] = E_{\mathbf{z}^- \sim p_Z}\left[e^{\mathbf{w}\cdot\mathbf{z}^-/\tau}\frac{q_Z^-(\mathbf{z}^-)}{p_Z(\mathbf{z}^-)}\right]$$
$$= E_{\mathbf{z}^- \sim p_Z}\left[e^{\mathbf{w}\cdot\mathbf{z}^-/\tau}e^{\beta\mathbf{z}^+\cdot\mathbf{z}^-}\right]. \tag{3}$$

Intra-image Correlation Loss L_{IC}. Patches at different positions have different representations. For example, in Fig. 3a, the central patch represents the stamen; other patches represent the petals or the background. Different patches have different similarity distributions. The (a, b) channels of this image (Fig. 3b) show a similar story. For the real-image (a, b) channels, any patch Z_k has a different similarity with the others, as captured by the similarity distribution P_k

$$P_k(i) = \frac{e^{\mathbf{z}_k \cdot \mathbf{z}_i}}{\sum_{j=1}^{K} e^{\mathbf{z}_k \cdot \mathbf{z}_j}}. \tag{4}$$

A patch $\mathbf{w}_k$ in the (a, b) channels of the generated image has the similarity distribution Q_k with the other patches $\mathbf{w}_i$ given by

$$Q_k(i) = \frac{e^{\mathbf{w}_k \cdot \mathbf{w}_i}}{\sum_{j=1}^{K} e^{\mathbf{w}_k \cdot \mathbf{w}_j}}, \tag{5}$$

which should match P_k as much as possible. Given the above, we define the intra-image correlation loss L_{IC} which measures intra-image patches correlations in terms of the Jensen-Shannon divergence

$$L_{\text{IC}} = \sum_{k=1}^{K} \text{JSD}(P_k \| Q_k). \tag{6}$$

3.2   Color Memory Module

The color memory module M consists of a feature extractor and a memory (see Fig. 2). Inspired by the memory module of [10], we design the memory of M as follows

$$\text{Memory} = (K_1, V_1, A_1), (K_2, V_2, A_2), \cdots, (K_m, V_m, A_m), \qquad (7)$$

where K and V represent the spatial and color features extracted from the training data, A tracks the ages of the infrequent (K, V) pairs, and m denotes the adjustable memory size. The model can retrieve the nearest color feature to guide the coloring process during testing, and the feature extractor extracts spatial features $s \in \mathbb{R}^{512}$ from grayscale images. The color features $c \subset \mathbb{R}^{313}$ are obtained from color images by using a quantized (a, b) value method [30].

The ability to extract spatial features determines whether the corresponding color can be found. We redefine the color memory module loss for unsupervised training to better extract spatial features. The triplet loss used in MemoPainter [28] optimizes the within-class similarity and between-class similarity by means of average force. We use the circle loss [23], which adds the weights to control the gradient contribution of the positive and negative keys, so as to obtain a more discriminative model than using the triplet loss. We describe the specific definition of the color memory module loss in Sect. 3.4.

3.3 Colorization Module

The colorization module C is built upon the baseline of CGAN [17] which consists of a generator and a discriminator.

Generator G. The input x is a grayscale image, *i.e.*, the L channel, and the output $\hat{y}$ predicts the real image y. Our generator (Fig. 2) contains an encoder consisting of downsample blocks and residual blocks, and a decoder consisting of residual blocks and upsample blocks. We concatenate the L channel and a duplicate L channel before feeding it to the encoder. This ensures that the encoder can be used directly by P to extract multi-scale features. We use AdaIN [5] to treat color features c retrieved from the color memory module M as a guide for the colorization module. Specifically, we compute the affine scaling y_1 and shift y_2 of AdaIN by MLP from c and let it act on the AdaIN layer as

$$\text{AdaIN}(x_{\text{now}}, c) = y_1 \left(\frac{x_{\text{now}} - \mu(x_{\text{now}})}{\sigma(x_{\text{now}})} \right) + y_2, \qquad (8)$$

where μ and σ denote average and standard deviation of the output of the previous convolutional layer x_{now}.

Discriminator D. The discriminator uses color features as a condition to distinguish between real images and output images. We use the Markovian discriminator [6] to pay attention to image details, avoiding extreme outputs of the discriminator. Given that our input images are 256×256 pixels, we use a receptive field of size 70×70. The discriminator D outputs a matrix of size 32×32 in which each element represents the classification (true/fake) of each patch.

3.4   Objective Functions

Color Memory Loss L_M. For the unsupervised learning of the feature extractor, we use the circle loss defined as

$$L_M(S_n, S_p) = \log\left(1 + \sum_{i=1}^{K}\sum_{j=1}^{L} e^{\gamma(\alpha_n^j S_n^j - \alpha_p^i S_p^i)}\right), \tag{9}$$

where S_n is the between-class similarity, and S_p is the within-class similarity. Negative and positive keys $K[n_b]$ and $K[n_p]$ are given by $\mathrm{KL}(V[n_b] \parallel v) > \delta_1$ and $\mathrm{KL}(V[n_p] \parallel v) < \delta_1$ respectively, where δ_1 is the user preset color threshold. K and L are the number of positive, respectively negative, keys; $\gamma = 256$ is a scale factor; and α_p^i and α_n^j are the weights of positive and negative samples, respectively, defined as

$$\alpha_p^i = [O_p - S_p^i]_+ \quad \text{and} \quad \alpha_n^j = [S_n^j - O_n]_+, \tag{10}$$

where $[\cdot]_+$ denotes 'cut off at zero' to ensure positive values, $O_p = 1 + m$, $O_n = -m$, and m is a hyperparameter set to 0.25. Minimizing L_M allows the feature extractor to extract a query q with the smallest possible between class similarity and the largest possible within-class similarity.

Colorization and Patch Sampling Loss. We combine four losses to jointly train C and P: (1) patch-wise contrastive loss L_{PC} (see Sect. 3.1); (2) intra-image correlation loss L_{IC} (see Sect. 3.1); (3) content loss L_{smooth}; and (4) adversarial loss L_{LSGAN}, as follows.

Content Loss L_{smooth}. We use the smooth L_1 metric between the generated $\dot{y}$ and the ground truth image y, *i.e.* ,

$$L_{smooth}(y, \hat{y}) = \begin{cases} \frac{1}{2}(y - \hat{y})^2 & \text{if } |y - \hat{y}| \leqslant \delta_2 \\ \delta_2|y - \hat{y}| - \frac{1}{2}\delta_2^2 & \text{otherwise,} \end{cases} \tag{11}$$

to make training more robust to outlier images.

Adversarial Loss L_{LSGAN}. LSGAN [15] uses a least squares loss to mitigate the vanishing gradient problem. We follow a LSGAN design with the discriminator and generator losses given by

$$L_{LSGAN}^D = \frac{1}{2}E_{y \sim P_{data}}[(D(y, c) - 1)^2] + \frac{1}{2}E_{x \sim P_{data}}[D(G(x, c), c)^2], \tag{12}$$

$$L_{LSGAN}^G = \frac{1}{2}E_{x \sim P_{data}}[(D(G(x, c), c) - 1)^2],$$

respectively. Putting it all together, the final loss functions of C and P amount to a generator loss L_G and a discriminator loss L_D which are defined as

$$L_G = \lambda_1 L_{PC} + \lambda_2 L_{IC} + \lambda_3 L_{smooth} + \lambda_4 L_{LSGAN}^G, \tag{13}$$

$$L_D = L_{LSGAN}^D.$$

4   Experiments

We now present datasets and metrics used to evaluate our method (Sect. 4.1), several implementation details (Sect. 4.2), and the results of our evaluation and comparisons (Sect. 4.3), and ablation studies (Sect. 4.4).

4.1   Datasets and Evaluation Metrics

We measure the performance of our model on four datasets, namely **Oxford102 Flowers** [18], **Bird100** [25], **Hero** [28], and **Pokemon**[1], where Hero performs few-shot colorization, and Pokemon performs one-shot or zero-shot colorization. The FID score [3] is used to evaluate the colorization image quality. LPIPS [31] evaluates the perceptual similarity which is more consistent with human perception. We provide the evaluation measured by PSNR as a reference, although experiments show that PSNR prefers grayish images. The colorfulness score [2] reflects the degree of color brightness.

4.2   Implementation Details

We implemented PCCNet with PyTorch and trained our models on an NVIDIA RTX 2060 GPU using the Adam optimizer with the learning rate decaying from 10^{-3} to 10^{-6}. We optimize the color memory module M first, then optimize the colorization and patch sampling modules C and P jointly. Please see the Supplementary Material for parameter settings.

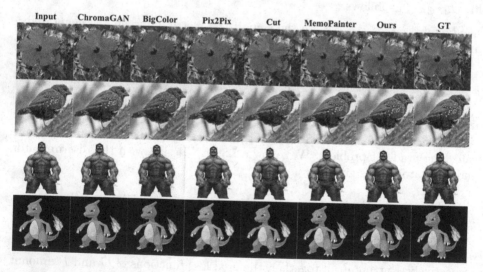

Fig. 4. Qualitative comparison of colorization results on four different datasets.

---

[1] https://www.kaggle.com/kvpratama/pokemon-images-dataset.

4.3   Evaluation

Qualitative Comparisons. We compare PCCNet with ChromaGAN [24], Big-Color [11], Pix2Pix [6], Cut [19], and MemoPainter [28]. Figure 4 shows that ChromaGAN and Cut generate images that are grayish, akin to old photos that are not restored well. BigColor and Pix2Pix produce more vibrant results, but the lack of supervision of image patches makes color transitions unnatural. Especially in the few-shot cases, *i.e.*, on the Hero datasets, severe unreasonable color fusion phenomena occur. In this case, MemoPainter yields better results due to color memory. However, the results still show color inconsistency and color deviations. Compared with the above methods, our method obtains better visual results. In line with the requirements listed in Sect. 1, our method improves the model's ability to maintain color consistency, color correctness, and color saturation. See the Supplementary Material for more qualitative results.

Table 1. Quantitative evaluation of colorization experiments

Dataset	Oxford102 Flowers				Bird100			
Metric	FID↓	LPIPS↓	PSNR↑	Colorful↑	FID↓	LPIPS↓	PSNR↑	Colorful↑
ChromaGAN	74.306	0.231	18.768	44.756	41.613	0.188	22.302	25.256
BigColor	59.464	0.217	19.031	65.287	38.866	0.229	18.633	48.883
Pix2Pix	46.899	0.217	19.182	52.319	44.495	0.205	21.546	23.413
Cut	44.174	0.213	18.956	59.674	45.266	0.218	20.193	27.146
MemoPainter	59.338	0.272	17.693	66.286	40.011	0.216	21.080	29.012
Ours	**41.206**	**0.211**	**20.142**	**66.868**	**29.836**	**0.181**	**22.321**	**36.278**
Dataset	Hero				Pokemon			
Metric	FID↓	LPIPS↓	PSNR↑	Colorful↑	FID↓	LPIPS↓	PSNR↑	Colorful↑
ChromaGAN	104.171	0.098	23.467	26.155	92.050	0.125	**21.811**	24.101
BigColor	143.791	0.147	21.238	21.841	111.534	0.168	18.233	34.626
Pix2Pix	133.237	0.109	21.981	**36.931**	94.265	0.140	21.217	10.897
Cut	130.329	0.116	22.052	24.709	90.807	0.136	20.762	28.180
MemoPainter	139.494	0.105	22.311	23.747	89.816	0.138	20.646	26.520
Ours	**90.252**	**0.081**	**24.372**	33.528	**64.023**	**0.124**	21.703	**32.416**

Quantitative Evaluation. Table 1 shows the results of our quantitative evaluation. For all datasets, our method achieves lower FID and LPIPS scores. This indicates that our method is able to generate more natural and realistic color images that are closer to the ground truth. The two exceptions to the above are Pix2Pix and ChromaGAN, where Pix2Pix achieves a higher Colorfulness score than our method on the Hero dataset and ChromaGAN achieves a higher PSNR score than our method on the Pokemon dataset. However, as mentioned earlier, Pix2Pix exhibits a 'color fusion' phenomenon for this dataset, and ChromaGAN exhibits a 'desaturation' phenomenon for the Pokemon dataset (see again Fig. 4

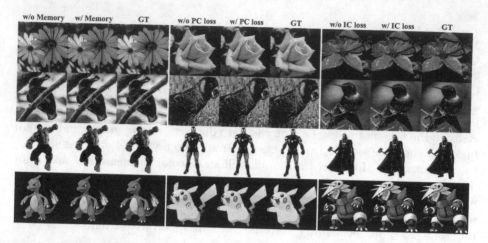

w/o Memory w/ Memory GT   w/o PC loss w/ PC loss GT   w/o IC loss w/ IC loss GT

Fig. 5. Qualitative comparisons of ablation studies on PCCNet.

Table 2. Quantitative comparisons for ablation studies.

Setting			Oxford102 Flowers			
Memory Module	PC Loss	IC Loss	FID↓	LPIPS↓	PSNR↑	Colorful↑
✗	✓	✓	42.101	0.213	19.888	58.450
✓	✗	✓	48.849	0.217	19.696	65.108
✓	✓	✗	42.789	0.214	20.126	66.209
✓	✓	✓	**41.206**	**0.211**	**20.142**	**66.868**

or more visual results in the Supplementary Material). While this leads to higher scores, we argue that the results of Pix2Pix and ChromaGAN are less similar to the ground truth than ours.

4.4 Ablation Study

As described in Sect. 3, our method has three main components which can be seen as the key heuristics we use to drive our colorization: the color memory module, the patch-wise contrastive loss L_{PC}, and the intra-image correlation loss L_{IC}. To further understand the effect of these components, we performed a series of ablation studies. Figure 5 visually shows the effect of each of our modules. M helps to memorize the colors, and the network without M generates images with biased colors. Further adding L_{PC} and L_{IC} leads to better handling of the details of the images. Hence, we argue that each individual module is of added value to the final colorization. In Table 2, the results show the meaningful improvements by our three components. Adding each component to our network results in varying degrees of improvement on the Oxford102 Flowers dataset. The best results are seen when all components are added. See supplementary material for more ablation experiments.

5 Conclusion

We have presented PCCNet, a new deep learning model for colorization with improved color consistency, color correctness, and color saturation. Our framework relies on a patch-wise contrastive learning mechanism and an intra-image correlation loss for distilling the learning process of the correlation between image patches in two aspects: inter-image and intra-image. We further drive our colorization by a memory module which favors the learning of outlier color patterns present in the training images. Qualitative and quantitative comparisons as well as ablation experiments illustrate its effectiveness on various benchmark datasets.

Acknowledgements. This work was partially supported by the Zhejiang Provincial Natural Science Foundation of China (LGF21F20012).

References

1. Deng, J., Dong, W., Socher, R., Li, L.J., Li, K., Fei-Fei, L.: Imagenet: a large-scale hierarchical image database. In: IEEE Conference on Computer Vision and Pattern Recognition, pp. 248–255 (2009)
2. Hasler, D., Süsstrunk, S.: Measuring colorfulness in natural images. In: IS&T/SPIE Electronic Imaging (2003)
3. Heusel, M., Ramsauer, H., Unterthiner, T., Nessler, B., Hochreiter, S.: GANs trained by a two time-scale update rule converge to a local nash equilibrium. In: NIPS (2017)
4. Hong, K., et al.: Joint intensity-gradient guided generative modeling for colorization. ArXiv arxiv:2012.14130 (2020)
5. Huang, X., Belongie, S.J.: Arbitrary style transfer in real-time with adaptive instance normalization. In: IEEE International Conference on Computer Vision (ICCV), pp. 1510–1519 (2017)
6. Isola, P., Zhu, J.Y., Zhou, T., Efros, A.A.: Image-to-image translation with conditional adversarial networks. In: IEEE Conference on Computer Vision and Pattern Recognition (CVPR), pp. 5967–5976 (2017)
7. Ji, X., et al.: Colorformer: image colorization via color memory assisted hybrid-attention transformer. In: European Conference on Computer Vision (2022)
8. Jin, X., et al.: Focusing on persons: colorizing old images learning from modern historical movies. In: Proceedings of the 29th ACM International Conference on Multimedia (2021)
9. Jin, Y., Sheng, B., Li, P., Chen, C.L.P.: Broad colorization. IEEE Trans. Neural Netw. Learn. Syst. **32**, 2330–2343 (2020)
10. Kaiser, L., Nachum, O., Roy, A., Bengio, S.: Learning to remember rare events. ArXiv arxiv:1703.03129 (2017)
11. Kim, G.Y., et al.: Bigcolor: colorization using a generative color prior for natural images. In: European Conference on Computer Vision (2022)

12. Kumar, M., Weissenborn, D., Kalchbrenner, N.: Colorization transformer. ArXiv arxiv:2102.04432 (2021)
13. Li, H., Sheng, B., Li, P., Ali, R., Chen, C.L.P.: Globally and locally semantic colorization via exemplar-based broad-GAN. IEEE Trans. Image Process. **30**, 8526–8539 (2021)
14. Lin, T.-Y., et al.: Microsoft COCO: common objects in context. In: Fleet, D., Pajdla, T., Schiele, B., Tuytelaars, T. (eds.) ECCV 2014. LNCS, vol. 8693, pp. 740–755. Springer, Cham (2014). https://doi.org/10.1007/978-3-319-10602-1_48
15. Mao, X., Li, Q., Xie, H., Lau, R.Y.K., Wang, Z., Smolley, S.P.: Least squares generative adversarial networks. In: IEEE International Conference on Computer Vision (ICCV), pp. 2813–2821 (2016)
16. Mardia, K.V., Jupp, P.E.: Directional Statistics. John Wiley & Sons, Inc., Hoboken (2000)
17. Mirza, M., Osindero, S.: Conditional generative adversarial nets. ArXiv arxiv:1411.1784 (2014)
18. Nilsback, M.E., Zisserman, A.: Automated flower classification over a large number of classes. In: Sixth Indian Conference on Computer Vision, Graphics & Image Processing, pp. 722–729 (2008)
19. Park, T., Efros, A.A., Zhang, R., Zhu, J.-Y.: Contrastive learning for unpaired image-to-image translation. In: Vedaldi, A., Bischof, H., Brox, T., Frahm, J.-M. (eds.) ECCV 2020. LNCS, vol. 12354, pp. 319–345. Springer, Cham (2020). https://doi.org/10.1007/978-3-030-58545-7_19
20. Robinson, J., Chuang, C.Y., Sra, S., Jegelka, S.: Contrastive learning with hard negative samples. ArXiv arxiv:2010.04592 (2020)
21. Su, J.W., kuo Chu, H., Huang, J.B.: Instance-aware image colorization. In: IEEE/CVF Conference on Computer Vision and Pattern Recognition (CVPR), pp. 7965–7974 (2020)
22. Sun, Q., et al.: A GAN-based approach toward architectural line drawing colorization prototyping. Vis. Comput. **38**, 1283–1300 (2021)
23. Sun, Y., et al.: Circle loss: a unified perspective of pair similarity optimization. In: IEEE/CVF Conference on Computer Vision and Pattern Recognition (CVPR), pp. 6397–6406 (2020)
24. Vitoria, P., Raad, L., Ballester, C.: Chromagan: adversarial picture colorization with semantic class distribution. In: IEEE Winter Conference on Applications of Computer Vision (WACV), pp. 2434–2443 (2020)
25. Wah, C., Branson, S., Welinder, P., Perona, P., Belongie, S.: The caltech-ucsd birds-200-2011 dataset. California institute of technology (2011)
26. Wu, Y., Wang, X., Li, Y., Zhang, H., Zhao, X., Shan, Y.: Towards vivid and diverse image colorization with generative color prior. In: IEEE/CVF International Conference on Computer Vision (ICCV), pp. 14357–14366 (2021)
27. Yeh, C.H., Hong, C.Y., Hsu, Y.C., Liu, T.L., Chen, Y., LeCun, Y.: Decoupled contrastive learning. ArXiv arxiv:2110.06848 (2021)
28. Yoo, S., Bahng, H., Chung, S., Lee, J., Chang, J., Choo, J.: Coloring with limited data: few-shot colorization via memory augmented networks. In: IEEE/CVF Conference on Computer Vision and Pattern Recognition (CVPR), pp. 11275–11284 (2019)
29. Zhang, J., et al.: Scsnet: an efficient paradigm for learning simultaneously image colorization and super-resolution. In: AAAI Conference on Artificial Intelligence (2022)

30. Zhang, R., Isola, P., Efros, A.A.: Colorful image colorization. In: Leibe, B., Matas, J., Sebe, N., Welling, M. (eds.) ECCV 2016. LNCS, vol. 9907, pp. 649–666. Springer, Cham (2016). https://doi.org/10.1007/978-3-319-46487-9_40
31. Zhang, R., Isola, P., Efros, A.A., Shechtman, E., Wang, O.: The unreasonable effectiveness of deep features as a perceptual metric. In: IEEE/CVF Conference on Computer Vision and Pattern Recognition, pp. 586–595 (2018)

Reference-Based Line Drawing Colorization Through Diffusion Model

Jiaze He[1], Wenqing Zhao[1], Ziruo Li[2], Jin Huang[1(✉)], Ping Li[3], Lei Zhu[4], Bin Sheng[5(✉)], and Subrota Kumar Mondal[6]

[1] Wuhan Textile University, Wuhan, China
derick0320@foxmail.com
[2] Wuhan University of Technology, Wuhan, China
[3] Hong Kong Polytechnic University, Hong Kong, China
[4] The Hong Kong University of Science and Technology, Hong Kong, China
[5] Shanghai Jiao Tong University, Shanghai, China
shengbin@sjtu.edu.cn
[6] Macau University of Science and Technology, Macau, China

Abstract. Line drawing colorization is an indispensable stage in the image painting process, however, traditional manual coloring requires a lot of time and energy from professional artists. With the development of deep learning techniques, attempts have been made to colorize line drawings by means of user prompts, text, etc, but these methods also seem to require some manual involvement. In this paper, we propose a reference-based colorization method for cartoon line drawings, which uses a more stable diffusion model to automatically colorize line drawings to improve the quality of the generated images. In addition, to further learn the color of the reference image and improve the quality of the colorized image, we also design a two-stage training strategy. To ensure the generality of the model, in addition to the 17,769 benchmark datasets shared on the Kaggle, we used the cartoon dataset provided by the competition in the fine-tuning stage and created a small garment dataset. Finally, we illustrate the effectiveness of the model in reference-based automatic coloring through a large number of qualitative and quantitative experiments.

Keywords: Line drawing colorization · Diffusion model · Referenced method · Cartoon and garment datasets

1 Introduction

The colorization of cartoon line drawing is the most crucial step in the anime production process, a perfect color combination is essential for a good anime, however, manual coloring is not simple, not only does it require a professional artist to operate it, but even professionals may spend a lot of time and effort to produce the right color combination, so it is valuable to devise an suitable automated coloring method. The task of coloring a given line drawing has attracted

Fig. 1. Given a line drawing and reference image as input, our model learns the input reference image to colorize the line drawing, thus generating a color result.

a lot of attention in computer vision due to its remarkable demand in practice (Fig. 1).

Early colorization tasks focused mainly on grayscale images [25]. However, line drawing images lack certain grayscale information, which makes their coloring inherently challenging. More automated colorization methods such as Scribble Colors-based [2], text-based [8], and palette-based [26]. However, some aesthetic art is still required to generate beautiful coloring images for amateur users. Reference-image-based approaches such as [5, 10, 12, 23] provides a more concise approach that shares semantic information through line drawings and reference images. To further improve coloring results, He et al. [5] proposed a deep learning approach for exemplar-based local colorization. However, due to the sparse line information carried by the line art, transferring the color correctly from the reference to the same semantic area is a challenge. GAN, a mainstream model for generative models, has been used as one of the main architectures in many image process tasks. Liu et al. [12] design a reference color style extractor and multi-scale discriminator to improve the reality of the output. Wen et al. [22] design a unsupervised image deblurring method based on a multi-adversarial optimized cycle-consistent generative adversarial network. However, the GAN-based models require multiple losses to be deployed in the training, which also makes the training process more difficult.

Recently, diffusion models have gained popularity [3] and demonstrated impressive results in various fields [20]. Building upon this, we propose a diffusion model for coloring line drawings, and design a two-stage training strategy.

Experiments demonstrate that our approach outperforms other GAN-based methods. Furthermore, we create a garment illustration dataset, consisting of garment line drawings paired with corresponding illustrations. Our approach successfully enables the colorization of garment line drawings. In conclusion, the contributions of this paper are summarized as follows:

- We propose a reference-based automatic coloring model that uses a more stable diffusion model as the baseline. Experiments show that the diffusion model we use outperforms most GAN-based models and achieves more advanced coloring of line drawings.
- We employ a two-stage training strategy. The model is initially pre-trained on a large dataset with similar features and then fine-tuned in downstream datasets. This approach improves model stability when training on limited datasets.
- To ensure the generality of the model, in addition to the dataset provided by the competition, we produced a small clothing dataset that has some cartoonish features.

2   Related Work

2.1   Line Drawing Colorization

Colorizing line drawing images in cartoon industry is a crucial yet time-consuming task. Directly applying grayscale image coloring methods is challenging due to the sparse grayscale values and limited semantic information present in the lines. A number of coloring methods customized for line drawings have been developed. Traditional coloring methods are based on optimization [11,16].

With the development of deep learning techniques, automated coloring of line drawings has become popular, and GANs show better results in line coloring compared to traditional optimization-based methods. Liu et al. [13] proposes a conditional GAN model that allows users to color animated line drawings using their favorite colors. There is also a reference based method, Lee et al. [10] designed a spatially corresponding feature transfer module to transfer the color information obtained from the reference to the corresponding spatial location of the line drawing. In addition, Zhang et al. [24] designed a correlation matching feature transfer module (CMFT) to improve the consistency and quality of color frames.

2.2   Diffusion Model

The diffusion model is a new generative model consisting of a forward process (signal to noise) and a reverse process (noise to signal). In recent years, the diffusion model demonstrates impressive results in generating high-quality samples [6], which uses the diffusion process to model the data distribution and has achieved good results in image generation tasks. Song et al. [19] built upon the success of DDPM and introduced the denoising diffusion implicit models (DDIM), which combines the benefits of both diffusion and implicit models. DDIM provides a more efficient sampling process by leveraging continuous denoising score matching, which allows flexible selection of the noise schedule.

Palette [17] proposed a unified framework for image-to-image translation based on conditional diffusion models, confirming the effect of L_2 versus L_1 loss in denoising diffusion targets on sample diversity.

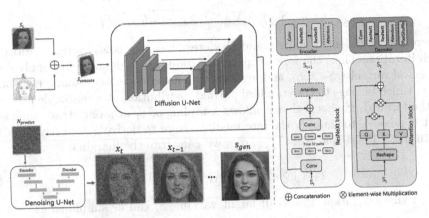

Fig. 2. The framework is based on a diffusion model that takes line drawings S_l and reference images S_t as input, adds noise through the U-Net network, denoises the process through our U-Net, and after layers of training, finally outputs a colored image that is consistent with the input in terms of content and with the reference in terms of style S_{gen}.

3 Method

3.1 Model Architecture

As shown in Fig. 2, the S_l is our input line drawing image and the S_t is the reference image, The forward diffusion goes from S_0 to S_t with random t step in the range of T(S_0 is mean the ground truth). Then, S_t, S_l are connected together as inputs. The reverse denoising process we build a U-Net network to predict the noise added to S_0. The U-Net network exhibits a remarkable adaptability, as it is not only well-suited for colorization tasks but also demonstrates promising capabilities in the domains of Virtual try-on [7] and segmentation [1,14].

The encoder and decoder in the forward diffusion process have similar structures with convolutional blocks and ResNeXt blocks ending with attention blocks. The base of ResNeXt module is 32 and upsampling in decoder is done by PixelShuffle. Attention blocks are optional as indicated by dashed boxes. In the shallow layer of the encoder, which mainly learns large features, we do not use attention blocks. The multi-head attention ones enable our model to efficiently capture global and local features in different convolution layers. The use of the attention mechanism allows the model to learn long range features and multi-scale features, which are essential for our colorization task. Lastly we use a denoising function to predict S_{t-1} iteratively until generate S_{gen}.

3.2   Pre-training

The forward diffusion process which is a Markov chain, gradually adds Gaussian noise to the S_0 according to a variance schedule $\beta_1...\beta_t$:

$$q\left(S_t \mid S_{t\text{-}1}\right) = \mathcal{N}\left(S_t; \sqrt{1-\beta_t}S_{t\text{-}1}, \beta_t\mathbf{I}\right) \tag{1}$$

where $\mathbf{I}$ is the identity matrix and β_t determines the noise variance added at each iteration. Thus, the forward process produces a series of increasingly noisy potential variables $S_1 \dots S_t$, and after enough noise steps, we obtain a pure noise $S_{1:T}$, which belongs to the standard normal distribution. A remarkable property of the forward process is that it allows sampling of S_t at an arbitrary time step t. It is possible to simplify the intermediate steps to derive S_t directly from S_0. With $\alpha_t := 1 - \beta_t$ and $\bar{\alpha}_t := \prod_{g=1}^{t} \alpha_g$, we can write the marginal

$$q\left(S_t \mid S_0\right) = \mathcal{N}\left(S_t; \sqrt{\bar{\alpha}}S_{t\text{-}1}, (1-\bar{\alpha})\mathbf{I}\right) \tag{2}$$

after t times iteration, the result latent variable S_t can be simplified as

$$S_t = \sqrt{\bar{\alpha}}S_0 + \sqrt{1-\bar{\alpha}}\epsilon, \epsilon \in \mathcal{N}(0, \mathbf{I}) \tag{3}$$

The training objective of the model is to predict the noise $\epsilon_\theta(S_l, S_t, t)$ with given noised data point S_t, time step t and condition S_l, and optimizing the objective

$$\mathbb{E}_{S_0, \epsilon \sim \mathcal{N}(0, I), S_l, t} \left\| \epsilon_\theta\left(S_l, S_t, t\right) - \epsilon \right\|_2^2 \tag{4}$$

3.3   Fine-Tuning

After the forward process, we will get the final noise S_t, and the distribution of $p(S_t)$ that is closed to the standard Gaussian distribution $\mathcal{N}(0, \mathbf{I})$, the reverse process starts by the Gaussian noise, which is then subjected to T rounds of denoising. After the model is pre-trained, we can enable it to fit various types of cartoon image generation tasks. This training strategy aims to learn useful representations by fine-tuning a pretrained model on a image for cartoon reconstruction. In this way, we can solve the problem of diffusion models that require a lot of arithmetic power and time. In addition, as the number of training iterations increases, the impact of guidance on the quality of generated images increases. Consequently, in the fine-tuning stage of the model, we utilize noise generated according to the reference image rather than random noise, according to Eq 3, S_0 is predicted as

$$\tilde{S}_0 = \frac{1}{\sqrt{\bar{\alpha}_t}}\left(S_t - \sqrt{1-\bar{\alpha}_t}\epsilon_\theta\left(S_l, S_t, t\right)\right) \tag{5}$$

$\mu_\theta(S_t, t)$ is used to predict the denoised observation, which is a prediction of S_0 given S_t, the mean value of reverse process $p_\theta\left(S_{t-1} \mid S_t, S_l\right)$ can be given by a reparameterization that depends only on S_t and ϵ_θ.

$$\tilde{\mu}_\theta\left(S_t, t\right) = \frac{(1-\bar{\alpha}_{t-1})\sqrt{\alpha_t}}{1-\bar{\alpha}_t} \cdot S_t + \frac{\sqrt{\bar{\alpha}_{t-1}}\beta_t}{1-\bar{\alpha}_t} \cdot \tilde{S}_0 \tag{6}$$

With the end of the reverse process, the denoising function ultimately produces the colored image S_{gen}. We employ the mean square error (MSE) metric to measure the dissimilarity between S_{gen} and the ground truth image S_0, thereby constraining the generated image to approximate the original image.

$$L_{rec} = \mathbb{E}_{S_0,\epsilon \sim \mathcal{N}(0,I),S_l,t} \left\| S_{gen} - S_0 \right\|_2^2 \tag{7}$$

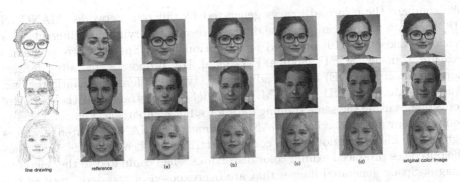

Fig. 3. Comparison with other methods, the input line drawing, the reference cartoon, (a) SCFT, (b) MANGAN, (c) SPADE, (d) our method and original color image.

4 Experiments

4.1 Experimental Setup

Dataset. For Pre-training stage, we trained our model with an anime dataset consisting shared on Kaggle website [9] and all images are resized to 256 × 256 resolution. In the fine-tuning phase, in addition to using the cartoon dataset provided by the competition, we also built our own garment illustrations and the corresponding line drawing datasets, which are also part of the cartoon style.

Implementation Details. During most of our experimental trials, we assigned hyper-parameters time step T in models to 1000. and set the forward process variances to constants increasing linearly from $\beta_1 = 1 \times 10^{-4}$ to $\beta_T = 0.02$ following. Adam optimizer with a learning rate of 1×10^{-5} is used to optimize learnable parameters. In pre-training we train the model with the batch size of 32 for 200 epochs. and we fine tune models with batchsize of 4 for 5 epoch. Pre-training spend 72 h and fine-tuning spend about 6 h. We implement our model with PyTorch. All experiments are performed on a single NVIDIA RTX 3090 GPU device.

Evaluation Metrics. To evaluate the generative ability of Diffusion-based network, FID [4] is adopted as our metric, it is used to assess the perceptual quality of generated images by comparing the distance between distributions of generated and real images. We also adopt the SSIM [21], which is used to calculate the similarity between the generated image and the reference image.

4.2 Qualitative Experiments

We compare the colorized images generated by different networks, MANGAN [18] based on CGAN can generate different results by trying out different color schemes, Lee et al. [10] proposed an attention based Spatial Correspondence Feature Transfer (SCFT) module, Park et al. [15] propose a spatially-adaptive normalization (SPADE) layer to adjust the style of different semantic regions. And evaluate using FID and SSIM. All models are pretrained to the extent of convergence using the same training data for a fair comparison. Figure 3 visually compares our method and other GAN-based methods. MANGAN often produces light colors inside a region with a common attribution. Lee et al. [10] sometimes the outcomes produced exhibit color distortions when compared to the reference images. Spade generated images that are overexposed or too dark, such as the second row where the right half of the girl's collar is all white. In comparison, our method propagates the reference color styles to the line drawing precisely.

4.3 Quantitative Experiments

We proceeded to conduct a quantitative evaluation, and we use FID and SSIM as evaluation metrics. For estimating the reconstruction quality, we randomly selected cartoon and line drawing pairs and set the cartoon as the guidance to colorize the line drawing. Ideally, the resulting colorized image should match the cartoon precisely. Table 1 shows that our method have the better reconstruction quality and colorization performance than other three GAN-based methods.

Table 1. Quantitative Comparison between our diffusion model and other three GAN-based methods

Methods	FID ↓	SSIM ↑
SPADE	65.23	0.70
SCFT	61.64	0.75
MANGAN	68.29	0.76
Ours	51.10	0.82

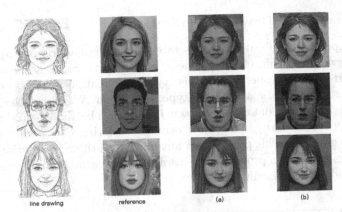

line drawing   reference   (a)   (b)

Fig. 4. The result of removing a part of the model: the input line drawing, the reference cartoon, (a) the result without Fine-tuning, (b) the result through Fine-tuning with 1 epoch.

Table 2. Quantitative Evaluation results for ablation study.

Methods	FID↓	SSIM ↑
Without Fine-tuning	58.69	0.76
Fine-tuning with 1 epoch	53.58	0.79
Fine-tuning with 5 epoches	51.30	0.81

4.4 Ablation Study

To further validate our two-stage strategy, we conducted an ablation study. We explored the effectiveness of colorization performance test based on random reference, as shown in Fig 4. The image without fine-tuning can not fully learn the color of reference image. After fine-tuning, the colorization effect obviously increase (Table 2).

Fig. 5. Garment line drawing coloring results.

4.5   Garment Line Drawing Colorization

Another important application of this work is the application of the model to the line drawing coloring of the garment illustrations. Since garment illustration has cartoon-like properties such as style and creation process, we consider clothing illustration to be a different type of cartoon. We tested the model on the produced clothing dataset as shown in Fig. 5. The model produced good coloring effects and had good control over the coloring of the characters and parts of the garment. This provides an automated method for coloring garment line drawings, which can provide more inspiration to garment designers, increase efficiency and reduce drawing costs.

5   Conclusion

In this paper, we have presented a novel diffusion models approach to generate colorization for cartoon line drawing. In order to solve the high consumption problem of diffusion model and the over-fitting problem when learning with limited data, we design a two-stage training strategy. Quantitative and qualitative experiments demonstrate that such a training method can indeed generate better results than other GAN-based methods. Eventually, we introduce our garment illustration and line drawing datasets, the results of our experiments show that the model is also applicable to the coloring of garment line drawing.

Although our method has better results in effectively learning the reference image colors, there are still several limitations and potential areas for improvement. One main challenge is fully capturing the color distribution of the reference image. Although our model shows improved color learning over previous methods, it does not yet achieve the richness of the reference fully. This points to difficulties in effectively learning color representations from limited data. Another limitation arises in complex backgrounds with multiple colors and textures, where blurring across boundaries can still occur during color transfer. Future work could focus on incorporating more semantic knowledge or text cues to help the model better understand the colors and objects to transfer. Interactivity may also help by allowing users to guide the model to desired colors.

References

1. Chen, L., Wan, L.: CTUNet: automatic pancreas segmentation using a channel-wise transformer and 3d u-net. Visual Comput. **39**, 1–15 (2022)
2. Ci, Y., Ma, X., Wang, Z., Li, H., Luo, Z.: User-guided deep anime line art colorization with conditional adversarial networks. In: Proceedings of the 26th ACM International Conference on Multimedia, pp. 1536–1544 (2018)
3. Dhariwal, P., Nichol, A.: Diffusion models beat GANs on image synthesis. Adv. Neural. Inf. Process. Syst. **34**, 8780–8794 (2021)

4. Dowson, D., Landau, B.: The fréchet distance between multivariate normal distributions. J. Multivar. Anal. **12**(3), 450–455 (1982)
5. He, M., Chen, D., Liao, J., Sander, P.V., Yuan, L.: Deep exemplar-based colorization. ACM Trans. Graph. (TOG) **37**(4), 1–16 (2018)
6. Ho, J., Jain, A., Abbeel, P.: Denoising diffusion probabilistic models. Adv. Neural. Inf. Process. Syst. **33**, 6840–6851 (2020)
7. Hu, X., Zhang, J., Huang, J., Liang, J., Yu, F., Peng, T.: Virtual try-on based on attention u-net. Vis. Comput. **38**(9–10), 3365–3376 (2022)
8. Kim, H., Jhoo, H.Y., Park, E., Yoo, S.: Tag2pix: line art colorization using text tag with secat and changing loss. In: Proceedings of the IEEE/CVF International Conference on Computer Vision, pp. 9056–9065 (2019)
9. Kim, T.: Anime sketch colorization paired dataset from danbooru (2018). https://www.kaggle.com/datasets/ktaebum/anime-sketch-colorization-pair
10. Lee, J., Kim, E., Lee, Y., Kim, D., Chang, J., Choo, J.: Reference-based sketch image colorization using augmented-self reference and dense semantic correspondence. In: Proceedings of the IEEE/CVF Conference on Computer Vision and Pattern Recognition, pp. 5801–5810 (2020)
11. Levin, A., Lischinski, D., Weiss, Y.: Colorization using optimization. In: ACM SIGGRAPH 2004 Papers, pp. 689–694 (2004)
12. Liu, X., Wu, W., Li, C., Li, Y., Wu, H.: Reference-guided structure-aware deep sketch colorization for cartoons. Comput. Visual Media **8**, 135–148 (2022)
13. Liu, Y., Qin, Z., Wan, T., Luo, Z.: Auto-painter: cartoon image generation from sketch by using conditional wasserstein generative adversarial networks. Neurocomputing **311**, 78–87 (2018)
14. Nazir, A., et al.: Ecsu-net: an embedded clustering sliced u-net coupled with fusing strategy for efficient intervertebral disc segmentation and classification. IEEE Trans. Image Process. **31**, 880–893 (2021)
15. Park, T., Liu, M.Y., Wang, T.C., Zhu, J.Y.: Semantic image synthesis with spatially-adaptive normalization. In: Proceedings of the IEEE/CVF Conference on Computer Vision and Pattern Recognition, pp. 2337–2346 (2019)
16. Qu, Y., Wong, T.T., Heng, P.A.: Manga colorization. ACM Trans. Graph. (ToG) **25**(3), 1214–1220 (2006)
17. Saharia, C., et al.: Palette: image-to-image diffusion models. In: ACM SIGGRAPH 2022 Conference Proceedings, pp. 1–10 (2022)
18. Silva, F.C., de Castro, P.A.L., Júnior, H.R., Marujo, E.C.: Mangan: assisting colorization of manga characters concept art using conditional GAN. In: 2019 IEEE International Conference on Image Processing (ICIP), pp. 3257–3261. IEEE (2019)
19. Song, J., Meng, C., Ermon, S.: Denoising diffusion implicit models. arXiv preprint arXiv:2010.02502 (2020)
20. Song, Y., Sohl-Dickstein, J., Kingma, D.P., Kumar, A., Ermon, S., Poole, B.: Score-based generative modeling through stochastic differential equations. arXiv preprint arXiv:2011.13456 (2020)
21. Wang, Z., Bovik, A.C., Sheikh, H.R., Simoncelli, E.P.: Image quality assessment: from error visibility to structural similarity. IEEE Trans. Image Process. **13**(4), 600–612 (2004)
22. Wen, Y., et al.: Structure-aware motion deblurring using multi-adversarial optimized cyclegan. IEEE Trans. Image Process. **30**, 6142–6155 (2021)
23. Zhang, L., Ji, Y., Lin, X., Liu, C.: Style transfer for anime sketches with enhanced residual u-net and auxiliary classifier GAN. In: 2017 4th IAPR Asian Conference on Pattern Recognition (ACPR), pp. 506–511. IEEE (2017)

24. Zhang, Q., Wang, B., Wen, W., Li, H., Liu, J.: Line art correlation matching feature transfer network for automatic animation colorization. In: Proceedings of the IEEE/CVF Winter Conference on Applications of Computer Vision, pp. 3872–3881 (2021)
25. Zhang, R., Isola, P., Efros, A.A.: Colorful image colorization. In: Leibe, B., Matas, J., Sebe, N., Welling, M. (eds.) ECCV 2016. LNCS, vol. 9907, pp. 649–666. Springer, Cham (2016). https://doi.org/10.1007/978-3-319-46487-9_40
26. Zhang, R., et al.: Real-time user-guided image colorization with learned deep priors. arXiv preprint arXiv:1705.02999 (2017)

Research of Virtual Try-On Technology Based on Two-Dimensional Image

Yan Wan, Yue Wang$^{(\boxtimes)}$, and Li Yao

Donghua University, Shanghai, China
18835739152@163.com

Abstract. Virtual try-on based on two-dimensional image refers to trying on the target clothing on a human image to generate the final fitting image. In order to solve the problems of blurred human images, body parts missing and clothing cannot be correctly warped according to the posture of human images after fitting, this paper improves the Flow-Style-VTON network structure and proposes a virtual try-on model A-VITON. This paper adds residual blocks and CBAM attention mechanism to the U-Net network of the try-on module to improve the network's feature extraction ability for target objects, making the generated try-on images more realistic. Secondly, this paper also proposes a layered virtual try-on method to provide consumers with more diverse fitting services. Finally, in order to reduce the interference of complex background on the try-on results, this paper proposes a virtual try-on method with background for the first time, which can generate high-quality try-on images while preserving the original image background. The try-on results on the VITON dataset show that the proposed method has great advantages in generating high-quality try-on images.

Keywords: Virtual try-on · Layered try-on · Attention mechanism

1 Introduction

At present, the research of virtual try-on is mainly divided into two categories, namely, virtual try-on based on 3D model and virtual try-on based on 2D model. Virtual try-on based on 3D model needs more accurate 3D measurement to capture the body shape, which is costly and has more difficulties in promotion and application. It hinders the development of virtual try-on technology, so virtual try-on technology based on 2D model is more convenient.

Virtual try-on based on 2D model is mostly divided into two stages: the first stage is the clothes warping module, which requires the clothing to be naturally warped according to the posture of the human body. At the same time, it also needs to clearly retain the texture of the clothing. VITON [1], CP-VTON [2], CP-VTON+ [3] and VINCT [4] deform clothing by calculating TPS parameters, which is a common 2D interpolation method. VTNCT combines feature with pixel transformation to obtain warped clothes. However, TPS interpolation

© The Author(s), under exclusive license to Springer Nature Switzerland AG 2024
B. Sheng et al. (Eds.): CGI 2023, LNCS 14496, pp. 373–384, 2024.
https://doi.org/10.1007/978-3-031-50072-5_30

is applicable to rigid objects and not to non-rigid objects such as clothing. At the same time, TPS interpolation has limited degrees of freedom and cannot cope with complex deformation situations. Compared with TPS interpolation, appearance flow has higher flexibility and accuracy. Appearance flow estimates the point-by-point correspondence between the original clothing and the try-on clothing. Each point is a two-dimensional vector to guide the clothing deformation. ClothFlow [5], AFSF-3DVTON [6], PF-AFN [7] and Flow-Style-VTON [8] deform clothing by predicting the appearance flow between the human image and clothing.

The second stage is the try-on module, which needs to generate try-on results. The difficulty lies in the need to preserve the features such as the face and posture of the human, as well as the need to generate real body parts. Most try-on modules use U-Net [9] network to fuse clothing and human images to generate fitting images. The deeper the network, the more complex features can be extracted. However, too many layers of the network will lead to the degradation of the deep network. Flow-Style-VTON adopts Res-UNet [10] network. To solve this problem, this paper adds the residual block of ResNetV2 [11] in the U-Net network. The CBAM attention mechanism is embedded in the above network to improve the feature extraction ability of the target objects.

At present, the study of virtual try-on only considers changing clothes, ignoring layered try-on. The difficulty is the lack of truth value and the inability to train the model. In order to solve this problem, this paper proposes a layered virtual try-on method.

Complex backgrounds can interfere with the feature extraction ability of the network. Therefore, in order to reduce the interference of complex backgrounds on try-on results, this paper proposes a virtual try-on method with background.

The research work of this paper has three main contributions. First, the residual block and CBAM attention mechanism [12] are added in the try-on module to improve the feature extraction ability of the network for the target object. In order to bring more rich experience to the buyer, a layered try on method is also proposed. Finally, in order to reduce the interference of background on the fitting results, a virtual try-on method for complex background is proposed for the first time. In this paper, a large number of experiments have been carried out to prove that the proposed model can generate more realistic images and is more robust by comparing with other baseline models.

2   Related Work

2.1   Virtual Try-On

CA-GAN [13] transforms virtual try-on into a graphical analogy problem. Both CP-VTON and CP-VTON+ use pose points and body mask as input to generate try-on images. The try-on images generated by these models are relatively blurry. HR-VITON [14], RT-VTON [15] and ACGPN [16] all generate try on results by transforming clothing through generated human parsing maps. However, the body parts will be lost when human parsing maps are not accurate.

WUTON [17] is a parser-free model, divided into a "teacher" network and a "student" network, using the "teacher" network to guide the "student" network in generating more realistic try on images. PF-AFN realizes that the try-on results of "teacher" network will have some errors, and using them as the truth value to supervise the training of "tudent" network will produce unsatisfactory results. Therefore, it adopts the method of self supervised learning, using real images for self supervision, so that network can generate high-quality images.

The Flow-Style-VTON model proposes an estimation of global appearance flow based on StyleGAN [18], which enables encoding using global style vectors. It consists of four modules, namely the parser-based clothes warping module and try-on module, as well as the parser-free clothes warping module and try-on module. As shown in Fig. 1, the fitting images generated by Flow-Style-VTON are the most realistic. However, its generalization ability is insufficient in the face of complex human postures.

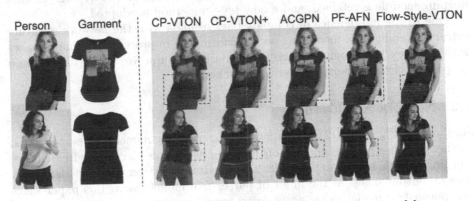

Fig. 1. Comparison of try-on results between virtual try-on models

2.2   U-Net Network

U-Net network belongs to encoder-decoder structure. Encoder is composed of convolution layer and down-sampling layer, which is mainly responsible for extracting input features. Decoder is composed of convolution layer and up-sampling layer, which is responsible for restoring original resolution. It is a symmetric U-shaped network structure, which is widely used in semantic segmentation.

2.3   Attention Mechanism

At present, attention mechanism has been widely used in many fields, such as image segmentation. Attention mechanism can make the network pay more attention to the target object, improve the feature extraction ability. Attention mechanism is mostly added to encoder-decoder network. In this paper, the

CBAM attention mechanism is embedded in the U-Net network to improve the network's feature extraction ability and output high-quality images.

3   Research Method

3.1   Main Content

This paper is based on the Flow-Style-VTON model for research and improvement, and proposes the virtual try-on method A-VITON. The network structure is shown in Fig. 2. In order to improve the convergence of the model, this paper embeds ResNetV2 residual blocks into U-Net. In order to generate high-quality images, this paper adds a CBAM module to learn important information during the network down-sampling process.

In order to further improve the virtual try-on experience, this paper proposes a layered try-on method. On the virtual try-on method A-VITON, the clothes warping module is retained, and a new try-on method is adopted.

Due to the interference of complex backgrounds with the network's feature extraction ability, the model has poor performance in processing human images with complex backgrounds. Therefore, this paper improves on A-VITON and proposes a virtual try-on method with background.

3.2   Network Architecture

As shown in Fig. 2, A-VITON consists of four modules, namely the parser-based clothes warping module and try-on module, as well as the parser-free clothes warping module and try-on module. The pre-trained parser-based model generates an output image as the input of parser-free model. Next, this paper takes the parser-free model as an example to provide a detailed explanation of the clothes warping module and the try-on module.

3.3   Clothes Warping Module

The purpose of clothes warping module is to make clothes deform according to the human posture. This module first pre-processes the human image, and needs to generate the human feature representation p^* from the given human image, which is composed of the 3D human dense pose points generated by the Densepose [19] , the skeleton joint points generated by the Openpose [20] and human parsing maps. p^* and clothes are input into the clothes warping module. Two feature pyramid networks are used to extract their features, and each feature pyramid network contains five stages. The Fig. 2 shows three stages. Use $\{p_i\}_{i=1}^5$ represents the features extracted from p^* , and use $\{c_i\}_{i=1}^5$ represents the features extracted from clothes. The extracted features are used to generate the corresponding appearance flow $\{f_i\}_{i=1}^5$, and the appearance flow f_5 generated in the last stage guides the warping of clothes.

$$\hat{c} = S\left(c, f_5\right) \tag{1}$$

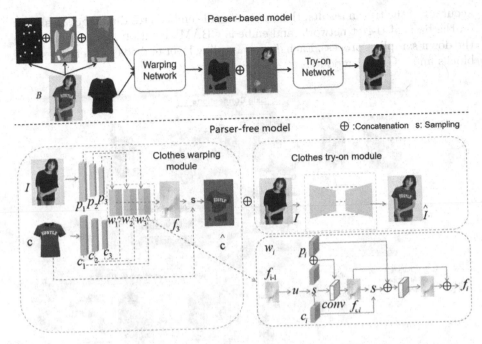

Fig. 2. The virtual try-on architecture of A-VITON

S represents the clothes warping network, and c represents clothes. $\hat{c}$ refers to warped clothes. In order to prevent excessive deformation from producing unnatural results, this paper uses second-order smooth constraint [7] to better preserve the features of clothes.

$$L_{sec} = \sum_{i=1}^{5} \sum_{t} \sum_{\pi \in N_t} P\left(f_i^{t-\pi} + f_i^{t+\pi} - 2f_i^t\right) \tag{2}$$

P means Charbonnier Loss [21], f_i^t represents the t-th point of the i-th flow chart. L_w is the target loss function of clothes warping module, and it is composed of the loss L_{w1} between $\hat{c}$ and clothing B_c on the human image B, perceptual loss L_{wp} and L_{sec}. ϕ_m is the m-th feature map in the pre-trained VGG-19 [22] network.

$$L_{w1} = \| \hat{c} - B_c \|_1 \tag{3}$$

$$L_{wp} = \sum_{m} \| \phi_m(\hat{c}) - \phi_m(B_c) \|_1 \tag{4}$$

$$L_w = \lambda_1 L_{w1} + \lambda_p L_{wp} + \lambda_{sec} L_{sec} \tag{5}$$

3.4 Clothes Try-On Module

In the clothes try-on module, both $\hat{c}$ and I are input into the network to generate try-on results. As shown in Fig. 3, in order to improve the authenticity and accuracy of the try-on results, the try-on module embeds residual block ResBlock on the basis of U-Net network, and embeds CBAM attention mechanism during the down-sampling process. Each down-sampling layer embeds two serial residual blocks and a CBAM module.

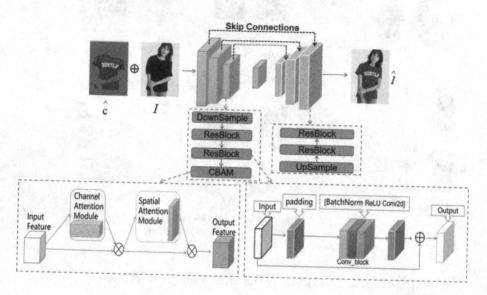

Fig. 3. The architecture of clothes try-on module

The residual block can retain the original input information and avoid network degradation in the deep level network. As shown in Fig. 3, the residual block of ResNetV2 is used, and the pre-activation method is adopted. The BatchNorm and ReLU activation function are placed before the convolution network. In pre-activated networks, identity mapping can achieve direct transmission of signals between units, making information transmission from the previous layer to the next layer more direct.

Due to the different importance of each layer in the network, the network needs to pay more attention to key information. In this paper, the attention mechanism CBAM is introduced into the try-on module. CBAM contains channel attention and spatial attention, which are combined in serial order. This paper improves feature extraction capabilities from both channel and spatial dimensions, improving the effect of fitting.

L_{g1} is the loss between the try-on result $\hat{I}$ and the human image B, and the target loss function of the clothes try-on module L_g by L_{g1} loss and perceptual loss L_{gp} composition:

$$L_{g1} = \| \hat{I} - B \|_1 \tag{6}$$

$$L_{gp} = \sum_m \| \phi_m\left(\hat{I}\right) - \phi_m(B) \|_1 \tag{7}$$

$$L_g = \lambda_1 L_{g1} + \lambda_p L_{gp} \tag{8}$$

3.5 Layered Try-On

As shown in Fig. 4, in order to provide consumers with a better experience, this paper proposes a layered try-on method, which has a significant effect. The clothes warping module in the layered try-on method is consistent with the A-VITON model. The input image undergoes a warping network to generate a deformed clothing $\hat{g}$ and a deformed clothing mask $\hat{gm}$. Then invert the color of $\hat{gm}$ and fuse it with the human image. $\hat{p_g}$ denotes a layered try-on result.

$$g\hat{m}o = 1 - \hat{gm} \tag{9}$$

$$\hat{p_g} = \hat{g} + p \times g\hat{m}o \tag{10}$$

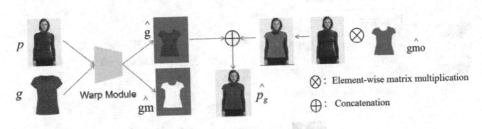

Fig. 4. The architecture of layered try-on

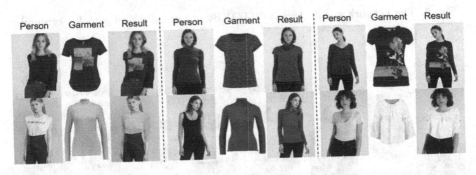

Fig. 5. Results of layered virtual try-on

Previous virtual try-on models hardly considered how to achieve layered try-on, and there were no corresponding evaluation indicators, so quantitative and comparative experiments cannot be conducted now. Therefore, this paper shows the results of layered try-on. As shown in Fig. 5, the first line is the results of fitting short sleeves on long sleeves, and the second line is the results of fitting long sleeves on short sleeves. The experimental results indicate that the method proposed can provide consumers with a variety of fitting services.

3.6   Virtual Try-On with Background

In practical applications, the original background of the human image can cause some interference to the virtual try-on model, resulting in poor fitting effect. Therefore, this paper proposes a virtual try-on model with background, which adds a background removal module and a background fusion module on the basis of the A-VITON model. The network structure is shown in Fig. 6. Module for removing background uses the U^2-Net [23] network to achieve target edge detection. The human image without background I_{bgo} and clothing are input into the A-VITON to generate $\hat{I}_{bgo}$. Finally, the background is extracted and fused with $\hat{I}_{bgo}$ to generate the final try-on image $\hat{I}_{bg}$.

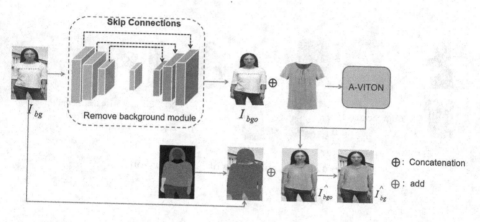

Fig. 6. The network architecture A-VITONBg of virtual try-on with background

Fig. 7. Comparison results of virtual try-on models with background

As shown in Fig. 7, for virtual try-on with background, this paper compares the fitting results of the Flow-Style-VTON model and the A-VITONBg model, highlighting the flaws in the fitting image with blue dashed border. It can be seen that the generated image of Flow-Style-VTON has issues with partially incomplete arms, exaggerated limbs, and partial background loss. The try-on image generated using the A-VITONBg model successfully solved the problem of background interference. Through this comparison, it can be concluded that the method proposed is feasible and generates more realistic fitting results.

4 Experiments

4.1 Dataset

This paper selects the VITON dataset, which is usually used to study virtual try-on. The dataset contains 16253 image pairs in total, of which 14221 image pairs are used for training, and 2032 image pairs are used for testing. Each image pair contains a human image and a top clothing image with the resolution of 256 × 192.

4.2 Qualitative Results

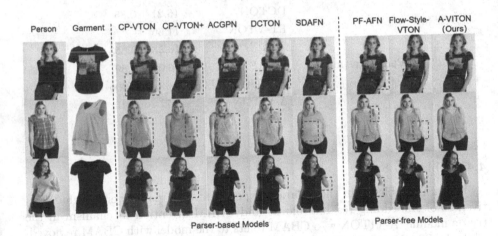

Fig. 8. Comparison results of virtual try-on models

As shown in Fig. 8, a visual comparison is conducted between the model proposed in this paper and other models. The red dashed border is used to mark the areas where the quality of the try-on results generated by other models is lower than that of A-VITON. Compared to other models, A-VITON is more capable of generating high-quality try-on results, and can well retain the texture and pattern of clothing. Especially when the arms intersect with the clothes, the ability to generate body parts is stronger.

4.3   Quantitative Results

In this paper, SSIM [24] and FID [25] are used as evaluation indicators. The larger the SSIM value, the more similar the two groups of images are. The lower the FID score, the more similar the two groups of images are. Table 1 shows the quantitative comparison results between virtual try-on models. Table 1 divides virtual try-on models into two categories, namely parser-based models and parser-free models . It can be concluded that A-VITON is optimal in both SSIM and FID evaluation metrics, whether compared with parser-based models or parser-free models.

Table 1. Quantitative comparison results of virtual try-on models.

Type	Methods	FID↓	SSIM↑
Parser-based models	VITON	55.71	0.74
	CP-VTON	24.35	0.72
	Cloth-flow	14.43	0.84
	CP-VTON+	21.04	0.75
	ACGPN	16.64	0.84
	OVNet [26]	-	0.852
	DCTON	16.21	0.85
	RT-VTON	11.66	-
	SDAFN	10.531	0.853
Parser-free models	PF-AFN	10.09	0.89
	Flow-Style-VTON	8.89	0.906
	A-VITON	8.77	0.91

4.4   Ablation Study

As shown in Table. 2, in the ablation experiment, this paper verifies the effectiveness of embedding residual blocks and CBAM attention mechanism in the try-on module. A-VITON w/o CBAM refers to the model with CBAM removed, while A-VITON w/o ResBlock refers to the model with ResBlock removed.

Table 2. Comparison of ablation models on FID and SSIM

Methods	FID↓	SSIM↑
A-VITON w/o CBAM	8.79	0.90
A-VITON w/o ResBlock	9.93	0.88
A-VITON	8.77	0.91

5   Conclusion

In this work, this paper proposes the A-VITON model based on the Flow-Style-VTON model. This paper combines ResNetV2 residual block and CBAM on the basis of the U-Net network to generate higher quality try-on images. Secondly, this paper proposes a layered virtual try-on method, which brings more rich experience to the buyers. Finally, this paper proposes for the first time a virtual try-on method with background, reducing the impact of the background on the try-on results. A large number of comparative results show that the method in this paper is more realistic and has great advantages.

References

1. Han, X., Wu, Z., Wu, Z., Yu, R., Davis, L.S.: Viton: an image-based virtual try-on network (2017)
2. Wang, B., Zheng, H., Liang, X., Chen, Y., Lin, L., Yang, M.: Toward characteristic-preserving image-based virtual try-on network. In: Proceedings of the European Conference on Computer Vision (ECCV), pp. 589–604 (2018)
3. Minar, M.R., Tuan, T.T., Ahn, H., Rosin, P., Lai, Y.K.: Cp vton+: clothing shape and texture preserving image-based virtual try-on. In: CVPR Workshops. vol. 3, pp. 10–14 (2020)
4. Chang, Y., Peng, T., Yu, F., He, R., Hu, X., Liu, J., Zhang, Z., Jiang, M.: Vtnct: an image-based virtual try-on network by combining feature with pixel transformation. Vis. Comput. **39**(7), 2583–2596 (2023)
5. Han, X., Huang, W., Hu, X., Scott, M.: Clothflow: a flow-based model for clothed person generation. In: International Conference on Computer Vision
6. Chen, Z., et al.: Three stages of 3D virtual try-on network with appearance flow and shape field. The Visual Computer, pp. 1–15 (2023)
7. Ge, Y., Song, Y., Zhang, R., Ge, C., Luo, P.: Parser-free virtual try-on via distilling appearance flows (2021)
8. He, S., Song, Y.Z., Xiang, T.: Style-based global appearance flow for virtual try-on (2022)
9. Ronneberger, O., Fischer, P., Brox, T.: U-Net: convolutional networks for biomedical image segmentation. In: Navab, N., Hornegger, J., Wells, W.M., Frangi, A.F. (eds.) MICCAI 2015. LNCS, vol. 9351, pp. 234–241. Springer, Cham (2015). https://doi.org/10.1007/978-3-319-24574-4_28
10. Diakogiannis, F.I., Waldner, F., Caccetta, P., Wu, C.: Resunet-a: a deep learning framework for semantic segmentation of remotely sensed data. ISPRS J. Photogramm. Remote. Sens. **162**, 94–114 (2020)
11. He, K., Zhang, X., Ren, S., Sun, J.: Identity mappings in deep residual networks. In: Leibe, B., Matas, J., Sebe, N., Welling, M. (eds.) ECCV 2016. LNCS, vol. 9908, pp. 630–645. Springer, Cham (2016). https://doi.org/10.1007/978-3-319-46493-0_38
12. Woo, S., Park, J., Lee, J.Y., Kweon, I.S.: Cbam: convolutional block attention module. In: Proceedings of the European Conference On Computer Vision (ECCV), pp. 3–19 (2018)
13. Jetchev, N., Bergmann, U.: The conditional analogy gan: Swapping fashion articles on people images. In: Proceedings of the IEEE International Conference on Computer Vision Workshops, pp. 2287–2292 (2017)

14. Choi, S., Park, S., Lee, M., Choo, J.: Viton-hd: high-resolution virtual try-on via misalignment-aware normalization. In: Proceedings of the IEEE/CVF Conference On Computer Vision And Pattern Recognition, pp. 14131–14140 (2021)
15. Yang, H., Yu, X., Liu, Z.: Full-range virtual try-on with recurrent tri-level transform. In: Proceedings of the IEEE/CVF Conference on Computer Vision and Pattern Recognition, pp. 3460–3469 (2022)
16. Yang, H., Zhang, R., Guo, X., Liu, W., Zuo, W., Luo, P.: Towards photo-realistic virtual try-on by adaptively generating-preserving image content. In: Proceedings of the IEEE/CVF Conference On Computer Vision and Pattern Recognition, pp. 7850–7859 (2020)
17. Issenhuth, T., Mary, J., Calauzènes, C.: Do not mask what you do not need to mask: a parser-free virtual try-on. In: Vedaldi, A., Bischof, H., Brox, T., Frahm, J.-M. (eds.) ECCV 2020. LNCS, vol. 12365, pp. 619–635. Springer, Cham (2020). https://doi.org/10.1007/978-3-030-58565-5_37
18. Karras, T., Laine, S., Aila, T.: A style-based generator architecture for generative adversarial networks. In: 2019 IEEE/CVF Conference on Computer Vision and Pattern Recognition (CVPR) (2019)
19. Guler, R., Neverova, N., DensePose, I.: Dense human pose estimation in the wild. In: Proceedings of the IEEE Conference on Computer Vision and Pattern Recognition, Salt Lake City, UT, USA, pp. 18–23 (2018)
20. Cao, Z., Simon, T., Wei, S.E., Sheikh, Y.: Realtime multi-person 2D pose estimation using part affinity fields. In: Proceedings of the IEEE Conference On Computer Vision And Pattern Recognition, pp. 7291–7299 (2017)
21. Sun, D., Roth, S., Black, M.J.: A quantitative analysis of current practices in optical flow estimation and the principles behind them. Int. J. Comput. Vision 106, 115–137 (2014)
22. Simonyan, K., Zisserman, A.: Very deep convolutional networks for large-scale image recognition. arXiv preprint arXiv:1409.1556 (2014)
23. Qin, X., Zhang, Z., Huang, C., Dehghan, M., Zaiane, O.R., Jagersand, M.: U2-net: going deeper with nested u-structure for salient object detection. Pattern Recogn. 106, 107404 (2020)
24. Wang, Z., Bovik, A.C., Sheikh, H.R., Simoncelli, E.P.: Image quality assessment: from error visibility to structural similarity. IEEE Trans. Image Process. 13(4), 600–612 (2004)
25. Heusel, M., Ramsauer, H., Unterthiner, T., Nessler, B., Hochreiter, S.: Gans trained by a two time-scale update rule converge to a local nash equilibrium. Adv. Neural Inform. Process. Syst. 30 (2017)
26. Li, K., Chong, M.J., Zhang, J., Liu, J.: Toward accurate and realistic outfits visualization with attention to details. In: Proceedings of the IEEE/CVF Conference on Computer Vision and Pattern Recognition, pp. 15546–15555 (2021)

Synthesis and Generation

Investigation on the Encoder-Decoder Application for Mesh Generation

Marco Mameli[1]([✉])(iD), Emanuele Balloni[1](iD), Adriano Mancini[1](iD),
Emanuele Frontoni[2](iD), and Primo Zingaretti[1](iD)

[1] Department of Information Engineering (DII), Università Politecnica delle Marche,
Via Brecce Bianche 12, Ancona, Italy
m.mameli@pm.univpm.it

[2] Department of Political Sciences, Communication and International Relations
(SPOCRI), Università degli Studi di Macerata, Via Don Minzoni 22/A, Macerata,
Italy

Abstract. In computer graphics, 3D modeling is a fundamental concept. It is the process of creating three-dimensional objects or scenes using specialized software that allows users to create, manipulate and modify geometric shapes to build complex models. This operation requires a huge amount of time to perform and specialised knowledge. Typically, it takes three to five hours of modelling to obtain a basic mesh from the blueprint. Several approaches have tried to automate this operation to reduce modelling time. The most interesting of these approaches are based on Deep Learning, and one of the most interesting is Pixel2Mesh. However, training this network requires at least 150 epochs to obtain usable results. Starting from these premises, this work investigates the possibility of training a modified version of the Pixel2Mesh in fewer epochs to obtain comparable or better results. A modification was applied to the convolutional block to achieve this, replacing the classification-based approach with an image reconstruction-based approach. This modification uses a configuration based on constructing an encoder-decoder architecture using state-of-the-art networks such as VGG, DenseNet, ResNet, and Inception. Using this approach, the convolutional block learns how to reconstruct the image correctly from the source image by learning the position of the object of interest within the image. With this approach, it was possible to train the complete network in 50 epochs, achieving results that outperform the state-of-the-art. The tests performed on the networks show an increase of 0.5% points over the state-of-the-art average.

Keywords: Computer graphics · Pixel2Mesh · 3D Modelling

1 Introduction

In Computer Graphics (CG), 3D modelling is a crucial step in the design process. It is the process of creating a virtual representation of a physical object or scene

B. Sheng et al. (Eds.): CGI 2023, LNCS 14496, pp. 387–400, 2024.
https://doi.org/10.1007/978-3-031-50072-5_31

using specialized software [1]. This technology has become increasingly popular and has revolutionised industries such as architecture [2], videogame development [3], product design [4], and more [5]. With 3D modelling, designers can easily create intricate and complex shapes, textures, and animations. It allows them to visualize their ideas in a way that was previously impossible with traditional 2D methods. There are many types of 3D modelling techniques, including polygonal modelling, spline modelling, and digital sculpting. Each technique has its own unique advantages and is best suited for different applications. Overall, 3D modelling is an incredibly powerful tool that has transformed the way we create and design in various fields. Starting from a 2D representation (i.e., an image or a series of images) of an object, 3D artists are required to create a three-dimensional representation of it; this is usually done by modifying a basic mesh, manually shaping it in the desired form, and using images as references. This can be a very time-consuming process. This is why Artificial Intelligence (AI) and, more specifically, Deep Learning have started to be leveraged in this process, as they significantly reduce the creation time of 3D models. AI has been leveraged for both 2D [6] and 3D [7] tasks; one of the state-of-the-art networks in the 3D area is Pixel2Mesh, which, starting from an input image, can create a 3D model of it. Pixel2Mesh is a deep learning technique used for 3D shape reconstruction from a single 2D image. It was introduced in a research paper by Wang et al. [8]. The technique involves generating a coarse 3D mesh of an object from a 2D image using a convolutional neural network (CNN) and then refining the mesh using a graph convolutional neural network (GCNN) [9]. Pixel2Mesh is particularly useful for applications such as computer vision, robotics, and augmented reality, where the ability to reconstruct a 3D model from a 2D image is essential. The technique has shown promising results in generating high-quality 3D meshes of objects with complex shapes and varying topologies. It has the potential to significantly advance the field of 3D shape reconstruction and pave the way for new applications and technologies. One of the main drawbacks of Pixel2Mesh is that it requires a large amount of training data to produce accurate and high-quality results. This is because the model needs to learn to generalize to a wide range of 3D shapes and to account for variations in lighting, texture, and other environmental factors.

Another drawback of Pixel2Mesh is that it can be computationally expensive and time-consuming to train and apply. The model involves multiple processing steps, including convolutional neural networks, Graph Convolutional networks (GCN), and iterative refinement, which can take a significant amount of time and resources. This downside which is the training time (about 150 epochs to obtain acceptable results); this is why this work explored the possibility of changing the Pixel2Mesh architecture to achieve similar or better results in a shorter amount of time. The proposed solution is described in Sect. 3. The state-of-the-art network is presented, and the modification applied to it consists of replacing the convolutional block, which had the task of classifying the input image, with an encoder-decoder block, which has the purpose of reconstructing the input image. In this way, during the training of the feature extraction network from the picture, the encoder will be able to learn in a more detailed way the position of the dominant features of the image to separate the content from the background and recognize the contour of the object more precisely. Furthermore, this approach requires fewer training epochs.

The paper is organized as follows: Sect. 2 gives details on the state of art on 3D models generation; Sect. 3 describes the methodology used in this approach. Section 4.2 presents the results and some discussions. Section 5 is devoted to the conclusions and future works in this direction.

2 State of the Art

The generation of 3D models can be viewed according to the data structure used for data representation, the main ones being:

- **Point Cloud**: 3D representation based on the position of points in 3D space based on the use of coordinates (x, y, z).
- **Voxel**: 3D representation based on the usage of a basic block represented by a 3D cube of unit size. Created structures are based on this element.
- **Mesh**: 3D representation based on primitives of three types: a point with 3D coordinates, an edge joining two points, and faces (or planes) that consist of at least 3 points and 3 edges.

The data structure used as the basis in early approaches of 3D construction and early works using it include Wu, Zhang, Xue, Freeman, and Tenenbaum [10], Wu et al. [11], Brock, Lim, Ritchie, and Weston [12], Guan, Jahan, and Kaick [13], Wu, Zhuang, Xu, Zhang, and Chen [14], Xie et al. [15]. In Wu, Zhang, Xue, Freeman, and Tenenbaum [10], the authors present an approach called 3D-GAN; with this approach, 3D objects are generated from a representation in a reduced-dimensional space, and volumetric convolution and the GAN framework are used for construction. Also, the same framework from Brock, Lim, Ritchie, and Weston [12] proposes a similar approach to the framework proposed by Wu, Zhang, Xue, Freeman, and Tenenbaum [10], again relying on volumetric convolution. GANs have also been leveraged in 3D reconstruction from sketches (e.g., [16]). Using an encoder-decoder-based structure, Wu et al. [17] presented SAG-Net in which the encoder is a Variational Autoencoder that extracts structure from a 3D object and uses its latent representation to generate a new 3D shape of the same class. Point Clouds as data representation structures have gained relevance in Cultural Heritage as they are often used to represent data collected using devices such as Lidar. The data collection, however, is complex and time-consuming, so researchers proposed solutions to generate synthetic data in this area. The most widely used frameworks are based on GANs; some relevant examples include Achlioptas, Diamanti, Mitliagkas, and Guibas [18], Shu, Park, and Kwon [19], Li, Zaheer, Zhang, Poczos, and Salakhutdinov [20], Zamorski et al. [21], Gal, Bermano, Zhang, and Cohen-Or [22], Ramasinghe, Khan, Barnes, and Gould [23], Li, Li, Hui, and Fu [24].

Meshes are data structures that allow for a 3D representation to be adapted to be more similar to the real 3D shape. Mesh representation is the most memory-intensive data structure, as three pieces of information must be saved for each representation. Still, it is the most widely used representation method for 3D content. Among the works that have demonstrated the feasibility of using this data structure is the work of Wang *et al.* [25], in which Pixel2Mesh is presented: an approach that exploits the encoder-decoder structure based on VGG16 to extract features from a single RGB image and create a representation of it in a latent space from which then, via the decoder, the reconstruction of the 3D Mesh is obtained. The later evolution of it is Wen, Zhang, Li, and Fu [26], in which a multiview approach is used, i.e., no longer a single RGB image is used, but the same object is acquired from different viewpoints. Other studies have been based on mesh reconstruction from 3D data, such as point clouds by Lv, Lin, and Zhao [27] to generate meshes composed of voxels or face reconstruction from a single image [28].

2.1 Relationship Between Meshes and Graphs

From graph theory, a Connected Graph is defined as a graph in which pairs of vertices are all connected; that is, there is at least one edges path that connects them directly or indirectly. In addition, a k-connected graph is said if there are k different paths between all pairs of vertices. Each graph is embedded in R^d if each vertex is assigned to a position in R^d. Next, a Planar Graph is defined as a graph whose vertices and edges can be embedded in R^2 and such that its edges do not intersect. Each Planar Graph can be represented as a straight-line plane graph. Triangulation is a Planar Graph in which all faces are triangles.

Starting from these definitions, we can define a Mesh as a Straight-line graph embedded in R^3 in which we recognise:

– Boundary edge: edges that are adjacent only and only to one face;
– Regular edges: edges that are adjacent to exactly two faces;
– Singular edge: edges adjacent to more than two faces.

A Closed Mesh is a mesh with no boundary edges, while a Manifold Mesh is a mesh with no singular edges. We can use these definitions to represent a Closed Mesh as a connected graph.

3 Methods

In generating 3D content from a single input image, extracting features from pictures, such as VGG and similar, is necessary. One of the most exciting approaches is Pixel2Mesh, which applies a single view generation approach. The goodness of the original network was assessed by Brocchini *et al.* [29].

The Pixel2Mesh pipeline is based on the VGG [30]. From the convolutional block, information is extracted from the high-level image and used within a block called the *"Deformation Block"*, which takes an input from a base mesh and deformations removed from the image features are applied to it via Graph Convolutional Layers.

This approach requires a time-consuming fine-tuning process of the VGG, and in real-case scenarios, a mesh must be ready to use in the shortest possible time. It is then fundamental to speed up the training process; this is why the application of an encoder-decoder architecture is investigated.

The application of the encoder-decoder architecture allows the network to learn how to observe the content of an image. More specifically, the idea of applying this architecture originates from the results seen in the field of image segmentation, as shown in [31] for U-Net network. Indeed, this architecture is widely used in this field and has produced exceptional results. For this reason, it was decided to investigate its application as a replacement for the convolutional block for classification in this work. The idea behind using an encoder-decoder approach is that the network learns by reconstructing the input image, where the object is positioned in the source image and then correctly identifies its position, separating it from the background and accurately identifying the shape.

In this work, a novel variation of the pixel2mesh was studied in which the image reconstruction task is added using an encoder-decoder approach.

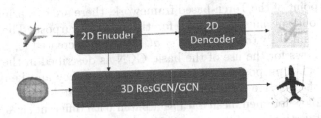

Fig. 1. Pixel2Mesh Network with a modified structure based on the encoder and decoder

In addition, four convolutional network models were used to study how different convolutional configurations can affect the generation of 3D content from 2D images. In particular, encoder-decoder architectures were constructed based on the VGG16, ResNet50, DenseNet121 and InceptionV3 models. To train the encoder-decoder, L1-Loss was used to evaluate its reconstruction, while the following metrics were used to train the Graph Convolutional Network for mesh generation. The use of a mesh as a starting point graph in combination with the projection layer of the pixel2mesh allows for it to move and establishes the node's position in the R^3 space, thanks to the Graph Convolutional network.

3.1   Network Configuration

The changes to the pixel2mesh original work are applied to the extraction features block. As expressed before, that block was changed with the use of an encoder-decoder architecture based on the basic state-of-the-art deep learning approach for the image analysis: VGG16 by Simonyan and Zisserman [30],

ResNet by He, Zhang, Ren, and Sun [32], InceptionNet by Szegedy *et al.* [33], DenseNet by Huang, Liu, Van Der Maaten, and Weinberger [34]. In particular, for each base network, the decoder block is based on the same number of inverted blocks of the base network. Each inverted block uses the transposed convolution. For the DenseNet, the decoder block uses three transposed convolutional blocks with the same densely connected approach; for the InceptionNet, the decoder block uses three transposed convolutional blocks with the same method of the horizontal profundity, and the ResNet use four transposed convolutional block with the simple residual connection.

3.2   Implementation Limits

The Graph Convolutional Network will become very useful for future approaches in the 3D Mesh tasks. In this section, the practical use is going to be analysed because it has some limitations. One possible framework is TensorFlow Graphics[1]. It contains the basic GCN block but not the latest released one. This library is created for the Computer Graphics application, not the General Graph application. More general is TensorFlow Graph Neural Network[2] (in the alpha state), which contains the generalisation of the previous framework.

From the point of the Torch-based framework, there are two principal frameworks, again one specialised and one for the general purpose. The generalised framework is named PyTorch3D Ravi *et al.* [35]. It was created for Mesh manipulation and allows for the use of the basic GCN as described in the pixel2mesh but for the general purpose called PyTorch Geometric Fey and Lenssen [36].

But both these frameworks have a common issue: batch data usage. In particular, they allow for open mesh data as a batch with different sizes (in terms of the number of vertices and faces); but the graph network configuration based on images and meshes does not allow for the usage of batches for training, because the generated graph from the GCN, if developed in the collection from the input image, can't be well managed due to the projection layer.

4   Results

The network training is done with 50 epochs instead of the 150 required for the original version. Moreover, as shown in Table 1, the VGG and DenseNet proved to be the most valuable features extractor for mesh generation.

4.1   Metrics

Chamfer Distance (CD) is an evaluation metric for two-point clouds. It takes the distance of each point into account. For each point in each cloud, CD finds the nearest point in the other point set and sums the square of distance up. It

---

[1] https://www.tensorflow.org/graphics.
[2] https://github.com/tensorflow/gnn.

Table 1. F1-Score Results of the Pixel2Mesh with Encoder-Decoder architecture used to train the feature extractor. The threshold was fixed to 10^{-4}

Category	Original	MPixel2Mesh with VGG	MPixel2Mesh with ResNet	MPixel2Mesh with DenseNet	MPixel2Mesh with Inception
plane	71.12	71.98	71.68	71.79	71.66
bench	57.57	58.23	57.77	58.33	57.86
cabinet	60.39	59.88	60.19	60.46	59.89
car	67.86	68.45	67.92	68.43	67.88
chair	54.38	55.64	54.74	55.56	54.58
monitor	51.39	51.87	51.68	51.76	51.42
lamp	48.15	49.62	48.78	49.64	48.73
speaker	48.84	49.97	48.93	49.87	48.93
firearm	73.20	73.89	73.31	73.83	73.29
couch	51.90	52.86	51.92	52.92	51.93
table	66.30	67.21	66.62	67.35	66.35
cellphone	70.24	70.88	70.31	70.86	70.37
watercraft	55.12	56.02	55.35	55.87	55.42
mean	59.72	60.5	59.94	60.51	59.87

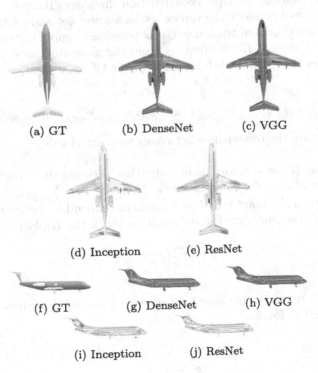

(a) GT   (b) DenseNet   (c) VGG

(d) Inception   (e) ResNet

(f) GT   (g) DenseNet   (h) VGG

(i) Inception   (j) ResNet

Fig. 2. The generated plane from all the network configurations. Numerical result are reported to Table 1

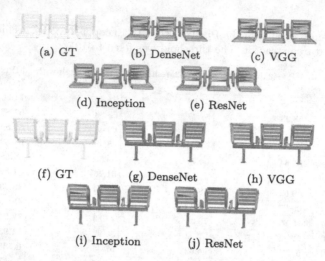

Fig. 3. The generated bench from all the network configurations. Numerical result are reported in Table 1

is used in the Shapenet's shape reconstruction challenge. To apply that function to a mesh, we can consider the vertex set as a point set and on that set, from the generated and ground truth mesh, it is possible to apply the computation of the Chamfer Distance. If the point set from the generated mesh is S_1 and the point set from the ground truth mesh is S_2, the CD can be written as reported in Eq. 1

$$CD(S_1, S_2) = \frac{1}{|S_1|} \sum_{x \in S_1} min_{y \in S_2} ||x - y||_2^2 + \frac{1}{|S_2|} \sum_{y \in S_2} min_{x \in S_1} ||x - y||_2^2 \quad (1)$$

The CD measure the discrepancy between two point clouds.

Laplacian Loss (L) is a smoothing measure that prevents the vertices from moving too freely after a deformation block. If the $\delta_p = -\sum_{q \in N(p)} \frac{1}{|N(p)|} q$ is the distance between the point p and its Laplacian Embedding before the deformation, and δ_p' is the one after the deformation block the Laplacian Loss can be defined in Eq. 2

$$L = \sum_p ||\delta_p' - \delta_p||^2 \quad (2)$$

Edge Loss (E) is used to penalise long edges in the mesh by minimising the L_2 norm expressed in Eq. 3

$$E = \sum_p \sum_{q \in N(p)} ||p - q||^2 \quad (3)$$

As shown in Fig. 2, the results for the plane generation showed the main difference between the two configurations, with better results based on the presence

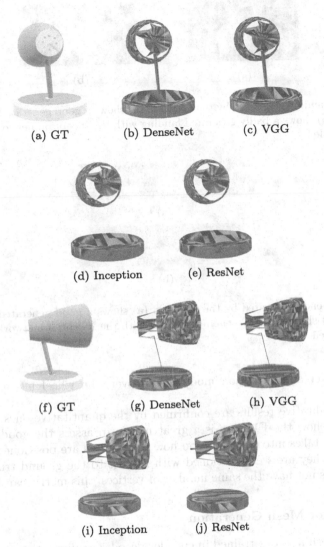

(a) GT   (b) DenseNet   (c) VGG

(d) Inception   (e) ResNet

(f) GT   (g) DenseNet   (h) VGG

(i) Inception   (j) ResNet

Fig. 4. The generated lamp from all the network configurations. Numerical result are reported in Table 1.

of the connection between the aeroplane landing gear and plane. The generation of the bench, as shown in Fig. 3, for the ResNet and InceptionNet, has less quality. In particular, the corner of the bench is not well defined, as depicted in detail in Fig. 6.

Figure 4 shows the result of the generation of the lamp; it is immediately noticeable that there is a missing connection between the two pieces of the mesh

(a)   (b)

Fig. 5. The landing generated by the network. (a) shows a good generated landing with DenseNet. (b) shows a badly generated landing with the Inception network. Numerical result in Table 1

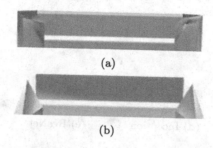

(a)

(b)

Fig. 6. The bench generated by the network. (a) shows a good generated bench with DenseNet. (b) shows a badly generated bench with the Inception network. Numerical result in Table 1

for the ResNet and Inception models. Moreover, the wheel has a generation problem.

These qualitative results are confirmed by the quantitative ones in Table 1, also showing how the F1-score is a great metric to assess the goodness of the method, as it takes into consideration how the vertices are positioned in the 3D space and if they are well-positioned with respect to the ground truth; also, if the mesh does not have the same number of vertices, this metric can be shallow.

4.2   Time for Mesh Generation

The Pixel2Mesh network trained in encoder-decoder configuration, presented in Sect. 3, was tested to measure mesh creation times with the Pixel2Mesh based on the DenseNet network. As part of the test, the decoder section was deactivated as it was not required for mesh generation. Two test configurations used were:

- **Configuration 1**: Intel i7 10th generation with 64GB DDR4 RAM, SSD 1TB, NVIDIA RTX 2070 Super with 8GB GDDR6 video memory, OS Ubuntu Linux 21.04.
- **Configuration 2**: Intel Xeon E5 Silver, 128GB RAM DDR4, 4TB HDD and NVIDIA RTX 2080 Ti with 11GB GDDR6 video memory, OS Ubuntu Linux 20.04.

Two types of tests were performed:

- **Test 1**: The generation of a single mesh is requested to simulate the result of a spot request to the network, obtaining the resulting mesh in 4 s using configuration 1 and 3 s using configuration 2.
- **Test 2**: Mesh generation with successive requests is requested. In particular, we wanted to simulate a working environment where a modeller requests the network to create several basic meshes consecutively. To simulate this context, the request to generate a mesh was repeated 25 consecutive times. The average generation times are 4.16 s on configuration 1 and 3.27 on configuration 2.

5 Conclusions and Future Development

This work showed that Deep Learning can have exciting applications in mesh generation. This is confirmed by the results obtained and the possibility of decreasing the times of the tasks analyzed. In particular, the modification made to the Pixel2Mesh network allowed for an increase in the F1-Score over the state-of-the-art for all the networks used in the experiments with a 0.78 for the VGG and 0.79 for the DenseNet. The modified Pixel2Mesh, using the DenseNet121, took 4 s to create a mesh of an aeroplane, the result of which is shown in Fig. 1. Considering the experiments done in Sect. 4.2, it can be stated that it takes 1/3600 of the time required for an operator to create a mesh, which must be finished from the same image. An example of the result is shown in Fig. 1.

Although some recent networks (i.e., Get3D [37], Magic123 [38]) that leverage generative approaches can perform more accurately in terms of quantitative metrics, they are far more complex in terms of structure and require more computational resources to train and test effectively. In this regard, the Pixel2mesh model is much lighter, performing effectively and efficiently while maintaining relatively low memory usage; these factors can result in higher ease of use and the possibility of adaptation of the network to different types of hardware.

Regarding future development, it could be interesting to apply networks entirely based on Graph Convolution both for extracting information from images and constructing meshes. An example of an application is the use of Simple Linear Iterative Clustering (SLIC), such as Kim, Zhang, Kang, and Ko [39], extracting the Graph representing the image content clustered and applying the Graph convolution to convert it to a mesh.

Also, it could be interesting to study the possible applications of attention-based mechanisms to improve the results obtained. In addition, it could be helpful to direct interest towards Deep Learning approaches for mesh reconstruction, since incomplete meshes are often obtained from 3D scans due to data loss or scanning errors. These approaches could decrease the time required for re-scanning.

References

1. Verykokou, S., Ioannidis, C.: An overview on image-based and scanner-based 3D modeling technologies. Sensors **23**(2), 596 (2023)
2. Bevilacqua, M.G., Russo, M., Giordano, A., Spallone, R.: 3D reconstruction, digital twinning, and virtual reality: architectural heritage applications. In: 2022 IEEE Conference on Virtual Reality and 3D User Interfaces Abstracts and Workshops (VRW), pp. 92 96. IEEE (2022)
3. Moradi, M., Noor, N.F.B.M., Abdullah, R.B.H.: The effects of problem-based serious games on learning 3D computer graphics. Iran. J. Sci. Technol. Trans. Electr. Eng. **46**(4), 989–1004 (2022)
4. Huang, H., Lee, C.-F.: Factors affecting usability of 3D model learning in a virtual reality environment. Interact. Learn. Environ. **30**(5), 848–861 (2022)
5. Okura, F.: 3D modeling and reconstruction of plants and trees: a cross-cutting review across computer graphics, vision, and plant phenotyping. Breed. Sci. **72**(1), 31–47 (2022)
6. Liu, R., et al.: TMM-Nets: transferred multi- to mono-modal generation for lupus retinopathy diagnosis. IEEE Trans. Med. Imaging **42**(4), 1083–1094 (2023). 36409801[PMID], ISSN 1558-254X. https://doi.org/10.1109/TMI.2022.3223683. https://pubmed.ncbi.nlm.nih.gov/36409801
7. Xiao, B., Da, F.: Three-stage generative network for single-view point cloud completion. Vis. Comput. **38**(12), 4373–4382 (2022). https://doi.org/10.1007/s00371-021-02301-4
8. Wang, N., et al.: Pixel2mesh: generating 3D mesh models from single RGB images. In: Proceedings of the European Conference on Computer Vision (ECCV), pp. 52–67 (2018)
9. Zhang, S., Tong, H., Xu, J., Maciejewski, R.: Graph convolutional networks: a comprehensive review. Comput. Soc. Netw. **6**(1), 1–23 (2019)
10. Wu, J., Zhang, C., Xue, T., Freeman, B., Tenenbaum, J.: Learning a probabilistic latent space of object shapes via 3D generative-adversarial modeling. In: Advances in Neural Information Processing Systems, vol. 29 (2016)
11. Wu, J., et al.: Marrnet: 3D shape reconstruction via 2.5D sketches. In: Advances in Neural Information Processing Systems, vol. 30 (2017)
12. Brock, A., Lim, T., Ritchie, J.M., Weston, N.: Generative and discriminative voxel modeling with convolutional neural networks, arXiv preprint arXiv:1608.04236 (2016)
13. Guan, Y., Jahan, T., van Kaick, O.: Generalized autoencoder for volumetric shape generation. In: Proceedings of the IEEE/CVF Conference on Computer Vision and Pattern Recognition Workshops, pp. 268–269 (2020)
14. Wu, R., Zhuang, Y., Xu, K., Zhang, H., Chen, B.: PQ-NET: a generative part Seq2Seq network for 3D shapes. In: Proceedings of the IEEE/CVF Conference on Computer Vision and Pattern Recognition, pp. 829–838 (2020)
15. Xie, J., et al.: Learning descriptor networks for 3D shape synthesis and analysis. In: Proceedings of the IEEE Conference on Computer Vision and Pattern Recognition, pp. 8629–8638 (2018)
16. Nozawa, N., Shum, H.P.H., Feng, Q., Ho, E.S.L., Morishima, S.: 3D car shape reconstruction from a contour sketch using GAN and lazy learning. Vis. Comput. **38**(4), 1317–1330 (2022). https://doi.org/10.1007/s00371-020-02024-y
17. Wu, Z., et al.: Sagnet: structure-aware generative network for 3D-shape modeling. In: ACM Transactions Graphic Proceedings of SIGGRAPH 2019, vol. 38, no. 4, pp. 91:1–91:14 (2019)

18. Achlioptas, P., Diamanti, O., Mitliagkas, I., Guibas, L.: Learning representations and generative models for 3D point clouds. In: International Conference on Machine Learning, pp. 40–49. PMLR (2018)
19. Shu, D.W., Park, S.W., Kwon, J.: 3D point cloud generative adversarial network based on tree structured graph convolutions. In: Proceedings of the IEEE/CVF International Conference on Computer Vision, pp. 3859–3868 (2019)
20. Li, C.-L., Zaheer, M., Zhang, Y., Poczos, B., Salakhutdinov, R.: Point cloud GAN, arXiv preprint arXiv:1810.05795 (2018)
21. Zamorski, M., et al.: Adversarial autoencoders for compact representations of 3D point clouds. In: Computer Vision and Image Understanding, vol. 193, p. 102921 (2020)
22. Gal, R., Bermano, A., Zhang, H., Cohen-Or, D.: MRGAN: multi-rooted 3D shape generation with unsupervised part disentanglement, arXiv preprint arXiv:2007.12944 (2020)
23. Ramasinghe, S., Khan, S., Barnes, N., Gould, S.: Spectral-GANs for high-resolution 3D point-cloud generation. In: 2020 IEEE/RSJ International Conference on Intelligent Robots and Systems (IROS), pp. 8169–8176. IEEE (2020)
24. Li, R., Li, X., Hui, K.-H., Fu, C.-W.: SP-GAN: sphere-guided 3D shape generation and manipulation. ACM Trans. Graph. (TOG) 40(4), 1–12 (2021)
25. Wang, N., et al.: Pixel2mesh: generating 3D mesh models from single RGB images. In: Proceedings of the European Conference on Computer Vision (ECCV) (2018)
26. Wen, C., Zhang, Y., Li, Z., Fu, Y.: Pixel2mesh++: multi-view 3D mesh generation via deformation. In: Proceedings of the IEEE/CVF International Conference on Computer Vision, pp. 1042–1051 (2019)
27. Lv, C., Lin, W., Zhao, B.: Voxel structurebased mesh reconstruction from a 3D point cloud. IEEE Trans. Multimedia 24, 1815–1829 (2021)
28. Deng, Z., et al.: Fast 3D face reconstruction from a single image combining attention mechanism and graph convolutional network. Vis. Comput. (2022). https://doi.org/10.1007/s00371-022-02679-9
29. Brocchini, M., et al.: Monster: a deep learning-based system for the automatic generation of gaming assets. In: Mazzeo, P.L., Frontoni, E., Sclaroff, S., Distante, C. (eds.) ICIAP 2022. LNCS, vol. 13373, pp. 280–290. Springer, Cham (2022). https://doi.org/10.1007/978-3-031-13321-3_25
30. Simonyan, K., Zisserman, A.: Very deep convolutional networks for large-scale image recognition, arXiv arXiv:1409.1556 (2014)
31. Ronneberger, O., Fischer, P., Brox, T.: U-Net: convolutional networks for biomedical image segmentation. In: Navab, N., Hornegger, J., Wells, W.M., Frangi, A.F. (eds.) MICCAI 2015. LNCS, vol. 9351, pp. 234–241. Springer, Cham (2015). https://doi.org/10.1007/978-3-319-24574-4_28
32. He, K., Zhang, X., Ren, S., Sun, J.: Deep residual learning for image recognition. In: Proceedings of the IEEE Conference on Computer Vision and Pattern Recognition, pp. 770–778 (2016)
33. Szegedy, C., et al.: Going deeper with convolutions. In: Proceedings of the IEEE Conference on Computer Vision and Pattern Recognition, pp. 1–9 (2015)
34. Huang, G., Liu, Z., Van Der Maaten, L., Weinberger, K.Q.: Densely connected convolutional networks. In: Proceedings of the IEEE Conference on Computer Vision and Pattern Recognition, pp. 4700–4708 (2017)
35. Ravi, N., et al.: Accelerating 3D deep learning with PyTorch3D, arXiv:2007.08501 (2020)
36. Fey, M., Lenssen, J.E.: Fast graph representation learning with PyTorch geometric. In: ICLR Workshop on Representation Learning on Graphs and Manifolds (2019)

37. Gao, J., et al.: GET3D: a generative model of high quality 3D textured shapes learned from images (2022). arXiv: 2209.11163
38. Qian, G., et al.: Magic123: one image to high quality 3D object generation using both 2D and 3D diffusion priors (2023). arXiv: 2306.17843
39. Kim, K.-S., Zhang, D., Kang, M.-C., Ko, S.-J.: Improved simple linear iterative clustering superpixels. In: 2013 IEEE International Symposium on Consumer Electronics (ISCE), pp. 259–260 (2013). https://doi.org/10.1109/ISCE.2013.6570216

Arbitrary Style Transfer with Style Enhancement and Structure Retention

Sijia Yang and Yun Zhou(✉)

National University of Defense Technology, Changsha 410000, China
zhouyun@nudt.edu.cn

Abstract. Arbitrary style transfer is to transfer the style of any reference image to another image by a trained neural network, while preserving its content as much as possible. So far, a lot of work focused on reducing training costs without achieving sufficient style transfer, while some other work has neglected image frequency domain alignment. Balancing style presentation and content retention is no doubt challenging, we therefore propose a style transfer method that introduces frequency domain alignment and style secondary embedding, which is mainly embodied in two parts: style enhancement module (SEM) and content retention module (SRM). SEM aligns the stylistic image and stylized image statistics in the feature space. SRM reduces the loss of content by mapping the original and stylized images into the frequency domain and airspace for synchronous alignment. This new approach works well in terms of both style transfer and content retention. Experimental and questionnaire results show that this method can generate satisfactory stylized images without loss of content information.

Keywords: style transfer · high-frequency information · neural networks

1 Introduction

With the development of computer vision, machines can also "paint art" like humans. As a technique used to output images combining the content of the input image and the style of a reference image, Art style transfer, becomes a hot research topic in computer vision. In addition to studying the performance of new technologies on style transfer, we believe that the balance between content retention and style transfer of generated images is significant, which will affect its downstream applications.

Since Gatys et al. [8] successfully used a convolutional neural network to represent styles with a Gram matrix of feature maps, more and more CNN-based methods have improved the speed, generation quality, and generalization of style transfer. One of the classical approaches, led by Li et al. [18], efficiently implemented real-time style transfer by designing a linear feed-forward network that aligns the statistics (mean and standard deviation) of content and style images.

B. Sheng et al. (Eds.): CGI 2023, LNCS 14496, pp. 401–413, 2024.
https://doi.org/10.1007/978-3-031-50072-5_32

This method is less difficult to train, but the generated image is not sufficiently stylized, as shown in Fig. 1(a). Other studies based on model optimization, such as Park et al. [23] use attention to make content and style features close to each other semantically, and Zhang et al. [32] capture the color distribution and specific style details through a contrastive learning framework. Even though these methods can generate various high-quality images, they have difficulty in balancing style integration and content preservation, while taking too much time to train.

Moreover, we find that few studies on artistic style transfer pay attention to the structure and detail retention of content images, while most of the studies focus on capturing styles, resulting in the generated images may be over-adapted to the style field. For example, MCCNet [5] fuses the features of both styles by calculating the correlation matrix of style images and content images on different channels in the feature space. Although this approach makes most use of style features, it can lead to the blurring of content features (as shown in Fig. 1(b)).

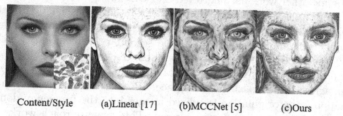

Content/Style   (a)Linear [17]   (b)MCCNet [5]   (c)Ours

Fig. 1. The stylization degree will affect the quality of the resulting image. Here, we show the results of some classical methods compared with ours.

To solve the above limitations, we proposed an improved arbitrary style transfer method with style and content enhancement in this paper, which can both generate fascinating stylized images and preserve content details well. Specifically, our model consists of an encoder-decoder network, a style enhancement module (SEM), and a structure retention module (SRM). Inspired by [13,18], The SEM extracts the feature maps of the pre-trained VGG encoder and computes the covariance of style features to capture cross-channel dependence. We then map the features to the spatial domain by Gaussian kernel, and Fourier domain by Fast Fourier Transformation separately to obtain the high-frequency components of images. Clearly, the high-frequency components of the picture represent the parts where the gray value changes sharply, which contain the edge information of the image. The low-frequency components refer to the regions where the gray value changes gently, corresponding to the style and texture information. By filtering out low-frequency components, we can calculate the Gaussian loss and Fourier loss in the spatial and frequency domains during the style transfer process.

The main contributions of our work can be summarized as follows:

- We propose a new style enhancement framework for arbitrary style transfer, which aligns the second-order statistics of the feature maps of style images and content images twice in the feature space for the style enhancement purpose.

- We then introduce a structure retention module for pixel, frequency and spatial domain transformation, which regulates the consistency of content images and generated images in the frequency domain.
- We conducted both qualitative and quantitative experiments, demonstrating that our method can generate high-quality stylized images with relatively good efficiency, compared to state-of-the-art methods.

2 Related Work

2.1 Previous Style Transfer

Before the emergence of convolutional neural networks, relevant studies used non-realistic rendering methods to study style transfer, such as stroke-based rendering methods [7,12] and image analogy methods. These algorithms are designed for specific styles and are also difficult to extract high-level semantic information from images, leading to a poor effect on synthesized images. Gatys et al. [8,9] multiplied the feature expression of a layer of VGG with its transpose matrix to obtain the Gram matrix and then updated the pixel value of the reconstructed image in the way of gradient descent. Although this work can solve the problem, it is computationally expensive and time costly, while inevitably losing low-level information such as edges and structures. Subsequent related algorithms have been developed to solve the above problems, from the Per-Style-Per-Model Fast Neural Methods [14,26] which train a specific network to generate fixed-style images, to the Multiple-Style-Per-Model Fast Neural Methods [6,19,30] which generate multiple styles of images. So far, current methods can almost transfer any style to the content image.

2.2 Arbitrary Style Transfer

To realize real-time arbitrary style transfer, AdaIN [13], inspired by CIN [6], firstly replaced the parameters of affine transformation in the CIN layer with the statistics of style features and content features. Wang et. [27] used two pre-trained VGG networks to separately achieve the style transfer and detail reconstruction. Park et al. [23] used the spatial correlation of style features and content features to strengthen the integration of style and proposed the Identity Loss to maintain the content structure. Lee et al. [16] used the histogram analogy in image transfer and used the extracted color feature of the reference image to modulate the color of the source image. Deng et al. [5] proposed MCCNet, which calculates multi-channel correlations of style features and integrates them with content features to achieve effective style transfer. Liu et al. [22] regard style features as the weighted statistical sum of all style feature pixels and then use the normalization module to make the model adaptive for attention normalization. In addition, some researches based on GAN [4,25,28] also achieved good results. Choi et al. [4] proposed StarGAN to simultaneously train multiple datasets with different domains within a single network. However, these GAN-based methods have too many parameters that makes them time-consuming for training.

2.3   Style Transfer in Frequency Domain

Image can be processed in both spatial and frequency domains. The spatial domain directly processes pixels in the pixel space, and the frequency domain processes pixels in the image transformation domain (namely frequency domain) and then get results after inverse transformation. At present, many studies adopt image enhancement methods in the frequency domain and spatial domain to improve the acquisition of structure edge information. Li et al. [20] used a digital Gaussian low-pass filter to deal with cross-domain problems in computer vision. Yang et. [29] devised the difference-of-Gaussian filter approach to correct line shift between image drawing. Li et al. [17] adopted the Laplacian filtering method to add the difference of filtering results between content images and stylized images as a loss function, so as to compensate for the loss of high-frequency information caused by calculation in abstract high-dimensional feature space.

3   Method

Our new style transfer method includes two major modules: 1) the style enhancement Module (SEM), designed to improve the integration of style into the content image, and 2) the structure retention module (SRM), designed to preserve more structural information of the content images. The whole training procedure is illustrated in Fig. 2.

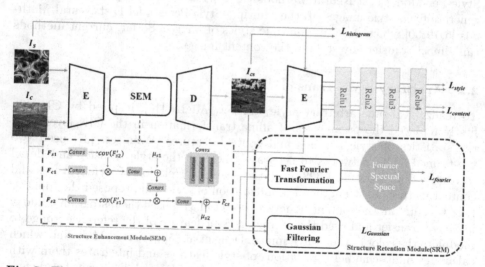

Fig. 2. The proposed architecture with a style enhancement module (SEM) and a structure retention module (SRM).

3.1   Style Enhancement Module

Figure 2 demonstrates the structure of the style enhancement module (SEM), which takes the feature maps of the VGG-19 encoder as inputs and embeds the information of style images into content images.

Inspired by Linear [18] and SANet [23], we adopt the covariance matrix to focus on the relationship between channels. To be specific, after the content image and style image are encoded by a fixed VGG-19 network, we obtain the features of two layers $ReLU3\_1$ and $ReLU4\_1$ and name them as F_{c1}, F_{c2} and F_{s1}, F_{s2} respectively. In addition, we normalize the standard deviations and means of channels of F_{c1} and means of channels of F_{s1}, F_{s2} to get $\overline{f_c}$, $\overline{f_{s1}}$ and $\overline{f_{s2}}$. Compared to directly using the results of layers of encoder, it will reduce the computational cost.

Then we divide SEM into two parts: in the first part, we send $\overline{f_c}$ and $\overline{f_{s1}}$ to a pair of compress blocks (both contain 3 convolutional layers and 2 $ReLU$ layers, just like Linear [18]) to reduce the dimension of channels and get exact global information. In order to get the correlation of inter-channels features, we calculate the covariance matrix $cov(\cdot)$ of $\overline{f_{s1}}$. After simply fusing the features through an element-wise multiplication between $cov(\overline{f_{s1}})$ and $\overline{f_c}$, we choose a single convolution layer $conv(\cdot)$ to convert to the original dimension of channels and add $\overline{f_{s1}}$ afterwards. In the second part, we take the results of the first part as input and follow the same procedure as in the first part, which further enhances the style features to align with content features, therefore the overall calculation process is:

$$F_{cs} = conv(cov(\theta(Norm(F_{s2}))) \otimes \theta(Std(F'_{cs}))) + \mu_{s2}, \tag{1}$$

where the $\theta(\cdot)$ denotes the 3-layers convolution, $Norm(\cdot)$ and $Std(\cdot)$ refers to the mean-variance normalization and the standard deviation normalization, $\otimes$ is the matrix multiplication, F'_{cs} denotes the results of the first part.

3.2   Structure Retention Module

As SEM effectively improves the quality of style integration, we then design a simple module including 2 loss functions to guarantee structural consistency.

Gaussian Highpass Filtering (GHPF). In contrast to the Gaussian lowpass filter, by suppressing the low-frequency information of the image, the Gaussian highpass filter (GHPF) is sensitive to the high-frequency component, which corresponds to the edges of the structure in the image:

$$H_{Gaussian}(i, j) = 1 - \frac{1}{2\pi\sigma^2} e^{-\frac{i^2+j^2}{2\pi\sigma^2}}, \tag{2}$$

where $H_{Gaussian}(i, j)$ denotes the high-frequency value of pixel spatial location (i, j) in the image, σ^2 is the variation of the Gaussian function, which also represents the "smoothing degree". σ^2 is determined by the size of the Gaussian kernel, and we set it to 27. In order to obtain the high-frequency value, we subtract the Gaussian lowpass filtering function by 1.

Through GHPF, we then transform the content image I_c and output image I_{cs} into spatial domain and align them. Noting that Gaussian filtering only processes the grayscale value of pixels, we first convert RGB images I_c and I_{cs} to grayscale images:

$$\mathcal{L}_{Gaussian} = \mathbb{E}[\| H(Gray(I_c)) - H(Gray(I_{cs})) \|_1]. \tag{3}$$

Fourier Fast Transformation (FFT). Another way to preserve the structural details is Fourier transformation. Inspired by Cai et al. [3], we convert the content image and the output image into the Fourier spectral space by FFT, then obtain the spectrum and centralize it, and obtain the high frequency extended from the center of the spectrum through a mask. Therefore, we can calculate the loss:

$$\mathcal{L}_{fourier} = \mathbb{E}[\| \mathcal{M}(F(I_c)) - \mathcal{M}(F(I_{cs})) \|_1], \tag{4}$$

where $F(\cdot)$ denotes the Fourier fast transformation function, and $\mathcal{M}(\cdot)$ is the mask of the Fourier spectrum. Since the high frequencies are distributed around the spectrum, the mask should be a circle whose radius is set to 27[1].

3.3   Objective Function

Although GHPF and FFT are adopted to ensure image reconstruction, the network still sometimes outputs images with small color differences, which is caused by the emphasis of the style enhancement module on the overall statistical results of the style. To make the global color distribution of the generated image more aligned with the style image, we use the histogram loss proposed by [1]:

$$\mathcal{L}_{histogram} = \frac{1}{\sqrt{2}} \| H_s^{\frac{1}{2}} - H_{cs}^{\frac{1}{2}} \|_2, \tag{5}$$

where $H^{\frac{1}{2}}$ is an element-wise square root, and $\| \cdot \|_2$ denotes the standard Euclidean norm.

Apart from the loss functions above, the content $\mathcal{L}_c$ and the style loss $\mathcal{L}_s$ are also introduced, Following the former approach in [8]. Generally, both $\mathcal{L}_c$ and $\mathcal{L}_s$ are measured by the Euclidean distance of the stylized features and the features of the content image or style image in the decoder. the content loss $\mathcal{L}_c$ and the style loss $\mathcal{L}_s$ are defined as follows:

$$\mathcal{L}_c = \| \overline{E(I_{cs})_{ReLU4\_1}} - \overline{E(I_c)_{ReLU4\_1}} \|_F, \tag{6}$$

$$\mathcal{L}_s = \sum_{l=1}^{L} [\| \mu(\phi_l(I_{cs})) - \mu(\phi_l(I_s)) \|_F + \| \sigma(\phi_l(I_{cs})) - \sigma(\phi_l(I_s)) \|_F], \tag{7}$$

---

[1] Following the setting of [3], we tried several mask sizes and chose 27, which generated good results.

where ϕ_l represents the output feature map of layer l in VGG, $\mu(\cdot)$ and $\phi(\cdot)$ denote the mean and variance of the feature map respectively.

The content loss $\mathcal{L}_c$ is directly determined by the difference between the mean-variance normalization results of the $ReLU4\_1$ layer content feature and the $ReLU4\_1$ layer generated feature, while the style loss $\mathcal{L}_s$ is the sum of the difference between the mean and standard deviation of generated feature and style feature for all layers within $\{ReLU1\_1, ReLU2\_1, ReLU3\_1, ReLU4\_1\}$.

Combining the above loss functions, our overall objective function is:

$$\mathcal{L}_{total} = \lambda_s\mathcal{L}_s + \lambda_c\mathcal{L}_c + \lambda_h\mathcal{L}_{histogram} + \lambda_f\mathcal{L}_{fourier} + \lambda_{hf}\mathcal{L}_{hf}, \tag{8}$$

where λ_s, λ_c, λ_h, λ_f, λ_{hf} are the weights of the loss respectively which we set to $\lambda_s = 5$, $\lambda_c = 1$, $\lambda_h = 2$, $\lambda_f = 2$, $\lambda_{hf} = 2$ by default.

4   Experimental Result

4.1   Experimental Settings

We used 100,000 artistic images randomly selected from WikiArt [24] as the style dataset for training, and 80,000 images from MS-COCO [21] as the content dataset. We used Adam [15] as the optimizer. Specifically, we set the learning rate to 0.0001 and the momentum to 0.9, and a batch size of 8 to train the model for 160,000 iterations by default. We feed the reference and content image into the network, which resizes the smaller dimension of both images to 512, then randomly crops a 256×256 patch as the final input during the training. In the testing phase, our model can tackle pictures of any size for its fully convolutional architecture. We conducted the experiments on a server with an NVIDIA GeForce RTX 2080 Ti GPU.

4.2   Quantitative Evaluation

To reflect the effects of various methods and give fair quantitative results, we use several indicators to evaluate the stylization effect and the degree of structure retention. The competing algorithms are Gatys. [8], AdaIN [13], Linear [18], Artflow [2], MCCNet [5], and AdaAttN [22]. We select LPIPS [31], originally used to measure the diversity of generated images, and SSIM [11] as evaluation indicators. For LPIPS [31], we calculate the perceptual distance between the content image and the stylized image in the deep feature space through a pre-trained AlexNet. To verify that our method can promote the retention of structure and detail, we use SSIM [11] to evaluate the similarity between the content image and the stylized image in terms of brightness, contrast, and structure.

We also introduce human evaluation here. We randomly selected four art paintings and four photographs, then generated four stylized images using the methods mentioned above. Then we invited 30 participants (aged 13 to 45) to select their favorite stylized image from the results generated by all approaches. A total of 120 questionnaire survey results were collected and then counted,

Table 1. Quantitative comparison with other arbitrary style transfer methods. We make the first-place scores bold and the second-place scores underlined.

Method	Ours	Gatys. [8]	Linear [18]	AdaIN [13]	Artflow [2]	MCCNet [5]	AdaAttN [22]
LPIPS [31]↓	0.331	0.401	0.352	0.337	0.339	**0.303**	0.382
SSIM [11]↑	**0.369**	0.214	0.238	0.269	0.243	0.227	0.304
User Study↑	**0.283**	0.059	0.100	0.133	0.033	0.225	0.167

"User Study" evaluation results are presented as percentages in the last row of Table 1. The results show that our method can generate acceptable and favorite artworks for users, which proves that our approach has the potential to apply in practice.

4.3 Qualitative Evaluation

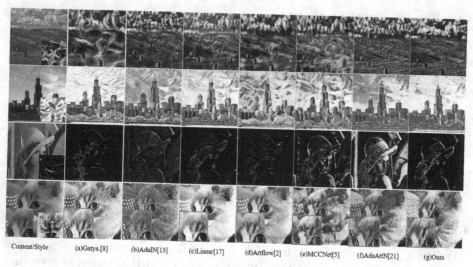

Content/Style   (a)Gatys.[8]   (b)AdaIN[13]   (c)Linear[17]   (d)Artflow[2]   (e)MCCNet[5]   (f)AdaAttN[21]   (g)Ours

Fig. 3. Visual comparisons with several state-of-the-art arbitrary style transfer methods.

Figure 3 shows the visual comparison results of our approach with other competing state-of-the-art methods. Gatys [8] successfully used CNN to separate the content and style and realized the style transfer through image iteration. But the images it produces are sometimes too blunt and artificial (e.g., the 1st, 4th rows) while performing poorly in retaining detail (e.g., the 3rd rows). AdaIN [13] achieves style transfer by adaptive global adjustment of the mean and variance of content and style features. Because it adjusts globally and is adaptive, the stylized image often cannot align with the style images (e.g., the 2nd, 4th rows), leading to the loss of some details. Linear [18] performs better in detail retention than the previous methods, but is less satisfactory in style realization, with artifacts (e.g., the 3rd rows) and missing details (the 4th rows). The images generated by Artflow [2] have some surface textures on the whole, which affect the image quality (e.g., the 2nd, 3rd, and 4th rows). In addition, the method produces some colors (e.g., the 2nd rows) and edge artifacts (e.g., the 1st, 4th rows) that are not present in the style image. The results of MCCNet [5] sometimes are too "stylized", resulting in some brush strokes and colors that do not exist in the style image, and the structural details of the image are lost. AdaAttN [22] cannot well capture the color of the reference image and then transfer it to the content image (e.g., the 2nd and 4th rows), and fail to semantically aligned with it. Compared with the above methods, our method ensures the retention of the structure while style transfer. In each task, the color of the style image is evenly distributed in the generated image combined with semantic information, such as our results in the 1st, 2nd and 3rd rows in Fig. 3 (Fig. 4).

Content/Style   (a)Artflow[2]   (b)Linear[17]   (c)MCCNet[5]   (d)Ours

Fig. 4. Comparison of depth maps with other style transfer methods, the brighter areas (such as the yellow areas) represent the closer to the shooting camera. Each depth image in the second row is the generation result of the corresponding image in the first row. (Color figure online)

We further evaluate the structural consistency between generated images and content images. The depth map takes the distance from the image collector to each point in the scene as the pixel value, which directly reflects the structure and geometry of the picture. We use Monodepth2 [11] to predict the depth map of a single image. Specifically, we randomly select a test image from the KITTI dataset [10] and then use a publicly available pre-trained model to generate the visual results and depth error (RMSE and RMSE log) for that image. The degree of similarity between the depth map of the generated image and the depth map of the content image partly reflects the retention of information inherent in the content image, which allows the converted image to still be used for practical operations, such as object recognition. The experiment results show that our method can preserve more landscape structure than other methods (Table 2).

Table 2. Quantitative results of depth estimation. We used two depth error evaluation indexes RMSE and RMSE log, and the left column is the depth estimation of the original image.

Content Image	Method	Artflow [2]	Linear [18]	MCCNet [5]	Ours
4.141	RMSE↓	4.592	4.242	16.935	**3.994**
0.176	RMSE log↓	0.202	0.193	0.651	**0.190**

4.4   Ablation Study

In Fig. 5, we explore the role of the style enhancement module, the content retention module, and other loss functions. Figure 5(b) shows the result without $\mathcal{L}_{fourier}$, in which the details, such as the suspension line of the bridge, are too thick. Figure 5(c) shows the result of fixing $\mathcal{L}_c$, $\mathcal{L}_s$, $\mathcal{L}_{histogram}$, $\mathcal{L}_{fourier}$ and abandoning $\mathcal{L}_{Gaussian}$. The suspension line of the bridge is as thin as the content image, but some vertical lines on the bridge disappear. Figure 5(d) shows the result of discarding the content retention module, the heavy yellow rendering in the messenger wire. For Fig. 5(e), the sky appears green. In terms of the effect of the style enhancement module, Fig. 5(f) shows the training results of only fixing $\mathcal{L}_c$, $\mathcal{L}_s$, in which both the bridge part and the sky part also appear a lot green, and the edge of the bridge distorts a little bit. Figure 5(g) is the result generated using the complete model, the seawater is blue and purple, and the edge structure is relatively intact, which is very consistent with the semantic expression of the original figure.

Fig. 5. Ablation study results, all weights are the default values mentioned in Sect. 3. From left to right: (a) content and style images; (b) result only without loss $\mathcal{L}_{fourier}$; (c) result only without loss $\mathcal{L}_{Gaussian}$; (d) result without $\mathcal{L}_{fourier}$ and $\mathcal{L}_{Gaussian}$; (e) result only without $\mathcal{L}_{histogram}$; (f) result only with $\mathcal{L}_c$ and $\mathcal{L}_s$; (g) result with full losses.

4.5   Application

In the aspect of the application, in Fig. 6, we simply show the result of style interpolation for a single content image given two different style images. On the feature map of the input decoder, we adjust the weights of the two style images to achieve different degrees of interpolation.

Figure 7 shows the results of controlling the degree of stylization. Specifically, we interpolate content features of different degrees by features that have not been fed into the decoder. In this way, we can control the level of stylization during testing without having to train a new model.

Fig. 6. Style interpolation results of two different style images.

Fig. 7. The results of controlling the degree of stylization using a style image.

5 Conclusion

In this paper, we propose a new style transfer approach, which tries to solve the balance between style capture and content consistency during the transfer process. We design a style enhancement module to enhance style by utilizing second-order statistics of feature maps of style images and content images. To avoid over-adapting to the reference image, we then designed a structure retention module, which mapped the content images and the transferred images to the frequency domain and the spatial domain simultaneously, captured the high-frequency information for comparison and calculation of loss, and realized the alignment of the two. In addition, we also conducted experiments to verify that our method can generate high-quality stylized images with preserved structure, and showed some application scenarios of our method.

Acknowledgements. This work was supported in part by the National Natural Science Foundation of China under Grant 62276262; Science and Technology Innovation Program of Hunan Province under Grant 2021RC3076; Training Program for Excellent Young Innovators of Changsha under Grant KQ2009009.

References

1. Afifi, M., Brubaker, M.A., Brown, M.S.: Histogan: controlling colors of GAN-generated and real images via color histograms. In: Proceedings of the IEEE/CVF Conference on Computer Vision and Pattern Recognition, pp. 7941–7950 (2021)
2. An, J., Huang, S., Song, Y., Dou, D., Liu, W., Luo, J.: Artflow: unbiased image style transfer via reversible neural flows. In: Proceedings of the IEEE/CVF Conference on Computer Vision and Pattern Recognition, pp. 862–871 (2021)

3. Cai, M., Zhang, H., Huang, H., Geng, Q., Li, Y., Huang, G.: Frequency domain image translation: more photo-realistic, better identity-preserving. In: Proceedings of the IEEE/CVF International Conference on Computer Vision, pp. 13930–13940 (2021)

4. Choi, Y., Choi, M., Kim, M., Ha, J.W., Kim, S., Choo, J.: Stargan: unified generative adversarial networks for multi-domain image-to-image translation. In: Proceedings of the IEEE Conference on Computer Vision and Pattern Recognition, pp. 8789–8797 (2018)

5. Deng, Y., Tang, F., Dong, W., Huang, H., Ma, C., Xu, C.: Arbitrary video style transfer via multi-channel correlation. In: Proceedings of the AAAI Conference on Artificial Intelligence, vol. 35, pp. 1210–1217 (2021)

6. Dumoulin, V., Shlens, J., Kudlur, M.: A learned representation for artistic style. arXiv preprint arXiv:1610.07629 (2016)

7. Fišer, J., et al.: Stylit: illumination-guided example-based stylization of 3D renderings. ACM Trans. Graph. (TOG) **35**(4), 1–11 (2016)

8. Gatys, L.A., Ecker, A.S., Bethge, M.: Image style transfer using convolutional neural networks. In: Proceedings of the IEEE Conference on Computer Vision and Pattern Recognition, pp. 2414–2423 (2016)

9. Gatys, L.A., Ecker, A.S., Bethge, M., Hertzmann, A., Shechtman, E.: Controlling perceptual factors in neural style transfer. In: Proceedings of the IEEE Conference on Computer Vision and Pattern Recognition, pp. 3985–3993 (2017)

10. Geiger, A., Lenz, P., Urtasun, R.: Are we ready for autonomous driving? The kitti vision benchmark suite. In: 2012 IEEE Conference on Computer Vision and Pattern Recognition, pp. 3354–3361. IEEE (2012)

11. Godard, C., Mac Aodha, O., Firman, M., Brostow, G.J.: Digging into self-supervised monocular depth estimation. In: Proceedings of the IEEE/CVF International Conference on Computer Vision, pp. 3828–3838 (2019)

12. Hertzmann, A.: Painterly rendering with curved brush strokes of multiple sizes. In: Proceedings of the 25th Annual Conference on Computer Graphics and Interactive Techniques, pp. 453–460 (1998)

13. Huang, X., Belongie, S.: Arbitrary style transfer in real-time with adaptive instance normalization. In: Proceedings of the IEEE International Conference on Computer Vision, pp. 1501–1510 (2017)

14. Johnson, J., Alahi, A., Fei-Fei, L.: Perceptual losses for real-time style transfer and super-resolution. In: Leibe, B., Matas, J., Sebe, N., Welling, M. (eds.) ECCV 2016. LNCS, vol. 9906, pp. 694–711. Springer, Cham (2016). https://doi.org/10.1007/978-3-319-46475-6_43

15. Kingma, D.P., Ba, J.: Adam: a method for stochastic optimization. arXiv preprint arXiv:1412.6980 (2014)

16. Lee, J., Son, H., Lee, G., Lee, J., Cho, S., Lee, S.: Deep color transfer using histogram analogy. Vis. Comput. **36**, 2129–2143 (2020)

17. Li, S., Xu, X., Nie, L., Chua, T.S.: Laplacian-steered neural style transfer. In: Proceedings of the 25th ACM International Conference on Multimedia, pp. 1716–1724 (2017)

18. Li, X., Liu, S., Kautz, J., Yang, M.H.: Learning linear transformations for fast image and video style transfer. In: Proceedings of the IEEE/CVF Conference on Computer Vision and Pattern Recognition, pp. 3809–3817 (2019)

19. Li, Y., Fang, C., Yang, J., Wang, Z., Lu, X., Yang, M.H.: Diversified texture synthesis with feed-forward networks. In: Proceedings of the IEEE Conference on Computer Vision and Pattern Recognition, pp. 3920–3928 (2017)

20. Li, Z., Zhao, X., Zhao, C., Tang, M., Wang, J.: Transfering low-frequency features for domain adaptation. In: 2022 IEEE International Conference on Multimedia and Expo (ICME), pp. 1–6. IEEE (2022)
21. Lin, T.-Y., et al.: Microsoft COCO: common objects in context. In: Fleet, D., Pajdla, T., Schiele, B., Tuytelaars, T. (eds.) ECCV 2014. LNCS, vol. 8693, pp. 740–755. Springer, Cham (2014). https://doi.org/10.1007/978-3-319-10602-1_48
22. Liu, S., et al.: Adaattn: revisit attention mechanism in arbitrary neural style transfer. In: Proceedings of the IEEE/CVF International Conference on Computer Vision, pp. 6649–6658 (2021)
23. Park, D.Y., Lee, K.H.: Arbitrary style transfer with style-attentional networks. In: Proceedings of the IEEE/CVF Conference on Computer Vision and Pattern Recognition, pp. 5880–5888 (2019)
24. Phillips, F., Mackintosh, B.: Wiki art gallery, inc.: a case for critical thinking. Issues Account. Educ. **26**(3), 593–608 (2011)
25. Sanakoyeu, A., Kotovenko, D., Lang, S., Ommer, B.: A style-aware content loss for real-time HD style transfer. In: Proceedings of the European Conference on Computer Vision (ECCV), pp. 698–714 (2018)
26. Ulyanov, D., Lebedev, V., Vedaldi, A., Lempitsky, V.: Texture networks: feed-forward synthesis of textures and stylized images. arXiv preprint arXiv:1603.03417 (2016)
27. Wang, L., Wang, Z., Yang, X., Hu, S.M., Zhang, J.: Photographic style transfer. Vis. Comput. **36**, 317–331 (2020)
28. Xu, W., Long, C., Wang, R., Wang, G.: DRB-GAN: a dynamic resblock generative adversarial network for artistic style transfer. In: Proceedings of the IEEE/CVF International Conference on Computer Vision, pp. 6383–6392 (2021)
29. Yang, H., Min, K.: Importance-based approach for rough drawings. Vis. Comput. **35**(4), 609–622 (2019)
30. Zhang, H., Dana, K.: Multi-style generative network for real-time transfer. In: Proceedings of the European Conference on Computer Vision (ECCV) Workshops (2018)
31. Zhang, R., Isola, P., Efros, A.A., Shechtman, E., Wang, O.: The unreasonable effectiveness of deep features as a perceptual metric. In: Proceedings of the IEEE Conference on Computer Vision and Pattern Recognition, pp. 586–595 (2018)
32. Zhang, Y., et al.: Domain enhanced arbitrary image style transfer via contrastive learning. arXiv preprint arXiv:2205.09542 (2022)

Zero3D: Semantic-Driven 3D Shape Generation for Zero-Shot Learning

Bo Han[1]([⊠]), Yixuan Shen[2], and Yitong Fu[1]

[1] College of Computer Science and Technology, Zhejiang University, Hangzhou, China
borishan815@zju.edu.cn
[2] National University of Singapore, Singapore, Singapore

Abstract. Semantic-driven 3D shape generation aims to generate 3D shapes conditioned on textual input. However, previous approaches have faced challenges with the single-category generation, low-frequency details, and the requirement for large quantities of paired data. To address these issues, we propose a multi-category diffusion model. Specifically, our approach includes the following components: 1) To mitigate the problem of limited large-scale paired data, we establish a connection between text, 2D images, and 3D shapes through the use of the pre-trained CLIP model, enabling zero-shot learning. 2) To obtain the multi-category 3D shape feature, we employ a conditional flow model to generate a multi-category shape vector conditioned on the CLIP embedding. 3) To generate multi-category 3D shapes, we utilize a hidden-layer diffusion model conditioned on the multi-category shape vector, resulting in significant reductions in training time and memory consumption. We evaluate the generated results of our framework and demonstrate that our method outperforms existing methods. The code and more qualitative samples can be found at website.

Keywords: 3D Shape Generation · Point-Cloud · Diffusion Model

1 Introduction

As a core element in the Metaverse world [30], 3D objects play a vital role in enhancing user interactivity. With the rapid development of AIGC technology [7,11,16,22], it has become increasingly easy to create images, audio, and video through text prompts. However, the design of 3D objects still relies on manual modeling software such as Blender and Maya3D, which requires significant time and expertise. As such, the generation of high-quality 3D objects through semantic information has become a practical challenge.

Unlike 2D images, which can be represented as arrays of pixel values, 3D objects have diverse and complex representations, including voxels [35], point clouds [18], grids [14], and implicit representations [3]. Each representation has its own advantages and limitations, and different representations require different processing methods, adding to the challenge [27]. Text to 3D shape generation is also challenging [9,29] due to the difficulty of jointly understanding 3D shapes

B. Sheng et al. (Eds.): CGI 2023, LNCS 14496, pp. 414–426, 2024.
https://doi.org/10.1007/978-3-031-50072-5_33

and text and representing them in a common space. Furthermore, unlike text to image generation where paired data is abundant, text to 3D shape generation lacks large-scale paired text and 3D shape data.

Recent work on 3D shape generation [13,17,18,21] has yielded promising results. DreamFusion [21] transforms the diffusion and denoising processes in pixel space into operations in the NeRF parameter space [19]. However, due to the use of low-resolution images (64×64) as supervision signals, DreamFusion is unable to synthesize high-frequency 3D geometric and texture details. DPM [18] trains an encoder to generate a shape vector representing a point cloud shape, which is then used to train a flow model. The pre-trained flow model can then convert noise into a shape vector, and the diffusion model utilizes this shape vector as a condition for 3D shape generation. However, since DPM is trained on a specific category, it can only generate point cloud data of one type.

To address these challenges, we first pre-train a CLIP model [7] to establish a superior correspondence between text and 2D images. We can also obtain a large number of high-resolution 2D images corresponding to 3D objects through Blender. As such, the CLIP model bridges text, 2D images, and 3D objects, mitigating the problem of limited large-scale paired text-3D shape data. We then apply a conditional flow model [6] to generate a multi-category shape vector conditioned on the CLIP embedding. Subsequently, we employ a conditional diffusion model to generate the 3D point cloud data conditioned on the multi-category shape vector. Specifically, during training, the CLIP model is used to encode the 2D image as a condition, allowing the model to learn the correspondence between the 2D image and the 3D point cloud. During inference, the CLIP model encodes semantic information as a condition, enabling the generation of 3D point cloud corresponding to the semantic information. Additionally, to address the high time and memory consumption of the diffusion model itself, we implement the diffusion process and denoising operation on the hidden layer.

To summarize, our main contributions are:

- Considering the superior correspondence between 2D images and texts in the CLIP model, We establish a connection between texts and 3D shapes by using 2D images as a medium, thereby enabling zero-shot learning.
- We propose a multi-category diffusion framework capable of generating 3D point cloud data for multiple categories using a single network model.

2 Background

2.1 3D Shape Generation

Some widely used generative models currently include the Variational Autoencoder (VAE) [15], Generative Adversarial Network (GAN) [8], Flow model [24], and Diffusion model [10]. 3D-GAN [32] first employs a 3D-CNN to gradually map a high-dimensional hidden vector into a 3D object represented by voxels. r-GAN [31] utilizes Graph Convolutional Network as the generator, effectively leveraging local information within point cloud data. However, due to the inherent uncertainty of GAN [5], the results are not always ideal. PointFlow [33] introduces a flow model to generate the shape distribution of point clouds, using a hidden vector representing the shape distribution as a condition to guide point cloud generation. However, since point clouds are typically distributed on a two-dimensional manifold, it is difficult to obtain better results using a flow model that assumes the point cloud follows a three-dimensional prior distribution. In the 3D domain, DPM [18] and PVD [35] use diffusion models to generate point cloud data. Although they can produce satisfactory results, they are both trained in specific categories.

2.2 Semantic-Driven 3D Shape Generation

Text2Shape [2] proposes an end-to-end association learning framework that separately encodes text and 3D shapes into the same latent space. However, large-scale text-3D shape data is still difficult to obtain, so recent work has proposed several zero-shot learning methods [1] leveraging the CLIP model. Clip-Forge [25] depends on an unlabelled shape dataset and CLIP model. CLIP-Mesh [20] employs the CLIP model to assess the degree of correspondence between images and text, enabling direct optimization of mesh model parameters. Similarly, AvatarCLIP [12] utilizes the CLIP model to facilitate the semantically driven generation of 3D human body models. This is achieved by optimizing SMPL parameters through the learning of correspondences between differentiable rendered images and input text. Dreamfields [13], DreamFusion [21], and Magic3D [17] all use NeRF [19] as an implicit representation of 3D objects and render images through differentiable renderers. They utilize the degree of match between images and text to optimize the entire network and ultimately extract the 3D mesh model from the optimized implicit neural field representation.

3   Method

The schematic overview of our proposed architecture is illustrated in Fig. 1. The left side of the figure shows the training architecture, which consists of four main components: a shape encoder, a CLIP model, a conditional flow model, and a conditional diffusion model. We use the DPM model as our backbone, which samples noise data from a Gaussian distribution and generates point cloud data through a denoising process under the given condition. Specifically, during training, we divide our model into two tasks. First, we render 3D objects to obtain high-resolution 2D images, which are then used as input to the pre-trained CLIP model. We use the shape encoder to obtain the shape parameter vector of multi-category 3D point cloud data, and then the conditional flow model is trained to establish the relationship between the CLIP embedding and the multi-category shape vector. Next, we use the multi-category shape vector as a condition to guide 3D shape generation in the diffusion model. During inference, the text is used as input to the CLIP model. Based on the bi-directionality of the flow model, we can obtain the shape vector guided by the CLIP embedding. Subsequently, the shape vector guides the diffusion model to generate multi-category point clouds. In this way, we use readily available 2D images as a medium to establish the connection between 3D point cloud data and text data, enabling zero-shot learning.

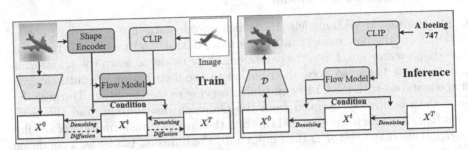

Fig. 1. The left image represents the training stage, while the right image represents the inference stage. The gray modules ε and $\mathcal{D}$, representing the encoder and decoder in the point cloud autoencoder, respectively, are pre-trained in advance. The CLIP model uses the Visual Transformer [7] ViT-B/32 checkpoint. During the training phase, the conditional flow model and point cloud diffusion model are jointly trained on 2D image and 3D point cloud data. During the inference stage, text data is used to drive and generate corresponding 3D point cloud data.

3.1 Shape Encoder

The model maps point cloud data to a distribution of shape vectors, namely the shape mean and shape variance, and then samples a shape vector from the shape mean and variance. The overall network comprises a feature extraction layer and a distribution mapping layer. For the feature extraction layer, we use a series of 1D convolutional layers to increase the dimensionality of the point cloud data, followed by selecting the maximum value of each dimension feature to perform feature dimension reduction. For the distribution mapping layer, the data after feature dimension reduction is mapped to the shape mean and variance, respectively, to represent the distribution of the point cloud shape vector. Subsequently, an offset value ε is randomly generated to sample a shape vector $s = \mu + \epsilon * \exp\left(0.5 * \log\left(\sigma^2\right)\right)$.

3.2 CLIP Model

The CLIP model encodes text and 2D images into the same latent space, enabling the matching of images and text. Based on the CLIP model, we learn the correspondence between 3D point clouds and text using images as an intermediary. The CLIP model is based on the VisualTransformer [7] and uses the ViT-B/32 model to match images to 16×16 text vectors. During the training and inference stage, images or text are passed through the CLIP model to obtain a one-dimensional vector of length 256, which is normalized and input into the conditional flow model as a condition.

3.3   Conditional Flow Model

Unlike traditional VAE models [15], which encode data into a standard normal distribution, the flow model can learn a more flexible and variable distribution. The shape vector is fed into the conditional flow model to learn the transformation from the Gaussian noise distribution to the distribution of multi-category shape features, with the CLIP embedding serving as the condition. During inference, data is directly sampled from the Gaussian distribution, and the corresponding shape vector is obtained through the inverse transformation of the flow model. This shape vector is then input into the diffusion model as a condition. We use the affine transformation layer in the RealNVP network architecture [6] to construct the flow model. The affine transformation layer divides the input into two parts: the first part remains unchanged, while the second part is transformed using scale and offset coefficients. For an input x that is D-dimensional, the forward calculation for the output y of the affine coupling layer is as follows:

$$
\begin{aligned}
y_{1:d} &= x_{1:d} \\
y_{d+1:D} &= x_{d+1:D} \odot \exp\left(s\left(x_{1:d}\right)\right) + t\left(x_{1:d}\right)
\end{aligned}
\tag{1}
$$

The inverse calculation for the output x is as follows:

$$
\begin{aligned}
x_{1:d} &= y_{1:d} \\
x_{d+1:D} &= \left(y_{d+1:D} - t\left(y_{1:d}\right)\right) \odot \exp\left(-s\left(y_{1:d}\right)\right)
\end{aligned}
\tag{2}
$$

Since the first part of the input is directly the output, if each layer is divided into two parts in the same way, the first part of the input and output of the entire flow model will remain unchanged. To enhance the model's ability to process data and produce a more balanced output, we adopt an alternating mask approach. In this approach, odd-numbered layers use the first d-dimensional data as the first part and the last $D - d$ dimensional data as the second part, while even-numbered layers do the opposite.

3.4   Point Cloud Autoencoder

To reduce the computational time and memory consumption of the diffusion model, we first train a point cloud autoencoder, with the encoded hidden vector serving as input to the subsequent diffusion model for 3D shape generation. The output of the denoising process diffusion model is decoded into point cloud data by the point cloud decoder. The point cloud autoencoder comprises an encoder and a decoder. The encoder is primarily based on the PointNet network architecture [23] and the graph-based max pooling layer [26], while the decoder

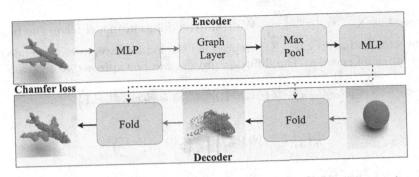

Fig. 2. Point Cloud Autoencoder network architecture

is primarily based on FoldingNet [34]. Figure 2 shows the network architecture of the point cloud autoencoder.

The goal of the point cloud autoencoder is to restore the original point cloud shape as accurately as possible. To achieve this, we use the point cloud reconstruction loss, calculated using the Chamfer Distance. The Chamfer Distance between two point sets S_1 and S_2 in 3D point cloud reconstruction is calculated by finding the closest point in S_2 for each point in S_1 and then calculating the L2 distance. The average of the distances calculated for each point in S_1 is then taken, as shown in the following Eq. 3:

$$Ch\left(S_1, S_2\right) = \sum_{p_1 \in S_1} \min_{p_2 \in S_2} \|p_1 - p_2\|_2 \tag{3}$$

For two point sets, the mutual Chamfer Distance must be calculated, resulting in the final distance formula shown in Eq. 4. In this formula, N_{S_1} and N_{S_1} represent the number of points in the two point sets, respectively.

$$
\begin{aligned}
d_{ch}\left(S_1, S_2\right) &= \frac{1}{N_{S_1}} Ch\left(S_1, S_2\right) + \frac{1}{N_{S_2}} Ch\left(S_2, S_1\right) \\
&= \frac{1}{N_{S_1}} \sum_{p_1 \in S_1} \min_{p_2 \in S_2} \|p_1 - p_2\|_2 + \frac{1}{N_{S_2}} \sum_{p_2 \in S_2} \min_{p_1 \in S_1} \|p_2 - p_1\|_2
\end{aligned}
\tag{4}
$$

3.5   Conditional Diffusion Model

The diffusion model consists of a diffusion process and a denoising process. The diffusion process gradually adds noise to the point cloud hidden vector, converting a point cloud distribution of a specific shape into a random noise Gaussian distribution. The denoising process transforms noisy data into the point cloud hidden vector, with the shape vector s serving as the condition. Based on the diffusion model, point cloud data can be considered as a set of points randomly sampled from a specific distribution. These points follow the same distribution but are independent of each other, meaning that point cloud data can be expressed as $\mathbf{X}^{(0)} = \left\{ x_i^{(0)} \right\}_{i=1}^{N}$. We train the diffusion model using the hidden layer vector, so in this case, $\mathbf{X}^{(0)}$ represents the hidden layer vector encoded by the point cloud encoder. The diffusion process can be expressed as follows:

$$q\left(x_i^{(t)} \mid x_i^{(t-1)} \right) = \mathcal{N}\left(x_i^{(t)} \mid \sqrt{1 - \beta_t} x_i^{(t-1)}, \beta_t \mathbf{I} \right) \tag{5}$$

$$q\left(x_i^{1:T} \mid x_i^{(0)} \right) = \prod_{t=1}^{T} q\left(x_i^{(t)} \mid x_i^{(t-1)} \right) \tag{6}$$

where $\beta_1 ... \beta_T$ are hyperparameters at each time step that controls the noise addition process.

The denoising process aims to recover the original point cloud hidden vector from the noise data. First, the point cloud hidden vector is sampled from the noise distribution, and then, through a reverse Markov chain, the noise is gradually subtracted. Under the condition of the shape vector s, the denoised diffusion process can be expressed as follows:

$$p_\theta \left(x^{(t-1)} \mid x^{(t)}, s \right) = \mathcal{N}\left(x^{(t-1)} \mid \mu_\theta \left(x^{(t)}, t, s \right), \beta_t \mathbf{I} \right) \tag{7}$$

$$p_\theta \left(x^{(0:T)} \mid s \right) = p\left(x^{(T)} \right) \prod_{t=1}^{T} p_\theta \left(x^{(t-1)} \mid x^{(t)}, s \right) \tag{8}$$

Among them, μ_θ is a mean value estimated by the neural network, s is the conditional shape vector, and the initial data of inverse diffusion obeys the standard normal distribution $N(0, I)$.

Since the overall point cloud data can be considered as a collection of sampling points that follow the same distribution, the probability of the overall point cloud data can be expressed by the probability of each individual point:

$$q\left(\mathbf{X}^{(1:T)} \mid \mathbf{X}^0 \right) = \prod_{i=1}^{N} q\left(x_i^{(1:T)} \mid x_i^{(0)} \right)$$

$$p_\theta \left(\mathbf{X}^{(0:T)} \mid s \right) = \prod_{i=1}^{N} p_\theta \left(x_i^{(0:T)} \mid s \right) \tag{9}$$

The training objective is to maximize the likelihood function of the generated point cloud data $E\left[\log p_\theta \left(\mathbf{X}^{(0)} \right) \right]$. Similar to the VAE model, the specific optimization goal is still to maximize its variational lower bound (ELBO):

$$\mathbb{E}[\log p_\theta(\mathbf{X}^{(0)})] \geq \mathbb{E}\left[\log \frac{p_\theta(\mathbf{X}^{(0:T)}, s)}{q(\mathbf{X}^{(1:T)}, s \mid \mathbf{X}^{(0)})} \right]$$

$$= \mathbb{E}\left[\log p(\mathbf{X}^T) + \sum_{t=1}^{T} \log \frac{p_\theta(\mathbf{X}^{(t-1)} \mid \mathbf{X}^{(t)}, s)}{q(\mathbf{X}^{(t)} \mid \mathbf{X}^{(t-1)})} - \log \frac{q_\phi(s \mid \mathbf{X}^{(0)})}{p(s \mid c)} \right] \tag{10}$$

In the above equation, c represents the condition of the flow model, i.e., the embedding encoded by the CLIP model, while s represents the condition of the diffusion model, i.e., the shape vector. In the last step of the denoising process, the resulting data, denoted as $\mathbf{X}^{(0)}$, is known and thus treated separately.

This training process is parameterized by a squared L2 loss. To simplify the above variational bound, the above training process can be simplified by directly predicting the accumulated noise [10]. The following objectives are easier to train, similar to denoising score matching [28], and have been found to produce higher-quality samples:

$$L(\theta) = \left\| \epsilon - \epsilon_\theta \left(x_i^{(t)}, t, s \right) \right\|^2, \epsilon \sim \mathcal{N}(0, \mathbf{I}) \tag{11}$$

where t is sampled uniformly from $[1, T]$, and ϵ_θ is the learned diffusion model.

4   Experiments

4.1   Experimental Setup

Dataset.   We use the ShapeNet V2 processed dataset [4], which contains 13 categories of data, with each sample comprising point cloud data and corresponding 2D rendered images of each 3D object. To ensure a fair comparison, we adopt the same dataset-splitting approach. **Evaluation Metrics.** For single-class generation, we use the Chamfer Distance (CD) and Earth Mover's Distance (EMD) to evaluate the quality following prior works [31,33,35]. (1) **CD.** It calculates the average minimum distance between each generated point and its closest point in the ground-truth point cloud. (2) **EMD.** It measures the dissimilarity between two distributions, taking into account both their shape and relative position. For semantic-driven generation, Zero3D enables zero-shot training, eliminating the need for 3D data with associated compound text labels.

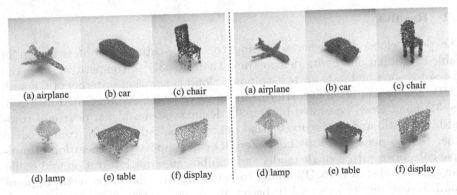

(a) airplane   (b) car   (c) chair   (a) airplane   (b) car   (c) chair

(d) lamp   (e) table   (f) display   (d) lamp   (e) table   (f) display

Fig. 3. Point cloud generated from the corresponding word. On the left is the result generated by our method, on the right is the result generated by PVD [35]

While this offers significant advantages in terms of training and application scalability, it also results in the absence of real data corresponding to the text during evaluation. In line with previous research, we assess composite text-driven point cloud data using the CLIP R-precision employed in DreamFields [13]. (3) **CLIP R-precision.** It evaluates the generation effect with composite text by ranking results between textual descriptions and generated images. The higher the ranking of the real text, the higher the quality of the generated data.

Implementation Details. For the point cloud autoencoder, we pre-trained the model using the Adam optimizer with a learning rate of 1e-6 and set the number of point cloud sampling points to 2025. For the conditional diffusion model, both the input and output data dimensions were set to 128. We employed the Adam optimizer with a learning rate of 2e-3. The conditional flow model consisted of 14 affine transformation layers, with consistent input and output dimensions for each layer. The diffusion model had a time step of 100, with hyperparameters β_1 and β_t set to 1e-4 and 0.02, respectively. The time step sampling strategy utilized a linear calculation method.

Table 1. Compared with SOTAs. CD, EMD and CLIP R-precision metrics results.

Method	Airplane		chair		Car		CLIP -precision ↑		
	CD↓	EMD↓	CD	EMD	CD	EMD	CLIP B/32	CLIP B/16	CLIP L/14
r-GAN [31]	97.3	95.2	86.2	89.6	91.7	98.7	-	-	-
PointFlow [33]	78.2	78.1	67.2	67.2	58.1	54.7	-	-	-
PVD [35]	76.8	67.8	60.5	56.9	59.0	54.5	-	-	-
DreamFusion [21]	-	-	-	-	-	-	42.5	44.6	58.5
Ours-P	80.1	71.2	64.8	58.2	65.3	61.7	31.5	35.1	40.8
Ours	77.3	**65.7**	61.8	**54.4**	**57.1**	**54.0**	32.8	34.1	41.5

4.2 Results

The point cloud data generated using the single-category word is shown in Table 1. Evaluation results demonstrate that Zero3D is competitive with the state-of-the-art methods for text-to-point cloud generation in terms of CD and EMD metrics and often outperforms in terms of EMD. As illustrated in Fig. 3, the 3D point cloud generated by Zero3D demonstrates a higher degree of compatibility with single-category textual descriptions. Additionally, compared to other text to point cloud methods, Zero3D can support the generation of multiple categories with a single model and exhibits superior integration and scalability. This is due to Zero3D's ability to better capture the shape vector of point cloud. In contrast to other CLIP-based 3D shape generation approaches, such as CLIP-Forge [25] and CLIP-Mesh [20], which represent 3D shapes using voxel and mesh formats respectively, our method employs 3D point clouds. Due to this difference in representation, a fair comparison cannot be made, and thus we have excluded these two methods from our comparative analysis.

The point cloud data generated using composite text is shown in Table 1. As there are no open-source works on composite text-to-point cloud generation for comparison, we can only compare our results to DreamFusion [21]. DreamFusion employs NeRF parameters to represent 3D scenes, whereas our approach utilizes 3D point clouds for the same purpose. In comparison to NeRF parameters [19], our rendered 2D images exhibit lower fidelity. As a result, when using the CLIP-R metric to evaluate the correspondence between images and text, our approach is outperformed by DreamFusion in terms of CLIP-R scores. However, as demonstrated in Fig. 4, our approach is capable of generating high-fidelity 3D shapes from composite textual descriptions.

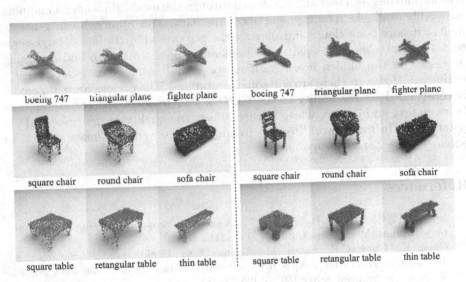

Fig. 4. Point cloud generated from composite text. On the left is the result generated by our method, on the right is the result generated by Our-P.

4.3   Ablation Study

To validate the efficacy of our approach in enhancing results through the implementation of a point cloud diffusion model on the hidden layer, we conducted ablation experiments. The diffusion model based on the original point cloud, denoted as Our-P, involves directly inputting 3D point cloud data into the diffusion model for training without passing through the point cloud autoencoder. As demonstrated in Tables 1, the point cloud diffusion model based on the hidden layer outperforms the diffusion model based on the original point cloud in both single-category and composite text-driven point cloud generation tasks.

Furthermore, Our-P and Ours required 280,000 and 220,000 epochs, respectively, to reach convergence. The time taken for a single iteration was 0.09 s and 0.03 s, respectively, and the memory usage during training was 11,057MB and 8,102MB, respectively. Therefore, the point cloud diffusion model based on the hidden layer exhibits superior performance compared to the diffusion model based on the original point cloud.

5 Conclusion

In this paper, We have developed a zero-shot learning framework that leverages a pre-trained CLIP model to establish associations between text, 2D images, and 3D shapes. By utilizing this association, we are able to transfer the mapping relationship between text and 3D shapes through the establishment of a mapping on readily available 2D image and 3D shape data. This approach can generate multi-category point clouds and alleviate the gap caused by the lack of large-scale text-3D point cloud data pairs. By implementing the diffusion and denoising processes on the hidden layer, training speed and memory usage are greatly optimized. However, there are still some limitations. The performance of Zero3D is constrained by the ability of the CLIP model to learn the correspondence between text and images, which in turn affects the quality of the generated 3D point cloud. In future work, we aim to employ improved text-image models to enhance the generation capabilities.

References

1. Bhagat, P., Choudhary, P., Singh, K.M.: A study on zero-shot learning from semantic viewpoint. Vis. Comput. **39**(5), 2149–2163 (2023)
2. Chen, K., Choy, C.B., Savva, M., Chang, A.X., Funkhouser, T., Savarese, S.: Text2shape: generating shapes from natural language by learning joint embeddings. arXiv preprint arXiv:1803.08495 (2018)
3. Chiang, P.Z., Tsai, M.S., Tseng, H.Y., Lai, W.S., Chiu, W.C.: Stylizing 3D scene via implicit representation and hypernetwork. In: Proceedings of the IEEE/CVF Winter Conference on Applications of Computer Vision, pp. 1475–1484 (2022)
4. Choy, C.B., Xu, D., Gwak, J.Y., Chen, K., Savarese, S.: 3D-R2N2: a unified approach for single and multi-view 3D object reconstruction. In: Leibe, B., Matas, J., Sebe, N., Welling, M. (eds.) ECCV 2016. LNCS, vol. 9912, pp. 628–644. Springer, Cham (2016). https://doi.org/10.1007/978-3-319-46484-8_38
5. Creswell, A., White, T., Dumoulin, V., Arulkumaran, K., Sengupta, B., Bharath, A.A.: Generative adversarial networks: an overview. IEEE Signal Process. Mag. **35**(1), 53–65 (2018)
6. Dinh, L., Sohl-Dickstein, J., Bengio, S.: Density estimation using real NVP. arXiv preprint arXiv:1605.08803 (2016)
7. Dosovitskiy, A., et al.: An image is worth 16x16 words: transformers for image recognition at scale. In: ICLR (2020)
8. Goodfellow, I., et al.: Generative adversarial networks. Commun. ACM **63**(11), 139–144 (2020)

9. Han, Z., Shang, M., Wang, X., Liu, Y.S., Zwicker, M.: Y2seq2seq: cross-modal representation learning for 3D shape and text by joint reconstruction and prediction of view and word sequences. In: AAAI, vol. 33, pp. 126–133 (2019)
10. Ho, J., Jain, A., Abbeel, P.: Denoising diffusion probabilistic models. Adv. Neural. Inf. Process. Syst. **33**, 6840–6851 (2020)
11. Ho, J., Salimans, T., Gritsenko, A., Chan, W., Norouzi, M., Fleet, D.J.: Video diffusion models. arXiv preprint arXiv:2204.03458 (2022)
12. Hong, F., Zhang, M., Pan, L., Cai, Z., Yang, L., Liu, Z.: Avatarclip: zero-shot text-driven generation and animation of 3D avatars. ACM Trans. Graph. (TOG) **41**(4), 1–19 (2022)
13. Jain, A., Mildenhall, B., Barron, J.T., Abbeel, P., Poole, B.: Zero-shot text-guided object generation with dream fields. In: CVPR, pp. 867–876 (2022)
14. Jiang, C., Sud, A., Makadia, A., Huang, J., Nießner, M., Funkhouser, T., et al.: Local implicit grid representations for 3D scenes. In: Proceedings of the IEEE/CVF Conference on Computer Vision and Pattern Recognition, pp. 6001–6010 (2020)
15. Kingma, D.P., Welling, M.: Auto-encoding variational bayes. arXiv preprint arXiv:1312.6114 (2013)
16. Li, S., Wu, F., fan, Y., Song, X., Dong, W.: PLDGAN: portrait line drawing generation with prior knowledge and conditioning target. Vis. Comput. 1–12 (2023)
17. Lin, C.H., et al.: Magic3D: high-resolution text-to-3D content creation. arXiv preprint arXiv.2211.10440 (2022)
18. Luo, S., Hu, W.: Diffusion probabilistic models for 3D point cloud generation. In: CVPR, pp. 2837–2845 (2021)
19. Mildenhall, B., Srinivasan, P.P., Tancik, M., Barron, J.T., Ramamoorthi, R., Ng, R.: NeRF: representing scenes as neural radiance fields for view synthesis. Commun. ACM **65**(1), 99–106 (2021)
20. Mohammad Khalid, N., Xie, T., Belilovsky, E., Popa, T.: Clip-mesh: generating textured meshes from text using pretrained image-text models. In: SIGGRAPH, pp. 1–8 (2022)
21. Poole, B., Jain, A., Barron, J.T., Mildenhall, B.: Dreamfusion: text-to-3D using 2D diffusion. arXiv preprint arXiv:2209.14988 (2022)
22. Presnov, D., Berels, M., Kolb, A.: Pacemod: parametric contour-based modifications for glyph generation. Vis. Comput. 1–14 (2023)
23. Qi, C.R., Su, H., Mo, K., Guibas, L.J.: Pointnet: deep learning on point sets for 3D classification and segmentation. In: CVPR, pp. 652–660 (2017)
24. Rezende, D., Mohamed, S.: Variational inference with normalizing flows. In: International Conference on Machine Learning, pp. 1530–1538. PMLR (2015)
25. Sanghi, A., et al.: Clip-forge: towards zero-shot text-to-shape generation. In: CVPR, pp. 18603–18613 (2022)
26. Shen, Y., Feng, C., Yang, Y., Tian, D.: Mining point cloud local structures by kernel correlation and graph pooling. In: CVPR, pp. 4548–4557 (2018)
27. Shi, Z., Peng, S., Xu, Y., Liao, Y., Shen, Y.: Deep generative models on 3D representations: a survey. arXiv preprint arXiv:2210.15663 (2022)
28. Song, Y., Ermon, S.: Generative modeling by estimating gradients of the data distribution. In: Advances in Neural Information Processing Systems, vol. 32 (2019)
29. Tang, C., Yang, X., Wu, B., Han, Z., Chang, Y.: Part2word: learning joint embedding of point clouds and text by matching parts to words. arXiv preprint arXiv:2107.01872 (2021)
30. Upadhyay, A.K., Khandelwal, K.: Metaverse: the future of immersive training. Strateg. HR Rev. **21**(3), 83–86 (2022)

31. Valsesia, D., Fracastoro, G., Magli, E.: Learning localized generative models for 3D point clouds via graph convolution. In: International Conference on Learning Representations (2019)

32. Wu, J., Zhang, C., Xue, T., Freeman, B., Tenenbaum, J.: Learning a probabilistic latent space of object shapes via 3D generative-adversarial modeling. In: NeurIPS, vol. 29 (2016)

33. Yang, G., Huang, X., Hao, Z., Liu, M.Y., Belongie, S., Hariharan, B.: Pointflow: 3D point cloud generation with continuous normalizing flows. In: ICCV, pp. 4541–4550 (2019)

34. Yang, Y., Feng, C., Shen, Y., Tian, D.: Foldingnet: point cloud auto-encoder via deep grid deformation. In: CVPR, pp. 206–215 (2018)

35. Zhou, L., Du, Y., Wu, J.: 3D shape generation and completion through point-voxel diffusion. In: ICCV, pp. 5826–5835 (2021)

Seeing is No Longer Believing: A Survey on the State of Deepfakes, AI-Generated Humans, and Other Nonveridical Media

Andreea Pocol[1]([envelope]) [ID], Lesley Istead[1,2] [ID], Sherman Siu[1] [ID], Sabrina Mokhtari[1], and Sara Kodeiri[1]

[1] University of Waterloo, Waterloo, ON, Canada
apocol@uwaterloo.ca
[2] Carleton University, Ottawa, ON, Canada

Abstract. Did you see that crazy photo of Chris Hemsworth wearing a gorgeous, blue ballgown? What about the leaked photo of Bernie Sanders dancing with Sarah Palin? If these don't sound familiar, it's because these events never happened–but with text-to-image generators and deepfake AI technologies, it is effortless for *anyone* to produce such images. Over the last decade, there has been an explosive rise in research papers, as well as tool development and usage, dedicated to deepfakes, text-to-image generation, and image synthesis. These tools provide users with great creative power, but with that power comes "great responsibility;" it is just as easy to produce nefarious and misleading content as it is to produce comedic or artistic content. Therefore, given the recent advances in the field, it is important to assess the impact they may have. In this paper, we conduct meta-research on deepfakes to visualize the evolution of these tools and paper publications. We also identify key authors, research institutions, and papers based on bibliometric data. Finally, we conduct a survey that tests the ability of participants to distinguish photos of real people from fake, AI-generated images of people. Based on our meta-research, survey, and background study, we conclude that humans are falling behind in the race to keep up with AI, and we must be conscious of the societal impact.

Keywords: deepfakes · AI image synthesis · text-to-image synthesis

1 Introduction

Computer science is constantly advancing, but are we putting the same amount of effort into researching the ethics behind the technology? With the advent of amazing technology, we are given the power to do bad things – and with great power comes great responsibility. The impact of scientists may be both negative and positive, hence the importance of responsible AI development. Deepfakes, which are synthetic media wherein one person's face is replaced with another, have both good and bad applications. Similar tools, such as generative image

© The Author(s), under exclusive license to Springer Nature Switzerland AG 2024
B. Sheng et al. (Eds.): CGI 2023, LNCS 14496, pp. 427–440, 2024.
https://doi.org/10.1007/978-3-031-50072-5_34

technologies (i.e., DALL-E 2 [24] and other text-to-image tools), provide the ability to replace faces, replace or insert people/items, or generate completely fictitious images with the likeness of real or artificial humans. Both methods present users with the ability to produce beautiful images or art–but also fake news, blackmail, and propaganda. These technologies are already being used in many films and television shows, including Star Wars, The Mandalorian, and Sassy Justice. Applications such as using the likeness of actors to profit after their death, are more of a gray area rather than definitively good or bad. Note that the internet is rife with nonveridical media. While there is nothing new about disinformation (150 years ago, disinformation was even easier to propagate except for the latency), the medium keeps changing. AI image synthesis is one of the latest threats to the truth.

The utilitarian school of thought would argue that technology should march forward despite the potential negative impacts, but we take a step back to examine how far AI has come and whether society is still equipped to handle it. Several over-arching questions motivate our study. Has AI gotten so good at generating realistic nonveridical, or fake, media that we can no longer distinguish what is real? Is society prepared? More importantly, *can we still trust our own eyes?*

We begin this investigation with a background study of the history and development of deepfakes. We use bibliometric data to produce insightful visualizations of trends and impact. We then assess the ability of 260 participants to distinguish real images from fake, AI-generated images in a user study that provides insight into how good the state-of-the-art tools (e.g., Stable Diffusion [26], DALL-E 2) have gotten.

2   Background

Several years ago, [3] published a paper on video rewriting with the aim of smoother dubbing. Many consider this to be the first publication on deepfakes, or at least the groundwork. What we know as deepfakes today can be traced back to 2014 when researchers began exploring the use of Generative Adversarial Networks (GANs) [9] for image and video generation. GANs are a neural network consisting of two competing models: a generator and a discriminator. The generator produces synthetic images or videos, while the discriminator determines whether the media is real or fake. The two models are trained together, with the generator attempting to create synthetic media that the discriminator cannot distinguish from real media.

It is difficult to determine the exact first deepfake ever created, as the term "deepfake" only emerged in 2017, and the technology behind it has been in development for much longer. However, some early examples of generative AI art include the "DeepDream" images[1] created by Google engineer Alexander Mordvintsev in 2015 and the "ThisPersonDoesNotExist"[2] website created by software engineer Philip Wang in 2019, which generated realistic-looking images of people

---

[1] https://www.tensorflow.org/tutorials/generative/deepdream.
[2] https://thispersondoesnotexist.com/.

using GANs. Deepfakes as we understand them today, however, emerged in 2017 with the creation of a Reddit user named "deepfakes," who used GANs to generate synthetic celebrity pornography [14]. The user's creations quickly gained attention and sparked a discussion about the potential consequences of deepfake technology.

However, it was not until the release of the Deepfake Detection Challenge [6] in 2019 that the use of GANs for deepfake creation gained widespread attention. The challenge, which was sponsored by AWS, Facebook, and Microsoft, aimed to encourage the development of algorithms that could detect deepfakes.

Since then, deepfakes have become more sophisticated and easier to create, leading to concerns about their potential impact on society [11]. While deepfakes, as a tool, can be used for positive (e.g., entertainment) purposes, most researchers have raised concerns about what they can do in the long run. They believe there is more damage to be done than problems to solve [20,28]. Some even consider the damage already uncontrollable; so far, nefarious applications have included fake news, impersonating individuals online for propaganda and other malicious purposes, blackmail, and orchestrating public behavior and opinion. These effects aren't necessarily raised from widespread and viral content; even one instance is enough to convince an individual [21]. Some have even pointed out the possibility of deepfakes being used to manipulate elections or spread disinformation [20]. Because of this, there have been proposals of appropriate frameworks [13] and robust tools [27] to better handle this technology. For example, in 2019, the U.S. government passed the Deepfake Report Act, which requires the Science and Technology Directorate in the Department of Homeland Security to report at specified intervals on the state of digital content forgery technology. They have defined digital forgery as "including artificial intelligence and machine learning techniques, to fabricate or manipulate audio, visual, or text content with the intent to mislead."[3]

Another problem that deepfakes inherently contribute to is discrediting media as a whole. Over time, this causes videos and other media to carry less perceived weight than they did before [7]. In order to address the epistemic threat of deepfakes, it is important for individuals to be able to critically evaluate the information they encounter and to verify the authenticity of media before they share it.

In addition to addressing and trying to prevent the negative consequences, there have also been efforts to try and detect deepfakes after the damage is done. Detecting them could be perceptual, computational, or provenance-based [8].

3   Meta-research of Deepfake Research

We felt that there was a lack of meta-research in the field of AI image synthesis, particularly deepfakes. This section is devoted to filling this gap. We assess the number of deepfake papers published per year, the top contributing researchers

---

[3] https://www.congress.gov/bill/116th-congress/house-bill/3600/all-info.

and research institutions to deepfake research, and key metrics such as the number of monthly downloads of key tools in deepfake generation and detection. All of our code is available on GitHub.

3.1 The Evolution of Deepfakes

We used Semantic Scholar's keyword search engine to search for the number of 'deepfake' paper publications over the years. The results in Fig. 1a show an increasing trend in deepfake-related publications.

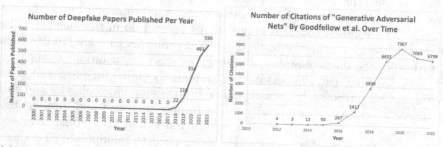

(a) The explosive rise in the number of deepfake papers published over the years.

(b) Number of citations of the "Generative Adversarial Nets" over the years.

Fig. 1. Publication and citation frequencies.

The rise of deepfake models can be traced to academia, such as CihaNet [19], FaceController [30], FaceInpainter [15], SimSwap [4], FaceShifter [16], FSGAN [22], IPGAN [2], and FaceSwap [23].

More importantly, many of the underlying tools and technologies used to create deepfakes and other realistic, artificially-generated images stem from academia. For example, the paper "Generative Adversarial Nets" is the 2014 NIPS paper that gave rise to generative-adversarial-network-based deepfakes, including tools like Deep Nostalgia and MoCoGAN, though it does not mention deepfakes. It has 34,200 citations. As shown in Fig. 1b, the citations of this paper have increased drastically over time.

According to DBLP, the top contributing authors to the field of deepfakes (and their corresponding number of papers) are:

- Simon S. Woo, 18 publications
- Siwei Lyu, 15 publications
- Yuezun Li, 12 publications
- Shahroz Tariq, 11 publications

Note that DBLP is a very restrictive dataset focused on a select few, top computer science conferences.

The top dedicated deepfake papers (by citation count) in this research area are: [5, 6, 10, 17, 18]. Note that they are all about detection rather than generation, in the wake of rising concerns.

According to CS Rankings, the top AI/ML institutions around the world in terms of acceptance to major conferences from 2000–2022 are Carnegie Mellon University (8.6%), Tsinghua University (5.6%), University of Alberta (4.7%), and Technion (4.4%). Unsurprisingly, that suggests the countries outputting the most significant AI/ML research – the AI/ML 'hotspots' – are the US, China, Canada, and Israel.

3.2   Deepfake Software

One of the most significant applications of GANs is image creation. These models have played a critical role in the advent of deepfake applications. Therefore, in addition to the usage of deepfake applications, we also studied the usage of GAN libraries in Python, which is generally considered to be the best programming language for AI because of its rich, open-source machine learning frameworks (e.g., Pytorch, Tensorflow). We used the data from Python Package Index (PyPI) which was available on Google Cloud BigQuery to retrieve information about various Python packages that are used for generating deepfake images.

In addition, with the growth of deepfake applications, a large body of research has focused on designing deepfake/face detection mechanisms to distinguish between real and fake images. Therefore, there has been a growing number of applications and software packages on the internet that help detect fake images. As a result, we also study some of the most famous packages and libraries from Pypi, again by querying BigQuery database. We found increasing usage trends in all, beginning in 2019. Academia itself has produced a lot of software related to the recognition of nonveridical images, such as [1, 12], and [29].

4   User Study

The goal of our user study was to assess the ability of participants to discern real photos from fake, artificially-generated photos, and thereby further our understanding of the societal implications of such nonveridical, AI-generated media. We define per-image classification accuracy as the overall accuracy of participants' guesses with respect to a given image. We define per-user classification accuracy as the user's overall correctness score. We felt that if the overall per-image classification accuracy exceeded 85%, then the data would suggest that humans are currently quite adept at differentiating real images from fake images.

The survey[4] was disseminated on Twitter, Reddit, Instagram, and other communication channels. In total, 260 members of the public chose to complete our study.

Participants were asked to view a series of images on their personal devices. For each image, they were asked whether they believe it to be real or fake. If

---

[4] https://forms.gle/CnzQN9BbmWMEuHn99.

they wished to provide any commentary justifying their belief, they were able to enter it. Note that each image was shown on its own separate page of the survey.

Importantly, the survey reminded participants:

Try not to overthink your answers. A brief glance, similar to the attention you'd afford a news headline photo, is encouraged. Note that heavily photoshopped models would still count as 'real,' as they are edited versions of real subjects. In essence, you are being asked to answer whether you believe this person exists.

We used 20 test images, 10 real and 10 fake, randomly ordered. The fake images are shown in Table 1. Stable Diffusion (Wavyfusion) was used to generate 9 of them; DALL-E 2 was used to generate 1. The reason we did not use DALL-E 2 more is given in Sect. 5. We procured 2 from Reddit.[5] The real images, selected via Google Image search, are shown in Table 2. Each image is accompanied by its corresponding classification accuracy. The numerical label is its placement in the survey list.

Note that the images used in this study are not specifically deepfakes. While we certainly can give Stable Diffusion and DALL-E 2 a seed image that is someone's actual face—as in Figs. 2 and 3—it was not the best choice for this study. Generative AI tools such as Stable Diffusion, which turn text into images, provide us with the ability to produce *completely fake* people in *completely fake* situations in addition to replacing a face or body. This ability is far more powerful than traditional deepfake tools. Generative, text-to-image AI tools are also more prevalent, as they are more plentiful, affordable, and accessible in our experience. Furthermore, dedicated deepfake tools available on the web tend to be costly and primarily operate on video.

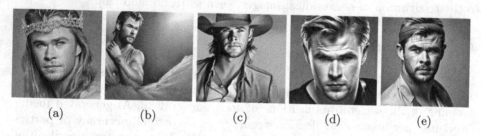

(a)   (b)   (c)   (d)   (e)

Fig. 2. A few deepfake images we generated using Stable Diffusion 2.1 of actor Chris Hemsworth in less than 5 s each. They may seem ridiculous, but this becomes dangerous when a more plausible premise is used.

---

[5] https://www.reddit.com/r/StableDiffusion/comments/zhfre0/realistic_portraits_wi
th_an_unexpected_model/.

Table 1. Fake test images.

Image	Classification Accuracy
(a) 1	• % Guessed Right • % Guessed Wrong
(b) 2	• % Guessed Right • % Guessed Wrong
(c) 5	• % Guessed Right • % Guessed Wrong
(d) 9	• % Guessed Right • % Guessed Wrong
(e) 11	• % Guessed Right • % Guessed Wrong
(f) 12	• % Guessed Right • % Guessed Wrong
(g) 13	• % Guessed Right • % Guessed Wrong
(h) 15	• % Guessed Right • % Guessed Wrong
(I) 17	• % Guessed Right • % Guessed Wrong
(j) 18	• % Guessed Right • % Guessed Wrong

Table 2. Real test images.

Image	Classification Accuracy
(k) 3	• % Guessed Right • % Guessed Wrong
(l) 4	• % Guessed Right • % Guessed Wrong
(m) 6	• % Guessed Right • % Guessed Wrong
(n) 7	• % Guessed Right • % Guessed Wrong
(o) 8	• % Guessed Right • % Guessed Wrong
(p) 10	• % Guessed Right • % Guessed Wrong
(q) 14	• % Guessed Right • % Guessed Wrong
(r) 16	• % Guessed Right • % Guessed Wrong
(s) 19	• % Guessed Right • % Guessed Wrong
(t) 20	• % Guessed Right • % Guessed Wrong

(a) The original.   (b) The deepfake (Stable Diffusion 2.1.)

Fig. 3. A deepfake image we generated using swapping, which may be more controversial.

4.1   Results

The overall image classification accuracy is 61%. This is also the average per-user classification accuracy, as shown in Fig. 4c. The average correctness for fake images is 52.6% (variance 0.0198) and 68.5% (variance 0.0187) for real images. Our results indicate that participants were more likely to correctly classify images of real people, as shown in Fig. 4a. The lack of overlapping confidence intervals in Fig. 4b indicates that there is a statistically significant difference between the classification of real and fake images amongst participants, proven using an ANOVA test (Table 3).

A confusion matrix, presented in Table 4, further illustrates participants' classification accuracy by illustrating the occurrences of false positives (fake images classified by participants as real) and negatives (real images classified as fake). These results demonstrate that people are *not* good at separating real images from fake ones, easily allowing the propagation of false and potentially dangerous narratives. Notable exceptions include obviously fake images such as Table 1(c) – image 5 in the survey.

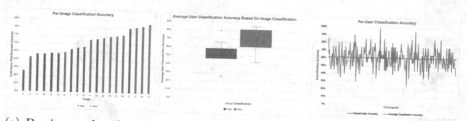

(a) Per-image classification accuracy.   (b) Average user classification accuracy.   (c) Per-user classification accuracy.

Fig. 4. Classification accuracy by image, type, and participant.

Next, we wanted to know which gender—male, female, or other—is better at the recognition task. Our results suggest that individuals identifying as female performed best, which is backed by previous scientific studies [25]. Figure 5a shows the results in a box-and-whiskers plot. Note that the number of male, female and other participants is not equal. We performed an ANOVA test on the results, which indicated that there is no statistically significant difference in classification accuracy between any of the genders.

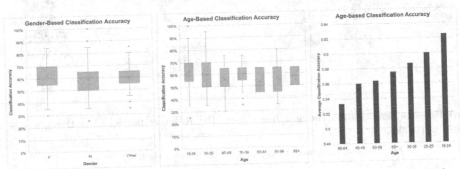

(a) Average gender-based classification accuracy.

(b) Average age-based classification accuracy.

(c) Average age-based classification accuracy, sorted.

Fig. 5. Classification accuracy based on age and gender.

We also evaluated classification accuracy by age. Overall age-based classification accuracy is shown in Fig. 5b and 5c. The results suggest the most adept age group is the 18–24 bracket. However, we note that the distribution of participants was not equal between age brackets—51.3% of participants were between the ages of 18 and 24, 20.7% were between the ages of 25 and 29, 16.1% were between the ages of 30 and 39, and the remaining age brackets had less than 6% each. Furthermore, even if the sample sizes were equal, there is no guarantee that the sample would be representative of the population. Overall, as the largely-overlapping confidence intervals in Figs. 5b and 5a show, there is no statistically significant difference in real/fake image recognition across genders or age groups and an ANOVA test agrees with this conclusion.

4.2 Participant Comments

Participants were asked to provide comments on why they selected real/fake for each image. We analyzed their responses using text mining and keyword extraction and produced word clouds to visualize the common justifications participants provided for real and fake responses (Fig. 6a and 6b).

Further analysis of the fake justifications for keywords of interest suggests that eyes were the primary indicator of whether an image was real or fake, as shown in Fig. 6c.

(a) Reasons participants thought images were fake.

(b) Reasons participants thought images were real.

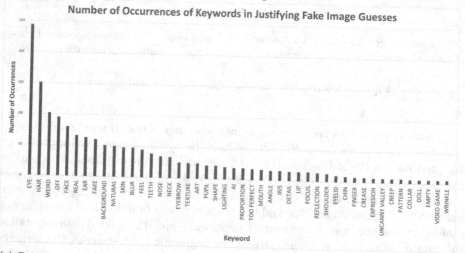

(c) Prominent, interesting keywords extracted from reasons participants thought images were fake.

Fig. 6. Survey participant justifications.

Table 3. A condensed confusion matrix format.

		Predicted Classification	
		Positive (PP)	Negative (PN)
Actual Condition	Positive (P)	True Positive (TP)	False negative (FN)
	Negative (N)	False positive (FP)	True negative (TN)

Table 4. A condensed confusion matrix indicating the number of images that were identified into each category.

		Predicted Classification	
		Positive (PP)	Negative (PN)
Actual Condition	Positive (P)	8	2
	Negative (N)	5	5

5   Discussion

Overall, we found that generative AI struggles to produce realistic eyes and teeth. In particular, a common sign that an image is AI-generated is the presence of heterochromia. Another common indicator is white pixels around the eyes. Empirically, we found Stable Diffusion to produce more realistic eyes than DALL-E 2. A tell-tale sign of an AI-generated image is heterochromia, whereas a real photo would contain detailed, homochromatic irises. White pixels around the eyes are another indicator. Empirically, we found that Stable Diffusion produced more realistic images than DALL-E 2. For example, Fig. 7 shows some images we generated with DALL-E 2, focused on the eyes. People generally fared well at identifying real images when they contained flaws like skin imperfections. It is worth noting, however, that we can artificially generate such imperfections with well-chosen prompts, so this is no consolation. Overall, we received feedback from many participants after the survey, saying that they 'had a really hard time' figuring out which images were real, and at some point they just 'randomly guessed.' Some reached out directly via email to request the answers. At the outset of our experiment, we theorized that a classification accuracy of over 85% would indicate that humans are still ahead of AI. The survey results showed that classification accuracy is, on average, 61%, which falls short. This suggests that we are failing to stay afloat with AI advancements.

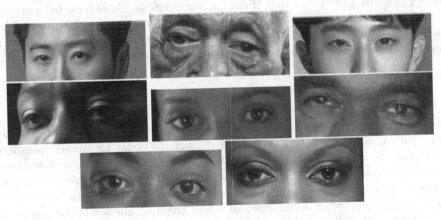

Fig. 7. Unrealistic eyes generated with DALL-E 2.

6   Limitations and Future Work

Image compression, device/screen size and resolution, and a plethora of other similar factors may all affect user perception of the images in our study. As this was not a supervised study, distractions in the environment may have also affected participants' concentration and discernment.

Moreover, we used a diverse/representative dataset but chose images arbitrarily rather than systematically. This prevents observant participants from categorizing the data into demographic-based real-fake pairs, which would enhance their performance on the test. This arbitrary selection means that some demographics are underrepresented, however. On the one hand, this does not matter very much because we are not studying per-subject-demographic classification accuracy. On the other hand, the question of bias comes into play. We are unsure if classification accuracy may be affected by unconscious bias. Future work could seek to control and balance subject demographics as well as other aspects of the image, like background, jewelry, fabrics, etc. The challenge will be to somehow obscure the aforementioned real-fake pairs. Discrimination is always possible and may depend on the participant's culture and ethnicity. In future studies, we will collect more demographic information about our participants. However, the more selective our groups are, the smaller they will be, which makes statistical analysis challenging.

A future study will explore adding the faces of celebrities to the study to see if subject recognition impacts the participant's guess. It should also ask two additional questions: "how successful do you think you'll be?" at the start, and "how successful do you think you were?" at the end.

Finally, in the future, we would like to conduct natural language processing on Twitter data to extract deepfake concerns, perhaps studying the number of retweets or likes of deepfake posts. In general, we would like to examine the number of issues raised over time. Perhaps, for example, there have been articles decrying mass dissemination of an AI-generated image/video of a presidential candidate in some compromising context around election time, raising the alarm that it's fake, but the image/video was still widely believed by the masses.

7 Conclusion

It is our responsibility, as scientists, to assess our work from an ethical standpoint, with consideration for its societal impact. In order to answer questions like *where are we in this research field?* or *how far have we come?*, we need concrete data, which can be accrued via surveys. In this paper, we present the results of a survey we conducted to answer precisely those questions. We gave 260 participants a set of 20 images and asked them to guess whether each was real or fake, optionally providing justification for their guess. Average classification accuracy was 61%, with users faring better at classifying real photos than fake ones. The results of the survey show that AI has come a frighteningly long way, making it difficult for the average internet user to gauge whether an image that comes across their screen is real or fake. In lieu of ground truth, we must exercise caution. Seeing is no longer believing, and probably never will be again.

References

1. Afchar, D., Nozick, V., Yamagishi, J., Echizen, I.: MesoNet: a compact facial video forgery detection network. In: 2018 IEEE International Workshop on Information Forensics and Security (WIFS). IEEE, December 2018. https://doi.org/10.1109/wifs.2018.8630761
2. Bao, J., Chen, D., Wen, F., Li, H., Hua, G.: Towards open-set identity preserving face synthesis. In: 2018 IEEE/CVF Conference on Computer Vision and Pattern Recognition, pp. 6713–6722 (2018). https://doi.org/10.1109/CVPR.2018.00702
3. Bregler, C., Covell, M., Slaney, M.: Video rewrite: driving visual speech with audio. In: Proceedings of the 24th Annual Conference on Computer Graphics and Interactive Techniques, SIGGRAPH 1997, pp. 353–360. ACM Press/Addison-Wesley Publishing Co., USA (1997). https://doi.org/10.1145/258734.258880
4. Chen, R., Chen, X., Ni, B., Ge, Y.: SimSwap: an efficient framework for high fidelity face swapping. In: Proceedings of the 28th ACM International Conference on Multimedia, MM 2020, New York, NY, USA, pp. 2003–2011. Association for Computing Machinery (2020). https://doi.org/10.1145/3394171.3413630
5. Dolhansky, B., et al.: The deepfake detection challenge dataset. arXiv:2006.07397 (2020)
6. Dolhansky, B., Howes, R., Pflaum, B., Baram, N., Canton-Ferrer, C.: The deepfake detection challenge (DFDC) preview dataset. arXiv:1910.08854 (2019)
7. Fallis, D.: The epistemic threat of deepfakes. Philos. Technol. **34**(4), 623–643 (2021). https://doi.org/10.1007/s13347-020-00419-2
8. Farid, H.: Creating, using, misusing, and detecting deep fakes. J. Online Trust Saf. **1**(4), September 2022. https://doi.org/10.54501/jots.v1i4.56. https://tsjournal.org/index.php/jots/article/view/56
9. Goodfellow, I.J., et al.: Generative adversarial networks (2014)
10. Guera, D., Delp, E.J.: Deepfake video detection using recurrent neural networks. In: 2018 15th IEEE International Conference on Advanced Video and Signal Based Surveillance (AVSS), pp. 1–6 (2018)
11. Hancock, J.T., Bailenson, J.N.: The social impact of deepfakes. Cyberpsychol. Behav. Soc. Netw. **24**(3), 149–152 (2021). https://doi.org/10.1089/cyber.2021.29208.jth. pMID: 33760669
12. Huh, M., Liu, A., Owens, A., Efros, A.A.: Fighting fake news: image splice detection via learned self-consistency. In: Ferrari, V., Hebert, M., Sminchisescu, C., Weiss, Y. (eds.) ECCV 2018. LNCS, vol. 11215, pp. 106–124. Springer, Cham (2018). https://doi.org/10.1007/978-3-030-01252-6_7
13. Kietzmann, J., Lee, L.W., McCarthy, I.P., Kietzmann, T.C.: Deepfakes: trick or treat? Bus. Horizons **63**(2), 135–146 (2020). https://doi.org/10.1016/j.bushor.2019.11.006. https://www.sciencedirect.com/science/article/pii/S0007681319301600. Artificial Intelligence and Machine Learning
14. Korshunov, P., Marcel, S.: Deepfakes: a new threat to face recognition? Assessment and detection (2018)
15. Li, J., Li, Z., Cao, J., Song, X., He, R.: FaceInpainter: high fidelity face adaptation to heterogeneous domains. In: Proceedings of the IEEE/CVF Conference on Computer Vision and Pattern Recognition (CVPR), pp. 5089–5098, June 2021
16. Li, L., Bao, J., Yang, H., Chen, D., Wen, F.: FaceShifter: towards high fidelity and occlusion aware face swapping (2019). https://doi.org/10.48550/ARXIV.1912.13457. https://arxiv.org/abs/1912.13457

17. Li, Y., Lyu, S.: Exposing deepfake videos by detecting face warping artifacts. arXiv:1811.00656 (2018)
18. Li, Y., Yang, X., Sun, P., Qi, H., Lyu, S.: Celeb-DF: a large-scale challenging dataset for deepfake forensics. In: 2020 IEEE/CVF Conference on Computer Vision and Pattern Recognition (CVPR), pp. 3204–3213 (2019)
19. Liu, Y., Xiang, M., Shi, H., Mei, T.: One-stage context and identity hallucination network. In: Proceedings of the 29th ACM International Conference on Multimedia, MM 2021, New York, NY, USA, pp. 835–843. Association for Computing Machinery (2021). https://doi.org/10.1145/3474085.3475257
20. Mirsky, Y., Lee, W.: The creation and detection of deepfakes: a survey. ACM Comput. Surv. (CSUR) **54**(1), 1–41 (2021). https://doi.org/10.1145/3425780
21. Nguyen, T.T., et al.: Deep learning for deepfakes creation and detection: a survey. Comput. Vis. Image Underst. **223**, 103525 (2022). https://doi.org/10.1016/j.cviu.2022.103525. https://www.sciencedirect.com/science/article/pii/S1077314222001114
22. Nirkin, Y., Keller, Y., Hassner, T.: FSGAN: subject agnostic face swapping and reenactment (2019). https://doi.org/10.48550/ARXIV.1908.05932. https://arxiv.org/abs/1908.05932
23. Nirkin, Y., Masi, I., Tran, A., Hassner, T., Medioni, G.G.: On face segmentation, face swapping, and face perception. In: 2018 13th IEEE International Conference on Automatic Face & Gesture Recognition (FG 2018), pp. 98–105 (2017)
24. Ramesh, A., Dhariwal, P., Nichol, A., Chu, C., Chen, M.: Hierarchical text-conditional image generation with clip latents. arXiv:2204.06125 (2022)
25. Rennels, J., Cummings, A.: Sex differences in facial scanning: similarities and dissimilarities between infants and adults. Int. J. Behav. Dev. **37**, 111–117 (2013). https://doi.org/10.1177/0165025412472411
26. Rombach, R., Blattmann, A., Lorenz, D., Esser, P., Ommer, B.: High-resolution image synthesis with latent diffusion models. In: Proceedings of the IEEE/CVF Conference on Computer Vision and Pattern Recognition, pp. 10684–10695 (2022)
27. Tolosana, R., Vera-Rodriguez, R., Fierrez, J., Morales, A., Ortega-Garcia, J.: Deepfakes and beyond: a survey of face manipulation and fake detection. Inf. Fusion **64**, 131–148 (2020). https://doi.org/10.1016/j.inffus.2020.06.014. https://www.sciencedirect.com/science/article/pii/S1566253520303110
28. Westerlund, M.: The emergence of deepfake technology: a review. Technol. Innov. Manag. Rev. **9**, 40–53 (2019). https://doi.org/10.22215/timreview/1282. https://timreview.ca/article/1282
29. Wu, Y., AbdAlmageed, W., Natarajan, P.: Mantra-Net: manipulation tracing network for detection and localization of image forgeries with anomalous features. In: Proceedings of the IEEE/CVF Conference on Computer Vision and Pattern Recognition (CVPR), June 2019
30. Xu, Z., et al.: FaceController: controllable attribute editing for face in the wild (2021). https://doi.org/10.48550/ARXIV.2102.11464. https://arxiv.org/abs/2102.11464

Diffusion-Based Semantic Image Synthesis from Sparse Layouts

Yuantian Huang[⊠], Satoshi Iizuka, and Kazuhiro Fukui

University of Tsukuba, Ibaraki 305-8577, Japan
huang_yuantian@cvlab.cs.tsukuba.ac.jp, {iizuka,kfukui}@cs.tsukuba.ac.jp

Abstract. We present an efficient framework that utilizes diffusion models to generate landscape images from sparse semantic layouts. Previous approaches use dense semantic label maps to generate images, where the quality of the results is highly dependent on the accuracy of the input semantic layouts. However, it is not trivial to create detailed and accurate semantic layouts in practice. To address this challenge, we carefully design a random masking process that effectively simulates real user input during the model training phase, making it more practical for real-world applications. Our framework leverages the Semantic Diffusion Model (SDM) as a generator to create full landscape images from sparse label maps, which are created randomly during the random masking process. Missing semantic information is complemented based on the learned image structure. Furthermore, we achieve comparable inference speed to GAN-based models through a model distillation process while preserving the generation quality. After training with the well-designed random masking process, our proposed framework is able to generate high-quality landscape images with sparse and intuitive inputs, which is useful for practical applications. Experiments show that our proposed method outperforms existing approaches both quantitatively and qualitatively. Code is available at https://github.com/sky24h/SIS_from_Sparse_Layouts.

Keywords: Semantic Image Synthesis · Sparse Input · Diffusion Models

1 Introduction

Semantic image synthesis refers to a subfield of image synthesis, which aims to generate new images conditioned on semantic layouts that contains required features and structural information of the image. It can be utilized for a variety of applications, including image editing, content creation, and artificial intelligence art. The earliest attempt at this task goes back at least to image analogies [8], where they automatically learned filters from training data based on a simplistic multi-scale autoregression.

This study was supported by the Japan Science and Technology Agency Support for Pioneering Research Initiated by the Next Generation (JST SPRING); Grant Number JPMJSP2124.

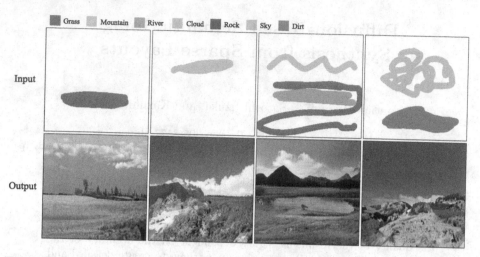

Grass   Mountain   River   Cloud   Rock   Sky   Dirt

Input

Output

Fig. 1. Our approach can synthesize landscape images from more sparse and intuitive semantic layouts rather than detailed and precise layouts while maintaining the same level of generation quality.

With the recent success of generative adversarial networks (GANs [7]), data-driven generation approaches have become a dominant trend. Several GAN-based methods have achieved good results by directly learning image-to-image mapping, such as pix2pixGAN, which first established a common framework for learning the mapping of paired data and successfully generated realistic images. Furthermore, Park *et al.* [17] proposed SPatially-ADaptive DEnormal-ization (SPADE), which outperforms previous methods on the task of seman-tic image synthesis. Subsequent models, including SEAN [34], SMIS [35], and OASIS [28], extend the SPADE model in different aspects. Recently, Wang *et al.* [30] developed a semantic image synthesis approach based on Denoising Dif-fusion Probabilistic Models (DDPMs) [11]. This method integrates SPADE into the residual blocks of the decoder networks to better leverage the information in the input semantic mask, leading to improvements in the overall quality of the generated images.

Existing approaches for semantic image synthesis have focused on process-ing a comprehensive semantic layout that captures the entire scene, which is equivalent to the reverse task of semantic segmentation. However, in real-world applications that rely on human-authored layouts as input, creating detailed and precise layouts that accurately represent real-world scenes can be quite challeng-ing. To address this issue, we carefully design a random masking process that enables the simulation to mimic actual user input, thereby making the inputs better suited for use in real-world settings.

Our generator is constructed based on the Semantic Diffusion Model (SDM) [30]. It feeds noisy images to the encoder of the U-Net structure, similar to other diffusion-based image generation methods. Additionally, the semantic layouts are injected into the SPADE [17] layers of the decoder. By progressively refining the generated results, it achieves state-of-the-art performance on the task of semantic image synthesis. Moreover, we find that the methodology of diffusion is most appropriate for our masking design and achieves the best results for more sparse and intuitive inputs. We also accomplished comparable inference speed to GAN-based models through a model distillation process while preserving generation quality.

After training with the well-designed random masking process, our proposed framework can generate high-quality landscape images with sparse and intuitive inputs (Fig. 1), which enables the practical application of semantic image synthesis in scenarios that require human-authored layouts. We evaluate our approach quantitatively with both automatic metrics and a perceptual user study, in addition to qualitative results. Results demonstrate that our approach outperforms existing approaches in all metrics.

This study presents the following contributions:

- A well-designed masking strategy that simulates human-authored sparse layouts, improving the practical application of semantic image synthesis.
- A diffusion-based generator with a model distillation process that enables fast sampling while preserving better generation quality compared to GAN-based models.
- In-depth evaluation of our method with both qualitative and quantitative comparisons with existing approaches.

2   Related Work

2.1   Semantic Image Synthesis

Semantic image synthesis focuses on generating new images conditioned on semantic image maps and is mainly dominated by GAN-based [7] approaches in recent years. For example, the pix2pixGAN [12] established a common framework for learning the mapping of paired data and successfully generated realistic images. This approach has been extended in the following research [3,18,29,31]. Furthermore, Park et al. [17] proposed the SPatially-ADaptive DEnormalization (SPADE) approach, which outperforms previous methods in generating photorealistic images conditioned on semantic layouts. Various improvements have been made to the SPADE architecture in different aspects, such as SMIS [35], which produces semantically multimodal images by replacing all regular convolution layers in the generator with group convolutions, and SEAN [34], which uses style input images to create spatially varying normalization parameters per semantic region. Additionally, OASIS [28] surpasses SPADE in diversity while maintaining similar quality by redesigning the discriminator. Besides GAN-based models, Chen et al. [2] proposed the Cascaded Refinement Network (CRN) for high-resolution semantic image synthesis. It has been extended by subsequent methods [14,18]. However, these approaches still underperform compared to state-of-the-art GAN-based models. Recently, with the advent of diffusion models, SDM [30] has incorporated SPADE with Denoising Diffusion Probabilistic

Models (DDPMs), enabling better generation fidelity and diversity simultaneously. We construct our generator based on SDM, which outperforms GAN-based methods in terms of generation quality and is most appropriate for our masking design.

2.2   Sparse and Intuitive User Input on Image Synthesis

In real-world computer graphics applications, users often prefer to provide intuitive inputs rather than comprehensive ones, as producing the latter can be highly challenging. Intuitive inputs may include text, sketches, scene graphs, and semantic layouts for image synthesis tasks. For instance, text-to-image synthesis models [19–21,32] generate photorealistic images from text descriptions, while other works focus on generating images from edges and sketches [5,6,12,15,33] and scene graphs [1,13]. These inputs are easy to create but lack precise control and struggle to produce high-quality results due to the difficulty of training. Among the many types of inputs, we believe that semantic layouts offer the most control and interactivity while providing plausible results, as the semantic labels provide precise shape and content. However, creating a semantic layout that perfectly matches the inputs to the training set is always challenging. In contrast to previous methods that require users to reproduce detailed semantic label maps, in this paper, we propose simulating human-authored semantic layouts during training using a well-designed random masking strategy. Notably, our proposed method still provides precise control if the input semantic layout is dense enough, unlike sketches-based models and scene graphs-based models that only accept sparse inputs, as discussed in Sect. 3.1.

2.3   Diffusion Probabilistic Models

Diffusion Models (DMs) can be defined as Markov chains trained using variational inference that gradually transition from random noise to the target distribution through a series of diffusion steps [26]. Ho et al. [11] proposed Denoising Diffusion Probabilistic Models (DDPMs), establishing an explicit connection between diffusion models and denoising score matching, which leads to improved image generation quality. Subsequently, many studies [23,27] have explored the potential of DMs in various aspects, such as unconditional image synthesis [4], image-to-image translation [22,25], and text-to-image generation [19,21]. These studies demonstrate the superiority of DMs over GAN-based models in terms of both quality and stability. Recently, Wang *et al.* [30] developed a semantic image synthesis approach that integrates SPADE [17] into the residual blocks of the decoder networks to better leverage the information in the input semantic mask, leading to improvements in overall quality on the task of semantic image synthesis. In this paper, we utilize a network structure similar to the SDM model and modify it to accommodate the requirements of progressive distillation [24]. This modification results in a significant boost in inference speed, making the approach more practical for real-world applications.

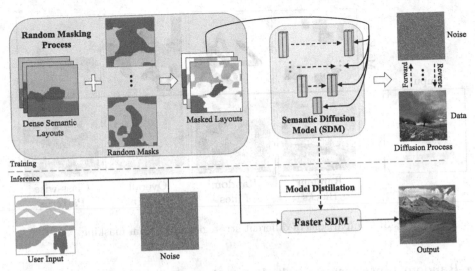

Fig. 2. Our proposed framework. The semantic layout is processed by our random masking process to simulate the actual user input and then passed to our generator, which learns to predict a landscape image from random noise through the diffusion process. During the inference phase, after the model distillation process, a distilled generator can quickly sample an output landscape corresponding to the sparser user input.

3   Proposed Framework

Our proposed framework consists of three components: a) a random masking process that simulates actual user input, improving generation quality in practical applications; b) a diffusion-based generator that we found to be most suitable for our masking design while also surpassing previous GAN-based models in both fidelity and diversity; and c) a progressive model distillation process that significantly reduces diffusion steps during the inference stage, making our framework interactive and broadly applicable.

During training, a detailed semantic layout is processed by our random masking process for each iteration to simulate user input. The masked layout is then passed to our generator, which learns to predict a landscape image from random noise through the diffusion process while conditioning on the masked layout. In the inference phase, a distilled generator can quickly sample an output landscape image from random noise, corresponding to the sparser input semantic layouts provided by the users. An overview of the model is depicted in Fig. 2.

3.1   Masking Strategy

We try to simulate user input in different strategies as follows:

- **Random Blocks** generate multiple coordinates, with random width and height.

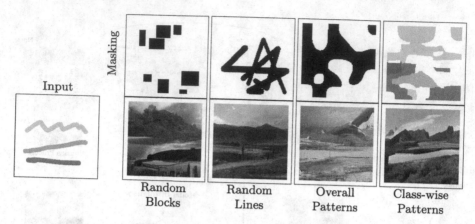

Fig. 3. Comparisons of different strategies of random masking.

- **Random Lines** generate multiple paired coordinates as the start and end points of a stroke line, then generate random middle points. Finally, draw lines with random stroke width.
- **Random Patterns** generate a low-resolution random pattern to meet an average percentage of binary masks. For example, we set the average masking percentage of our generated patterns from 15%~75%, which is also randomized in every iteration.
- **Class-wise Random Patterns** are similar to the previous one but generate a different mask for each class at the same percentage to avoid disregarding classes that are smaller than the average size, such as trees and rocks. These smaller-sized classes are more likely to be completed masked if we use an overall mask, which may lead to biased learning. Examples of different random masking strategies are shown in Fig. 3.

Based on our experiments, we find that class-wise random patterns achieve the most appropriate simulation for actual user inputs. Thus, we adopt this masking strategy in the following experiments for our proposed model and baseline models. Additionally, to improve performance when the input semantic is dense, we set a random 15% of the input semantic to be left intact, enhancing the stability of the training and providing more precise control over the generated images. For a fair comparison, we apply the same settings during the training of all baseline models.

3.2   Diffusion-Based Generator

We use the same network architecture as Semantic Diffusion Model [30], which builds upon DDPMs [11]. This architecture features a U-Net structure comprising an encoder and a decoder. It is specifically designed for the diffusion process, incorporating attention blocks, skip-connections, and a timestep embedding module. Most importantly, in contrast to previous models that feed both input

Table 1. Evaluation of Model Distillation (MD). We evaluate the models before and after model distillation in different scales. Notably, we substantially increase inference speed to 64 times while maintaining a consistent FID metric.

	Diffusion Steps	Inference Time (s)	FID↓
Original	1024	183.84	38.37
MD×16	64	10.27	39.60
MD×64	16	2.49	41.94

semantic layouts and random noise into the encoder, the SDM injects semantic label maps into the decoder to condition the semantic information. This is achieved by introducing SPADE (SPatially-ADaptive DEnormalization) [17], a highly effective normalization technique for the task of semantic image synthesis, into the decoder part of the networks.

Our generator has been modified in two aspects that have been proven to be more effective for the progressive distillation [24] process, which we conduct after the training. Firstly, we adopt a cosine noise schedule where $\alpha_t = \cos(0.5\pi t)$ and $\sigma_t^2 = 1 - \alpha_t^2$ similar to that introduced by improved DDPMs [16]. Furthermore, our generator is modified to predict $v = \alpha_t \epsilon - \sigma_t x$ instead of a random noise ϵ that is sampled from the standard Gaussian distribution, where $x \sim p(x)$ denotes the input image and $t \in [0, T]$ indicates timestep. We set $T = 1024$ in our proposed framework for better alignment during the distillation.

Training Objective. Given a sample image x, a noisy sample $\tilde{x}$ is produced as follows:

$$\tilde{x} = \sqrt{\alpha_t}x + \sqrt{1 - \alpha_t}v \tag{1}$$

Our objective function during the training includes a simple mean-squared error loss L_{simple} to predict v described above, which can be defined as:

$$L_{simple} = \mathbb{E}_{x,v,t}\left[\|v - v_\theta(\sqrt{\alpha_t}x + \sqrt{1 - \alpha_t}v, l, t)\|_2\right], \tag{2}$$

where l indicates the input semantic layout.

3.3 Model Distillation

One of the main limitations of diffusion-based models is the extremely slow sampling process, which requires simulating a Markov chain for numerous steps to generate a sample. To address this concern, we apply progressive distillation [24] to our proposed model. We briefly review the concept of progressive distillation, which is quite simple and straightforward. Assume we have a teacher model, which is the model obtained after the main training. We establish a student model initially copied from the teacher model and attempt to learn one student diffusion step to match two teacher diffusion steps. After the first distillation training, we obtain a student model that takes $T/2$ sampling steps to replace the original teacher model that required T sampling steps. This process can be conducted repeatedly until the final model only requires a few steps to generate a sample of similar quality to the original one.

As mentioned in Sect. 3.2, our generator is modified to meet the necessary requirements discovered by the authors of the progressive distillation, enabling it to accelerate the sampling process significantly while still preserving plausible generation quality. A brief evaluation of our distillation process in terms of generation quality and inference time cost are shown in Table 1. In addition to the distillation loss used in the original progressive distillation paper, we incorporate an additional simple loss, as defined in Eq. 2, to evaluate how well the student model matches the initial training. This strategy is widely used in distillation and was first introduced by Hinton et al. [10].

4   Results

We evaluate our approach and compare it with other methods both qualitatively and quantitatively.

4.1   Experiments Setup

We adopt this masking strategy in the following experiments for our proposed model and baseline models.

Datasets. We conduct experiments on Flickr Landscapes. We first collect 50,000 landscape photos that include various outdoor scenes from Flickr. We then remove 19,000 samples according to their generated label maps if they have irrelevant labels, such as people or animals. We are left with 31,000 images, of which 1,000 are left as a validation set.

Baselines. We chose three existing models as baselines for semantic image synthesis: the SPADE [17], the SEAN [34] model, and the OASIS [28] model. All of the baseline models are trained with the implementations provided by the authors. In the inference phase, we note that the SEAN model requires a style code as input, which we pre-compute from the mean style codes for all the training data. It is important to note that the same masking process is applied to all baseline models and our proposed model, ensuring a fair comparison.

4.2   Implementation Details

We train all networks from scratch. Specifically, we set the learning rate to 0.0001 in the first 600,000 iterations, which is then reduced to 0.00002 for the subsequent 200,000 iterations. To better facilitate the progressive distillation process, we set the diffusion steps to 1024 instead of the original 1000 steps. We adopt a cosine scheduler instead of a linear one for the same reason. The image size is set to be 256×256 pixels in all training.

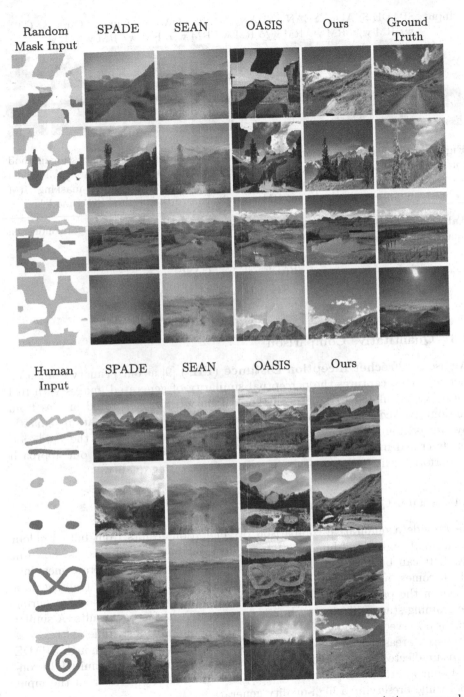

Fig. 4. Qualitative comparison. We compare our approach against existing approaches in both random mask input using our random masking strategy and actual human input.

Input SPADE SPADE SEAN SEAN OASIS OASIS Ours Ours GT
       w/ RM w/o RM w/ RM w/o RM w/ RM w/o RM w/ RM w/o RM

Fig. 5. Examples from ablation study. We compare our approach with existing methods for generating images conditioned on unmasked dense semantic layouts. All models are trained under two different settings: with or without our random masking (RM) process, and ours trained without RM is equivalent to the original SDM model.

Table 2. Quantitative evaluation. We compare with existing approaches for conditional image generation using the FID metric.

	SPADE	SEAN	OASIS	ours
FID↓	57.82	148.32	44.47	**38.37**

4.3   Quantitative Comparison

We use the **Fréchet Inception Distance (FID)** [9] as our primary evaluation metric, which captures the perceptual similarity of generated images with real ones. We calculated FID between the real images and generated images from random masked semantic layouts. We use a total of 4,000 validation semantic layouts as input, which are randomly masked four times based on the validation set described in Sect. 4.1. As shown in Table 2, we can see that our approach outperforms existing approaches in terms of generating quality.

4.4   Visual Quality Comparison

We provide a qualitative comparison of generation results from both random mask input and actual human input, against our baseline models, as shown in Fig. 4. It can be observed that the results of SEAN fail to generate meaningful outcomes, as it generates an average style derived from the training data based on the paired label maps. However, due to the random masking during the training stage, this approach fails to generate satisfactory results. A similar issue is observed for OASIS, which tends to generate obviously different textures in masked areas due to its semantically-aware discriminator. Although SPADE seems unaffected by the random masks, the generation quality is limited. In contrast, our approach automatically completes the missing areas from the input label while preserving a high-quality generation.

Table 3. Perceptual user study results. The numbers indicate the percentage of users that prefer our method with respect to existing approaches.

vs.	SPADE	OASIS	Real
Ours	73.42%	65.22%	24.56%

Table 4. Abalation Study. We compare our approach with existing methods for generating images conditioned on unmasked dense semantic layouts. All models are trained under two different settings: with or without our random masking (RM) process, and ours trained without RM is equivalent to the original SDM model.

Method	trained w/ RM	FID↓	Increase↓
SPADE [17]	✗	38.70	
	✓	55.49	43.39%
SEAN [34]	✗	143.20	
	✓	152.86	6.75%
OASIS [28]	✗	32.31	
	✓	40.46	25.22%
ours	✗	32.67	
	✓	**36.41**	**11.45%**

4.5 Perceptual User Study

We evaluate our method with a perceptual user study conducted with 10 participants. We use all 4,000 generated images from each approach and their paired real images, which are the same settings used in the quantitative comparisons. In each round of the study, two images are shown to the user, both randomly selected from different approaches or real images. Participants are asked to choose which image appears more realistic for a total of 500 rounds per user. As shown in Table 3, our approach is preferred over existing approaches. Furthermore, when compared against real images, our approach is considered better 24.56% of the time, consistent with the quantitative comparison results.

4.6 Ablation Study

We also conduct an ablation study to verify the effectiveness of our masking design, as shown in Table 4 and Fig. 5. All models are trained under two different settings: with or without our random masking process. During the inference phase, only complete semantic layouts are used as input to generate results for evaluation. We are able to evaluate how it affects generation quality by observing the increase in FID when utilizing our random masking strategy. Notably, our proposed model is minimally affected by the masking process, indicating its robustness and effectiveness in handling masked inputs.

(a) Input   (b) Output

Fig. 6. Generation conditioned on unnatural inputs. When provided inputs are unnatural, such as clouds beneath mountains on the left or 90° rotations, the model might face difficulty in producing results as the input is significantly different from anything seen during training.

4.7 Limitations and Discussion

Although our framework can generate high-quality landscape images from sparse and intuitive semantic label maps, it comes with several constraints due to the data-driven approach. Specifically, the application is limited to known labels, and new data must be acquired to extend the model to new labels, such as animals. Furthermore, the model learns a mapping from realistic semantic maps to artwork images and can fail if the input semantic maps diverge significantly from the training data, as shown in Fig. 6.

5   Conclusion

We have presented a novel framework for generating landscape images from sparse semantic layouts. Our approach consists of a well-designed masking strategy that simulates actual user input, thereby avoiding the challenging task of producing detailed semantic layouts and improving generation quality in real-world applications. We employ a diffusion-based generator tailored to our masking design, which outperforms existing models in terms of both fidelity and diversity Furthermore, an additional model distillation process makes our framework more interactive and applicable for practical use.

References

1. Ashual, O., Wolf, L.: Specifying object attributes and relations in interactive scene generation. In: Proceedings of the IEEE/CVF International Conference on Computer Vision (ICCV), October 2019
2. Chen, Q., Koltun, V.: Photographic image synthesis with cascaded refinement networks. In: Proceedings of the IEEE International Conference on Computer Vision, pp. 1511–1520 (2017)
3. Choi, Y., Choi, M., Kim, M., Ha, J.W., Kim, S., Choo, J.: StarGAN: unified generative adversarial networks for multi-domain image-to-image translation. In: Proceedings of the IEEE Conference on Computer Vision and Pattern Recognition, pp. 8789–8797 (2018)
4. Dhariwal, P., Nichol, A.: Diffusion models beat GANs on image synthesis. In: Advances in Neural Information Processing Systems 34, pp. 8780–8794 (2021)
5. Gao, C., Liu, Q., Xu, Q., Wang, L., Liu, J., Zou, C.: SketchyCOCO: image generation from freehand scene sketches. In: Proceedings of the IEEE/CVF Conference on Computer Vision and Pattern Recognition, pp. 5174–5183 (2020)
6. Ghosh, A., et al.: Interactive sketch & fill: multiclass sketch-to-image translation. In: Proceedings of the IEEE International Conference on Computer Vision (2019)
7. Goodfellow, I.J., et al.: Generative adversarial networks (2014)
8. Hertzmann, A.: Can computers create art? Arts 7(2), 18 (2018)
9. Heusel, M., Ramsauer, H., Unterthiner, T., Nessler, B., Hochreiter, S.: GANs trained by a two time-scale update rule converge to a local nash equilibrium. In: Advances in Neural Information Processing Systems, pp. 6626–6637 (2017)
10. Hinton, G., Vinyals, O., Dean, J.: Distilling the knowledge in a neural network. arXiv preprint arXiv:1503.02531 (2015)
11. Ho, J., Jain, A., Abbeel, P.: Denoising diffusion probabilistic models. In: Advances in Neural Information Processing Systems 33, pp. 6840–6851 (2020)
12. Isola, P., Zhu, J.Y., Zhou, T., Efros, A.A.: Image-to-image translation with conditional adversarial networks. In: Proceedings of the IEEE Conference on Computer Vision and Pattern Recognition, pp. 1125–1134 (2017)
13. Johnson, J., Gupta, A., Fei-Fei, L.: Image generation from scene graphs. In: Proceedings of the IEEE Conference on Computer Vision and Pattern Recognition (CVPR), June 2018
14. Li, K., Zhang, T., Malik, J.: Diverse image synthesis from semantic layouts via conditional IMLE. In: Proceedings of the IEEE/CVF International Conference on Computer Vision, pp. 4220–4229 (2019)
15. Li, L., Tang, J., Shao, Z., Tan, X., Ma, L.: Sketch-to-photo face generation based on semantic consistency preserving and similar connected component refinement. Vis. Comput. 38(11), 3577–3594 (2022)
16. Nichol, A.Q., Dhariwal, P.: Improved denoising diffusion probabilistic models. In: International Conference on Machine Learning, pp. 8162–8171. PMLR (2021)
17. Park, T., Liu, M.Y., Wang, T.C., Zhu, J.Y.: Semantic image synthesis with spatially-adaptive normalization. In: Proceedings of the IEEE Conference on Computer Vision and Pattern Recognition, pp. 2337–2346 (2019)
18. Qi, X., Chen, Q., Jia, J., Koltun, V.: Semi-parametric image synthesis. In: Proceedings of the IEEE Conference on Computer Vision and Pattern Recognition, pp. 8808–8816 (2018)
19. Ramesh, A., Dhariwal, P., Nichol, A., Chu, C., Chen, M.: Hierarchical text-conditional image generation with clip latents. arXiv preprint arXiv:2204.06125 (2022)

20. Razavi, A., van den Oord, A., Vinyals, O.: Generating diverse high-fidelity images with VQ-VAE-2. In: Wallach, H., Larochelle, H., Beygelzimer, A., d' Alché-Buc, F., Fox, E., Garnett, R. (eds.) Advances in Neural Information Processing Systems, vol. 32. Curran Associates, Inc. (2019)

21. Rombach, R., Blattmann, A., Lorenz, D., Esser, P., Ommer, B.: High-resolution image synthesis with latent diffusion models. In: Proceedings of the IEEE/CVF Conference on Computer Vision and Pattern Recognition (CVPR), pp. 10684–10695, June 2022

22. Saharia, C., et al.: Palette: image-to-image diffusion models. In: ACM SIGGRAPH 2022 Conference Proceedings, pp. 1–10 (2022)

23. Saharia, C., Ho, J., Chan, W., Salimans, T., Fleet, D.J., Norouzi, M.: Image super-resolution via iterative refinement. IEEE Trans. Pattern Anal. Mach. Intell. **45**(4), 4713–4726 (2022)

24. Salimans, T., Ho, J.: Progressive distillation for fast sampling of diffusion models. In: International Conference on Learning Representations (2022)

25. Sasaki, H., Willcocks, C.G., Breckon, T.P.: UNIT-DDPM: UNpaired image translation with denoising diffusion probabilistic models. arXiv preprint arXiv:2104.05358 (2021)

26. Sohl-Dickstein, J., Weiss, E., Maheswaranathan, N., Ganguli, S.: Deep unsupervised learning using nonequilibrium thermodynamics. In: International Conference on Machine Learning, pp. 2256–2265. PMLR (2015)

27. Song, Y., Sohl-Dickstein, J., Kingma, D.P., Kumar, A., Ermon, S., Poole, B.: Score-based generative modeling through stochastic differential equations. arXiv preprint arXiv:2011.13456 (2020)

28. Sushko, V., Schönfeld, E., Zhang, D., Gall, J., Schiele, B., Khoreva, A.: You only need adversarial supervision for semantic image synthesis. arXiv preprint arXiv:2012.04781 (2020)

29. Wang, T.C., Liu, M.Y., Zhu, J.Y., Tao, A., Kautz, J., Catanzaro, B.: High-resolution image synthesis and semantic manipulation with conditional GANs. In: Proceedings of the IEEE Conference on Computer Vision and Pattern Recognition, pp. 8798–8807 (2018)

30. Wang, W., et al.: Semantic image synthesis via diffusion models (2022)

31. Yu, Y., Li, D., Li, B., Li, N.: Multi-style image generation based on semantic image. Vis. Comput. 1–16 (2023). https://doi.org/10.1007/s00371-023-03042-2

32. Zhang, H., et al.: StackGAN: text to photo-realistic image synthesis with stacked generative adversarial networks. In: Proceedings of the IEEE International Conference on Computer Vision (ICCV), October 2017

33. Zhang, Z., et al.: Stroke-based semantic segmentation for scene-level free-hand sketches. Vis. Comput. **39**, 6309–6321 (2022). https://doi.org/10.1007/s00371-022-02731-8

34. Zhu, P., Abdal, R., Qin, Y., Wonka, P.: SEAN: image synthesis with semantic region-adaptive normalization. In: Proceedings of the IEEE/CVF Conference on Computer Vision and Pattern Recognition, pp. 5104–5113 (2020)

35. Zhu, Z., Xu, Z., You, A., Bai, X.: Semantically multi-modal image synthesis. In: Proceedings of the IEEE/CVF Conference on Computer Vision and Pattern Recognition, pp. 5467–5476 (2020)

FoldGEN: Multimodal Transformer for Garment Sketch-to-Photo Generation

Jia Chen[1,2], Yanfang Wen[1], Jin Huang[1,2(✉)], Xinrong Hu[1,2], and Tao Peng[1,2]

[1] Wuhan Textile University, Wuhan 430200, Hubei, China
derick0320@foxmail.com
[2] Engineering Research Center of Hubei Province for Clothing Information,
Wuhan 430200, Hubei, China

Abstract. Garment sketch-to-photo generation is one of the most crucial steps in garment design. Most existing methods contain only single conditional information, and it is challenging to combine multiple condition information. At the same time, these methods cannot generate garment folds based on sketch strokes and face a low-fidelity problem. Therefore, this paper proposes a two-stage multi-modal framework, FoldGEN, to generate garment images with folds using sketches and descriptive text as conditional information. In the first stage, we combine feature matching of discriminators and semantic perception of Convolutional Neural Network in vector quantization, which can reconstruct the details and folds of the garment images. In the second stage, a multi-conditional constrained Transformer is used to establish the association between different modality data, which allows the generated images to contain not only text description information but also folds corresponding to the strokes of the sketch. Experiments show that our method can generate garment images with different folds from sketches with high fidelity while achieving the best FID and IS on both unimodal and multi-modal tasks.

Keywords: Garment · Sketch-to-photo · Fold Generation · Transformer · Multi-modal

1 Introduction

Garment sketch-to-photo generation is vital in the garment design industry. Many methods have been proposed to achieve garment sketch-to-photo generation. Most existing approaches [1,7,8,11,20,22], such as generative adversarial networks, treat the conditional image generation task as an image-to-image translation task. However, these methods are unimodal and focus only on the translation between two image domains, thus ignoring the semantic information, which makes the generated garment images relatively homogeneous; Some other two-stage image generation methods [3,5,6,15] achieve cross-mode image generation. However, garment images usually contain rich folds and textures, and these methods cannot learn these details in the first stage of vector quantization, facing the problem of low fidelity (Fig. 1).

Supported by organization x.

B. Sheng et al. (Eds.): CGI 2023, LNCS 14496, pp. 455–466, 2024.
https://doi.org/10.1007/978-3-031-50072-5_36

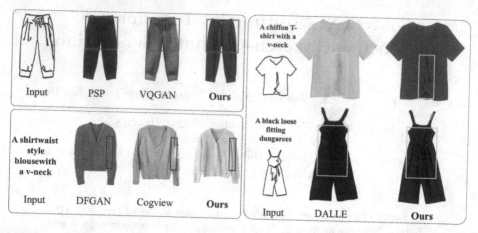

Fig. 1. The proposed method allows users to controllably generate corresponding images from text and sketch, while being able to generate corresponding folds from the strokes of the sketch.

Therefore, in this paper, we propose a vector quantization encoding method for garment images. We incorporate feature matching of the discriminator and semantic awareness of Convolutional Neural Network in VQGAN to learn the textures and folds information of the garment images. In the second stage, we take text and sketch as input to guide the generation of garment images. In order to make the garment image generate corresponding folds according to the strokes of the sketch, we propose a multi-conditional constraint Transformer to constrain the folds as well as the semantic information. The semantic constraint can give the generated images better semantics, while the fold constraint can make the generated images contain the corresponding textures and folds. The main contributions of this paper are summarized as follows:

- We design FoldGEN, a multi-modal framework for garment sketch-to-photo generation, to collaboratively control image generation by inputting textual description and sketch information.
- We propose a simple and effective strategy to improve the existing vector quantization encoding method to reconstruct the folds of garment images.
- We introduce a multi-conditional constrained Transformer to enable collaborative control between text and sketch information, which can generate the corresponding folds precisely according to the strokes of the sketch.

2   Method

In this section, we present the framework of our model, as shown in Fig. 2. Our approach is divided into two main stages: in the first stage: encoding the data for the different modalities, and in the second stage, using the Transformer to learn the associations between the different modal information.

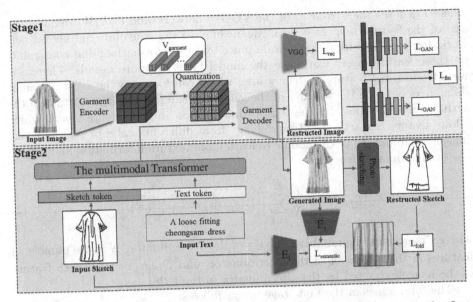

Fig. 2. The framework of FoldGEN. Our model consists of two stages. In the first stage, we encode the data of each modality. As shown in Stage1, for garment images, we combine the semantic perception of VGG and the feature matching of the discriminator to encode them with vector quantization; for sketches and text, the encoding method will be introduced in Sect. 2.1. In the second stage, we establish the association between different modal data by a multi-conditional constrained Transformer.

2.1 Encoding of Multimodal Information

Encoding of Condition Information. The text and the garment sketch together form conditional information. For the encoding of text, we use Word2vec [13] directly. For garment sketches, since they contain only simple black lines that carry less practical information, we do not need to focus on their detailed information, and therefore it is easy to obtain an image representation of them; we use the VQ-GAN model to encode them directly as a series of discrete sequences.

Encoding of Garment Images. For garment images, we improve the encoding strategy of vector quantization by incorporating feature matching of the discriminator and semantic awareness of the VGG network, which can significantly preserve the detailed information of garment images during vector quantization. Specifically, we incorporated two losses in VQ-GAN: the perceptual loss L_{rec}, and the feature matching loss L_{fm}. The perceptual loss uses a pre-trained classification network to measure the semantic difference between images (the Euclidean distance between high-level features of two images), and we use the VGG19 [18] network. The loss of i-th layer is as follows:

$$L_{rec} = \frac{1}{C_i H_i W_i} \|\phi_i(x) - \phi_i(x')\|_2^2 \tag{1}$$

where i denotes the i-th layer of the VGG19 network and $C_i H_i W_i$ denotes the size of the feature map at layer i. Meanwhile, In the convolutional neural network, low-level feature maps contain more texture information, and constraints on these feature layers can make the model focus on more details. Therefore, we introduce the feature matching loss, which can focus on the most apparent differences between the features of the generated samples and the features of the actual samples, especially the texture information in the feature space, which allows feature extraction and "matching" from different scales of real and fake images, enabling the GAN module to learn more texture information and restore the original image structure:

$$L_{fm}(t) = \frac{1}{N} \sum_{i=1}^{N} \left[\left| Dis_t^{(i)}(x) - Dis_t^{(i)}(x') \right| \right] \tag{2}$$

where t represents the number of layers of the discriminator, N is the number of features in the t-th layer of the discriminator, and $Dis_t^{(i)}(x)$ is the i-th feature of the image extracted by the discriminator in the t-th layer.

The total losses in the first stage are as follows:

$$L_{stage1} = L_{VQ} + \lambda_1 L_{rec} + \lambda_2 L_{fm} \tag{3}$$

where L_{VQ} denotes the training losses used in VQ-GAN.

2.2   The Multimodal Transformer

In the second stage, we use the autoregressive generation approach. In contrast to existing cross-modal image generation approaches [2,4,9,12] that can only accomplish text-to-image generation or image-to-image generation, our FoldGEN framework is a versatile model that can process data from different modalities in a unified network. The backbone of the model is a unidirectional autoregressive Transformer that can collectively accept different control signals as input and predict the discrete sequences used to generate the images. The model structure is shown in Fig. 3; the control signals in our model consist of text and sketch, where the text token sequences are obtained from the text encoder, and the image token sequences are obtained from the image encoder introduced in Sect. 2.1. Meanwhile, different token sequences are combined. The FoldGEN then predicts the token sequences and feeds them to the image decoder to generate the images. In order to make the garment images generate folds in the area corresponding to the sketch strokes, we add fold constraints to the model. Specifically, we reconstruct the generated images as sketches via the Photosketching [10] network and then calculated the $L2$ loss between them and the input sketches using the following loss function:

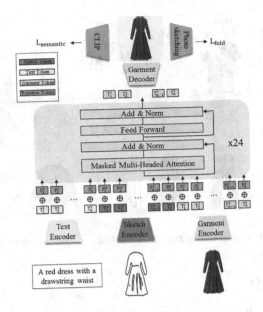

Fig. 3. The multi-conditional constrained Transformer.

$$L_{fold} = \|s - F(D(t, s))\|_2^2 \qquad (4)$$

where F is the PhotoSketch network, s is the input sketch and t is the input text. At the same time, to make the generated garment images have better semantics, we also make the corresponding constraint on the text. We use the CLIP [14] model, which is a pre-training neural network model for matching images and texts trained on 400 million pairs of image text. We have conducted small-scale migration training on the garment dataset sets to improve the matching accuracy. Then, we use the trained model to calculate the cosine similarity between the generated image and the input text. The loss function is as follows:

$$L_{semantic} = 1 - cos(E_i(D(s, t)) - E_t(t)) \qquad (5)$$

where E_i is the image encoder of the CLIP [14] model and E_t is the text encoder of the CLIP model.

The overall loss function in the second stage is as follows:

$$L_{stage2} = L_{Transformer} + L_{fold} + L_{semantic} \qquad (6)$$

where $L_{transformer}$ is the log-likelihood of the data.

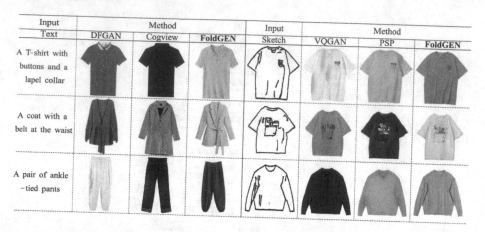

Input	Method			Input	Method		
Text	DFGAN	Cogview	FoldGEN	Sketch	VQGAN	PSP	FoldGEN
A T-shirt with buttons and a lapel collar							
A coat with a belt at the waist							
A pair of ankle −tied pants							

Fig. 4. Comparison results with the uni-modal methods

3   Experiments

In this section, we validate our proposed network model and evaluate our model by comparing it with various existing generative image generation methods.

3.1   Data Preparation

Research on garment image generation has been limited by the lack of high quality garment datasets. Therefore, we collect and produce our dataset. We collect a dataset of approximately 150,000 garment images and corresponding text descriptions from competing platforms on Taobao and AliTianchi. Then, we expand the data in five ways: cropping, flipping, one text corresponding to multiple images, one image corresponding to multiple texts, and brightness adjustment. We then use the Photo-Sketching [10] network to convert all the garment images into corresponding sketches and remove the noise using binarization.

3.2   Comparison Results with the Uni-modal Methods

We select four unimodal methods for comparative experiments. Among them, the text-to-image generation method selects Cogview and DF-GAN [19] models, and the sketch-to-image generation method selects VQGAN and PSP [17] models. DF-GAN and PSP are traditional methods based on Generative Adversarial Network, and VQGAN and Cogview use a two-stage generation method. We train on our dataset with different methods, and the generated results are shown in Fig. 4. The results show that the fidelity of the image generated by DF-GAN is relatively low, and the generated images have some white spots in details such as neckline and folds, and the color is also very monotonous; the PSP model generates better results for short sleeves, but for shirts and pants, there are no folds; the images generated by the Cogview model have artifacts at edges and

Table 1. The evaluation results of various methods under different tasks

Task	Text-to-image			Sketch-to-image		Text+Sketch-to-image		
Metric	FID	IS	R-prec	FID	IS	FID	IS	R-prec
Cogview	42.368	2.99	**72.36**	—	—	—	—	—
DF-GAN	121.477	2.17	62.85	—	—	—	—	—
VQGAN	—	—	—	30.239	3.42	—	—	—
PSP	—	—	—	68.743	3.04	—	—	—
DALLE	37.494	3.62	54.08	32.575	3.31	35.374	3.55	53.62
ControlNet	31.244	3.47	64.92	28.635	3.27	28.021	3.51	62.59
FoldGEN	**29.211**	**3.74**	70.42	**26.395**	**3.67**	**25.459**	**3.69**	**71.74**

folds; the VQGAN model generates images that ignore many strokes in sketches, such as the lines of the pant legs and the shoulders of the sleeves, while our method generates relatively high-quality images and can generate corresponding folds from sketched strokes.

The first four rows of Table 1 show the evaluation results for the four methods, with our method obtaining the best FID and IS in both text-to-image generation and sketch-to-image generation but slightly below Cogview in the R-precision metric; this is because Cogview uses the three-region sparse attention in training to generate text-to-image sparse attention and uses only text as conditional information. In contrast, our input uses three combinations of tokens.

3.3 Comparison Results with State-of-the-Art Methods

In this section, we validate the effectiveness of our model on multimodal generation, and the generated samples are shown in Fig. 6. The images generated

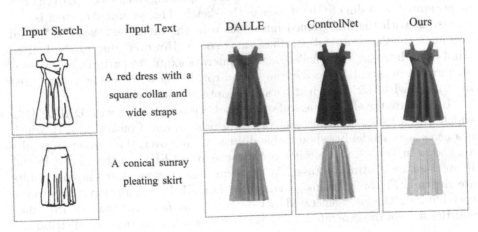

Input Sketch   Input Text   DALLE   ControlNet   Ours

A red dress with a square collar and wide straps

A conical sunray pleating skirt

Fig. 5. Comparison results with the multi-modal methods

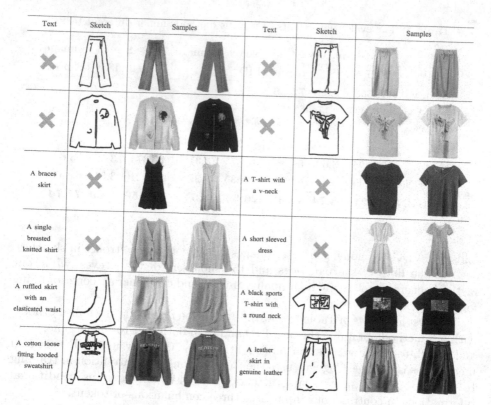

Fig. 6. Examples of multimodal information generation

by our method are of high quality and can generate garment images consistent with the input sketch and text. At the same time, the details of the input sketch have been given sufficient attention, and corresponding creases or patterns can be generated according to the strokes of the sketch. The generated content is also consistent with the fine-grained information in the input text, such as "round neckline", "leather material", "ruffles", and so on. However, due to the limited number of datasets, it is challenging to generate exquisite patterns or patterns on garment images. As shown in the second row in Fig. 6, the patterns generated from areas with thick sketch strokes will contain motley colors.

To validate the effectiveness of our model, we compared it with DALLE [16], which uses a two-stage image generation approach, and ControlNet [21], which is a generative model based on stable diffusion. Moreover, the evaluation results are shown in Table 1. Our method obtains the lowest FID and the highest IS and R-precision on multimodal tasks. At the same time, the generated sample results are shown in Fig. 5. The folds generated by DALLE have many artifacts and are very blurred. The folds generated by ControlNet are more random and irregular, and the style of the generated image is more dependent on the color distribution of the dataset. In contrast, our method can generate the corresponding folds according to the strokes in the sketch.

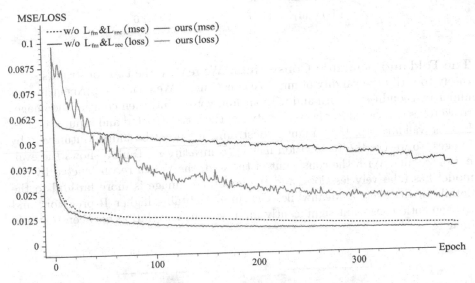

Fig. 7. Comparison of results for different losses

3.4 Ablation Studies

In this section, we perform the ablation studies of the improved vector quantization encoding method as well as the multi-constraint Transformer to verify their effectiveness.

The Improved Vector Quantization: To investigate the effectiveness of the improved vector quantization encoding method, we use the same configuration with different types of losses in our experiments. Figure 7 shows the MSE and loss during the training for different methods.

Table 2 shows the FID of the reconstructed images for the different models, and our model shows a relatively significant improvement on both the training and test sets. Figure 8 shows an example of the results of the different models, and the first row shows the original input image, the second row shows the reconstructed image after removing feature matching and semantic perception, and the third row shows the image reconstructed by our method, with the red boxes highlighting the areas of significant improvement. Our method can more clearly reconstruct the detailed information of garment images, such as folds, patterns, and quilting. It can reduce artifacts and reproduce finer texture details, further improving the quality of the reconstructed images.

Table 2. The FID of the reconstructed images

method	w/o L_{fm} and L_{rec}	**ours**
FID (train)	39.43	**27.74**
FID (val)	44.57	**31.36**

The Fold and Semantic Constraints: We remove the two constraints separately to verify the validity of multiple constraints. We generate garment images under two conditions, with and without fold constraint, then convert the images to sketches and calculate the MSE between the reconstructed and input sketches. For the validation of the semantic constraint, it cannot be judged intuitively by images, so we use the R-precision metric to measure it. Table 3 shows the evaluation results. With the constraint of the fold, the sketch reconstructed by our model has relatively less loss, and the generated image is more faithful to the details of the sketch. Meanwhile, Our model obtains higher R-precision, and the semantic constraint significantly improves the correlation between text and images.

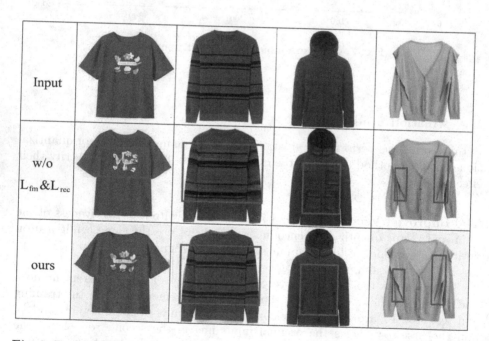

Fig. 8. Examples of reconstruction results for different methods (Color figure online)

Table 3. The evaluation of the fold and semantic constraints

Metric	R-precision		MSE	
Condition	Text	Text+Sketch	Sketch	Text+Sketch
w/o $L_{semantic}$	63.62	54.39	—	—
w/o L_{fold}	—	—	0.091	0.114
ours	**70.42**	**71.74**	**0.047**	**0.062**

4 Conclusion

In this paper, we propose FoldGEN, a multimodal framework for garment fold sketch-to-image generation, which collaboratively controls the generation of images by inputting textual description and sketch information. We improve the vector quantization encoding strategy for garment images by combining feature matching of discriminators and semantic awareness of Convolutional Neural Network, which can reconstruct the details and folds of garment images during vector quantization. At the same time, we constrain the folds and semantics separately, allowing the model to generate high-fidelity garment images with rich folds guided by text and sketch. Experiments show that FoldGEN can capture the fold information of garment images and outperform previous methods in unimodal and multimodal image generation tasks.

Acknowledgements. Chen's research was sponsored by the National Natural Science Foundation of China (Grant No. 62202345).

References

1. Bai, J., Chen, R., Liu, M.: Feature-attention module for context-aware image-to-image translation. Vis. Comput. **36**, 2145–2159 (2020). https://doi.org/10.1007/s00371-020-01943-0
2. Chang, H., Zhang, H., Jiang, L., Liu, C., Freeman, W.T.: MaskGIT: masked generative image transformer. In: Proceedings of the IEEE/CVF Conference on Computer Vision and Pattern Recognition, pp. 11315–11325 (2022)
3. Chen, M., et al.: Generative pretraining from pixels. In: International Conference on Machine Learning, pp. 1691–1703. PMLR (2020)
4. Ding, M., et al.: CogView: mastering text-to-image generation via transformers. In: Advances in Neural Information Processing Systems, vol. 34 (2021)
5. Dong, X., et al.: PeCo: perceptual codebook for BERT pre-training of vision transformers. arXiv preprint arXiv:2111.12710 (2021)
6. Esser, P., Rombach, R., Ommer, B.: Taming transformers for high-resolution image synthesis. In: 2021 IEEE/CVF Conference on Computer Vision and Pattern Recognition (CVPR), pp. 12868–12878 (2021). https://doi.org/10.1109/CVPR46437.2021.01268
7. Huang, L., Wang, Y., Bai, T.: Recognizing art work image from natural type: a deep adaptive depiction fusion method. Vis. Comput. **37**, 1221–1232 (2021). https://doi.org/10.1007/s00371-020-01995-2

8. Huang, X., Liu, M.-Y., Belongie, S., Kautz, J.: Multimodal unsupervised image-to-image translation. In: Ferrari, V., Hebert, M., Sminchisescu, C., Weiss, Y. (eds.) ECCV 2018. LNCS, vol. 11207, pp. 179–196. Springer, Cham (2018). https://doi.org/10.1007/978-3-030-01219-9_11

9. Lee, D., Kim, C., Kim, S., Cho, M., Han, W.S.: Autoregressive image generation using residual quantization. In: Proceedings of the IEEE/CVF Conference on Computer Vision and Pattern Recognition, pp. 11523–11532 (2022)

10. Li, M., Lin, Z., Mech, R., Yumer, E., Ramanan, D.: Photo-sketching: inferring contour drawings from images. In: 2019 IEEE Winter Conference on Applications of Computer Vision (WACV), pp. 1403–1412. IEEE (2019)

11. Li, S., Wu, F., Fan, Y., Song, X., Dong, W.: PLDGAN: portrait line drawing generation with prior knowledge and conditioning target. Vis. Comput. **39**, 3507–3518 (2023). https://doi.org/10.1007/s00371-023-02956-1

12. Li, Z., Zhou, H., Bai, S., Li, P., Zhou, C., Yang, H.: M6-fashion: high-fidelity multimodal image generation and editing. arXiv preprint arXiv:2205.11705 (2022)

13. Mikolov, T., Sutskever, I., Chen, K., Corrado, G.S., Dean, J.: Distributed representations of words and phrases and their compositionality. In: Advances in Neural Information Processing Systems, vol. 26 (2013)

14. Radford, A., et al.: Learning transferable visual models from natural language supervision. In: International Conference on Machine Learning, pp. 8748–8763. PMLR (2021)

15. Razavi, A., van den Oord, A., Vinyals, O.: Generating diverse high-fidelity images with VQ-VAE-2. In: Wallach, H., Larochelle, H., Beygelzimer, A., d'Alché-Buc, F., Fox, E., Garnett, R. (eds.) Advances in Neural Information Processing Systems, vol. 32. Curran Associates, Inc. (2019). https://proceedings.neurips.cc/paper/files/paper/2019/file/5f8e2fa1718d1bbcadf1cd9c7a54fb8c-Paper.pdf

16. Reddy, M.D.M., Basha, M.S.M., Hari, M.M.C., Penchalaiah, M.N.: DALL-E: creating images from text. UGC Care Group I J. **8**(14), 71–75 (2021)

17. Richardson, E., et al.: Encoding in style: a StyleGAN encoder for image-to-image translation. In: Proceedings of the IEEE/CVF Conference on Computer Vision and Pattern Recognition, pp. 2287–2296 (2021)

18. Simonyan, K., Zisserman, A.: Very deep convolutional networks for large-scale image recognition. arXiv preprint arXiv:1409.1556 (2014)

19. Tao, M., Tang, H., Wu, F., Jing, X.Y., Bao, B.K., Xu, C.: DF-GAN: a simple and effective baseline for text-to-image synthesis. In: Proceedings of the IEEE/CVF Conference on Computer Vision and Pattern Recognition, pp. 16515–16525 (2022)

20. Yoshikawa, T., Endo, Y., Kanamori, Y.: Diversifying detail and appearance in sketch-based face image synthesis. Vis. Comput. **38**(9–10), 3121–3133 (2022). https://doi.org/10.1007/s00371-022-02538-7

21. Zhang, L., Agrawala, M.: Adding conditional control to text-to-image diffusion models. arXiv preprint arXiv:2302.05543 (2023)

22. Zhou, X., et al.: CoCosNet v2: full-resolution correspondence learning for image translation. In: Proceedings of the IEEE/CVF Conference on Computer Vision and Pattern Recognition, pp. 11465–11475 (2021)

Light Accumulation Map for Natural Foliage Scene Generation

Ruien Shen[1] , Chi Weng Ma[1] , Deli Dong[2] , and Shuangjiu Xiao[1]([envelope])

[1] School of Software, Shanghai JiaoTong University, Shanghai, China
xiaosj@sjtu.edu.cn
[2] Shanghai JiaoTong University, Shanghai, China

Abstract. Foliage scene generation is an important problem in computer graphics. Realistic virtual floras require simulation of real plant symbiotic principles. Among the factors that affect the spatial distribution of plants, lighting is the most important one. The change of seasons, geographic locations, and shading from higher plants will greatly affect the sunlight conditions for different plants in floras, which cannot be easily described with parameters. In order to generate natural foliage scene that accurately reflects the sunlight condition while maintaining efficiency, we propose a novel method named Light Accumulation Map (LAM) which stores sunlight receiving and occlusion information of each tree model. By calculating sunlight accumulation during one year at different latitudes, we simulate the sunlight occlusion effect of the tree model and store the occlusion result as LAM. Then, a LAM-based foliage generation algorithm is brought out to simulate accurate foliage distribution with different latitudes and seasons. The evaluation shows that our method exhibits strong adaptability in creating a lifelike distribution of foliage, particularly in undergrowth areas, across various regions and throughout different seasons of the year.

Keywords: Modeling and simulation · Foliage scene generation · Natural phenomena

1 Introduction

Foliage scene is an important part in visual applications such as games and VR apps, and its authenticity plays an essential role in the immersion of users. Among all factors that affect the cover and richness of foliage, sunlight is considered to be the major one [2]. Sunlight changes with time and location, resulting in various effects on plants in different temporal and spatial locations. Sunlight is also affected by the distribution of foliage layers and canopy structure. For example, the shade from large broad-leaved trees will have a certain impact on the distribution of undergrowth.

Supplementary Information The online version contains supplementary material available at https://doi.org/10.1007/978-3-031-50072-5_37.

At the same time, different plants respond differently to the change in light. Species that have a lower tolerance to shade typically exhibit a more limited distribution and smaller size due to inadequate access to light. In the case of trees, light is a critical determinant of their growth, and they tend to grow towards sources of ample light to optimize photosynthesis efficiency. Similarly, light availability plays a significant role in determining the distribution and growth conditions of undergrowth, thereby exerting a pivotal influence on the overall composition of the scene.

Previous vegetation scene generation methods often assumed that lighting parameters are fixed and the cost area is evenly distributed surrounding the tree which does not match the actual situation. In order to generate foliage scenes with real distribution affected by the sunlight, we propose a method to store the sunlight info in Light Accumulation Maps (LAM) with the simulation on plant models and use them to realize the distribution of vegetation under real light.

In summary, our contributions are:

- a novel method called Light Accumulation Map to numerically analyze light occlusion effect on undergrowth in different time and place
- a LAM-based foliage generation algorithm for natural distribution with accurate lighting effect handling

2   Related Work

While significant progress has been made in simulating forest fog [1] and avalanches [15], tackling foliage scenes remains a formidable challenge. There have been many studies around this topic, including the generation of plant models [14,27], the distribution of plants, and the integration of the overall scene and plants, covering from individual foliage to the full ecosystem.

Tradition foliage scene generation methods mainly focus on two aspects: one is the simulation method and the other is the distribution analysis method.

Methods focusing on simulation usually model and simulate the growth of plants according to real-world growth environments. Former works use radial interaction [5] and L-system [13] to simulate the foliage growth. Měch and Prusinkiewicz [17] build a simulation and visualization framework for the interaction between plants and the environment. More recent work [8] considers how to balance simulation fidelity and performance. Makowski et al. [16] presented a novel ecosystem modeling framework that simulates the influence of tree branches on their neighbors.

Methods focusing on distribution analysis usually require manual input to parameters of the ecosystem and use different distribution methods to meet these parameters. The basic method of distribution synthesis is to determine the generated location through a density map [5], or to divide different foliage communities through a species map. Machine learning is also used to generate more detailed foliage distribution. Zhang et al. [26] use a CNN network to generate foliage details with high efficiency, Kapp et al. [11] use a GAN network to refine plant distribution. By enhancing ecological features of foliage and combining procedural distribution generation method, Ecormier et al. [6] expand the 2D distribution analysis into 3D and give a more accurate result.

Sunlight is one of the most important factors affecting the growth of foliage, especially in tropical rainforests [4] and for undergrowth [2]. The distribution and growth of undergrowth are heavily influenced by the amount of shadow coverage. This is evidenced by the significant impact that shadows have on species distribution and growth [25]. Several studies on tree modeling have investigated the role of light in plant growth. For example, Bene et al. [3] incorporated the local shadow effect in their simulation of plant development. Soler [22] developed a highly precise lighting simulation system for rendering vegetation scenes. Other researchers have focused on the impact of light intensity on tree growth. Hadrich [9] utilized light as a driving force for the growth of climbing plants. Prik [19,20] considered the effect of light from obstacles and the tree itself in his tree stress model, while Stava [24] regarded light as a critical factor in his procedural tree modeling work.

In previous procedural foliage scene generation work, the parameters of sunlight are usually taken in the form of maps [5]. In procedural foliage generation, trees are often considered as a consumer which consumes light energy in a disk range [11]. Under this method, there will be a threshold sunlight resource value for tree growth. However, these distribution analysis methods do not take into account the occlusion of sunlight from plants of higher levels. This will cause the problem of lacking spatial interaction between foliage caused by sunlight occlusion which is particularly evident in the undergrowth.

3 Methodology

In order to generate natural foliage scenes with realistic distribution reflecting sunlight conditions while ensuring efficient generation, we propose a LAM generation algorithm to store the sunlight occlusion effect of trees and a LAM-based foliage generation algorithm that makes use of LAM to generate foliage scenes under realistic sunlight condition as shown in Fig. 1.

3.1 Tree LAM Generation

The first step of our foliage generation pipeline is tree LAM generation. In this step, the light occlusion information of a tree model in a specified time period will be encoded into a Light Accumulation Map. The LAM is used to identify how much light will be occluded by the corresponding tree. This process can be divided into three parts: a Sunlight Direction Sampler, a Light Map Generator, and a Light Map Composer.

Sunlight Direction Sampler. In order to calculate the occlusion effect of the tree model on sunlight, we need to sample the direction of sunlight at any time period in a coordinate system formed by the three axes of longitude, latitude, and

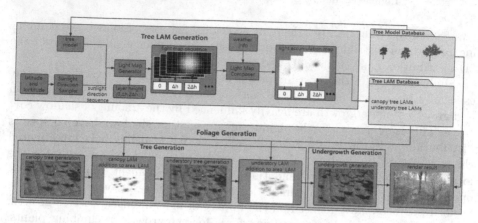

Fig. 1. The framework of LAM-based foliage generation algorithm

vertical axis to the ground. Given the target location (latitude and longitude) and the time of a typical day, we can calculate the sunlight direction. The declination angle δ is calculated using Spencer's [23] equation. The solar position is estimated using Eq. (1) provided by Preetham [21] where θ_s is the solar angle from zenith, ϕ_s is the solar azimuth, l is the latitude, δ is the declination and t is the solar time.

$$
\theta_s = \frac{\pi}{2} - \arcsin\left(\sin l \sin \delta - \cos l \cos \delta \cos \frac{\pi t}{12}\right),
$$
$$
\phi_s = \arctan\left(\frac{-\cos \delta \sin \frac{\pi t}{12}}{\cos l \sin \delta - \sin l \cos \delta \cos \frac{\pi t}{12}}\right) \tag{1}
$$

Light Map Generator. Light Map Generator uses real-time ray tracing to obtain the occlusion condition of a typical tree model in a specified sunlight direction and at a specified height. The input of the Light Map Generator is a tree model, the heights of each layer, and a sunlight direction sequence. The output of the Light Map Generator is multiple light map sequences stored in 2d float arrays that represent the light occlusion condition at different chosen heights over a period of time.

Figure 2 shows our pipeline for light map generation which is a modification on traditional ray-tracing shadow method [10]. We employ the ray generation shader for generating rays to trace the path of light in a designated square area. Given the predominantly directional nature of sunlight, we produce directional rays that consistently align with a particular orientation within the square area. We utilize the miss shader and the closest hit shader to simulate the intensity of light emanating from distinct directions and account for the attenuation of light as it traverses through forested areas. Considering that a tree model usually uses the alpha channel of leaf textures to represent the actual area of the leaf, we directly return the result when the alpha value is one, and a certain attenuation value is added to the result as compensation when the alpha is zero.

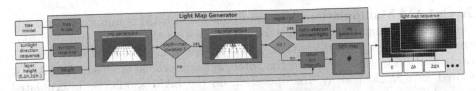

Fig. 2. Light Map Generator

The Light Map Generator will generate light maps of different height levels for each tree model. The delta height between each level is decided by the user according to the need for height precision, computational cost, and height of the foliage.

Light Map Composer. By utilizing the sequence of light maps produced by a tree model as input, our Light Map Composer amalgamates the light maps within a defined time frame to obtain an average sunlight occlusion effect. The output of this process is the light map of different height layers, which corresponds to the impact of the tree's sunlight influence on different plane heights.

In Light Map Composer, according to the selected time period, the light maps in this time period are selected for accumulation, and the average light of trees in this time period is obtained. The images that record the occlusion effect of sunlight are named Light Accumulation Map. When the sampling frequency of the Sunlight Direction Sampler is low for a period of time, the obtained LAM will still have obvious traces of tree occlusion and stacking. In this case, our Light Map Composer adds a Gaussian blur to the image to get a smooth LAM and more natural result.

$$LAM_{direct} = \frac{\sum_{i=1}^{N} lightmap_i}{N} \tag{2}$$

$$LAM = LAM_{direct} * p + \alpha_{damp} * LAM_{indirect} * (1 - p) \tag{3}$$

$$LAM_{normalized} = \frac{LAM}{light\text{-}intensity} \tag{4}$$

As light map and LAM are presented using a 2d float array and stored as image, all the operation below is the 2d float array operation. Equation (2) is the process of combining N light maps under a specified time period into one LAM, the values on the LAM_{direct} indicates the average sunlight intensity in this period of time. In order to accurately model the effect of sunlight under varying weather conditions, Eq. (3) incorporates a parameter, denoted by p, which represents the proportion of user-specified sunny periods, and serves to balance the contribution of direct sunny and indirect overcast sunlight [18]. The $LAM_{indirect}$ here we use the light intensity on an overcast day to populate the 2D array to account for indirect light conditions caused by weather and other effects. To ensure that the final LAM generated accurately reflects the degree of light occlusion, we applied a normalization process, the LAM is normalized by the non-occluded light intensity to get the average occlusion condition.

Area LAM Manipulation. The manipulation of LAM is mainly about addition and sampling. The sampling of LAM gives us the correct sun occlusion condition at the specified location. The addition of LAM accumulates the sun occlusion effect of one tree into the total area sun occlusion effect. As LAM is stored as a 2d float array, the operation on the LAM should be interpolated using bilinear interpolation when the enquired coordinates do not accurately align with integer coordinates.

Algorithm 1 is the process of sampling light intensity in a specific position from the area LAM. (x, y, z) is the coordinate we want to sample, LAM_a is the area LAM, z_f and z_c denote the heights of two adjacent layers, such that height z satisfies $z_f < z < z_c$.

Algorithm 1. LAM sampling

1: **function** LAM-SAMPLING(LAM_a, x, y, z)
2:     find two layer heights $z_f = n \times \Delta h$ and $z_c = (n+1) \times \Delta h$ in LAM_t that make $z_f + z < z_l < z_c + z$
3:     calculate the pixels $[p]$ that the tree model should occupy
4:     $n_p = num([p])$
5:     **for** every p_s in $[p]$ **do**
6:         $occ\mathbin{+}= \frac{LAM_a[x,y,z_f] \times (z_c - z) + LAM_a[x,y,z_c] \times (z - z_f)}{\Delta h * n_p}$
7:     **end for**
8:     **return** occ
9: **end function**

When a tree is placed, we add the LAM of the tree to the total LAM map of the whole area. In Algorithm 2, LAM_a is the LAM of the specified area, LAM_t is the LAM of the chosen tree model, (x, y, z) is the coordinate of the tree, and r is the range we want to add.

Algorithm 2. LAM addition

1: **procedure** LAM-ADDITION(LAM_a, LAM_t, x, y, z)
2:     **for** every z_l in LAM_a **do**
3:         **for** every pixel coord (x_a, t_a) that $dis((x_a, y_a), (x, y)) < r$ **do**
4:             transfer LAM_a coord (x_a, y_a, z_l) into LAM_t coord (x_t, y_t, z_t)
5:             $occ = LAM_t[x_t, y_t, z_t]$
6:             $LAM_a[x_a, y_a, z_l] = LAM_a[x_a, y_a, z_l] \times occ$
7:         **end for**
8:     **end for**
9: **end procedure**

3.2   Foliage Generation

The foliage generation process can be divided into two stages: the canopy and understory tree generation stage and the undergrowth generation stage. Before placing foliage, LAMs that represent the average sunlight intensity will be built for this area at multiple different heights.

Tree Generation. The placement of canopy trees is similar to other competitive models. In this stage, our generation method uses lighting, terrain, and water resource factors to determine whether the canopy tree should be placed in a specific location. For constraints in ecosystems, our method takes into account the necessary parameters such as competitive distance between trees, settlements between species, etc.

When all canopy tree is placed, our method uses LAM addition to add LAM of each placed tree model into the area LAM. After adding all the canopy tree LAMs into the area LAM, the area LAM contains all the sun-occluding conditions affected by the canopy trees in multiple height levels.

During the placement of understory trees, the information of sunlight occlusion should be considered carefully. In order to decide whether a location is suitable for trees, the floor space of the tree is calculated to decide how many coordinates on the area LAM should we sample. LAM can also determine the density distribution of leaves for the understory tree. From a botanical point of view, trees grow in the direction where the light source is more abundant and the leaves in this direction will be denser than in other directions. By sampling the occlusion values of the area LAM near the tree, the gradient direction of the light intensity can be obtained, which also corresponds to the growth direction of trees. Equation (5) shows the detailed calculation of the growth direction.

$$dir_g = \begin{bmatrix} LAM[x+dx,y,z] - LAM[x-dx,y,z] \\ LAM[x,y+dy,z] - LAM[x,y-dy,z] \\ LAM[x,y,z+dz] - LAM[x,y,z-dz] \end{bmatrix} \tag{5}$$

Undergrowth Generation. The undergrowth has the largest number within the entire foliage ecology, with some being vulnerable to sunlight while others are not. Therefore, LAM has the greatest impact on the underlying foliage. In the generation process of the undergrowth (see Algorithm 3), our method uses a sigmoid function with different parameters for each undergrowth to describe the probability that a species can grow normally under a certain light intensity. By sampling the LAM values of different positions, we can get the growth probability of a certain plant in a certain position to decide whether it can grow or not. With the function that describes the relationship between growth potential and LAM, our method can easily generate undergrowth foliage following natural distribution accordingly.

Algorithm 3. Grass Generation

```
 1: procedure GRASS GENERATION(LAM_a, n_s)
 2:     for i in n_s do
 3:         pos=uniform-random()
 4:         l=LAM-sampling(LAM_a, pos_x, pos_y, 0)
 5:         s_g = getspecie(pos) ▷ decide specie s_g from the location and species cluster
 6:         p_g = probability_{s_g}(l)
 7:         p_c = random(0, 1)
 8:         if p_c < p_g then                    ▷ check if the undergrowth can grow
 9:             generate grass
10:         end if
11:     end for
12: end procedure
```

4   Result

4.1   Implementation and Performance

We use the DirectX ray tracing API to build a system that can generate the light map automatically. The tree LAM generation work is deployed on a desktop with intel core i7-13700k, 64 GB of RAM, and Nvidia RTX3070. The foliage generation part is implied using python. An exhibiting program is built using Unreal Engine [7] to show the final scene with a detailed rendering effect.

Our research focuses on generating medium-range foliage. The landscape size we are working with is approximately 0.5 km × 0.5 km. A single layer of the tree LAM is represented by a 128×128 2D float array, and the LAM size of the entire area is 512×512. This means that each value in both the tree LAM and area LAM corresponds to one square meter in the real world.

Table 1. Performance of scene generation

scene	canopy	understory	undergrowth	time cost	map size
rainforest	300	1313	189422	2.6 s	0.5 km × 0.5 km
broadleaf forest	250	436	84464	2.7 s	0.5 km × 0.5 km
alder forest	250	455	28993	0.7 s	0.5 km × 0.5 km

Our sunlight direction sampling frequency is one day per month and per hour of that day. During ray tracing, every pixel will generate four rays to compute the intersection. We modeled and generated three different vegetation scenes using our LAM approach. The amount of each kind of species is shown in Table 1. As LAM is precomputed and stored in the database, the time cost in the tree generation stage is significantly low.

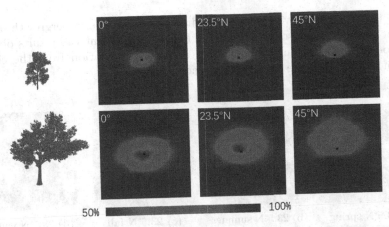

Fig. 3. LAM generated in different latitudes using different models

4.2   Results and Evaluation

The normalized LAM generated by our pipeline is presented in Fig. 3. This figure displays the average shadow cover under the influence of trees in different latitudes, represented by different models with varying sizes and shapes. In order to show shadow overlays more obviously, we change the grayscale LAM into HSV color space. It is evident that the shadow cover area and its impact vary depending on the tree model used, with larger trees producing a greater shadow cover area than smaller ones. Furthermore, as latitude increases, the shadow cover area shifts towards the north, corresponding to the actual movement of the sun in the real world.

Fig. 4. Foliage distribution comparison between the real and generated scene

It is well-known that grass will grow differently under trees due to the shade they provide [25]. Numerous studies have indicated that the morphology of trees can significantly impact the distribution of shade [12]. The left image of Fig. 4 is a photograph of Kentucky Bluegrass in America, the shadows of the trees do not form an approximately circular distribution extending from the center of the tree. Consequently, the sparse area of grass is concentrated in the north of the tree, where shadows cover a longer period of time. The middle image of Fig. 4 illustrates the undergrowth generated using a previously proposed method by

Kapp et al. [11]. It is evident that the distribution of the undergrowth forms a circular shape. On the right side of the figure, we present the results obtained using our method, which demonstrates a distinct deviation from the circular pattern exhibited in the previous approach.

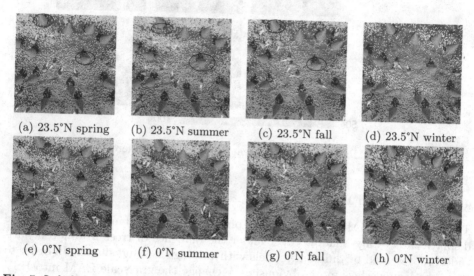

(a) 23.5°N spring   (b) 23.5°N summer   (c) 23.5°N fall   (d) 23.5°N winter

(e) 0°N spring   (f) 0°N summer   (g) 0°N fall   (h) 0°N winter

Fig. 5. Labeled scene in different latitudes. Canopy trees are labeled in red, understory trees in blue, sun-loving undergrowth in green and shadow-tolerant undergrowth in yellow. The yellow arrow indicates the direction of denser leaves. (Color figure online)

As depicted in Fig. 5, the images illustrate the seasonal changes in plants at 23.5° north and 0° north. The comparison demonstrates the effectiveness of our method at different latitudes using the same plants. Our findings reveal that grasslands at 0° latitude do not change significantly with the seasons, which aligns with our understanding that illumination changes are relatively minor near the equator. During spring and autumn, light resources are most abundant, and tree shadows are more evenly dispersed. Since the grass we set has a tendency towards the sun, it grows most abundantly during these periods and is more evenly distributed around the trees. Conversely, at 23.5° north, the grass undergoes significant seasonal changes. Our results show that grass growth is most extensive in the summer, with the largest number of grasses and the most widespread distribution. In the winter, the overall number of grasses decreases due to the decrease in light intensity.

4.3 Discussion and Limitation

Our framework can easily reinforce plant distribution under realistic light occlusion simulation. However, this method still has some limitations.

Firstly, the LAM generation highly depends on the quality of a tree model. If the model's level of detail is too low or the model does not fit the actual size of the foliage in real life, it will be time-consuming to adjust the model.

Secondly, although the LAM can solve the problem of inaccurate light estimation and complex manual lighting parameters, there are still many factors like temperature and humidity that need to be modeled in a more efficient way.

5 Conclusion and Future Work

This paper describes a LAM-based natural foliage scene generation algorithm. This algorithm can simulate the real foliage light occlusion through a pre-computed method with low cost to generate a numerical-based light analysis map, and complete the construction of the prepared ecology. At the same time, this system avoids the complex setting of plant lighting parameters in the traditional methods.

For future work, we plan to implement this algorithm using CUDA for better performance. We aim to generate and measure more foliage growth factors using automated methods to free foliage generation from redundant parameters.

References

1. Abbas, F., Babahenini, M.C.: Forest fog rendering using generative adversarial networks. Vis. Comput. **39**(3), 943–952 (2022). https://doi.org/10.1007/s00371-021-02376-z
2. Barbier, S., Gosselin, F., Balandier, P.: Influence of tree species on understory vegetation diversity and mechanisms involved-a critical review for temperate and boreal forests. For. Ecol. Manag. **254**(1), 1–15 (2008)
3. Beneš, B.: An efficient estimation of light in simulation of plant development. In: Boulic, R., Hégron, G. (eds.) Computer Animation and Simulation 1996, pp. 153–165. Springer, Vienna (1996). https://doi.org/10.1007/978-3-7091-7486-9_11
4. Chazdon, R.L., Pearcy, R.W., Lee, D.W., Fetcher, N.: Photosynthetic responses of tropical forest plants to contrasting light environments. In: Mulkey, S.S., Chazdon, R.L., Smith, A.P. (eds.) Tropical Forest Plant Ecophysiology, pp. 5–55. Springer, Boston (1996). https://doi.org/10.1007/978-1-4613-1163-8_1
5. Deussen, O., Hanrahan, P., Lintermann, B., Měch, R., Pharr, M., Prusinkiewicz, P.: Realistic modeling and rendering of plant ecosystems. In: Proceedings of the 25th Annual Conference on Computer Graphics and Interactive Techniques, pp. 275–286 (1998)
6. Ecormier-Nocca, P., Memari, P., Gain, J., Cani, M.P.: Accurate synthesis of multi-class disk distributions. In: Computer Graphics Forum, vol. 38, pp. 157–168. Wiley Online Library (2019)
7. Epic Games: Unreal engine. https://www.unrealengine.com
8. Gain, J., Long, H., Cordonnier, G., Cani, M.P.: EcoBrush: interactive control of visually consistent large-scale ecosystems. In: Computer Graphics Forum, vol. 36, pp. 63–73. Wiley Online Library (2017)
9. Hädrich, T., Benes, B., Deussen, O., Pirk, S.: Interactive modeling and authoring of climbing plants. In: Computer Graphics Forum, vol. 36, pp. 49–61. Wiley Online Library (2017)

10. Haines, E., Akenine-Möller, T.: Ray Tracing Gems: High-Quality and Real-Time Rendering with DXR and Other APIs. Apress (2019)
11. Kapp, K., Gain, J., Guérin, E., Galin, E., Peytavie, A.: Data-driven authoring of large-scale ecosystems. ACM Trans. Graph. (TOG) **39**(6), 1–14 (2020)
12. Kuuluvainen, T., Pukkala, T.: Effect of crown shape and tree distribution on the spatial distribution of shade. Agric. For. Meteorol. **40**(3), 215–231 (1987)
13. Lane, B., Prusinkiewicz, P., et al.: Generating spatial distributions for multilevel models of plant communities. In: Graphics Interface, vol. 2002, pp. 69–87. Citeseer (2002)
14. Li, B., et al.: Learning to reconstruct botanical trees from single images. ACM Trans. Graph. (TOG) **40**(6), 1–15 (2021)
15. Liu, X., Chen, Y., Zhang, H., Zou, Y., Wang, Z., Peng, Q.: Physically based modeling and rendering of avalanches. Vis. Comput. **37**(9–11), 2619–2629 (2021). https://doi.org/10.1007/s00371-021-02215-1
16. Makowski, M., Hädrich, T., Scheffczyk, J., Michels, D.L., Pirk, S., Pałubicki, W.: Synthetic silviculture: multi-scale modeling of plant ecosystems. ACM Trans. Graph. (TOG) **38**(4), 1–14 (2019)
17. Měch, R., Prusinkiewicz, P.: Visual models of plants interacting with their environment. In: Proceedings of the 23rd Annual Conference on Computer Graphics and Interactive Techniques, pp. 397–410 (1996)
18. Mousavi Maleki, S.A., Hizam, H., Gomes, C.: Estimation of hourly, daily and monthly global solar radiation on inclined surfaces: models re-visited. Energies **10**(1), 134 (2017)
19. Pirk, S., Niese, T., Hädrich, T., Benes, B., Deussen, O.: Windy trees: computing stress response for developmental tree models. ACM Trans. Graph. (TOG) **33**(6), 1–11 (2014)
20. Pirk, S., et al.: Plastic trees: interactive self-adapting botanical tree models. ACM Trans. Graph. (TOG) **31**(4), 1–10 (2012)
21. Preetham, A.J., Shirley, P., Smits, B.: A practical analytic model for daylight. In: Proceedings of the 26th Annual Conference on Computer Graphics and Interactive Techniques, pp. 91–100 (1999)
22. Soler, C., Sillion, F.X., Blaise, F., Dereffye, P.: An efficient instantiation algorithm for simulating radiant energy transfer in plant models. ACM Trans. Graph. (TOG) **22**(2), 204–233 (2003)
23. Spencer, J.W.: Fourier series representation of the position of the sun. Search **2**(5), 172 (1971)
24. Stava, O., et al.: Inverse procedural modelling of trees. In: Computer Graphics Forum, vol. 33, pp. 118–131. Wiley Online Library (2014)
25. Strong, W.: Lateral Picea shadow effects on Populus tremuloides understory vegetation in central Yukon, Canada. For. Ecol. Manag. **261**(11), 1866–1875 (2011)
26. Zhang, J., Wang, C., Li, C., Qin, H.: Example-based rapid generation of vegetation on terrain via CNN-based distribution learning. Vis. Comput. **35**(6), 1181–1191 (2019). https://doi.org/10.1007/s00371-019-01667-w
27. Zhao, Y., Barbič, J.: Interactive authoring of simulation-ready plants. ACM Trans. Graph. (TOG) **32**(4), 1–12 (2013)

DrawGAN: Multi-view Generative Model Inspired by the Artist's Drawing Method

Bailin Yang[1]([✉])[ID], Zheng Chen[1][ID], Frederick W. B. Li[2][ID], Haoqiang Sun[1][ID], and Jianlu Cai[1][ID]

[1] Zhejiang GongShang University, Hangzhou, China
ybl@zjgsu.edu.cn
[2] University of Durham, Durham, UK
frederick.li@durham.ac.uk

Abstract. We present a novel approach for modeling artists' drawing processes using an architecture that combines an unconditional generative adversarial network (GAN) with a multi-view generator and multi-discriminator. Our method excels in synthesizing various types of picture drawing, including line drawing, shading, and color drawing, achieving high quality and robustness. Notably, our approach surpasses the existing state-of-the-art unconditional GANs. The key novelty of our approach lies in its architecture design, which closely resembles the typical sequence of an artist's drawing process, leading to significantly enhanced image quality. Through experimental results on few-shot datasets, we demonstrate the potential of leveraging a multi-view generative model to enhance feature knowledge and modulate image generation processes. Our proposed method holds great promise for advancing AI in the visual arts field and opens up new avenues for research and creative practices.

Keywords: Unconditional GANs · AI art · few-shot dataset · multi-view generative model

1 Introduction

GANs have revolutionized machine learning by generating novel visual content through modeling high-dimensional distributions They have excelled in various applications such as image translation, motion deblurring, frame prediction, and text-to-image synthesis [3,15,28,33]. However, training GANs is challenging due to the non-convex game nature and high-dimensional parameter space, leading to mode collapse and training instability [1,31].

While unconditional GANs perform well on class-specific datasets, they struggle with generating outline, gray, and color views simultaneously [19,30], which limits the generality of image generation. State-of-the-art methods like

Supported by National Natural Science Foundation of China NO. 62172366.
Supported by Key Laboratory of Electronic Business and Logistics Information Technology of Zhejiang Province KF202201.

B. Sheng et al. (Eds.): CGI 2023, LNCS 14496, pp. 479–490, 2024.
https://doi.org/10.1007/978-3-031-50072-5_38

StyleGAN and StyleGAN2 offer reliable performance but require significant computational resources [13,14]. FastGAN addressed this by proposing a skip-layer excitation module and a self-supervised discriminator [18].

However, current GANs have limitations in evaluating a single view of an image, leading to mode collapse and neglect of important image features. To address this, we propose DrawGAN, an unconditional generative model inspired by the artist's drawing process. In the artist's process, coloring is applied on top of object shapes, indicating that line drawing and shading contain valuable knowledge for coloring. DrawGAN aims to enhance the detection of diverse descriptors and capture more image features by utilizing a multi-component approach.

Our approach models the image generation process using outline, gray, and color components, with outline and gray integrated into the color component. We believe these components are mutually dependent and complementary. The DrawGAN model incorporates a novel multi-view generator capable of generating images at three levels: outline, gray, and color. This approach aims to produce high-quality synthesized images with improved diversity and fidelity. Our main contributions are as follows:

1. Proposal of the integration of the artist's painting concepts into the unconditional generative adversarial network, resulting in the novel DrawGAN model structure.
2. Development of DrawGAN, which incorporates a three-view generator and a multi-discriminator. This architectural design empowers the model to effectively capture diverse image information, including multiple view features, and mitigate the mode collapse issue.
3. Execution of experiments on few-shot datasets to validate and demonstrate the robustness of DrawGAN in generating good-quality images.

2   Related Work

2.1   Image Generation and Synthesis

In recent years, the field of image generation and synthesis has witnessed numerous variations of Generative Adversarial Networks (GANs) aiming to improve the quality of generated samples.

Few-Shot Image Generation: Generating high-quality images with GANs in a few-shot scenario is challenging due to the need of large datasets during training (typically 50,000 to 100,000 images). When training data is limited, the discriminator can easily overfit, leading to inadequate feedback for the generator.

To address this challenge, DiffAug and StyleGAN-Ada rely on data augmentation techniques to prevent discriminator overfitting [12,34]. ContraD introduced a strong data augmentation strategy by learning a contrastive representation compatible with GANs [10]. Another recent approach utilizes LeCam divergence, minimizing an f-divergence through modulation of discriminator predictions [26]. However, while these methods have shown success in capturing information from single views, they do not support the generation of multiple image versions (e.g., outline and gray) within the same GAN architecture.

Image-to-Image Translation: Image-to-image translation involves converting an input image into a different output form. Establishing the correlation between input and output images is a significant challenge. When the network fails to capture this correlation, the generator may cheat by ignoring the input, resulting in output images similar to the truth images. StarGAN and its successor, StarGAN v2, propose a single network model for image-to-image translations across multiple domains, requiring paired image datasets from these domains [4,5]. Nazeri et al. divide image inpainting into two steps: predicting missing region edges and completing the image using the predicted edges [21]. While DrawGAN shares similarities with their idea, we differ by generating three views (outline, gray, and color) using a single generator, whereas they employ two separate generators.

Differing from the aforementioned works, our focus lies in unconditional image generation, which removes the constraint of paired images as inputs. Notably, our work introduces a novel multi-view generative network capable of simultaneously generating outline, gray, and color versions of images. This advancement enables the synthesis of diverse and comprehensive images.

2.2   AI Art

AI technology advancement for digital art was marked by the milestone of image style transfer [7]. This technique utilized CNNs to generate stylized images by separating and recombining the "content" and "style" of an image.

Building upon GAN for generating creative images, Elgammal et al. introduced Creative Adversarial Networks (CAN) [6]. CAN incorporates two feedback signals from the discriminator to the generator: classification of "art or not art" and the ability to classify the generated art into established styles. By optimizing these signals, CAN enables the generation of creative images that deviate from established styles while conforming to the distribution of art.

Yi et al. proposed APDrawingGAN, a GAN-based approach for generating artistic portrait drawings from face images [29]. This method employs hierarchical generators and discriminators, leveraging both global and local convolutional networks to extract facial features. These features are then fused to produce the final output. In contrast, Li et al. presented a two-stage method for colorizing line drawings using GANs [16]. The initial stage generates a color draft that aggressively applies colors to enrich variety, despite potential errors such as color mistakes, bleeding, and blurring/distortion. The second refinement stage utilizes a synthetic paired image dataset to address these errors.

The novelty of our DrawGAN lies in its ability to generate three distinct representations of an image (outline, grayscale, and color) using a single multi-view generative network. Unlike existing methods that produce only one representation, DrawGAN expands the possibilities of image synthesis and offers the exploration of diverse visual representations. This advancement in AI art facilitates new creative possibilities and opens avenues for artistic expression.

3   Method

Inspired by the art drawing process, we propose DrawGAN, an architecture capable of generating outline, gray, and color images (Fig. 1). Training our network requires datasets with all three views, but existing datasets typically provide only the color view. To overcome this limitation, we apply traditional algorithms to extract the outline and gray views from color images, creating our own dataset. We use the canny algorithm for edge extraction to generate the outline view and the Floyd-Steinberg dithering algorithm to approximate brightness and obtain the gray view.

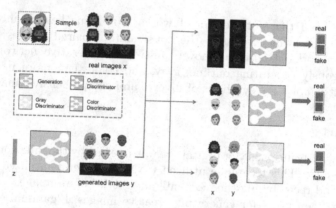

Fig. 1. DrawGAN utilizes a multi-view generator with three outputs, feeding to three corresponding discriminators, which are trained with distinct loss functions for discriminating real and fake outputs of the outline, gray, and color views of images, respectively.

3.1   Loss Formation

In a vanilla GAN, the discriminator D and the generator G engage in a minimax game to guide the generator in synthesizing noise vectors into realistic images. For the sake of simplicity, the equation can be expressed as:

$$\mathcal{L}_D = \underset{x \sim P_d}{\mathbb{E}}[\log D(x)] + \mathbb{E}_{z \sim p_z}[\log(1 - D(G(z)))] \tag{1}$$

$$\mathcal{L}_G = \underset{z \sim N}{\mathbb{E}}[\log D(G(z))] \tag{2}$$

There have been numerous studies on GAN loss functions since the introduction of GAN, including wgan [2], wgan-gp [8], and hinge loss [17]. According to various experiments, hinge loss is generally considered the most stable and efficient approach for unconditional image generation [17, 25]. Therefore, we use the hinge version of the adversarial loss to train our D and G iteratively.

$$\mathcal{L}_D = -\mathbb{E}x \sim P_d[\min(0, -1 + D(x))] - \mathbb{E}_{z \sim N}[\min(0, -1 - D(G(z)))] \quad (3)$$

$$\mathcal{L}_G = -\mathbb{E}z \sim N[D(G(z))] \quad (4)$$

Our proposed architecture, in contrast to existing GAN architectures, includes a multi-view generator that produces three distinct outputs. This model architecture not only follows the artist drawing process but also adheres to the GAN training mechanism. As shown in Fig. 1, our model comprises a generator with three outputs that are linked to three distinct discriminators.

The generator in our proposed DrawGAN architecture is different from traditional GAN generators, which usually generate a single-view image y. Instead, our generator produces an image set y_1, y_2, y_3 for the outline, gray, and color views, respectively, from a noise vector $z \sim N$, where $y_1, y_2, y_3 = G(z)$. Similarly, for training our network, we use image sets of outline, gray, and color views x_1, x_2, x_3 from real images. Corresponding discriminators D_1, D_2, and D_3 are constructed to distinguish real and fake views, respectively. Hence, Eq. 3 can be rewritten as:

$$\mathcal{L}_{D_i} = -\mathbb{E}[\min(0, -1 + D_i(x_i))] - \mathbb{E}[\min(0, -1 - D_i(y_i))] \quad (5)$$

FastGAN [18] proposed reconstructive training to ensure that D can extract more comprehensive representations from inputs, covering both overall composition and detailed textures, with minimal additional computational cost. Our discriminator has adopted this reconstructive training technique, such that:

$$\mathcal{L}_{recon} = \mathbb{E}[|\ |\ g(f) - T(x)\ |\ |] \quad (6)$$

Therefore, Eq. 5 is further rewritten as:

$$\mathcal{L}_{D_i} = -\mathbb{E}[\min(0, -1 + D_i(x_i))]$$
$$-\mathbb{E}[\min(0, -1 - D_i(y_i))] + \mathcal{L}_{recon} \quad (7)$$

The final losses for generators and discriminators are formulated as follows:

$$\mathcal{L}_D = \mathcal{L}_{D_1} + \mathcal{L}_{D_2} + \mathcal{L}_{D_3} \quad (8)$$
$$\mathcal{L}_G = -\mathbb{E}[D(y_1)] - \mathbb{E}[D(y_2)] - \mathbb{E}[D(y_3)] \quad (9)$$

3.2   Model Architecture

Based on the equations provided, we propose a multi-view generator architecture with three outputs, as illustrated in Fig. 2. The input noise vector z is first transformed into a 4×4 feature space through a Transpose Convolution (4×4) and a Convolution (3×3). We then employ a process of upsampling followed by two 3×3 convolutions to improve the feature space resolution, which is commonly

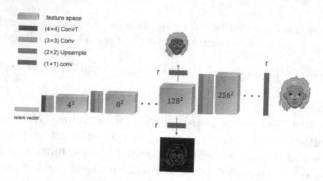

Fig. 2. The generator architecture uses nearest-neighbor interpolation and a 3×3 convolution for upsampling. The feature space of 128 is processed by function r to generate outline and grayscale views, while the final feature space is for color view generation.

used in most GAN architectures [11,18,22]. Finally, we define a mapping function r to generate the output images corresponding to the outline, gray, and color views. The mapping function r is implemented using a convolution (1×1) layer to project the feature space onto the image space. To enhance the stability of the training, we apply spectral normalization [20] to all of the convolutional layers.

Our generator is designed to mimic the artist's drawing process by first generating the line drawing (outline) view and shading (gray) view, and then generating the color view, as shown in Fig. 2. We use a 128×128 resolution feature space to output the outline and gray views and the final feature space to output the color view of the image. The design of our model follows the forward propagation mechanism of neural networks.

As shown in Fig. 1, our DrawGAN multi-discriminator comprises three modules, namely outline discriminator, gray discriminator, and color discriminator. They provide useful feedback to the generator by comparing the generated image set y_i with the real image set x_i. We adopt the FastGAN model [18] to construct the architecture of our multi-discriminator, where the color discriminator remains unchanged, and the number of channels for outline and gray discriminator is reduced to half that for the color discriminator.

In terms of the discriminator's auto-encoding reconstruction, we adopt different reconstruction loss functions for different views. The color image reconstruction loss uses the perceptual similarity metric [32], while the outline and gray image reconstruction loss use the structural similarity index (SSIM) [27]. The DrawGAN generator G produces three fake samples Y_i from a noise vector z, where the number of output channels for outline and gray is 1. X_i and Y_i are then fed into the multi-discriminator for training DrawGAN using the loss functions defined in Eq. 8 and Eq. 9.

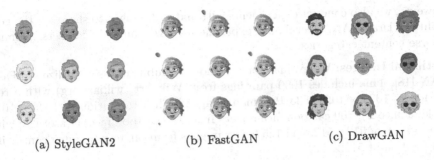

(a) StyleGAN2   (b) FastGAN   (c) DrawGAN

Fig. 3. The qualitative results of the cartoon face dataset clearly demonstrate that both StyleGAN2 [14] and FastGAN [18] are plagued by mode collapse, while our DrawGAN produces more realistic results. These findings indicate that DrawGAN achieves state-of-the-art performance on this dataset.

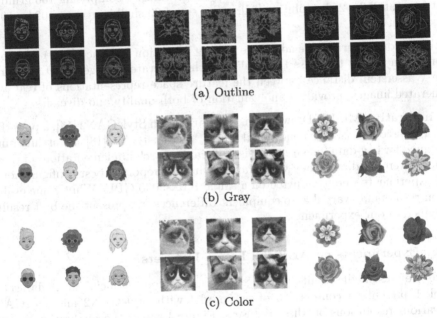

(a) Outline

(b) Gray

(c) Color

Fig. 4. The comparison between real images (top rows) and the generated images (bottom rows) highlights DrawGAN's ability to generate random and uncurated images with three different views (outline, gray, and color) on high-resolution datasets.

4   Experiment

4.1   Datasets and Evaluation Metrics

To align with the artist drawing process, our model focuses on extracting clear line drawings (outlines) from the datasets. While line drawings from natural images tend to be chaotic, those from artificial images are typically clearer. Consequently, our image generation task primarily concentrates on artificial images.

However, we also conduct experiments with natural images to showcase the generality of DrawGAN. Overall, our experiments cover multiple datasets spanning diverse content categories.

Artificial Images: We evaluate our method on public datasets utilized in Fast-GAN [18]. This includes 1000 paintings from WikiArt (wikiart.org) with a resolution of 1024×1024, 833 Pokemon images with a resolution of 1024×1024 (pokemon.com), 500 cartoon face images from the cartoon face dataset [23] with a resolution of 512×512, and 125 flower images from pngimg (pngimg.com) with a resolution of 512×512.

Natural Images: DrawGAN is evaluated on datasets, including the widely-used AFHQ Cat dataset [24], consisting of 160 cat face images at 256×256 resolution, the 100-Shot-Panda dataset, containing 100 panda face images at 256×256 resolution, the 100-Shot-Grumpy-cat dataset, comprising 100 grumpy cat faces at 256×256 resolution [34], and a set of 60 shell images at 1024×1024 resolution.

Evaluation Metrics: We adopt the Fréchet Inception Distance (FID) [9] as our evaluation metric to assess the quality of the generated images. FID measures the Wasserstein distance between the feature space representations of real and generated images, providing an evaluation of both quality and diversity.

Comparative Model: DrawGAN is compared with StyleGAN2 [14], a powerful but resource-intensive unconditional model, and FastGAN [18], an architecture designed for low-data image synthesis. Official PyTorch implementations of these models were used, and they were trained with the reported best configurations. All experiments were conducted on a single RTX-3060 GPU. While some evaluation results may vary due to equipment differences, we present the best results obtained in our experiments.

4.2   Experiments on Artificial Image Datasets

Here, we present the results of our experiments on four artificial image datasets. Table 1 presents a comparison of our model with StyleGAN2 and FastGAN at various resolutions on these datasets. Figure 3 shows the qualitative results of cartoon faces, where we observe that both StyleGAN2 and FastGAN suffer from mode collapse, while DrawGAN generates more realistic results. In other words, with artificial datasets that have clear outlines, DrawGAN significantly outperforms state-of-the-art methods in terms of image synthesis quality. However, DrawGAN still outperforms state-of-the-art methods, albeit with smaller improvements, when dealing with datasets that lack clear outlines.

4.3   Experiments on Natural Image Datasets

We present our experiment results conducted on four natural image datasets. The results between our model and StyleGAN2 and FastGAN at various resolutions on multiple datasets are summarized in Table 2. Our model demonstrates

Table 1. Comparing with state-of-the-art models over artificial image datasets trained with 500 (cartoon face), 1000 (painting), 125 (flower), and 833 (pokemon) samples, DrawGAN consistently outperforms them and mitigates mode-collapse on generator.

Datasets	Cartoon face	Painting	Flower	Pokemon
Image Number	500	1000	125	833
Resolution	512	1024	512	1024
StyleGAN2	65.4	74.56	112.10	60.12
FastGAN	145.08	45.08	81.66	57.19
Our Method	**27.4**	**42.35**	**75.32**	**46.90**

impressive performance in generating images of natural scenes, showcasing its versatility. However, as shown in the middle section of Fig. 4, the outline extraction for natural images is not as clear, indicating that the lack of clarity in line drawing might be a contributing factor to the relatively modest improvement achieved by our method. It is important to note that the artist drawing process, which is the focal point of our paper, may not entirely align with the process of creating natural scene images. In reality, natural objects may lack explicit outlines, and the outlines we perceive are often formed by variations in environmental illumination or disparities in colors among foreground and background objects, as well as different parts of an object. Such outlines are implicitly created by gray and color features, which can be ambiguous or untidy in nature.

Table 2. Comparing with state-of-the-art models over natural image datasets trained with 100 (Grumpy Cat and Panda), 160 (AFHQ Cat), and 60 (shell) samples, DrawGAN's performance slightly outperforms the state-of-the-art.

Datasets	AFHQ Cat	Shell	Panda	Grumpy cat
Image Number	160	60	100	100
Resolution	256	1024	256	256
StyleGAN2	42.44	220.45	12.06	27.08
FastGAN	35.11	155.47	10.03	26.65
Our Method	**34.32**	**114.62**	**9.56**	**24.48**

4.4 Discussion

Unconditional GAN models typically generate images from a single view, which may result in limited contour and shading information. In contrast, our multi-view approach captures diverse information, enhancing the image representation. The outline and gray components play crucial roles, with the outline capturing strong gradient changes and the gray conveying color intensity and shading. Our model effectively incorporates both features, enabling a wider range of image information to be considered. Figure 4 provides a visual comparison of the generated data types with real data.

We conducted an experiment to explore an alternative approach of extracting outline and gray features directly from the final generated image, after the color view. However, the results in Fig. 5 demonstrate that the original setting of DrawGAN outperforms this alternative approach in generating high-quality results. This finding confirms the rationality of following the artist's drawing process. However, generating the outline and gray views after the color view requires adjusting the color feature space, resulting in a decrease in color richness.

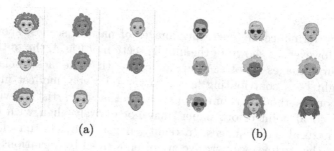

(a)   (b)

Fig. 5. Right group of 9 color images: Best results obtained by generating outline and gray views after the color view (FID 65.5). Left group of 9 color images: Best results obtained based on original setting of DrawGAN (FID 27.4).

5   Conclusion

DrawGAN, a novel multi-view generative model, addresses the challenge of over-fitting in limited data image generation tasks by introducing a multi-view generator and three discriminators. The multi-view design enriches the feature space, allowing the generator to capture complex structures and patterns. The discriminators focus on different views, providing diverse information to mitigate over-fitting. The sequential generation of outline, gray, and color views enhances model stability and gradient flow. Experimental results on multiple few-shot datasets demonstrate that DrawGAN outperforms state-of-the-art methods, showcasing its effectiveness in image generation. However, limitations are observed in generating backgrounds with diverse colors, due to limitations in outline and gray views. The equal weighting of views in the loss function dilutes background color information. DrawGAN introduces a novel approach to GANs, with potential for driving advancements in the field of digital art.

References

1. Arjovsky, M., Bottou, L.: Towards principled methods for training generative adversarial networks. arXiv preprint arXiv:1701.04862 (2017)

2. Arjovsky, M., Chintala, S., Bottou, L.: Wasserstein generative adversarial networks. In: International Conference on Machine Learning, pp. 214–223. PMLR (2017)

3. Cheema, M.N., et al.: Modified GAN-cAED to minimize risk of unintentional liver major vessels cutting by controlled segmentation using CTA/SPET-CT. IEEE Trans. Ind. Inform. **17**(12), 7991–8002 (2021)

4. Choi, Y., Choi, M., Kim, M., Ha, J.-W., Kim, S., Choo, J.: StarGAN: unified generative adversarial networks for multi-domain image-to-image translation. In: Proceedings of the IEEE Conference on Computer Vision and Pattern Recognition, pp. 8789–8797 (2018)

5. Choi, Y., Uh, Y., Yoo, J., Ha, J.-W.: StarGAN v2: diverse image synthesis for multiple domains. In: Proceedings of the IEEE Conference on Computer Vision and Pattern Recognition, pp. 8188–8197 (2020)

6. Elgammal, A., Liu, B., Elhoseiny, M., Mazzone, M.: CAN: creative adversarial networks, generating "art" by learning about styles and deviating from style norms. arXiv preprint arXiv:1706.07068 (2017)

7. Gatys, L.A., Ecker, A.S., Bethge, M.: Image style transfer using convolutional neural networks. In: Proceedings of the IEEE Conference on Computer Vision and Pattern Recognition, pp. 2414–2423 (2016)

8. Gulrajani, I., Ahmed, F., Arjovsky, M., Dumoulin, V., Courville, A.C.: Improved training of wasserstein GANs. In: Advances in Neural Information Processing Systems, vol. 30 (2017)

9. Heusel, M., Ramsauer, H., Unterthiner, T., Nessler, B., Hochreiter, S.: GANs trained by a two time-scale update rule converge to a local Nash equilibrium. In: Advances in Neural Information Processing Systems, vol. 30 (2017)

10. Jeong, J., Shin, J.: Training GANs with stronger augmentations via contrastive discriminator. arXiv preprint arXiv:2103.09742 (2021)

11. Karnewar, A., Wang, O.: MSG-GAN: multi-scale gradients for generative adversarial networks. In: Proceedings of the IEEE/CVF Conference on Computer Vision and Pattern Recognition, pp. 7799–7808 (2020)

12. Karras, T., Aittala, M., Hellsten, J., Laine, S., Lehtinen, J., Aila, T.: Training generative adversarial networks with limited data. In: Advances in Neural Information Processing Systems, vol. 33, pp. 12104–12114 (2020)

13. Karras, T., Laine, S., Aila, T.: A style-based generator architecture for generative adversarial networks. In: Proceedings of the IEEE/CVF Conference on Computer Vision and Pattern Recognition, pp. 4401–4410 (2019)

14. Karras, T., Laine, S., Aittala, M., Hellsten, J., Lehtinen, J., Aila, T.: Analyzing and improving the image quality of StyleGAN. In: Proceedings of the IEEE/CVF Conference on Computer Vision and Pattern Recognition, pp. 8110–8119 (2020)

15. Kwon, Y.-H., Park, M.-G.: Predicting future frames using retrospective cycle GAN. In: Proceedings of the IEEE/CVF Conference on Computer Vision and Pattern Recognition, pp. 1811–1820 (2019)

16. Li, C.: Two-stage sketch colorization. ACM Trans. Graph. **37**(6), 1–14 (2018)

17. Lim, J.H., Ye, J.C.: Geometric GAN. arXiv preprint arXiv:1705.02894 (2017)

18. Liu, B., Zhu, Y., Song, K., Elgammal, A.: Towards faster and stabilized GAN training for high-fidelity few-shot image synthesis. In: International Conference on Learning Representations (2020)

19. Liu, Z., Luo, P., Wang, X., Tang, X.: Deep learning face attributes in the wild. In: Proceedings of the IEEE International Conference on Computer Vision, pp. 3730–3738 (2015)

20. Miyato, T., Kataoka, T., Koyama, M., Yoshida, Y.: Spectral normalization for generative adversarial networks. arXiv preprint arXiv:1802.05957 (2018)

21. Nazeri, K., Ng, E., Joseph, T., Qureshi, F.Z., Ebrahimi, M.: EdgeConnect: generative image inpainting with adversarial edge learning. arXiv preprint arXiv:1901.00212 (2019)
22. Radford, A., Metz, L., Chintala, S.: Unsupervised representation learning with deep convolutional generative adversarial networks. arXiv preprint arXiv:1511.06434 (2015)
23. Royer, A., et al.: XGAN: unsupervised image-to-image translation for many-to-many mappings. In: Singh, R., Vatsa, M., Patel, V.M., Ratha, N. (eds.) Domain Adaptation for Visual Understanding, pp. 33–49. Springer, Cham (2020). https://doi.org/10.1007/978-3-030-30671-7_3
24. Si, Z., Zhu, S.-C.: Learning hybrid image templates (HIT) by information projection. IEEE Trans. Pattern Anal. Mach. Intell. **34**(7), 1354–1367 (2011)
25. Tran, D., Ranganath, R., Blei, D.M.: Deep and hierarchical implicit models **7**(3), 13 (2017). arXiv preprint arXiv:1702.08896
26. Tseng, H.-Y., Jiang, L., Liu, C., Yang, M.-H., Yang, W.: Regularizing generative adversarial networks under limited data. In: Proceedings of the IEEE/CVF Conference on Computer Vision and Pattern Recognition, pp. 7921–7931 (2021)
27. Wang, Z., Bovik, A.C., Sheikh, H.R., Simoncelli, E.P.: Image quality assessment: from error visibility to structural similarity. IEEE Trans. Image Process. **13**(4), 600–612 (2004)
28. Wen, Y., et al.: Structure-aware motion deblurring using multi-adversarial optimized CycleGAN. IEEE Trans. Image Process. **30**, 6142–6155 (2021)
29. Yi, R., Liu, Y.-J., Lai, Y.-K., Rosin, P.L.: APDrawingGAN: generating artistic portrait drawings from face photos with hierarchical GANs. In: Proceedings of the IEEE/CVF Conference on Computer Vision and Pattern Recognition, pp. 10743–10752 (2019)
30. Yu, F., Seff, A., Zhang, Y., Song, S., Funkhouser, T., Xiao, J.: LSUN: construction of a large-scale image dataset using deep learning with humans in the loop. arXiv preprint arXiv:1506.03365 (2015)
31. Zhang, D., Khoreva, A.: PA-GAN: improving GAN training by progressive augmentation (2018)
32. Zhang, R., Isola, P., Efros, A.A., Shechtman, E., Wang, O.: The unreasonable effectiveness of deep features as a perceptual metric. In: Proceedings of the IEEE Conference on Computer Vision and Pattern Recognition, pp. 586–595 (2018)
33. Zhang, Y., Han, S., Zhang, Z., Wang, J., Bi, H.: CF-GAN: cross-domain feature fusion generative adversarial network for text-to-image synthesis. Vis. Comput. **39**(4), 1283–1293 (2022). https://doi.org/10.1007/s00371-022-02404-6
34. Zhao, S., Liu, Z., Lin, J., Zhu, J.-Y., Han, S.: Differentiable augmentation for data-efficient GAN training. In: Advances in Neural Information Processing Systems, vol. 33, pp. 7559–7570 (2020)

A Two-Step Approach for Interactive Animatable Avatars

Takumi Kitamura[2], Naoya Iwamoto[2], Hiroshi Kawasaki[1],
and Diego Thomas[1(✉)]

[1] Kyushu University, Fukuoka, Japan
thomas@ait.kyushu-u.ac.jp
[2] Huawei Technologies Japan K.K., Tokyo, Japan

Abstract. We propose a two-step human body animation technique that generates pose-dependent detailed deformations in real-time on standard animation pipeline. In order to accomplish real-time animation, we utilize the template-based approach and represent pose-dependent deformations using 2D displacement maps. In order to generalize to totally new motions, we employ a two-step strategy: 1) the first step aligns the topology of the Skinned Multi-Person Linear Model (SMPL) [25] model to our proposed template model. 2) the second step models detailed clothes and muscles deformation for the specific motion. Our experimental results show that our proposed method can animate an avatar up to 30 times faster than baselines while keeping similar or even better level of details.

Keywords: Animatable avatars · Real time · Clothes animation · Non-rigid fitting

1 Introduction

Digitizing humans is crucial for various applications ranging from entertainment to autonomous driving and medical support. One key challenge to create digital humans is to give the avatars the ability to be animated in the digital worlds at interactive time with realistic motions of muscles and clothes. Currently, only professionals and artists can make realistic animatable avatars by using offline softwares like Maya or Blender, because it requires special skills such as skeleton construction, skinning weights and physics (e.g. hair, clothes, etc.). A wide variety of techniques have been proposed to automate the process of generating animatable avatars, such as using examples of 3D posed meshes [4,18–22], captured 4D data [3,13,33,36] or multi-view images [8,15,23,31,32,34]. However, these methods require either heavy data preparation steps or time consuming post-process to transform the output into usable 3D meshes. What we really

_____

Supplementary Information The online version contains supplementary material available at https://doi.org/10.1007/978-3-031-50072-5_39.

B. Sheng et al. (Eds.): CGI 2023, LNCS 14496, pp. 491–509, 2024.
https://doi.org/10.1007/978-3-031-50072-5_39

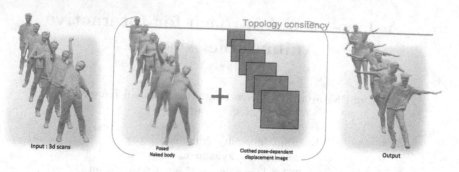

Fig. 1. Our proposed method takes as input raw 3D scans and learn animatable avatars that can be used to synthesized new realistic animations from a sequence of 3D skeletons.

need, instead, is (1) a robust and automatized data preparation pipeline; (2) output that is generated at interactive frame-rate; (3) consistent topology. We address these three challenges simultaneously in this paper for the first time.

We propose a two-step method for real-time clothed human body animation synthesis. The first step (Step 1) is to generate a posed naked body shape from a skeletal pose with up-sampling SMPL mesh [25]. The SMPL model is a statistical model of the naked human body that is controlled by pose and shape parameters. The second step (Step 2) predicts the pose-dependent clothed body deformations using a deep neural network. The network generates a displacement map from a 3D skeletal pose to add pose-dependent geometric detail to the output mesh of the first step (see Fig. 1 for an overview). For training, we also propose an automation technique to generate training dataset from topology inconsistency mesh sequences (Sect. 4). Our method generates animation in real-time, ensuring smoothness at joint locations and capturing intricate details such as wrinkles in clothes and muscle movements.

The key idea in our proposed method is to represent the 3D displacements with 2D images. Then, by utilizing efficient 2D convolutional layers, we can achieve rapid animation synthesis. This also allows us to better preserve spatial consistency. In addition, we learn the pose-dependent clothes and muscles deformations directly in the pose space, instead of learning in the canonical space [33,36]. As a consequence, predicting skinning weights is no longer required, speeding up inference and improving reconstruction accuracy.

Our method is trained using a sequence of 3D scans that are topologically aligned to a template mesh. One difficulty is that fitting a detailed human template model to 3D scans without manual intervention does not work [2] or require additional training process [5,6,38]. We propose a new SDF gradient-based method in a tetrahedralized volumetric hull to make the non-registration process fully automatic, robust and accurate.

We evaluate our proposed method both quantitatively and qualitatively with 3D and 4D datasets. We use both public datasets [28,37], purchased dataset [12] and our own 4D dataset. Our network is trained independently for each subject and we evaluate interpolation, extrapolation and retargeting ability of our proposed method compared with baselines SCANimate[1] [33], Fast-SNARF[2] [9] and POP[3] [29]. Results show that our proposed method achieves realistic animation at least 30 times faster than other methods while keeping similar or better level of details. Our ablation study demonstrates the advantage of using two stages in the animation, which allows generating smooth animations at joints locations. All our code and own data are available at https://github.com/diegothomas/Interactive-Animatable-Avatar.

In summary, our key contributions are: (1) Building a network to obtain detailed displacements considering clothing from a posed skeleton. (2) Constructing a framework to automatically generate training data from scanned data. (3) Demonstrating a system that generates detailed clothed human body animations in real-time from input skeletal pose sequence.

2   Related Works

The most popular 3D representation of a human avatar is a 3D mesh that is animated with using either blendshapes [11,35] or skinning [16]. SMPL [25] and then SMPL-X [30] are popular human body templates that combine both blendshapes and skinning. Linear blend skinning is used to animate the 3D mesh and errors are compensated with using pose-dependent shape deformation correctives. SMPL and SMPL-X use blendshapes to adapt the template model to a large variety of people, but they cannot model clothes, hair, face details or muscles.

A solution to model clothes and detailed geometry is to augment the SMPL model with displacement vectors. These approaches are referred to as SMPL+D, and we also follow this idea. Deep neural networks can be used to learn to predict displacement vectors for an input 3D pose. SCALE[4] [27] and POP [29] proposed to use the point cloud representation. POP proposed to use an implicit neural network that predicts the displacement vector for any point in space. Then the resolution of the output can be freely adjusted. However, calling the network on each point independently takes time, and the output must be post-processed to generate a 3D mesh. This method cannot generate real-time animations. In addition, the topology of the output mesh changes at every frame, which does not satisfy the requirements of standard graphics pipeline. By using user specific template models, real-time, topologically consistent and high resolution 3D animation can be generated [3]. But preparing the training data becomes excessively time consuming and requires strong expertise.

Template-free methods allows to significantly simplify the training data generation process. Representing detailed 3D shape with implicit neural functions was proven to be very efficient for 3D shape reconstruction. These ideas have

---

[1] Skinned Clothed Avatar Networks.
[2] Skinned Neural Articulated Representations with Forward skinning.
[3] Power of Points.
[4] Surface Codec of Articulated Local Elements.

been applied to create animatable avatars in SCANimate [33] and SNARF [10]. The networks are trained to simultaneously fit the signed distance field in a rest pose and learn skinning weights to reproduce the detailed animation. Fast-SNARF [9] speeds up the original network with using optimised CUDA implementation. LoopReg [6] uses weakly supervised learning to deform the input 3D scans in the neutral pose. Tiwari et al. [36] proposed Neural-GIF[5] to improve surface details with a combination of canonical map network and displacement field network. Shaofei et al. [39] and Bruno et al. [7] proposed to combine monocular RGB and depth images to improve details reconstruction. However, to output a 3D mesh, the networks must be called on each summits of a uniform grid, followed by applying Marching Cubes algorithm [26]. These approaches are not suited for real-time application. In addition, the topology of the output mesh changes at every frame, which does not satisfy the requirements of standard graphics pipeline.

3   A Two Step Approach for Pose-Dependent Deformation

We employ a two-step approach to achieve animation at interactive frame-rate with accurate geometry even for totally new motions. The first step (STEP 1) up-samples the posed skinned SMPL mesh to match the common topology of the 3D meshes used for training. The second step (STEP 2) generates local displacement maps that are applied to the up-sampled version of the posed skinned SMPL mesh. We propose to model pose-dependent deformations in local coordinate systems with a normalization process. We design a skeleton-aware encoder-decoder network that learns to generate detailed displacement maps from input human body poses. Figure 2 shows an overview of our method.

3.1   Pose-Dependent Deformation Model

Key to our method is the displacement map $D(\Theta)$ that depends on the input pose Θ and is computed in pose space. $D(\Theta)$ is obtained by assigning to each pixel in the UV texture space the 3D displacement between the corresponding 3D vertex in the up-sampled posed SMPL mesh and the ground truth (GT) mesh[6]. The displacement vectors between the naked body and the clothed body are first transformed into the local coordinate systems before being recorded in the displacement map. Important is that the local coordinate systems vary smoothly with respect to the shape of the template mesh. As a consequence the values of neighboring pixels in the displacement images also vary smoothly, which helps the training process and facilitates any post-process such as smoothing.

For the ith vertex B_i of the template mesh and pose Θ, the local coordinate system $L_i(\Theta)$ is computed as

$$L_i(\Theta) = [L_i(\Theta)_0^\mathsf{T}, L_i(\Theta)_1^\mathsf{T}, L_i(\Theta)_2^\mathsf{T}]^\mathsf{T}, \tag{1}$$

$$L_i(\Theta)_j = LBS((e_j + B_i), \Theta) - LBS(B_i, \Theta), \tag{2}$$

---

[5] Neural Generalized Implicit Functions.
[6] How to generate registered GT meshes is explained in Sect. 4.

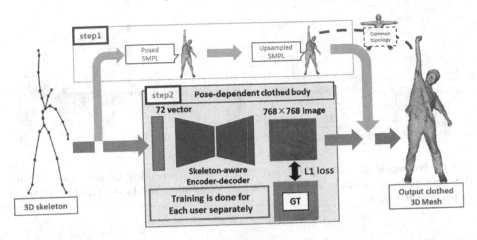

Fig. 2. We reconstruct detailed full body animation in two steps. (1) We reconstruct pose-dependent naked deformations from input pose and (2) we add clothes, muscles and subject specific pose-dependent deformations from the posed naked body.

where $e_0 = [1,0,0]$, $e_1 = [0,1,0]$, $e_2 = [0,0,1]$ and LBS is the linear blend skinning function.

The displacement image $\mathbf{D}(\Theta)$ is calculated between the posed template mesh mesh $LBS(B, \Theta)$ and the GT mesh M in the local coordinate systems. The raw displacement texture $\mathbf{D^{src}}(\Theta)$ is normalized using the per-pixel mean images $\hat{\mathbf{D}}$ and the accumulated standard deviation σ so that most of the displacements in the distribution fall within the range 0 to 1. This normalisation step is critical because it reduces the range of the displacement image and direct the network to focus on the pose-dependent deformation rather than the subject's shape. The normalized displacement map $\mathbf{D}(\Theta)$ is computed as follows for each pixel (x, y).

$$\mathbf{D^{src}_{(x,y)}}(\Theta) = (M_i - LBS(B_i, \Theta))\mathbf{L_i}(\Theta)^{-1} \tag{3}$$

$$\mathbf{D_{(x,y)}}(\Theta) = \frac{\mathbf{D^{src}_{(x,y)}}(\Theta) - \hat{\mathbf{D}}_{(x,y)}}{3\sigma}. \tag{4}$$

Note that assuming a normal distribution, 99.73% of the data fall within the interval $[0, 1]$ for 3σ.

To summarize, the formula to reconstruct the avatar $M(\Theta)$ from the displacement map $\mathbf{D_{(x,y)}}(\Theta)$ at the pose Θ is

$$\mathbf{M}(\Theta) = LBS(\mathbf{B}, \Theta) + (\mathbf{D}(\Theta)3\sigma + \hat{\mathbf{D}})\mathbf{L_i}(\Theta) \tag{5}$$

3.2   Step 1: Mesh Conversion from Skeletal Pose

We introduce our own template mesh to facilitate the training data generation process. The key idea is to remove details of the SMPL model like fingers and facial details that may trap the fitting process into local minima. We also inflate

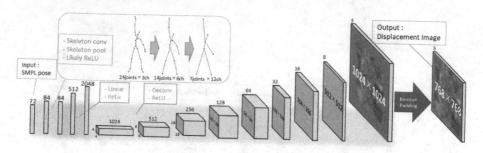

Fig. 3. Network Details. The input SMPL pose is encoded by skeleton convolution and skeleton pooling, and the inverted convolution produces a $1024 \times 1024 \times 3$ displacement image.

the template mesh to make the fitting process more robust. The template mesh is constructed as follows.

1) SMPL in a canonical pose is encoded in a Signed Distance Field (SDF) discretized in a 512^3 voxel grids of 0.005 m width. The template mesh is obtained from the SDF with using the Marching Cubes algorithm for the τ level-set (where $\tau = 0.1$).
2) We manually assign texture coordinates to each vertex on the surface of the template mesh using Blender. This operation to define the UV coordinates is required only once for the first time, and the defined UV coordinates can be used for any subject.

The final template mesh is a high-resolution mesh with 93894 vertices and 187784 faces.

All the ground truth meshes are registered to our template mesh (Sect. 4), which has a different topology than the posed SMPL mesh. As a consequence it is not possible to directly calculate the displacement between the ground truth meshes and the posed SMPL mesh. Therefore, we use an up-sampling process (STEP 1) that matches the topology of the posed SMPL mesh to the same topology as our template mesh. The up-sampling process involves the following pre-processing steps: (1) Fitting the template mesh to the SMPL mesh in the canonical pose. (2) Determining the barycentric coordinates of each vertex in the fitted template mesh with respect to the summits of the triangle in the SMPL mesh that contains the vertex. Then at training/prediction times, up-sampling the posed SMPL meshis done by computing the vertices positions of the template mesh using the pre-computed barycentric weights.

3.3   Step 2: Pose-Dependent Displacement Map Generation

We show an overview of our proposed displacement network in Fig. 3. The input of the network is a 3D human skeletal pose following SMPL format. The skeletal is represented by 24 rotations, defined as $3 + 23 \times 3 = 72$ parameters of root joint rotation and rotations relative to the parent joints. Following recent studies, our proposed network uses the skeleton-aware graph convolution [1]. Concretely, a skeleton aware encoder consisting of skeleton convolution and skeleton pooling is used to extract latent feature codes at time t from the input skeleton. These latent feature codes are subsequently decoded into 3-channel displacement maps. The displacement maps are encoded in the UV space of the template mesh. (Details are described in Sect. 4). By decoding the latent pose features on a two-dimensional 3-channel instead of decoding them on a one-dimensional vector, it is possible to better train the network while keeping spatial consistency.

Note that to reduce artifacts such as candy wrapping around joints, it is preferable to apply displacements on the deformed human body that is the output of the first step, rather than directly on the template mesh. Our network is trained independently for each user given 3D scans in various poses. Each scan holds a completely different topology, and in order to train with consistent data, it is necessary to register all data to a common template and then generate a displacement texture for each 3D scan. The process of generating displacement maps is described in detail in Sect. 4.

3.4   Implementation

We implemented our method using Pytorch. The network takes a tensor of size $(72, 1)$ as input and outputs a tensor of size $(768, 768, 3)$. The network uses two skeleton convolution layers with skeleton pooling process, which allows encoding the input into latent feature vectors. Latent feature vectors with size $(84, 1)$ are combined into vectors with size $(2048, 1)$ by the full concatenation layer and passed to the decoder. The method weights of the network are optimized using the L_1 loss. The learning rate varies from $1.0e^{-3}$ to $1.0e^{-6}$ with a scheduler.

The network takes about 1 h to train on a sequence of about 200 scans and generates pose-dependent textures in about 3 ms. Applying the displacement map to the mesh can be done efficiently on a GPU, and with a straightforward Numba implementation, animation can be performed in real-time at about 30 fps.

4   Training Data Generation

Our proposed method is trained with ground-truth displacement maps that represent pose-dependent deformations of the clothed human body. Each pixel of the displacement maps represent the deformation of a specific vertex of the template mesh. This means that all 3D meshes used for training must be aligned to a consistent topology.

Such a non-rigid registration process is a difficult task and typically requires manual work by experts using computer graphics tools, which takes prohibitive time and resources. Bagautdinov et al. [3] reported that pre-processing a single data set required about 14 days of work on 160 GPUs, with 10% of the processed data being rejected. Therefore, automatic methods using template models such as SMPL are preferred, but identifying the correct point correspondences

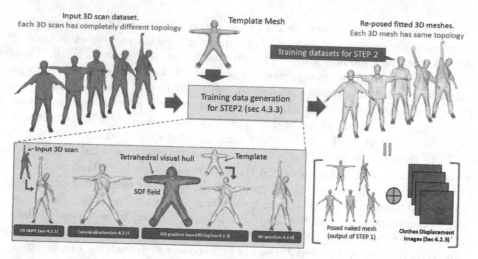

Fig. 4. Overall view of training data generation for a clothed avatar. The template mesh is non-rigidly fitted to the input scan embedded in a tight tetrahedral signed distance field (SDF).

between SMPL meshes and 3D scans often fails, even with highly accurate 3D pose estimation. This requires manual work to clean up the dataset, and some data is lost [2]. Recently, a network [5,38] has been proposed to predict point correspondences between the SMPL model and the input 3D scan but the resolution of the fitted mesh is limited to about 6000 vertices in the SMPL model. It also requires retraining the network for any new template model, which is not a flexible approach. Therefore, there is a need for an accurate method that is fully automatic, robust to input poses, and able to adapt to any template.

We propose a robust SDF gradient-based non-rigid registration method to automatically generate training displacement images that are consistent through all the observed poses. Figure 4 illustrates our proposed process of generating the training data. The process consists of: SMPL fitting in Sect. 4.1; canonicalization in Sect. 4.2; SDF gradient-based fitting in Sect. 4.3; reposing in Sect. 4.4; local displacement mapping in Sect. 3.1. Compared to the conventional data generation process that requires a great deal of labor, the data generation process of our proposed method is automated and can effortlessly produce the displacement images necessary for training the network.

4.1 SMPL Fitting

We fit the SMPL model to the input posed scans using Chumpy[7]. We carefully fit the shape parameters of SMPL only for the first scan, then keep the shape parameters fixed and only optimize the pose parameters. We make two observations: (1) jointly fitting the pose and shape parameters does not work in most

---

[7] In extreme poses SMPL add-on for Blender was used for manual initialisation.

poses when the person is wearing loose closes; (2) even with good initialisation existing tools struggle to estimate accurate SMPL pose parameters. This is possibly due to non-Euclidean space of pose parameters and the fact that there is no perfect fit of the (naked) SMPL model to the (clothed) input scans. These observations are in line with recent works [2, 24, 40, 41].

4.2   Canonicalization

We center the scan using the root joint and assign skinning weights for each point of the centered scan from the closest point on the fitted SMPL model. Each point is deformed using linear blend skinning to make the canonical mesh. Note that this operation is reversible: we can reproduce the posed mesh by using the inverse transformations. The goal is to bring all scans into a same 3D pose to facilitate the registration process. After registration, the fitted mesh is re-posed by using the inverse transformations of the corresponding vertices. Displacement maps are computed in the pose and skinning weights do not matter. The canonical mesh contains holes or wrong topology (if an arm is touching the body for example), so we re-mesh the canonical point cloud using the Poisson mesh reconstruction [17].

4.3   SDF Gradient Base Fitting

We propose a non-rigid registration technique that uses the gradients of a tetrahedral SDF field to guide the deformation of the source mesh to match the 0 level set that defines the target surface.

The template mesh is discretized with tetrahedra to create a tetrahedral volumetric hull. The template mesh and volumetric hull are scaled using the ratio of bone lengths between neutral SMPL skeleton and SMPL skeleton of the subject to ensure that the 3D scan is fully contained inside the tetrahedral volume. We encode the canonical 3D mesh in an SDF field that is sampled at each summit of the tetrahedra. Then we fit the template mesh to the 0 level-set of the SDF field. Using tetrahedra instead of voxels to discretize the volume is critical to achieve accurate fitting. Evaluation of our fitting method is in the supplemental video.

Our proposed method iterates between moving the vertices toward the 0 level-set by combining gradient vector and normal vector and regularizing the mesh by redistributing the vertices on the surface using the tangential barycentric coordinates. Specifically, at each iteration, for each vertex v_i of the template mesh with normal n_i, we compute the SDF value sdf_i and corresponding gradient g_i from the tetrahedral grid. Then,

$$v_i = v_i - \alpha g_i + \delta \|g_i\| sdf_i n_i \quad \text{if } g_i \cdot n_i < 0, \tag{6}$$
$$v_i = v_i - \alpha g_i - \delta \|g_i\| sdf_i n_i \quad \text{otherwise,}$$

where $\cdot$ denotes the scalar product. We use $\alpha = 0.01$ and $\delta = 0.003$ in our experiments.

After moving the vertices, we smooth the mesh by moving each vertex in its tangent plane using projected neighboring summits and barycentric coordinates computed in the canonical pose. Specifically,

$$\mathbf{v_i} = \sum_{s \in N(v_i)} w_s^i \pi(\mathbf{v_s}|\mathbf{v_i}, \mathbf{n_i}), \tag{7}$$

$$\text{where } \pi(\mathbf{v_s}|\mathbf{v_i}, \mathbf{n_i}) = \mathbf{v_s} - (\mathbf{n_i} \cdot (\mathbf{v_s} - \mathbf{v_i}))\mathbf{n_i}.$$

$N(v_i)$ is the set of neighbors of $\mathbf{v_i}$ in the template mesh and w_s^i are the barycentric weights of $\mathbf{v_i}$ in the template mesh in rest pose with respect to $\mathbf{v_s}$. Note that normal vectors are updated at each iteration.

4.4   Re-posing

To warp a 3D mesh from its canonical pose to a given pose, skinning weights at each vertex are required. These skinning weights depend on the shape of the 3D mesh, but also on the type of each vertex: skin or cloth. For example, a vertex on the sleeve of a shirt will not move in the same way as the corresponding vertex on the skin. This means that depending on the 3D position of the vertex and its type, the skinning weight of that vertex changes. In other words, if the method output displacement maps in the canonical pose, then for each predicted displacement vector a corresponding skinning weight would need to be also predicted. This means more parameters in the networks (i.e., more computational time) and less stability in the training (i.e., higher probability of seeing artifacts).

We propose to re-pose the fitted template mesh in the original pose before computing the displacement maps. This is important because then the network does not need to predict the pose-dependent skinning weights. For each vertex in the fitted template mesh: 1) we identify in the canonical mesh the closest face that intersects the ray emitted from the vertex and oriented by the normal vector; 2) we compute the corresponding skinning weights by linear interpolation in the face. We transfer the skinning weights from the canonicalised mesh to the fitted template mesh and use these skinning weights to warp the mesh into the original pose.

5   Experiments

We trained and tested our method on a Windows machine equipped with a TiTAN RTX GPU. In order to evaluate the advantage of our method over previous studies, we performed extensive quantitative and qualitative comparisons with state-of-the-art methods and ablation studies. More results are in the supp. video[8].

---

[8] https://github.com/diegothomas/Interactive-Animatable-Avatar.

5.1   Datasets

We used two publicly available datasets in our experiments: MIT dataset [37] and CAPE dataset [28]; one purchased dataset: 3D scan dataset [12], and our newly generated 4D dataset.

The MIT dataset contains high-quality 4D data with multi-view images. We use the I_{crane} dataset for our experiments. The CAPE dataset contains raw 3D scan data (RAW) and SMPL-fitted meshes (CAPE). While it is a high-quality dataset with rich motion, the Raw 3D scan data also contains missing data such as holes in the mesh, which is challenging. The 3D scan dataset contains high quality scan data with color for 4 subjects in a few poses, including complex postures such as dance scenes. The 4D dataset was captured in a 4DView studio, a green background space equipped with a volumetric video capture system capable of synchronous shooting with 32 cameras at 30 fps. The data set contains a motion sequence of 210 high quality 3d meshes.

5.2   Comparative Methods

We compare our method with ground truth GT and three other state-of-the-art methods: SCANimate [33], POP [29], and Fast-SNARF [10]. We ran the SCANimate code provided by the authors on a desktop machine with an RTX 2080 GPU and 32GB memory. The input was a centered scan mesh and paired SMPL pose parameters.

We ran the codes of POP and Fast-SNARF [9] provided by the authors on a desktop machine with a TiTAN RTX GPU and 32 GB of memory. Fast-SNARF is an implicit representation-based method for learning forward deformation fields, and like SCANimate, it is trained using 3D scans. POP takes as input the SMPL mesh, which is the mesh of the human body part, instead of the SMPL pose and outputs a cloud of points. We converted the output of POP to a 3D mesh using Poisson Surface Reconstruction [17].

5.3   Quantitative Evaluation

We conducted quantitative evaluations on the MIT, CAPE and 4D datasets. We performed three kind of experiments: Interpolation, Extrapolation and retargeting. (1) For the interpolation tests, we used the $(i*10)^{th}$ frames for training and the $(i*10+5)^{th}$ frames for testing. (2) For the extrapolation tests, we used the first 30% frames for training and the remaining 70% frames for testing. (3) For

Table 1. Comparison of average running time to generate the sequence of animated 3D meshes.

	SCANimate	Fast-SNARF	POP	Ours
Speed	1 fps	0.7 fps	1.1 fps	**30 fps**

Table 2. Comparative evaluation of our method with SCANimate [33]. We compute point to surface Chamfer distances and normal consistency from the predicted mesh to the ground truth and from the ground truth mesh to the predicted one.

	Interpolation				Extrapolation			
	GT2Pred		Pred2GT		GT2Pred		Pred2GT	
	Ds2m($\downarrow$)	Dn($\uparrow$)	Ds2m($\downarrow$)	Dn($\uparrow$)	Ds2m($\downarrow$)	Dn($\uparrow$)	Ds2m($\downarrow$)	Dn($\uparrow$)
4D dataset								
Base-O	10.257	0.857	11.205	0.827	12.561	0.822	13.788	0.792
SCANimate	**2.530**	0.122	12.626	0.856	**2.573**	0.115	14.900	**0.811**
Ours(1path)	5.463	**0.925**	**6.720**	**0.880**	10.773	0.846	11.955	0.793
Ours(2path)	6.200	0.921	7.432	0.876	10.268	**0.853**	**11.216**	0.801
MIT								
Base-O	9.770	0.819	10.486	0.787	10.441	0.804	11.468	0.773
SCANimate	**2.349**	0.136	10.431	0.827	**2.239**	0.128	11.000	0.805
Ours(1path)	6.810	**0.886**	**7.175**	**0.842**	8.490	0.855	8.987	**0.820**
Ours(2path)	6.994	0.885	7.268	0.841	8.514	**0.860**	**8.775**	**0.820**
CAPE								
Base-O	7.625	0.912	10.741	0.813	8.221	0.913	12.787	0.802
SCANimate	**1.593**	0.240	6.011	**0.909**	1.774	0.110	9.805	0.881
Ours(1path)	2.634	**0.959**	**4.548**	0.881	5.412	0.948	8.783	0.849
Ours(2path)	2.762	**0.959**	4.696	0.880	**1.066**	**0.971**	**3.606**	**0.883**

the retargeting tests, we used all data for training and a totally new motion for testing.

We measured the accuracy score of the reconstructed 3D meshes with using the Chamfer distance D_{s2m}^{p2g} between the vertices on the output mesh of each method and the nearest neighbor faces on the ground-truth mesh and the completeness score with using the Chamfer distance D_{s2m}^{g2p} between the vertices on the ground-truth mesh to the nearest neighbor face on the output mesh of each method. We also compute the cosine similarity score D_n between the normal vectors of the corresponding vertices and faces.[9]

Table 1 shows comparative run times for the different methods. For all methods, the fps value measures the average computational time to output the final 3D mesh from the input 3D skeletal pose. We have measured the fps values for all methods on the same machine with the same environment. Our method runs in average at 30 fps with a straightforward implementation. This is 30 times faster than POP [29], Fast-SNARF [9] and SCANimate [33].

---

[9] We used the Kaolin [14] library to compute these scores.

Table 3. Comparative evaluation of our method with Pop [29]. We compute point to surface Chamfer distances and normal consistency from the predicted mesh to the ground truth and from the ground truth mesh to the predicted one.

	Interpolation				Extrapolation			
	GT2Pred		Pred2GT		GT2Pred		Pred2GT	
	Ds2m(↓)	Dn(↑)	Ds2m(↓)	Dn(↑)	Ds2m(↓)	Dn(↑)	Ds2m(↓)	Dn(↑)
03375_blazerlong_volleyball_trial1 (RAW)								
POP	**3.827**	**0.959**	**3.617**	**0.940**	4.760	**0.949**	4.581	**0.933**
Ours	5.120	0.931	4.278	0.885	5.208	0.933	**4.447**	0.896
03375_blazerlong_climb_trial1 (RAW)								
POP	**4.914**	**0.933**	**4.625**	**0.917**	5.595	**0.934**	4.948	**0.913**
Ours	5.746	0.914	4.722	0.874	6.106	0.906	5.143	0.863
00096_shortlong_squats (RAW)								
POP	**2.093**	**0.982**	**2.020**	**0.975**	3.325	**0.969**	3.221	**0.958**
Ours	2.900	0.959	2.719	0.928	4.069	0.950	3.616	0.917
00215_poloshort_punching (RAW)								
POP	**2.408**	**0.976**	2.435	**0.971**	**3.131**	**0.969**	3.024	**0.958**
Ours	2.541	0.962	**2.321**	0.933	3.648	0.952	3.314	0.914

Table 4. Comparative evaluation of our method with Fast-SNARF [9]. We compute point to surface Chamfer distances and normal consistency from the predicted mesh to the ground truth and from the ground truth mesh to the predicted one.

	Interpolation				Extrapolation			
	GT2Pred		Pred2GT		GT2Pred		Pred2GT	
	Ds2m(↓)	Dn(↑)	Ds2m(↓)	Dn(↑)	Ds2m(↓)	Dn(↑)	Ds2m(↓)	Dn(↑)
03375_blazerlong_volleyball_trial1 (CAPE)								
SNARF	6.715	0.901	4.962	**0.903**	33.251	0.719	20.944	0.706
Ours(2path)	**3.778**	**0.909**	**3.131**	0.882	**5.749**	**0.894**	**4.717**	**0.876**
03375_blazerlong_climb_trial1 (CAPE)								
SNARF	8.483	**0.866**	8.066	**0.861**	38.521	0.660	22.756	0.617
Ours(2path)	**4.844**	0.857	**3.965**	0.840	**10.463**	**0.804**	**8.314**	**0.753**
00096_shortlong_squats (CAPE)								
SNARF	77.969	0.606	29.422	0.675	124.015	0.467	40.029	0.468
Ours(2path)	**2.448**	**0.927**	**2.133**	**0.918**	**4.901**	**0.902**	**4.323**	**0.878**
00215_poloshort_punching (CAPE)								
SNARF	96.914	0.419	55.867	0.424	14.176	0.819	10.911	0.831
Ours(2path)	**2.929**	**0.925**	**2.526**	**0.898**	**4.126**	**0.913**	**3.564**	**0.888**

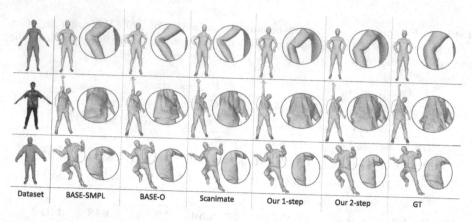

| Dataset | BASE-SMPL | BASE-O | Scanimate | Our 1-step | Our 2-step | GT |

Fig. 5. Comparison of BASE-SMPL, BASE-O, SCANimate, our method with one step, and our method with two steps.

Table 2 shows the average error between the generated meshes and the ground-truth meshes for the 1-step method, 2-step method and SCANimate. The 1-step method applies the displacement maps directly to our proposed template mesh. Errors were computed for both interpolation and extrapolation tests. In addition to the comparison with SCANimate, we also compare the results with the baseline method Base-O. In the baseline method the template mesh is fitted to the first frame of the input sequence and animated using linear blend skinning. As can be seen in the table, our method always generates the 3D motion more accurately than SCANimate. In addition, SCANimate runs at about 1.2 fps while our proposed method runs at about 30 fps, which is about 30 times speed up, and directly outputs topologically consistent 3D meshes. Table 2 also shows that our two-step method is particularly effective for extrapolation tests. The CAPE dataset contains many poses with bent elbows and knees, which indicates that our proposed two-step method efficiently reduced artifacts around the joints. The baseline method Base-O could not generate detailed deformations. Note that reconstruction errors vary significantly across different datasets. This is because each dataset has a completely different range of motion. As a consequence, the difficulty of the extrapolation task changes depending on how similar motions in the training set are.

Table 3 shows the comparative results with POP. Note that the input of our proposed method is SMPL pose, whereas the input of POP is the SMPL human body mesh, which gives significant advantage to POP. Although our method had slightly worse results than those obtained with POP (about 1 mm difference) our method has a clear advantage when taking into account the computational time (about 30 times faster). POP requires more than one second to complete, making it impossible to generate a mesh in real time.

Table 4 shows the comparative results with SNARF. Despite our best efforts, the errors obtained with SNARF were large for most cases. This is because

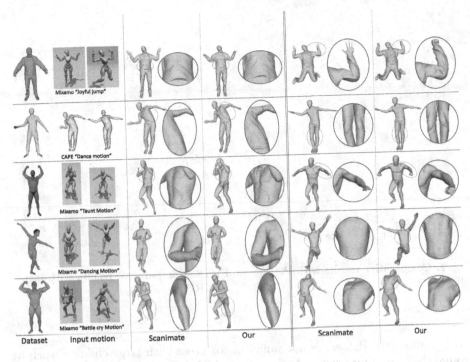

Fig. 6. Representative Comparison of CAPE Data with SCANimate in Retargeting Sequences Using 3D Scan Data.

SNARF needs to be trained with a large amount of example 3D scans (hundreds to tens of thousands of input poses) but in this test we used only a few dozen poses for training. On the other hand, our method produces consistent results for all meshes, indicating that it can be successfully trained even with few input scans.

5.4   Qualitative Evaluation

Figure 5 shows the qualitative interpolation results obtained with using our method and SCANimate, including the 3d scan of the ground truth. From this figure, it can be seen that the results generated by our method reproduce more accurate and realistic clothing deformations than SCANimate, with fewer artifacts around joints, such as around the elbows.

We also performed a qualitative evaluation of the trained animatable avatar with a new motion obtained from Mixamo[10]. Figure 6 shows the results obtained with using our method and SCANimate. As shown in the red box, the wrinkles and shaking of the clothes due to movement were reproduced in detail. Results obtained with the CAPE dataset (first row) show that SCANimate and the one-step method generate volume loss. These problems may be caused by insufficient

---

[10] https://www.mixamo.com/.

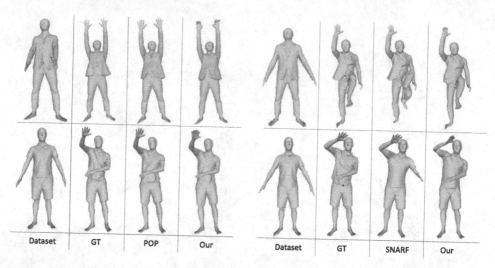

Fig. 7. Comparative results with POP [29].

Fig. 8. Comparative results with fast-SNARF [9]

learning when the dataset is not sufficient for areas with large changes, such as around the arms. Our proposed two-step method provides more robust results by predicting the adding the naked human body animation in addition to predicting the clothing.

Figure 7 shows the results of the comparison between the proposed method and the POP method. Our proposed method was able to generate animation in real-time with similar level of quality as the offline-based POP method. In particular, for the data 00215_poloshort_punching, the predicted direction of wrinkles obtained with our proposed method is closer to the ground truth than that of POP, and the deformation of the clothes hidden by the left hand is also closer to the ground truth.

Figure 8 shows the comparison results between our proposed method and Fast-SNARF [9]. In the experiments, interpolation and extrapolation tests were performed on a total of eight datasets, but most of the SNARF-generated motions failed, and only a few successful cases are shown in the figure. Even in these results, there are failures, such as multiple outputs of hands and different positions of generated hands. This is because of the few number of training data. Our proposed method was able to output stable and accurate results even with a small amount of training data without.

6   Conclusion

We proposed a two-step approach for animating avatars with consistent topology in real-time. We trained a network that predicts pose-dependent displacement maps that are mapped to the animated and up-sampled SMPL model. The network is implemented with CUDA, which allows for real-time mesh generation. To generate training data that are with consistent topology through all input poses, we propose our own template model and an SDF-based non-rigid alignment method. Training data generation is done automatically and robustly. Experimental results show that our proposed method runs in real-time and maintains the same or better score than previous offline methods, demonstrating the effectiveness of our proposed method. Our proposed method matches the standard graphics pipeline and opens new possible concrete applications.

References

1. Aberman, K., Li, P., Lischinski, D., Sorkine-Hornung, O., Cohen-Or, D., Chen, B.: Skeleton-aware networks for deep motion retargeting. ACM Trans. Graph. (TOG) **39**(4), 62:1 (2020)
2. Alldieck, T., Pons-Moll, G., Theobalt, C., Magnor, M.: Tex2shape: detailed full human body geometry from a single image. In: Proceedings of the IEEE/CVF International Conference on Computer Vision, pp. 2293–2303 (2019)
3. Bagautdinov, T., et al.: Driving-signal aware full-body avatars. ACM Trans. Graph. **40**(4) (2021). https://doi.org/10.1145/3450626.3459850
4. Bailey, S.W., Otte, D., Dilorenzo, P., O'Brien, J.F.: Fast and deep deformation approximations. ACM Trans. Graph. **37**(4), 119:1–119:12 (2018). https://doi.org/10.1145/3197517.3201300. Presented at SIGGRAPH 2018, Los Angeles
5. Bhatnagar, B.L., Sminchisescu, C., Theobalt, C., Pons-Moll, G.: Combining implicit function learning and parametric models for 3D human reconstruction. In: Vedaldi, A., Bischof, H., Brox, T., Frahm, J.-M. (eds.) ECCV 2020. LNCS, vol. 12347, pp. 311–329. Springer, Cham (2020). https://doi.org/10.1007/978-3-030-58536-5_19
6. Bhatnagar, B.L., Sminchisescu, C., Theobalt, C., Pons-Moll, G.: LoopReg: self-supervised learning of implicit surface correspondences, pose and shape for 3D human mesh registration. In: Neural Information Processing Systems (NeurIPS) (2020)
7. Burov, A., Nießner, M., Thies, J.: Dynamic surface function networks for clothed human bodies (2021)
8. Chang, Y., et al.: VTNCT: an image-based virtual try-on network by combining feature with pixel transformation. Vis. Comput. **39**(7), 2583–2596 (2023)
9. Chen, X., et al.: Fast-SNARF: a fast deformer for articulated neural fields. arXiv:2211.15601 (2022)
10. Chen, X., Zheng, Y., Black, M.J., Hilliges, O., Geiger, A.: SNARF: differentiable forward skinning for animating non-rigid neural implicit shapes. In: International Conference on Computer Vision (ICCV) (2021)
11. Chuang, E., Bregler, C.: Performance driven facial animation using blendshape interpolation. Computer Science Technical Report, Stanford University, vol. 2, no. 2, p. 3 (2002)
12. Scan Dataset. https://www.3dscanstore.com
13. Deng, B., et al.: NASA neural articulated shape approximation. In: Vedaldi, A., Bischof, H., Brox, T., Frahm, J.-M. (eds.) ECCV 2020. LNCS, vol. 12352, pp. 612–628. Springer, Cham (2020). https://doi.org/10.1007/978-3-030-58571-6_36

14. Fuji Tsang, C., et al.: Kaolin: a pytorch library for accelerating 3d deep learning research (2022). https://github.com/NVIDIAGameWorks/kaolin
15. Habermann, M., Liu, L., Xu, W., Zollhoefer, M., Pons-Moll, G., Theobalt, C.: Real-time deep dynamic characters. ACM Trans. Graph. **40**(4), 1–16 (2021)
16. Kavan, L., Collins, S., Žára, J., O'Sullivan, C.: Skinning with dual quaternions. In: Proceedings of the 2007 Symposium on Interactive 3D Graphics and Games, pp. 39–46 (2007)
17. Kazhdan, M., Bolitho, M., Hoppe, H.: Poisson surface reconstruction. In: Proceedings of the Fourth Eurographics Symposium on Geometry Processing, vol. 7 (2006)
18. Le, B.H., Lewis, J.P.: Direct delta mush skinning and variants. ACM Trans. Graph. **38**(4) (2019). https://doi.org/10.1145/3306346.3322982
19. Le, B.H., Villeneuve, K., Gonzalez-Ochoa, C.: Direct delta mush skinning compression with continuous examples. ACM Trans. Graph. **40**(4) (2021). https://doi.org/10.1145/3450626.3459779
20. Li, P., Aberman, K., Hanocka, R., Liu, L., Sorkine-Hornung, O., Chen, B.: Learning skeletal articulations with neural blend shapes. ACM Trans. Graph. (TOG) **40**(4), 1 (2021)
21. Li, T., Shi, R., Kanai, T.: MultiResGNet: approximating nonlinear deformation via multi-resolution graphs. Comput. Graph. Forum **40**(2), 537–548 (2021). https://doi.org/10.1111/cgf.142653
22. Li, X., Li, G., Li, T., Lv, J., Mitrouchev, P.: Remodeling of mannequins based on automatic binding of mesh to anthropometric parameters. Vis. Comput. **39**, 6435–6458 (2022)
23. Liu, L., Habermann, M., Rudnev, V., Sarkar, K., Gu, J., Theobalt, C.: Neural actor: neural free-view synthesis of human actors with pose control. ACM Trans. Graph. (ACM SIGGRAPH Asia) **40**, 1–16 (2021)
24. Loper, M., Mahmood, N., Black, M.J.: Mosh: motion and shape capture from sparse markers. ACM Trans. Graph. (ToG) **33**(6), 1–13 (2014)
25. Loper, M., Mahmood, N., Romero, J., Pons-Moll, G., Black, M.J.: SMPL: a skinned multi-person linear model. ACM Trans. Graph. (Proc. SIGGRAPH Asia) **34**(6), 248:1–248:16 (2015)
26. Lorensen, W.E., Cline, H.E.: Marching cubes: a high resolution 3d surface construction algorithm. ACM SIGGRAPH Comput. Graph. **21**(4), 163–169 (1987)
27. Ma, Q., Saito, S., Yang, J., Tang, S., Black, M.J.: SCALE: modeling clothed humans with a surface codec of articulated local elements. In: Proceedings IEEE/CVF Conference on Computer Vision and Pattern Recognition (CVPR) (2021)
28. Ma, Q., et al.: Learning to dress 3D people in generative clothing. In: Computer Vision and Pattern Recognition (CVPR) (2020)
29. Ma, Q., Yang, J., Tang, S., Black, M.J.: The power of points for modeling humans in clothing. In: Proceedings of the IEEE/CVF International Conference on Computer Vision (ICCV) (2021)
30. Pavlakos, G., et al.: Expressive body capture: 3d hands, face, and body from a single image. In: Proceedings IEEE Conference on Computer Vision and Pattern Recognition (CVPR) (2019)
31. Prokudin, S., Black, M.J., Romero, J.: SMPLpix: neural avatars from 3D human models. In: Proceedings of the IEEE/CVF Winter Conference on Applications of Computer Vision, pp. 1810–1819 (2021)

32. Raj, A., Tanke, J., Hays, J., Vo, M., Stoll, C., Lassner, C.: ANR: articulated neural rendering for virtual avatars. In: Proceedings of the IEEE/CVF Conference on Computer Vision and Pattern Recognition (CVPR), pp. 3722–3731 (2021)
33. Saito, S., Yang, J., Ma, Q., Black, M.J.: SCANimate: weakly supervised learning of skinned clothed avatar networks. In: Proceedings IEEE/CVF Conference on Computer Vision and Pattern Recognition (2021)
34. Shysheya, A., et al.: Textured neural avatars. In: Proceedings of the IEEE/CVF Conference on Computer Vision and Pattern Recognition (CVPR) (2019)
35. Thomas, D., Taniguchi, R.I.: Augmented blendshapes for real-time simultaneous 3d head modeling and facial motion capture. In: Proceedings of the IEEE Conference on Computer Vision and Pattern Recognition, pp. 3299–3308 (2016)
36. Tiwari, G., Sarafianos, N., Tung, T., Pons-Moll, G.: Neural-GIF: neural generalized implicit functions for animating people in clothing. In: International Conference on Computer Vision (ICCV) (2021)
37. Vlasic, D., Baran, I., Matusik, W., Popović, J.: Articulated mesh animation from multi-view silhouettes. ACM Trans. Graph. **27**(3), 1–9 (2008). https://doi.org/10.1145/1360612.1360696
38. Wang, S., Geiger, A., Tang, S.: Locally aware piecewise transformation fields for 3d human mesh registration. In: Proceedings of the IEEE/CVF Conference on Computer Vision and Pattern Recognition, pp. 7639–7648 (2021)
39. Wang, S., Mihajlovic, M., Ma, Q., Geiger, A., Tang, S.: MetaAvatar: learning animatable clothed human models from few depth images. In: Advances in Neural Information Processing Systems (2021)
40. Zanfir, M., Zanfir, A., Bazavan, E.G., Freeman, W.T., Sukthankar, R., Sminchisescu, C.: THUNDR: transformer-based 3d human reconstruction with markers. In: Proceedings of the IEEE/CVF International Conference on Computer Vision, pp. 12971–12980 (2021)
41. Zhang, Y., Black, M.J., Tang, S.: We are more than our joints: predicting how 3d bodies move. In: Proceedings of the IEEE/CVF Conference on Computer Vision and Pattern Recognition, pp. 3372–3382 (2021)

Author Index

B. Sheng et al. (Eds.): CGI 2023, LNCS 14496, pp. 511–513, 2024.
https://doi.org/10.1007/978-3-031-50072-5

Author Index

Printed in the United States
by Baker & Taylor Publisher Services

Printed in the United States
by Baker & Taylor Publisher Services